SCHOOL SOCIAL WORK

Practice and Research Perspectives

Also available from Lyceum Books, Inc.

CLINICAL ASSESSMENT FOR SOCIAL WORKERS: QUANTITATIVE AND QUALITATIVE METHODS, by Catheleen Jordan and Cynthia Franklin

MODERN SOCIAL WORK THEORY: A CRITICAL INTRODUCTION, by Malcolm Payne, foreword by Stephen C. Anderson

STRUCTURING CHANGE: EFFECTIVE PRACTICE FOR COMMON CLIENT PROBLEMS, edited by Kevin Corcoran

WORKING WITH CHILDREN AND THEIR FAMILIES, by Martin Herbert, introduction by Charles Zastrow

POLICY ANALYSIS AND RESEARCH TECHNOLOGIES: POLITICAL AND ETHICAL CONSIDERATIONS, by Thomas M. Meenaghan and Keith M. Kilty

THE NEW POLITICS OF WELFARE: AN AGENDA FOR THE 1990s?, edited by Michael McCarthy, preface by Thomas M. Meenaghan

SOCIAL WORK EDUCATION IN EASTERN EUROPE: CHANGING HORIZONS, edited by Robert Constable and Vera Mehta

ADOLESCENTS IN FOSTER FAMILIES, edited by Jane Aldgate, Anthony Maluccio, and Christine Reeves

MARKETING STRATEGIES FOR NONPROFIT ORGANIZATIONS by Siri Espy

SCHOOL SOCIAL WORK

Practice and Research Perspectives

Third Edition

Edited by

ROBERT CONSTABLE
School of Social Work
Loyola University of Chicago

JOHN P. FLYNN
School of Social Work
Western Michigan University

SHIRLEY McDONALD
Jane Addams College of Social Work
University of Illinois at Chicago

Dedicated to children in the American public school system, past, present, and future;
to the families and communities whose hopes they bear;
to teachers who nourish and protect the unique and living spark in each child;
to school social workers who struggle to make the partnership alive and effective.

© Lyceum Books, Inc., 1996

Published by

    LYCEUM BOOKS, INC.
    5758 S. Blackstone Ave.
    Chicago, Illinois 60637
    312/643-1903 (Fax)
    312/643-1902 (Phone)

All rights reserved. No part of the publication may be reproduced, stored in a retrieval system, copied, or transmitted in any form or by any means without written permission from the publisher.

Library of Congress Cataloging-in-Publication Data

School social work : practice and research perspectives / edited by
  Robert Constable, John P. Flynn, Shirley McDonald. — 3rd ed.
    p.   cm.
  Includes bibliographical references and index.
  ISBN 0-925065-11-0
  1. School social work—United States.   I. Constable, Robert T.
II. Flynn, John P.   III. McDonald, Shirley, 1934–
LB3013.4.S365   1996   95-32132
371.4′6—dc20   CIP

Florence Poole (1904–1980): In Appreciation

—

Florence Poole died suddenly on June 23, 1980. To those of us who were closely associated with Florence, the news came as a shock. The significant contributions that she made to both social work and education and the outpouring of time and energy she had invested in the work for which she was so fitted—the education of social workers—cannot be forgotten.

With careful deliberation I perused Florence's resume to cull some of the things that might be of interest to social workers. I recalled a phrase written by Heinrich Heine: "The actions of persons are like the index of a book; they point out what is most remarkable in them." Everything Florence Poole has done has been valuable to us and truly has pointed out what was most remarkable in her—elementary school teacher, camp counselor, social worker, supervisor, and finally the coveted titles of associate professor at the University of Pittsburgh School of Social Work, and professor at the University of Illinois School of Social Work in Urbana and at the Jane Addams School of Social Work in Chicago. For a half-century of her life, Florence Poole offered dedicated service to children, parents, teachers, social workers, and administrators in some capacity, and her writings have inspired all of us to perform more effectively.

Florence was an unusual person. In a profession that has been graced by so many wonderful people, she was still exceptional—in her shy, unassuming, and gentle ways. One of her outstanding characteristics was her belief that the dignity and worth of every human being were living, consuming realities, and this guided her every action. She possessed a fundamental commitment to social work as a service profession. If she wanted the best from her students, it was only that they might bring the best to the people they would serve.

Her accomplishments in the field of social work and education are many, and any attempt to recapitulate their significance would scarcely allow her the exemplary credits she deserves. Few in the field of social work have been as prolific in writing articles of such value to the field. Few have so graciously and unstintingly given of their time and talents. Florence wrote thirteen publications and papers and at least twenty-five unpublished papers and speeches. She had the enviable record of more than thirty-nine institutes and workshops that have given insight and impetus to social workers, teachers, parents, and administrators and have allowed us to profit immensely from what she has done. Universities sought her leadership and knowledge when having their schools of social work accredited. National and state organizations sought her help by asking her to assume an officer's position, to be a consultant, or to be involved in some capacity to assist them in functioning more appropriately. Many universities requested that she teach in their summer programs. Florence, who I am sure never knew what she was getting into when she entered a helping profession, was constantly engaged in making social work, and especially school social work, the profession it ought to be and did grow to be.

Among her memorabilia was found a Japanese proverb that was representative of Florence's outlook in life: "When I dig another out of trouble, the hole from which I left him is the place where I bury my own." Another article, entitled "Thought for Today," exemplified her pattern for daily living. It read:

> On this day ...
> Mend a quarrel,
> Search out a forgotten friend,
> Dismiss a suspicion and replace it with trust,
> Write a letter to someone who misses you,
> Encourage a youth who has lost faith,
> Keep a promise,
> Forget an old grudge,
> Examine your demands on others and how to reduce them,
> Fight for a principle,
> Express your gratitude,
> Overcome an old fear,
> Take two minutes to appreciate the beauty of nature,
> Tell someone you love them,
> Tell them again,
> And again,
> And again.

The personal and professional tribute that should be accorded to Florence can never be written adequately; out debt of gratitude can never be repaid; the generosity and support she has offered us cannot be duplicated. School social work will succeed in its undertakings because of the exemplary designs that Florence fashioned for us from its crude beginnings.

Few persons have spent as enriched a life as Florence did in her service to others. Few have made such dedicated contributions and left such a precious imprint on the social work profession. Few have so influenced the lives of others. The memory of Florence's conscientious and devoted efforts will always be enshrined in our hearts, and for these we are grateful.

Margaret Quane

CONTENTS

Preface   xiii

Section I   General Perspectives on Theory and Practice in School Social Work   1

Chapter 1.   General Perspectives on Theory and Practice   *Robert Constable*   3

Chapter 2.   The Contribution of Social Workers to Schooling—Revisited   *Paula Allen-Meares*   17

Chapter 3.   An Ecological Perspective on Social Work in the Schools   *Carel B. Germain*   26

Chapter 4.   The Characteristic Focus of the Social Worker in the Public Schools   *Marjorie McQueen Monkman*   38

Chapter 5.   The Wonderland of Social Work in the Schools, or How Alice Learned to Cope   *Sally G. Goren*   57

Chapter 6.   The Economic, Politcal, and Social World of School Social Work   *Isadora R. Hare and Kathleen Sullivan Allen*   66

Section II   Mandated Foundations for Service Delivery   85

Chapter 7.   Mandated Foundations for Service Delivery: An Overview   *Robert Constable*   87

Chapter 8.   Foundations for Values in Special Education   *John A. McLaughlin and Ruth Ann Protinsky*   95

Chapter 9.   Educational Mandates for Children with Disabilities: Educational Program Development   *Vaughn W. Morrison, Marguerite Tiefentha, and David Moorman*   103

Chapter 10.   Part H of the Individuals with Disabilities Education Act: Analysis and Implications for Social Workers   *Kathleen Kirk Bishop*   116

Chapter 11.	Social Work and the Special Education System: Overview of Recent Cases Affecting Professional Decisions *Brooke R. Whitted*	132
Chapter 12.	The Trend toward Inclusion *Shirley McDonald*	147

Section III Service Delivery in the Schools 157

Chapter 13.	Service Delivery in the Schools: An Overview *Robert Constable*	159
Chapter 14.	The School Social Worker's Role: A Three-Decade Chronology *Renee Shai Levine*	166
Chapter 15.	The Dynamics of Systems Involvement with Children in School: A Case Perspective *Helen S. Wolkow*	174
Chapter 16.	School Social Work: Facilitating Home-School Partnerships *Robert Constable and Herbert Walberg*	182
Chapter 17.	The Social Developmental Study *Marguerite Tiefenthal and Rita S. Charak*	197
Chapter 18.	The Individualized Education Program and the IFSP: Content, Process, and the Social Worker's Role *Robert Constable*	209
Chapter 19.	The Least Restrictive Environment and the School Social Worker *Mary Lou Rogoff and Robert Constable*	225
Chapter 20.	School-To-Work Transition Programs *Kevin Hollenback and Bridget F. Timmeney*	237
Chapter 21.	Promoting Children's Social Competence in the Schools *Craig Winston LeCroy and Kerry B. Milligan*	253
Chapter 22.	Developing School Social Work Consultation Programs in the Context of Special Needs Children *Christine Anlauf Sabatino*	267
Chapter 23.	Student Forums: Addressing Racial Conflict in a High School *Rita McGary*	282
Chapter 24.	Conflict Resolution *Shirley McDonald and Anthony Moriarty*	290
Chapter 25.	Mediation as a Form of Peer-Based Conflict Resolution *Anthony Moriarty and Shirley McDonald*	299
Chapter 26.	The No-Fault School: Understanding Groups— Understanding Schools *Joy Johnson*	307
Chapter 27.	Analyzing the Organizational Context of Schools *Edith M. Freeman*	328

Chapter 28.	Resource Development and Coordination of Services *Robert Constable*	343
Chapter 29.	Child Protection and the School Social Worker *Sally G. Goren*	355

Section IV   Research and Evaluation   367

Chapter 30.	Research and Evaluation of Practice and Services in the Schools: An Overview *John P. Flynn*	369
Chapter 31.	Initiating Change through Research and Evaluation *John P. Flynn*	374
Chapter 32.	An Ethnic-Sensitive Approach to Empirical School Social Work Practice *Lester B. Brown*	387
Chapter 33.	Practical Approaches to Conducting and Using Research in the Schools *Sun Sil Lee Sohng and Richard Weatherley*	400
Chapter 34.	Needs Assessment in a School Setting *Lyndell R. Bleyer and Kathryn Joiner*	414
Chapter 35.	Differential Ethical Orientations to Practice and Research in School Social Work *Joseph R. Steiner and Thomas Pastorello*	428
Chapter 36.	Research in School Social Work: To Survive and Thrive *Christine Anlauf Sabatino and Elizabeth March Timberlake*	444

Appendix	Taxonomy of Terms and Jargon Which School Social Workers Encounter	461

Index   465

Preface

As in its initial edition, this book addresses the common elements of the role unique to school social work. Building on the knowledge, values, and skills common to all fields of social work practice, our focus is on school social work, its response to the needs of school children, and the forces that shape this response. Reflecting the living, growing edge of this complex field, this book is meant to be useful both to school social work practitioners and to students. It is adaptable to a variety of education formats. Bringing together theory and practice, research and policy development, and focusing on the school milieu, it is comprehensive. It looks forward to elements of school social work functions, which are still developing, within a field of practice whose contributions to the public schools are still only partially identified. As an edited book, it reflects the development of the field through the views and professional wisdom of those who are closest to its emerging development. One of the lasting contributions of the first edition was its balance of practice specificity within a clearly developed theoretical model. The second and this third edition have been constructed to reflect how the field of school social work is emerging through a complex relation of theory, practice, policy, and research. This emergent whole is greater than any of its parts. The elements of school social work practice, which we first outlined in 1982, have proved to be lasting components. The decades of 80s and 90s have affirmed and furthered this developmental process and evermore effectively demonstrated the contribution of school social work to the educational process. The third edition of *School Social Work: Practice and Research Perspectives* also looks forward to further developments in the field in the final decade of the twentieth century. The coming challenges to young people and to the field of education will require a more developed partnership between home and school and educational programs which focus on the interdependent relations between families and institutions.

School Social Work: Practice and Research Perspectives is designed for school social workers, educators, school social work students, and the general social work readership. This book's concentration on applied research material reflects the renewed interest in the relations between practice and research and makes it particularly useful to social work students and practitioners alike. The emphasis on the legal and organizational base will be valuable to school social workers and educators who are still struggling with the unique relationship between school social work and the institution of public education.

The two unifying concepts in the book are: school social work makes the educational process reasonably effective for vulnerable youngsters and their families; and the rich correspondence of the fields of social work and education creates a unique field of practice in social work, a field that stands on its own. These concepts and their practices have been developed consistently since the beginning of the twentieth century, but were most clearly enunciated by Florence Poole. Her conceptual clarity and the soundness of her approach to the school social worker's role can best be seen in the following passage from her work:

> At the present time we no longer see social work as a service appended to the schools. We see one of our most significant social institutions establishing social work as an integral part of its service, essential to the carrying out of its purpose. We recognize a clarity in the definition of the services as a social work service.

She saw this clarity and uniqueness of social work service coming from the societal function of the school.

> [The worker] must be able to determine which needs within the school can be appropriately met through school social work service. She must be able to develop a method of offering the service which will fit in with the general organization and structure of the school, but which is identifiable as one requiring social work knowledge and skill. She must be able to define the service and her contribution in such a way that the school personnel can accept it as a service which contributes to the major purpose of the school.[1]

Some changes have taken place over forty years in the societal mandate given the schools. Florence Poole's approach to practice was built upon the parameters of the mission of the school, the knowledge and skill of social work, and the worker's professional responsibility to determine what needs to be done and to develop an appropriate program for doing it. The "givens" of school social work have been the rich interaction between the mission of the school and the knowledge and skill of social work. Built upon these givens, the worker's professional judgment was the crucial ingredient in determining professional function. The issues that Florence Poole helped clarify so soundly are scarcely less important today: the legal and institu-

---

1. Florence Poole. An analysis of the characteristics of the school social worker. *Social Service Review* 23, December 1949, 454–59.

tional base for practice; the institution as a target for service; the interprofessional team cooperation; and the relation of all of these filtered through professional judgment to determine the resultant action taken by the worker.

The chapters in this book were chosen and arranged keeping in mind this theory base. Undoubtedly the shadows of the 1980s have pointed out the types of issues that will be faced by school social workers through the 1990s and well into the millennium. The challenges of family breakdown, addiction, AIDS, homelessness, and the struggle to find values that bring together the natural diversity of society will undoubtedly continue, and perhaps become more serious. They will be reflected in the social institution of education and in all of its processes. School social work will grow and develop in relation to each of these problems. Although this book cannot fully address the richness and diversity of school social work's response to these problems or channel its future development, the process through which this will happen will not significantly change: the interaction between the mission of the school, the needs of the school community and the knowledge, skill, and professional judgment of the school social worker.

School Social Work: Practice and Research Perspectives is divided into four sections. The first section, "General Perspectives on Theory and Practice in School Social Work," is concerned with general statements of practice theory, the school social worker's role, and the process of learning this role. The second section, "Mandated Foundations for Service Delivery," deals with the legal and value foundations of the education system. The third section, "School Social Work Practice and Service Delivery," develops the differing functions of the school social worker, the practice theory, and the literature base for these functions. This is the largest section in the book; its seventeen articles range in an ever-expanding framework to focus on the individual school child, on children in the classroom, on parents, on the multidisciplinary team, on the school itself as an organization, and on the community. Special attention is given to the social work functions that arise out of legal entitlement of children with disabilities to a free, appropriate public education. New topics, e.g., current political environment, trend toward inclusion, transition programs, developing consultation programs, conflict resolution, research evaluation as a means of effecting change, school needs assessment development, and a taxonomy of educational terms, focus on current issues in school social work. They are exemplars of application of theory in practice. In every case, the practice papers develop the unique components and possibilities of social work in an education setting.

The fourth section, "Research and Evaluation," deals with issues of accountability and knowledge development. Research is not treated as an enterprise for researchers within university walls, but, rather, as one for practicing school social workers. This practical approach to research is made possible by sharpening the focus through knowledge of the school social worker's role and accountability. The authors address the practitioner's potential contribution to research-based knowledge and ways in which this contribution can be made, as well as practice issues involved in doing research in a school setting.

The book comprises thirty-six chapters. Eight have been written especially for this edition; one is a reprint from material that was developed over the last four years and is new to the third edition. Most of the remaining articles were substantially rewritten to reflect the current state of knowledge in the field.

The third edition of *School Social Work: Practice and Research Perspectives* is a joint product of thirty-eight authors, including the three editors. Each of us acknowledges the patience and forbearance of our families, spouses, children, grandchildren, and friends, who made the endeavor possible. Two schools of social work, Loyola University of Chicago and the University of Illinois at Chicago, allowed the editors to employ significant parts of their work week to bring the book to completion. To this list we can only add the many readers of the first and second editions, who supported us in the belief that the content is worthwhile and usable, and who urged us to refine and develop these ideas in a third edition.

Robert Constable
John P. Flynn
Shirley McDonald

SECTION ONE
General Perspectives on Theory and Practice in School Social Work

CHAPTER 1

General Perspectives on Theory and Practice

Robert Constable
Professor, Loyola University of Chicago

Public education is a social movement scarcely a century-and a-half-old, conceived in the optimism of a young country and born in the still unrealized conviction that every human being had a right to the means to realize individual potential. The vision of Horace Mann and others would become clouded by the immense task of bringing the idea of democracy and equality to reality in a culturally diverse society where professed dedication to equal opportunity masks the realities of discrimination. The profundity of the charge to education in our society is succinctly expressed in the landmark case of *Brown v. Board of Education of Topeka, Kansas.*

> If education is a principal instrument in helping the child to adjust normally to his environment, it is doubtful that any child may reasonably be expected to succeed in life if he is denied the opportunity of an education. The opportunity of an education, where the state has undertaken to provide it to any, is a right which must be made available to all on equal terms.

It is perfectly consistent with the ideology of democracy that education should eventually be considered a civil right. However, the quotation lays bare a broader inherent mission for education. In a society based on individual achievement, education is necessary to adjust normally to an environment and to succeed in life. The court faced squarely what has in fact been the function of education for many years in an increasingly complex and individualistic society. The almost instinctive commitment and belief in education may seem naive to some observers. The manifest inequalities of our society seem to belie its promise. Nevertheless, the institution of education is closely linked to the energy and the dynamics of its society. In the twentieth century, the state of education is very much a reflection of the state of society.

SCHOOL SOCIAL WORK AS A FIELD OF PRACTICE

This chapter introduces the field of school social work practice and, in all of their diversity, the themes developed in the remainder of the book. Building on an historical analysis of the dynamic relation of social work with education, we will define the theoretical foundations for this unique and highly differentiated social work practice. Our analysis continues into the future, analyzing the broadening definition of schooling, the developing community of partnership of parents, students, and school personnel, and finally the mission of inclusion of all children, particularly those more vulnerable, in the common work of education with its promise for the present and future. This broadened definition and indeed mission of education, so well-adapted to postmodern conditions and challenges, invites the school social worker to participate in developing theory, practice, and research that is more differentiated to meet this challenge. This is the overriding purpose of the third edition of this book.

During the past eighty years of its existence, school social work as a field of practice has addressed the increasing societal expectations of education in a complex and modernized society. The problems confronted by the education institution have ranged from the presence of old and continuing problems—such as a large immigrant population, truancy, and the tragic waste of potential in emotional disturbances of childhood—to newer problems, such as school disruption, homelessness, drugs, the new immigrants, and AIDS. The diversity of problems the school social worker has dealt with historically, and in the present moment, is immense and ever-changing. There is an equal diversity of methodology: work with individuals, groups, families, and the education institution itself, and with each of the above in relation to the other. School social workers play many different roles, depending on the needs of the particular school community and what they have negotiated with school personnel as an appropriate focus. There are even some regional differences in the school social worker's role, although this appears to be diminishing.

Despite, indeed because of, the diversity of the school social work role, *School Social Work: Practice and Research Perspectives* addresses the common elements of this role that are unique to the field of practice. Social work education provides foundation theory and skills that are applicable to all fields of practice. A more complete understanding of practice has demanded that theory and methods also develop around fields, such as school social work. This introductory section deals with school social work practice and theory; the following three sections deal with mandated foundations of practice, applications of theory to practice, and research as an integral part of practice. In each section our focus is not on the almost unlimited diversity of applications of practice, but on the unchanging essentials of school social work practice itself. These unchanging essentials are derived from a deepened understanding of the dynamic mission of education in a diverse, pluralistic, and changing society, and the mission education carries out in relation to the mission and competence of social work.

The function of the social worker in the school and the mandate for public education were closely intertwined from the beginning. Given the mandate of education for equal educational opportunity for all in a democracy, the exclusion of any person from participation in the opportunity for an education is both a societal and individual problem. The passage of the mandatory school attendance laws at the turn of the century is credited with beginning a revolution in secondary school education. Schools began to broaden their curricula to accommodate a greater diversity of students. The first social workers in schools, in 1907 in New York City, were hired in recognition of the fact that conditions which prevented the school from carrying out its mandate were its legitimate concern (Costin, 1978; Meares, 1986). School social work would draw its legitimacy and its function from its capability to make education work for groups of children who could not otherwise participate. It has reflected in its history the evolving awareness in education and in society of groups of children where education has not been effective—the child of the immigrant, the impoverished, the economically and socially oppressed, the delinquent, the disturbed, and the disabled. It drew its function from the needs and eventually the rights of these groups as they interfaced with the institution of education and confronted the expectation that they should achieve to their fullest potential. In each circumstance, as school social workers defined their roles, there was a match of the social work perspective, its knowledge, values, and skills, and the missions and mandates of the school. Should school social work lose its connection with the broader mandates of the school and with these populations, it would quickly lose its place in the schools.

AN HISTORICAL ANALYSIS OF SCHOOL SOCIAL WORK

The first school social workers in Hartford, Connecticut and New York City carried with them in their models of practice the unresolved questions of the broader social work field, for example, the differences of Mary Richmond and Jane Addams in their respective visions of practice. The Hartford group, established at the same time as the New York group, became part of a psychological clinic and dealt with the psychosocial problems which children brought to school and which impeded their educational performance. They reflected Mary Richmond's approach to social work practice. In contrast, the New York group came from the settlement house tradition. They were primarily concerned with the environmental problems which prevented children of immigrants from using their opportunities for an education and reflected more the intellectual influence of Jane Addams than Mary Richmond. While these dichotomies still exist in the way many school social workers conceptualize their practice, for the most part they have long ago been resolved in practice, but without a language of theory.

The basic issues and possible future direction in the maturation of school social work practice and theory were laid out in the Milford Conference Report and later in the work of Harriett T. Bartlett who used the issues outlined in the Milford Report as the focus of her life work. It is worthwhile reviewing the issues and distinctions which came out of the Report and the following work of Harriet Bartlett, William E. Gordon, and others who have responded to these issues.

By the end of the 1920s a wide range of fields of practice had organized themselves based on different settings of school, hospital, court, settlement house, child welfare agency, family service agency, and so forth. Social work education followed an apprenticeship model, teaching what were perceived to be highly specialized and segmented fields of practice. The question of what all of these fields had in common became extremely important. In 1929, at the Milford Conference the basic distinction between fields of practice, the *specific* practice which emerged from these fields and the *generic* base for practice in these fields, that is, the knowledge, values, and skills of casework, was established. This distinction was extremely important for social work education and for the field of social work in that it allowed each field of practice to flourish and develop on a common foundation of casework. The emergent field was indeed diverse. Furthermore, no theory had emerged which could do more than offer a general orientation to helping. It still was up to the learner/practitioner and supervisor to find a way to relate theory to practice. This situation would continue in various permutations of the history of theory for more than half a century. The casework theory identified as *generic* would not refer to a concrete practice separable from its manifestation in different fields. It would be a foundation for a further differentiation of practice. This casework foundation did not focus simply on individuals, as later versions did, but on persons and family units together. It was much more than a simple base for methodology as it included knowledge and values, but it was still a conceptual foundation for specific practice. Freestanding practice took place in fields of practice which would develop from settings, but would also be reflected in academic and field preparation. Practice differentiation took place in relation to specific, identified fields, such as school social work, medical social work, psychiatric social work, child welfare, family services, and so on. Grace Marcus clarified the distinction between *generic* and *specific*:

> The term generic does not apply to any actual, concrete practice of an agency or field but refers to an essential, common property of casework knowledge, ideas and skills which caseworkers of every field must command if they are to perform adequately their specific jobs. As for our other troublemaking word, "specific", it refers to the form case work takes within the particular administra-

tive setting: it is the manifest use to which the generic store of knowledge has been put in meeting the particular purposes, problems, and conditions of the agency in dispensing its particular resources (Marcus, 1938-39).

The distinction was important, not only for its ability to permit professional differentiation on a common foundation, but also because later versions began to separate a body of method theory, such as casework, from its specific manifestation in fields of practice.

Considerable development of school social work as a field of practice had already taken place from the mid-1920s through 1955. This growth trailed off by 1955 with the consolidation of the National Association of Social Workers (NASW) which had merged then-existing organizations, representing different fields of practice, into one single professional organization. The *Bulletin* of the American Association of Visiting Teachers was merged into the new journal of the united social work profession, *Social Work*. The period of the 1950s and 1960s were centralizing years. School social work literature dropped off with the loss of the *Bulletin*. However, at that point, the major concern in the professional literature, in the profession and in social work education had to do with what social workers had in common, not what made them different in different sectors of the profession.

By the late 1950s, and through the following decade, Harriet Bartlett's and others' work built the foundation for a reorientation of methods and skills to a clarified professional perspective of the social worker. Bartlett (1959, 1970) worked with William E. Gordon (1964) to elaborate the concept of the transaction between individuals and their social environments into a common base and a fundamental beginning point for social work. Shifting the focus to the person-environment transaction, it was no longer assumed that the individual was the primary object of help. The development and diffusion of group and environmental interventions and the use of a range of helping modalities in richly differentiated areas of practice would make Gordon and Bartlett's work useful.

The parallel detachment of generic models of theory from specific practice led to a detachment of theory from practice as it took place in areas such as school social work. Dissatisfaction of practicing social workers in different areas with these centralizing tendencies which do not seem to reflect their own fields of practice led to a gradual redevelopment of literature, journals, and regional association of social workers in different fields of practice. School social workers, with large numbers of experienced practitioners who were encouraged to remain in direct practice by the structure and incentives of the school field, were some of the first and strongest advocates of this movement. With the development of state associations and then journals in the mid- to late-1970s the search for some balance between centralizing and standardizing thrusts and the thrust of specific practice began again. The profession in its development of theory revisited the balance of generic and specific as would each student as he or she would attempt to formulate a practice model which would match the conditions and demands they experience in a school social work field placement where practice is well developed.

At present school social work appears to be most developed in regions where it has been free to develop its distinct model of practice in relation to the mission, process, organizational and legal structure of *education* (as distinguished from a particular *school*).

The difficult demands on present day schools make school social work not a luxury, but a necessity, if schools are to accomplish their societal mandate. In special education, the rights of every child with disabilities to a free, appropriate, public education have been increasingly more explicitly defined over the past thirty years. The resulting role of the school social worker has shifted from a focus on youngsters who did not meet normative expectations to a focus on implementing individualized approaches to learning and influencing the norms themselves on behalf of youngsters. School social work service was a humane attempt on the school's part to help youngsters; it is now in many cases an entitlement, a civil right of every youngster with disabilities who needs this type of help in order to benefit from an education.

The societal expectations for the present day school have in turn demanded a more complete understanding and interpretation of the distinct contribution of the school social worker. It is no accident that a major portion of the literature has concerned itself with the parameters of the school social work role. The institution of education is not simply a backdrop for some type of standard practice. In the blending of social work with the mission of education, a distinct and different practice emerges. The characteristics of the education institution are as much an integral part of school social work practice as are the dynamics of the school community and the coping behaviors of the school's clientele.

A THEORETICAL INTRODUCTION TO SCHOOL SOCIAL WORK PRACTICE

The dynamic relation between school social work and education generates the purpose and scope of practice, and the techniques used. When this relationship is clarified, practice then becomes free to grow in the many different directions that are consistent with its purpose and the needs addressed at any given time. Social work education would develop beyond its focus on the foundation knowledge, values, and skills. Social work educators could educate students for the many ways in which a fundamental theoretical orientation is converted into practice and promote research into practice effectiveness. As with much other social work practice, without this dynamic relation of practice and theory in the development of a specific field of practice, practice would still develop, but it would be ahead of its theoretical base and without consciousness of its own rationale.

In order to develop a theoretical base for school social work, we first need to articulate a concept of the fundamental orientation of social work across all fields of practice. A major achievement of the past several decades has been that fundamental orientation to further professional differentiation has been clearly defined. This was done by a Task Force on Specialization of which Carol Meyer and William E. Gordon were members. The Task Force was jointly sponsored by NASW and the Council on Social Work Education:

> The fundamental zone of social work is where people and their environment are in exchange with each other. Social work historically has focused on the transaction zone where the exchange between people and the environment which impinge on them results in changes in both. Social work intervention aims at the coping capabilities of people and the demands and resources of their environment so that the transactions between them are helpful to both. Social work's concern extends to both the dysfunctional or deficient conditions at the juncture between people and their environment, and to the opportunities there for producing growth and improving the environment. It is the duality of focus on people and their environments that distinguishes social work from other professions (Garber, Gordon, Lewis, Meyer, and Williams 1979).

The duality of focus in the above statement involves the integration of *personal* tasks and *social* tasks in the characteristic perspective of social work. The personal and the social can be brought together with a concept of relational "work" as it takes place on an interpersonal level and in every institutional area of society. This relational work is done by client systems and institutions with the social worker as a coach for what is being done, moving person and systems toward reflective understanding and action. The work of the social worker is to facilitate the relational work taking place in the context of central human values. The practice of social work must *deal with values and in values*. It can never be comprised of pure techniques. Differentiation of social work is not based on different methods, but on a relation between method, social processes and human purposes and values.

Social workers practice in the arena where human beings work with others to perform life tasks and achieve fundamental human goods where achievement or provision is at risk and where human vulnerability or circumstances make it difficult for the outcome of the work to reflect the full worth of persons and their membership unit. Risk and vulnerability come for many people with the performance of life tasks and with life transitions. Vulnerability may come in utilizing personal and institutional resources for coping. Personal and developmental vulnerabilities are compounded by the inevitable deficiencies of institutions. As Paul Tillich put it in commenting on the philosophy social work in confronting the influx of refugees in 1940, legal and organizational arrangements will "inevitably fail" (Tillich, 1962). Changes and adjustments in persons and institutions in relation to each other become the province of the client system in concert with the social worker.

The social worker is a catalyst for the personal, familial, and institutional work to be done for the best match between resources and life tasks, in accord with the essential values of human nature. The practitioner is skillful to the extent that he or she can bring a person or a set of persons to work on a problem, in the process of that work to learn, to grow, and to change, while simultaneously influencing others in an altered transaction. Assessment of what is happening and what can happen between person and environment is the crucial skill in the change process. Personal and societal change comes from doing. Much of the catalytic effect of social work is through helping people to reflect and modify actions. This process of being a catalyst to action demands an assessment both of the process and of the limits of the possible within the situation in relation to purpose. Such assessment, used by the social worker, made available to the client, in fact jointly done with the client, objectifies for the social worker and for the client the nature of the tasks, the risks, the process and the persons. It thus begins to reconcile the subjective and objective aspects of helping, and indeed assessment could be seen as the master skill.

With this understanding of the practice of social work, how may we define school social work as a field of practice, related to other fields of social work practice, and to social work education and theory? The Task Force on Specialization defined specialization in relation to the institutions that society has evolved to meet common human needs. These needs and their institutions were seen to include:

The need for physical and mental well being—Health

The need to know and to learn—Education

The need for justice—Justice

The need for economic security—Work/public assistance

The need for self realization, intimacy and relationships—Family and child welfare (Garber, Gordon, Lewis, Meyer, and Williams, 1979)

In each area, the social worker works as a professional and mediates a relationship between persons and institutions. Fields of practice in social work grow around such transactions. Practice within each field of practice is defined by a *clientele*, a *point of entry*, a *social institution* with its institutional purposes and the *contribution of social work practice*, its knowledge, values, and appropriateness to the institutional purpose.

DEFINING THE PRACTICE OF SCHOOL SOCIAL WORK

How may we define the practice of school social work? The school social worker is concerned with every child whose coping capacity may not be well matched with the demands and resources of the educational institution. The mission of American education places a heavy responsibility on education, not merely to teach, but to prepare for the future, to be the vehicle for aspirations, not simply for children who may conform easily to external expectations, but for every child. There are responsibilities placed on the school, on the parent, and on the child to make the educational process work toward the maximal fulfillment of the potential for growth that resides within each child who goes to school.

The school social worker makes education possible for many children who otherwise would have difficulty coping with an educational process as it takes place and is defined in school. The close association with education is not a limitation or narrowing of focus; in reality, it broadens the functions of the school social worker with at least as explicit and developed a focus of the worker's efforts toward change in the school as an institution, as toward change in the child and family. Again, the changes in one will affect the other and vice versa. The nature of practice in school institutions brings social workers to accept fairly clearly a simultaneous dual focus on individuals and environments. The school provides a natural setting for social work intervention, a setting which calls forth a diversity of skills, working with individuals, neighborhoods, families, groups, teaching professionals, multi-disciplinary teams, and educational decision makers. Thus within this framework there is an integration point from theories of individual helping, groups, families, school teams and organizations, and communities. The role, with its foundation in social work values and the values of American education, with its consciousness of the natural strengths in the ecological position of the school with families and children, becomes the point of integration of theory from all of the above areas. They are all a part of the latent natural dynamics of the education process. The school social worker only needs to recognize them and work with them to create powerful tools for change processes, particularly when one sector of the ecosystem, the community, the school organization with its teams and with its classes, families, peer groups and school children, discover their own resources and the ways they can help each other accomplish goals. And the school social worker works with all of these systems, each in relation to each other. Versions of this role have existed since the earliest days of school social work and it is a magnificent mission!

To understand how change takes place we must understand the ecological position of the school. A social worker who operates in relation to the mandate of the school is part of an institution which, in the most profound way, mediates success and failure, belongingness and non-belongingness for children in our society. Only the family may have a more powerful influence. The centrality of the school to all natural ecosystems of childhood provides an opportunity for a unique blend of social work practice. The school is intertwined with just about everything which happens to children.

The image of self developed in the classroom, among other places, is carried throughout the person's lifetime. Problems outside of the school are reflected in the school environment. The ecological perspective is useful in developing an understanding of the child in school, in community, and in family precisely because it allows a focus on the interaction with the environment and not the person alone. Behavior in the classroom may be understood better by understanding its context, its relations to other settings, and the relation of these settings to each other. As one learns to develop an "ecological map" of the important transactions and relations between systems, one may build on the understanding developed. Choices can be made of where to intervene and, through an understanding of the developmental history of behaviors, *when* an intervention may be most effective.

Thus, theory for school social work practice grows out of this constant interaction of *clientele, point of entry, the institutional setting* and *social work knowledge,* and *values* in the context of human development and the education process. As it is practiced, such theory clarifies the meaning of its own activity and responds to changes in education and its mission, and the conditions and contexts of children's development. Thus theory grows from a self-conscious practice. Similarly, preparation for school social work practice grows from an increasingly more developed interaction between social work education and school social work as a field of practice. Much of the content of the professional degree is common to all fields of practice. This foundation content has well been defined in the Curriculum Policy Statement for Accreditation of School of Social Work (Council on Social Work Education, 1992). Following the distinction we have already made between generic and specific content, the learning of specific practice in the field of school social work would grow from the student's integration of a field experience in school social work, application of theory to specific tasks in the field, and generalization from the learning inherent in these tasks and from the learning processes of other students in the school social work concentration.

Building on generic social work knowledge and values, there are then three components of this learning of school social work practice. These three components are: a knowledge and theory base, integration of theory in practice, and the process of generalization from one's own and others experiences to a personal practice model in school social work.

The *knowledge and theory base* is drawn from:

1. *Knowledge of the educational institution,* its legal and sociological base as an expression of community values, knowledge of its organization, including financing; knowledge of the proposed parents to this institution; familiarity with and understanding of the language and concepts used by educators;

2. *Knowledge of programs for school children with special needs,* the philosophy and methodology of these programs, and the implications of different types of special education programs for pupil adjustment;
3. *Familiarity with principles of curriculum development* and teaching methods; understanding of the differential effect of teaching styles on children; ability to contribute helpfully as a social worker in a consultative relationship with teachers and school administrators;
4. Deepened *understanding of the nature of developmental crises* and children's responses to stress; understanding of familial, institutional, and community dynamics in relation to the behavior of children.

Integration of theory in practice would take place based on the practicum and course content. Again, building on generic practice theory, the student's integration of theory in practice should result in the following general outcomes:

1. *The ability to operate as a practitioner in the complex organization of the school* with parents, with teachers, and with school children, in carrying out a given intervention plan. The student should have tested experience working in the context of professional difference, familiarity with the role difference of other specialists, and ability to collaborate and communicate in a purposeful way.
2. *The ability to participate as a social worker in planning efforts* geared toward curriculum and program development; the ability to initiate planning efforts when necessary and provide professionally appropriate supervision and consultation; the ability to communicate regarding school needs from one's professional point of view to the community.

The integration of theory in practice and the process of generalization from one's own experience and that of their students into a *personal practice model* would take place through an integrative seminar in school which is closely related to the *field experience* and through the *field experience* itself.

SCHOOL SOCIAL WORK: TOWARD THE MILLENNIUM

Having defined the parameters of school social work as a field of practice, let us turn our analysis to the needs of the families and children in schools in the current postmodern society. As one coeditor has experienced in developing school social work in Lithuania, school social work grows in any place where families are reshaping the relational textures of their worlds, and where schools have become the essential community institution in the ecosystems of childhood, in the transition to young adulthood and in the world of work. While conditions may differ in the developed and the developing worlds, the conditions that families, schools, and children are facing have a certain similarity. Let us sketch out a few of these:

1. Aspirations continue to grow that families, society, and children themselves be included in education as a normalized process involving all students at different levels of need and capability and in different educational processes. This is a continuation of a trend with roots in the last century, still incomplete in the developed world and beginning in the developing world, where in some regions segregation of persons with different capabilities has been the norm. School reform experience in the United States carries with it increased expectations of performance by children who, in fact, are more at risk and often have fewer institutional, community, and family supports than their more advantaged peers (Mintzies and Hare, 1985).
2. The protections normally associated with childhood appear to be declining as government policies shift toward a market philosophy. This is discussed in the context of the United States in the final chapter of this book. The implications are that children more and more are living in worlds where societies permit and even passively construct increasingly greater risks. High rates of suicide, addiction, violence to and among children, early pregnancy, AIDS, and early exposure to the job market through economic necessity are among the risks which are passively constructed through the decline of support for protective institutions, such as family and school, and policies which address the situation of young people and young families. The inevitable and necessary response to such a constructed vacuum of policy in support of families and children would have to be a new construction of families and the institutions which assist families in carrying out their tasks. School social workers have much to contribute to this movement when it happens.
3. In the meantime, school social workers work at the crucial junction points in the ecosystems of childhood and transitional young adulthood to strengthen families and schools, burdened by the increases in risk and expectation discussed above. To facilitate this crucial work, a new model of school social work based on partnership of schools and families needs to develop based on a conception of school as a community of children and families and school personnel. Parents and teachers would work as a team, though with different roles. There would be a more balanced relation of interests on the part of home and school.

SCHOOL CONCEIVED OF AS A COMMUNITY OF FAMILIES AND SCHOOL PERSONNEL

Both concepts of partnership, influencing policy and being an educator of one's own child, depend on a radically different picture of school. No longer a building, nor simply a collection of classrooms with teachers and pupils working together, school is conceptualized as *a community of families and school personnel engaged in the education process.* The school community, no longer simply bounded by geography, comprises those who engage in the education process. As in any community, there are all sorts of varied concrete roles. People fit into such communities in very different ways. Parents and families are members through their children; but this membership needs to include other facilitative and policymaking involvements. Teachers and other school personnel are members with a complex accountability to parents, children, and the expectations of the broader community. The school social worker focuses on making education work to the fullest extent, drawing on each person's possible capacities. And so school social workers work with parents, teachers, pupils, and administrators on behalf of vulnerable children, or groups of children at risk. The success of the process is dependent upon the collective and individual involvement of parents as community, and whether directly or indirectly, the school social worker assists to make the school operate as a real community so that personal, familial, and community resources can be discovered and used for children's developmental needs.

In the process of helping schools to develop a broader concept of their own community, the social work role need not be discovered anew. There are bodies of experience and theory which can be drawn upon and adapted to this new and evolving focus. The traditional approach of connecting children with networks of community services has been evident from the earliest years of social work in schools. Beginning in the late 1960s, the parent involvement experiences through the War on Poverty and Project Headstart Program added a new dimension to the relationship. More recently, there are the parent-sponsored school movements of the 1970s and 1980s. Each movement found methodology to develop a "school-community", although goals differed according to the conceptions of the times.

FROM SPANNING BOUNDARIES TO ORGANIZING SCHOOL COMMUNITIES

As long as it was taken for granted that home would be isolated from school, the school social worker's role has historically been to span the boundaries between home and school as expeditiously as possible and this has taken place since the origins of public education. Schools have generally operated in relative isolation from their constituent families, protecting their functions from "interference" from the other. This isolation is, of course, counterproductive in situations of individual and family vulnerability or difficulty in coping, and thus a need for someone such as the school social worker to span these boundaries is created. Certainly, in some cases these boundaries have been challenged by school social workers and parents. From their conception, school is conceived as a *community* of families with teachers and parents in a partnership with each other, for socialization of their children, with both similar and different functions. The numerous and ongoing experiments with parent-sponsored schools are evidence of the popularity of the concept. Yet the conception of school as a community of parents, teachers, and children is a major departure from conventional thinking and practice. It represents the logical next step in responding to the defined goals and problems of American education.

This broadened concept of school social work function is capable of being adapted in different ways to different school and community situations. With school social workers developing agreements about their role in school communities, and as they clarify their services to these communities, they are in the process defining the school community. This concept is developed in a general way in the first section, with an overview of theory, and in the following sections of the book through the research functions of the school social worker in developing and documenting what is done. The role of the school social worker as it develops over the coming decades in this community of school and families is an appropriate and necessary response to the dilemmas of greater risks and expectations placed on children, shifts in resources and the need for new definitions of community and new policies more in the interest of children.

REFERENCES

Bartlett, H. 1959. "The generic-specific concept in social work education and practice," in Alfred E. Kahn, Issues in American social work. New York. Columbia University Press.

Bartlett, H. 1970. The common base of social work practice. New York. National Association of Social Workers.

Brown v. Board of Education, Topeka, KS. 347 US 483 (1954).

Council on Social Work Education. 1992. Curriculum policy statement for accreditation of school social work. Alexandria, VA. Council on Social Work Education.

Gordon, W.A., Lewis, H., Garber, R., Meyer, C., and Williams, C. 1979. "Specialization in the social work profession." National Association of Social Workers Document 79-310-08. Washington, D.C.

Marcus, G. 1938–39. "The generic and specific in social casework: recent developments in our thinking." *News-letter*. American Association of Psychiatric Social Workers, vol. 3/4.

Mintzies, P., and Hare, I. 1985. The human factor: a key to excellence in education. Washington, D.C. National Association of Social Workers.

Tillich, P. 1962. "The philosophy of social work." Social Service Review. 36, 1 (March).

CHAPTER 2

The Contribution of Social Workers to Schooling—Revisited*

Paula Allen-Meares
Professor and Dean, School of Social Work, University of Michigan;
Chair, NASW Communication Committee

INTRODUCTION

Many educators are unfamiliar with the services provided by social workers employed in the school setting. The purpose of this chapter is to describe the history of the service and those who shaped it, and its values and contribution to schooling with particular reference to entry level tasks required for professional practice. Relevant literature in education and social work is also reviewed.

The breadth and diversity of school social work is illustrated, to some degree, in the publication *Achieving Educational Excellence for Children at Risk* (Hawkins, 1987), which describes the goals and services offered by the profession. Examples include the provision of group work to gifted children, transitional programming for disabled children, forming partnerships with families of the disabled, early intervention to prevent truancy, a special project to prevent adolescent suicide, ways to facilitate racial integration, and expanding schooling to involve multicultural communities. A review of the history of school social work highlights its flexibility and adaptability as a field of practice.

HISTORICAL DEVELOPMENT OF SOCIAL WORK SERVICES IN SCHOOLS

Social work services in schools grew out of concern for underprivileged pupils. The service began during the school year of 1906–1907, indepen-

---

*SOURCE: *Urban Education*, 22(4), January 1988, 401–312. © 1988. Paula Meares. Reprinted by permission of Sage Publications, Inc. Adapted for this publication.

dently, in New York City, Boston, and Hartford. In New York City, settlement workers from Hartley House and Greenwich House thought that it was necessary to know the teachers of children who came to the settlements, so they assigned two workers to visit schools and homes in order to work more closely with schools and community groups to promote understanding and communication (Allen-Meares et al., 1986). In Boston, the Women's Education Association placed visiting teachers in the schools to foster harmony between school and home and facilitate the children's education.

The Psychological Clinic in Hartford initiated the first visiting teachers program (today frequently referred to as school social workers) in that area. It was the function of the visiting teacher to assist the psychologist to secure family and developmental histories of children and to implement the clinic's treatment recommendation (Lide, 1959). The first board of education to initiate and finance a visiting teachers program was in Rochester, New York, in 1913. The board of education at that time stated:

> This is the first step in an attempt to meet a need that the school system has been conscious of for some time. It is an undisputed fact that in the environment outside of school are to be found forces that will often thwart the school in its endeavors. The appointment of visiting teachers is an attempt on the part of the school to meet its responsibilities for the whole welfare of the child ... and to maximize cooperation between the home and the school (Lide, 1959: 108).

During the decades that followed, school social workers grew in number and the focus of the service changed in response to important influences of the times. For example, one significant influence in the field's early development was the passage of compulsory school attendance laws, which grew out of the concern for the illiteracy of immigrant children and brought needed attention to the child's right to at least a minimum education. The lack of effective enforcement of the school attendance laws led to such studies as that of Abbott and Breckinridge (1917) on nonattendance in Chicago schools. Their findings supported the need for attendance officers (another term to designate the school social worker) who understood the social ills of the community—poverty, ill health, and lack of secure family income—and their effects on attendance. Attendance workers played an important role, clarifying and sensitizing school personnel to the effects that children's out-of-school lives had on them. Thus the principal activity of the school social worker, at that time, was one of home-school-community liaison.

Oppenheimer (1925) carried out a study to obtain a detailed list of school social work tasks. The study involved the analysis of 300 case reports made by school social workers or visiting teachers, resulting in a list of 32 core functions. An appraisal of the nature of these tasks confirmed the school-family-community liaison as the primary role of these practitioners. Oppenheimer also concluded that the most important function of the school social workers was to aid in the reorganization of school administration and practices by supplying evidence of unfavorable conditions that underlie pupils' school difficulties and by pointing out needed changes.

As a result of the mental hygiene movement, the services expanded in the 1920s to include a therapeutic role (Lide, 1959). There was increasing interest on the part of the school social worker to understand behavior problems of pupils and techniques to prevent social maladjustment.

During the 1930s, the role of attendance officers gradually took on a new dimension: individual work with children and their families, later referred to as social casework. With the advent of the Great Depression, the provision of food, shelter, clothing, and emotional support for troubled pupils occupied much of the school social workers' attention. In addition, there were those at the time who saw the sources of problems not as inherent in the personality of the troubled pupil, but the result of a faulty school curriculum and policies (Reynolds, 1935).

During the 1940s to 1960s, home-school liaison and the attendance officer's role were essentially replaced by social casework. No longer would social change and neighborhood conditions be seen as targets of intervention.

The 1960s brought still another change in goals and methods of school social work practice (Sarri and Maple, 1972). Public schools were under attack. Several studies of public education documented adverse school policies. It was claimed that inequality of educational opportunity existed as a result of segregation; that public schools were reinforcing the myth that minority children and pupils from low-income backgrounds could not perform as well as their middle-class counterparts; and that the school was essentially a repressive institution (Kerner Report, 1968). Some parents claimed they felt alienated from the school. Simultaneously, the literature on school social work was advocating group work with parents and students, broader approaches to practice, drawing upon a social systems perspective, and methods and demonstration projects to bring the school and community closer together to facilitate the educational process (Sarri and Maple, 1972). The school was essentially singled out for the violence of the 1960s because it had failed to educate minority pupils.

For social work services in the schools, the 1970s were a time of great expansion. The numbers of programs and workers across the United States increased. There was an increased emphasis on family, community, and teaming with other school personnel, and broader models were encouraged (Alderson, 1972). One model, widely discussed in the literature and intended to address the problems of securing equal educational opportunity for all pupils, was the school-community-pupil relations model (Costin, 1975). This model emphasized the complexities of the interactions among students, the school, and the community. Its primary goal was to bring about change in the interaction of this triad and thus to modify to some extent those harmful school policies and practices and community conditions that undermined schooling.

Influences on the school social worker role have been explored by Constable, Flynn, and McDonald (1991), who found that litigation, federal legislation, and other influences have a profound impact on the activities of school social workers. Factors that have played a role include: legislation such as the Education for All Handicapped Children Act, 1975; changes in the theoretical perspective grounding social work practice; an increased emphasis placed on ecological and social systems approaches; and pressures from the social work profession to evaluate outcomes and to be accountable.

As the school setting became the institution targeted to rectify deprivation in the home, community, and family, once more its strategic position in the network of human services was recognized. A content analysis of social work literature over the period 1968–1978 found that school social workers were once again expanding their focus (Allen-Meares and Lane, 1982). Though more attention was given to children with disabling conditions, the liaison role was emphasized, as well as the role of promoting change in adverse school policies and practice. Consultation, teaming, and collaborative activities suggested a move away from long-term clinical treatment to an approach that had breadth in terms of tasks, and that was responsive to changing needs and conditions.

As social conditions (e.g., poverty, unemployment, and so forth) continued to place children and their families at greater risk and the federal government saw legislation as the mechanism to best address various groups who needed educational assistance, school social workers grew in number and so did their state associations. In response to this growth, the National Association of Social Workers held special school social work conferences as part of its annual meeting. A review of conference programs reaffirmed the expansion of the service and its resiliency to respond to changing needs. These special conferences focused on work with infants, the role of the school social worker in early childhood special education, school reform, how school social workers could facilitate a multicultural school environment, and social work practice with new populations (e.g., chemically exposed infants, youth infected with AIDS, and those who were homeless).

The debate about the quality of education from the report of the National Commission on Excellence in Education (1983) and the national cry to reform schooling led to a national study of state offices of education to identify reform initiatives to achieve excellence as well as conditions that were barriers to academic excellence (Allen-Meares, 1987). Allen-Meares (1987) maintained that the impetus for the study also evolved from concern about the erosion of federal support for social welfare programs for vulnerable children and their families. At the time, the call for school reform and improvement in the achievement of pupils ignored the consequences of racism, sexism, inadequate health care, poverty, and economic deprivation on the physical, emotional, psychological, and intellectual growth of children and adolescents. The study found that excellence was defined by having an effective school administrator; maintaining high expectations for students and staff; involving students in learning; and eradicating school problems. Reform initiates were: appointment of blue ribbon committees; pressure on the legislature to increase funding; an increase in scholastic requirements for teachers and pupils; and more attention to math and science. Barriers to excellence in education were: parental apathy, poverty, child abuse and neglect, family crisis; poor parenting skills; economic deprivation; poor parent-teacher relationships; lack of drop-out prevention programs and team work among school personnel; and lack of financial resources. It was clear that school social workers could play a variety of direct practice roles to minimize the impact of such barriers; however, systemic change was also in order.

During this time, the number of state associations of school social workers increased. Today there are 25 state associations, and many hold annual conferences and publish independent newsletters. Twenty state NASW chapters now have school social work committees. There are also four regional councils: the Midwest School Social Work Council; the Southern School Social Work Council; the Western Alliance of School Social Workers; and the Northeastern Coalition. In 1994, spearheaded by the school social work leadership, a School Social Work Association of America formed, independent of NASW. These state, regional, and national professional associations provide their members with educational opportunities for professional growth through the provision of yearly workshops, job networks, continuing education credit, and legislative advocacy. There are currently 12,000–15,000 school social workers nationally.

Also in 1994, NASW launched school social work as the first practice section. During the period of 1980 until the present, NASW has taken an active role in changing the credentialing requirements for school social workers. Many states upgraded their credentialing standards for school personnel as a part of their efforts to reform schooling. For example, in Illinois, social work practitioners seeking employment in the public schools must complete special graduate school social work courses and take two exams (one that tests knowledge of such areas as educational legislation, exceptional children, school code, models of school social work practice, social work values, ethics, and interventions, and another exam which tests for basic skills competencies, in reading, math, and English).

In anticipation of the proliferation of school social work credentialing exams, NASW, the Educational Testing Service in Princeton, New Jersey, and Allen-Meares developed the first national school social work credential examination. The exam was first administered in 1992. The content of the exam was developed from data obtained from a national sample of school social work practitioners (Allen-Meares, 1994). This study had essentially four purposes:

1. To collect information about the demographic and organizational contexts in which school social workers work;
2. To identify the most important job dimensions that school social workers must be able to perform as they begin their practice;
3. To ascertain whether these job dimensions correlate positively or negatively in terms of frequency performed; and
4. To identify and compare tasks school social workers prefer to perform and those that are mandated.

Preferred and Mandated Tasks

Respondents to the survey considered the following tasks in rank order as most important: 1) *administrative and professional tasks,* 2) *home-school liaison,* 3) *educational counseling with children,* 4) *facilitating and advocating families' use of community resources,* and 5) *leadership and policy-making.* The size of the employing school district significantly influenced the importance given to some tasks. An analysis of tasks contained in each job dimension was conducted to differentiate tasks that were mandated from those that were preferred. Mandated tasks would be to make home visits or to refer children and their families for service. Tasks school social workers preferred to perform would be to act as advocate with community agencies, to help new staff understand diversity, or to help develop prevention programs. Further analysis of these data led the researcher to conclude that the practice of school social work is influenced by a number of contextual variables that are beyond the control of the practitioner. Large caseloads, expectations by supervisors and administrators, multi-building assignments and too few workers were identified as variables that prevented practitioners from embracing their preferred tasks.

In 1994, known as the Year of Education Reform, school social workers were once more included in a major piece of legislation—Goals 2000: Educate America Act, P.L.102-227. This act was signed into law on March 31, 1994. The intent of the act is to promote research, consensus building, and systemic change to ensure quality of educational opportunities for all students.

This major piece of legislation targets reform initiatives particular to schools, but major social and technological-economic changes in the broader society may prevent it from achieving equity in educational opportunity. For example, an increasing number of children and female-headed households live in poverty; technological advancements require a more sophisticated labor force; reform in welfare and health care are still topics of debate

TABLE 1 Social Work Values

Social Work Values	Applications to Social Work in Schools
1. Recognition of the worth and dignity of each human being	1. Each pupil is valued as an individual regardless of any unique characteristic
2. The right to self-determination or self-realization	2. Each pupil should be allowed to share in the learning process
3. Respect for individual potential and support for an individual's aspirations to attain it	3. Individual differences (including differences in rate of learning) should be recognized; intervention should be aimed at supporting pupils' education goals
4. The right of each individual to be different from every other and to be accorded respect for those differences	4. Each child, regardless of race and socioeconomic characteristics, has a right to equal treatment in the school

SOURCE: Adapted from Allen-Meares et al. (1986)

without firm proposals for real change; there is a call for more community control of schools; and violence in the community and in schools is at an all-time high.

SOCIAL WORK VALUES

It can be readily seen from this brief account of historical development that the goals of the school social work profession have expanded greatly since its modest beginnings at the turn of the century. Examples of primary values of the social work profession and their applications in school social work practices are shown in Table 1.

Examples of other values compatible with those of the profession as a whole but having special relevance to school social work are (1) children are entitled to equal educational opportunities and to learning experiences adapted to their individual needs and (2) the process of education should not only provide the child with tools for future learning and skills to use in earning a living, but provide essential ingredients contributing to the child's positive mental health (Allen-Meares et al., 1986).

FUTURE DIRECTIONS AND CHALLENGES

Questions about the quality of schooling, reduced tax base, the increased demand on schools to serve a more diverse student population, increased poverty among children and families, and violence will challenge this field of practice to think critically and differently about school social work service delivery. For the twenty-first century, the integration of school social work and community services will be essential. It is clear that schools cannot respond to the social, emotional, and educational needs of all their pupils. The capacity of the community to devote its resources to enhance the availability and scope of social supports will be a decisive factor in the health and functioning of its children and families. Thus, collaboration between the different service delivery systems within the school, as well as those external to it, will also be essential.

What does this mean for school social work services? There will be an increased emphasis on developing a service delivery system involving collaboration between schools and community agencies both private and public. Clearly, practitioners will need to rethink and restructure their roles within the school. The challenge is to redefine school social work to meet such a major shift in our society.

REFERENCES

Abbott, E. and Breckenridge, S. 1917. *Truancy and non-attendance in the Chicago schools: A study of the social aspects of compulsory education and child labor legislation of Illinois.* Chicago: University of Chicago Press.

Alderson, J. 1972. Models of school social work practice. In R. Sarri and F. Maple (eds). *School in the community.* Washington, DC: National Association of Social Workers.

Allen-Meares, P. and Lane, B. 1982. A content analysis of school social work literature: 1968–1978. In R. Constable and J. Flynn (eds.). *School social work: Practice and research perspectives.* Homewood, IL: Dorsey Press. 39–49.

Allen-Meares, P., Washington, R.O., and Welsh, B. 1986. *Social work services in schools.* Englewood Cliffs, NJ: Prentice-Hall.

Allen-Meares, P. 1987. A national study of educational reform: Social work practice in schools. *Children and Youth Services Review* 9(3):207–19.

Allen-Meares, P. 1994. Social work services in schools: A national study. *Social Work* 39(4):560–67.

Constable, R., Flynn, J., and McDonald, S., (eds). 1991. *School social work: Practice and research perspectives.* Chicago, IL. Lyceum Books, Inc.

Costin, L. 1975. School social work practice: A new model. *Social Work* 20 (21): 135–39.

Education for All Handicapped Children Act. 1975. P.L. 94–142.

Goals 2000: Educate America Act. 1994. P.L. 103–227.

Hawkins, M. (ed.). 1987. *Achieving educational excellence for children at risk.* Washington, DC: National Association of Social Workers.

Kerner Report. 1968. The National Advisory Committee on Civil Disorder. Washington, DC: Government Printing Office.

Lide, P. 1959. "A study of historical influences of major importance in determining the present function of the school social worker." In G. Lee (ed.). *Helping the troubled school child in school social work, 1935–1955.* Washington, D.C. National Association of Social Workers.

National Commission on Excellence in Education. 1983. *A nation at risk: The imperative for educational reform.* Washington, DC: Government Printing Office.

Oppenheimer, J. 1925. *The visiting teacher movement, with special reference to administrative relationships.* 2nd ed. NY: Joint Committee on Methods of Preventing Delinquency.

Reynolds, B. 1935. "Social casework: What is it? What is its place in the world today?" *Family* 16 (December): 238.

Sarri, S. and Maple, F. (eds.). 1972. *School in the community.* Washington, D.C. National Association of Social Workers.

CHAPTER 3
An Ecological Perspective on Social Work in the Schools

Carel B. Germain
Emerita Professor of Social Work, School of Social Work,
University of Connecticut

One of the most difficult tasks for all of social work practice is to define its distinctiveness—what distinguishes the social worker from other professional helpers. In fact, this is not even a new task. In 1915 Abraham Flexner was invited to speak before the National Conference of Charities and Corrections. He was the social scientist who modernized medical education in this country, bringing it up from the depths of inadequate proprietary schools and into the universities. Because of his achievement and his resulting status in the arena of professional education, Flexner's appearance at the national conference was eagerly awaited. He would be speaking to an occupational group whose members called themselves social workers and who aspired to professional status. Imagine the consternation, then, as the speaker informed his audience that, indeed, they were not a profession nor could they reasonably aspire to becoming one because they did not have a distinctive professional knowledge base or skills that were transmissible (Flexner, 1915).

Furthermore, and this must have been the crowning blow, their only function was a mediating one for linking up their clients to other professions, and invoking their power in solving the client's problem. The impact on the audience can be sensed in the responses of those present as preserved in the conference proceedings. But the reponses echoed down the years as social work continually tried to define its distinctiveness and to establish its professional status. In particular, the casework segment devoted time, energy, and thought to developing a distinctive knowledge and value base and distinctive skills which then became confused with those of other pro-

---

SOURCE: Adapted from a paper presented at the New York State Conference of School Social Workers, White Plains, New York, May 22, 1978.

fessions on whom they were patterned, especially psychiatry. The efforts left undeveloped until the present day what might have been a truly distinctive function. Flexner's indictment of the mediating function, and Mary Richmond's refusal (1917) to accept it as a social work function, are particularly ironic in today's world. It is clear that what is needed in this dehumanized and depersonalized bureaucratic society is a profession that mediates between people in need—particularly the poor and other powerless groups such as children and the aged—and the institutions of society set up to serve them. Ironic, because this increasingly important function so ably performed by social work, does indeed rest upon an identifiable and transmissible base of knowledge, values, and skill.

In some ways, school social work followed the same historical trends of the larger professional group. Originally conceived as a response to problems of truancy created by free, compulsory public education, school social work was expected to uncover and to mitigate neighborhood and school conditions that gave rise to truancy (Costin, 1969). For many historical reasons, school social work, by the 1930s, had narrowed its focus to a casework service for children who were defined by the school as having emotional and behavioral disturbances attributable to early family experiences. The number of children thus served was necessarily small; there was little impact on adverse school structures and practices, and the service itself tended to become stigmatized.

By the 1960s and 70s, however, schools and school social work faced new imperatives generated by new social forces. The numbers of alienated pupils and high school dropouts increased. The school's ability to teach fundamental skills to many children declined, especially those pupils whose lifestyles and languages differed from the middle-class orientation of the school. Overt conflict between communities and schools for control of educational processes increased. The pain and stress accompanying the struggle for desegregation, the worry that schools might actually be undermining the creativity and spontaneity of all pupils, and the recognition that schools solidified the inequities of social class became salient forces in the field of school social work (Rist, 1970). In addition, every profession is now under attack on issues of effectiveness, ethical practice, and accountability. Insistence on public control of all professions is mounting and many of the consequent reforms, such as equal educational opportunities for the disabled, are long overdue. These reforms do pose new issues of formal and informal labeling, confidentiality, and even service provisions when so much time is required by the new accountability procedures and forms.

THE DUAL FUNCTION OF SOCIAL WORK

The profession's struggle for distinctiveness, that began in 1915, also influenced the development of school social work within this set of contemporary forces. William Gordon (1969) and Harriett Bartlett (1970), under the auspices of NASW, constructed a definition of social work practice that suggests social work's uniqueness lies in its location in the interface area where people's coping patterns interact with the qualities of their impinging environment. Thus, the social worker's function is to work in that interface with the person, the environment, or both, in order to secure a better match between coping needs and environmental requirements and people's coping abilities. This definition means that the social worker—in any field of practice—has a dual and simultaneous function: to strengthen people's coping patterns and their growth potential on the one hand, and to improve the quality of the impinging environment on the other. This interface position does not negate the importance of the personality and its motivational, emotional, cognitive, and sensory-perceptual elements. But neither does it overlook the complexity of the environment and its interacting physical, social, and cultural elements. Rather, it takes both into account simultaneously and seeks to improve the transactions between them. Thus the old polarity between social workers who favor social action, and social workers who favor service to people can become, instead, a complementarity of two essential functions. This view of professional purpose can correct the imperfections in our commitment to person-situation which are apparent whenever we overlook one or the other. Most often, it is the situation that is overlooked, perhaps because it is the more difficult of the two to change.

An ecological metaphor for practice can respond to this dual function in a way that the traditional medical or disease metaphor cannot do (Germain, 1979). Ecology is the science of organism-environment relations. It leads to a view of person and environment as a unitary, interacting system in which each constantly affects and shapes the other. This view directs our professional attention to the whole, so that we attend to the complexities of the environment just as we attend to the complexities of the person, developing skills for intervening with each and with their transactions. The ecological metaphor also shifts us from an illness orientation to a health orientation, and to engaging the progressive forces in people and situational assets, and effecting the removal of environmental obstacles to growth and adaptive functioning.

Most school social workers have been practicing in just this way, conceiving their social purpose to be helping children develop age-appropriate social competence, and influencing the school to be more responsive to the needs of the children. William Schwartz (1971) characterizes this as helping the children reach out to the school and helping the school reach out to the children since each needs the other. Perhaps the reason that school social workers seem to be ahead of other sectors of practice in fulfilling the distinctive dual function of social work is because the school is a real-life ecological unit, beyond the realm of metaphor or analogy. The child clearly is in intimate interaction with the school, second in intensity only to the interaction of the child and family. But the school social worker literally is located at the interface where school and child transact, in a way that the family agency social worker or child welfare social worker, for example, can never be located with respect to the child-family transactions.

Actually, the school social worker stands at the interface not only of child and school, but family and school, and community and school. Thus, s/he is in a position to help child, parents, and community develop social competence and, at the same time, to help increase the school's responsiveness to the needs and aspirations of children, parents, and community. Social competence as a human attribute or achievement is tied to ideas of self-esteem and identity. It includes effectiveness with respect to knowing and deciding when to take action in the environment, as opposed to a passive orientation to life and its events and processes. It is tied also to relative autonomy from internal pressures and external demands, while maintaining relatedness to other human beings, to the world of nature, and to one's own internal needs (Germain, 1978). This appears to be a nonnormative set of ideas fitting any cultural context in any historical era, for it is the culture and the times that define the actual substance of such competence.

Robert White (1959) speaks of competence as the human being's innate drive to have an effect on the environment. Piaget refers to competence when he describes how children's intellects develop through opportunities to take action upon the environment, assimilating and accommodating the external into internal cognitive structures (Evans, 1973). The ego psychologists, in tracing the development of integrated ego functioning, are describing competence. Erikson's notion (1959) of school children's tasks of industry is a case in point. How children deal with the task depends, in part, on what they bring to it, on how they handled the earlier tasks of trust, autonomy, and initiative, and on what their physical states provide in health, vigor, stature, coordination, and so on. It will also depend on their cognitive, sensory-perceptual, and motivational equipment for adaptation and coping. But, and this is the value of Erikson's formulation for social work, their ability to achieve competence will also depend upon the qualities of the impinging social and physical environments, particularly the family, the school, and the community. These environments must provide the growth-inducing conditions and the right stimuli at the right time and in the right amount if children are to achieve the tasks involved in establishing industry and competence. Otherwise, they may be left with residues of inferiority—social, intellectual, physical, or emotional inferiority—that may affect their ability to handle later tasks. Three examples of interface work on competence follow: First, an example from the child-school interface:

> Jim, age 13, a newcomer in a middle school, was referred to the social worker. He had no friends, rebuffed the other boys, and didn't return teachers' greetings. He often seemed angry in class, and he was failing several subjects. Yet,

he had been an average student in elementary schools and had had friends and interests. During our first few interviews there was little mutuality, and I learned the meaning of patience all over again. Then one day Jim told me the family secret that his mother is an alcoholic. He was very angry with her for drinking and for the way she treated him as a baby when she was drunk. He was afraid to make new friends and of bringing them to the house for fear he might divulge the secret. His interest in school work had all but disappeared. Mother had given Jim this permission to talk freely, which I interpreted as her call for help. I saw her alone, and with my encouragement she began attending AA. Soon Jim expressed interest in catching up at school, and we worked out a tutoring plan that seemed to go well. Yet, his teachers were not recognizing his efforts and his changed motivation and were treating him with seeming dislike and annoyance. This stimulated his anger, which then provoked their further negative responses. Jim's problems, though not caused initially by the school, were now being perpetuated by school staff. I asked the principal to call a conference in which I explained to his teachers that Jim had realistic problems in his family that were being handled. I wanted them to see that Jim had real courage in tackling his problems—first alone and now with help. He was trying hard, but marked change will require more time and patience. At the end, one teacher commented she had not really thought of Jim with such sympathy before. Jim's grades are now improving, the teachers' attitudes toward Jim and his attitudes toward them are more positive. He made several friends and was busy with them during the past four Saturdays. He also told me his mother drank only once over the last month, and my impression is that he is less involved now in his mother's behavior. His whole bearing reflects his returning self-esteem, sense of competence, and even autonomy (Shelling, n.d.).

Second, an example from the parent-school interface:

> The social worker in an inner city school in Brooklyn was concerned about poor relations between parents and the school which compounded the problems children were having in school. She persuaded the principal to turn over an unused room as a parents' drop-in lounge for those mothers bringing their small children to school each morning. She decorated it with plants and had coffee and doughnuts ready. She made each mother feel welcome and valued, and soon had a number of regulars who looked forward to the respite, the warmth, and attention given them by the school. After a bit she was able to engage two separate groups in meeting to talk to their shared needs and tasks as single parents living on limited budgets in a harsh environment. In the process, the mothers developed a mutual aid system, exchanging ideas, resources, and social support. Through social work intervention, the mothers' competence was enhanced and the school's responsiveness was increased. Anon.

A third example is from the community-school interface:

> The social worker induced the elementary school in a Hispanic neighborhood to extend its boundary beyond its doors and out into its neighborhood. It became, in effect, a community center. The parents planned family life educa-

tion and ethnic programs. They held evening forums for discussion of neighborhood issues of housing, welfare and health care. After-school recreational programs for the children were provided in the school yard, supervised by older siblings and adult volunteers. It is not surprising that this school enjoyed the full support of its community, and its children, parents, teachers, and community enjoyed a strengthened sense of competence, self-esteem, and identity (Phillips, 1978).

PRIMARY PREVENTION

There is another implication to be derived from the school social worker's distinctive dual function. As a profession, we feel pressed to move into the arena of life itself in order to prevent problems before they arise. The school social worker's location in the child's ecological context is critical to undertaking preventive tasks. The state of our knowledge does not yet permit us to claim the same preventive success that public health professionals achieve through vaccination and sanitation measures based on known etiology. Nevertheless, we have reason to believe that emotional innoculation and life-oriented growth experiences can stave off disorganization in the child, the family, and perhaps within the community.

From an ecological perspective, all organisms use adaptive processes to change their environments and/or to change themselves in order to reach and maintain a goodness-of-fit. In human beings, adaptation is the active, creative use of social and cultural processes to change environments so they will conform to human needs and aspirations. Humans also actively change themselves to conform to environmental requirements and expectations through biological and psychological processes. Human beings, however, never fully achieve a goodness-of-fit or adaptive balance with their environments because their needs and goals forever change, environments constantly change, and also because what people do to physical and social environments is often detrimental to their own functioning (Dubos, 1968).

This evolutionary, adaptive view of people and environments lends additional support to Gordon's (1969) formulation of the social work function as strengthening adaptive potential and improving environments. But it also points to the usefulness of a growing body of stress theory which has an important bearing on primary prevention (Coelho, Hamburg, and Adams, 1974). Stress theory suggests that when the usual adaptive balance is upset by external or internal processes and events, the person and/or the environment will experience the upset as stress and will institute coping strategies to eliminate or reduce the stress or to accommodate to it. Stress and coping are mediated by age, sex, culture, physical condition, particular vulnerabilities, and previous experience. Stress is a part of living, arises from all facets of life, and is not necessarily problematic. In fact, some stress is pleasurable, or is generated by desired events, or is even sought after to alleviate tedium. Stress theory suggests, however, that problematic stress must be understood as a transactional phenomenon occurring in the interface between person and environment—again the area where the school social worker is located.

Coping, too, is a transactional phenomenon located in the interface area because it depends upon personality variables that are in reciprocal relation to environmental variables (Mechanic, 1974; White, 1974). For example, cognition and problem-solving skills used in coping depend on the quality and quantity of information and on the training provided by the environment of family, school, and other social institutions. Coping rests on a minimal amount of self-esteem and psychic comfort, but those qualities depend on emotional supports from the social environment. Motivation for coping depends, in part, on the incentives and rewards provided by the family, school, and community. And finally, coping requires some degree of autonomy, or having enough space and time in the physical and social environments in order to make decisions and take action. This suggests, again, that the interface area is indeed a strategic location for the school social worker. Typically, s/he strengthens coping by supporting self-esteem and identity, rewarding motivation and coping efforts, providing information, teaching problem-solving skills, working to relieve anxiety, depression, and other threatening affects that interfere with coping, and providing opportunities for decision making and action. S/he also directs his/her efforts to reducing stress imposed on the child, the parents, or the community by the procedures or personnel of the school.

So far this discussion of adaptation, stress, and coping merely reformulates what was said earlier about the school social worker's dual function. I would now like to suggest that ideas of stress and coping bear also on issues related to the primary prevention of difficulties before they arise. In general, social work is most often engaged in secondary and tertiary prevention to prevent further disabling from already present and often entrenched problems. As a result, we often feel we are engaged also in picking up the pieces after the damage has been done and have little to do with preventing those problems in the first place. Yet, school social work is moving more and more toward primary prevention. It can also point the way for social workers in other fields of practice who are interested in primary prevention.

Primary prevention has been defined as specific actions directed at specific populations for specific purposes (Goldston, 1977). It seeks to prevent problematic stress and maladaptation and to promote adaptive functioning and positive development. To reach these goals, primary prevention engages the positive forces in individuals, families, and groups, and works to change environmental properties that have an adverse effect on growth and adaptive functioning.

Knowledge of the developmental stages and tasks of the child, adult, and family, and of the environmental provisions required for those tasks enables the school social worker to identify populations-at-risk. These might include, for example, children whose parents are considering or moving into separation or divorce, children experiencing the serious illness or death of a parent or sibling, or children not reaching their intellectual potential. Parental populations-at-risk might include single parents, unemployed parents, parents living in poverty, or socially isolated parents. School social workers frequently offer group meetings to parents of children entering school for the first time, because initial entry represents a transitional point in the life cycles of both parent and child. Thus it has potential for stress and maladaptive response.

> In one such program, the social worker included the kindergarten teacher as a group member because she could provide immediate observations of the child's reactions in the classroom. Her presence also facilitated communication between parent and teacher which could then foster mutual trust and mutual decision making and problem solving as the parents moved through the elementary grades. In this particular program, the parents who participated were engaged in planning the next year's groups and then served as their co-leaders. Thus the roles of parents changed from recipients of the program to planners, then to recruiters of other parents, eventually to group co-leaders, and thus to providers of the service now intended to reach the entire population-at-risk (Santos, 1977).

In a middle-class school, with bused-in children from the inner city, the school social worker—with the principal's consent—developed a project she called "Concern for Community," utilizing a team made up of a teacher and several volunteers including a retired social worker. The project involved a series of fifth grade field trips for firsthand learning about institutions and agencies set up to meet human needs, including hospitals, adolescent group homes, and geriatric facilities. The children learned the community's layout by locating their own homes on a map in relation to the homes of the other group members and classmates. The children also met with the social worker in small groups during the school year to talk about human needs in their community and resources for meeting them. The project's objectives were to stimulate a greater concern in the children for one another, for human need, and for their shared environment, and to increase the children's sense of interdependence and mutual caring. The trips, and especially the small group experiences, were evaluated by the school as having met the objectives.[1]

Early adolescence, ages 12 to 15, is a critical period of development that involves coping with unique biological, psychological, and social demands. Because of hormonal and bodily changes, especially in girls, and sudden

---

1. I am indebted to Edna Bernstein, MSW, Stamford, Connecticut, for this illustration.

entry into the teen culture with its new pressures and demands, early adolescence can be a period of stress and increased vulnerability. Yet, the educational structure in many communities superimposes additional stress by the transfer from elementary to junior high at this very time. The security achieved in a small, self-contained classroom with a single teacher can be lost in the larger population, larger campus, rotating classes, multiple teachers, and increased academic demands (Hamburg, 1974). This appears to be an appropriate population-at-risk for primary prevention programs by the social worker. Such programs might include meetings with teachers and administrators to educate the educators about the age-related stresses of their pupils. These would be based on the teachers' interests and work-related needs so that desired structural changes might be achieved. Anticipatory guidance groups for sixth graders, mutual support groups of seventh grade teachers on how to help their students deal with demands of the transition, and mutual aid groups for parents on their shared tasks in understanding the early adolescent could also be offered (Work Group E, 1977). While we do not know for sure, such primary prevention might contribute to reduced dropout, drug use, and pregnancy and lead to better grades, less absenteeism, and fewer court referrals. Preventive programs will need to be evaluated, particularly in the light of such real constraints as insufficient funding, insufficient staffing, and value systems that tend to resist prevention efforts as invasion of privacy.

Opportunities for preventive work will depend upon the social worker's skill in establishing an ecological niche in the school, so that services are not limited to children who are referred. One social worker reported on efforts to begin relationships before problems emerge by creating an atmosphere that allows all students to confer with him about concerns and difficulties confronting many or most children, such as management of adult authority, peer group disruptions, and pressures of competition. He uses an open-door policy for children to drop in. He accepts advisory roles in student activities and participates in playground and lunchroom duties so that he can provide on-the-spot or life-space helping efforts. He suggests that this increases children's awareness of the social work service and their right to it when and where needed or desired, and without stigma (McGarrity, 1975).

INFLUENCING THE SCHOOL

Throughout this chapter, I have referred to the social worker's function as including professional responsibility to influence the school to be more responsive to the needs of child, family, or community and changing school practices that undermine self-esteem, autonomy, and competence or that add to the burden of depression, anxiety, passivity, or alienation already present. Those tasks are hard—which may explain why many social workers tend to give short shrift to the "situation side" of our person-situation commitment. Nevertheless there are two reasons for optimism: First, we are understanding our commitment better so we are more ready to accept the dual, simultaneous function. Second, real help with environmental tasks is on the way. Anderson (1974), for example, has developed a team model in school social work which has many advantages in addressing problems that affect large numbers of pupils. The team consists of the social worker, psychologist, and often the secondary counselor and nurse, and sometimes the teacher and principal who are, in any case, included in the planning and action. A team can exert greater influence than an individual, although Anderson acknowledges there are severe difficulties in team management just as there are in medical and psychiatric settings where team practice is commonplace.

By virtue of the interface position, however, even the individual school social worker can serve as an early warning system to the school regarding undesirable consequences of its policies and procedures. This collaborative role assumes there is consensus between the school and the practitioner about what is good or bad for children, families, and communities. Where there is such consensus, efforts of the social worker to bring about change in organizational elements can be relatively easy and relatively successful. Sometimes, however, there may not be consensus—perhaps because of such issues as power, authority, prestige, competing interests, personal commitments, or fiscal and political constraints imposed by the outside environment. Assuming the advocacy role in such situations demands "influencing skills" in addition to our helping skills (Brager, 1975). Advocacy in one's own system is a delicate task, since it must be done in such a way that the practitioner does not alienate the very system that employs him/her. A social worker trying to introduce change into the organization, who loses his/her job in the process, is of little use to his/her clients. Thus, political skills of influencing are needed including persuasion, bargaining, mediation, negotiation, and conflict management. Knowledge of a specialized kind is required in order to understand and to utilize the formal and informal systems within the school, its seats of power and decision making, channels of communication, its norms, customs, rules, and policies. Organizational theory and skills of influencing are now taught in many social work schools and in many agencies' staff development programs. They are also set forth in journal articles and books (Brager and Holloway, 1978; Germain and Gitterman, 1980; Patti and Resnick, 1972; Wax, 1968). All practitioners, however, must work at integrating them into our practice. School social workers, like many practitioners in other fields, are effective in working within the system on behalf of one child or one parent, getting the school to bend a rule, make an exception, grant a privilege here, or withhold a sanction there. This very important activity must be continued, but we must also maintain constant vigilance about the impact of the school on all its pupils and, where necessary, undertake knowledgeable, well-planned, skillfully implemented efforts to change adverse structures and practices in the school. That is the implication of the distinctive dual function of social work. It is the implication of primary prevention, and it may be the 1990s response to Abraham Flexner.

REFERENCES

Anderson, R.J. 1974. School social work: The promise of a team model. *Child Welfare* 53: 524–530.

Bartlett, H. 1970. Seeking the strengths of social work. In *The common base of social work practice*. NY: National Association of Social Workers.

Brager, G. 1975. Helping vs. influencing: Some political elements of organizational change. Paper presented at the National Conference of Social Welfare, San Francisco, CA.

Brager, G., and Holloway, S. 1978. *Changing human service organizations: Politics and practice*. NY: Free Press.

Coehlo, G. B., Hamburg, D., and Adams, J. (eds.). 1974. *Coping and adaptation*. NY: Basic Books.

Costin, L. B. 1969. An analysis of the tasks in school social work. *Social Service Review* 43: 274–285.

Dubos, R. 1968. *So human an animal*. NY: Charles Scribner's.

Erikson, Erik. 1959. The healthy personality: Identity and the life cycle. *Psychological Issues*. NY: International Universities Press. 1 (1): 50–100.

Evans, R. I. 1973. *Jean Piaget, the man and his ideas*. NY: E. P. Dutton, 78–79.

Flexner, A. 1915. Is social work a profession? *National Conference Charities and Corrections, Proceedings*, 576–606.

Germain, C. 1978. General systems theory and ego psychology: An ecological perspective. *Social Service Review* 52(4): 535–550.

Germain, C. B. (ed.). 1979. *Social work practice: People and environments*. NY: Columbia University Press.

Germain, C. B., and Gitterman, A. 1980. *The life model of social work practice*. NY: Columbia University Press.

Goldston, S. 1977. An overview of primary prevention programming. In Donald Klein and Stephen Goldston (eds.). *Primary prevention: An idea whose time has come*. Rockville, MD: U.S. DHEW Publication No. (ADM) 77-447.

Gordon, W. E. 1969. Basic constructs for an integrative and generative conception of social work. In Gordon Hearn (ed.). *The general systems approach: Contribution toward an holistic conception of social work*. NY: Council of Social Work Education.

Hamburg, A. 1974. Early adolescence: A specific and stressful stage of the life cycle. In G. B. Coehlo, D. Hamburg, and J. Adams (eds.). *Coping and adaptation*. NY: Basic Books.

McGarrity, M. 1975. Building early relationships in school social work. *Social Casework* 56: 323–327.

Mechanic, D. 1974. Social structure and personal adaptation: Some neglected dimensions. In G. B. Coelho, D. Hamburg, and J. Adams (eds.). *Coping and adaptation*. NY: Basic Books.

Patti, R. J., and Resnick, H. 1972. Changing the agency from within. *Social Work* July, 48–57.

Phillips, M. H. 1978. The community school: A partnership between school and child welfare agency. *Child Welfare* 57: 83–92.

Richmond, M. 1917. The social caseworker's task. *National Conference of Social Work, Proceedings*, 112–115.

Rist, R. 1970. Student social class and teacher expectations: The self-fulfilling prophecy in ghetto education. *Harvard Education Review* 40: 411–451.

Santos, R. R. 1977. Developing primary prevention programs with major community institutions. In D. Klein and S. Goldston (eds.). *Primary prevention, an idea whose time has come*. Washington, DC: Department of Health, Education, and Welfare.

Schwartz, W. 1971. On the use of groups in social work practice. In W. Schwartz and S. Zalba (eds.). *The practice of group work*. NY: Columbia University Press.

Shelling, J. 1978. Unpublished case material. The University of Connecticut School of Social Work.

Wax, J. 1968. Developing social work power in a medical organization. *Social Work*, October.

White, R. 1959. Motivation reconsidered: The concept of competence. *Psychological Review* 66: 297–333.

White, R. 1974. Strategies of adaptation: An attempt at systematic description. In G. B. Coelho, D. Hamburg, and J. Adams (eds.). *Coping and adaptation*. NY: Basic Books.

Work Group E. 1977. Population at risk: Secondary school students. In D. Klein and S. Goldston (eds.). *Primary prevention: An idea whose time has come*. Washington, DC: Department of Health, Education, and Welfare.

CHAPTER 4

The Characteristic Focus of the Social Worker in the Public Schools

Marjorie McQueen Monkman
Professor Emerita of Social Work, University of Illinois at Urbana

Federal and state legislation and major legal decisions have given recognition to school social work services and provided an opportunity to broaden these services from the traditional roles. The recognition of school social work services in the laws and policies creates greater expectations for the worker and challenges the profession. The purpose of this paper is to conceptualize what is the focus of school social work and what is the role of the individual worker in utilizing this focus, in developing new techniques in practice, and in demonstrating desired change.

It is hard to overestimate the importance of the individual worker's contribution to change in the practice situation. Workers carry a heavy responsibility for what they bring to the practice situation. They bring a characteristic professional focus which is both broad and unique. The worker's focus makes it possible for him or her to identify knowledge needed for intervention. The worker brings activities and skills for bringing about desired changes. The worker brings values that lead to the selection of perspective, knowledge, and action. The worker brings the contribution of charisma and personal style. It is through the social worker that the professional focus, knowledge, values, and activities impinge on the practice situation. The role of the worker is formed from these attributes as they interact with the particular structure and expectations of the setting (see figure 1).

THE CHARACTERISTIC FOCUS OF SOCIAL WORK

From the beginning, the social work focus has been identified as resting on the person-in-the-situation, a dual focus. As a result of this focus, social

FIGURE 1 Contributions of the Worker

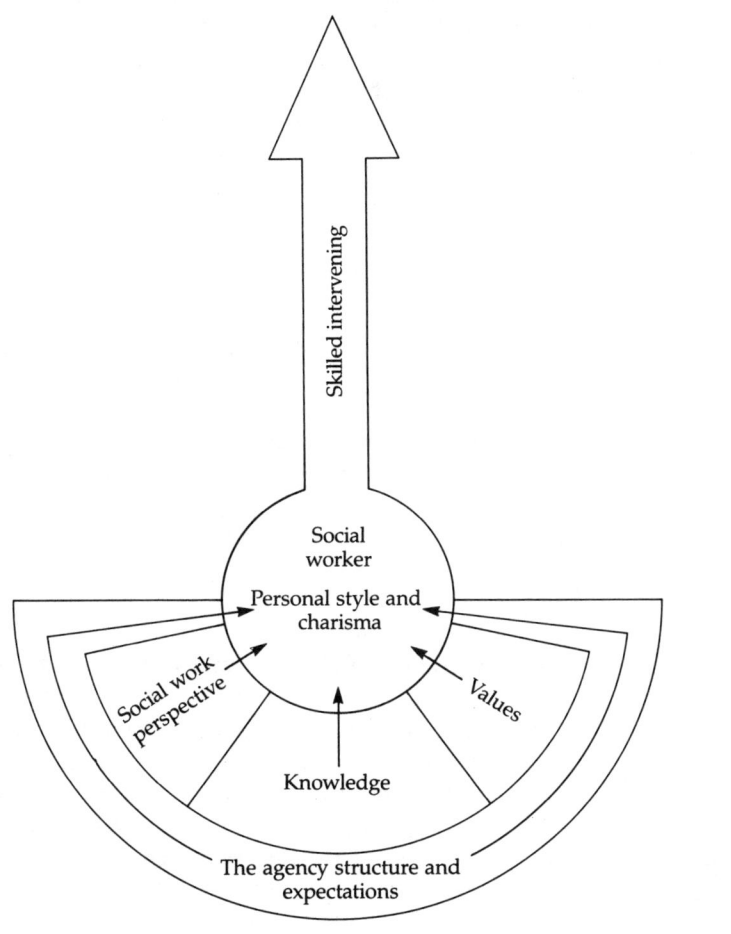

workers work with persons in diverse aspects of life, perhaps more than any other helping discipline. The conceptualization of the person-in-the-situation has been enhanced for social work by the work of Harriett Bartlett (1970), William E. Gordon (1969), and others (Gitterman and Germain, 1976; Germain and Gitterman, 1980; Monkman, 1976, 1978, 1981, 1983, 1984; Pincus and Minahan, 1972; Schwartz, 1969). These theorists have conceptualized the traditional focus in a manner that more accurately reflects the roots and multiple avenues of practice. Their approach to defining the point of intervention in social work is to emphasize phenomena at the point where the person and the environment meet. Social work interventions take place in the transactions between the coping behavior of the person and the qualities of the impinging environment. The purpose of the intervention is to bring about a better match between the person and the environment in a manner that induces growth for the person and at the same time is remediating to the environment (Gordon, 1969).

In order to understand more clearly the characteristic focus of the social worker the concepts, *transactions, coping behavior, quality of the impinging environment, practice target,* and *outcomes of intervention,* need to be more clearly explicated.

Transactions

The activities at the interface may be termed transaction(s) between the individual and the environment. Transactions embody exchange in the context of action or activity. This action or activity is a combination of a person's activity and impinging environment activity; thus, exchange occurs only in the context of activity involving both person and environment. The transaction is created by the individual's coping behavior on the one hand and the activity of the impinging environment on the other (Gordon, 1969).

Coping Behavior

Coping behavior is that behavior at the surface of the human organism which is capable of being consciously directed toward the management of transactions. Coping behavior excludes the many activities that are governed by neural processes below the conscious level. It includes the broad repertoire of behavior that may be directed to the impinging environment and that potentially can be brought under conscious control. Coping behaviors include not only the behaviors directed to the environment, but also those efforts of individuals to exert some control over their behaviors—to use themselves purposively.

Coping behaviors are learned behaviors and, once learned, they become established as coping patterns. Significant repetitions in coping behavior by individuals or groups of individuals suggest coping patterns that may at times become the focus of the interventive action. Looking for these patterns in what people are experiencing and how they are responding to a set of environmental conditions takes us beyond our traditional concern for the uniqueness and integrity of each individual. If we know something about the conditions and about human coping, we can say something in some detail and substance about the response of a clientele to a social institution such as education and from this we can develop the appropriate response of school social work. In a relationship with any one individual, we respond to that person as a unique human being and as a part of a larger collectivity. We respect and encourage the effort of an individual with disabilities to overcome adversity, and/or social discrimination, but we know that some of the adversity and discrimination is shared with other persons with disabilities. This knowledge is as much a base for action as is our knowledge of his or her unique response to adversity and discrimination.

People cope with themselves as well as with the environment and this is also learned behavior. These behaviors, as they are developed over time, incorporate expectations and feedback from the environment. The ways individuals and groups cope are related to the information they have about themselves or their environment—how they perceive self and environment. This information is patterned into a cognitive structure which directs the coping behaviors and could even direct the perception of the environment in a manner that will make it difficult to receive further information as feedback from the environment. There is a circular relation between what we usually do to cope with the environment and how we perceive things. An understanding of this relation is the crucial assessment tool. If coping behaviors and patterns are not in keeping with the environment as we perceive it, we may then examine the information and the perceptions of the coping persons. This assessment is directed toward patterns of perception and action rather than seeking some type of single cause within the individual.

Coping is an active, creative behavior which continually breaks the boundaries of "the given." Adapting is seen as a passive concept that implies that the person simply takes in the output from the environment. Some writers connect coping with stress in adapting and refer to coping as those behaviors emitted when there is stress in adapting. We would say that stress is inherent in any growing process, but that it is important to assess the degree of stress to understand the coping patterns adopted. The person is considered able to cope when he or she is dealing with the stress and "making a go of it" (Gordon, 1969).

Quality of the Impinging Environment

The other side of the transaction field is the environment. Social work practice has not confined its concern to the person in any particular situation, that is, at home, in the hospital, in school, or in any other situation. No other profession seems to follow people so extensively into their daily habitats. We have been interested in how the qualities of any of these situations interact with the coping behaviors. As in the case of the coping behaviors, Gordon (1969) has given a way of partializing the qualities of a situation. He has defined the qualities of the impinging environment as those qualities at the surface of the environmental system that the person is actually in contact with, rather than "below-the-surface" structures, which are inferred to be responsible for the nature of what the human organism actually confronts.

FIGURE 2 T.I.E. Framework: Transactions between Individuals and Environments

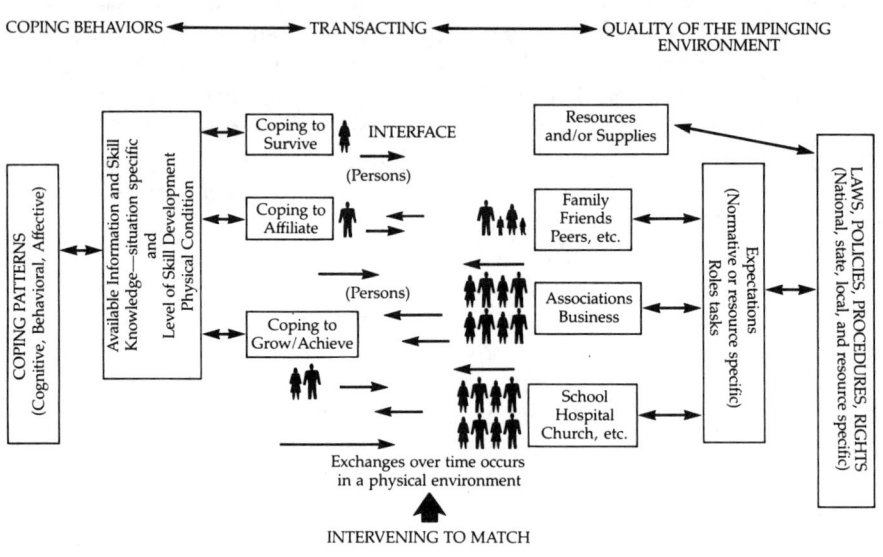

SOURCE: Monkman (1981).

While emphasis on the environmental side is on the impingements, it is recognized that it is through one's knowledge of what is back of the impingements that enables the person to arrange for changes in those impingements in desired directions. It is often necessary to work for change on several levels. For example, a worker may be working with a truant child in an effort to get the child to return to school. At the same time, he or she may find that the teacher is happier with the child truant and that the administration is indifferent. Intervention may be needed at all three levels if the child is to return and remain in school (see figure 2).

Practice Target

Transaction has been defined as activity which combines coping behaviors and the quality of the impinging environment. Through these transactions there is an exchange between the components of each side. The goal of social work practice is matching, that is, bringing about a fit which makes for positive outcomes both for the person and the environment. Professional intervention for bringing about a match may include efforts to change the coping behavior, the quality of the impinging environment, or both (Gordon, 1969).

Social work is concerned with what will happen to the coping behaviors and the quality of the impinging environment as a result of the exchanges between them. The relation of coping and environment is reciprocal. Thus coping behavior and/or quality of the impinging environment could become what we are seeking to change and thus our measures of outcome or dependent variables. To the degree that activity in the transaction changes, we may predict consequent changes in either or both the coping behavior and environmental side.

ECOLOGICAL PERSPECTIVE

We are essentially operating from an ecological perspective. Ecology seeks to understand the reciprocal relation between organisms and environment: how organisms shape the environment to its needs and how this shaping enhances the life-supporting properties of the environment (Germain and Gitterman, 1980). For social work, the ecological perspective appears to fit our historical view much better than the medical or disease perspective that we seemed to have adopted in past decades. The ecological perspective is essentially a perspective, a point of view, for relationships which take place in reality; it is a way of perceiving these relationships more clearly.

One of the reasons for the better fit of the ecological perspective to social work is that it is a multicausal rather than a linear causal perspective; that is, it makes possible a view of multifaceted relationships. From this perspective, our attention is called to the consequences of transactions between people and environment, but the metaphors, models, and/or theories we have previously borrowed have focused more on cause of action and have tended to be one-sided and unidirectional.

SOCIAL WORK KNOWLEDGE

A basic area of knowledge for social work is knowledge of the *needs of people and how these needs are met*. People individually and collectively have a need for physical well-being. These needs consist of food, shelter, and so on, which may be identified as needs for surviving. People have need for relationships, including intimacy and other forms of affiliating. People have need for growth, which may include their need to know, to learn, to develop their talents, and to experience mental and emotional well-being.

A second major area of knowledge for social work is knowledge of *the institutions or societal resources* which have been established to meet these needs. We need knowledge of the major structures and processes involved in resource provision and development. This area is quite complex and includes expectations, policies, procedures, and so on.

The third major area of knowledge is knowledge of *the match between these institutions and the needs of the people*. From the perspective of social work, this is knowledge of the transactions and the result of these transactions for people and their environments. For example, P.L. 94-142 and subquently P.L. 101-476 (IDEA, Individuals with Disabilities Education Act) is an environmental policy change that changes societal expectations and resources for exceptional children and, in turn, affects all children. The environmental impingements that individual children experience will change as these policies change. The difference in the transactions between pupils and their teachers, peers, and even the physical structure of the school have become a part of the general experience of children. However, these children continue struggling to cope with change and new events brought on by these policies. These transactions are particularized and occur in time and space (at a particular time and in a particular place), as do all living transactions.

The Purpose of Social Work Activity

The purpose of social work activity is to improve the match between coping behaviors and the quality of the impinging environment so that the stress in these transactions is not so great that it is destructive to the coping abilities of the individual or the environment. Changes are always occurring and people are always coping or striving to manage change. Not only is our purpose to bring a match that is not destructive but, if possible, one that makes the person better able to cope with further change and makes the environment less stressful to others.

As our focus becomes clearer, we could make the knowledge we have of transactions more explicit for social workers and other disciplines. To do this we need to develop our focus in a way that makes what we aim to change, coping behavior and the impinging environment, more explicit. Figure 2 illustrates the concepts we will be discussing.

T.I.E. FRAMEWORK: OUTCOME CATEGORIES

Coping Behaviors

Social workers basically deal with at least three categories of coping behaviors and three categories of the impinging environment (Monkman, 1978). This framework for dealing with the transactions between individuals and environments is called Transactions Individuals Environment (TIE). Surviving, affiliating, growing, and achieving form a continuum of coping. There are then three categories of coping behaviors: (1) coping behaviors for surviving, (2) coping behaviors for affiliation, and (3) coping behaviors for growing and achieving. These categories help us set priorities for practice intervention. Coping behaviors at any point in time are affected by information from past coping experience and build themselves over time. Our first consideration is whether the client has the capacity to obtain and use the necessities for surviving; second, for affiliating. Both surviving and affiliating skills seem to be prerequisites to growing and achieving.

Coping behaviors for surviving are those behaviors that enable the person to obtain and use resources that make it possible to continue life or activity. To survive we need to have the capacity to obtain food, shelter, clothing, and medical treatment, and to have access to these through locomotion.

Coping behaviors for affiliating are those behaviors that enable the person to unite in a close connection to others in the environment. Subcategories of affiliating behaviors are (1) the capacity to obtain and use personal relationships and (2) the ability to use organizations and organizational structure. Social workers would have great difficulty conceiving of a person apart from his or her social relations. Each individual experiences social relations through organizations and groups, families, schools, clubs, church, and such.

Coping behaviors for growing and achieving are those behaviors that enable the person to perform for, and to contribute to, him or herself and others. Subcategories of coping behaviors for growing are developing and using (1) cognitive capacities, (2) physical capacities, (3) economic capacities, and (4) emotional capacities.

Quality of the Impinging Environment

The environment can be seen as comprising: (1) resources, (2) expectations, and (3) laws and policies. The categories of the environment do not have a priority of their own. Rather, since our major value is the person, their priority gets established in the match with coping behaviors.

Resources. Resources are supplies that can be drawn on when needed or can be turned to for support. Pincus and Minahan (1972) have characterized resource systems as informal, formal, and societal. Informal resource systems consist of family, neighbors, co-workers, and the like. Formal resource systems could be membership organizations or formal associations that promote the interest of the member, such as AA, Association for Retarded Citizens, and so on. Societal resource systems are structured services and service institutions, such as schools, hospitals, social security programs, courts and police agencies, and so on. Resource systems may be adequate or inadequate and provide opportunities, incentives, or limitations. In many situations, there are no resources to match the coping behaviors for surviving, affiliating, and growing.

Expectations. Expectations are the patterned performances and normative obligations that are grounded in established societal structures. Expectations can involve roles and tasks. Social workers recognize these structures and recognize that a positive role complementarity usually leads to greater mutual satisfaction and growth. However, it is not our purpose as social workers simply to help people adapt to societal roles or perform all expected tasks. Roles are the patterned, functional behaviors which are performed by the collection of persons. Examples of roles are mother, father, social worker, physician, and so on. While these are normative patterns in our society, individuals do not always agree on the specific behaviors of a role. Roles do change, since they are socially defined and functionally oriented. Sometimes this societal change is not acceptable to the individual and creates a mismatch between coping behaviors and the environment.

The concept of task is a way of describing the pressures placed on people by various life situations. These tasks "have to do with daily living, such as growing up in the family, and also with the common traumatic situations such as bereavement, separation, illness, or financial difficulties" (Bartlett, 1970). These tasks call for coping responses from the people involved in the situation.

Laws and policies. Laws and policies are those binding customs or rules of conduct created by a controlling authority, such as legislation, legal decisions, and majority pressures. Subcategories of laws and policies are rights and responsibilities, procedures, sanctions, and inhibiting or restricting factors. As a category, laws and policies are seen as necessary and positive components of the environment. Yet, it is also recognized that many single laws or policies have negative effects for groups of people. Some of our policies make survival more difficult. In some cases, particularly for welfare clients, to receive assistance from welfare agencies may make affiliation almost impossible.

Expectations, laws, policies, and procedures are communicated through resources. The quality of output from a resource, such as a school, is very much affected by the state and national policies that have been adopted. The ultimate test of these policies is the match they make with coping behaviors of those persons with whom the school transacts, namely children. Thus, if these transactions are destructive to the coping behaviors of children, the procedure for implementing or the policy itself is in need of change. This is another way of saying that policy is a legitimate target for change. Social workers are often in the best position for evaluating the match between policy and coping. The classroom is an example that may make the interrelationship of the environmental categories clearer. The expectations for tasks to be accomplished in the classroom come to the child through the teacher (and others). The teacher is a resource to the child, but unless he or she is able to bring the expectations in line with the coping behaviors of the child, there is no match. In some cases, the coping behaviors are so different from the expectations that other resources are necessary. Social workers might intervene in the environment and/or in coping behaviors of school children, that is, in the resources, expectations, policies, procedures, and/or in the coping. In some situations, however, change might be indicated in all six outcome categories.

Research Evidence

An exploratory study (Monkman and Meares, 1984) using a random sample of Illinois school social workers and utilizing the focus described in this manuscript (TIE Framework) lends evidence to the fit of this framework to practice. The data show that coping behavior and environment outcome categories were selected in approximately equal amounts. A national study using a random sample of direct practice MSWs from a variety of practice settings (Monkman, 1989) gave additional evidence that social workers outcomes are located in the categories described in this framework.

Matching Person and Environment

The discussion to follow will be an oversimplification of the interrelation between transaction and the matching process, but it is a first step in utilizing the framework developed thus far. Two populations will be used as examples (see figure 3).

The first population to be considered comprises unmarried teenage parents. To be of help to this group it is important to consider the match between behaviors for surviving, affiliating, and growing and each of the categories on the environmental side. To give a few specific examples: placing the teenage mother on homebound instruction may enhance cognitive achievement but may be destructive to affiliation in interpersonal relationships and affiliation with society and/or organizations. The student may not be aware of laws and policies that can affect her decision to have her baby and keep her baby. Knowledge of the task of being a mother is important both for the mother and for the child.

Another population would be developmentally delayed children. Again, we are concerned with matching in all six categories. Many of the programs presently developed for developmentally delayed children are geared to maximizing cognitive development—or more specifically, academic achievement. Most of these programs do not develop affiliating or surviving skills. Very little energy is put into making a better match between the coping behaviors of the developmentally delayed child and the wide range of tasks for daily living.

It is important to remember that our outcome variables are both coping behaviors and the quality of the impinging environment. We may affect either or both. In the case of the teenage parent, the social worker may have helped to change her behavior in all three categories, as well as increasing resources. The worker may have made information about expectations,

FIGURE 3 The Characteristic Focus of School Social Work

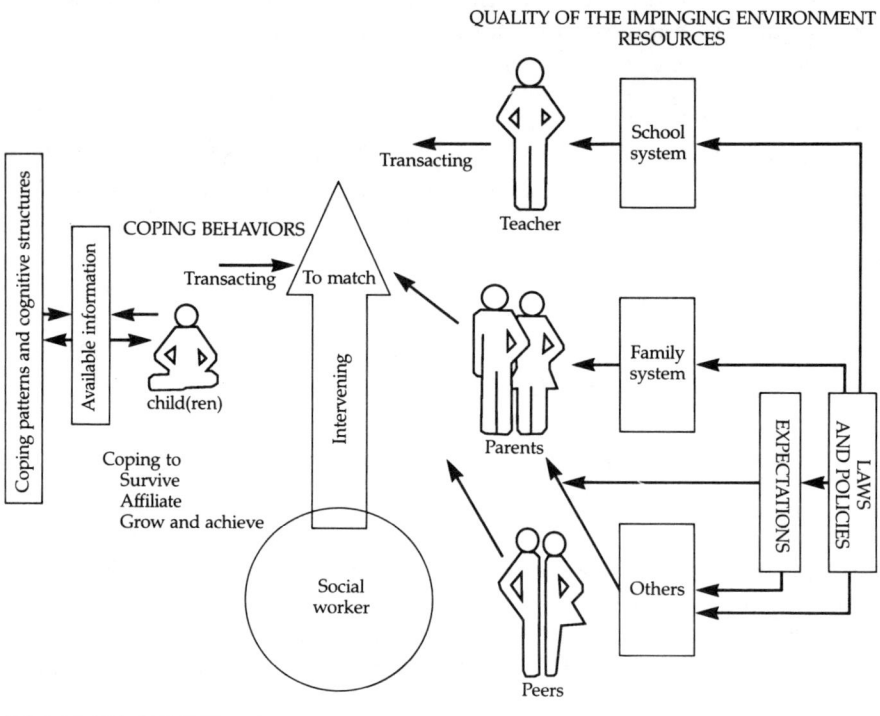

laws, and policies more available to her and may have changed some of the expectations emanating from her impinging environment; for example, the worker may have changed the demands to give up her baby or keep her baby. For the developmentally delayed child, he or she may have developed resources for increasing his or her affiliating behavior. He or she may even have measures of change in these behaviors. The worker may have helped his or her parents change their expectations so that they do not make impossible demands on the child.

Often, social work interventions include teaming with other social workers and other helping persons. For example, many growing and achieving behaviors for school children require teaming with teachers of these children. Teachers spend many more hours with children than social workers do. They have more direct opportunities to develop coping behaviors and skills in children. By teaming with teachers, social workers can increase their change possibilities for children. By bringing these two resources together, they can make a greater change in some aspect of the children's environment.

The point of these examples is to show that this framework makes it possible for us to partialize, generalize, and measure change in practice situations. It is possible to make each of these examples more explicit depending on the conditions of your practice situation. To bring about these changes a worker may, for instance, use knowledge of organizations, skills for working with groups, skills for data collecting, and skills for communicating. The worker must also determine the major critical exchanges in the transaction.

CONCEPTS FOR ANALYZING RESOURCES

Resources have been identified as a major component of the environment. Resources such as family, school, hospitals, and so on, may be viewed as systems. Concepts from the general systems model are useful for conceptualizing and organizing data in the various resource systems. These concepts may be used to call our attention to the skills necessary for the worker to get in and out of a resource system. This model calls to our attention such questions as (1) For what is the major energy in the system being used? (2) Is tension in the system a productive or destructive force? (3) What effect will change in one part of the system have on the other parts? Social workers, such as those employed in schools, become parts of systems. However, while the worker is a part of the system, the worker also intervenes in the system itself as a resource for children (Monkman, 1981).

Understanding Organizations

Workers need to understand what makes organizations operate if they will be able to use the school or other social agencies as a resource. For example, organizations have a managerial structure that is generally hierarchical. Organizational structure can be best understood in relation to organizational process. Workers need to understand the informal power that can be gained either from interpersonal relationships or from assuming responsibilities, as well as power that comes from the formal structural arrangements.

A second, but no less important, process variable is communication. Communication serves a linkage function. It links various parts of the organization by information flow. This may be individual to individual, individual to group, unit to unit, and unit to the supra structure, and so on. Communication has been called the "life blood" of organizations or systems. Social workers have a particular responsibility for developing and maintaining channels of communication if they are to accomplish their own missions.

The climate of an organization has a major effect on its productivity. Climate describes expectancies and incentives and represents a property that is perceived directly or indirectly by individuals in the organization. Climate is made up of such phenomena as warmth, support, conflict, identity, reward, and risk. For social workers, climate is seen as a major quality of resources and is often a target for change.

The earlier discussion makes clear that resources are dependent variables or targets for change for social workers. Resources for clients may take a variety of meanings and may in particular be the "setting" or places of employment for social workers. Thus, it is imperative for social workers to understand the systems or organizations of which they may be a part and to know and ask the essential questions for assessing resources.

In addition, organizational systems have external environments. The exchange between an organization and its environment is essential to the growth of the organization. Organizational environment may be thought of in two categories: (1) general environment, and (2) specific environment.

The general environment consists of conditions that must be of concern to all organizations. Examples of these would include political, economic, demographic, cultural, technological, and legal conditions. The specific environment includes other organizations with which the organization interacts frequently or particular individuals who are crucial to the organization. Examples of the specific environment of a school system are the parents of the children enrolled in the school, the local mental health center, the local child welfare services, the juvenile court, and so forth.

Social Networks

Environments are made up of networks of resources. An important, but sometimes neglected, network is the informal social network for the client: that is, peers, neighbors, friends, relatives, and so on. Each of the persons individually is an important resource for the client, but the linkage and relationship between these persons in the network is also important. Professionals are aware of the negative potential of peer influence on children. However, the positive aspects of these relationships are also useful to practice. Within these networks can be found members who serve as effective informal helpers. Knowledge of social networks and the ability to assess these in practice situations is becoming increasingly important as people become more mobile and lose continuing contact with their own roots. Mobility weakens these linkages, increases isolation and loss, and simultaneously makes network relationships more important.

Networks of Service Organizations

Social workers are often in the position of developing networks of service organizations for clients. Many of our practice situations involve a service network such as the school, family, state child welfare agency, and the courts or judicial system. Social workers are particularly concerned about the relations between these resource systems. This is a domain of social work practice. Social workers may develop and use these interresource linkages, establish channels of communication between these resources, and develop new resources. Thus, the school social workers are in the middle of a system, within an organizational structure, in an environment of social and environmental networks. In order to enhance the development of linkages between various human service organizations, they need to have knowledge of systems variables and organizational variables. Knowledge of the relations of change taking place in differing parts of the system, of the tendency of systems to maintain themselves, to tighten their boundaries, when threatened, can make the worker much more sensitive to the necessary steps in developing linkages between agencies.

We have reviewed concepts and knowledge applicable to the environmental aspects of school social work practice. Other areas of knowledge are equally applicable. These might be (1) knowledge of normal growth and development of children and the stress in coping that accompanies different growth stages, (2) knowledge of exceptional children, (3) knowledge of various learning processes, (4) knowledge of specific resources, (5) knowledge of major policy and policy issues affecting practices in the school setting, and (6) knowledge of positive and negative transaction patterns. Certainly, the earlier discussion gives evidence of the breadth of knowledge that social workers need to bring to practice in the school setting. While we borrow knowledge from psychology, sociology, economics, political science, education, and so on, we borrow from them in relation to our perspectives and to accomplish the purposes of social work.

VALUES

Values guide the action of social work from the preferred perspective to the preferred action. A clarification of types of values is helpful in determining the role of a specific value in practice. Siporin (1975) has defined ten different types of values; five of these are particularly useful to social work:

1. *Ultimate (conceived, or absolute) value* is a general, abstract formulation, such as liberty, justice, progress, self-realization, the worth of the individual.
2. *Instrumental value* is more specific and immediately applicable, such as acceptance of others, equality of opportunity for education, safeguarding the confidentiality of client information. This is also termed a utility value, in referring specifically to the property of things as good or beneficial because of their usefulness to an end.
3. *Personal value* refers to what an individual considers good and right for himself, or what is generally so considered as right or beneficial for an individual, such as individuality, self-respect, self-reliance, privacy, self-realization.

4. *Scientific value* is one to which scientists commit themselves and which they believe should govern scientific behavior: rationality, objectivity, progress, critical inquiry. Society is increasingly accepting these as general social values.
5. *Professional value* is one to which professional people commit themselves and accept as a basis for professional behavior, such as competence, impartiality, placing a client's interest first.

The primary and ultimate value in social work seems to be that "It is good and desirable for man(kind) to fulfil his/her potential, to realize himself/herself, and to balance this with essentially equal efforts to help others fulfill their capacities and realize themselves" (Gordon, 1962). This value represents our dual focus on people and their environment that has characterized social work practice from its beginning. From our ultimate values follow instrumental values that guide actions in practice. An example of an instrumental value is "the right to self-determination." This instrumental value guides our practice, unless it is in conflict with our ultimate value, that is, the individual's self-determination is destructive to himself/herself or others. Knowledge is usually required to make this determination. Thus, values and knowledge are different, but interrelated, in their application to practice. Values, however, give us purpose and ethical structure in social work.

We are careful not to inflict our personal values on others while we accept professional values as a basis for our professional behavior. Hopefully, our personal values are not in conflict with the professional and ultimate values. Yet, the professional values may not encompass all of our personal values. An example of this difference may be seen in relation to divorce. An individual worker may feel that divorce would be wrong for him or herself, but his or her professional values would enable the worker to help clients make this decision for themselves.

It is important to remember that social work has a philosophical base and continues to require judgment as to means and ends. The judgment, however, can be made with more explicit awareness of the *knowledge* and *value* implications.

Social workers must be able to understand the differences between knowledge and values and the relationship of the two. Value refers to what persons prefer or would want to be. This preference may involve all the devotion or sacrifice of which one is capable. Knowledge denotes the picture we have built up of the world and ourselves as it is, not necessarily as we would prefer it to be. It is a picture derived from the most rigorous interpretation we are capable of giving to the most objective sense data we are able to obtain (Gordon, 1962). The future of social work may be dependent on this discrimination. That is, if a value is used as a guide in professional action when knowledge is called for, the resulting action is likely to be ineffective. If knowledge is called on when a value is needed as a guide to action, the resulting action may be destructive. Thus:

> Both outcomes greatly reduce the potential for human welfare residing in the profession's heritage of both knowledge and values. Man's ability over time to bring some aspect of the world into conformity with his preferences (realize his values) seems to be directly proportional to his ability to bring his statements and perceptions into conformity with the world as it now is (develop the relevant science) (Gordon, 1962).

SOCIAL WORK ACTIVITIES

Social work activities involve assessing, relating, communicating, planning, implementing, and evaluating. *Assessing* is the bridging concept between action and knowledge and values. This does not mean to imply that assessing is a first step that occurs before any other activity. It is rather a continuous process as other data continue to be gathered. The social work perspective makes explicit the view of the phenomena into which we intervene. Knowledge gives us the most accurate picture of these phenomena that we are able to obtain in any one point in time. Values lead in the choice of perspectives, in the desire to obtain knowledge, and in the choice of action approaches. The first step in any practice situation is to assess that situation from our perspective, with our knowledge, and in relationship to our values. This step leads to change action.

In most practice situations, *assessing* occurs simultaneously with *relating*. The idea of establishing a relationship has been common in social work literature from the beginning. In more recent years, it has been discussed as a process activity that leads to an end change, resulting in the phenomena into which we intervene. At times in the past, it has been confused with an end in itself or an outcome variable. Certainly, to establish a relationship may be seen as an interim goal, but not as an outcome in the practice situation. Social work places considerable importance on the skill required to relate to the major factors involved in any practice situation, whether client or resource.

Communicating is an essential activity in practice. Most of our data is collected through communicating. To a large extent the accuracy of our data is dependent on our ability to ask questions and clarify answers. It is through communicating that we express our desire and ability to relate and to help.

Planning activities leads to change goals and tasks for each party involved in a practice situation. Plans need to be based on the assessment of the practice situation including the resources available to carry out these plans. Some plans include the development of other resources, as well as bringing about a match between person(s) coping behaviors and existing resources. Planning includes time lines and criteria for assessing change, and contracts are the tools used to bridge planning and implementation.

Implementing a change plan is the activity involved in accomplishing these various tasks and goals. Implementing may involve linking people with resources, changing expectations of the client or of the resource(s), developing or changing policy, changing the procedures in a resource system, or developing new or more effective coping behaviors in person(s), and so on.

Evaluating is part of the assessing process. In the beginning, we assess where the various parts of the practice situation are and, in the end, we evaluate or assess the changes in the various parts. We also evaluate activities that the change processes have accomplished. Evaluation is an assessment of both the outcome and the process. Assessment of outcome is not possible without a perspective that makes our outcome measures clear. It is because in the past this focus has not been explicit that we have been vague and inaccurate and/or confused the relating process with an outcome measure. Assessing and evaluating are continuous processes that should be linked to our characteristic focus, knowledge, and values. Our assessing and planning processes need to be done in a manner that makes evaluation possible.

Each of these process activities involves and includes many skills. They simply serve as a way of organizing our various skill areas. While there is a beginning and an ending to the change process, the steps in this process are not mutually exclusive or linear steps. They are rather interrelated and purposeful activities that together accomplish an end result.

THE WORKER

While workers may bring the characteristic focus, knowledge, values, and actions of the profession, they also bring themselves as resources to the change process. Workers, like clients, have past experiences, information, and cognitive structures or preferred views of transactions, and predictions about consequences of certain kinds of transactions. Each worker brings his or her own style of transacting. It is the responsibility of the worker to constantly change his or her perceptions in the light of new knowledge, more accurate facts from the situation, new resources, and so on.

Workers often tend to prefer particular practice activities. However, the workers' preferred skills should not blunt the awareness of what is needed in any particular situation. For example, some workers have knowledge of interventions to change coping behaviors of individuals. The specific knowledge, plus workers' preference for their individual activities, may lead to a limited practice. Various combinations of selected knowledge and individual preference may lead to a limited perspective for assessing and may lead workers to ignore the important aspects of the practice situation. Workers may fail to develop skills for working with groups, the school system, or other community resources.

Many school social workers were trained at a time when methods of practice were the major divisions of training. Workers were trained to do either casework, group work, community organization, and/or intervention at the policy or administrative level. The major method for a school social worker was casework. In more recent years, it has been recognized that there are many common activities in practice. It has also been recognized that change may be enhanced through collaboration and exchange with others who share common change goals. It is the responsibility of practitioners to keep up with changes in knowledge and to develop their skill level to incorporate new practice activities as they develop and are tested.

There is nothing, however, in the professional methodology or activities that can subordinate the unique, personal artistic contributions that each worker brings to the helping process. Certainly, the individual's sensitive capacity to experience and express empathy and caring are valued among social workers. It is, however, the responsibility of individual workers to evaluate the effects of their individual style on any change process. It is the worker's responsibility to recognize strengths and limitations. Unique qualities and personal style must be self-conscious and disciplined, just as discipline is inherent in the definition of art itself.

We have analyzed and specified the components, characteristic focus, the knowledge, the values, and the skills, that social workers contribute to the public schools. This contribution is significant and provides a response that can be uniquely useful to education in meeting the challenges of its changing mandate. In specifying the components of practice, we see the model developed as useful, both for clarification of the contribution of the social worker, and as a tool for building social work knowledge, and for research testing of theory. Since the construction of a model is the first step toward measurement and testing, we would see the elements of the model as a first step toward the measurement and testing of components of social work practice and we have developed them with that intention. For each social worker, the task of participating in the development of new knowledge is just as important as application of the characteristic focus of the profession and its knowledge, values, and skills. There is much creative work to be done. The responsibility may seem heavy, but the challenge is exciting.

REFERENCES

Bartlett, H. 1970. Seeking the strengths of social work. In *The common base of social work practice*. NY: National Association of Social Workers.

Germain, C. B., and Gitterman, A. 1980. *The life model of social work practice*. NY: Columbia University Press.

Gitterman, A., and Germain, C. 1976. Social work practice: A life model. *Social Service Review* December, 50: 601–610.

Gordon, W. E. 1962. A critique of the working definition. *Social Work* October, p. 9.

Gordon, W. E. 1969. Basic constructs for an integrative and generative conception of social work. In Gordon Hearn (ed.). *The general systems approach: Contributions toward an holistic conception of social work*. NY: Council on Social Work Education.

Monkman, M. M. 1976. A framework for effective social work intervention in the public schools. *School Social Work Journal* Fall, 1(1).

Monkman, M. M. 1978. A broader, more comprehensive view of school social work practice. *School Social Work Journal* Spring, 2(2).

Monkman, M. M. 1981. An outcome focus for differential levels of school social work practice. In *Professional issues for social workers in schools*. Conference Proceedings Silver Spring, MD: National Association of Social Workers, 138-150.

Monkman, M. M. 1983. The specialization of school social work and a model for differential levels of practice. In Miller, D. G. (ed.). *Differential levels of students support services: Including crisis remedial and prevention/developmental approaches*. MN: Department of Education.

Monkman, M. M., and Meares, P. A. 1984. An exploratory study of school social work and its fit to the T.I.E. framework. *School Social Work* 19(1): 9-22.

Monkman, M. M. 1989. A national study of outcome objectives in social work practice: Person and environment. Unpublished.

Pincus, A., and Minahan, A. 1972. *Social work practice, model and method*. IL: F. E. Peacock.

Schwartz, W. 1969. Private troubles and public issues: One social work job or two? *Social welfare forum*. NY: Columbia University Press.

CHAPTER 5

The Wonderland of Social Work in the Schools, or How Alice Learned to Cope

Sally G. Goren
Clinical Associate Professor, Jane Addams College of Social Work,
University of Illinois at Chicago

A social worker entering a school for the first time may feel a bit like Alice as she tumbled into the Rabbit Hole and landed in the long corridor, finding it lined with locked doors. Only when she discovered the means by which she could change her size and shape did she begin her adventures in Wonderland. Throughout her experience in the pages of Carroll's book, Alice used her judgment, her feelings, and her integrity to deal with the characters whom she met. This paper will attempt to offer some guidance to the social worker who finds him or herself in the Wonderland of a school system. The worker may initially feel that his/her district or building resembles a series of locked doors with bits of the madness of Wonderland emerging through the cracks. To function effectively, it is essential that the social worker named Alice (or Alex) learn to identify within his/her setting the means by which he/she can achieve that optimal effectiveness that will prove his/her value to the system and meet his/her own professional standards and personal needs. Therefore, an evaluation of the system will be based on some understanding of systems theory. It is this writer's belief that each social worker in a school constitutes a "mini-agency" complete in one person. On such an assumption, we will examine the roles the social worker might play, the various constituencies with whom the social worker interacts, and the question of accountability.

SOURCE: Reprinted with permission from *School Social Work Journal*, Vol. 6, Fall 1981, pp. 19–26.

SYSTEMS THEORY

To flesh out this view of school social work, it is important to share some common understanding of systems theory. If we view any system as a complex, adaptive organization which is continually generating, elaborating, and restructuring patterns of actions and interaction, we see that the school, as a system, must be understood as an entity which is greater than the sum of its parts. It has discrete properties that need to be evaluated if we are to identify the points in which social work interventions may be made to ensure the maximum effectiveness mentioned above. To view the school as an *adaptive* organization supports the social worker's theoretical underpinnings in which linkage, environmental impact, and enablement of each individual's maximum development is held in high value. The systems definition also emphasizes the *interactive* elements which may impede or aid goal achievement. Thus the social worker is led to identify the junctures of interactions which bridge or fragment the discrete elements within the system (Costin, 1995).

Looking further into one's own school system, it is important to estimate its openness. An open system receives input, produces output, and interacts with all the actors within and outside of the system. The interactions may not always be agreeable, but there must be the opportunity for the school, its administrators, teachers, support staff, students, parents, and community to be heard and to hear one another. An important element of a viable system is, in fact, *tension*. This becomes the impetus for change and growth, for negotiation, for development, and for effective, productive relationships. Another element of the open system is that of *feedback* (Fordor, 1976). This speaks to a communications system that generates action in response to information which is the basis for constructive change.

As an employee of the school, it is critically important that the social worker define him or herself within the system. The opportunity to be a significant interactor rests on the social worker's ability to inform the other actors of the social work role, to accept the input from others within and outside the school, and to respond, to produce output which is designed to meet needs that have been identified. A systems understanding speaks emphatically to the need for the social worker to be visible, viable, and valuable. We will examine next how these qualities may be evidenced within the school.

VISIBILITY

To whom is the social worker important? In what ways is the social worker significant? The answers to these questions are to everyone and in every way. The social worker has an impact on any person with whom he or she interacts. To look at the possible breadth of the assignment, we will examine several factors defined by Lela Costin (1972) as a guide to visibility. The effective social worker will function as:

1. Provider of direct counseling services to pupils;
2. Advocate for specific pupils or groups of pupils whose needs are underserved or unmet;
3. Consultant to administrators in their task of program development and policy change;
4. Consultant to teachers to enhance their ability to create a productive climate for maximum learning;
5. Link to community services and facilitator between the school and community in obtaining necessary services for pupils and their families;
6. Leader in coordination of interdisciplinary teams providing service to pupils; and
7. Assessor of needs of individual pupils and of the school system as related to program development. (Costin, 1972)

All of the above demand that the social worker becomes known to the administrators, the teachers, and pupil services personnel who function within the school or school district. The social worker also needs to create an identity with the pupils in the school and, from these contacts, with the families whose children may be the recipients of social work services. How one fleshes out his/her visibility will vary but may include:

1. Informal meetings with teachers and other school personnel over lunch or coffee, before or after the pupils are in the building;
2. Regularly scheduled conferences with administrators and with teachers with whom the social worker shares responsibility for a child's welfare;
3. Initiation of contact with community agencies to whom the social worker may refer children or families for service;
4. Explanation of services to families via attendance at meetings of the PTA or other parent groups;
5. Responsibility for presentations at in-service meetings for teachers and/or administrators;
6. Assumption of leadership at pupil services personnel team meetings; and
7. Attendance and presentations at school board meetings.

There are many ways that the social worker's visibility may be developed and the particular manner in which this is demonstrated will depend on the social worker's understanding of the politics of the school and the district. As early in one's entry into a district as possible, one must identify the power structure. Determining that will direct the worker toward the creation of relationships that will provide him or her with the support necessary for provision of service. To attempt to work without such support from the person or persons who wield power is an exercise in frustration and a sure diminution of the effectiveness of the efforts. These remarks are not meant to imply that all workers in all settings need to be allied with the power structure, but the worker does need to identify where the power lies in order to understand how his/her work may be enhanced or inhibited. The development of successful working relationships will depend on the clinical assessment skills and the use of relationship building skills that are in the educational and employment experience of all social workers. However, it must be stated that even the most highly skilled workers may be unable to achieve an alignment with the administrative power structure in some instances. Acknowledging that there may be more frustration than gratification in such settings, the social worker may still be able to function as an advocate for children and parents, particularly when the law supports necessary services. The social worker may be a mediator between teachers and administration on behalf of individual children or particular programs. In short, the social worker retains the responsibility to carry out the interventive roles fulfilled by workers in any field of practice (Compton and Gallaway 1979).

Visibility also implies availability. To be ready to assist a principal or nurse in handling a crisis such as child abuse is an excellent way to cement one's position in the school. To provide linkage to a neighborhood day-care center for a child whose parent has become seriously ill demonstrates the effectiveness of relationship building in the community. To educate parents regarding the symptoms of childhood depression or normal pre-adolescent behavior presents the social worker in an appropriate and useful educator role. To inform the school board of new legislation affecting the school and to present a plan for meeting the criteria demanded by the law again places the social worker in a position of enormous value to the school community. It is no longer possible to limit one's role to individual or group counseling of children, though only a few years ago studies indicated that many school social workers defined their responsibilities in just such limited terms (Costin, 1969). Fortunately, there has been a shift in this narrow definition and social workers in schools are engaging in the variety of tasks that have been mentioned above (Costin, 1969). All of this leads to an examination of the viability of the school social worker.

VIABILITY

Linked to visibility is viability. Not only does the school social worker need to be seen, the social worker needs to be seen in action. Creativity is the catch word and the ability to use oneself creatively with the interactors in the school system is imperative. No longer remaining in one's office counseling children, the worker must assess special needs of the system and develop programs to meet them. If a classroom appears to be out of control, how can the worker assist the teacher, the students, or their families? What will meet the needs of the greatest number? It might be regular consultation with the teacher or an effective education project with the class, or several small group meetings with a portion of the pupils in the classroom. Perhaps a need for systematic handling of truancy problems exists. The worker may develop a plan to meet this need in coordination with the principal or assistant principal. Families or some members of the school board may be included in the development of the plan. Time spent with community agencies may alter previous adversarial positions or simply establish a modus operandi that had not existed and which can be functional not only for the worker but also for other school personnel who identify children in need of particular services. We again see how assessment skills, organizational skills, and finally, treatment skills can be applied to a school system to provide maximum learning opportunities for the pupils served by that system.

Not only might the social worker be creative in relation to direct services to pupils with specific needs, he or she can be equally creative in identifying system needs and developing programs to address them.

A social worker who noted considerable distrust and low morale among teachers in a junior high school established a series of meetings and, assuming the role of facilitator, enabled the teachers to examine some of the system problems and the impact on their work. As concerns were shared and ideas for dealing with them were explored, the suspiciousness of the teachers declined and fruitful relationships soon developed. They admitted similar anxieties about their classroom performances and, as a unit, were able to prepare criteria for the evaluation of their work and advocate for their adoption by the administration.

In another instance, a social worker worked with a principal and pupil personnel staff to develop an enrichment program for minority first grade students. The social worker was able to provide some research expertise which aided the program's acceptance by the school board and by the families whose children attended the school.

Since Public Law 94-142 was passed in 1975 (now reformulated as PL 101-476, Individuals with Disabilities Education Act, IDEA) opportunities to expand social work services in the schools have increased. The law provides funding for districts to provide new services for children with disabilities and therefore has led to the hiring of new staff and the development of creative programs, to serve their target groups in ways previously not possible. In many instances, the guidelines of the law have been imaginatively and broadly interpreted in those districts which have seen the mandate as an opportunity rather than a burden. It behooves the school social worker to be in the lead in such program development and to take an active role in the execution of new programs.

Built into the law is the necessity for accountability, an ever increasing requirement in all fields of social work practice. Without minimizing the additional time this demands and recognizing that it can be regarded as a burden for an already overworked staff, there is also a chance to dramatically detail the breadth, content, and effectiveness of social work services. The law has provided us with the impetus to devise systems which can readily indicate who we serve, how we serve them, and the time allocation the various services require. This brings us to an examination of the final V: the value of the school social worker.

VALUE

Early in this paper the author commented upon the total agency concept implicit in each social worker in the schools. It is eminently clear to any reader who is employed in schools that this is true. Is it clear to teachers and administrators? As a professional working within a host setting, the requirement for interpretation of one's function is continual. This is so because the responsibilities are broad and change as needs of the school community change. Since the other professional staff is also continually changing, new staff need to be informed in order to best utilize our services. Implicit in the statement above is the responsibility of the social worker to have control of the definition of his/her role. While it will always be defined in relation to an accurate assessment of service needs, it is the social worker who has the most intimate knowledge of his/her own skills and training and this needs to be communicated to staff in a school setting. To expect that teachers, speech therapists, principals, psychologists, et al., know what one does is to permit any and all of the staff to dictate what to do, how to do it, and when to do it. Rather than allow the job to be defined by others, it behooves a social worker entering into practice in a school to view him or herself as that total agency with the intent of meeting the school and community needs. These needs will be addressed within the knowledge, skill, and ethics of the social work profession; therefore, it is incumbent on the social worker to have a comfortable professional identity that can be expressed soundly to delineate the functions the social worker may undertake in the setting.

Just as it is the responsibility of the worker to be visible and viable in the school building, it is even more important that the social worker, from the point of entrance into a school system, share in the control of the evaluation process. Defining one's role and the scope of the job establishes the basis on which an evaluation of the social worker will be made by the responsible administrator. If the social worker regards him or herself as that total agency he/she needs to think and act as administrator, supervisor, and line worker.

As an administrator, one partializes time to meet the needs of the organization. This determination of the allocation of one's resources should be cooperatively established with the school district official to whom the social worker is directly responsible. The breadth of function, client contact, and caseload management are all part of this role. In order to have realistic criteria upon which one's evaluation will be based, the social worker needs to be a participant in their development. If a district has a standard evaluation form for teachers, it might need to be adapted so that it is appropriate for a social worker or else another one be developed which will better judge the overall effect of social work services in the building. In the role of administrator, it might be well to establish regular conferences with the building principal, the special education coordinator, and/or any other administrative level personnel who might have an impact on the worker's position. This will continuously inform them of one's work, and, of course, of one's value.

There are a number of situations with which this writer is familiar, where administrators avoid contact with the social worker and reluctantly have any interaction. In other districts, the principal or assistant principals are intrusively involved in the case by case management of the social worker. In the first-mentioned situation, administrators must be informed via some method of one's overall work. This may be achieved by memos, weekly or monthly statistical and/or case reviews, and extensive written documentation of any cases wherein issues of legal responsibility may be a factor. The reasons for avoidance may be varied, but the worker must maintain professional linkage with administration by whatever means possible. In the case of the overly-involved administrator, some methods similar to those employed with the "absent" administrator may serve to satisfy the control needs of that person. If the administrator is convinced that the worker is sharing with him/her the case management issues which the administrator feels necessary to know, the worker may find him or herself freer to pursue the tasks as they have been assessed.

There are many suggestions for management of the system in this paper. Each may work in some situations and not in others. Many ideas have not been mentioned. Nonetheless, the message is to experiment with various means of engagement, reporting, integration of social work services within the educational milieu. Failure of one method does not foretell failure of another and perseverance will be rewarded in most circumstances.

As one's own supervisor, the social worker must determine individual and group needs of the pupils with whom he/she works. Judging the necessity of a referral, any indication of the need for consultation, and the type of interventive role which will most readily meet the assessed need are assists the line worker receives from a supervisor. In most school districts, the line worker must carry this dual responsibility. Some districts do provide social work supervision or consultation, some have access to psychiatric consultation, but many school social workers have no established avenue to obtain this kind of input. The need for input, feedback, and direction has led some social workers in schools to develop informal consultation groups. Without devaluing the autonomy the school social worker enjoys, the burden of such total responsibility for one's work can be shared with others. But the significance of the responsibility should be accorded adequate valuation by the district's administration.

There is no need to review the many, varied tasks the social worker, as line worker, undertakes. There is need, however, to account for them. The importance of *counting* contacts with children, with parents, with teachers, and with community resources cannot be overemphasized. Adding the time to fill out necessary reports and records is imperative. This kind of statistical record will provide the basis for the evaluation of effectiveness of service. Following the time keeping is the need to demonstrate effectiveness of one's action. If the social worker has shared in the development of goals with teachers and administrators, he/she will be able to share in the evaluation of his/her service. The fact that the social worker may not be effective in every instance should not deter him/her from creating an evaluation system which will demonstrate incremental change, diagnostic reassessments, and goal renegotiations. It is important to show that service plans are related to jointly-determined goals and to provide some rationale for success or failure of the plans. To reemphasize the importance of one's involvement in this evaluative process, one might consider designing a short form that could be used with any child, group, family, or teacher. The form might include goals, methods for achievement, and time spent in an effort to meet the goals.

This entire section on value may have been better entitled *evaluation*. It is the author's contention that one's value is best understood via evaluation of one's work and the plea is, therefore, for each school social worker to carry a major responsibility for the negotiation and creation of the criteria on which such an evaluation will be based. This is another way that one informs, educates, and indeed, determines the parameters of one's work. Control is shared, goals are shared, and power is shared. The social workers who can actively demonstrate their value will find that they have a strong advocate in the principal or other administrator and that kind of advocacy will agitate for more social work services and, hopefully, more social workers.

To be an effective participant in the creation of an atmosphere that will enhance learning opportunities for children, the social worker in the school must use all his/her best clinical and organizational skills. The social worker must first know who and what he/she is professionally. He/she must develop respect for the work of others. Trust will grow as hopes and expectations are shared and common goals are agreed upon. The social worker who creates a significant position for him or herself in a school system will have an accurate knowledge of the system and a clear knowledge of his/her position in it. The social worker will know the loci of power, the system needs, and the style of all the interactors within the system. This assessment will be the basis for the social worker's creation of an appropriate role. The social worker in a school, in essence, is always using professional skills. Whether meeting with a child or a teacher, arranging a contractual agreement with a family service agency, or consulting with a pupil services team, the effective social worker will be actively assessing and treating.

As Alice moved through her adventures in Wonderland and the Looking Glass, she became more assertive and gained control. Alice (or Alex) in the school system will find that active involvement in all aspects of that system will be the foundation for provision of service, acceptance within the system, and professional satisfaction for a job very well done. The social worker will also be very tired at the end of each day, recognizing that he/she has indeed used him or herself skillfully throughout every contact that he/she has had. The social worker will have been visible, viable, and of value to everyone he/she encountered during the day at school.

REFERENCES

Compton, B., and Galaway, B. 1979. *Social work processes*, 2nd ed. Homewood, IL: Dorsey Press.

Costin, Lela B. 1969. An analysis of the tasks of school social workers. *Social Service Review* 43: 274–285.

Costin, Lela B. 1972. Adaptations on the delivery of school social work services. *Social Casework* 53: 348–354.

Costin, Lela B. 1975. School social work practice: A new model. *Social Work* 20: 136.

Fordor, Anthony. 1976. Social work and system theory. *British Journal of Social Work* 6, Spring. Reprinted in Compton and Galaway, *Social work processes*, 2nd ed. Homewood, IL: Dorsey Press, 1979, 98–101.

CHAPTER 6

The Economic, Political and Social World of School Social Work

Isadora R. Hare
Director of Quality Assurance, NASW, Washington, D.C.

Kathleen Sullivan Allen, MSW
Masters Graduate of Virginia Commonwealth University, School of Social Work

INTRODUCTION

The education of the young is a matter of great concern to all societies. It is an important mechanism of socialization, of instructing the new generation in the ways of the culture, of preparing them for the future, and ensuring the continuation of the society. Education is therefore subject to many social, economic, and political forces. Since its inception more than eighty years ago, school social work's content and direction has also been influenced by its social environment: conditions and events within society itself and particularly within the education institution where the practice of school social work occurs.

This is particularly true in the decade of the 1990s, leading to the year 2000. In its beginning years (1993–94), the school reform movement resulted in Congress passing an ambitious and comprehensive education agenda, so much so that it was called "An Education Congress" ("An Education Congress," 1994). The months following the November 1994 elections, during which the Republican party gained control of both Houses, witnessed an intense debate in Congress about the course the nation would take in providing educational opportunities to its children and young people.

THE FIRST PHASE

A major feature of education policy in the first half of the decade was the enactment of Goals 2000: Educate America Act (P.L. 103-227), signed into law by the President on March 31, 1994. Goals 2000 put into place eight national education goals, the culmination of trends which began during George Bush's presidency. In September 1989, an historic summit was held in Charlottesville, Virginia at which President Bush and the nation's governors proposed six national education goals to guide schools during the coming decade. These were formally adopted by the National Governors' Association at its winter meeting in Washington, D.C. in February 1990, and were enacted into law, with two goals added during the 1993–94 congressional session. The goals are defined in the law as follows (with goals 4 and 8 added to the original six):

"*Goal 1: Readiness:* By the year 2000, all children in America will start school ready to learn." Objectives include ensuring access to high quality and developmentally appropriate preschool programs for all disadvantaged and disabled children, facilitating parent involvement in education and providing the training and support required to perform this function, and supplementing education with nutrition and health care.

"*Goal 2: School Completion:* By the year 2000, the high school graduation rate will increase to at least 90 percent." Objectives include reducing the dropout rate and eliminating the gap in high school graduation rates between students from minority backgrounds and their non-minority counterparts.

"*Goal 3: Student Achievement and Citizenship:* By the year 2000, all students will leave grades 4, 8, and 12 having demonstrated competency over challenging subject matter including English, mathematics, science, foreign languages, civics and government, economics, arts, history, and geography, and every school in America will ensure that all students learn to use their minds well, so they may be prepared for responsible citizenship, further learning, and productive employment in our modern economy."

"*Goal 4: Teacher Education and Professional Development:* By the year 2000, the nation's teaching force will have access to programs for the continued improvement of their professional skills and the opportunity to acquire the knowledge and skills needed to instruct and prepare all American students for the next century."

"*Goal 5: Mathematics and Science:* By the year 2000, United States students will be first in the world in mathematics and science achievement."

"*Goal 6: Adult Literacy and Lifelong Learning:* By the year 2000, every adult American will be literate and will possess the knowledge and skills necessary to compete in a global economy and exercise the rights and responsibilities of citizenship."

"*Goal 7: Safe, Disciplined and Drug-Free Schools:* By the year 2000, every school in the United States will be free of drugs, violence, and the unauthorized presence of firearms and alcohol and will offer a disciplined environment conducive to learning." Objectives include the implementation of firm and fair policies on drugs and alcohol, encouraging collaboration between parents, businesses, and community organizations, and developing comprehensive K–12 drug and alcohol prevention programs to be taught within health education, and organizing "community-based teams to provide students and teachers with needed support" (National Governors' Association, 1990).

"*Goal 8: Parental Participation:* By the year 2000, every school will promote partnerships that will increase parental involvement and participation in promoting the social, emotional, and academic growth of children." Objectives of this goal include developing policies and programs for increasing partnerships that respond to the varying needs of parents and the home, including parents of children who are disadvantaged or bilingual, or parents of children with disabilities; and engaging parents and families in a partnership that supports the academic work of children at home and shared educational decision making at school.

Background of the Goals 2000: Educate America Act

The enactment of this set of national education goals and objectives represented a radical development in American education. Its evolution was the logical outcome of trends within society, the economy, and education throughout the previous decade. During the eighties, a major education reform movement occurred in the United States. Several national studies were released that highlighted problems in the educational system such as declining test scores, high rates of functional illiteracy among teenagers and adults, and the fact that business and military leaders were required to spend millions of dollars on remedial training programs in basic skills. Initial proposals to counter the "rising tide of mediocrity" in American education focused on academic strategies such as higher graduation requirements, more homework, merit pay for teachers, and a general striving for excellence in education (Education Commission of the States, 1983; National Commission on Excellence in Education, 1983; The Twentieth Century Fund, 1983). The National Association of Social Workers (NASW) was one of the first organizations to focus on the psychosocial components that affected educational performance. In 1985, at its Third National Conference on School Social Work, NASW released a report that detailed human and social barriers to educational excellence and made recommendations to overcome them (Mintzies and Hare, 1985). Major recommendations included strengthening collaboration between school and community, strengthening pupil services, increasing parental involvement, emphasizing early intervention and prevention, and expanding use of the school building.

As other organizations and bodies also recognized the primacy of social factors in education, (National Coalition of Advocates for Students, 1985; Children's Defense Fund, 1986; National Education Association, 1987), a second wave of education reform focused on students-at-risk, that is, students vulnerable to educational failure because of social, economic, or personal problems. The national education goals of 1994 combine a focus on achieving academic excellence with concern for vulnerable students who are disadvantaged, disabled, abusing drugs, or at-risk of dropping out for these and other reasons.

Major Social Factors Influencing U.S. Education

Poverty. The educationally disadvantaged student population (mainly from low-income or minority families) is growing at a far more rapid rate than the rest of the population because of higher birth rates and immigration (Levin, 1986; Austin, 1992; Chavkin, 1993; Stewart, 1993). In 1991, one in every five (20 percent) of America's children lived below the poverty line (Annie E. Casey Foundation, 1994). For children under six, the poverty rate is significantly higher. In 1990, it was 23 percent, a total of 5.3 million (National Center for Children in Poverty, 1994). By 1993, the Census Bureau reported that it had risen to 25 percent (Annie E. Casey Foundation, 1994). Fifty-eight percent of poor children under six are from families of color, yet these children constitute only 32 percent of the total population of children in this group (National Center for Children in Poverty, 1994). Twenty percent of all U.S. public schools have student populations in which more than 50 percent are eligible for free or reduced price lunches; and in 6,500 schools (8 percent), 75 percent of students are below this poverty-indicator (Dryfoos, 1994). Nationwide, the rate of children reported for child abuse or neglect increased 50 percent from 1985 to 1992. In 1992, 2.9 million children were reported to Child Protective Services agencies as alleged victims of child maltreatment. Of these, the substantiation was 40 percent, indicating that 1.1 million children were found to be actual victims of child abuse and neglect. The rate of fatalities has risen steadily over the past seven years. In 1992, an estimated 1,261 children died from abuse or neglect (McCurdy and Daro, 1993).

Pregnancy and school dropout. Data for 1992 show that a slight decline occurred in the U.S. teen birth rate, from 62 in 1991 to 61 births for 1,000 females aged 15 to 19 in 1992. However, the teen birth rate remains 21 percent higher than it was in 1986, and is 50 percent or more higher than the rate in other industrial nations (Child Trends Inc., 1995). Over 10 percent of all births to African-American women in the U.S. occurred to women younger than 18 years of age (U.S. Dept. Of Health and Human Services, 1994). Research indicates that children born to single teenage mothers are more likely to drop out of school, to give birth out of wedlock, to divorce or separate, and to be dependent on welfare (Annie E. Casey Foundation, 1994). In 1991, only 68.8 percent of young people graduated from high school after four years (Annie E. Casey Foundation, 1994). Many of these complete their high school studies later. Between 1975 and 1992, the overall dropout rate for 16 to 24 year olds declined slightly from 14 percent to 11 percent. The gap between white and black narrowed during this period, but rates for Hispanic students remained consistently higher (National Education Goals Panel, 1993, Volume 1).

Substance-abuse. While over 90 percent of students report never being under the influence of alcohol or other drugs while at school, overall use is much higher. Alcohol was used by 77 percent of all high school students in 1992. This was down from 88 percent in 1980. Marijuana use increases while students are in school, reaching 22 percent in grade 12 (National Education Goals Panel, 1993, Volume 1). Furthermore, the University of Michigan's annual survey of drug use showed an alarming rise in marijuana and crack cocaine use during 1993 (Thomas, 1994). Fetal Alcohol Syndrome occurs in 1.9 per 1,000 live births or 7,000 cases per year in the United States. This makes FAS the leading known preventable cause of mental retardation (Troccoli, 1994; Vobejda, 1994).

Violence. Violence is emerging as a serious and escalating factor affecting young people in the United States. While the incidence of students being victimized at school appears to have declined modestly in recent years, the levels remain unacceptably high. About one in five eighth graders reported being threatened with a weapon in 1992, while almost one in ten reported carrying a weapon with them on to school grounds (National Education Goals Panel, 1993, Volume 1). School violence left students dead or seriously wounded in 41 percent of big American cities in 1993–94 ("School Survey," 1994). Homicide is the leading cause of death among male and female African-Americans aged 15 to 34 years. Between 1979 and 1991 nearly 50,000 children were killed by firearms, a total equal to the number of United States casualties in the Vietnam War (Lopez, 1993; Children's Defense Fund, 1994). In summer 1994, the number of inmates in United States prisons topped one million for the first time, and put the U.S. second only to Russia for rates of incarceration (Holmes, 1994). A 1989 study reported that 82 percent of America's prisoners are high school dropouts and it cost an average of $20,000 per year to maintain each one in jail (Hodgkinson, 1989).

Educational performance. As a result of such risk factors, as well as problems within our nation's schools, our educational performance continues to give cause for concern. In 1993, only 85 out of every 1,000 high school juniors and seniors took Advanced Placement exams in English, mathematics, science and history, and only approximately two-thirds of these received passing scores; universities are increasingly teaching remedial skills that should have been gained in high school; on a 1992 survey of adult literacy, just 11 percent of U.S. high school graduates could accurately restate in writing the main point of a newspaper article; many employers report they cannot find people to hire who have the skills, knowledge, attitudes, and habits needed to do the work (Finn, 1994). In 1991, American 13-year-olds were outperformed in mathematics and science assessments by students in Korea, Taiwan, France, and Hungary (National Education Goals Panel, 1994). The NEGP reported in 1993 that "the current rate of progress is wholly inadequate if we are to achieve the National Education Goals by the year 2000" (National Education Goals Panel, 1993, p. XV), and in 1994 it stated that our progress was "nowhere near the levels required" (National Education Goals Panel, 1994, p. 53).

Economic factors. The rising American trade deficit generated growing concern about U.S. competitiveness in world markets. The U.S. work force was not able to work cheaply enough to compete with workers of other nations, necessitating a more capable and more productive work force, and one that has the skill to "work smarter." Further, as the end of the century approaches, each worker will become more valuable. Between 1990 and 2030, as the proportion of elderly people in the population rises, the ratio of workers to the Social Security recipients they support through their tax dollars will drop by nearly one-third. In 1950, sixteen people worked for each person receiving social security benefits. In 1990, it was three workers for every recipient, and by the year 2030, it will be only two (Board of Trustees, Federal Old-Age and Survivors Insurance and Disability Insurance Trust Funds, 1995).

Minorities. Until recently, schools have shown the least success in educating minority students, who are disproportionately represented among people who are poor. Thus, the challenge to schools became clear. Educators were no longer able to blame the student and family background for educational failure; they had to devise strategies to educate all children effectively to equip them for an increasingly technologically complex society. A report issued by the Quality Education for Minorities Project (1990) emphasized the critical importance of successfully educating minority youth. By the end of the 20th century one-third of America's public school students will be members of racial and ethnic minorities. To continue to fail them is to place our nation and our economy at risk (Quality Education for Minorities Project, 1990).

FURTHER EDUCATION REFORMS

The education reforms of the first half of the decade were contained in a thorough and comprehensive legislative package to address these educational, social, and economic factors by covering the entire span of a child's school years, from preschool to college. Six major education bills, and two closely related bills passed the 103rd Congress:

1. Goals 2000: Educate America Act
2. Improving America's Schools Act
3. Head Start Program Reauthorization
4. Student Loan Reform Act
5. National and Community Service Trust Act
6. School-to-Work Opportunities Act
7. Omnibus Budget Reconciliation Act
8. Violent Crime Control and Law Enforcement Act

1. *Goals 2000: Educate America Act.* At the center of the educational reform package was the Goals 2000: Educate America Act that, in addition to the goals previously outlined, also authorized a bipartisan National Education Goals Panel (NEGP), which had in fact existed since July 1990. The Panel is made up of Governors, members of the Administration, and members of both houses of Congress. Each year since 1992, on the anniversary of the Charlottesville summit, the NEGP has issued the National Education Goals Report in which it monitors the nation's progress toward the attainment of the goals. The Act also provides for grants to states and local education agencies for school improvement plans. Title VII of Goals 2000 was the Safe Schools Act of 1994. It was enacted to provide grants to local education agencies to establish programs to include violence prevention, community education, comprehensive planning strategies for addressing school violence, and counseling programs for victims of school violence.

2. *Improving America's Schools Act (IASA).* A second significant achievement was the passage and enactment of the Improving America's Schools Act (IASA) of 1994 (P.L. 103-382), signed into law on October 5, 1994. IASA reauthorized the Elementary and Secondary Education Act (ESEA), first passed in 1965 as part of President Johnson's Great Society, and last reauthorized in 1988 as the Augustus F. Hawkins–Robert T. Stafford Elementary and Secondary School Improvement Amendments of 1988 (P.L. 100-297). Title I of IASA is the largest federal education program and provides compensatory education for low income, educationally disadvantaged children. Prior to its passage, the law was reformulated to provide a greater proportion of resources to poorer school districts, with a requirement that the children in Title I programs attain the same high standards of performance now demanded of students in the general population. IASA also provides for the Dwight D. Eisenhower Professional Development Program (for which school social workers are eligible), and for educational technology, gifted and talented pro-

grams and charter schools. Title IV covers Safe and Drug-Free Schools and Communities, and Title V promotes equity through magnet schools assistance and programs for women. Native American Education and bilingual education are found in Titles VI and VII. IASA also amends the Stewart B. McKinney Homeless Assistance Act, making provision for local grants which can include the provision of pupil services (NASW, Office of Government Relations, Issue Brief, 1994).

3. *Head Start Program Reauthorization.* To address the early education years for students-at-risk, Congress reauthorized the Head Start program in 1994 (P.L. 103-252), and in doing so expanded this popular program and set aside funds to strengthen its quality. Head Start is a child development program for preschool children who are economically disadvantaged. It began in the 1960s as part of President Lyndon Johnson's Great Society program, part of which was called the War on Poverty (Ginsberg, 1995). Unfortunately, despite the program's bipartisan support, it has never been funded at a high enough level to reach all eligible children. The National Commission on Education (cited in Ginsberg, 1995) reported that fewer than one-fourth of the children who are eligible for Head Start are enrolled.

4. *Student Loan Reform Act.* College level education was aided in 1993 by the passage of the Student Loan Reform Act (P.L. 103-66), which restructured the existing student loan program by offering students the advantage of borrowing directly from the federal government, thereby decreasing the government's administrative costs, and by providing more flexibility for repayment.

5. *National and Community Service Trust Act.* Building on the National and Community Service Act of 1990, the National and Community Service Trust Act of 1993 (P.L. 103-82) was enacted to provide financial assistance for higher education and training, or repayment of student loans, to individuals who perform community service that addresses unmet needs in the areas of education, the environment, and human and public safety. A central feature of this act is the Americorps Program, designed to provide participants with a limited wage and a monetary service award for use toward education expenses in exchange for a full year of community service.

6. *School-to-Work Opportunities Act.* The last of the six major education bills passed in the first half of the decade was the School-to-Work Opportunities Act of 1994 (P.L. 103-239), which authorized funding for state grants to establish job training programs, apprenticeships, and vocational education systems so that students who do not attend college can be helped to make a smooth transition from high school to the labor market.

Also of significance to school social work are two bills related to education that were signed into law during the 103rd Congress: the Omnibus

Budget Reconciliation Act (OBRA) of 1993 (P.L. 103-66), and the Violent Crime Control and Law Enforcement Act of 1994, popularly known as "The Crime Bill" (P.L. 103-322).

The Omnibus Budget Reconciliation Act. OBRA provides support for a range of social services in newly created empowerment zones and enterprise communities, and for family preservation and support programs.

A) Empowerment Zones and Enterprise Communities: This initiative aims to revive decaying neighborhoods and stimulate jobs through a combination of social service aid, tax incentives, and better coordination of federal resources. Schools are expected to participate in the planning and delivery of needed services to revitalize both urban and rural areas receiving grants.

B) Family Preservation and Support Programs: These are services designed to help families at risk or in crisis, and community-based services to promote the well-being of children and families. OBRA provided one billion dollars over five years to fund the planning and implementation of comprehensive programs to improve child welfare and emphasize prevention. The planning for these programs must be broad-based, and include schools, and professional and advocacy organizations.

The Violent Crime Control and Law Enforcement Act (The Crime Bill). As passed by Congress, this is a comprehensive anti-crime package banning 19 types of assault weapons, toughening sentencing provisions, and authorizing funding to hire police officers, construct prisons, and initiate or expand a variety of school-based, school-linked, crime prevention programs.

DEVELOPMENTS IN SPECIAL EDUCATION

During the first half of the decade there were significant changes in special education which affected school social workers. The year 1995 marked the twentieth anniversary of the passage of the landmark Education for All Handicapped Children Act (P.L. 94-142) which (as Part B of the Education of the Handicapped Act) legislated a free, appropriate public education (FAPE) in the least restrictive environment (LRE) for all children with disabilities. It also provided for related services required to assist a child to benefit from special education. School social work services were not initially named in the statute, but in 1977 were referenced and defined in the Federal regulations to the Act. In various amendments to the Education of the Handicapped Act (EHA) in recent years, several provisions relating to social work services were added. The title of the Act was also amended to the Individuals with Disabilities Education Act (IDEA) by P.L. 101-476 in 1990, substituting the term "disabilities" for "handicaps" throughout the Act.

Early Intervention for Infants and Toddlers. The extension of services downward in age to birth was legislated by the Education of the Handicapped Act Amendments of 1986 (P.L. 99-457). A new Part H was added to the Act which provided for early intervention services for infants and toddlers from birth to their third birthday, and increased incentives for states to provide more extensive services for three- to five-year-olds. The Act named social workers as one of the qualified providers of early intervention services, and regulations issued later defined these services as including home visits, preparing psychosocial assessments, providing counseling, working with environmental problems, and identifying, mobilizing, and coordinating community resources.

Recognition of School Social Workers. The Individuals with Disabilities Education Act, P.L. 101-476, significantly added "social work services" to the list of related services named in the Act, and also to the list of early intervention services. In 1991, IDEA was amended again by P.L. 102-119 which changed the term "case management" to "service coordination." In report language interpreting the change, the U.S. Senate recognized that provision of social work services was critical and social workers' training equipped them to perform service coordination. Because social work services were added to the statute by the 1990 amendments, the regulations in place since 1977 were reviewed and revised by the Department of Education in 1992. After intensive lobbying by school social workers, the final regulations retained the title "social work services in schools" and made only minor changes to the definition itself (Federal Register, 29 September 1992). The number of school social workers employed in special education programs has increased from 7,643 in 1989, to 9,309 in 1994, an increase of 22 percent over five years (U.S. Department of Education Office of Special Education and Rehabilitation Services, 1989 and 1994).

EFFECTS OF EDUCATION AND HEALTH CARE REFORM ON SCHOOL SOCIAL WORK

The ferment of activity in education and health care during the eighties and nineties has affected school social work. Although many challenges remain, and the context of practice is changing, the profession is winning increasing national recognition.

Education Reform

School social work is included both in the Goals 2000: Educate America Act, and in the Improving America's Schools Act (IASA) of 1994. Goals 2000 utilizes the definition of "related services" found in the Individuals with Disabilities Education Act, in which school social workers are specifically mentioned. Related Services Personnel are cited as participating in many school reform activities at the state and local levels.

The Improving America's Schools Act remains the definition of "pupil services" and "pupil services personnel" that was first formulated in the Hawkins-Stafford Amendments in 1988. "Pupil Services" and "Pupil Services Personnel" are defined as "school counselors, school social workers, school psychologists, and other qualified professional personnel involved in providing assessment, diagnosis, counseling, educational, therapeutic, and other necessary services (including related services as such term is defined in section 602(A)(17) of the Individuals With Disabilities Education Act) as part of a comprehensive program to meet student needs; and the services provided by pupil services personnel."

The Act contains many provisions that will provide greater understanding and support of pupil services programs and the role of social workers and other pupil services professionals in education reform and a host of other programs (National Association of Social Workers Office of Government Regulations, 1994). In addition, until Title X—Programs of National Significance, the Elementary School Counseling Demonstration Act authorizes grants for schools to establish or expand comprehensive elementary school counseling programs. Such programs must use school social workers (defined as "an individual who holds a masters degree in social work and is licensed or certified by the state in which services are provided or holds a school social work specialist credential"), school counselors, or school psychologists. This extensive recognition of pupil services in federal legislation is partly the result of the cooperative relationships among national professional organizations of pupil services providers which have been established in Washington D.C.

Florence Poole (1954) stressed the importance of school social worker participation in professional teams to provide coordinated and integrated services. This goal is even more applicable today, both in direct service delivery at the school level, and in macro-level activities. The National Alliance of Pupil Services Organizations, first established in 1979 by NASW in conjunction with the National Association of School Psychologists, has strengthened the ties among organizations representing pupil services and related services providers, as well as teachers and special educators. It has also increased the visibility of pupil services in the education community.

School-Linked Services

The context of school social work practice is changing with the emergence of new models of delivering health and social services to children and families. Usually called "school-linked services," these models have emerged in reaction to two forces: first, education's growing concern with the 40 percent of children at risk of educational failure because of complex social, economic, and emotional problems (National Commission on Children, 1991); and secondly, the concern that services to children and families in general are inefficient because the delivery system is fragmented, difficult to access, confusing, and uncoordinated. In January 1994 more than fifty national organizations concerned with the well-being of children, youth, and families gathered in Washington, D.C. and developed a consensus regarding principles for developing integrated service systems. Such systems should be community-based, school-linked, family-centered, culturally competent, comprehensive, and prevention-focused. They should also feature on-going needs assessment and program evaluation, and should be collaborative in nature, merging categorical funding streams for most efficient service delivery to families and children.

Both Goals 2000 and IASA contain provisions relating to coordinated services designed to give students and their families better access to the social, health, and educational services necessary for success in school. Both state and local plans for restructuring and improving schools must include strategies for establishing sites in or near schools that provide "one-stop shopping" for parents and students. These developments provide both a challenge and an opportunity for school social workers. Models such as school-based health centers (National Health and Education Consortium, 1995) and family resource centers (Cohen, 1995) are evolving in many states (Hare, 1995). Often they bring social workers and other professionals from community agencies into the schools. Ironically problems of coordination have arisen between practitioners hired by outside agencies and those employed by the schools. School social workers are "strategically placed to act as bridges connecting agencies and schools, to provide a 'glue factor' in collaborative work" (Pennekamp, 1992). They should be pro-active in demonstrating this capability if and when such services are organized (National Alliance of Pupil Services Organizations, 1992; Carlson, Clark and Marx, 1992).

Health Care Reform

School social work will also be increasingly affected by other developments in the health arena. Medicaid (Title XIX of the Social Security Act) funding for students living in poverty is being utilized in many school systems to finance those school social work services which can be classified as part of the Early and Periodic Screening, Diagnosis and Treatment (EPSDT) provisions of the Medicaid law, or the targeted case management provisions (Farrow and Joe, 1992). This may require that school social workers have clinical credentials to enable them to be recognized as providers of Medicaid funded services. As Medicaid patients are mandated to utilize managed care health services in order to stem the rising costs of Medicaid on a fee-for-service basis, and as managed care plans develop so-called behavioral health services to provide mental health and substance abuse services, it is likely that these developments will cause social work services in schools to evolve in different and challenging ways in the years ahead.

The expansion of Comprehensive School Health Programs will also alter the focus of school social work in the years ahead. Initially concentrated on HIV-AIDS prevention programs in the schools, the evolving model of Comprehensive School Health being developed by the federal Centers for Disease Control and Prevention (CDC) now comprises an eight-component system. This system is designed to prevent and combat priority health risk behaviors among children and adolescents that would potentially result in HIV, STD or pregnancy, alcohol and other drug use, unintentional and intentional injuries, tobacco use, and risky patterns of diet and insufficient exercise. The eight components are: health education; health services; physical education; nutrition services; health promotion for staff (staff wellness); healthy school environment; and counseling, psychosocial and social services (Kolbe, 1994).

THE POTENTIAL REPUDIATION OF FEDERAL SCHOOL REFORM

Following the legislative initiatives outlined above, in January 1995 the 104th Congressional session commenced. The priorities of deficit reduction and reduced federal involvement, as stated by the leadership of the newly composed majority of the Congress, promise to affect profoundly the education legislation previously passed. Budget rescissions, totaling $1.7 billion, threaten to completely eliminate the Safe and Drug-Free Schools Program (part of IASA), "technical preparation" education, state student incentive grants, adult education literacy programs, and education for homeless children and youth, and to decimate Goals 2000, Title I grants, and school-to-work opportunities. Though federal financing for education on average accounts for only seven percent of a local district's total budget, education analysts believe the proposed cuts, in tandem with state and local budget problems, would particularly affect urban schools.

The "Contract With America," signed by 300 Republican members of the House of Representatives, established an ambitious legislative agenda to be completed during the first 100 days of the 104th Congress (1995). Federal involvement in social programs would be reduced through block grants. Block grants are funding mechanisms created from the consolidation of scores of categorical federal programs. The federal government proposes to provide a fixed lump sum to each state to use for their programs in several broad categories. Controversy surrounds the block grant funding mechanism. Some believe it would provide the states with greater flexibility and less federal oversight so that they may run innovative and less costly programs. While critics agree that this may be true, they argue that providing block grants would remove the safety net of support in the event of a recession, and that less federal oversight and requirements would result in reduced outcomes. For example, the Personal Responsibility Act establishes five block grants including those relating to Aid to Families with Dependent

Children (AFDC), Child Protection, Child Care, Family Nutrition (Food Stamps), and the school-based Nutrition Block Grant. All of these relate in various ways to families and children, and would therefore impact the school population. The most direct effects will come from the proposal to convert the school lunch and breakfast programs into block grants. Originally signed into law in 1946 by President Truman, the school lunch program today serves lunch to 25 million children, and the breakfast program, first legislated in 1966, now provides nutrition to 4.8 million children every school day. The block grant proposal cuts significantly the number of children that states would be able to feed (Geiger, 1995). The Police-or-Prevention Block Grants Bill, passed by the House in February 1995, replaces the Crime Bill's authorization of $8.8 billion for hiring new police officers over six years, and $3.9 billion for crime prevention programs, with $10 billion in block grants that give local authorities the choice of hiring more police or funding crime prevention programs.

PRIVATE REFORM EFFORTS

Apart from federal legislative activities for education reform, private innovations, and investments are being implemented at state and local levels to encourage entrepreneurial schools. Numerous innovative programs are developing: charter schools, defined by Finn (1994) as "independent public schools, often run by a group of teachers or parents, innovative or traditional in content, and free from most regulations and external controls;" public-private partnerships; performance testing for students and teachers; a merit-pay system for teachers and administrators; and school choice. These are all actions being taken to foster excellence in the education systems (Bennett, 1995). For example, The Edison Project, a for-profit venture initiated by media entrepreneur Christopher Whittle, announced $30 million in new investments that will guarantee the opening of the first phase of its for-profit plan to run public schools. The Edison Project's model focuses on high academic standards, use of technology, and parental involvement (Walsh, 1995). Other public and private ventures in education reform include the New American Schools Development Corporation, supporting several break-the-mold experimental schools, and the Coalition of Essential Schools (Finn, 1994). Another for-profit company, Minneapolis-based Education Alternatives Inc. (EAI), has been managing nine schools in Baltimore, Maryland, and has won a contract to manage all 32 public schools in Hartford, Connecticut.

Other innovative models include that of James Comer (1988) which involves a model of broad-based governance and management teams who focus on creating a desirable climate of social-relationships in both the school and the academic program. His model also involves groups of support staff (including social workers) who focus on preventing problem behaviors as well as modifying them (Comer, 1988; Hare, 1988; Winters and Easton, 1983).

CERTIFICATION

Poole (1954) emphasized the need to establish certification requirements for school social workers similar to those in other areas of education. This need remains acute as educators promote competency testing and credentialing of teachers to advance the goals of the education reform movement. In 1994, the National Board for Professional Teaching Standards awarded its first certificates to a small group of teachers who had met rigorous national standards formulated by the National Board. In 1992, almost two thousand school social workers qualified to receive a credential developed by NASW, the School Social Work Specialist credential (SSWS), which indicates that they have met national standards of knowledge and work experience. The credential involves passing a school social work test administered by the Educational Testing Service (E.T.S.) as part of the National Teachers Examination. Developed jointly by E.T.S. and NASW, this test was based on a national survey of school social workers conducted in 1989.

Constable (1979) stated that "There is a new thrust to school social work practice which is broad in its method base but more specific to the school . . . an integrated blend of change-oriented efforts directed to both individuals and systems" (p. 140). This statement remains relevant as we approach the end of the twentieth century. As the United States confronts its social, economic, and educational problems in a rapidly-changing world, and is being constantly transformed by developing technologies, school social workers must demonstrate and interpret the profession's relevance, and contribute creatively as new programs and paradigms are developed and implemented. School social workers must stand together being both proactive and reactive to the evolving economic, political and social world. Knowledge of such developments, and participation in their design, is essential to a healthy practice and to a healthy profession.

REFERENCES

An Education Congress. 1994, October 18. *The Washington Post*, p. A16.

Annie E. Casey Foundation. 1994. *Kids count data book: State profiles of child well-being*. Baltimore, MD: Annie E. Casey Foundation.

Augustus F. Hawkins–Robert T. Stafford Elementary and Secondary School Improvement Amendments of 1988, P.L. 100-297.

Austin, G. 1992. *School failure and alcohol and other drug use*. Madison, WI: Wisconsin Clearinghouse, University of Wisconsin-Madison.

Bennett, W.J. 1995, March. What to do about the children. *Commentary*, pp. 23–28.

Board of Trustees, Federal Old-Age and Survivors Insurance and Disability Insurance Trust Funds. 1995. *1995 annual report of the board of trustees of the federal old-age and survivors insurance and disability insurance trust funds*. Washington, D.C.: Social Security Administration.

Carlson, S., Clark, J.P., and Marx, D. 1992. *School and community resource collaboration* (Position paper). Des Moines, IA: Midwest School Social Work Council.

Chavkin, N. F., (ed.). 1993. *Families and schools in a pluralistic society*. Albany: State University of New York Press.

Children's Defense Fund. 1994. Press Release on Youth Violence, January 20, 1994. Washington, D.C.: Children's Defense Fund.

Children's Defense Fund. 1986. *Preventing children having children*. (Available from Children's Defense Fund, 122 C Street, NW, Washington, DC 20001.)

Child Trends, Inc. 1995. *Facts at a glance: 1992 data on teen fertility in the United States*. Washington, DC: Child Trends, Inc.

Cohen, D. 1995, March 29. Going the extra mile is hallmark of family-resource centers in Ky. *Education Week*, p. 6.

Comer, J. P. 1988. Is "parenting" essential to good teaching? *NEA Today: Issues '88*. 6: 34–40.

Constable, R. T. 1979. Toward the construction of role in an emergent social work specialization. *School Social Work Quarterly* 1:139–148.

Contract With America. 1994.

Dryfoos, J. G. 1994. *Full-service schools: a revolution in health and social services for children, youth, and families*. San Francisco, CA: Jossey-Bass, Inc.

Education Commission of the States. 1983. *Action for excellence*. Denver: Education Commission of the States.

Education for All Handicapped Children Act. P.L. 99-457.

Education of the Handicapped Act Amendments of 1986. P.L. 99-457.

Farrow, F., and Joe, T. 1982. Financing school-linked, integrated services. In *School-Linked Services, The Future of Children* 2:1, Spring 1992, pp. 56–57. Los Altos, CA: The David and Lucile Packard Foundation.

Federal Register. 1992. 57 (189): 44803.

Finn, C. E. 1994, October. What to do about education 2: the schools. *Commentary*, pp. 30–37.

Geiger, K. 1995, March 19. Thin gruel with an onion. *The Washington Post*, p. C4.

Ginsberg, L. 1995. *Social work almanac*. 2nd ed. Washington, DC: NASW Press.

Goals 2000: Educate America Act. P.L. 103-227.

Hare, I. 1995. School-linked services. In *Encyclopedia of Social Work*, 19th ed. Vol. 3. p. 2100–2109, Washington, DC: NASW Press.

Hare, I. 1994. School social work in transition. *Social Work in Education* 16(1):64–68.

Hare, I. 1988. School social work and effective schools. *Urban Education* 22:413–428.

Head Start Reauthorization of 1994. P.L. 103-252.

Hodgkinson, H. L. 1989. *The same client: The demographics of education and service delivery systems.* Washington, D.C.: Institute for Education Leadership.

Holmes, S. A. 1994, October 28. Ranks of inmates reach one million in a two decade rise. *The New York Times,* pp. A1 and A25.

Improving America's Schools Act of 1994. P.L. 103-382.

Individuals with Disabilities Education Act, P.L. 101-476.

Johnston, R. C. 1995, February 15. Clinton urges 3.8 percent increase for E. D. programs. *Education Week,* pp. 16, 18.

Kolbe, L. J. 1994. An essential strategy to improve the health and education of Americans. In P. Cortese and K. Middleton (eds.). *The comprehensive school health challenge: promoting health through education* (pp. 55–80). Santa Cruz: ETR Associates.

Levin, H. M. 1986. *Educational reform for disadvantaged students. An emerging crisis.* Washington, D.C.: National Education Association.

Lopez, H. D. 1993. Violence as a health and mental issue. *Testimony presented to the Committee on Government Operations. Subcommittee on Human Resources and Intergovernmental Relations of the U.S. House of Representatives.* November 1, 1993. Washington, DC.

Manegold, C. S. 1995, February 21. Republicans skeptical of Education Department's worth would like to eliminate it. *The New York Times,* p. A15.

McCurdy, K., and Daro, D. 1993. *Current trends in child abuse reporting and fatalities: the results of the 1992 annual fifty state survey.* Chicago: The National Committee for Prevention of Child Abuse.

Mintzies, P., and Hare, I. 1985. *The human factor: a key to excellence in education.* Silver Spring, MD: National Association of Social Workers.

National Alliance of Pupil Services Organizations. 1992. *Policy statement on school-linked integrated services.* Washington, DC: National Alliance of Pupil Services Organization.

National Association of Social Workers (NASW) Office of Government Relations 1994. Issue Brief: *The Improving America's Schools Act of 1994, Public Law 103-382.* Unpublished.

National and Community Service Trust Act of 1993. P.L. 103-82.

National Center for Children in Poverty. 1994. *National Center for Children in Poverty: a program report on the first five years 1989–1993.* NY: Columbia University School of Public Health, National Center for Children in Poverty.

National Coalition of Advocates for Students. 1985. *Barriers to excellence: our children at risk.* Boston: National Coalition of Advocates for Students.

National Commission on Children. 1991. *Beyond rhetoric: A new American agenda for children and families.* Washington, DC: National Commission on Children. (Available from U.S. Government Printing Office.)

National Commission on Excellence in Education. 1983. *A nation at risk: the imperative for education reform*. Washington, DC: National Commission on Excellence in Education.

National Education Association. 1987. *Estimate of school statistics 1986–87*. Washington, DC: National Education Association.

National Education Goals Panel. 1994. *National education goals report: Building a nation of learners, Volume I*. Washington, DC.

National Education Goals Panel. 1993. *National education goals report: Building a nation of learners. Volumes 1 and 2, 1994*. Washington, DC.

National Governors' Association. 1990. *National education goals*. Washington, DC: NGA (unpublished version dated January, 1990).

National Health and Education Consortium. 1995. *Eat to learn, learn to eat: the link between nutrition and learning in children*. Washington, DC: National Health and Educational Consortium.

Omnibus Budget Reconciliation Act of 1993. P.L. 103-66.

Pennekamp, M. 1992. Toward school-linked and school-based human services for children and families. *Social Work in Education* 14(2):125–30.

Poole, F. 1954. An analysis of the characteristics of school social work. In G. Lee (ed.). *Helping the troubled school child* (pp. 46–51). NY: National Association of Social Workers.

Quality Education for Minorities Project. 1990. *Education that works: an action plan for the education of minorities*. Cambridge, MA: Massachusetts Institute of Technology.

School Survey Finds Violence All Over; Big Cites are Worst. 1994, November 2. *Washington Post*, p. A17.

School-to-Work Opportunities Act of 1994. P.L. 103-239.

Stewart, D. W. 1993. *Immigration and education*. NY: Lexington Books. An Imprint of MacMillan Inc.

Student Loan Reform Act of 1993. P.L. 103-66.

Thomas, P. 1994, December 13. Use of drugs by teenagers is increasing. *The Washington Post*, pp. A1 and A17.

Troccoli, Karen B. 1994. *Fetal alcohol syndrome: The impact on children's ability to learn*. Washington, DC: National Health/Education Consortium, Occasional Paper #10.

The Twentieth Century Fund. 1983. *Making the grade*. NY: The Twentieth Century Fund.

U.S. Department of Education Office of Special Education and Rehabilitation Services. 1994. *Sixteenth annual report to Congress on the implementation of the Individuals With Disabilities Education Act*. Washington, DC: U.S. Department of Education Office of Special Education and Rehabilitation Services.

U.S. Department of Education Office of Special Education and Rehabilitation Services. 1989. *Eleventh annual report to Congress on the implementation of the*

Individuals With Disabilities Education Act. Washington, DC: U.S. Department of Education Office of Special Education and Rehabilitative Services.

U.S. Department of Health and Human Services, Maternal and Child Health Bureau. 1994. *Child health USA '93.* Washington, DC: U.S. Department of Health and Human Services, Maternal and Child Health Bureau.

Violent Crime Control and Law Enforcement Act of 1994. P.L. 103-322.

Vobejda, Barbara. 1994, April 20. Sobering look at alcohol and pregnancy. Doctors face the facts on drinking's effects. *The Washington Post,* p. A3.

Walsh, M. 1995, March 22. Edison Project announces $30 million in investments. *Education Week,* p. 6.

Winters, W. G., and Easton, F. 1983. *The practice of social work in schools: An ecological perspective.* NY: The Free Press.

SECTION TWO
Mandated Foundations for Service Delivery

CHAPTER 7
Mandated Foundations for Service Delivery: An Overview

Robert Constable
Professor, Loyola University of Chicago

The articles by Meares, Hare, and Germain in the previous section examined the past, the present, and the possible future of the relation between social work and education. This relation is made concrete and systematic through the development of social policy within and around the education institution and function. Social policy in a social institution, such as education, is formulated through societal and professional values, through a developing and growing body of law, expressing political realities. Social policy is manifested through the practice of the myriad professionals in a school in their daily encounters with students and through the concrete organization of the school itself. Thus the concrete organizational and economic realities of the school reflect the merging of law, public expectation, and what is humanly and organizationally possible. There is usually a gap between what is expected and valued and what at any given time becomes possible, but even the identification of such a gap is an important spur to change and may be prophetic of the future.

Over the past twenty years, laws and policies have been developed that clarify the civil rights of children with disabilities to a free, appropriate public education. Social work has found itself at the center of the decision-making and procedural safeguards for these children. The extension of these rights to the area of early childhood through P.L. 99-457 in 1986 opens the opportunity for early intervention with families as well as with children. Finally, the Regular Education Initiative (REI) encourages movement back into the regular classroom for youngsters with mild disabilities. Although the focus is on children with special needs, the thrust toward involvement with regular education is a trend that inevitably involves, in one way or another, all children and the school as a whole.

THE LAW OF SPECIAL EDUCATION

In 1970-72, two court decisions were made that were destined to revolutionize the delivery of services to pupils with disabilities in schools. The effects of these decisions would reverberate for many years and in the process change the fundamental nature of social services to children in schools. These decisions, *Pennsylvania Association of Retarded Children (PARC) v. Commonwealth of Pennsylvania*[1] and *Mills v. District of Columbia*,[2] each contributed to the revolution by defining the concept of rights of persons with disabilities to an appropriate education and to access to the same opportunities enjoyed in our society by the nondisabled. These court decisions acknowledged a set of civil rights for persons with disabilities and sketched out the boundaries in giving shape to those rights. In the several years following those decisions, other laws were passed, such as the Vocational Rehabilitation Act of 1973[3] and the Education of All Handicapped Children Act (P.L. 94-142) and the Individuals with Disabilities Education Act (P.L. 101-476).[4] These laws would define the rights more precisely and set down the mechanism for enforcement.

By the end of the decade and the beginning of the 1980s, there had gradually emerged a refined body of court decisions, laws, ensuing regulations, Office of Special Education policies, and Office of Civil Rights findings that have defined what is an irreversible direction toward the enforcement of the rights of people with disabilities. The thrust of this cumulative body of law is becoming more clear. Whether it is clarified by a body of regulations that may serve to avoid litigation, or whether the clarification is achieved through court decisions, the direction becomes the same. The overall direction of judicial decisions and regulations is toward the broadening of the traditional focus of the school in the process of providing and facilitating a free, appropriate, public education for all children. This right, to a free, appropriate, public education, was to consist of more than equal access to education or even compensatory education. For people with disabilities, neither opportunities nor objectives could be the same as for the regular education student. The new concept of the right to an education was to encompass, as Weintraub and Abeson clarified, "equal access to differing resources for differing objectives."[5]

Two major federal district court decisions dominate the many right-to-education decisions of this period and illustrate the definitive change taking place: *Pennsylvania Association for Retarded Children (PARC) v. Commonwealth of Pennsylvania*[6] and *Mills v. Board of Education*.[7] The PARC case was taken on behalf of thirteen school-aged children with developmental disabilities placed in state institutions and the class of all other children with developmental disabilities in the state denied free access to public education opportunity by public policy as expressed in law, policies, and practices of the state education agency and school districts throughout the state that would postpone, terminate, or deny children with developmental disablities access to a publicly supported education, including a public school program, tuition or tuition maintenance, and homebound instruction. The order struck down sections of the state school code and set dates by which the plaintiff children and all other children with developmental disablities in the state were to be reevaluated and provided a publicly supported education. Local districts that provided programs of preschool education were required to provide the same for children with developmental disablities. Furthermore, the court urged that these children be educated in a program most like that provided to nondisabled children.

Mills v. Board of Education followed the PARC case by several months and was basically similar except that a wider range of disabilities were represented and some of the children were residing at home. As in the PARC case, the court ordered that the plaintiffs and all others of the class were to receive a publicly supported education; the decision also specified that the plaintiffs would be entitled to due process of law prior to any change in educational program. The District of Columbia Board of Education failed to comply with the court order, stating that it did not have the necessary financial resources and that to divert money from regular education programs would deprive regular education children of their rights. The court was not persuaded by that contention. The school has an obligation to provide a free, public education to these exceptional children. Failure to provide this education could not be excused by the claim that there are insufficient funds. "The inadequacies of the District of Columbia public school system cannot be permitted to bear more heavily on the 'exceptional' or disabled child than on the normal child." The resultant court order, which was quite comprehensive, could be summarized under two basic sections:

1. A declaration of the constitutional right of all children, regardless of any exceptional condition or disability, to a publicly supported education.
2. A declaration that the defendant's rules, policies, and practices, which excluded children without a provision for adequate and immediate alternative educational services, and the absence of prior hearing and review of placement procedures, denied the plaintiffs and class rights of due process and equal protection of the law.

With these two cases the rights of child with disabilities to a free and appropriate public education and many of the procedural safeguards which were to find their way into later legislation and regulations were already manifest. Shortly following the court decisions, two closely related laws were to clarify further the rights of the disabled to an education. The first, Section 504 of the Vocational Rehabilitation Act of 1973, prohibited discrimination on the basis of disability in programs and activities receiving federal financial assistance.[8] The second, Public Law 94–142, a "bill of rights for the people with disabilities," gave further definition to the right to a free, appropriate, public education for all children with disabilities aged 3 to 21. The latter also provided for education in the environment of least restriction and spelled out the accountability and procedural safeguards which would ensure this right.[9] States that request funding under P.L. 94-142 now must file a state plan that assures that the state will comply with the requirements set forth in the P.L. 94-142 legislation. The Office of Special Education and Rehabilitative Services reviews these state plans and conducts onsite visits to determine whether educational programs comply with P.L. 94-142. Furthermore, all states that accept federal funds for any educational purpose must comply with Section 504. A state may decide to reject funding under P.L. 94-142 but must still comply with Section 504 unless the state decides to reject all federal educational funds. The Office of Civil Rights enforces Section 504 by investigating complaints and coordinating compliance reviews.

P.L. 94-142 covers a wide range of disabilities comprising approximately 12 percent of the school-age population. Educational objectives for children with disabilities are arrived at by the multidisciplinary team and parents, following a "complete, multifaceted, nondiscriminatory evaluation." These objectives, together with the special education and related services needed to achieve them, become part of a written Individualized Education Program (IEP). The IEP needs to contain "appropriate objectives, criteria and evaluation procedures, and schedules for determining, on at least an annual basis, whether instructional objectives are being achieved." The IEP is a statement of resources necessary to achieve a goal, an agreement on what an appropriate education for the child is to be, and the central management tool for ensuring accountability and compliance with the purposes of P.L. 94-142.[10]

Children with disabilities have the right to special education and related services. Related services are defined in the regulations as "those additional services required to assist a child to benefit from special education." Without establishing a limit, the regulations of P.L. 94-142 provided a long list of possible related services. This list includes psychological and school social work services and excludes medical services, except those needed for diagnostic and evaluation purposes. The concept of related services is also treated in the educational regulations of Section 504 of the Vocational Rehabilitation Act of 1973. The Section 504 regulations define nondiscrimination in education as "the provision of a free, appropriate public education to qualified persons with disabilities regardless of the nature and severity of the person's disability." These regulations extended the concept of related aids and services to apply to regular education as well as special education. Two passages from these regulations point out the purpose of "aids, benefits, and services" in regular education:

> For the purpose of this report, aids, benefits and services, to be equally effective are not required to produce the identical result or level of achievement for

disabled or for nondisabled persons but must afford disabled persons equal opportunity to obtain the same result, to gain the same benefit or to the same level of achievement, in the most integrated setting appropriate to the person's needs. . . .

A recipient shall place a disabled person in the regular educational environment operated by the recipient unless it is demonstrated by the recipient that the education of the person in the regular environment with the use of supplementary aids and services cannot be provided satisfactorily.[11]

There has been considerable discussion as to how extensive the term *related services* should be. To what extent would the term include ongoing services, medical in nature? Would a language board or a hearing aid be related service? Is psychotherapy a related service? How extensive this right was to be would be a matter for the courts and ongoing federal regulations. In the following five years a body of judicial decisions and regulations would emerge that clarified the meaning and direction of this right. As in the Mills case, prior to P.L. 94-142, the child's right to a free, appropriate public education, and to related services, as defined in the IEP, could not be abridged by ability or availability in the local district. In many cases, the needed special education and related services would be purchased from the outside, from special education districts designed to meet needs that the local schools could not meet, and from private schools and institutions. The development of ways to share costs for services between districts quickly followed the enunciation of the right.

According to the Office of Civil Rights, Congress did not intend to restrict the definition of the term *related services* to any list or category. What the child with disabilities needs to assist him or her in benefiting from an education is the essential criterion of related services. Developmental, corrective, or supportive services (such as artistic and cultural programs, art, music, and dance therapy) could be related services if they are required to assist a disabled child to benefit from special education. An ongoing medical service would be considered a related service if it is needed to enable a qualified student with disabilities to obtain the same result, to gain the same benefit, or to reach the same level of achievement as a nondisabled student to the maximum extent possible.[12]

The issue of payment for psychotherapy as a "related service" for youngsters with emotional disturbances in residential facilities was joined in 1980. In a landmark decision in the federal district court in Northern Illinois, *Gary B. v. Cronin*,[13] the court ruled that psychotherapy and a number of other services given to children in a residential treatment center should be considered "related services" and should be made available at no cost to youngsters and their parents. The district court decision took place about six months after an Office of Civil Rights finding that the state was out of compliance with federal guarantees of equal access in withholding payment for psychotherapy for children in institutions.[14] The agreement in response to the Office of Special Education and the District Court released $48 million of federal funding that had been withheld. In agreeing that psychotherapy and other services should be available at no cost to the parents, the state made it clear that the cost would not necessarily be borne by the state education agency, but that planning for each placement would involve participation of other state agencies that would share whatever parts of the cost for the youngster as might be appropriate. The only solution to the potential cost liability to the schools alone would be a degree of coordination of services and collaboration not hitherto possible in a segmented system. The school in many cases would only be responsible for purchase of special education services from the residential school, with other state agencies picking up other parts of the bill.[15]

An Office of Civil Rights ruling in the case of a Connecticut regulation on related services sheds light on whether a clear distinction between *educational* and *noneducational* could be made. The regulation would have allowed school districts to avoid payment for certain related services if they determined residential placements were for noneducational reasons. In this particular case, the school district refused to pay for room and board and the cost of psychological counseling as "other than educationally related aids and services." The Office of Civil Rights' finding was that the "critical element" in determining whether a local educational agency is responsible for paying the cost of related services is whether the disabling condition adversely affects the child's educational performance. As soon as the school district decided that a residential placement was necessary for the student "to meet with success in school," it became obligated to provide that education at no cost to the parents.[16]

Whether educational policy is made through regulations or through the courts, the effect of such policies and the direction taken by the courts in interpreting P.L. 94-142 and Section 504 is becoming fairly clear. It is crucial to analyze the effect of these provisions on school social work practice, on delivery of services to children with disabilities, and on the school itself as it has traditionally conceived of its mission. Along with the question of the effect of these developments on schools and on school services is the larger and related question of implementation. How might schools absorb the changes in their traditional mission? How may the current service delivery system adapt to the current reality of entitlement to services through the schools? What models of school social work practice emerge from these mandates which cover areas where school social workers have been serving for seventy years? What role might school social work play in the implementation of services to children based on educational rights?

In Section Two, John McLaughlin and Ruth Ann Protinsky examine values in education, particularly as developed over the previous thirty years in special education. Schools reflect to some degree the changing relations of society toward children with disabilities and the changing legal base of special education. They also reflect values that have developed among educators in the struggle to define their craft. Social workers will see in values such as zero reject a striking similarity to their personal values. In many respects these values are a reaction to the potential destructiveness to children with disabilities of certain mainstream societal values, such as individualism and competition. Maintaining such values becomes further justification for collegial relations with education and for the extension and development of social work skills in the service of these familiar commitments. Such values help to define the development of practice methods and techniques.

Three papers in Section Two review how the landscape of schools is changing as a result of the explication of rights of children with disabilities to free, appropriate, public education. Marguerite Tiefenthal, Dave Moorman, and Vaughn Morrison review in detail of the parts of the law and its regulations that continue to have a profound effect on school social work practice. Kathleen Kirk Bishop extends the discussion of the preceding chapter to the Early Childhood Amendments (P.L. 99-457). These amendments extend the right to a free, appropriate, public education to youngsters with disabilities three to five years of age and encourage the development of early intervention programs for youngsters from birth through two years of age. A family focus is central to serving these youngsters. Parents and siblings need to realize what the child with disabilities brings to and asks of the family. The family, not the school, is where learning takes place at this age, and the most important person in education for families of very young children with special needs is the social worker, not the teacher.

Changes in the expectations of schools and in school structure are profoundly influencing the purposes and functions of school social work. Furthermore, as the school social worker becomes more deeply involved with consultation on issues that have implications, not simply for single cases, but for entire school districts, an understanding of the roots of policy development in the schools will be essential. Even now, in many locales the knowledge and skills of school social work and its understanding of the school clientele are proving useful to the policy-development process. Any further development will depend upon the commitment of school social workers to seeing policy development as a natural direction of practice and to preparing themselves for the implications of this role.

In summary, the articles in this section provide in-depth explorations into crucial aspects of the school as an institution and its complex task of coping and interfacing with other institutions around human service issues. There is no pretense of providing a comprehensive review of all aspects of the institution or all the vulnerable populations and institutions with which the school deals. Rather, the articles provide models for the type of thinking necessary if school social work is to achieve its appropriate match with the institution of education and provide a link to other elements in the community as a system.

REFERENCES

1. *Pennsylvania Association of Retarded Children (PARC) v. Commonwealth of Pennsylvania*, 334 F. Supp. 1257. (E.D. Pa. 1971).
2. *Mills v. Board of Education of the District of Columbia*, 348 F. Supp. 866 (DDC, 1972).
3. 29 U.S.C. 794.
4. 20 U.S.C. 1401 et seq.
5. Weintraub, F. J., and A. Abeson. 1976. New education policies for the handicapped: the quiet revolution. In F. Weintraub, A. Abeson, J. Ballard, and M. LaVor, *Public policy and the education of exceptional children.* Washington, D.C.: Council for Exceptional Children. pp. 7-13.
6. *PARC v. Commonwealth of Pennsylvania.*
7. *Mills v. Board of Education of the District of Columbia.*
8. 29 U.S.C. 794.
9. 20 U.S.C. 1401 et seq.
10. Department of Health Education and Welfare. Education of handicapped children. *Federal Register* August 23, 1977: 121a340-42.
11. Department of Education. Nondiscrimination on the basis of handicap in programs and activities receiving or benefiting from federal financial assistance. *Federal Register* May 19, 1980: 33(6)(1) (34CFR part 104).
12. Office of Civil Rights, Letter of Findings, February 27, 1980, Illinois Board of Education, *Education of the Handicapped Law Report* (Washington, D.C., CRR Publishing, 1980), 257:176. See also Education of the Handicapped Law Report, Analysis and Comment, EHLR Perspective: Related Services, Supplement 28, July 25, 1980 (Washington, D.C.: CRR Publishing, 1980), A/C 20-21, *Tatro v. Texas*, U.S. Dist. Court, N. Dist. Texas, 12-21-79, and *Tatro v. Texas*, 625 F. 2nd 557 (5th Cir. 1980).
13. *Gary B. v. Cronin*, 79c5383 (N.D. Ill) 1980; see also: *North v. D.C. Board of Education*, 466 F. Supp. 136 (D.D.C. 1979); *In the Matter of the "A" Family*, 602 P. 2d 157 (Supreme Court of Montana) 1979, for parallel decisions on psychotherapy services.
14. Office of Civil Rights, Letter of Findings, February 27, 1980, Illinois Board of Education, op. cit.
15. Illinois State Board of Education, *Management Bulletin*, Fall 1980; D. G. Gill, Illinois State Superintendent of Education, Letter to Dr. E. W. Martin, Assistant Secretary for Special Education and Rehabilitative Services, September 3, 1980.
16. Office of Civil Rights, Simsbury, Connecticut Public Schools, Letter of Findings, June 16, 1980, *Education of the Handicapped Law Review*, 257:178. (Washington, D.C.: C.R.R. Publishing.)

CHAPTER 8

Foundations for Values in Special Education

John A. McLaughlin
Associate Professor and Director, Institute for the Study of Exceptionalities,
Virgina Tech, Blacksburg, Virginia

Ruth Ann Protinsky
Research Associate, Curriculum and Instruction Department, Virgina Tech,
Blacksburg, Virginia

The purpose of this chapter is to examine the relation of values to the delivery of special education and related services to learners with disabilities. The passage of P. L. 94–142, the Education for All Handicapped Children Act, and subsequently P.L. 101–476, Individuals with Disabilities Education Act (IDEA), have brought many educational reforms. Among these have been the multidisciplinary approach to the identification, diagnosis, planning, and delivery of special education and related services. Professions such as psychology, medicine, social work, education, and others which, in pockets of excellence, had previously worked together, were now given federal impetus to join together to meet the needs of learners with disabilities. Working together brings forth a number of value issues. The authors attempt to define some of the values typically related to special education and discuss some issues around value conflict.

WHY VALUES?

Values play an integral part in people's day-to-day interactions with their environments. Education is a key component of this environment and, as such, is impacted upon by the values of those involved with the planning, implementing, and evaluation of its activities. Goodlad and Richter (1977), focusing on the importance of values in education, indicate that when curriculum planners consider the characteristics of society which will be addressed in the school's curriculum, the values of planners are likely to dictate which characteristics will be included. Indeed, values probably enter into all phases of curricular planning.

The various curriculum strategies that are then operationalized within school systems also are impacted upon by the values of the curriculum implementors (administrators, teachers, and support staff), those who interact with the curriculum (students and parents), those who provide fiscal support and appropriate funds for education (taxpayers and school board members), and those who interpret the legal implications of the curriculum (court systems).

Further, values in education certainly are not limited to the visible curriculum operating within school systems. Fraenkel (1980, pp. 95-96) suggested that research has shown that the hidden curriculum of our schools "socializes children to various expectations that may or may not be in accord with what the visible curriculum teaches . . . and which is far more powerful and longer lasting than anything that the visible curriculum can present."

Corrigan (1978), in discussing the implications of P. L. 94-142 for classroom teachers, suggests that teaching and teacher training has placed its sights too frequently on means rather than ends. He states further that there are only two options open to educators: to be conscious of and positive about their values, or to hide and confuse them.

Another set of values that influence the school system are those values that have been mandated into laws by local, state, or federal legislative bodies. Regulations associated with these legislative policies force schools to interpret and enforce values inherent in the laws.

Values also play a role in the design, delivery, and evaluation of special education and related services. This delivery system, by law and practice, has become multidisciplinary in nature. One of the key figures in the system is the school social worker. According to Costin (1981), the purpose of the profession of social work is based in the values of its members. The values held by school social workers and their colleagues from other professions are often similar, but when they are not, conflict may arise.

VALUES TYPICALLY ASSOCIATED WITH SPECIAL EDUCATION

Values are highly personalized. However, it is possible to identify some values clearly associated with the delivery of special education and related services to learners with disabilities. The preamble to the NEA Code of Ethics sets forth the general values which educators profess. The statement begins with general standards of belief in the worth and dignity of people, recognition of the importance of the pursuit of truth, the encouragement of scholarship, the promotion of democratic citizenship, the protection of the freedom to teach and the responsibility to practice according to the highest ethical standards. Following these general statements are a set of values which relate more specifically to the education institution and the process of education.

> We measure success by the process of each student toward achievement of his maximum potential. We, therefore, work to stimulate the spirit of inquiry, the acquisition of knowledge and understanding, and the thoughtful formulation of worthy goals. We recognize the importance of cooperative relationships with other community institutions, especially the home (pp. 67–68).

Many of the values associated with today's special education programming are found in the language of P. L. 94-142 and IDEA. Some of these are:

1. *Zero reject.* All children regardless of the type or severity of their disability must be afforded an opportunity to benefit from a public education at no cost. School personnel must actively seek out the disabled learner and inform him or her or the child's advocate of his/her rights.
2. *Nondiscriminatory testing.* When identified through child-find or school-based referral systems, the learner potentially in need of special educational services is entitled to be evaluated, using fair practices which lead to valid and useful educational planning and placement decisions.
3. *Individualized education.* Educational programs for learners with disabilities will be judged meaningful only when they are based on the individual's strengths and needs, as identified through nondiscriminatory testing.
4. *Least restrictive placement.* Whenever possible, special educational services are to be provided in an environment conducive to the maximum interaction between disabled and nondisabled.
5. *Evaluation.* At least annually, the learner's individual program is to be evaluated to determine the degree to which that program has met his/her needs and to identify areas where special educational services must be continued or added.
6. *Procedural due process.* At all times, the individual or his/her advocate or the school may protest or challenge an intended action, which threatens the loss of an entitlement.
7. *Consumer involvement.* This value is basic to our democratic society. It infers that the individual values the opportunity to participate in planning and programming which affects him/her. In special education such participation can come at any phase in the child-centered processes of referral, diagnosis, planning, placement, instruction, or evaluation. Further, public participation is called for on advisory panels when LEAs and SEAs prepare programwide service plans.
8. *Qualified staff.* Federal and state regulations require that services be provided to learners with disabilities by qualified professionals. These regulations also call for inservice education to promote this concept.

9. *Early identification.* We value the early identification of a disability and subsequent provision of appropriate services. This is evident not only in our federal and state laws, but also in the literature. The number of textbooks and commercially produced instructional packages designed to impact on preschool-aged learners far exceeds the number for other age groups.

10. *Multidisciplinary involvement.* Providing appropriate special educational and related services requires input from a variety of professionals at all points in the system, from referral through evaluation. No longer does the special education teacher have sole responsibility for the learner with disabilities. Program planning, implementation, and evaluation is now a team effort and the members respect the viewpoints and counsel of other members.

Turnbull and Turnbull (1978, pp. 249-251) set forth a comprehensive list of beliefs which they consider important to guide social, educational, and political changes as they relate to the person with disabilities.

1. We believe that education makes a difference in a person's life.
2. We know and believe that children with disablities can profit from an education appropriate to their capabilities.
3. We believe in equity, that is, in equal educational opportunity.
4. We believe in the value of an education for all people—the universality of education.
5. We believe that governmental benefits should not be parceled out on the basis of unalterable characteristics of the recipients.
6. We believe in the essential sameness of all persons.
7. We believe that the economic investment of furnishing a person with disabilities with an education appropriate to his needs will yield long-term returns in the increased productivity and decreased dependency of that person.
8. We believe that the ample evidence of longstanding state and local neglect of the educational claims of children with disabilities will not be abated in the foreseeable future.
9. We believe that, because we choose who governs us, we have the right to ask our representatives to be accountable to us.
10. We believe that people should treat each other fairly and decently and that government should deal fairly and decently with the governed. Alternatively stated, we believe that a fair process of governing will produce fair and acceptable results.
11. We believe in participatory democracy in the education of children.

Values play an important part in the establishment of categories of disabling conditions. According to Bartel and Guskin (1980), the distinctiveness of the disabled is dependent, not on their characteristics, but rather on the characteristic responses of others to them. Professionals have created labels, organizations, and treatments which reflect their values and those of society.

Costin (1981) cited the standards for social work services in the schools, which were approved by the National Association of Social Workers in 1978, as reflecting the basic values which influence school social workers. She presented a model for understanding those values which divided them into three levels: (1) the ultimate values, (2) valued qualities of a well-functioning person, and (3) operational values. An example of an ultimate value held by school social workers might be equality of educational opportunity. Thus, equal access to the school resources for the learner with disabilities would be supported. A valued quality of a well-functioning person might be "readiness to seek and use opportunities." Here the school social worker might value the ability of the learner with disabilities to use and/or benefit from resources made available to him or her. Finally, "equal treatment within the school setting" might be a valued principle. In this case the social worker would promote a school environment where the disabled learner is given the same opportunity as his or her nondisabled peer.

Conflicts with other values in society and with other values we ourselves hold is to be expected. However, these need not be viewed negatively. Werkmeister (1970) implied that growth can occur through value conflicts. According to that author, innovations evolve from value judgments that challenge existing values. Filley (1975, pp. 4–7) suggested that conflict in itself is neither bad nor good. Rather it is the outcome of conflict to which one should look for value. Some positive outcomes of conflict identified are:

1. The diffusion of more serious conflict.
2. The stimulation to search for new facts or solutions.
3. An increase in group cohesion and performance.
4. The measure of power or ability.

In order for conflict to emerge as a positive factor in the decision-making process, it must be dealt with openly. A problem-solving approach must be utilized. Avoidance, withdrawal, or authoritarian strategies will rarely lead to positive ends. Rather, an approach to conflict management, which results in some gain or benefit for all participants, is necessary.

Filley (1975) outlines nine broad antecedent conditions which might precipitate conflict in organizations. These are applied to the special education arena.

1. *Ambiguous jurisidictions.* These conditions are likely to generate conflict when roles are not clearly defined. For example, the school social worker

and guidance counselor may both potentially provide counseling to the learner with disabilities.
2. *Conflicts of interest.* This potential for conflict is exemplified in monitoring of local special education programs by SEA staff. The local program wants to get on with the business of serving learners and views the preparation for and participation in the monitoring visit as an impediment.
3. *Communication barriers.* Here two examples will suffice. First, the school social worker may be located in a different building from the school psychologist, with infrequent conjoint visits to a particular learner's classroom. Little opportunity exists for sharing. An associated problem is the lack of understanding of the role and function of other coworkers. For example, the regular classroom teacher may not know why the social worker is involved in the disabled learner's program. He may not understand the rationale (values) underlying the social worker's strategies.
4. *Dependance on one party.* Whenever the work of the group is ordered, the possibility of slippage exists if one member does not complete his task. How often is the eligibility decision delayed because the school psychologist has a backlog of clients? Or the delivery of family counseling withheld because the school social worker has too many clients to serve?
5. *Differentiation in organization.* The more complex an organization is, the greater the potential for conflict. In recent years, passage of federal and state laws regulating special education has led to an increased complexity in service delivery systems. With such complexity may come conflicts associated with items one through four.
6. *Association of parties.* As the decisions to be made become more dependent on cooperation between and among group members, the opportunity for conflict increases. The multidisciplinary nature of special education reinforces this occurrence. Hyman et al. (1973) found considerable conflict in school-based child study teams charged with arriving at classification decisions.
7. *Need for consensus.* Closely associated with condition six, the need for consensus requires the group to come up with one decision. Here a potential conflict may arise when members from similar disciplines cannot agree on an approach to a learner need. For example, the psychologist may want to use behavior management while the psychiatrist may see group therapy as the most appropriate method to change antisocial behavior.
8. *Behavior regulations.* Filley indicates that regulations may reduce conflict because they restrict alternatives. However, they can produce conflict when the group members resist or disagree with the regulations. How

often have we observed in special education the cry for local and, at times, individual autonomy?

9. *Unresolved prior conflict.* In this case, the group interaction was probably doomed before it got underway. Prior unresolved conflicts serve as barriers to productive group decision making. The frustration of regular classroom consultants is an exemplar here. How frequently have you heard in the IEP meeting, "The last time you placed a learner with disabilities in my class I never saw you until the end of the year evaluation"?

There are many values which may guide programmatic decision making in special education. There are just as many opportunities for conflict. However, conflict in itself is not necessarily bad. The outcomes of the conflict must be evaluated. Several potentially positive outcomes were presented. For these to occur positive action on the part of the conflict participants must be undertaken. In the opinion of these authors, the first step in reaching a positive resolution to the conflict is to gain an understanding of the value systems which are driving or restraining the actions of the participants in the conflict.

Delivery of special education and related services involves a multidisciplinary approach. Hopefully this discussion will set the beginnings of fruitful future discussions between educators and social workers on values. We have reviewed some of the values which educators subscribe to and which guide special education programming. These are values in conflict and in development. Social workers, who are no strangers to value conflicts, can find some similar resonance to some of the values to which educators subscribe. This is not purely accidental. Social reformers, such as Jane Addams and her associates, have influenced education as well as social welfare. There are ample reasons for social workers and educators to collaborate on shared commitments and similar visions for the future.

REFERENCES

Bartel, N., and Guskin, S. 1980. A handicap as a social phenomenon. In R. L. Burgdorf (ed.). *The legal rights of handicapped persons.* Baltimore, MD: Brooks.

Corrigan, D.C. 1978. Political and moral contexts that produced P. L. 94–142. *Journal of Teacher Education* 29(6).

Costin, L. B. 1981. School social work as a specialized practice. *Social Work* 26(1).

Filley, A. C. 1975. *Personnel management problem solving.* Glenview, IL: Scott, Foresman.

Fraenkel, J. R. 1980. Goals of teaching values and value analysis. *Journal of Research and Development in Education* 13(2).

Hyman, E., Carroll, R., Duffey, J., Manni, J., and Winikur, D. 1973. Patterns of interpersonal conflict resolution in school child study teams. *Journal of School Psychology* 11(3) Fall.

Turnbull, H. R., and Turnbull, A. P. 1978. *Free, appropriate, public education: Law and implementation.* Denver, CO: Love Publishing.

Werkmeister, W. H. 1970. *Historical spectrum of value theories* (Vol. 1). *German Language Group.* Lincoln, NB: Johnson Publishing.

CHAPTER 9

Educational Mandates for Children with Disabilities: Educational Program Development

Vaughn W. Morrison
School Social Work Consultant, Illinois State Board of Education, Past President, Illinois Association of School Social Workers, Past President, National Board of State Consultants for School Social Work Services

Marguerite Tiefenthal
Retired School Social Worker, School District 181, Hinsdale, Illinois

David Moorman
School Social Worker, Downers Grove Elementary Schools, Downers Grove, Illinois

This chapter reviews the Individuals with Disabilities Education Act (IDEA) P.L. 101-476, originally passed as PL 94-142, including the evaluation of children with disabilities, delivery of special education services, due-process hearing procedures, parent participation, accountability, and other facets of the education of children with one or more disabilities. The law is quite comprehensive and specific (the rules and regulations for its implementation total forty-nine pages in the Federal Register printed in small type).[1] We can only scratch the surface in this chapter. To be fully informed, obtain your own copy. The more you understand the letter and spirit of the law, the greater your efforts can impact its implementation.

As you read the law, you will realize that many sections are subject

---

SOURCE: This paper originally appeared in Robert Constable and Marguerite Tiefenthal, eds., *The School Social Worker and the Handicapped Child: Making P.L. 94-142 Work* (DeKalb, Ill.: Illinois Regional Resource Center, 1979).

to a variety of interpretations. Since its enactment, many of the originally confusing discrepancies in the statute and its attendant regulations have been clarified by the courts and administrative policy documents. One of the most helpful is the Code of Federal Regulations as Part 300 Appendix C. However, the area of special education is a much more complex area of the law than is the regular education aspect, and therefore, it is constantly being clarified by the courts.

THE PURPOSE OF THE INDIVIDUALS WITH DISABILITIES EDUCATION ACT (IDEA)

The intent of the law is to see that in all cases children with disabilities receive a free and appropriate public education which allows them to develop their abilities. By law, children with disabilities can no longer be ignored or under-served. Special educational services and related services must be provided. Specifically, the purpose of the act is:

1. To insure that all children with disabilities have available to them a free, appropriate, public education which includes special education and related services to meet their unique needs.
2. To insure that the rights of children with disabilities and their parents are protected.
3. To assist states and localities to provide for the education of all children with disabilities.
4. To assess and insure the effectiveness of efforts to educate those children.[2]

THE CHILD WITH DISABILITIES

The act defines *children with disabilities* as:

> Those children evaluated ... as being mentally retarded, hard of hearing, deaf, speech impaired, visually handicapped, seriously emotionally disturbed, orthopedically impaired, other health impaired, deaf-blind, multihandicapped, or as having specific learning disabilities, who because of those impairments need special education and related services.[3]

Children with autism and traumatic brain injury are included in a later amendment (P.L. 101-476).

SERIOUSLY EMOTIONALLY DISTURBED CHILDREN

IDEA makes provision for disabling conditions and each of these conditions is defined separately. One definition of particular significance to school social workers is "seriously emotionally disturbed." This term is defined as a condition exhibiting one or more of the following characteristics over a long period of time and to a marked degree, which adversely affects educational performance:

An inability to learn which cannot be explained by intellectual, sensory, or health factors.

An inability to build or maintain satisfactory interpersonal relationships with peers and teachers.

Inappropriate types of behavior or feelings under normal circumstances.

A general pervasive mood of unhappiness or depression.

A tendency to develop physical symptoms or fears associated with personal or school problems.[4]

Children who are mentally or physically impaired and who face the chronic stress of being disabled in a competitive world which values "normality" can easily become depressed and fail in relationships with others. Such children need our support and skill in accessing the resources they need to the greatest extent possible.

SPECIAL EDUCATION

According to IDEA, special education means:

Specially designed instruction, at no cost to the parent, to meet the unique needs of a disabled child, including classroom instruction, instruction in physical education, home instruction, and instruction in hospitals and institutions. The term includes speech pathology, or any other related service, if the service consists of specially designed instruction, at no cost to the parents, to meet the unique needs of a disabled child, and is considered "special education" rather than a "related service" under State standards.[5]

A child is not disabled unless he or she needs special education. The definition of "related service" also depends on this definition, since a related service must be necessary for a child to benefit from special education. Therefore, if a child does not need special education, there can be no "related services" and the child (because not "disabled") is not covered under the act.[6]

RELATED SERVICE

The term *related services* means transportation and such developmental, corrective, and other supportive services as are required to assist a child with a disability to benefit from special education, and includes transportation, speech pathology and audiology, psychological services, physical and occupational therapy, recreation, early identification and assessment of disabilities in children, counseling services, and medical services for diagnostic or evaluation purposes. The term also includes [7] school health services, social work services in schools, and parent counseling and training.[8]

"Social work services in schools" include:

1. Preparing a social or developmental history on a child identified as possibly having disabilities.
2. Group and individual counseling with the child and family.
3. Working with those problems in a child's living situation (home, school, and community) that affect the child's adjustment in school.
4. Mobilizing school and community resources to enable the child to receive maximum benefit from his or her educational program.[9]

SPECIAL EDUCATION "AT NO COST" TO PARENTS

"At no cost" means that all specially designed instruction is provided without charge, but does not preclude incidental fees which are normally charged to nondisabled students or their parents as part of the regular education program, such as book fees.[10]

EVALUATION

IDEA is quite specific in requiring a complete, multifaceted, nondiscriminatory evaluation. Testing and evaluating materials and procedures used for the purposes of evaluation and placement of children with disabilities must be selected and administered so as not to be racially or culturally discriminatory.[11]

Preplacement Evaluation

Before any action is taken with respect to the initial placement of a child with disabilities in a special education program, a full and individual evaluation of the child's educational needs must be conducted in accordance with the requirements (stated below).[12]

Evaluation procedures mean state and local educational agencies shall insure, at a minimum, that:

1. Tests and other evaluation materials:
   a. Are provided and administered in the child's native language or other mode of communication, unless it is clearly not feasible to do so.
   b. Have been validated for the specific purpose for which they are used.

c. Are administered by trained personnel in conformance with the instructions provided by their producer.
2. Tests and other evaluation materials include those tailored to assess specific areas of educational need and not merely those which are designated to provide a single general intelligence quotient.
3. Tests are selected and administered so as best to insure that when a test is administered to a child with impaired sensory, manual, or speaking skills, the test results accurately reflect the child's aptitude or achievement level or whatever other factors the test purports to measure, rather than reflecting the child's impaired sensory, manual, or speaking skills (except where those skills are the facets which the test purports to measure).
4. No single procedure is used as the sole criterion for determining an appropriate educational program for a child.
5. The evaluation is made by a multidisciplinary team or group of persons, including at least one teacher or other specialists with knowledge in the area of suspected disability.
6. The child is assessed in all areas related to the suspected disability, including, where appropriate, health, vision, hearing, social and emotional status, general intelligence, academic performance, communicative status, and motor abilities.[13]

Although the law implies that not every child need be assessed in all areas, there are some areas which must be checked with every student, such as vision and hearing. The stress of a disabling condition would generally dictate that some social and emotional evaluation may be necessary.

PROVISIONS FOR THE INDEPENDENT EVALUATION

Parents have the right to an independent educational evaluation, and under certain conditions, this may be carried out at public expense:

> A parent has the right to an independent educational evaluation at public expense if the parent disagrees with an evaluation obtained by the public agency. However, the public agency may initiate a hearing ... to show that its evaluation is appropriate. If the final decision is that the evaluation is appropriate, the parent still has the right to an independent educational evaluation, but not at the public expense.[14]

If the parent obtains an independent educational evaluation at private expense, the results of the evaluation:

> Must be considered by the public agency in any decision made with respect to the provision of a free, appropriate public education to the child.

May be presented as evidence at a hearing under this subpart regarding that child.[15]

Thus, the parents are guaranteed that results of an independent evaluation will be considered by the school in the evaluation of their child. This is a natural outcome, since P.L. 94-142, and subsequently IDEA, came into being as the result of many parents' frustration in their attempts to obtain an appropriate education for their children with disabilities. The bill's origin in parent concerns and child advocacy comes through strongly in this procedural safeguard.

PLACEMENT PROCEDURES

In interpreting evaluation data in making placement decisions, each public agency shall:

1. Draw upon information from a variety of sources, including adaptive and achievement tests, teacher recommendations, physical condition, social or cultural background, and adaptive behavior.
2. Insure that information obtained from all of these sources is documented and carefully considered.
3. Insure that the placement decision is made by a group of persons including persons knowledgeable about the child, the meaning of the evaluation data, and the placement options.
4. Insure that the placement decision is made in conformity with the least restrictive environment rules.
5. If a child ... needs special education and related services an individualized education program must be developed for the child.[16]

MULTIDISCIPLINARY TEAM

As mentioned in the placement procedures (point three), the evaluation, eligibility, and placement decisions are made by a multidisciplinary team or group of persons, including persons knowledgeable about the child, the meaning of the evaluation data, and the placement options. The basic procedure which public agencies are required to use in evaluating all children with disabilities requires that ... the evaluation be done by a multidisciplinary team.[17]

MEETINGS

After the meeting, or portion of the meeting, has determined that a student is eligible for special education and related services, an Individualized Education Program (IEP) must be developed. This discussion must occur only after the student has met all three requirements for eligibility: 1) verification of a disability; 2) proof of adverse effect in the educational environment; and 3) the need of special education and related services as the only remaining approach left for the school to serve the student. "A student merely requiring accommodations or who has no adverse effect is not, by definition, eligible under IDEA."[18]

The meeting to develop a child's Individualized Education Program must be held within 30 calendar days of the determination that the child needs special education and related services.[19] The following guidelines specify who may participate in the multidisciplinary staff conferences.

1. *General.* The public agency shall insure that each meeting includes the following participants:
    a. A representative of the public agency, other than the child's teacher, who is qualified to provide, or supervise the provision of special education.
    b. The child's teacher.
    c. One or both of the child's parents.
    d. The child, where appropriate.
    e. Other individuals at the discretion of the parent or agency.
2. *Evaluation personnel.* For a child with disabilities who has been evaluated for the first time, the public agency shall insure:
    a. That a member of the evaluation team participates in the meeting
    or
    b. That the representative of the public agency, the child's teacher, or some other person is present, who is knowledgeable about the evaluation procedures used with the child and is familiar with the results of the evaluation.[20]

Each public agency is responsible for initiating and conducting meetings to develop, review, and revise each child's IEP. A meeting must be held for this purpose at least once a year.[21]

WHAT IF NEITHER PARENT CAN ATTEND?

The school must make a good faith effort to see that at least one parent comes to the meeting.

1. Each public agency shall take steps to insure that one or both of the parents of the child with disabilities are present at each meeting or afforded the opportunity to participate, including:
    a. Notifying parents of the meeting early enough to insure that they will have an opportunity to attend.
    b. Scheduling the meeting at a mutually agreed upon time and place.

2. The notice under paragraph 1a of this section must indicate the purpose, time, and location of the meeting, and who will be in attendance.
3. If neither parent can attend, the public agency shall use other methods to insure parent participation, including individual or conference telephone calls.
4. A meeting may be conducted without a parent in attendance if the public agency is unable to convince the parents that they should attend. In this case, the public agency must have a record of its attempts to arrange a mutually agreed on time and place.
5. The public agency shall take whatever action is necessary to insure that the parents understand the proceedings at a meeting including arranging for an interpreter for parents who are deaf or whose native language is other than English.[22]

Note that the meeting is at a "mutually agreeable" time and place and that the parents need not come if they are determined not to do so.

PARENTS' RIGHT TO REVIEW EVALUATION MATERIAL

The parents have a right to review the evaluation material prior to the multidisciplinary staff conference and at any point during the child's education.

> Each participating agency shall permit parents to inspect and review any education records relating to their children which are collected, maintained, or used by the agency under this part. The agency shall comply with a request without unnecessary delay and before any meeting regarding an individualized education program or hearing relating to the identification, evaluation, or placement of the child and in no case more than 45 days after the request has been made.[23]

WHAT HAPPENS IF THE SCHOOL AND PARENTS DO NOT AGREE ON A PLACEMENT?

IDEA provides for the resolution of differences between parents and agencies through an impartial due process hearing procedure as described in Subpart E of the Rules and Regulations. In the Comment following No. 300.56, reference is made to the success of mediation as an intervening step prior to conducting a formal due process hearing: "In many cases, mediation[24] leads to resolution of differences between parents and agencies without the development of an adversarial relationship and with minimal emotional stress. However, mediation may not be used to deny or delay a parent's right...."[25]

The formal due process hearing may be initiated by either a parent or a public educational agency on any of the matters described in 300.504. The hearing must be conducted by the state educational agency or the public agency directly responsible for the education of the child, as determined under state statute, state regulation, or a written policy of the state educational agency.[26]

For details of hearing rights, the qualifications of an impartial hearing officer, the timelines and procedures of hearings and reviews, as well as details of the Administrative Appeal and Civil Action, see Subsection E of Rules and Regulations.

WHO CAN BECOME AN "IMPARTIAL HEARING OFFICER"?

People with a wide variety of backgrounds may become impartial hearing officers. However, restrictions are specified.

1. A hearing may not be conducted:
   a. By a person who is an employee of a public agency which is involved in the education or care of the child.
   b. By any person having a personal or professional interest which would conflict with his or her objectivity in the hearing.
2. A person who otherwise qualifies to conduct a hearing under paragraph 1 of this section is not an employee of the agency solely because he or she is paid by the agency to serve as a hearing officer.
3. Each public agency shall keep a list of the persons who serve as hearing officers. The list must include a statement of the qualifications of each of those persons.[27]

HOW ARE HEARINGS CONDUCTED?

Written evidence (such as test results, academic records, and evaluation reports) is introduced and witnesses are asked to share their knowledge and points of view. The hearing officer reviews the evidence and testimony and reaches a decision. This decision must be reached no more than forty-five days after the school has received a request for a hearing.

1. Any party to a hearing has the right to:
   a. Be accompanied and advised by counsel and by individuals with special knowledge or training with respect to the problems of children with disabilities.
   b. Present evidence and confront, cross-examine, and compel the attendance of witnesses.
   c. Prohibit the introduction of any evidence at the hearing that has not been disclosed to that party at least five days before the hearing.

d. Obtain a written or electronic verbatim record of the hearing if there is to be an appeal.
   e. Obtain written findings of fact and decisions.
2. Parents involved in hearings have the right to:
   a. Have the child who is the subject of the hearing present.
   b. Open the hearing to the public.[28]

APPEALS PROCESS

If either party is dissatisfied with the decision of the impartial hearing officer, they may appeal. A hearing officer, appointed by the state educational agency, reviews the evidence and must allow both parties the opportunities for oral or written arguments, or both. His or her decision is final unless either party decides to bring civil action against the other. If the hearing is conducted by a public agency other than the state education agency any party aggrieved by the findings and decision of the hearing may appeal to the state educational agency.

WHAT HAPPENS TO THE CHILD DURING DUE-PROCESS PROCEEDINGS?

The child's placement stays the same as it was before the disputed action took place. If the parents are disputing an initial placement in special education, the child remains in regular education. The following pertains to the child's status during proceedings:

1. During the pendency of any administrative or judicial proceedings regarding a complaint, unless the public agency and the parents of the child agree otherwise, the child involved in the complaint must remain in his or her present educational placement.
2. If the complaint involves an application for initial admission to public school, the child, with the consent of the parents must be placed in the public school program until the completion of all the proceedings.[29]

WHAT IF THERE ARE NO PARENTS WHO MAY SPEAK FOR THE CHILD?

IDEA has provisions for surrogate parents to be appointed when no parent can be identified or located, or if the child is a ward of the state. The surrogate parent must have the knowledge and skills to represent the child and have no interest which conflicts with the best interests of the child. He or she represents the child in all facets of the provision of special education.[30]

CAN SCHOOL PERSONNEL BE SUED IF THE CHILD DOES NOT MAKE THE PROGRESS OUTLINED IN THE IEP?

The IEP is a written agreement to provide services with specific goals and objectives. It is not a guarantee that the child will make a certain amount of progress. Specifically, P.L. 94-142 states:

> Each public agency must provide special education and related services to a handicapped child in accordance with an individualized education program. However, Part B of P.L. 94-142 does not require that an agency, teacher, or other person be held accountable if a child does not achieve the growth projected in the annual goals and objectives.[31]

It is reasonable to make goals and objectives realistic and achievable and to keep parents informed of the child's progress or lack of it. If it appears that goals will need to be altered, parents/guardians must be informed of the need for and the proposed time and place of an IEP meeting to discuss any changes and develop a new IEP for the child. IDEA allows for no substantial alterations to a child's IEP without following the required process of reconvening the IEP meeting. The term *substantial alteration* has been defined by the courts to include new/revised goals and additional short term objectives which constitute a change in the goal expectations.

SUMMARY

We have reviewed some of the major provisions of P.L. 94-142 and subsequently IDEA. These and other provisions are discussed in detail in other chapters herein. In addition, funding procedures, requirements for personnel development, timelines for implementation, and a host of other issues await your detailed investigation in the federal regulations.

A rigid application of the law, without consideration of the uniqueness of the child, could lead to an inflexible educational program with a mechanical flavor lacking the empathy and creativity which is essential to learning. Because of his or her concern for and orientation toward understanding the whole child, the school social worker can make many contributions toward the humane implementation of the law.

With an increased parental role in special education, communication between school and home becomes significant in a legal sense. If school policies and programs are interpreted to parents clearly and if parents are accorded their proper rights in the planning for the child, the education of children with disabilities will have taken a giant step forward.

REFERENCES

1. *Federal Register,* Education of Handicapped Children, Tuesday, August 23, 1977, Part II. Also *Federal Register,* Assistance to States for Education of Handicapped Children, December 29, 1977, Part III.
2. 45 C.F.R. 300.1.
3. 45 C.F.R. 300.5.
4. 45 C.F.R. 300.5(A–E)
5. 45 C.F.R. 300.14
6. 45 C.F.R. 300.14 Comment
7. Note that throughout P.L. 94–142, the term *include* means that "the items named are not all of the possible items that are covered, whether like or unlike the ones named." (*Federal Register,* Education of Handicapped Children, August 23, 1977, Part II, Subpart A, 121a.6.)
8. 45 C.F.R. 300.13.
9. 45 C.F.R. 300.13(b)(11).
10. 45 C.F.R. 300.14(b)(1).
11. 45 C.F.R. 300.530(b).
12. 45 C.F.R. 300.531.
13. 45 C.F.R. 300.532.
14. 45 C.F.R. 300.503(b).
15. 45 C.F.R. 300.503(c).
16. 45 C.F.R. 300.533.
17. 45 C.F.R. 300.532(e).
18. 45 C.F.R. 300.343(a).
19. 45 C.F.R. 300.343(c).
20. 45 C.F.R. 300.344.
21. 45 C.F.R. 300.343(d).
22. 45 C.F.R. 300.345.
23. 45 C.F.R. 300.562(a).
24. An excellent article on mediation which goes far beyond the scope of the current chapter may be found in C. B. Gallant, Mediation: A unique due process procedure which utilizes social work skills, in R. J. Anderson, M. Freeman & R. L. Edwards, (Eds.), *School social work and P.L. 94–142: The Education for All Handicapped Children Act* (Washington, D.C.: National Association of Social Workers, 1977).
25. 45 C.F.R. 300.506 (Comment).
26. 45 C.F.R. 300.506(b).

27. 45 C.F.R. 300.507.
28. 45 C.F.R. 300.508.
29. 45 C.F.R. 300.513.
30. 45 C.F.R. 300.514.
31. 45 C.F.R. 300.349.

CHAPTER 10

Part H of the Individuals with Disabilities Education Act: Analysis and Implications for Social Workers

Kathleen Kirk Bishop
Associate Professor, Department of Social Work, University of Vermont

INTRODUCTION

When Public Law 99-457 was signed into law on October 8, 1986, it provided an opportunity to take a giant step forward in developing the kinds of comprehensive service systems that can make a real difference in the lives of infants and toddlers with disabilities and their families. Reauthorized on October 7, 1991 as the Individuals with Disabilities Education Act (IDEA), most recently authorized as Public Law 102-119, this law continues to pose new challenges to all professionals and parents to go beyond their traditional roles and to work collaboratively with those in health, education, social services, mental health, and other public and private agencies in order to realize the potential of this landmark legislation (Bishop, 1987). Social workers are essential partners in the implementation of this legislation.

This presentation of P.L. 102-119, Part H, is a brief extrapolation of key parts of the law which potentially have the most relevancy for social workers. There are significant revisions in this later version which require careful study and thoughtful action, such as the provision for infants and toddlers with disabilities and their families who are American Indian and live on reservations.

WHAT IS THE PURPOSE OF P.L. 102-119, PART H?

The Individuals with Disabilities Education Act (IDEA), Part H, reauthorizes the newly established federal program for infants and toddlers with disabilities and their families. It provides formula funding on a voluntary basis for all states to fully implement a comprehensive, multidisciplinary, interagency, statewide system of early intervention services. According to Part H, Congress finds that there is an urgent and substantial need:

1. To enhance the development of infants and toddlers with disabilities and to minimize their potential for development delay;
2. To reduce the educational costs to our society, including our nation's schools, by minimizing the needs for special education and related services after infants and toddlers with disabilities reach school age;
3. To minimize the likelihood of institutionalization of individuals with disabilities and maximize the potential for their independent living in society; and
4. To enhance the capacity of families to meet the special needs of their infants and toddlers with disabilities (P.L. 102-119, Part H, Section 671[a]).

Based on these needs, Congress established a policy of providing financial assistance to states:

1. To develop and implement a statewide, comprehensive, coordinated, multidisciplinary, interagency program of early intervention services for infants and toddlers with disabilities and their families;
2. To facilitate the coordination of payment for early intervention services from federal, state, local, and private sources (including public and private insurance coverage); and
3. To enhance their capacity to provide quality early intervention services and expand and improve existing early intervention services being provided to infants and toddlers with disabilities and their families (Section 671[b]).

WHO WILL BE SERVED?

According to the law, the term "infants and toddlers with disabilities" means individuals from birth to the age of 2, inclusive, who need early intervention services because they fit one of the following criteria:

1. They are experiencing developmental delays, as measured by appropriate diagnostic instruments and procedures in one or more of the following areas: cognitive development, physical development, language and speech development (hereafter in this part referred to as "communication development"), psychosocial development (hereafter in this part referred to as "social or emotional development"), or self-help skills (hereafter in this part referred to as "adaptive development"); or

2. They have a diagnosed physical or mental condition that has a high probability of resulting in developmental delay. Such terms may also include, at a state's discretion, individuals from birth to age 2, inclusive, who are at risk of having substantial developmental delays if early intervention services are not provided (Definitions, section 672).

The law, therefore, requires each state to adopt a definition of "developmental delay" that will be used in implementation; however, each state may define this term to be as comprehensive or restrictive as wished. The term "developmental delay" has the meaning given such term by a state. Perhaps the most pressing challenge for each state continues to be the inclusion of "at risk" children and their families in the definition of the population—particularly with the expansion of this term into such categories as biologically, socially, emotionally, and medically at-risk statuses.

WHAT ARE EARLY INTERVENTION SERVICES?

According to the IDEA, the term "early intervention services" are developmental services that:

1. Are provided under public supervision;
2. Are provided at no cost except where federal or state law provides for a system of payments by families, including a schedule of sliding fees;
3. Are designed to meet the developmental needs of an infant or toddler with a disability in any one or more of the following areas: (a) physical development, (b) cognitive development, (c) communication development, (d) social or emotional development, or (e) adaptive development;
4. Meet the standards of the state, including the requirements of this part;
5. Include: (a) family training, counseling, and home visits, (b) special instruction, (c) speech pathology and audiology, (d) occupational therapy, (e) physical therapy, (f) psychological services, (g) case management services, hereafter in this part referred to as "service coordination services," (h) medical services only for diagnostic and evaluation purposes, (i) early identification, screening, and assessment services, and (j) health services necessary to enable the infant or toddler to benefit from the other early intervention services, (k) social work services, (l) vision services, (m) assistive technology devices and assistive technology services, and (n) transportation and related costs that are necessary to enable an infant or toddler and the infant's or toddler's family to receive early intervention services;
6. Are provided by qualified personnel, including: (a) special educators, (b) speech and language pathologists, and audiologists, (c) occupational therapists, (d) physical therapists, (e) psychologists, (f) social workers, (g)

nurses, (h) nutritionists, (i) family therapists, (j) orientation and mobility specialists, and (k) pediatricians and other physicians;
7. To the maximum extent appropriate, are provided in conformity with an individualized family services plan adopted in accordance with section 677 (section 672).

WHAT ARE THE REQUIREMENTS FOR A STATEWIDE SYSTEM?

In general, a statewide system of coordinated, comprehensive, multidisciplinary, interagency programs providing appropriate early intervention services to all infants and toddlers with disabilities and their families, including American Indian infants and toddlers with disabilities living on reservations, would include fourteen minimum components.

1. A definition of the term "developmentally delayed" that will be used by the state in carrying out programs under this part;
2. Timetables for ensuring that appropriate early intervention services will be available to all infants and toddlers with disabilities, including those Indians on reservations, in the state before the beginning of the fifth year of a state's participation under this part;
3. A timely, comprehensive, multidisciplinary evaluation of the functioning of each infant and toddler with a disability in the state and the needs of the families to appropriately assist in the development of the infant or toddler with a disability.
4. For each infant and toddler with a disability in the state, an individualized family service plan in accordance with section 677, including service coordination services in accordance with such service plan;
5. A comprehensive child-find system, including a system for making referrals to service providers that includes timelines and provides for the participation by primary referral sources;
6. A public awareness program focusing on early identification of infants and toddlers with disabilities including the preparation and dissemination of information materials for parents on early intervention services, and procedures for determining the extent to which primary referral sources, especially hospitals and physicians, disseminate information on the availability of early intervention services to parents of infants with disabilities;
7. A central directory that includes early intervention services, resources, and experts available in the state, and research and demonstration projects being conducted in the state;
8. A comprehensive system of personnel development;

9. A single line of responsibility in a lead agency designated or established by the governor for carrying out: (a) the general administration, supervision, and monitoring of activities receiving assistance, (b) the identification and coordination of all available resources within the state from federal, state, local, and private sources, (c) the assignment of financial responsibility to the appropriate agency, (d) the development of procedures to ensure that services are provided to infants and toddlers with disabilities and their families in a timely manner pending the resolution of any disputes among public agencies or service providers, (e) the resolution of intra- and interagency disputes, and (f) the entry into formal interagency agreements that define the financial responsibility of each agency for paying for early intervention services (consistent with state law) and procedures for resolving disputes including all additional components necessary to ensure meaningful cooperation and coordination;
10. A policy pertaining to the contracting or making of other arrangements with service providers to provide early intervention services in the state;
11. A procedure for securing timely reimbursement of funds expended;
12. Procedural safeguards;
13. Policies and procedures relating to the establishment and maintenance of standards to ensure that personnel are appropriately and adequately prepared and trained, including: (a) the establishment and maintenance of standards that are consistent with any state-approved or recognized certification, licensing, registration, or other comparable requirements that apply to the area in which such personnel are providing early intervention services, and (b) to the extent such standards are not based on the highest requirements in the state applicable to a specific profession or discipline, the steps the state is taking to require the retraining or hiring of personnel that meet appropriate professional requirements in the state; and
14. A system for compiling data on the numbers of infants and toddlers with disabilities and their families in the state in need of appropriate early intervention services (which may be based on a sampling of data), the numbers of such infants and toddlers and their families served, and the types of services provided. (Section 676[a][b]).

WHAT IS AN INDIVIDUALIZED FAMILY SERVICE PLAN?

Assessment and Program Development

Each infant or toddler with a disability and the infant's or toddler's family would receive:

1. A multidisciplinary assessment of unique strengths and needs, and the identification of services appropriate to meet such needs; and
2. A family-directed assessment of the resources, priorities, and concerns of the family, and the identification of the supports and services necessary to enhance the family's capacity to meet the developmental needs of their infant or toddler with a disability; and
3. A written individualized family service plan developed by a multidisciplinary team, including the parent or guardian.

Periodic Review

The individualized family service plan would be evaluated once a year and the family would be provided a review of the plan at six-month intervals; the evaluation could concur more often where appropriate, based on infant or toddler and family needs.

Promptness after Assessment

The individualized family service plan shall be developed within a reasonable time after the assessment is completed. With the parental consent, early intervention services may commence prior to the completion of such assessment.

Content of Plan

The individualized family service plan must be in writing and contain:

1. A statement of the infant's or toddler's current levels of physical development, cognitive development, communication development, social or emotional development, and adaptive development, based on acceptable objective criteria;
2. A statement of the family's resource, priorities, and concerns relating to enhancing the development of the family's infant or toddler with a disability;
3. A statement of major outcomes expected to be achieved for the infant or toddler and the family, and the criteria, procedures, and timelines used to determine the degree to which progress toward achieving the outcomes is being made and whether modifications or revisions of the outcomes or services are necessary;
4. A statement of specific early intervention services necessary to meet the unique needs of the infant or toddler and the family, including the frequency, intensity, and the method of delivering services;

5. A statement of the natural environments in which early intervention services would be provided;
6. The projected dates for initiation of services and the anticipated duration of such services;
7. The name of the case manager, hereafter referred to as "service coordinator," from the profession most immediately relevant to the infant's or toddler's and family's needs, or any qualified person who will be responsible for the implementation of the plan and coordination with other agencies and persons; and
8. The steps to be taken supporting the transition of the toddler with a disability to services provided by schools for free, appropriate public education for all children with disabilities aged three to five to the extent such services are considered appropriate (Section 677).

WHAT ARE THE PROCEDURAL SAFEGUARDS?

The procedural safeguards required to be included in a statewide system would provide, at minimum, the following:

1. The timely administrative resolution of complaints by parents. Any party aggrieved by the findings and decisions regarding an administrative complaint would have the right to bring a civil action with respect to the complaint; such action may be brought in a court of appropriate jurisdiction. In any action brought under this paragraph, the court would receive the records of the administrative proceedings, would hear additional evidence at the request of a party, and basing its decision on the preponderance of the evidence would be able to grant relief;
2. The right to confidentiality of personally identifiable information, including the rights of parents or guardians to written notice of, and written consent to, the exchange of information among agencies;
3. The right of the parents or guardians to determine whether they, their infant or toddler, or other family members will accept or decline any early intervention service without jeopardizing other early intervention services;
4. The opportunity for parents or guardians to examine records relating to assessment, screening, eligibility determinations, and the development and implementations of the individualized family service plan;
5. Procedures to protect the rights of the infant or toddler with a disability whenever the parents or guardians of the child are not known or are unavailable or the child is a ward of the state, including the assignment of an individual (who shall not be an employee of the state agency providing services) to act as a surrogate parent or guardian;

6. Written prior notice to the parents or guardians of the infant or toddler whenever the state agency or service provider proposes to initiate or change, or refuses to initiate or change, the identification, evaluation, placement, or the provision of appropriate early intervention services to the infant or toddler;
7. Procedures designed to assure that the notice fully informs the parents or guardians, in the parents' or guardians' native language, unless it clearly is not feasible to do so, of all procedures available pursuant to this section; and
8. While any proceeding or action involving a complaint is taking place, unless the state agency and the parents or guardians otherwise agree, the child shall continue to receive the appropriate early intervention services currently being provided, or if applying for initial services shall receive the services not in dispute (Section 680).

WHAT IS THE STATE INTERAGENCY COORDINATING COUNCIL?

Any state that desires to receive financial assistance under this law would need to establish a state Interagency Coordinating Council composed of at least fifteen members but not more than twenty-five members. This council and the chairperson of the council usually are appointed by the governor. In making appointments to the council, the governor needs to ensure that the membership of the council reasonably represents the populations of the state.

The council shall be composed of:

1. At least 20 percent of the members shall be parents, including minority parents, of infants or toddlers with disabilities, aged 12 or younger, with knowledge of or experience with programs for infants or toddlers with disabilities. At least one such member shall be a parent of an infant or toddler or a child with a disability aged 6 or younger;
2. At least 20 percent of the members shall be public or private providers of early intervention services;
3. At least one member from the State legislature;
4. At least one person involved in personnel preparation;
5. At least one member from the state education agency responsible for preschool services to children with disabilities with the authority to engage in policy planning and implementation;
6. At least one member shall be from the agency responsible for the state governance of insurance, especially health insurance; and
7. Other members representing each of the appropriate agencies involved

in the provision of or payment for early intervention services to infant and toddlers with disabilities and their families and others selected by the governor, such as a representative from agencies or tribal councils working with American Indian infants, toddlers and their families.

Meetings

The council will meet at least quarterly as deemed necessary. The meetings must be publicly announced, open, and accessible to the general public.

Subject to the approval of the governor, the council may prepare and approve a budget using funds under this part to hire staff, conduct hearings and forums, reimburse members for expenses, and obtain the services of such professional, technical, and clerical personnel as may be necessary to carry out its function.

Functions of the Council

The council would:

1. Advise and assist the lead agency in the identification of the sources of fiscal and other support for early intervention programs, assignment of financial responsibility to the appropriate agency, and the promotion of the interagency agreements, and advise and assist the lead agency in the preparation of applications and amendments;
2. Advise and assist the state education agency regarding the transitions of toddlers with disabilities to other public school and private agency services;
3. Prepare and submit an annual report to the governor and to the secretary on the status of early intervention programs for infants and toddlers with disabilities and their families operated within the state (Section 682).

ANALYSIS OF SELECTED ASPECTS OF THE LAW

Although the entire law and regulations have implications for social workers in the many areas of practice where they are serving infants and toddlers with disabilities and their families, this section will focus on two key components of the law which have major implications for social work practice: the individualized family service plan—Section 676(b)(4), Section 677 (a through d)—and case management services (referred to as "service coordination services)—Section 676(b)(4), Section 677(d)(6).

Before discussing particular foci for social workers, it is important to understand the philosophy of Part H, as originally authorized and subsequently revised as P.L. 102-119. Perhaps the philosophy is best reflected in the fact that families are mentioned at least thirty-one times in the legislation, beginning with the opening policy statement in which "Congress finds that there is an urgent and substantial need to enhance the capacity of *families* to meet the special needs of infants and toddlers with disabilities . . ." (Section 671,4). The clarifying regulations also contain main statements (Federal Register, Executive Order 12606, 303.344[b]) such as "parents retain the ultimate decision in determining whether, they, their child, or other family members will accept or decline services under this part (IFSP) (303,344, note 1). These statements directed to the needs of families throughout the legislation (e.g., Section 672[E] [i], Section 676[a] [b,3,4], Section 677) appear to signal a change in the philosophy—from a child-centered approach—to a family-centered approach to early intervention services—that is, services to infants and toddlers with disabilities must be provided within the context of their families and other natural environments.

This family-centered philosophy recognizes that the family is the constant in the child's life while service systems and personnel fluctuate. It suggests recognition, respect, and support for the pivotal role that families play in the care (and nurturance) of their children (Shelton, Jeppson, and Johnson, 1987). If a family-centered approach describes the philosophy of Part H, then this philosophy directs professionals to work as partners in securing the best possible early intervention services for families who have infants and toddlers with disabilities.

This philosophical approach, which includes a family-centered approach and family/professional partnerships, should guide the social workers as she/he participates in the development of an individualized family service plan and case management services.

Individualized Family Service Plan

As stated in the legislation, a requirement of the individualized family service plan (IFSP) is a statement of the family's resources, priorities, and concerns relating to enhancing the child's development. It also requires that the major outcomes expected for the child and family be written into the plan (Section 680,2,3).

Perhaps a major issue with the IFSP is to assure that the family is an integral part of the plan. It is important to conceptualize the IFSP very differently from the individualized education plan (IEP) required in P.L. 94-142. The IFSP is not an IEP with a couple of family goals added. It is not a group of plans from a variety of agencies located in a single folder termed the IFSP.

The IFSP is revolutionary in its conception. It is a single plan which addresses the total child and family as a unit, regardless of who delivers and who pays for the services. It is a plan that reflects a strong component of parent-family and professional collaboration in a manner that honors the wishes of the family.

Social workers have a long history of concern for families (see Richmond, 1919; Scherz, 1954; Germain, 1968, 1983). Family-centered practice is a model of social work practice which locates the family in the center of the unit of attention or field of action (Germain, 1968). As conceptualized within the life model of social work practice (Germain and Gitterman, 1980), the domain of family-centered social work practice is the transactions between families and their environments. Within this framework, social workers have a leadership role and major contribution to make as they assume a partnership role with families in the development and implementation of an IFSP that reflects a family's concerns and desires for their child with a disability as well as the concerns and desires of the entire family. In addition, social workers have a role to play in assisting other professionals in understanding the values, knowledge, and skills needed to work with families in a family-centered manner.

Service Coordination

As a result of discussions with family members and professionals, the section of the law that refers to case management services and the name of those services has been replaced by the term, *service coordination services*. This name change reflects comments from families that can be summarized as "I'm not a case and I don't want to be managed." Within the regulations (303.22.,a,2) it is stated that each child eligible for services and the child's family must be provided with one service coordinator who is responsible for coordinating all services across agency lines, and for serving as a single point of contact in helping families obtain the services and assistance they need.

Service coordination is described as an active, ongoing process that involves: (a) assisting parents of eligible children in gaining access to early intervention services and other services identified in the individualized family service plan; (b) coordinating the provision of early intervention services (such as medical services for other than diagnostic and evaluation purposes) that the child needs or is being provided; (c) facilitating the timely delivery of available services; and (d) continuously seeking the appropriate services and situations necessary to benefit the development of each child being served for the duration of the child's eligibility.

Specific service coordination activities include (303.22[b]):

1. Coordinating the performance of evaluations and assessments;
2. Facilitating and participating in the development, review, and evaluation of individualized family service plans;

3. Assisting families in identifying available service providers;
4. Coordinating and monitoring the delivery of available services;
5. Informing families of the availability of advocacy services;
6. Coordinating with medical and health providers; and
7. Facilitating the development of a transition plan to preschool services, if appropriate.

These service coordination activities recognize the interagency nature of the services that are required for this population of children and families, and emphasize the importance of the coordinative function necessary to implement the services effectively.

Some qualifications of service coordinators (303.22[d]) include meeting the specification of the individualized family service plan, demonstrating knowledge and understanding about the infants and toddlers eligible for service, understanding Part H and its regulations, and having knowledge of the nature, scope, and system of payment for early intervention services in their state.

For social workers, the service coordination functions and activities described in the law and regulations are a natural and expected component of social work services (see Weil and Karis, 1985; Roberts-DeGennaro, 1987). Social work as a profession traditionally has supported the values of client self-determination and participation in the planning and development of plans for service. Social workers are recognized in many settings as the link between clients and community. It would seem then that social workers are a natural choice to assist families within the service coordination activities they identify as useful for their child and family.

IMPLICATIONS FOR SOCIAL WORKERS

Within the context of P.L. 102-119 Part H, the responsibilities of service providers in all areas of early intervention services have been defined as: 1) consulting with parents, other service providers, and representatives of appropriate community agencies to assure the effective provision of services; 2) training parents and others regarding the provision of those services; and 3) participating in the multidisciplinary team's assessment of a child and the child's family, and in the development of integrated goals and outcomes for the individualized family service plan (Federal Register, 303.12, [c]).

Social workers (unlike in P.L. 94-142) have been defined as qualified providers of early intervention services (Definitions, Section 672,F,vi). Social work services are defined in the regulations as including:

1. Making home visits to evaluate a child's living conditions and patterns of parent-child interaction;

2. Preparing a social or emotional development assessment of the child within the family context;
3. Providing individual and family-group counseling with parents and other family members, and appropriate social-skill building activities with the child and parents;
4. Working with those problems in a child's and family's living situation (home, community, and any center where early intervention services are provided) that affect the child's maximum utilization of early intervention services; and
5. Identifying, mobilizing, and coordinating community resources and services to enable the child and family to receive maximum benefit from early intervention services (Hare, 1983).

The children and families to be served under P.L. 102-119 Part H will need a great variety of services from many different providers and agencies. Because social work focuses on the child and family as a unit (Laphan and Shevlin, 1986), social workers are in an excellent position to join in partnership with families, other disciplines, public and private agencies, and the community in implementing P.L. 99-457 (Bishop, 1987) and securing all of the services which families identify for the child with a disability and other family members.

Social workers have a leadership role and major contributions to make as advocates for individual families as well as for system changes. The social work responsibility could be conceived as three-fold within the context of families, with other service providers and agencies, and at the systems change/legislative level.

Within the context of families, social workers should:

1. Provide early intervention services to families that reflect a family-centered, community-based, coordinated approach;
2. Develop and model family/professional partnerships (Bishop, Woll, Arango, 1993) in all aspects of service provision, especially in the development of an individualized family services plan and the provision of case management services;
3. Assure that family support services are available to all families who desire them, including such services as respite care, sibling support, parent-to-parent support, and fathers' groups;
4. Provide services to families that reflect the principle of normalization—as close to home as possible—in the most facilitating environment;
5. Support families' participation in all meetings which concern their child and family;
6. Develop individual family service plans in partnership with families and other service providers;

7. Serve as service coordinators at the request of the family;
8. Assure the participation of families in all aspects of the development of early intervention services; and
9. Advocate for services that are accessible, flexible, culturally sensitive, and responsive to the diversity of family desires and styles (Rounds, Weil, and Bishop, 1994).

With other service providers and agencies, social workers should:

1. Assist other professionals in understanding the cultural and social experience of the child in the family and community (Clark, 1989);
2. Assure that services are family-centered, not agency-centered or provider-centered;
3. Facilitate collaboration between and among service providers and agencies;
4. Identify service gaps and work with agencies to fill the gaps;
5. Work on confidentiality procedures that will assure maximum protection of families while facilitating information-sharing that will benefit families and protect them from duplicative procedures and services;
6. Participate with other providers and agencies in the multi-disciplinary assessment of families;
7. Work with providers and agencies to assure that infants, toddlers and their families are offered a menu of services that reflects a variety of choices and options; and
8. Develop collaborative training programs in which parents and professional have opportunities to educate each other.

Within the context of legislative and systems change, social workers should:

1. Call the contact person at the designated lead agency in the state and volunteer to participate in the discussion of the state's plan for implementation of P.L. 102-119 Part H;
2. Offer consultation on such issues as the state's definition of who is served, on personnel training and standards, and on the range of services offered to families;
3. Identify parent, provider and agency groups who are concerned about infants, toddlers and their families and develop coalitions to monitor and evaluate all phases of Part H;
4. Provide recommendation to the governor on the composition of the state interagency coordinating council;
5. Advocate for the necessary financial resources to facilitate full implementation of the law;

6. Request review of all policies and procedure for Part H to insure that a family-centered approach is implemented.

Social workers have a special responsibility to this population of children and families. Infancy and toddlerhood are critical and vulnerable times in the lives of children and their families—a time of rapid growth and change. The provision of family-centered, appropriate and timely intervention services is essential and urgent.

No single provider and no single agency can provide all of the services that families with infants and toddlers with disabilities will identify as needed. Therefore, P.L. 101-119, Part H, presents an important opportunity for social workers to join hands with families and other providers and agencies within health, education, mental health, and social services in assuring that this law will improve the quality of life of infants and toddlers with disabilities and their families.

REFERENCES

Bishop, K. K., Rounds, K., and Weil, M. 1993. P.L. 99-457: The preparation of social workers for practice with infants and toddlers with handicapping conditions and their families. *Journal of Social Work Education* 29(1):36-45.

Bishop, K. K. 1987. The new law and the role of social workers. *Early Childhood* 3(2):6-7.

Bishop, K. K., Woll, J., and Arango, P. 1993. Family/professional collaboration for children with special health needs and their families. Department of Social Work, University of Vermont.

Campbell, P. H., Bellamy, G. T., and Bishop, K. K. 1988. Statewide intervention systems: An overview of the new federal program for infants and toddlers with handicaps. *Journal of Special Education* 22(2):25-40.

Clark, J. 1989. Proposed roles and mission for professionals working with handicapped infants and their families. Unpublished comments, January 17, 1989, Iowa.

Early intervention program for infants and toddlers with handicaps: Final regulations (Federal Register 34 CFR part 3030, July 30, 1993).

Germain, C. B. 1968. Social study: Past and future. *Social Casework* 49:403-409.

Germain, C. B., and Gitterman, A. 1980. *The life model of social work practice.* NY: Columbia University Press.

Hare, I. 1983. NASW Commission on Education, Regulations 303.12(d), 12.

McCann, J. 1986. Early childhood achieving autonomy. In E. V. Laphan and K. M. Shevlin (eds.). *The impact of chronic illness on psychosocial stages of human development* (pp. 29-37). National Center for Education in Maternal in Child Health, Washington, D.C.

Public Law 102-119. Infants and Toddlers with Disabilities, Part H, sections 671, 672, 676, 677, 680, 682.

Richmond, M. 1917. *Social Diagnosis*. NY: Russell Sage Foundation.

Roberts-DeGennaro, M. 1987. Developing case management as a practice model. *Social Casework. The Journal of Contemporary Social Work* 68:466–470.

Rounds, K., Weil, M. O., and Bishop, K. K. 1994. Practice with culturally diverse families of infants and toddlers with handicapping conditions. *Families in Society* 75(1):3–15.

Scherz, F. 1954. What is family-centered casework? *Social Casework* 34(8):343–348.

Shelton, T. L., Jeppson, E. S., and Johnson, B. H. 1987. Family-centered care for children with special health care needs. *Association for the Care of Children's Health*, 2nd ed.

Weil, M., and Karls, J. 1985. *Case management in human service practice*. San Francisco: Jossey-Bass.

CHAPTER 11

Social Work and the Special Education System: Overview of Recent Cases Affecting Professional Decisions

Brooke R. Whitted
Attorney, Whitted and Associates, P.C.

INTRODUCTION

The Education of the Handicapped Act, otherwise called the Individuals with Disabilities Education Act, and its accompanying regulations requires that every state, and the District of Columbia, ensure that a free, appropriate, public education is available to all children with disabilities. The education of unserved or underserved children with disabilities has priority over the education of children already receiving adequate services. Services must be provided to all qualifying children with disabilities without regard to their particular ability to benefit from special education. The Act is heavily parent/guardian oriented, and requires states to maximize parental involvement in educational decision making. A formal administrative system for the resolution of disputes may be invoked by the schools or the parents of pupils with disabilities. Throughout this system, detailed steps of identification, evaluation, determination of eligibility, planning, service, and administrative appeals are set forth. The social worker, both as a school staff member and as an outside consultant, is an important figure throughout. Working knowledge of the requirements of the Act is a must for those in the social work profession who will have regular contact with the special education system.

HOW DOES THE SPECIAL EDUCATION SYSTEM WORK?

To qualify for federal financial assistance under the Individuals with Disabilities Education Act (hereafter referred to as IDEA), a state must demonstrate that it "has in effect a policy that assures all handicapped children the right to a free, appropriate, public education."[1] That policy must be written in the form of a "state plan" and is subject to reapproval every three years by the U.S. Department of Education.[2] Children receiving no education are to have priority over those receiving some form of education.[3] Children with disabilities must be educated to the maximum extent appropriate with children who are not disabled. This is called the "least restrictive environment" mandate and is commonly referred to as "LRE."[4] The free, appropriate, public education (hereafter "FAPE") required by IDEA must be tailored to the unique needs of the child, through a document called an "individualized education program" (hereafter "IEP") prepared at a formal meeting between a qualified representative of the local education agency (hereafter "LEA"), the child's teacher, the child's parents or guardian, and, where appropriate, the child.[5] Parental involvement and consultation in this process must be maximized.[6] IDEA also imposes upon the states detailed procedural requirements, that is, a set of rules outlining exactly how the educational rights of children with disabilities are to be protected. The rights of parents to consent to the provision or termination of special education services, to question the decisions of educational personnel, and to invoke a highly specific administrative hearing process are all outlined in IDEA.[7] Parents or guardians may request an "impartial due process hearing," which in most instances must be granted, to consider their grievances against the school.[8] Any party dissatisfied with the results of the initial due process hearing may request and receive an impartial review by the state agency,[9] and if not satisfied with that review, may then go to court.[10]

Although IDEA leaves many details to the states concerning the development and implementation of particular programs, it imposes substantial requirements to be followed in the discharge of the states' responsibilities. Noncompliance with federal procedural requirements—either in the state plan document or in implementation of federal requirements—may be sanctioned by the withholding of federal dollars flowing to the offending agency.[11] For example, a state's educational system might be investigated by the U.S. Department of Education for failing to educate children in the least restrictive environment. Such a failure would be evidenced by a pattern of education of physically disabled children in separate, "segregated," facilities even though the children in question may have no problems other than the physical ones that challenge them. The federal law requires education of children with disabilities to the maximum extent appropriate with nondisabled children. The failure of a particular state to meet this requirement raises the risk of sanctions.

ROLE OF THE LOCAL SCHOOL SYSTEM

The impact of the law is ultimately to obligate the LEA to provide a free, appropriate, public education with *related services* to all children with disabilities. Related services are services required to assist a child with disabilities to benefit from special education. The implications of this assumption of responsibility is for the LEA to become the center for service, funding, and service provision for children with disabilities. Local school districts ultimately bear the responsibility for the education of each child within their jurisdiction. This is especially apparent when children with disabilities are concerned. Although other child welfare agencies might engage in interagency squabbles among themselves concerning who should pay or provide services, LEAs and the respective state board of education are not able to engage in such fingerpointing.[12] Under the Illinois school code, special education services not provided by another agency must be provided by the LEA or the state board of education.[13] Thus, the education sector—even in a time of shrinking resources—is and has been a consistent source of dollars for children's services and is indeed becoming the center for provision.

THE IDENTIFICATION OF CHILDREN WITH SPECIAL NEEDS

Local school districts must engage in ongoing activities to discover individuals who are not yet served, or who are underserved.[14] This is the "identification" process. Social workers are often in the forefront of this with their connections with families in the community and with teachers at the point of referral. The identification and evaluation process is mandated by statute in every state and constitutes the entry gate to the special education system. Social workers are crucial to this process, because they generally perform most of the required social developmental studies, interview the family and collateral contacts, attend staffings, and make recommendations.

Educational staff often need training and consultation to become aware of disabling conditions, to appropriately discriminate between the need for immediate referral in certain cases, or, in the case of the mildly disabled child, to try different approaches within the classroom to remediate perceived problems prior to referral.[15] Examples include children who seem depressed, hostile, or constantly afraid, or children who are not learning at the same rate as others, instances where the delay cannot be explained by mere situational factors.[16] The federal statute lists the various disabling conditions that determine special education eligibility.[17] All fifty states have their own statutes, which implement the federal mandate and may, at times, vary slightly from the federal scheme.[18] The state schemes must substantially comply with the federal scheme before the states may obtain the millions allocated for programs for the disabled.[19] Recent literature outlines a lack of coordination between the educational system and related systems, such as state and local mental health agencies and child welfare agencies.[20] Frequently, parents are forced to surrender their parental rights to state child welfare systems in order to obtain funding resources for needed residential treatment and other services, because the educational sector has, improperly, refused to assume these responsibilities. An awareness by the social worker of the real responsibilities of the educational sector serves the best interests of children with disabilities, especially when the social worker assists in the collaboration among agencies to obtain the required full continuum of services.[21] IDEA also affects social workers in practice outside the school system.[22] These professionals, in order to serve the best interests of the pupil involved, may act voluntarily as experts on behalf of the family for the purpose of providing a clinical opinion as to what is necessary to meet the student's educational needs. The social worker may testify, either at the administrative level or in court, in direct opposition to the opinion and/or recommendations of the school social worker.[23]

WHAT SERVICES MUST THE SCHOOLS PROVIDE?

Social work professionals are often ill-informed concerning just what kinds of services must be provided by the public schools. Under IDEA, the educational sector is required to pay for "related services," which include any services required to assist a child to benefit from special education.[24] The *Rowley* case involved a hearing-impaired girl who understood only about half of what was occurring in class, but who nevertheless received As and Bs because of her high intelligence.[25] Her parents wanted the school to provide a full-time sign language interpreter to attend class with her, but the Supreme Court held that the student was not so entitled, as she was already receiving an "educational benefit" without the interpreter.

Rowley generally is used by schools to back up the argument that they are not required to provide the "best" education—only that which is minimally appropriate and available. Social workers should likewise be aware that the recommendations contained in their reports should address services necessary to minimally enable the child to "benefit" from educational programming. For instance, some depressed students may need nonmedical psychotherapy to attend to instructional tasks. Such psychotherapy has been held to be a "related service" that must be provided by the schools.[26]

A law review article has stated that there are several thousand children in the United States so lacking in brain capacity that they are unable to benefit from any educational services, no matter how elementary they are.[27] The United States Supreme Court has declined to review a hotly contested case in which a child "lacking any cortex" was held to be entitled to related services even though he was unlikely to benefit from services.[28] The *Timothy W.* case originated in Rochester, New Hampshire, where the school district argued that providing *any* services to such a hopelessly disabled child would be a waste of tax dollars that were better spent on less disabled children.[29] In their pleadings to the U.S. Supreme Court, the attorneys for the schools, astonished by the decision of the Appellate Court, said that such decisions requiring school personnel to provide services to children who cannot benefit from any services "may have unfortunate consequences for families of uneducable children because [they] raise false hopes, which in turn often lead to bitterness and disillusionment" and ultimately to intensive family therapy or marital counseling.[30] The U.S. Supreme Court will not, however, "read in" any exceptions to IDEA that are not present—and no exception was drawn for so-called uneducable disabled children.[31]

If a child needs a residential setting in order to benefit from educational programming, the schools must pay for such a setting, and there can be no charges to the parents or guardian.[32] If other agencies are active and are able to pay part of the cost, such payments are allowed as long as such agencies do not charge the parents.[33] When a school district writes an IEP stating that another agency is to provide some of the services, the school district is still the "agency of last resort," and parents may rightfully turn to the schools for recompense.[34]

A well-known U.S. Supreme Court case has held that clean intermittent catheterization ("CIC") is a related service.[35] In the *Tatro* case, a female pupil needed CIC several times daily in order to stay in class and to benefit from educational services. The schools argued that CIC was a medical service and therefore not a related service. The U.S. Supreme Court did not agree, noting that CIC was not exclusively within the province of physicians, but could be administered easily by the school nurse. The school district was thus required to provide this service.

SUSPENSION AND EXPULSION OF STUDENTS WITH DISABILITIES

On January 20, 1988, the U.S. Supreme Court issued its opinion in *Honig v. Doe*.[36] This strongly worded case set forth guidelines that educators have actively and hotly debated ever since. The two related California cases involved violent, acting-out pupils who were suspended "indefinitely" and later expelled under the California statute that allowed indefinite suspensions. The school district's attorneys argued, when the cases finally reached the judicial level, that Congress could not possibly have intended that the schools be required to keep serving dangerous, emotionally disturbed pupils, when other staff members and students were at peril. The Court held that Congress "very much meant to strip schools of the unilateral authority they had traditionally employed to exclude disabled students, particularly emotionally disturbed students, from schools."[37] The U.S. Supreme Court, in this case, demonstrated clearly its reluctance to read into IDEA meanings never expressed by Congress.

The net effect of this case is that schools may not remove pupils with disabilities from school for behavior that is a manifestation of the disabling condition, without the consent of the parents. If the parents refuse to consent to a relocation of the child, the schools' only recourse is to have their attorneys file a petition in a court of proper jurisdiction to obtain the permission of a judge. Although it has been argued that school authorities may make some attempt to determine the "relatedness" of the behavior to the disability, any attempts at expulsion or exclusion for behavior claimed to be unrelated to the disabling condition leaves educators on very unstable legal ground.[38] Almost invariably, a court will determine that the exclusion was a "change of placement" outside the mandatory multidisciplinary process and therefore in violation of federal law. The Supreme Court has clearly expressed its feeling that allowing schools to suspend pupils who are dangerous to themselves and others for up to ten days cumulatively per school year gives education authorities sufficient time to seek parental consent, negotiate other alternatives, or go to court.

Social workers should become familiar with the basic law of suspension and expulsion of pupils with disabilities, as they may find themselves increasingly in the position of mediating disputes between schools and families of disabled students.[39] Moreover, social workers are commonly called as experts in due process hearings for the purpose of establishing whether the behavior in question was or was not related to the pupil's disabling condition. Finally, current law relating to suspension and expulsion is a powerful tool for families of the disabled in persuading school authorities to consider more restrictive alternatives for the child, such as private extended-day school programs or residential placement, when appropriate.

THE USE OF ATTORNEYS AND "PARENT ADVOCATES"

With increasing frequency, attorneys and other advocates have been present not only at administrative due process hearings, but also at multidisciplinary staffings. In the special education system, parents may be represented by any person or professional they choose, and that person need not be an attorney. Often, so-called parent advocates are themselves parents of a child with a disability who have been through a dispute with the schools and are now helping other parents. Sometimes parents will be represented by a cleric or friend of their choice, or by the social worker or other clinical professional working with the family. Such representation is perfectly legitimate, and some advocates are frequently more knowledgeable than attorneys in general practice. It is imprudent for educational personnel to attempt to bar an advocate from assisting the parent in any special education staffing or hearing, given advocates' substantial statutory backing. Although advocates' presence may be somewhat burdensome for the LEA, parents are entitled to use them, and in the long run advocates are useful when they assume the position of "buffer" between parents and school in an emotionally attenuated situation.[40]

The only drawback to using an "advocate" is the Handicapped Children's Protection Act of 1986. This new law amends IDEA to allow for reimbursement of all attorneys' fees and expert costs to parents who employ these professionals in administrative due process hearings and/or judicial review of those hearings, and "prevail." To "prevail" for the purposes of the Protection Act, all parents need to do is to prevail on an important issue in the case; they need not necessarily prevail on the central issue.[41] In contrast, school districts that "prevail" are not entitled to attorneys' fees reimbursement from the parents.[42] Obviously, if parents are represented by a non-attorney, the Protection Act cannot be utilized. Experience has taught that school districts are more receptive to realistic settlement negotiations when they are aware of the presence of an attorney representing the parents.[43]

DUE PROCESS AND JUDICIAL REVIEW

If mediation has failed and the parents have requested a due process hearing, the case eventually goes to hearing. Due process hearings in special education are "administrative" in nature and do not occur in a courtroom setting.[44] The rules of evidence do not apply, and the parents' representative need not be an attorney. If either the parents or the school district are dissatisfied with the outcome of the initial due process hearing, they have a right to proceed with an administrative appeal, as described by IDEA.[45] This second administrative level may include a new hearing, or it may simply involve a paper review of the materials and arguments considered at the lower level. If a review of the first decision is requested by the parents, a transcript of that hearing must be provided to them at no charge.[46]

Once the second review is completed, any party dissatisfied with the result may appeal it to either state or federal court,[47] by filing a lawsuit against the other party, requesting appropriate relief.[48] It is important to note that the "stay-put" provision operates while all proceedings are taking place.[49] This provision requires that the child remain in his or her then-current placement during such time as due process proceedings are pending. During this time, the district must pay for all educational services in the then-current placement, and the *Burlington* case clearly provides that even if the parent loses at each stage of the process, the district cannot obtain reimbursement from the parent.[50] The stay-put provision is thus a powerful tool if the proceedings commence at a time when the pupil is in an educational setting that satisfies the parents. The most common situation is where the child is in a school-funded residential placement and the district seeks to return him or her to a local or mainstream setting which it is important to note is one of the goals of the "inclusion" trend. If the parents request due process at this point, the child must remain in the residential setting at district expense during the pendency of all proceedings, through and including appellate court review.

Conversely, when the current placement is one that the parents feel is not appropriate, the stay-put provision operates to the benefit of the school district. In this instance, the parents' goal is to effect an alternative placement that they and their experts feel is more appropriate than the current setting, whereas the school district usually seeks to maintain the status quo. The school district continues to pay the cost of the child's educational placement, regardless of who requests due process.[51] For younger pupils entering school for the first time, the "current" placement is seen by most states as the setting in which the child would be placed in the absence of any disability. For pupils with disabilities transferring from one school district to another, the current placement is determined by the most recent Individualized Education Program (IEP).

INDIVIDUALIZED EDUCATION PROGRAMS

The IEP is the blueprint for all that happens in the education of a child with disabilities. School districts must write an IEP before they can provide services.[52] IDEA is quite detailed in its specification of the contents of this document.[53] All IEPs must be reviewed at least annually, and parents or guardians, as outlined previously, are always entitled to question IEPs through the due process procedures.[54] Many state boards of education publish manuals on how to write an IEP,[55] and all states have organizations and resource centers to assist parents and guardians in understanding the process of writing an IEP.[56] Social workers who intend to have ongoing contact with the special education system should avail themselves of the many resources concerning IEP drafting, as the input of the social worker during the drafting of the IEP often has a substantial effect on the recommendations made.

School districts often make the mistake of listing their recommendations for the pupil prior to drafting an IEP. This is a significant procedural error. IDEA requires the IEP to be written first on the logical assumption that recommendations for a particular educational setting and specific services cannot possibly be made until the needs of the child are determined. When recommendations occur before the IEP, this is sometimes a good indicator that school authorities are simply offering the program they have available, rather than creating a customized program to meet all of the needs of the child. It is legally improper and a violation of IDEA for recommendations to be based on administrative convenience, costs, waiting lists, or any factor other than the needs of the child with disabilities in question.[57]

The parent or guardian of a child covered by IDEA must be given prior written notice whenever a school district proposes a change in the educational placement of a child, or a change in its provision of a free, appropriate, public education for a child.[58] This notice must, at the minimum, contain a complete description of available procedural safeguards, an official explanation for the change(s) being proposed, and the reasons why other less restrictive options were rejected.[59] Although the consent of a parent or guardian is required for the initiation or termination of educational benefits, consent is not required when a district seeks to change the program for a child already in special education.[60] Notification of proposed changes, regardless of their magnitude, is required in all instances under IDEA because the right to demand a hearing is always vested in the parent or guardian who disagrees with the changes.[61] A "complete failure" to implement an IEP has been held to constitute a change in the child's educational placement, as well as a failure to provide a free, appropriate public education.[62] An IEP is not, however, a contract, nor is it a guarantee that the child will achieve the results contemplated. An IEP is a blueprint; a series of guidelines for educators to follow in conferring educational benefits; and a useful document for parents to follow in determining whether those benefits are being made available.

CONCLUSION

Legislation and case law on the civil right to a free, appropriate, public education for children with disabilities have created new structures of service for these children. The social worker's services are framed in a developing body of law. It is important to understand this law, not simply as a set of procedures, but as a mandate placed upon the school district and on the social worker to provide services that will enable children with disabilities and their families to survive in an initially unequal struggle. Here the language of the law can be translated into the language of service. The more familiar social workers are with both languages, the more able they will be to translate them into services that can redress this inequality.

In recent years, some advocates have said that the special education system is not working and that to benefit from educational services, students must be "fully included" in the mainstream. Many have gone so far as to present this concept as a "part of the law," and to tell parents this new "law" says they must cooperate in the full mainstreaming of their child. Nothing could be further from the truth. The law governing the least restrictive environment has not changed and merely requires that to the maximum extent *appropriate,* children with disabilities should be educated with nondisabled children. No law mandated "full inclusion," and in fact the expression is not to be found in the federal law. In fact, the statute still requires all school districts to make available a full continuum of alternatives from least restrictive (such as all mainstreaming with one resource period per day) to most restrictive (such as private residential placement).

REFERENCES

1. 20 USC 1412(1).
2. 20 USC 1412; 20 USC 1413—describing the goals, programs, and timetables under which the states intend to educate children with disabilities within their borders.
3. 20 USC 1412(3).
4. 20 USC 1412(5).
5. 20 USC 1401(18). The document must include at the minimum statements of present levels of educational performance, annual goals, short term instructional objectives, the specific services to be provided to the child, the extent to which the pupil will be able to be educated with non-disabled students, the projected date of initiation and anticipated duration of services, a statement of needed transition services, and various criteria for evaluating progress. 20 USC 1412(3), 1412(5), 1401(1), (19).
6. *Board of Education of the Hendrick Hudson Central School District Bd. of Ed., Westchester County, et al, vs. Amy Rowley, et al.,* 458 U.S. 176, 73 L Ed 2d 690, 102 S Ct 3034 (US Supreme Court June 28, 1982). Excluding parents from the process has, pursuant to *Rowley,* often been held by courts to be a "fatal flaw" committed by educators. *Spielberg v. Henrico County,* E.H.L.R. 441:178.
7. 20 USC 1415 et seq.
8. 20 USC 1415(b)(1)(D) and (E)—complaints can be brought "about any matter relating to" the child's evaluation and education.
9. *Mayson by Mayson v. Teague,* 749 F. 2d 652 (1984).
10. 20 USC 1415 (b)(2) and (c); 20 USC 1415(e)(2)—a party may go to either state or federal court. Recently, plaintiffs filing in state court have been "removed" by the school district to the federal district court. This is only a good strategy where a state board of education seeks removal, as these entities are protected by Eleventh Amendment sovereign immunity, while local school districts are not protected. *Dellmuth v. Muth,* 109 S. Ct. 2397 (1989), *Gary A. v. New Trier High School District and the Illinois State Board of Education,* 796 F. 2d 940 (1986).

11. 1414(b)(2)(A)—also by judicial review. 20 USC 1416.
12. *Parks v. Pavkovic*, 753 F. 2d 1397 (7th cir. 1985). In the district court opinion, Judge Prentice Marshall said that such finger pointing was one of the most heinous violations of Federal law he could imagine.
13. *Ill. Rev. Stat.* Ch. 122 [14-8.02.]
14. Certain federal dollars are earmarked in the Education of the Handicapped Act as set-asides for underserved or unserved populations of handicapped persons [20 U.S.C. 1412(3)]. LEAs must engage in affirmative efforts on an ongoing basis to make the general population aware of available services. A small ad placed on an annual basis on the last page of the local legal newspaper is not enough.
15. 34 C.F.R. 300.5 et seq.
16. 34 C.F.R. 300.5 et seq.
17. 20 U.S.C. [1401 et seq.]
18. For example, Indiana only serves children with disabilities aged five to twenty-one. The federal scheme provides for "seriously emotionally disturbed" children, while the Illinois scheme has no such category, and in its place utilizes the "behavior disorder" classification.
19. Current appropriations for fiscal year 1990 have been increased by Congress by 7 percent. There has never been a year in which appropriations have declined, although the population of disabled has grown faster than funding levels have increased, resulting in shrinking per-capita expenditures.
20. *NMHA Speaks*, June, 1989: "Students with Serious Emotional Disturbance Underserved in Special Education."
21. 20 USC 1412(7)(A); 34 CFR [300.344.]
22. As defined at 20 U.S.C. [1401 et seq.], 34 C.F.R. [77.1.]
23. The administrative level is the "due process" level that, pursuant to the Education of the Handicapped Act, must be pursued prior to such time as the family is able to file a formal complaint in court. It is usually required that the pupil and his/her family "exhaust" their administrative due process remedies prior to acquiring standing to proceed in court. The rationale behind this requirement is that frequently the parties settle the matter before they are able to access the court system. The requirement thus conserves judicial resources.
24. Except non-diagnostic medical services, such as ongoing medical treatment. The federal government says medical services are defined by who must provide the services, not by the specific service. If a particular non-diagnostic medical service can be provided only by a physician, the LEA need not cover it as a related service. 20 USC [1401(17)]; also see *Kelly McNair v. Oak Hills Local School District*, 1988–89 EHLR 441:381 (US Court of Appeals, 6th Cir.), in which the Court held that special transportation need not be provided to a deaf child because the need for it was not related to her disabling condition. The statute specifically required a connection between the related service and the unique needs of the child.

25. *Rowley*, 458 US at 184.
26. *Max M. v. Thompson*, 592 F.Supp. 1450 (1984). This student's neurotic anxieties prevented him from attending school, and the school social worker, among others, recommended psychotherapy. The school district did not provide the therapy. The parents paid for two years of treatment and then asked for reimbursement from the district. The court held that the school was responsible for the services to the extent that a non-physician could provide them. The district, then, had to reimburse parents the equivalent of psychologist-provided therapy, a lower amount than the actual cost, since a psychiatrist had been the therapist. See also *In the Matter of "A" Family*, 602 P. 2d 157 (Supreme Court of Montana): holding family therapy is a related service, and *Gary B. v. Cronin*, 625 F. 2d 563, n.15: ". . . while psychotherapy may be related to mental health, it may also be required before a child can derive *any benefit from education.*" (Emphasis added.)
27. Rothstein, *Educational Rights of Severely and Profoundly Handicapped Children*, 61 Nebraska Law Review 586 (1982). See also *Parks v. Pavkovic*, 753 F.2d at 1405, in which the Court speculated about what type of child might not ever be able to benefit—and concluded that such a child would have to be in a coma.
28. (1990). "Current Decisions." *Education of the Handicapped Law Review*. Washington, D.C.: CRR Publishing Company. (Hereafter called EHLR) 441:393, *Timothy W. & Cynthia W. vs. Rochester, N.H. School District*, EHLR Summary and Analysis, Pages SA 265–66 (December, 1989). Federal Appellate Court citation: 875 F. 2d 954 (1989); US District Court citation: EHLR 509:141 (1987). See also article by this author, "Educational Benefits After *Timothy W.*: Where Do We Go From Here?" Winter 1990 edition, Illinois Administrators of Special Education Newsletter.
29. 875 F. 2d at 954.
30. *Petition for Writ of Certiorari to the United States Supreme Court of Rochester NH School Dist. v. Timothy W. and Cynthia W.*, EHLR Summary & Analysis pg. 226, November 3, 1989.
31. *Honig v. Doe*, 484 US 305, 108 S. Ct. 592 (1988). Note that the Supreme Court, in refusing to review a decision, does not in the process issue an opinion covering its reasons. The citation in this note refers to the Court's tendency to rigidly read IDEA, and in *Honig*, it refused to read in a dangerousness exception to the principle that restricts exclusion of pupils with disabilities from school.
32. *Parks v. Pavkovic*, 753 F. 2d 1397 (7th Cir. 1985), cert. denied at 473 U.S. 906 (1985). Interprets 34 C.F.R. 300.302, among other regulatory provisions.
33. See, for example, the Disabled Children's Program of the Social Security Act, 42 USC 1382 et seq.
34. *Kattan vs. District of Columbia*, EHLR 441:207.
35. *Amber Tatro et al v. Irving (Tx.) Independent School District et al.*, 468 US 883 (1984).
36. *Honig v. Doe*, 484 US 305, 108 S. Ct. 592 (1988), interpreting the "stay-put" provision of the Education of the Handicapped Act, 20 USC 1415(e)(3). The

author strongly recommends that social work students read this case in its entirety. *Honig* is a powerful tool for advocates, and a thorough knowledge of the procedures set forth by the Supreme Court is crucial.

37. 484 U.S. at 321.
38. Yell, M. L. (1989). "Honig v. Doe: the Supreme Court addresses the suspension and expulsion of handicapped students." *Exceptional Children,* 56, 69; also see: Yell, M. L. (1990). "The use of corporal punishment, suspension, expulsion, and time out with behavioral disordered students in public schools: legal considerations." *Journal of Behavioral Disorders.* 15, 2.
39. For further information on mediation, see C. B. Gallant. (1980). "Mediation: A Unique Due Process Procedure Which Utilizes Social Work Skills," in R. J. Anderson, M. Freeman and R. L. Edwards (Editors), *School Social Work and P. L. 94-142: The Education for All Handicapped Act.* Washington, DC: National Association of Social Workers. Many states have implemented the mediation process as a technique for lowering the volume of hearings, and most of the mediation systems have been quite effective. Frequently, social workers are called upon to act as impartial mediators as well as utilize their skills in facilitating communication between the school and the family.
40. This is not to say that some advocates are incompetent to serve, and that some do not assist but instead increase the hostility level. The real problem is that in most states parent advocates in the special education system are unregulated. Thus, anyone can become an advocate, without any standardized training, and charge for his or her services. Regulation and licensing of advocates is being discussed in some states. The legal limitations of parent advocates are determined by the respective state boards of education. There is a good discussion in the *Education of the Handicapped Law Report* (EHLR) at Page 211:129.
41. 20 U.S.C. [1415(e)(4)(B)].
42. *Town of Burlington v. Dept. of Education,* 471 US 359, 105 S. Ct. 996 (1985).
43. This statement only applies, however, if the attorney is known to the district as having some expertise in the esoteric area of special education. Often, families will bring a friend or relative who is an attorney to a staffing or hearing. This is a mistake, as the individual's lack of knowledge of the system becomes apparent to the educators in a very short time. See, for further information on the Protection Act, "The Handicapped Children's Protection Act of 1986: Time to Pay the Piper?" by Mitchell L. Yell and Christine A. Espin, *Exceptional Children* Vol. 56, No. 05, February, 1990. This is an excellent article from the perspective of the educators, not the lawyers.
44. See 20 USC 1415 et seq. and the applicable statutory mandate for the state in question. Every state has a statute that is readily accessible which implements the requirements of IDEA. For example, in Illinois, the statute is located at *Ill. Rev. Stat.* [14-8.02] (the section on due process).
45. 20 USC [1415(c)].
46. 20 USC [1415(d)(3)].
47. 20 USC [1415(e)(2)].

48. A practical note: If the parents lose and can afford an attorney, there is no reluctance to sue the district. If the district loses, there is a fair degree of reluctance on the part of school boards to proceed with a lawsuit. One of the reasons for this is the fact that the child usually has to be sued as a "necessary party." This does not look good in local papers, especially if the child is very young. Another reason is expense. Insurance carriers for districts are resisting coverage for these matters, so a school board must vote to proceed knowing they will expend precious local dollars with no hope of recoupment. Finally, even if the district wins on the administrative level, if they are sued by the parents, the insurance carrier will resist coverage for any reimbursement costs or Protection Act attorney fees, since these are not 'damages'. *Tonya K. v. Chicago Public Schools et al*, 551 F.Supp. 1107 (1988). The greatest pressure on a district for settlement, then, is at the end point of the administrative proceedings.

49. 20 USC 1415(e)(3).

50. *Burlington* at page 370.

51. Note here that it is not just parents who can request due process. Schools are often faced with situations in which they seek to provide a service that the parents oppose. For instance, the district may want to place the child in a classroom for the retarded, while the parents may feel that their child is not retarded, but learning disabled. The parents' refusal to consent to the "MR" placement may be met with a district response of requesting due process. From a liability point of view, the only alternative for districts in this position is to request due process against the parents. Frequently, parents may not be able to accept that their child is so low-functioning. The social worker is called upon to assist the parents in working through their shame and guilt, among other feelings.

52. 20 USC [1401(18)].

53. Section 1401(19) of the US Code:
    1. Present levels of educational performance
    2. Annual goals and short-term objectives
    3. Services to be provided
    4. Extent of participation in 'regular' educational program ("least restrictive")

54. US Code Sections 1414(a)(5) and 1413(a)(11).

55. One of the best is (1984) *The IEP Primer*, published by the Illinois State Board of Education, Springfield. This is a simple but detailed "cookbook" manual and is required reading for Illinois parents and advocates.

56. An excellent parent-oriented organization in Illinois is the Coordinating Council for Handicapped Children at 20 E. Jackson Boulevard, Chicago 60603, telephone: 312/939-3513. This organization was founded over a decade ago by the parent of a child with disabilities who encountered hostility from school authorities when she demanded the services to which her child was entitled. Other sources of information include the Guardianship and Advocacy or Protection and Advocacy groups in most state capital cities, as well as the Legal

Assistance Foundation of the state. Law schools, more often than not, have clinics staffed by students and supervised by attorney-professors which accept special education cases free of charge.

57. *Timothy W.* id.
58. 20 USC [1415(b)(1)(C)]; 34 CFR [300.504].
59. 20 USC [1415(b)(1)(D)]; 34 CFR [300.505].
60. 34 CFR [300.504(b)].
61. 20 USC [1415(b)(1)(E) to (d)]; 34 CFR [300.506-.510].
62. *Lunceford v. District of Columbia Board of Education,* 745 F.2d 1577, 1582 (D.C. Cir. 1984).

CHAPTER 12

The Trend toward Inclusion

Shirley McDonald
Assistant Professor, Jane Addams College of Social Work,
University of Illinois at Chicago

The Regular Education Initiative (REI), currently known as "inclusion," is a call for reform of the current special education system. This reform movement has been defined narrowly as encompassing a review of the best educational practices as outlined in the Education for All Handicapped Children Act of 1975 (Public Law P.L. 94-142 and subsequently P.L. 101-476 Individuals with Disabilities Act [IDEA]). It has been defined broadly as calling for the total restructuring of all special education programs and the return of children in need of special education services to the regular classroom.

In whatever way inclusion is interpreted and implemented, as multidisciplinary conferences focus more on the concept of ensuring the least restrictive environment in placement considerations for children identified as being disabled and eligible for special education services, the role of the school social worker will evolve in significant ways. As more children with disabilities return to regular classrooms with support services brought into the classroom, there will be a great demand and need for consultative services (for a detailed discussion of consultation in school settings see Chapter 22). Professionals working with these students in the classroom will require preparation to help understand the needs of the child with the disability, not only his or her learning needs, but also what is the optimal learning environment and what social and emotional concerns have been identified. Such information is especially crucial so that all involved are prepared to help the child adapt to the new environment, and conversely to assure that the environment adapts to the new child, so that there can be an optimal transaction between the two parties. This is especially true for children being returned to a regular classroom who have been in a more restrictive special education environment. In addition, there will be an on-going need for mediation of differences that sometimes may take place in problem conferences (see Chapter 24 on conflict resolution) between the various professionals attempting to develop a cooperative working environment. In spite of the many obvious benefits gained through the cross-fertilization of ideas and skills that may be shared in such an environment, the actual delivery of services in the milieu of the classroom can have many coordination problems such as use of space, time, and ultimately, authority regarding classroom management. Finally, administration at times will struggle in seeking ways to efficiently, yet effectively, serve all students requiring services of professionals whose schedules are ever more delicately balanced as they move between their offices and classrooms to deliver services to both mandated and non-mandated students on the social work caseload. The attendant frustrations around these issues felt by both staff and administration may regularly need skilled intervention from the social worker to maintain a sense of fairness and balance in the decision-making process, as well as the final decisions made in these administrative areas. (An extended discussion of this model of intervention is found in Chapter 25.) Of course, providing direct social work service either to special education or mainstream students in the classroom will become a larger component of the social worker's focus, with its attendant potential for benefit or conflict within this environment. Social workers may well find themselves in the role as mediator in others' disagreements, and conversely, as the disputant in other conflicts needing resolution.

The rest of this chapter defines in more detail the potentials for increased academic success by this new emphasis on inclusion of disabled students in regular education environments; it also discusses several pitfalls. School social workers as advocates for all children, but especially for children with disabilities, need to be alert to the potential benefits and pitfalls that may be inherent in the proposed redesigning of the delivery of special education services to students with disabilities.

Arguments against the current centralized special education system, which is essentially administered, funded, and staffed separately from the regular education system, hinge primarily on the separateness of the regular and special education systems. Opponents of this separateness claim it prevents special education children from experiencing normal social development tasks by separating them from the chaos and anxieties experienced by the regular education child and protecting them from life's normal frustrations (Illinois State Board of Education, 1989). Opponents also state that the diversion of much-needed special education funds from the total education budget, especially in times of financial distress in school districts, encroaches on regular education funding (National Council on Disabilities, 1989). Proponents of the separate system, however, argue that decentralization would remove the legal protection and accountability factors built into the separate system and that special education as it currently exists, therefore, would quickly erode in times of financial entrenchment.

HISTORY OF THE REI: EDUCATION FOR ALL HANDICAPPED CHILDREN ACT

Understanding of the REI/inclusion controversy can be heightened by a review of the mandate issued to the education system to serve special populations of students. Chapter 33, subchapter 11, section 1412(5) of the Education for All Handicapped Children Act of 1975 states the following:

> The State has established procedures to assure that, to the maximum extent appropriate, handicapped children, including children in public or private institutions or other care facilities, are educated with children who are not handicapped, and that special classes, separate schooling, or other removal of handicapped children from the regular education environment occurs only when the nature of the severity of the handicap is such that education in regular classes with the use of supplementary aids and services cannot be achieved satisfactorily.

Federal regulation (34 C.F.R. 300.550 [1977]) requires the local school districts to ensure that these "least restrictive environment" provisions (which call for placement of students in the environment most similar to a regular education classroom) are adhered to when students are placed in education settings for special education ("Serving Those with Severe Handicaps," 1989). This act certainly is not a call for routine separation of special education and regular education children. It is a call for as much collaboration and as little programmatic disruptions for the student as is possible, consistent with the educational need of students.

REPORT TO U.S. DEPARTMENT OF EDUCATION

The document generally cited as the declaration for the REI is *Educating Students with Learning Problems—A Shared Responsibility* (Will, 1986). Will, who was then assistant secretary of the Office of Special Education and Rehabilitative Services, U.S. Department of Education, wrote:

> Although for some students the "pull-out" approach (taking a child out of class to receive special education and then returning the child to the regular classroom) may be appropriate, it is driven by a conceptual fallacy: that poor performance in education can be understood solely in terms of deficiencies in the learning environment. (p. 10)

Furthermore, she stated,

> The challenge is to take what we have learned from the special programs and begin to transfer this knowledge to the regular education classroom.... There is increasing evidence that it is better academically, socially and psychologically to educate mildly handicapped children with non-handicapped children, preferably within the regular classroom. (pp. 11–12)

Thus, the REI/inclusion originally focused on the mildly disabled child. Interpretations of inclusion that include returning all or most children in special education to regular education classrooms probably expand this concept beyond what Will originally intended.

Will explained that the REI/inclusion does not intend to deprive special education students of institutional protections or to place regular and special education students in the same classroom without redeploying resources and strategies. New instructional approaches, such as "the availability of consulting teacher models, Teacher Assistance Teams, and cooperative learning strategies, are intended to provide sufficient options to accommodate all children with learning problems in the regular classroom" (p. 18). She emphasized that "in no case should existing protections be diminished, nor should the rights of individual children be denied" (p. 19).

Will's admonishment is important. One of the concerns of those observing the outcomes of emerging regular education initiatives is whether it is more difficult to monitor special education students receiving required services when these services are incorporated into the general classroom routine than when they are delivered in the admittedly more restrictive arena of the special education setting. Once a student must share the educational setting with higher functioning students, the service provider is less able to focus on the special education component of the lesson because of the discrepancy in need. Even if time were not a factor, this monitoring would be difficult for the classroom teacher and/or social worker.

There is a tendency in regular education to "split the difference" in considering student abilities when presenting or reinforcing materials, but this tendency is challenged in special education by the demand for individualization of instruction as written into the student's individualized educational plan. Also, the motive of sparing a child the embarrassment of directly addressing discrepancies in their learning abilities may cause professionals to downplay specific educational needs in a regular education setting. In any case, maintaining the needed level of intervention and reinforcement of learning for a special education student adds programmatic and planning complications to the regular education settings.

ILLINOIS STATE BOARD OF EDUCATION RESPONSE

A draft paper by the Illinois State Board of Education (1988) that enthusiastically responded to Will's report stated that greater attention must be paid to alternatives to removing children from their regular education classroom for special education services if these services can be delivered in the classroom. This document stated that P.L. 94-142 resulted in unexpected "by-products," including "the diminished role of regular education programs in providing direct services, and the creation of a dichotomous delivery system where students receive services in settings other than the regular classroom setting" (p. 2).

PARALLELS WITH THE MENTAL HEALTH MOVEMENT

The Illinois State Board of Education (1988) document also made parallels between the REI/inclusion and the deinstitutionalization movement in the mental health field: "A unitary education system . . . is referred to as the Regular Education Initiative. The roots of this regular education initiative can be found in earlier antilabeling-deinstitutionalized movements" (p. 2). The lessons learned from deinstitutionalization in mental health may well be applicable to inclusion. The mental health system was identified as being too centralized and deinstitutionalization became the new thrust. The legitimacy of returning institutionalized patients to their communities was based on the expectation that communities would provide the needed range of services and care in surroundings more familiar to and comfortable for the patient. Family members and friends, it was reasoned, would have easier access to patients, making visits less costly in both time and money, and the patient's transition to community living also would be less traumatic and less costly. Like the deinstitutionalization movement, inclusion would keep children in their neighborhood schools to normalize social experiences and to facilitate identification with and support by the home school.

The deinstitutionalization movement's flaw has been that, with few exceptions, local communities have not developed the range of housing, support, and mental health services necessary to care for and maintain the mentally ill population, let alone to improve their quality of life. The increase in the homeless population is partly attributed to this movement.

Returning children to classrooms without proper supports would be a breach of trust and professional ethics. When implementers of inclusion pilot projects ask regular education teachers to absorb students into their classes who require specific professional expertise, advance planning is essential. Otherwise, the inclusion movement may dismantle the special education system in a district without allocating or reassigning adequate responsibility for the population served.

IMPLEMENTATION GUIDELINES

In 1989, the Illinois State Board of Education published the *Illinois Special Education Policy and Procedures Training Manual* that prescribes the process for determining placement and access to regular education experiences. The manual includes the following guidelines:

- Handicapped children must, to the maximum extent appropriate to their needs, be educated with children who are not handicapped.

- Removal of a handicapped child from the regular educational environment may only occur when the nature or severity of the child's handicap is such that education in regular classes cannot be achieved satisfactorily, even with the use of supplementary aids and services.
- Each handicapped child shall participate in nonacademic and extracurricular services and activities with non-handicapped children to the maximum extent appropriate to the needs of the child. If the child is unable to participate in nonacademic and extracurricular activities with non-handicapped peers, comparable activities must be provided.
- The handicapped child should be placed in the least restrictive environment.

CONSEQUENCE OF DECENTRALIZATION

Centralizing the administration and delivery of service to special education students has benefits that may be lost through decentralization. Although centralization is isolating, and thus arguably counterproductive to students' need to experience as many normal living conditions and educational experiences as possible, it is efficient in terms of time and money. Centralization facilitates fulfillment of the mandate in the laws, codes, rules, and regulations that services be delivered in a timely manner; generally, 60 days is the time span mandated between determination of a need and delivery of services. In these times of diminished public funds, efficient use of available resources is one of the major public policy thrusts of local, state, and national government. Many special education personnel who currently deliver "itinerant" services (that is, services on a small group or individual basis in regular education settings) report that they spend nearly as much time traveling from site to site as they do delivering services.

In the long run, possibly the greatest concern regarding a decentralized system will be the difficulty in monitoring the quality of services delivered to the population in need. Monitoring service delivery across settings could be impeded potentially by a hidden agenda for long range policy on the part of state and national governments. Returning responsibility for services to the local communities is the rally to action of those who long for less government control and, therefore, lower taxes. Difficulty in monitoring accountability for service delivery in a decentralized system would likely result in uneven, and thus unequal, access to services. The availability of such services could become more a function of local commitment than of need, because services must compete for resources with all other local, political, and economic issues.

Thus, the monitoring of the delivery of services to children with disabilities may frequently become an informal part of the job description of social workers in schools where they serve as advocates for children. When a problem begins to surface, it behooves the social worker as a mediator to request a conference to discuss possible options that will better supply needed services to the student. Early intervention in such situations will probably be the best tactic. Parent involvement at all points in the child's education would also create a strong impetus for maintaining the intent of the service delivery outlined in the child's Individualized Education Plan, as well as serve as a regular reminder to the team that the Individualized Education Plan must always govern actual service delivery decisions. So encouragement of increased parent participation in the child's school experience may have the added advantage of supplying an additional advocate for appropriate service delivery.

AVOIDING THE PITFALLS OF DECENTRALIZATION

Returning special education students to regular education classrooms without diminishing services will be expensive as well as time-consuming (Wilmette School District Pilot Project, 1990). For inclusion to be effective, the following is necessary:

- Ongoing teacher training about the specific needs of each disabled child in the classroom;
- Regular instruction for teachers regarding the appreciation of differences in students, and ways to understand and enjoy working with disabled children;
- Additional teacher's aides to support the functioning of seriously disabled children in regular education classes;
- Smaller class sizes determined by a formula that accounts for the increased challenge to the teacher due to the additional needs of disabled students;
- Increased special education staff to offset the loss in efficiency (for example, due to increased travel time to and from each school, complexities of maintaining a home office or satellite offices) of itinerant service providers;
- Parent education about the strengths and weaknesses of program and placement changes that focuses on parents' fears and concerns about the changes;
- A sophisticated and carefully monitored system of accountability for the delivery of quality services to special education students.

The danger is that few or none of these preparations will occur and that students will reenter the regular education system and eventually drop out or fall far behind. Planning entries and reentries into different settings and systems within the school are, of course, crucial tasks to school social work service delivery. Perhaps the students most at risk for failure are those with what are sometimes labeled "invisible handicaps"—learning disabilities, behavior disorders, communication deficits, or mild fine motor dysfunctions. Such students have previously experienced significant difficulties in the regular education setting and will be understandably anxious about reentering the system.

If adequate preparation is made for returning special education students to regular classrooms, inclusion will benefit students in the following ways:

- Children who now receive special resource services will experience less disruption created by regular leave-taking from the classroom;
- Provision of in-class services may spill over and benefit children who do not currently receive services but are identified as having some need and may fall through the cracks of the current system;
- More frequent monitoring by special education personnel of all classroom students would allow for the initiation of interventions when symptoms first appear;
- Increased understanding by regular and special education personnel of problems the other students encounter would potentially generate increased consultation and cooperation;
- A broadened exposure to other methods, techniques, and knowledge bases may increase the repertoire of interventions of all personnel;
- Impetus toward greater professionalism may occasionally encourage regular and special education personnel to return to college for additional knowledge and skills in new areas.

CONCLUSION

Federal and state laws, rules, and regulations that govern special education seek to ensure the placement of children in the least restrictive environment to support their educational needs. Monitoring of placement decisions and careful review of a child's need for special education services are essential. Pilot projects are currently being developed or implemented to test alternative methods of delivering services. It is essential that the safeguards listed above be in place before reentry to the regular education system occurs.

A special emphasis on accountability is crucial for quality service delivery to special education students. Special education is expensive and large-scale plans to revamp the system must be examined carefully for ulterior political and financial motives. Professionals working with children with disabilities must ensure that safeguards at the federal, state, and local level are securely in place before major changes are attempted in order to prevent the curtailment of services to the most vulnerable children.

REFERENCES

Illinois State Board of Education 1988. *Relationship/partnerships for achievement* (draft) Springfield, IL.

Illinois State Board of Education. 1989. Serving those with severe handicaps: Interview with Ed Sontag. *Illinois Special Education Forum* 2(2):1-6.

Illinois State Board of Education, Division of Educational Programs, Department of Special Education. 1989. *Illinois special education policy and procedures training manual.* Springfield, IL.

National Council on Disabilities. 1989. *The education of students with disabilities: Where do we stand?* (A Report to the President and Congress of the United States). Washington, DC.

Will, M. 1986. *Educating students with learning problems—A shared responsibility. A report to the secretary* (Monograph). Washington, DC: U.S. Department of Education, Office of Rehabilitative Services.

Wilmette School District Pilot project. 1990. Report presented at Illinois Education Partners, Skokie, IL.

FURTHER READING

Janney, Rachel E., Snell, Martha E., and Beers, Mary K. 1995. Integrating students with moderate and severe disabilities into general education classes. *Exceptional Children* 61(5):425-439. Council for Exceptional Children.

SECTION THREE
Service Delivery in the Schools

CHAPTER 13

Service Delivery in the Schools: An Overview

Robert Constable
Professor, Loyola University of Chicago

School social work practice models have tended to reflect the dominant methods of the broader social work profession as well as the needs, conditions, and strengths of the school setting. Social workers coming into a school setting usually feel that there is a gap between what they were trained to do and the demands of the setting. The school social work role is often quite fluid and involves a heavy emphasis on transactions with schools and school people on behalf of groups of students as well as traditional direct services to individual children in schools. When school social workers enter the school, they give up the security of conducting a practice with individuals within the confines of an office. They find themselves in a broader practice arena where there is a need to understand both individuals and the broader system of the school, family, and community. If change takes place, it takes place within these many systems as well as on the individual level. The diverse needs of the school and its pupils appropriately generate multiple avenues of response by school social workers. The traditional focus on helping individual pupils to cope remains strong and seems to run parallel to the widening breadth of school social work interventions, in the classroom, within the multidisciplinary team, in school policy development, and with families. Practitioners themselves have different proficiencies, whether with individuals, classroom groups, families, consultation relationships, and the community of resources. There is a match between pupil needs as the school defines them and the practice modalities with which the individual school social worker feels most capable.

THE FUNCTION OF THE SCHOOL SOCIAL WORKER

Florence Poole noted that the traditional function of the school social worker is derived from the rights of every child to an education. Pupils who could not use what the school had to offer are, as she put it almost fifty years ago, "children who are being denied, obscure though the cause may be, nevertheless denied because they are unable to use fully their right to an education." Educators have turned to social workers for help with children who were "having some particular difficulty in participating beneficially in a school experience." The function of the school social worker is to use his or her professional skill to help the school fulfill its primary purpose. Poole (1950) is shifting from a focus on the problem pupil, who could not adjust and adapt, to the dynamic relation of pupil and school in a context of each child's right to an education. The conditions that interfere with the pupil's ability to connect with the educational system are diverse, and the school social worker's role is correspondingly broad. Poole's explication of the function of the school social worker through analysis of the societal function and the mandates of the school in relation to the practice of social work was an essentially sound and farsighted approach. Her concept of multiple roles taken by the school social worker on behalf of a single pupil and of working with the school, as well as with the child, is still valid. What has changed has been the school itself and its consciousness of its mandates. In special education, for example, the right of every child with a disability to a free, appropriate public education has been more powerfully defined. Over the past thirty years, the role of the social worker has shifted from a focus on children who did not meet normative expectations to a focus on influencing the norms themselves on behalf of children, developing and implementing individualized approaches to learning. The service itself has shifted from a humane attempt on the school's part to help children who were out of the mainstream to an entitlement, a civil right of every child who needs help to benefit from education. With these changes has also come a concern for whole groups of children encountering similar conditions as well as for individuals.

The function of the school social worker is developed from the dynamic encounter of the social work perspective with the problem and needs to be addressed and the mandates given the social institution of education. Changing school conditions and conceptions of social work have led to many different definitions of what the school social worker should do, but the elements of this encounter have remained the same over many years. When the school was concerned mainly with cognitive development and the meeting of fixed expectations, social workers worked with pupils who could not meet these expectations or whose needs required careful planning with family, medical, or other systems in the community in meeting existing expectations. Social work is the only profession that has the depth of experience in dealing with all of these systems while remaining in close, intimate, and sensitive contact with the pupil and family, helping them to choose, to discover, and to use community, family, and personal resources. P.L. 94-142 and subsequently P.L. 101-476 (Individuals With Disabilities Education Act, IDEA) clarified the mandate of the school in relation to a vulnerable population to be provided an education. The profession is responding by the gradual development of a clearly rationalized set of tasks that can assist the individual and the school in carrying out this mission.

The school social work function that emerges from the present legal commitments and needs of the school and its pupils is a complex one. It can be divided into two main responsibilities: (1) a responsibility for helping pupils to use available services and resources to develop a workable connection with school, family, and community environments; and (2) a responsibility for developing networks of services and support systems in school, community, and family. In either case, at whatever level the school social worker is involved, with individuals or larger environments or both, the concern with the match between individual and environment remains the same. A focus on the larger environment is still related to individual coping and a focus on individual coping is still related to quality of the environment.

If school social workers are to succeed in the complex challenges of integrating children into communities and helping to maintain social integration, an ecological perspective must be taken. Within this perspective, there is a dual focus on the individual and his or her transaction with an environment. This characteristic perspective of the social worker has been developed in considerable detail in Paula Allen-Meares's, Carol Germain's, and Marjorie Monkman's chapters in this volume. This perspective leads to the social worker making a situational assessment that addresses the transaction of individuals with the environment. What conditions in the individual, in the environment, and in their transaction may be causing breakdown? What networks of services, what support systems, might make it possible for the individual to survive, to cope, to form satisfactory interpersonal relationships, and to experience some level of success in the community and family environment? The answers will depend upon individual needs and capacities. Individual survival, affiliation, and achievement are dependent on the sum total of what individuals may be experiencing in their living situation, at school, and in the community. Work with individuals to help them take hold must relate to how they are coping with these conditions. In many cases no amount of individual work can counterbalance what may be taking place in these crucial sectors of a person's life. The school social worker often has the best access to these sectors, as well as to individual pupils. This access to individuals and to major sectors of life activity allows for a practice approach that emphasizes interaction with the individual and with important sectors of the environment. The social worker does problem solving with teachers, administrators, and parents to help them to cope with the implications of their relations with the pupil and, when necessary, with pupils to help them to cope with the challenges of home, school, and community. The social worker knows that intervention may only be a temporary support in the situation and can at best help individuals discover their own resources for coping. The social worker needs most of all to have a broad understanding of the many acceptable ways people can discover and use their capabilities and can communicate with each other and be resources one to the other. It is the social worker's willingness to help people discover the many possibilities for healthy relationships and to facilitate this process with crucial resource systems and agencies as well as the individual and family that can make the difference between survival and breakdown in the relations of vulnerable individuals.

The Case of Jorge Oliverez

To illustrate the emergent function of the school social worker, we take a deliberately simplified example of social work services to a child with a moderate disability in a regular education setting, Jorge Oliverez. Jorge is a twelve-year-old with physical disabilities who has just moved into a different school district and is seeking entry into Blake Junior High School. Partly responding to the manifest anxiety of Jorge's middle-aged parents, for whom Jorge is the youngest child by eight years, and partly responding to Jorge's own irascible behavior, the previous school, Dorian Elementary, gave Jorge considerable attention but protected him from the effects that his hostile, demanding behavior had on others. Jorge did not understand his own specific needs and experienced them as all or nothing. His demands for attention from adults led to estrangements from other children. The problem tended to be reinforced by the parents who, in their unqualified support for Jorge's demands, were undercutting any positive, socializing effects the school might have. Jorge's new seventh-grade homeroom teacher, Mrs. Beall, found his constant demands for attention difficult to deal with in an active classroom.

From the beginning in the new situation, she responded by ignoring Jorge in the hope that he would modify his behavior. Jorge responded with increased self-destructive alienation or by looking for support from other places. He found allies in his parents and his gym teacher. With the implicit approval of his parents, Jorge had not turned in an assignment in language arts for several weeks and was beginning to fail the subject despite a close-to-average ability. His classmates were reacting to what they saw as Jorge's increasingly unusual behavior. The teacher felt that he must learn to take the consequences of his behavior but remained aloof from him. The principal was informed that Jorge's parents have been using the incident to mobilize other parents of children with disabilities in a parents' organization around the issue of districtwide neglect of programs for children with disabilities. Mrs. Beall decided that, if the principal backs the parents, she, in turn, would file a union grievance. She took the step of referring Jorge for placement out of his current regular class into a special class that generally has children with more severe disabilities. The parents, although conflicted, were partially in agreement with the idea of placement. What would a social worker, who had a specific responsibility for doing a social study, do in this situation? How would a worker make recommendations regarding school placement to the multidisciplinary team?

We can map out four components in this case: Jorge's actual behavior, the conditions behind Jorge's behavior, the impinging environment in the classroom, and the conditions behind the impinging environment (see table 1). Social workers have a dual focus on person and situation. A variety of methods may be used to provide a better match with their environment. A social worker could conceivably work with Jorge, his family, or the teacher, in program development in the school and in the community. At one point or another the social worker would probably have some direct or indirect influence on all of these systems and could intervene selectively in a few of them, according to the estimate of the situation, the worker's competence, and what the economy of time allows.

The predominant investment or the locus of concern of the social worker may rest on Jorge as an individual or children with disabilities as a group. The social worker may elect to make a predominant investment of time with Jorge and his parents to help them find different ways of managing the situation. One might work with the Oliverez parents and other parents of children with disabilities to promote greater awareness of the needs of children with disabilities in the school district. One might work with school administrators to plan better services for children with disabilities or with legislators to develop better laws to protect the child with disabilities' right to an appropriate education. One might act as a consultant to Jorge's teacher, Mrs. Beall, helping her to come to a better understanding of the other students in the class. The social worker might develop a close collaborative relationship between homeroom teacher and gym teacher so that Jorge can move more freely and use his relationship to the gym teacher as a support system without incurring the resentment of his homeroom teacher. The school social worker's focus will depend on an assessment of the needs of the situation. One's competence in different areas, time availablity, and the extent of development of the social work program in the school—in other words the realistic limitations and opportunities of the situation as perceived following a professional assessment—may affect the focus.

Jorge's example illustrates the transaction that can develop with a moderate disability with an intact and concerned family. A more severe disability and a more vulnerable family would demand other responses on the part of the social worker. The child with a severe disability is usually more vulnerable and more dependent on complex relations with systems external to the family as well as the family to meet his emergent needs. These external systems provide special education, physical and mental health services of different sorts, job training, transportation, and a variety of temporary or permanent care arrangements when family care is no longer adequate. The family of the child with disabilities is under considerable pressure and cannot really function without some assistance from the outside. The school social worker will need to negotiate networks of service agreements with the family and the appropriate providers. Considerable professional skill is necessary to keep such a network going, but these

TABLE 1 Transactions, Impingement, and Source Environments in the Case of Jorge

Source Environment (conditions behind behavior)	Transaction		Source Environment (conditions behind behavior)
	Coping Behavior	Classroom Impingement	
Jorge: Fearful; dependent; compensates by demands for attention; uses disability to control and manipulate adults around him.	Irascible; inordinate demands for attention; isolate; physical limitations; turns in no work; "building a case" against teacher.	Teacher: Ignores; has referred to special class placement	Likes independent children; feels should achieve at class level without special attention; resents Jorge's demands.
Parents: Disability has had deep impact on own feelings of adequacy, feel guilty also; react by overprotection; but basically feel quite helpless and angry to have this responsibility.	Alternate between high defensiveness and helplessness	Peers: Steal pencils; call him names	Don't understand Jorge's behavior or rejection of them; his disability bothers them.
		Gym teacher: Sympathetic to Jorge, spends time with him	Had a minor disability that he overcame when he was young; has had special training to prepare for working with physically disabled; feels competitive with Jorge's home room teacher.
			Principal: Concerned about image of school in community and with parents' organization; schools are being closed; tax revolt on.
			Parents' organization: Looking for test case to express concern about needs of children with disabilities.

networks could make the difference between remaining in the community and going to an institution.

The emergent school social work function with children having moderate to severe disabilities is a blend of the social and the individual. To ignore people's own very personal ways of coping and the complex needs of the child and family for services is to court certain failure. These needs, of course, are not merely individual but are shared with other children and families, and the social worker, planning with the school or appropriate educational resource and with external agencies, can affect large populations of pupils. It is undoubtedly in the exchange of individual and social, in the unique and personal transaction with the resources and systems that are available, that the social work function can most clearly find itself.

In the chapters that follow, authors will explore the multiple and complex dimensions of the function of the social worker in the school. The chapters follow a continuum of intervention from individual through organization and community. Renee Levine and Helen Wolkow, in two separate chapters, examine the role of the school social work practitioner, first from the life history of one practitioner focusing on three decades, and then from a case history spanning a child's elementary school years. There is a direct link between the theoretical discussion in the first section of this book and practice as it emerges in this third section. Building on this base, the following chapters treat social skills development; partnership between home, school, and community; and the social work role in the implementation of the right to a free, appropriate, public education for students with disabilities. The picture broadens to include the development of consultation skills. The school and its networks of people becomes the setting for change in the following chapters on conflict resolution, mediation, student forums, the no-fault school, and the organizational context of schools. Finally, the section ends with the relations of school and community networks and the child protection functions of the school social worker.

Each chapter in this section discusses in depth one aspect of the application of the theoretical base developed in the first section and the emergent function of the school social worker. For the school social worker, these aspects and the emergent function represent a development beyond generic practice theories. The school social worker in actual practice will shape and hew his or her practice to meet the needs and possibilities of the actual situation, the school, and its community environment. As a result of this shaping and hewing, the practice of one social worker will emphasize resource development and teamwork facilitation; another will emphasize the traditional treatment model, and so on, each becoming an adaptation to an environment of expectations and a professional decision on the worker's part about what is the most efficient, effective, and timely investment of self in service to a common social work commitment and perspective.

CHAPTER 14

The School Social Worker's Role: A Three-Decade Chronology

Renee Shai Levine
School Social Worker, Centennial School District, Warminster, Pennsylvania;
Past-President, Pennsylvania Association of School Social Work Personnel

The purpose of the following chronology is to explore the extent to which the professional social worker in the school influences the development of services for children. The school social work literature has emphasized several assumptions in the creation of a professional model for practice. The social worker has an ongoing role of interpreting the school to the *family* and the family's culture to the school. This assumption is that this role is not static; it evolves in response to changing population demographics in the community and the knowledge of the impact that psychosocial and biological forces have on the performance of children in the school. The role has expanded from direct service, identified with social casework, to the inclusion of group work with pupils and their families, work with parents, and work with the school and community as well. School social workers have become identified as the support personnel who reach out to mobilize and coordinate the services of community agencies that have the potential to augment the programs offered in the school and that may promote a pupil's increased school attendance and performance.

Research has documented that the social work role, besides giving direct service to students, involves consultation with teachers and administrators, who serve on multidisciplinary and other instructional support teams and participate in staff training and development as well as policy and decision making (Costin, 1969; Meares, 1977; Carr, 1976; Chavkin, 1985; Lambert and Mullaly, 1982; Poole, 1949; Timberlake, Sabatino, and Hooper, 1982). Research also has underscored the importance of working with parents to establish a home and school partnership to create the changes needed to influence a pupil's achievement in the school (Kurtz and Barth, 1989).

CHRONOLOGY OF A SCHOOL SOCIAL WORKER

The history of a school social worker in one school district from 1964 to 1995 permits an in-depth exploration of this evolving role and the extent to which the assumptions of the professional model were reflected in her practice. During the three decades in which this chronology occurred, a wealth of legislative mandates created imperatives for new programs and services in the schools. This period included the efforts for the War on Poverty in the Johnson Administration; the impact of the civil rights movement and its call for addressing the educational needs of all oppressed groups; the rights of the family to know and control the information schools circulated about their children; the rights of children with disabilities to a free, appropriate public education; and the rights of parents to participate in their child's experience in the school. The role of the social worker was also affected by legislation in response to the "battered child syndrome" and the part the school should play in identifying, reporting, and protecting children who have been abused or neglected. Other factors affecting the role have occurred with efforts to reform schools to integrate home, school, and community resources and include children and youth with different needs in education backgrounds (Constable, 1992; Streeter and Franklin, 1993). As we move from the 1980s to the 1990s, multiple levels of problems impacting the lives of families with children in the schools have required the social worker to assist in serving the homeless, children and youth who experiment with substance-abuse, those who have serious mental health problems, and those who are found to be ungovernable. In providing services for these children the social worker finds that she becomes involved with parents who are struggling with substance abuse and mental health problems and who are having difficulty coping with the responsibilities of caring for their family. The school social worker increasingly has been asked to assist parents unable to utilize community resources to support them in meeting the needs of their children. In the present decade the thrust to reduce categorical funding and promote a single point of contact for children and families in need of services has provided support for creating school-site Family Service Centers (Mintzies, 1993).

The social worker whose career we are following began her service in the schools in 1964. Her training and experience were essentially clinical. She was the first professionally trained social worker hired in her district, and in the beginning she served primarily as a liaison for families with children living in poverty. Her practice included group work with fifth-grade boys who acted out, community organizing to help families participate in the education of their children, advocacy for adequate housing maintenance and repairs, and gaining access to needed resources in community agencies.

In one year, the social worker served as director of a preschool and primary education project that was developed as an early intervention and prevention program to reduce the drop-out rate in low socioeconomic groups. Four months later, her responsibilities were extended to include directorship of the Head Start program. The Head Start program required the social worker to supervise a multidisciplinary staff, develop a budget, write proposals, coordinate and supervise the use of consultants, develop parent programs, empower parents to participate in the governance and management of the programs, recruit and train staff, select teaching materials, and develop curriculum (Mellor, 1967; Muller, 1970). Liaison work that the social worker performed involved assisting poor people in the community to develop their own resources, including development of a community center. This community center had programs and services for both children and their parents (Warminster Area Child Day Care Association, 1965). In this activity, the social worker served as a community organizer, a broker, and an enabler.

Throughout the social worker's involvement with poor people and minorities an increasing number of bilingual-bicultural families who lived in the housing project was revealed. Concerns for sensitivity to ethnicity caused the social worker to send four staff members (including the social worker) to visit these families' former communities in Puerto Rico. The visit resulted in the four staff members' participation in policy decisions for the development of classroom curriculum, the selection of staff, and the choice of teaching materials to meet the special needs of Hispanic students (Mellor, 1972a, 1972b).

Her work in the low-income community further sensitized the social worker to the mental health needs of its residents. She wrote proposals for funding that resulted in psychiatric training for the Head Start staff, and she also assisted staff from a local mental health service in developing a day treatment program. The social worker had increased her networking and liaison roles to integrate these services with the school programs (Centennial School District, 1970, 1973). While working on this assignment, the social worker became aware of the many youths who dropped out of school. She gathered data for a needs assessment, brought the problem to the attention of the school administrators, and participated in providing an alternative experience for those children whose skills were not in concert with mainstream education. The social worker agreed to prepare a grant proposal; the proposal was funded, and the grant became the seed money for the development of alternative school, which still is serving high school age students in that school district (Mellor et al., 1975).

With the opening of a new school building in the 1970s, the social worker participated in providing in-service training to teachers on the special needs of children from low socioeconomic and minority families, on the importance of gaining a partnership with parents, on developing interview skills, and on managing a mix of socioeconomic levels in the classroom. During that time, she also served as administrator of the newly created social work department in the district. About this time, the social worker became a field instructor for students from three local schools of social work. These students were offered opportunities to develop in-service programs for teachers and to initiate needs assessment for special groups of children. The social work students worked with school administrators, thereby influencing policy decisions in the schools, and they had the satisfaction of seeing their policy decisions implemented (Adams and Mellor, 1972).

A decline in school population during the late 1970s was accompanied by the emergence of children whose school performance was impaired by pain experienced when their parents divorce, whose school experiences were affected by drugs and alcohol, and who attempted suicide. The social worker resumed direct practice with individual children, families, and groups. With the implementation of P.L. 94-142, the social worker's practice took on new forms; she became a member of a child-study team and served as a consultant to school administrators, teachers, and members of the multidisciplinary team in the schools. She assisted a school board committee in developing the guidelines for the procedures and practices to be observed in the district regarding such mandates. These activities placed the social worker in the position of screening referrals to child protective services while preserving long-term working relationships with parents.

During the early 1970s, pregnant adolescent girls were no longer excluded from schools, and the school developed educational support programs that were separate from the mainstream. After the passage of Title IX, as part of the Education Amendments of 1972, pregnant adolescent girls no longer were excluded from schools in the district. The school social worker became the coordinator of a comprehensive support program for the pregnant and parenting teens in the district. In this program, students remained in their mainstream classes, had school-site day care for their children, a support class for their pre-natal, parenting, and child development educational needs, and counseling. The social worker collaborated with public and non-profit agencies to extend the supports available to these students during the summer. This would result in a six-week summer program to reinforce the employment preparation of parenting students, maintain their school achievement, and continue supporting their parenting and child development educational needs.

As we continue the discussion of the social work role in the school, it is important to acknowledge that schooling takes place in a building, each dominated by a particular culture, and that the principal plays a critical part in determining the extent to which the school social worker contributes to the support services available in a particular building (Dupper, 1994;

Gross, Giacquinta, and Bernstein, 1971; Streeter and Franklin, 1993). As the district restructured the junior high to a middle school program, the social worker was asked by a principal responsible for one of these buildings to play a role in preparing the staff for this change. She was asked to contribute by examining the issues in change and in working with groups. The principal also involved the social worker in the development of planning and prevention training focusing on sexual harassment.

During this same period, this worker assisted parents at a building and district level to reduce the barriers to their child's educational achievement. The social worker was active in curriculum development, in identifying community service and in collaborating with community agencies in parent education.

AN ANALYSIS OF THE CHRONOLOGY

The significant factors influencing this school social worker's practice have proved to be:

- The institution's mission
- The changing demographics in the community
- The courts, legislation, and administrative branch of government
- Professional values, knowledge, and relationships
- The willingness of administrators to include support services in their building

Her approach to practice, a process approach, is consistent with the model promoted by Poole (1949). It requires that a school social worker be sensitive to the priorities of school administrators and staff and attend to the needs of emerging client groups. The social worker's approach to practice included an appreciation for the structure provided by the ecological framework and resulted in an ongoing assessment of the ways in which collaboration between the home, school, and community agencies need to be integrated to reduce the obstacles to school attendance and learning (Germain, 1982; Monkman, 1982).

The social worker's contribution to change was based on practice skills, such as gathering data, making assessments, participating on committees, and writing reports and grant proposals to further new projects. Her professional knowledge of the influence of family dynamics on the child's behavior in school and of the impact of socioeconomic forces on the quality of family life allowed her to participate in the development of meaningful curriculum and classroom programs for special needs students. The social worker made others in the school aware of the significance of home experience in the attitudes and behaviors of children, and of the importance of involving parents in the schools to promote effective teaching and learning environments (Bettelheim, 1961, 1962; Chilman, 1965; Elheis, 1964; Erikson, 1963; Lee, 1959; Lippman, 1962; Reissman, 1962).

The social work role has evolved to include staff development and program development, as well as direct service. These multiple levels of activity interact to shape the services provided at each level and contribute to the effectiveness of the social worker in the district. These are effective in direct relationship to the credibility his/her work has established.

Given the changes occurring in the structure of our schools (Constable, 1992; Streeter and Franklin, 1993), it is important to note that if social work services are to be appreciated and seen as an integral part of the school setting, social workers themselves must create an awareness and appreciation of the contributions they have to offer in being members of the school staff. A significant part of this social worker's activity has been in her professional school social work organization and collective bargaining unit on a state level. This has meant organizing to create legislation for school social workers to be included as members of the professions listed in the school code. This step is necessary if there is to be a certification for school social workers in the State Department of Education. This has meant working together with colleagues from other parts of the state to identify and lobby those constituent groups whose support is essential, but who may be unaware or misinformed as to the role the school social worker plays in providing supports for at-risk children in creating changes that help them to succeed in the classroom; and the implications this carries for drop-out prevention, substance abuse prevention, and healthy growth and development for the entire student population.

REFERENCES

Adams, J., and Mellor, B.K. 1972. Report on Contributions of Graduate Students in Social Work. Warminster, PA.: Centennial School District, February.

Bettelheim, B. 1961. *Paul and Mary: Two case histories.* Garden City, NY: Anchor Books.

Bettelheim, B. 1962. *Dialogues with mothers.* NY: The Free Press.

Carr, L. 1976. *Summary of the preliminary report on the survey of social workers in the schools.* Washington, D.C.: National Association of Social Workers.

Centennial School District. Special Services. 1970. *Centennial schools psychiatric services.* Warminster, PA: Betty K Mellor. (Available from Centennial School District, Special Services, Warminster, PA 18974.)

Centennial School District. 1973. *Minutes of task force meeting to implement transfer of the day treatment program.* Warminster, PA. (Available from Centennial School District, Special Services, Warminster, PA 18974.)

Chavkin, N.F. 1985. School social work practice: A reappraisal. *Social Work in Education* 8(1): 3–13.

Chilman, C.S. 1965. Child rearing and family relationship patterns of the very poor. *Welfare in Review* 3(1): 9–17.

Constable, R.T. 1992. The new school reform and the school social worker. *Social Work in Education* 14(2): 106–112.

Costin, L.B. 1969. An analysis of the tasks in school social work. *The Social Service Review* 43(3): 274–285.

Dupper, D.R. 1994. Reducing out-of-school suspension: A survey of attitudes and barriers. *Social Work in Education* 16(2): 118.

Ehleis, H. (ed.). 1964. *Crucial issues in education.* NY: Holt, Rinehart, and Winston.

Erikson, E. 1963. *Childhood and society* (2nd ed.). NY: W.W. Norton.

Germain, C.B. 1982. An ecological perspective on social work in schools. In R. Constable and J.P. Flynn (eds.). *School social work: Practice and research perspectives*, pp. 72–84. Homewood, IL: Dorsey Press.

Gross, N., Giaquinta, J.B., and Bernstein, M. 1971. *Implementing organizational innovations*, pp. 196–198, 203. NY: Basic Books, Inc.

Jenson, J.M., and Howard, M.O. 1991. Risk-focused drug and alcohol prevention: Implications for school-based prevention programs. *Social Work in Education* 13(4): 351–257.

Kurtz, P.D., and Barth, R.P. 1989. Parent's involvement: Cornerstone of school social work practice. *Social Work* 34: 407–413.

Lambert, C., and Mullaly, R. 1982. School social work: The congruence of task importance and level of effort. In R. Constable and J.P. Flynn (eds.). *School social work: Practice and research perspectives*, pp. 72–84. Homewood, IL: Dorsey Press.

Lee, G. (ed.). 1959. *Helping the troubled school child: Selected readings in school social work.* NY: National Association of Social Workers.

Lippman, H.S. 1962. *Treatment of the child in emotional conflict* (2nd ed.). NY: McGraw-Hill.

Meares, P.A. 1977. An analysis of tasks in school social work. *Social Work* 22: 196–208.

Mellor, B.K. 1967, June 14. *Annual report: Preschool programs at Centennial schools.* (Available from Centennial School District, Special Services, Warminster, PA 18974.)

Mellor, B.K. 1972a. *Program for Spanish-speaking children.* (Available from Centennial School District, Special Services, Warminster, PA 18974.)

Mellor, B.K. 1972b. February. *Recommendation for future development of Centennial School's program for Spanish-speaking children.* (Available from Centennial School District, Special Services, Warminster, PA 18974.)

Mellor, B.K. 1975. *Memo to school administrators from school social workers and graduate students re: developmental of an alternative.* (Available from Centennial School District, Special Services, Warminster, PA 18974.)

Mintzies, P.M. 1993. The continuing dilemma: Finding a place for the social work profession in the schools. *Social Work in Education* 13(4): 251–251.

Monkman, M.M. 1982. The specialization of school social work and a model for differentiated levels of practice. In Differential levels of student support services, p. 139 Minnesota Department of Education.

Muller, R.R. 1970. *In . . .or out: An attack on the dropout problem through the preschool and primary education project.* (Available from Centennial School District, Special Services, Warminster, PA 18974.)

Poole, F. 1949. An analysis of the characteristics of school social work. *Social Service Review* 23: 454–459.

Poole, F. 1950. The social worker's contribution to the classroom teacher. *Journal of Exceptional Children* 17: 73–77, 87.

Radin, N. 1989. School social work practice: Past, present and future trends. *Social Work in Education* 11: 213–225.

Reissman, F. 1962. *The culturally deprived child.* NY: Harper & Row.

Streeter, C.L., and Ranklin, C. 1993. Site-based management in public education: Opportunities and challenges for school social workers. *Social Work in Education* 15(2): 72–80.

Timberlake, E.M., Sabatino, C.A., and Hooper, S.N. 1982. School social work practice and P.L. 94–142. In R. Constable, and J.P. Flynn (eds.). *School social work,* pp. 49–72. Homewood, IL: The Dorsey Press.

Warminster Area Child Day Care Association. 1965. *Proposal for funding under economic opportunities act, Title II-A.* Warminster, PA: Community Action Programs.

CHAPTER 15

The Dynamics of Systems Involvement with Children in School: A Case Perspective

Helen S. Wolkow
School Social Worker, Southwest Cook County,
Cooperative for Special Education

INTRODUCTION

If we are to view students in their environment, then we must examine the many facets of that environment: academic, social, developmental, and emotional. It is often difficult for educators and administrators to recognize that all parts of that environment must be attended to if learning is to proceed effectively. If a student is having difficulty at home, or with peers, his or her academics almost invariably will suffer. Working with a student on emotional needs when there is also an academic problem is not enough. Working on academics when a student is emotionally upset is not enough. If we are to view the child as a whole, then we must attend to all of his or her needs so that he or she may develop and function at his or her optimum.

The following is an example of a case quite common to the caseload of the school social worker. It involves a child with whom the social worker worked over a period of three years (second through fourth grade), his parents, his teachers, the school administration, and outside agencies.

REASON FOR REFERRAL

Alan was referred for evaluation by his second-grade classroom teacher toward the end of September, about five weeks after the start of school. He was a transfer student from another school district and was experiencing great difficulty with reading and spelling. He also had difficulty following directions and concentrating on his work, he was easily distracted, and he had poor fine motor coordination and poor visual perception. Alan often would try to copy from his neighbors, or just sit and not attempt to do his work. At times he would sit and suck his fingers. Teachers described him as shy and withdrawn.

The teacher presented the situation to the pupil personnel service team, and they agreed testing should be done. The parents were contacted and agreed to the evaluation. As part of this evaluation, or case study, I completed a Social Developmental Study. This provided us with some insight into possible etiology for some of his academic development and social difficulties.

CASE STUDY FINDINGS

Alan, a nice looking, blond, blue-eyed Caucasian male, was age seven at the time of our initial interview. When interviewed, he had a very quiet and shy manner, almost withdrawn. He spoke very softly, and at times it was difficult to understand what he said. A lot of his emotional energy seemed to be tied up with his parents' divorce, which had occurred a year-and-a-half earlier. He felt school was rather difficult, especially reading, but math was okay. He believed his older brother had learned to read as a baby. Later I found out his older brother had been retained, had reading difficulties, and still seemed to be having some academic problems. He felt that his parents yelled a lot, both at him and his brother. He talked quite a bit about this and many of his answers to my questions referred to this. He was able to say that he felt angry when he could not get his way.

FAMILY HISTORY

Alan, at the time of the evaluation, lived with his mother, his ten-year-old brother, and his three-year-old sister. His mother and father had separated at the end of Alan's kindergarten year. Initially, the mother stayed home with the children during the day, but went to her parents' home for the night when the father returned from work. The mother attended school at a local junior college at the time. The father works as an accountant and recently had become a born-again Christian; the mother is Catholic and attends church on a weekly basis. The divorce became final the summer after Alan completed first grade. That summer, mother and children moved to the same mobile home park where her parents resided. This move placed them within our district boundaries. The park had many children in residence and was comprised mostly of working-class people. The family fit within the norms of that community. During this time, the father usually would take the children on weekends. He was most consistent in doing so, and both children and father seemed to enjoy the time very much. Both sets of grandparents were involved with Alan and supportive of the family situation. Alan often would visit a country cottage with the maternal grandparents, and he was quite fond of those times.

EDUCATIONAL BACKGROUND AND EVALUATION

Alan attended preschool a few days a week at age four and then kindergarten and first grade in a standard educational placement. He came to his present district at the beginning of second grade, and he was evaluated shortly after entry.

The assessment pointed out that his support systems were eroding and that his self-concept was rapidly deteriorating, along with his academic performance. To shore up this deterioration and to assist in rebuilding him to former levels of functioning, resources needed to be utilized within the educational system, within the family, and within the community. Coordination of resources would be essential, or there was the potential for systems to impact negatively on the efforts of the others, even when each support system is working within its individual sphere toward the best interests of the child. Such a case normally requires an extended period of time, both because of the amount of work indicated and also because of the nature of the goals of the service delivery plan. This case extended over two years, during which this student was enrolled in the second through the fourth grade.

As a result of the evaluation, Alan was placed on a learning disabilities watch status, which meant that the learning disabilities specialist consulted with his classroom teacher weekly about possible interventions in the classroom for the perceived problems. Also, Alan was placed with the reading specialist in a small group to see if this would strengthen his reading skills. The social worker was identified as the interim case manager because it was clear that case management was going to be crucial to Alan's case. As a case manager, I met jointly with the classroom teacher, learning disabilities specialist, and reading specialist to arrange mutual consultation. With regard to direct social work service, Alan needed help with divorce issues, self-esteem, socialization skills, and learning appropriate ways to express his needs. I explored the possibility of outside counseling with his parents. They did not agree to this, so I monitored him on a consultative basis until further direct work could be arranged.

It is important to look at the developmental stage Alan had been moving through in order to understand his sense of failure and defeat. Considering Erikson's model of developmental stages, Alan would be well within the stage described as industry versus inferiority (Erikson, 1963). If we look at Piaget's stages of cognitive development, he would be in the middle of the concrete operations stage (Campbell, 1978, p. 8). According to some developmental theorists, he has been in a stage of fear. The five-year-old is fearful that his mother will not return home. Age six is also a fearful stage, in particular that something may happen to mother and she may not be there or may die. (Ilg et al., 1981, p. 160). Alan had been wrestling with events in his life with which his cognitive abilities were not yet capable of dealing. Efforts to soothe himself or put events in perspective generally had met with failure. Thus, he was becoming increasingly overwhelmed and anxious, and as a result some regressive behavior was noted (finger sucking, passivity, and disengagement). Emotionally he had been challenged by events that went right to the core of his worst fears, both in terms of potential abandonment and of his sense of self-competence.

SERVICES OFFERED, PROGRESS, AND RESULTS

Alan's second-grade teacher was highly structured and somewhat inflexible. She was not, initially, very encouraging with him, nor did she recognize his artistic and creative strengths and his good problem-solving skills. She found his slow pace of working, which was part of his perfectionistic need, difficult to relate to. This teacher was not particularly receptive to direct suggestions from me, so I had to develop some alternative strategies to implement through our already established consultation with the reading specialist. In these meetings, by explaining what my goals were in my work with Alan and discussing some parallel goals that might be implemented by the reading specialist, the classroom teacher was able to discuss her approach. She was able to draw upon an approach that she had used with a similar student a few years back. In fact, the earlier situation was close enough to be useful, and she felt she could use the same approach with Alan. By seeing the similarities between students she was able to accept other suggestions.

At the end of February of second grade, Alan's classroom teacher went on maternity leave. Alan's new teacher was very warm, caring, and creative. She liked Alan and wanted suggestions on how to help him. The consultation meetings continued. We soon agreed that Alan needed more intensive academic support. We requested a new Individualized Educational Program conference to amend the findings of the original case conference. Alan was changed from the learning disabilities watch list to direct learning disabilities services and started with thirty to sixty minutes a week in a small group. In order to arrange this meeting in a timely manner, the school administration had to be consulted about Alan's high-priority status. Given this information, the special education director in particular put in extra effort to reschedule the team and the parents so we could meet within the following week.

A week after this meeting and Alan's being placed in the learning disabilities program, his teacher brought to my attention a picture Alan had drawn of himself with a noose around his neck. When I questioned him about it, he said he had just been kidding around, but then did admit he had some very sad feelings. I told him that I wanted to check in with him every day for a while because his being this sad concerned me. I also told him I needed to talk to his mother and father because it was important that they also know about it. When I approached his mother regarding my concerns, she said that she felt it really was not serious and that in fact Alan seemed to be doing much better. His father felt it was serious and wanted Alan in outside counseling. I suggested to both that I continue to work with him until school was out in June and that then he should see an outside therapist. Both agreed. I felt that I needed to have another conference with his mother to support her awareness that in many ways Alan was doing much better, but that this new development was still something I hoped she would take seriously. She listened attentively, asked some very perceptive questions, and although she did not seem as convinced about the seriousness of Alan's situation as I had hoped, her attitude did seem to be much more open and cooperative.

Alan started to do much better after he started seeing the learning disabilities teacher. She continued to consult with me and the classroom teacher until the end of the year, and the classroom teacher began implementing similar strategies in the classroom to speed his progress. Likewise, he became more outgoing and started displaying improved social skills, first in our group and then in the classroom setting. When it was determined that he was starting to generalize the skills he was learning in our small group, I met with each of the personnel who worked with him to request that they encourage his fledgling efforts to become more assertive and outgoing. Most of them were indeed cooperative and actively helped him with this. They regularly reported to me informally. Retention still was considered at the end of the year because his academic progress was not as great as we had hoped, but the parents agreed that they wanted to wait to see how things would progress for him in third grade. I then went to the principal to encourage him to consider placing Alan with the more flexible and care giving third-grade teachers. He said he would take my request into consideration when making class assignments.

When the school year was nearly ended, I contacted the mother and father about making arrangements for Alan to see an outside therapist and gave them some names I could recommend. I asked that when they had made arrangements, they give the therapist permission to call me regarding Alan's case, and that they give me permission to discuss the case with the new therapist. The mother was very uncomfortable about the whole arrangement, stating that Alan would not be comfortable talking with a stranger, just as she would not be. Because I felt that my relationship with the mother was fairly strong by this time, I encouraged her to at least meet with the people I had recommended; then, if she wished, she could call me to talk further about her concerns. She thanked me, but did not act on this offer. In two weeks, just at the end of the school year, I received a call from the therapist whose named topped the list, who mentioned that the father had made the arrangements for the meeting, and only the father had come. However, the therapist had called the mother, and she had agreed to cooperate in getting Alan to his appointments. At the beginning of third grade, I met with Alan and his parents separately after discussing his progress with his outside therapist. We all agreed that, following a few visits to assist in his adjustment to the new school year, direct social work service would not be indicated at this time.

Third grade generally went well for Alan. He made good academic progress. He was seen by the reading specialist and the learning disabilities specialist two times a week, with one other student. I had regular contact with his classroom teacher to make sure he was progressing both academically and socially. Initially, I discussed with her his previous struggles, and alerted her to watch for signs of depression. I also helped her to institute a behavior modification plan for the whole class, focused on positive social interaction, as a way of keeping a handle on Alan's real social progress, aside from his teacher's impressions. Alan finished third grade on a positive note and was promoted to fourth grade.

Alan continued doing well in fourth grade. He had a male teacher whom he seemed to enjoy. The teacher noted that Alan improved greatly in his academic, organizational, and social skills after entering fourth grade. Alan improved several grade levels in reading, health, and social studies. Grades in other subject areas stayed the same or went up slightly. He became more organized and began writing his assignments down each day; his homework assignments were consistently completed daily. My work with his teacher that year was less intense than previously. I consulted with his teacher weekly for the first few weeks of school, giving him essentially the same background information as I had done for the third-grade teacher, though not in such detail. This was followed by monthly check-ins, except when the occasional brief concern arose.

Alan became more involved in class discussions, although he still was shy about sharing experiences. One thing he did share, slowly, with each of us involved with him, was his mother's remarriage at the end of the summer. He was beginning to enjoy his stepfather, although he felt the stepfather sometimes was not confident when problems arose, but, as Alan suggested, perhaps this was because he had never had children before. I learned of this by asking Alan if he would like to come to talk with me a few times once I learned from his teacher of this new development. I also asked him for permission to contact his mother and stepfather to ask them if they would like to come in to talk to me about any issues surrounding their relationship with the children, especially with Alan. Surprisingly, they agreed and came in the following week. We decided to keep in contact throughout the rest of the year. I also agreed to start seeing Alan again in a small group of boys. He interacted with the other students, but he still needed work on social skills. At times he reacted in a negative way physically to others when annoyed; however, he eventually learned to walk away from those situations. I thus recommended that Alan return to therapy for the summer months, given those latest developments, more to prevent backsliding than because of the former concerns regarding serious depression.

Alan became more comfortable with his academics and the school setting. He would have liked more friends. He enjoyed being with his stepfather and no longer thought so much about the divorce. He visited with his father every weekend and also became involved with outside activities, such as Boy Scouts. His mother then started to work part-time in the office of one of the district schools.

Alan completed his middle and junior high school years successfully. He was placed on a consult basis for LD/R services the last two years of junior high, and continued in the Chapter I reading program through sixth grade. Socially he interacted well with others and was involved in the chess club. He was very involved with the youth group at his father's church.

CURRENT PROGRESS

Alan is now a freshman in high school and doing well academically. He does not seem to have many friends in the mobile home park but does have friends in his father's neighborhood, which he visits regularly. He is still somewhat shy and a "loner." Mother states he may move in with his father, after his junior year, as did his oldest brother. The move will be prompted by the fact he would be attending a much smaller and more personal high school in a small town setting. Alan continues to maintain the progress he made, academically, socially, and emotionally—the progress begun when he first came to the attention of the multidisciplinary team many years ago.

SUMMARY

Alan is a good example of the importance of having several subsystems of the larger educational system work together. Success never would have been achieved by attacking only one component of this case. Alan needed to have his academics attended to, via the reading specialist, the learning disabilities specialist and the homeroom teacher. He needed the social work component to address his emotional and social needs, as well as to make his parents aware of those needs. He needed the outside support of the therapist at the mental health agency to carry on the therapeutic goals identified by the school when school was not in session. He needed the cooperation of the administration and staff to have these needs met appropriately and in a timely manner. Any of these component parts without the others would have compromised the outcome, with potentially serious results for Alan.

REFERENCES

Campbell, Sarah F. 1976. *Piaget Sampler*. New York: John Wiley & Sons, Inc. pp. 8–11.

Erikson, Erik. 1963. *Childhood and Society*. New York: W. W. Norton.

Ilg, Frances L., Louise Bates Ames, and Sidney M. Baker. 1981. *Child Behavior* (revised edition from Gesell Institute of Human Development from Birth to Ten). New York: Barnes & Noble.

Perlman, Helen Harris. 1974. *Social Casework*. Chicago: University of Chicago Press.

CHAPTER 16

School Social Work: Facilitating Home-School Partnerships

Robert Constable
Professor, Loyola University of Chicago; Former Editor, *Social Work in Education*

Herbert Walberg
Research Professor of Education, University of Illinois at Chicago

The family and school, two critical institutions in the ecology of childhood, have long lived with studied disregard for each other, paying cautious inattention to the extent of their real interdependence. Such cautious and strategic inattention works well when family and school are in implicit agreement, when the pupil is succeeding in school, and when the family is in control of the socialization processes outside of school hours. However, assumptions that such an ideal type of family life is the usual case are no longer valid for a great many pupils. Changes in the structure of families and fragmentation and atomization of communities have increased the incidence of vulnerable children and pupils at risk in the educational process. The school has the responsibility to meet the often considerable educational needs of all children. Schools have long claimed to work in partnership with parents, and it has been assumed that the family is essential to educational success. This belief is confirmed by the literature on school effectiveness and parent involvement. If excellence is to be achieved, the partnership of school and home must be developed. The school social worker functions at a critical point in the ecology of children, families, and community. The school social worker is positioned to work with the school, the parents,

---

SOURCE: Portions of this paper have been adapted from Robert Constable and Herbert Walberg, *Urban Education*, Vol. 22 No. 4, January 1988, 154-164. Copyright 1988 Sage Publications, Inc. Reprinted by permission of Sage Publications, Inc.

and the community in helping pupils develop the competence to use this environment in the process of learning (Germain, 1982).

STRESS AND VULNERABILITY IN FAMILIES

Loss of significant family members, such as the absence of a parent, or situational factors, such as poverty, or the disability of a child can significantly increase stress in families. Stress frequently plays a role in subsequent decisions to retreat from open relationships with others in the family, with friends, with neighbors, and with teachers. In reacting to stress, this chain of decisions can block family members from using the particular support that is openly available. Families of children with disabilities may experience a particularly heavy amount of stress and thus isolation. Reviews of research point out increased divorce and suicide rates; a higher incidence of child abuse; increased financial difficulties; and a variety of emotional manifestations, such as depression, anger, guilt, and anxiety in these families. Different types of disabling conditions may create different types of secondary problems. But all such conditions are exacerbated with increased age and caregiving demands as the child develops physically and emotionally (Gallagher, Beckman, and Cross, 1983). Parents of children with disabilities go through a mourning process with stages of anger, guilt, depression, and grief over loss of the "ideal child who never came." A realistic acceptance of the child may be reached. Yet chronic sorrow is often experienced in the day-to-day struggle to meet the needs of the child while maintaining personal self-esteem, integrity as a family, and a meaningful place in the community (Bristol and Gallagher, 1982; Olshansky, 1962; Lachney, 1982; Turnbull and Turnbull, 1978).

Intense and unrelieved involvement in caretaking for a special needs child can create severe pressures on parents and siblings. If family members cannot maintain an adaptive sharing of caring roles, the results are rejection of the child, or a split in the family into caregivers and noncaregivers, with the child empowered only by the disability itself, or simple empowerment of the child above others in the family. Tavormina and Associates noted four major parent styles of adapting to the reality of raising a child with disabilities. In the first case, one parent emotionally distances him/herself from the child, leaving the care of the child entirely up to the other parent and involving him/herself fully in outside activities, such as job and organizations unrelated to the child. A second style of adapting occurs when the parents draw together in rejection of the child. The child in this type of family is most apt to be institutionalized, regardless of the severity of his or her disability. In the third instance, the parents make the child the center of their universe, subordinating all of their own desires and pleasures to the service of the child with disabilities. A final style is one in which the parents join in mutual support of the child and of each other, but maintain a sense of their own identities and a semblance of a normal life (Bristol and Gallagher, 1982).

Bristol and Gallagher (1982) suggest a number of different ways in which schools can develop effective partnerships with parents. Programs can be made more flexible, with individualized family plans, the establishment of meaningful parent roles, and the involvement of the father as well as mother. Programs should focus on goals important to the family and expect something of the parents. Parents often need help to see the importance of the often small gains made. The school social worker might help the parents develop their own support network of friends and relatives or assist them in building an expanded network.

THE FAMILY AND ITS INSTITUTIONAL ECOLOGY

There is increasing evidence that we are far less independent than we ever imagined. We depend on one another first of all through family units, and also through informal support systems, networks of friends and neighbors, and membership in informal groups in the workplace. Family, friends, work groups, and neighbors can be "mediating systems" that connect and stand between public and private life. These systems help us relate to the necessary institution worlds of modern life, such as schools, workplaces, and health care, and they supply the preconditions for our doing and acting in a fully human sense. Family, the most important of the mediating systems, has been expected to contain within itself the primary means to supply human needs. Although the family still is delegated this mission in modern society, the family's own support systems or structural adequacy are often sorely lacking. The combination of family, informal support systems, and the formal, institutional structure constitutes a network that allows each person to cope with the complexity of modern society. Coping and adaptation are clearly related to one's access to and ability to call upon and use such support systems. The comparative social isolation of the modern family, together with breaks in generational linkages, may cut off access to support and collective experience and create social pathologies. When a society is composed of relatively privatized family units, close connections with friends, extended family, and neighbors can deteriorate.

School is the essential institution in the institutional ecology of a family with children. Schools may not accomplish their particular missions without their own connections with families and informal support systems. There are often mismatches between a social institution, such as health care, education, or justice, and the needs of the school's clientele of individuals in families. Hospitals, courts, and schools can forget that their clientele are members of families, but only at their own risk. The renewed stress on the family has led institutions to begin shifting orientation from clients as individuals or consumers to the family unit.

SCHOOL EFFECTIVENESS AND PARENT INVOLVEMENT

The ideal that schools work as partners with parents becomes a necessity when one considers the demands on today's schools. In the Supreme Court decision that defined education as a civil right, there is a clear statement of school mission:

> If education is a principal instrument in helping the child adjust normally to his environment, it is doubtful that any child may reasonably be expected to succeed in life if he is denied the opportunity of an education. The opportunity of an education, where the state has undertaken to provide it to any, is a right that must be made available to all on equal terms. (Brown v. Board of Education).

The thirty years following the decision have brought enormous changes in families as well as an expanding mandate for American schools to educate vulnerable children. Educators have become involved in child socialization, for which they are unprepared. In addition, evidence has recently begun to show that schools simply cannot accomplish their mission effectively without developing connections to families. Parents, the first educators of children, continue to have major influence on later development. In research on national assessment samples of adults, stimulating educative experience in families and schools predicted adult knowledge more decisively than did adult motivation and effort. Those who had an educative beginning gained knowledge at a faster rate as adults and attained cumulative advantages throughout their lives (Walberg and Tsai, 1983). Those who did not were correspondingly disadvantaged. An important corollary is that early work at the interface of family and school might reverse the otherwise inevitable disadvantage of some children. Through the formative years until the end of high school, parents nominally control 87 percent of the student's waking time. There are surprisingly large differences in family time investments in children. Even before school age, children differ by as much as five to one in the imputed value of parental care invested.

Recent findings from a poll of 568 parents, done for the national PTA, *Newsweek*, and Chrysler Corporation, suggest the involvement of parents in school may be more extensive than originally imagined. Seven in ten parents talk to their children about school and more than a third help with homework every day. Seventeen percent talk at least weekly with their child's teacher, and 71 percent attend parent teacher conferences (Ordevensky, 1990). Paradoxically, school social work experience does not seem to confirm this level of involvement for more vulnerable children. Kurtz's review of the literature points out that parent participation in public education has produced some notable benefits in terms of improved preschool pupil achievement, better parent emotional well-being, and increased childcare skills (Kurtz, 1988). Such differences may go a long way in accounting for children's varying capacities to profit from schooling and other educational experiences.

EDUCATIONAL PRODUCTIVITY

Syntheses of 2,575 empirical studies of academic learning show that parents directly or indirectly influence the eight chief determinants of cognitive, affective, and behavioral learning (Walberg, 1984). These determinants include four essential factors: student ability and motivation, and the quality and amount of instruction. Four indirect or supportive factors are the psychological climate of the class, academically stimulating conditions in the home environment, the characteristics of the student's peer group outside school, and, inversely, exposure to low-grade mass media, in particular, television.

Student ability and motivation and the amount and quality of instruction all appear necessary for classroom learning. Without a minimum level of each, the student learns little. Large amounts of instruction and high degrees of ability, for example, may count for little if students are unmotivated or instruction is unsuitable. The other determinants—the psychological climate of the classroom group, enduring affection and stimulation from adults at home, a peer group with academic interests, goals, and activities, and minimal exposure to low-grade television programs—influence learning in two ways. Students learn from them directly, and these factors indirectly benefit learning by raising student ability, motivation, and responsiveness to instruction. Other social and economic factors influence learning in school, but less directly. These factors, such as class size, financial expenditures per student, and private governance (independent or sectarian, in contrast to public control of schools) weakly correlate with learning, especially if the initial abilities of students are considered.

Improvements by parents and educators in the eight factors described above hold the best hope for improving learning. Because children spend so much time at home or under the nominal control of parents, it appears that altering home conditions and the relationship between homes and schools produces large effects on learning, particularly in the early grades. Analysis of the *High School and Beyond* national survey data shows that during the school year American high school students average about four or five hours of homework and about twenty-eight hours of television per week (Walberg and Shanahan, 1983). An obvious place where home and school come together is in the area of assigned homework, with the amount, quality, and usefulness potentially determined jointly by educator, parents, and students.

Home Environment

In addition to partnership on homework, school-parent programs to improve academic conditions in the home have an outstanding record of success in promoting achievement (Walberg, 1984). In twenty-nine controlled studies of the past decade, 91 percent of the comparisons favored children in such programs over nonparticipant groups. Although the average effect of school-parent programs on achievement was twice that of socioeconomic status, some programs had effects ten times as great. The programs appear to benefit older as well as younger students. Because few of the programs lasted more than a semester, the potential for programs sustained over the years of schooling is great. What might be called "the curriculum of the home" is twice as predictive of academic learning as family socioeconomic status.

This curriculum refers to informed parent-child conversations about everyday events; encouragement and discussion of leisure reading; monitoring and joint analysis of television viewing and peer activities; deferral of immediate gratifications to accomplish long-term goals, such as school achievement; and expressions of affection and interest in the child as a person and in his or her academic achievements (Walberg, 1984). Some research suggests other roles for parents, such as audience for the child's work, home tutor, co-learner with child, school-program supporter, advocate before school boards and other officials, committee member, and paid school-staff worker (Walberg, 1984).

Conception of the School as a Community of Families

From the origins of public education, school has generally operated in relative isolation from its constituent families, thus protecting their functions from "interference." This isolation is counterproductive in situations of individual and family vulnerability or difficulty in coping. As long as this isolation was taken for granted, the school social worker's role has historically been to span the boundaries as expeditiously as possible. In some cases the boundaries themselves have been challenged by school social workers and parents. The alternative is to conceive of school as a community of families with teachers and parents in a socializing partnership with one another, having both shared and separate functions. Parents have challenged barriers to this process in numerous and ongoing experiments with parent-sponsored schools. The conception of school as a community of families is a major departure from conventional thinking and practice. However, it is a trend that will shape the thinking in the 1990s.

Social workers have used a species of "community organization" skills to create a community around the learning process composed of families. The results reinforce partnership and appear to generally enhance the effectiveness of each child's education. In the late 1960s Project Headstart, reflecting a general philosophy governing community action programs, was the first to initiate planned parent participation as an essential dimension of schooling. Schraft and Comer (1979) reflect on the experience of parent involvement in an impoverished community where parents were perceived as "unmotivated" or "hard to reach." They reviewed how social workers took the lead in developing activities that, over time, involved a community of parents in the schools. In their review of their experience in New Haven, Connecticut, there were three levels of parent participation. The first level comprised general activity geared to involving the majority of the parent body, such as potluck suppers and fun fairs. The second level was designed to involve parents specifically in the daily life of the school, as classroom assistants or as participants in workshops to make materials for teachers. The third level enabled parents to participate meaningfully in the decision-making process in the school. Parents might move from level to level, but Schraft and Comer caution against expecting involvement in the third level without much development of the first two levels over a relatively long period of time.

Adolfi-Morse (1982) applied the above concepts to her work in a school for emotionally disturbed children in Fairfax County, Virginia. The school, which comprised a wide geographic area with many ethnic differences, is conceived of as a community of families. Events such as back-to-school night, potluck dinner, and parent-teacher organization meetings are used to reinforce this concept. Parents of children with disabilities, who may have been less involved than others, were often able to find important roles for themselves with their children as they were making the community work. Their involvement would bring about a change in their children's estimate of their own roles.

More recently, one of the authors did qualitative research at Argonne, a parent-run private school in Milan, Italy. The school is emblematic of a trend and of a restructured concept of family solidarity that appears to have enormous potential consequences for social policy in Italy and in Europe and the United States (Donati, 1989). Argonne School is first of all a community of families, and in its own way carries out all of Bristol and Gallagher's recommendations for parent involvement, although with relatively normal children. Children of these families are admitted to the school on the condition that the parents agree to involvement with the school and its activities in a partnership in the education of their child. Educational goals are individualized for each pupil in a process that is shared by parent, pupil, and school.

The resultant goals build toward developmentally appropriate strengths and capacities of children, which are much broader than the academic. Some children need help in developing friendships; others need to develop more consistent work habits. The effect of one child's changing and developing positive qualities is felt by classmates in many different ways, and this diffusion of the one child's changing is reinforced through peer friendship networks. The same friendship networks are encouraged among parents. Most parents needed to overcome the fear and reluctance involved in becoming friends with and resources to each other. The normality of development with all of its pitfalls and small triumphs is the theme of the shared experience of systematically organized friendship networks. Each child (ages ranging from six through nineteen in three schools) attends class with teachers, but works with a tutor on individual goals geared to normal developmental stages. The tutor coordinates the educational program with the parents, the teachers, and another set of parents that is more experienced and has a child at the same grade level. This other couple is specifically delegated to assist the family through their friendship, support, and ability to be candid about their own struggles in being parents and the normality of developmental crises. In the course of my study, I observed that tutors, when asked to describe a particular pupil, automatically, without being asked, also described the family situation. The emergent structure presents exciting possibilities for a very different conception of education. It is one that appears, allowing for growing pains, to be working well and producing good results. Parent involvement is estimated by the teachers at 90 percent, and the author consistently in his research saw that both parents were generally coming to conferences and involving themselves in school meetings.

A Necessary Arrangement of Relations between Family and School

There appears to be a necessary arrangement of relationships among families, other mediating systems, and societal institutions such as schools. Families cannot educate their children in a complex modern society without the assistance of schools, and schools cannot educate without the cooperation of families. Each can prevent the other from accomplishing its proper function. This is particularly true of vulnerable children and families. There is a necessary order in the relationship of family and school. Family functions of education come prior to the school functions. School functions exist to assist the family in carrying out its prior functions in a manner in keeping with the needs and standards of society and the rights of members of the family.

Children are in a recognized position of vulnerability and require protection from their environments. They have a right to receive adequate nurturance and socialization whenever possible in their own family. The community, often represented by the school, is obligated to ensure that families have all those aids—economic, social, educational, political, and cultural assistance—that they need to face all their responsibilities in a human way. It is not the role of the school to take away from families the child-rearing functions that families can perform on their own or in cooperative associations.

The relationship of the family unit to the school and the community can be expressed by three principles:

1. The family's primary functions are the care and socialization of its children. It has rights and responsibilities derived from this function. These responsibilities include the economic, social, educational, and cultural provision for the needs of its members. As such, the family is the basic social unit of society.
2. The school's primary functions are helping the family to accomplish its responsibilities and supplying certain cognitive instruction that the family cannot take on. The work of the family is always personal. Transactions *en famille* are expected to be based on affection and respect for the other person. Particular types of learning would be distorted if they excluded the personal dimension. In families this personal dimension is experienced and learned in work, worship, gender roles, respect for others in social relations, and respect for one's developing sexuality. When affection and respect break down, the partnership of home and school can be developed through social work services that assist the family in developing or redeveloping respect and affection among members.
3. A secondary function of the school (and in a broader sense, the community) is to monitor the potential abridgment of rights of children as pupils and citizens, when external conditions of society or internal conditions within the family make it impossible for the family to accomplish its primary function. This must be done, as in the first discussed principle, without inappropriately abridging the family's exercise of those functions it is able to accomplish.

These principles involve a balance between family and school, an order and a defined relation to each in its respective functions. The increased awareness of the importance of effective families, the increasing numbers of vulnerable families, and the increasing school responsibility for the education of vulnerable children inevitably lead to the need for more integrated relationships between school and family. On the other hand, the development of increased school services closing the gap between family and school could pose a threat to family autonomy and effectiveness. When services take over, rather than empowering families to carry out their duties, they limit the effectiveness of the partnership. North American schools need to redefine their relationship with families so that a truly collaborative relationship emerges with all families and so that vulnerable children in vulnerable families are helped to make the most of what school has to offer. Balancing the need for this collaborative relationship is the need for protection of the rights of children to appropriate family nurturance and socialization. Both need to be done in such a way that the family is appropriately supported in carrying out its responsibility.

RECENT EMPIRICAL FINDINGS REGARDING THE SCHOOL SOCIAL WORK ROLE

There is a good fit between the school's need for a specialist in promoting a partnership with families and the school social work role as it has emerged in the research of the previous two decades. In a period of great role specialization in the schools, the social worker's role has remained quite broad. School social workers are involved with pupils, teachers, parents, and the broader community and use methodologies as diverse as casework, group work, family intervention, consultation, and community organization. Practice theory in school social work has generally pointed out a broad role linked to the mission of the public school. The constants in this picture are the person-environment perspective of social work and the mission of the school. The match between the two in the context of changing societal conditions allows for a flexible use of methodology in the service of the broadly conceived education process.

Recent studies have found a similar richness of focus in actual practice. Building on the traditional focus on school children and their families, the areas of consultation to administrators, resource development and community change, student's rights, group work, and general consultation with and on behalf of students are very much a part of the school social work role (Chavkin, 1985). The breadth of this role definition is not only perceived by and agreed upon by school social workers but also by school administrators who work with social workers (Constable and Montgomery, 1985).

CHOOSING THE UNIT OF ATTENTION

The social worker is in the school to facilitate family, school, and community in working with one another and with the pupil and to assist the pupil in discovering his or her own resources and making use of what the pupil's family, school, and community have to offer. To accomplish this, a most important part of the role of the school social worker is choosing the unit of attention, discovering where to be and what to do to enable the best match to take place between pupil-family needs and school-community resources. The unit of attention is chosen as the point of most effective change, a point in the system where, if change takes place, other positive change will also become possible. The social worker may work with a pregnant adolescent and her family on issues of planning and coping with the pregnancy, with her teachers on issues of inclusion in an appropriate instructional program, and with community resources to provide appropriate child care—all so that she is able to carry out a plan of continuing school through graduation. In another community the social worker may work with other combinations of the groups in this picture. In another, work with individual children and families is the major focus. In another, the school social worker may spend time developing a truancy program or out-of-school resources for latchkey children. Again, the emphasis may be on helping teachers to be more effective with socially vulnerable children. In each school the role as developed differs somewhat and these differences are geared to the circumstances of each school and to agreements worked out between the social worker and the school administrators. Whatever the major thrust of the school social worker's role, the components of working with pupils, teachers, families, and community need to be there. Methods of working with each of these systems have been clearly established in social work education for many years, and over the past two decades much of the theory development has focused on integrating these essential components.

Using this framework, each unit of attention determines its own special demands on the social worker. Choosing the most effective focus, in the context of the time available, is a complex professional task for the school social worker. However, it is by no means a random process. There is a certain logical progression to it, reflecting principles of efficiency and family partnership with the school. In the following discussion, a case study is provided to highlight each unit of attention described and relate it to the school/family constellation.

THE SCHOOL PROGRAM AS A UNIT OF ATTENTION

The first unit of attention of the school social worker is the school program offered to pupils. Here the school social worker may work with others in the school to develop programs for particular groups, such as pregnant adolescents or children being mainstreamed from special education programs, or for individual students. In individual circumstances the social worker will work as a consultant to teachers. Many times developing a program or consulting with teachers may be enough to accomplish desired change. The change in the classroom affords the pupil an opportunity to accomplish learning and social developmental tasks. Nothing further is needed in this case. Extending intervention to the parents or pupil would be unnecessary and therefore intrusive. On the other hand, when intervention with parents and pupil is necessary, it should first of all be built on continuing work with the teachers and other resources in the school.

Jimmy B. is a seven-year-old boy with learning disabilities whose parents were going through a divorce. Jimmy was having great difficulty staying on task in class. He cried readily and was very dependent on adults in his environment. His classroom teacher, Ms. T., found him quite difficult and believed that he was simply avoiding the expectations of her class. His resource room teacher, Mr. G., saw more of what Jimmy could do in individual sessions, but seemed to be protecting him from the expectations of Ms. T.'s class. The social worker, in consultation with both teachers and after observing Jimmy in class, saw a child who was withdrawing from learning tasks, probably related to generally slow development, and the inconsistent, sometimes conflicting school theme expectations. Working with both teachers, tasks that could be expected of Jimmy in both classes were worked out. Both teachers developed a better understanding of the problems by sharing perspectives and by a better understanding of the relation of the divorce to Jimmy's effort to concentrate. Both agreed on a program of support to encourage more mature functioning with gradually increased expectations of more independent functioning. The social worker agreed to contact the home, help the parents understand the education goals, and solicit their help in supporting the new plan, especially when helping with Jimmy's homework.

THE FAMILY AS A UNIT OF ATTENTION

The second unit of attention is the family of the pupil. In harmony with the work begun by the teacher, the potential alliance of the school with the family may need to become explicit. With many students the contact with family and some ongoing work with teachers is enough to accomplish a goal. In any case, the family's involvement is usually necessary before going on to the next step.

In her contact with Jimmy's home, the social worker learned that the parents had separated in the summer. Mrs. B., a bakery clerk, felt herself very close to Jimmy, who was her youngest child. The mother had always enjoyed his sweet and babyish qualities, whereas the father tended to have high expectations of him. This difference was a cause of marital difficulty. Mrs. B. had relied on Mr. B. to set limits and was having difficulty setting controls of her own. The social worker had several contacts with Mrs. B. and one with both parents together. She helped them see some of the effects of their conflict on Jimmy and referred the couple to a family service agency for more extensive family counseling. Both parents became concerned about the extent to which Jimmy was reacting to their difficulties. Mrs. B. worked out an agreement so that she could be reached by phone at somewhere other than her place of employment, and, building on this, Mrs. B. was able to work more closely with the school regarding expectations of Jimmy. Mr. B. was willing to support this work. Both parents requested that Jimmy be seen by the social worker, and the social worker agreed to do this, providing she could remain in contact with both parents regarding developments at home and school. In her observations of Jimmy and in her contacts with the parents, the social worker noticed that

Jimmy himself drew out either protectiveness or rejection from people around him in the same way he had experienced this division from his parents. This is not unusual in children experiencing marital conflict. She decided to develop a contract between the parents and the teachers so that their efforts to work together and set common rules and expectations were supported.

THE PUPIL AS A UNIT OF ATTENTION

The third unit of attention is the pupil. Whatever changes take place in the classroom environment and in what the school is able to offer, the pupil needs help to utilize them and to deal with personal issues of change. Building on the sound base of a connection with both home and school, the combination of a small amount of home, school, and pupil changes is often much more powerful than an intensive focus on simply one or the other.

Jimmy was willing to see the social worker after his parents discussed it with him. He enjoyed working with clay, making elaborate log houses and little people, but could get teary-eyed if the social worker made any association in the play with home or with a mother or father. He eventually was able to talk about his feelings regarding school. The social worker was able to involve Jimmy in the contract with his teacher and his parents on assignments and expectations and reinforce improvements with him. She decided that she would go slowly with Jimmy, helping him to deal with the positive changes in the classroom and home that she had been encouraging.

THE COMMUNITY AS THE UNIT OF ATTENTION

A fourth unit of attention is the agencies and resources in the community. The community provides a variety of resources, such as child care, health care, employment, and so on, that may make it possible to achieve certain goals. In most cases, the social worker would have difficulty making the connection without first establishing a firm base with school, family, and pupil.

Jimmy's parents requested marital counseling at a family service agency. The school social worker collaborated with the counselor they were seeing. Jimmy was clearly triangulated and inappropriately involved with the marital issues, and only with considerable effort were they able to refocus their discussion. Both parents were concerned about Jimmy's reaction to their problems, but the school's work with Jimmy gave them insights that enabled them to get to issues more related to their actual marital problems.

In addition to helping people to use existing resources, frequently the school social worker is in a position to develop resources in the community. An example is the use of a student volunteer in a park system to help an extremely isolated thirteen-year-old move into group game activities and eventually get reinvolved in the school environment, which he had not attended for many years. Social workers frequently advocate for the client to secure services or act as the coordinator of a network of services.

SUMMARY

The new aspirations for excellence in education cannot be satisfied without family involvement. Family units, however, have become generally more vulnerable to multiple social pressures. School social workers have a wealth of experience in working with vulnerable families and vulnerable children in the context of the education process. These skills can be applied to the development of partnerships between school and parents, not only for the most vulnerable, but for the general condition of family vulnerability experienced today, a vulnerability that can defeat efforts to achieve excellence.

REFERENCES

Adolfi-Morse, B. 1982. Implementing parent involvement and participation in the educational process and the school community. In Constable, R. T. and Flynn, J. P. (eds.). *School social work: Practice and research perspectives.* Homewood, IL: The Dorsey Press, pp. 231–234.

Bristol, M. M., and Gallagher, J. J. 1982. A family focus for intervention. In Ramey, C. T., and Trohanis, P. L. (eds.). *Finding and educating high risk and handicapped infants.* Baltimore: University Park Press, pp. 137–161.

Chavkin, N. F. 1985. School social practice: A reappraisal. *Social Work in Education* 8, 1.

Constable, R. T. 1982. The educational system and the community as a context for social work practice. In Constable, R. T. and Flynn, J. P. (eds.). *School social work: practice and research perspectives.* Homewood, IL. Dorsey Press.

Constable, R. T., and Montgomery, E. 1985. Perceptions of the social worker's role. *Social Work in Education* 7, 4 (Summer): 244–257.

Donati, P. 1989. Personal interview with R. T. Constable. Argonne School, Milan, Italy.

Gallagher, J. J., Beckman, P., and Cross, A. H. 1983. Families of handicapped children: Sources of stress and its alleviation. *Exceptional Children* 50, 1:10–18.

Germain, C. G. 1982. An ecological perspective on social work in the schools." In Constable, R. T. and Flynn, J. P. (eds.). *School social work: Practice and research perspectives.* Homewood, IL. Dorsey Press.

Kurtz, P. D. 1988. Social work services to parents: Essential to pupils at risk. *Urban Education* 22, 4:444–457.

Lachney, M. E. 1982. Understanding families of the handicapped: A critical factor in the parent-school relationship. In Constable, R. T., and Flynn, J. P. (eds.). *School social work: Practice and research perspectives.* Homewood, IL: The Dorsey Press.

Olshansky, S. 1962. Chronic sorrow: A response to having mentally defective children. *Social Casework* 43: 190–192.

Ordonevsky, P. 1990. Parents report high involvement in school. *USA Today*, March 5, 1990.

Turnbull, A. P., and Turnbull, H. R. 1978. *Parents speak out: Views from the other side of the two-way mirror.* Columbus, Ohio: Charles E. Merrill.

Walberg, H. J. 1983. Improving the productivity of America's schools. *Educational Leadership* 41, 8: 19–27.

Walberg, H. J., and Shanahan, T. 1983. High school effects on individual students. *Educational Researcher* 53: 75–92.

CHAPTER 17

The Social Developmental Study

Marguerite Tiefenthal
School Social Worker, Retired, District 181, Hinsdale, Illinois

Rita Charak
School Social Worker, District 102, LaGrange, Illinois

Studying the social functioning of the child in his or her home, school, and community environment is an essential part of the total assessment of a student's functioning when the student is referred for a case study evaluation. This information along with an investigation into the child's general development, learning achievement, and his or her behavior patterns creates a relatively complete picture. A decision about the quality and extent of the child's special education needs are based upon these findings. This entire assessment satisfies the original mandate of P.L. 94-142, the Education for All Handicapped Children Act, and the subsequent Individuals with Disabilities Education Act, P.L. 101-476. This legislation places a strong emphasis on the non-biased assessment of children assured in part by the requirement for multidisciplinary input. Also it requires an assessment of the cultural milieu of the family and emphasizes the information obtained during a consultative interview with the parents about the child's background and current functioning outside of school (adaptive behavior assessment).

Both state and federal legislation further mandated the use of trained professionals in evaluating children referred and accepted for evaluation, including multidisciplinary input into the educational planning for children with special needs. This chapter will discuss the social developmental study used in public school settings, how information generated through the study is integrated into the child's background and current functioning, as well as the component of a comprehensive social developmental study, and the integration of the adaptive behavior assessment as an integral part of the study.

Although the Social Developmental Study (SDS) is sometimes referred to as the Social History, a tool often used by social workers to understand the dynamics of a client's difficulties, the SDS has additional required components making it more comprehensive and thus should not be confused with one of its component parts which is the child's "social history." The SDS includes minimal identification of essential information, the assessment of the child's adaptive behaviors, the cultural background, the events preceding the problem, the significant life experiences of the child, and current abilities. It is a compilation of information that broadly assesses the child's current and previous social/emotional level and provides a baseline for future planning and treatment.

The thrust of current legislation is for greater emphasis and a need for such a report for a truly non-biased assessment of each referred child. To fulfill this mandate, the social developmental study must provide information on the cultural background of the child's family, an evaluation of his/her adaptive behaviors, and a deepened understanding of the student's background and abilities compiled from the interview with the parents. According to Illinois regulations, the social developmental study includes assessment information from many sources including parents, foster parents, teachers and other involved staff, significant people outside the school such as extended family or other significant caretakers, involved agencies—each significant in developing a profile of the student's social and developmental capabilities. A thorough assessment of the student's adaptive behaviors, often using a formal assessment instrument, is also required regarding the child's intellectual performance for a balance of information presented by others on the multidisciplinary team. Hereafter, "parents" refers to parent(s), guardians, or foster parents (whatever adult or agency has legal custody of the child).

In a document published by the Illinois State Board of Education for parents, the SDS is described as ISBE form 34-57 B. (5-87).

> This study allows the evaluation team to understand you child by assessing in-school and out-of-school behavior and assessing how the environment affects your child's ability to learn. This study includes an assessment of adaptive behavior (how your child functions independently and meets standards of personal and social responsibility) and cultural background. This (adaptive behavior) study may include formal (tests) and informal procedures.

PURPOSES OF THE SOCIAL DEVELOPMENTAL STUDY

Since the SDS is a compilation and analysis of information concerning those life experiences of the child, both past and present, which pertain to the child's problems and/or to the possible alleviation of those problems, it serves several purposes in the school setting. One major purpose is to assist the parents and school personnel (and the child) in understanding life circumstances as related to the child's school performance or behavior. A second major purpose is to assist in selecting an educational environment conducive to optimum learning and the development of the child.

The SDS, by including information from sources outside the school, helps to assess the whole child, focusing on multiple strengths and areas in need of support. It brings into focus factors in the family and the home which affect the child's learning and behavioral patterns. This involvement with the family permits the school social worker to begin a working relationship between parents and the school that may not have been established earlier. Thus begins the process of developing an appropriate educational plan for their child with special needs.

In addition, a relationship may be established through which counseling, emotional support, information about community resources, and legal rights can be explained and the mediation of significant differences can begin. The beginning relationships with the family formed by the social worker when compiling a social developmental study should continue through placement of the student and implementation of the program. This relationship frequently has a therapeutic impact on the parent(s) or at least may ameliorate feelings of inferiority and/or alienation from their child's educational experience. During this process the social worker helps parents to 1) gain a clear understanding of the implication of the assessment, and 2) obtain a clear understanding of their due process rights under state and federal laws and regulations. The social worker needs the parents' help in the following areas:

1. Providing an overview of the child outside the school setting, including strengths and special needs,

2. Obtaining a clearer view of how the child perceives himself or herself,

3. Evaluating the needs of the parents in relation to their care and support of their child in the areas of coping skills, identifying their strengths and special needs, and/or support for respite, and

4. Assessing needed environmental changes (Henry, DeChristopher, Dowling, and Lapham, 1981, p. 10).

In the schools, the social developmental study is a diagnostic tool to help guard against inappropriate labeling of a child; this can occur when there is exclusive use of test scores and school performance without consideration of cultural differences, as well as other significant environmental influences and competencies (Goldstein, Askell, Aschcroft, Hurley and Lilley, 1976). The SDS provides relatively nondiscriminatory assessment of children evaluated for special education, since a broad variety of information is considered, including social or cultural background, and adaptive behavior (Reschly, 1980).

REFERENCES TO SOCIAL DEVELOPMENTAL STUDY IN P.L. 94-142 AND P.L. 101-476

Although P.L. 94-142 does not specifically refer to a "social developmental study," its regulations state that "the comprehensive evaluation of children necessarily involves the collection of a variety of information from the parents concerning their perception of the child's behavior. Such a practice is considered routine and basic to any evaluation and, therefore, unnecessary to be specifically listed" (U.S. Department of Health, Education, and Welfare, December 1977b, 121a. 540-543). The following guidelines for assessment are particularly important:

- The child must be assessed in all areas related to the suspected disability, including, where appropriate, health, vision, hearing, social and emotional status, general intelligence, academic performance, communicative status, and motor abilities.

- The team may not identify a child as having a specific learning disability if the severe discrepancy between ability and achievement is primarily the result of a visual, hearing or motor handicap, mental retardation, emotional disturbance, environmental, cultural or economic disadvantage.

- Testing and evaluation material and procedures used for the purpose of evaluation and placement of children with disabilities must be selected and administered so as not to be racially and culturally discriminatory.

- In interpreting evaluation data and in making placement decisions, each public agency shall draw upon information from a variety of sources, including aptitude and achievement tests, teacher recommendations, physical condition, social or cultural background and adaptive behavior, and ensure that information obtained from all of these sources is documented and carefully considered.

- No single procedure or test can be used alone to evaluate...

- Evaluation materials are to be administered by appropriately trained personnel...

- Evaluation must be made by a multidisciplinary team... (Department of Health, Education, and Welfare, August 1977a, 121a. 533-541).

COMPONENTS OF A SOCIAL DEVELOPMENTAL STUDY

Through the social developmental study, the evaluation done by the school social worker are assembled into a single written assessment statement. With the infusion of professional judgment, the bases for the social worker's recommendations emerge. The social developmental study should be written in educational language and should include information that relates to what the educational system should do, in the social worker's view, to assist the child in gaining the most benefit from the available educational system from the social/developmental perspective. Please note that in the SDS report, specific recommendations for class placement are not appropriate and must be avoided. This is because placement in a specific program is the result of the compilation of the child's learning needs and the Multidisciplinary Conference Team's (including the parents and all other contributors of the case study) determination of eligibility, and then the most appropriate placement in which these needs can be met.

The following are components of a social developmental study:

1. Interview with the child
2. Consultation with the child's parent(s)
3. Cultural background
4. Assessment of the child's learning environment
5. Observation of the child in the classroom
6. Observation of the child in the home environment
7. Adaptive behavior assessment
8. Consultation with the child's current and previous teachers
9. Consultation with other staff and/or agencies who would have knowledge of the child and/or family

Only information which directly impacts the child's educational progress should be included in the written report. The elements of this report are as follows:

I. Identifying Information
   1. The child's name, birthdate, school, grade, teacher
   2. Each family member's name, age, relationship to the child, educational background, occupation, employment/unemployment, address, marital status
   3. Names of other persons living in the home and their relationship to the child

II. Reasons for Referral
1. The stated reasons for the referral and any specific questions which should be addressed
2. The problem (the child's learning or behavior) as described by the teacher, parent, or others
3. What has been done to try to correct the situation (should include at least three significant interventions)
4. What the immediate precipitating events were which prompted the referral
5. A checklist citing specific behaviors which interfere with the learning process

III. Sources of Information
A list of the dates and sources of the data obtained should include, but not be limited to:
1. Home visit(s) or alternative modes of interviewing "parents"
2. Contacts with other relatives
3. Social worker's or other's interview(s) with the child
4. Review of school records
5. Outside evaluations
6. Formal or informal adaptive behavior assessment
7. Other observations of the student

IV. Developmental History
Developmental milestones which took place before the age of six may be significant and can include problems which occurred during pregnancy or delivery, and any unusual condition(s) at birth.

In addition, for a child between ages 3 and 5, the social/emotional profile may include an assessment of:
1. Degree of independence
2. Quality of and types of interpersonal relationships experienced
3. Self image
4. Adaptability
5. Play behavior

For a child 5 years and older:
1. Level of independence
2. Interpersonal relationships, including quality of:
   a. Peer interaction
   b. Adult interaction
3. Range and intensity of play activity
4. Self image
   a. Self-awareness
   b. Self-esteem
   c. Self-confidence
5. Coping and effectiveness in social situations
6. Sensitivity to others

7. Adaptability/appropriate persistence
8. Problem-solving abilities

In addition, any traumas, hospitalizations, accidents, health problems or chronic conditions, disabilities, unusual problems, or need for medication should be noted if significant regarding the child's educational functioning. The reason for absences from school need to be considered if known. The child's stamina, energy level, and length of attention span in specific situations can be significant. The child's physical appearance and conduct while in the presence of the social worker should be noted.

These items of observation can form the basis for listing a child's strengths and weaknesses and be useful information for the school, particularly if they are different from what was observed in class. Special attention is given to a child's interests at home, how he or she seems to learn best, areas of giftedness, hobbies, and special opportunities the child has for learning.

Developmental history would include tolerance for frustration from infancy on, causes of frustration, and what the parental reaction has been. Emotional development would include ability to successfully get his/her needs met and to develop satisfying age appropriate relationships. Also, any maladaptive tendency toward temper tantrums, fears, impulsivity, enuresis, sleep disturbances, stealing, lying, and so on should be noted.

A child's role in the family, family expectations, opportunities for friends outside of school, and sense of humor can all have meaning in the evaluation.

School History

The school history for young children begins with day care, nursery school, preschool, and early childhood classes and experiences. Increasingly, more children experience group learning and day-care facilities from infancy on. This section should include a chronological account of the informal and formal learning experiences, including their changes and interruptions and the progress or lack of progress the child has made to date.

School records now show fewer comments by teachers than in the past, but do reveal attendance records, retention, special instructional assistance, and testing results. Parents frequently recall significant changes, problems, traumatic experiences, etc., which have affected their child's learning progress over the years which are extremely helpful in assessment. Parental attitudes toward these early learning situations, their involvements with their child's learning, their expecions of the school and their child, their values, their ability and willingness to cooperate with the school are all significant data. The educational system's understanding of, and sensitivity

TABLE 1 Informal Adaptive Behavior Assessment: A Conceptual Model

Environmental Setting	Areas of Functioning		
	Independent Functioning	Personal Responsibility	Social Responsibility
	Does she/he have/can she/he acquire the necessary skills	Does she/he use skills	Does she/he use the skills appropriate (time and place)
Academic school: subject areas			
Nonacademic school: playground, halls, gym, to and from school and classes			
Out of school: home, neighborhood, peers, parents, other adults			

to, parental feelings and level of willing support may make the difference between a successful plan for their child and one in danger of failure.

Family Background

This section includes family history and family dynamics, separations, divorces, deaths, remarriages, moves, transfers, changes in child caretakers, absence of various family members, and significant other events. Also, the atmosphere within the family (which may be temporarily in crisis) needs to be noted along with the family's methods and abilities, individually, and as a unit, to cope with stressful situations.

Sensitivity and caring of family members to the child's problem and the family's ability, time, temperament, and willingness to be of assistance is important. The parent's view of the child's personality, the interrelationships between family members, the interests, activities, hobbies, and leisure activities all give clues to possible recommendations to help the child.

Adaptive Behavior Assessments

It is important to examine the extent to which the presenting problem influences the general behavior of the child. A simplified definition of adaptive behavior is the effectiveness with which the individual functions independently and meets culturally imposed standards of personal and social responsibility. The concept of adaptation, as it differentiates from measures of intelligence and specific handicaps, was well known before the term "adaptive behavior" was formulated.

A state regulation in Illinois requires the social worker to include an assessment both of the child's cultural background and adaptive behavior in the social developmental study (Illinois Office of Education, 1979). The social worker is identified as the person to conduct this assessment because of the social worker's formal training in patterns of normative behavior and cultural diversity. This information is typically gathered either through formal instruments measuring adaptive behaviors, or informally through observation and interview. In any case, the parents are interviewed for the purpose of collecting data for the social developmental study.

Informal and formal adaptive behavior assessments are used depending on the degree of the problem. Informal assessments compare the child's functioning in the classroom with his or her functioning out of the classroom, e.g., home, community, and external school activities. The areas of functioning include independent functioning, personal responsibility, and social responsibility. When addressing independent functioning, the assessment will answer the question, "Does he/she have (or can he/she acquire) the necessary skills" in each area? When assessing his or her personal responsibility, the assessment will answer the question, "Does he/she use the skills in each behavior setting?" When assessing social responsibility, the question to be answered is, "Does he/she use the skill appropriately," that is, in the appropriate place and at the appropriate time? Table 1 gives a conceptual model which may be used in acquiring this information systematically. The age of the child and the sociocultural background are, of course, essential ingredients in such an informal assessment, as they are formal assessments.

Since adaptive behavior assessments are intended to be as nondiscriminatory as possible in areas of culture, race, and ethnicity, assessing the child's level of adaptive behavior is extremely important in order to assure 1) that children from minority and culturally diverse groups are not represented disproportionately in special education classes because of cultural influences rather than adaptive deficits; and 2) that children of all ages and cultural backgrounds are appropriately diagnosed and placed. Generally speaking, formal adaptive behavior assessments cover the following areas: perception, gross and fine coordination motor, communication, self-help skills, socialization skills, intellectual functioning outside the school environment, and independence. There are several well-researched instruments, some more appropriate to assess particular presenting conditions, such as retardation.

There are formal instruments that have been developed commercially for assessing adaptive behavior. Formal instruments are developed from sample populations to derive "normal" or average age scores which are then converted to standard scores, whereas informal or even screening instruments are not. Most formal instruments are administered through interviews and most recommend that the person interviewed be the adult that is most familiar (i.e., parent or other caretaker) with the child's performance in environments other than the school. The choice of which instrument to use depends on the child's age and the areas to be evaluated. It is inappropriate to use one instrument for all ages and situations. There are and will continue to be constant development and refinements instruments.

A formal instrument for measuring adaptive behavior should be used if there is a possibility that a child may be categorized as mentally retarded or otherwise developmentally delayed. A formal instrument will more effectively exclude the biases inherent in even the most careful informal instrument assessment and will yield valuable information for the determination of learning needs.

Evaluation—Summary, Conclusions, and Recommendations

The final part of the social developmental study is a brief, concise summary of the meaningful information, including how these experiences affect the child's educational progress. This forms the basis for the social worker's recommendations regarding the educational needs of the child, the best learning environment, parent counseling, available school-based services, and further diagnostic evaluations. Specific recommendations about how parents can be helpful and supportive are appropriate. Since the social developmental study is a diagnostic tool and is often essential in assessing severity of emotional problems and mental retardation, the data must be carefully collected and assessed to ensure its accurate contribution to a differential diagnosis.

A frequent concern in writing social developmental studies is a matter of confidentiality. Some sensitive information may be shared with the social worker and may have a direct bearing on the child's problem, but may be inappropriate to share with other school personnel. "Sometimes social data is very personal and its potential prejudicial effect may outweigh its diagnostic values" (Byrne, Hare, Hooper, Morse and Sabatino, 1977, p. 52). One approach to this problem is to assure the parent(s) early in the initial interview that this confidential information will not be shared with the school unless permission is given, or unless withholding such would endanger the health or welfare of the child. A procedure in keeping with such assurance is that of preparing the study in the form in which it will be presented and giving the parent(s) the opportunity to read and correct factual inaccuracies.

In rare cases, information may need to be included to which the parents object. This would be true only if the information is accurate and critical to decisions to be made about the child's educational needs. In addition to the technical fulfillment of confidentiality commitments, this procedure gives the parents concrete emotional assurance that confidentiality will be honored and adds trust to the social worker–parent relationship. Often the social worker and parent can collaborate on wording that will convey concern without revealing sensitive details.

Social workers may be pressured to complete social developmental studies at the expense of direct service to students and may question the use of their time. The SDS is usually time consuming, so this dilemma is common among practitioners. Reserving time for these studies on a regular basis may help alleviate this pressure. Also, carefully drafting recommendations from the study so that they are useful in developing a treatment plan will make the work more relevant, and the time spent seem more reasonable. Forms mailed to parents are sometimes considered, but good practice dictates securing additional information through direct interviewing.

CONCLUSION

This chapter has discussed the social developmental study as a dynamic instrument, a diagnostic tool, a compilation of data from many sources, and a required component in the evaluation of the child. The purpose of the study is to assist the school, the special education team, and the parents in providing the best, both educationally and emotionally, for the child.

REFERENCES

Byrne, J.L., Hare, I., Hooper, S.N., Morse, B.J., and Sabatino, C.A. 1977. The role of a social history in special education evaluation. In Anderson, R.J., Freeman, M., and Edwards, R.L. School Social Work and P.L. 94-142 The Education for All Handicapped Act. NASW. 47-55.

Goldstein, H., Askell, C., Ashcroft, S.C., Hurley, O., and Lilley, M.S. 1976. In N. Hobbs (ed.), *Issues in the classification of children*. San Francisco: Jossey-Bass.

Gottlieb, B., and Gottlieb, L. 1971. An expanded role for the school social worker. *Social Work* 16:12–21.

Henry, D.L., DeChristopher, J., Dowling, P., and Laphan, E.V. 1981. Using the social history to assess handicapping conditions. *Social Work in Education* 3(3): 7–19.

Illinois Office of Education. 1980. *Rules and regulations to govern the administration and operation of special education*, effective February 1, 1979. Springfield, IL: Illinois Office of Education.

Reschly, D.J. 1980. *Non-biased assessment.* Ames, IA: Department of Psychology, Iowa State University.

U.S. Department of Health, Education, and Welfare. 1977a. Education of handicapped children. *Federal Register,* August 23.

U.S. Department of Health, Education, and Welfare. 1977b. Procedures for evaluating specific learning disorders. *Federal Register,* December 29.

CHAPTER 18

The Individualized Education Program and the IFSP: Content, Process, and the Social Worker's Role

Robert Constable
Professor, Loyola University of Chicago;
Former Editor, *Social Work in Education*

The Individualized Education Program (IEP) and the Individualized Family Service Plan (IFSP) are central to the school social worker's work with any disabled child or infant. The IEP grows out of P.L. 94-142 and P.L. 101-476 and focuses on the disabled child from birth to twenty-one and even beyond through transition planning and his or her right to a free, appropriate, public education. Parents are essential partners with the school in education. The IFSP grows out of the early intervention part of P.L. 99-457 and then P.L. 101-476, passed a decade later than P.L. 94-142 and dealing with infants with disabilities, birth through two years of age. In the IFSP, the family is more than just a partner; it is a principal agent in management and implementation of a plan that may use a variety of resources to meet the very young child's educational needs. The education of the child with disabilities from birth through age two is not at this point conceived to be a civil right. Nevertheless, the procedure and the involvement of the IFSP could certainly be adopted in the IEP. In both cases the social worker plays an important role, and the greater the need and complexity of family involvement, the more important this role becomes.

SOURCE: Parts of this article are adapted from Robert Constable, "The Individualized Education Program: Content, Process, and the Social Worker's Role," in Robert T. Constable and John P. Flynn (eds.), *School Social Work: Practice and Research Perspectives*, 1st ed. (Homewood, IL: The Dorsey Press, 1982).

THE INDIVIDUALIZED EDUCATION PROGRAM (IEP)

The IEP is the central management tool used to ensure the child with disabilities the right to a free, appropriate, public education. The IEP assembles recent evaluation, present decision making, and future expectations in one document. It is a synopsis of the service efforts of the multidisciplinary team. It is built upon and thus reflects the evaluation effort that has previously taken place and the areas of need identified in the multidisciplinary conference (MDC). It involves the people who have interest in the child's education and who attend the IEP staffing: the parents, differing members of the multidisciplinary team (e.g., the teacher, administrator, psychologist, and other specialized personnel), when appropriate, and the child. It would be a mistake to view the IEP as merely another document. It is the living record of a process. The success of the IEP is dependent on the process itself. It is important to note that only when the students learning needs are determined, and special services required to meet these needs are determined, can possibility of placement be entertained.

The IEP is a record of the completion of a number of complex evaluative and decision-making processes and is a product of common collaboration. The social worker's input into the decision-making process will be based in part on the social developmental study. The social worker who participated in the IEP staffing generally has important responsibilities, which go beyond the report and which address the decision-making process itself.

The decision-making process aims for an agreement in five crucial areas. These are (1) the child's present level of performance; (2) annual goals and short-term objectives; (3) the special education and related services to be provided the child; (4) the means of evaluation; and (5) the needed transition services, including a statement of the interagency responsibilities or linkages, before the student completes his/her school experience. The IEP is more than a set of reports of plans. It encapsulates the entire provision of special education and related services as well as the evaluation of effectiveness. It is ultimately a list of services to be provided to reach agreed-upon goals. Although the IEP cannot guarantee the child will actually reach these particular goals, it is an agreement on the school's part to provide or purchase (if it cannot directly provide) the special education and related services listed in the document. The completed agreement reflects that a complex evaluation and goal-setting process has taken place among parents, school, and child—and, if signed and not contested, is concrete evidence that consensus has been reached among all parties.

The full potential of what social work can offer to children in schools cannot be achieved without some significant level of participation by the social worker in the IEP process. No social worker can expect to offer services to children with disabilities in the school without IEP involvement. Although survival in the schools demands participation, the unique contribution of the social worker to the IEP process needs to be well understood. This contribution takes place in at least three major areas. The social worker (1) participates in the process of setting annual goals and short-term objectives; (2) helps the multidisciplinary team to develop sufficient consensus among itself and with parents to proceed; and (3) is involved with case management and integration of school and outside agency resources.

THE PROCESS OF SETTING ANNUAL GOALS AND SHORT-TERM OBJECTIVES

The social worker makes the education system work for children where it might not otherwise be effective. The education of the child with disabilities is in large part a preparation for his or her best level of social functioning outside of the school situation. Particularly for the severely disabled, a large part of this preparation has to do with the learning of life skills: those skills that promote appropriate independence, appropriate and satisfying interpersonal relationships, problem-solving skills, an appropriate self-image, and tolerance for unavoidable stress. These are areas where social workers have particular expertise and can make a crucial contribution to the educational process. For many children with disabilities, education is dependent upon achievement of these goals. The general areas listed earlier can be broken down into instructional objectives shared by teacher and social worker. These shared objectives can be achieved through consultation with the teacher, direct intervention with the child and parents, and through the social worker's involvement in the classroom itself. The instructional objectives often reflect the confluence of educational and social goals.

DEVELOPING AGREEMENTS AND INTEGRATION OF RESOURCES

Many school districts routinely use the social worker as a coordinator of the multidisciplinary team and in the IEP staffing with the parents. Most social workers have developed problem-solving and consensus-building skills through their professional education. These skills are often crucial to the successful completion of the IEP process. The high level of professional specialization within the school and the different interests often represented by parent and school create the potential for conflict. Agreements, if reached, are frequently perceived as accommodations between weaker and stronger sets of interests. The social worker, who is the most likely member of the school team to have a holistic perspective on the child, generally has the best contact with all elements of the process and is quite accustomed to working with potential conflict.

Attainment of IEP goals, particularly with the more seriously disabled children, often demands coordination and integration of a variety of services outside the school as well as inside. Disabled children receive services from a variety of agencies: medical services, respite care, child welfare, mental health, financial assistance, transportation, vocational education, and so on. In addition to formal agency services, they can receive a variety of helps from neighbors, kin, informal groups in the community, and so on. The social worker is usually the only member of the multidisciplinary team who, as a matter of choice, is in everyday contact with these resources and whose educational preparation does include concepts of problem solving and coordination among these services.

The U.S. Department of Education in a document discussing the IEP listed the social worker as one of three professionals (the others were counselor and psychologist) who might serve as coordinator or case manager of the IEP process for an individual child or all disabled children served by an agency. Examples of the kinds of activities that case managers might carry out are (1) coordinating the multidisciplinary evaluation; (2) collecting and synthesizing the evaluation reports and other relevant information about a child that might be needed at the IEP meeting; (3) communicating with the parents; and (4) participating in or conducting the IEP meeting itself (U.S. Department of Education, 1981).

THE CONTENTS OF AN INDIVIDUALIZED EDUCATION PROGRAM

The IEP for each child must include:

A statement of the child's present level of educational performance. The child's baseline levels in various areas of educational performance (for example, academic performance, classroom behavior, social skills) are used in determining the appropriate goals and objectives for that child. The comparison of the present levels of performance with the levels at which the child should be functioning reveals the areas of deficit. It is the responsibility of the multidisciplinary team to provide input that establishes the child's present levels of performance. These baseline data are the result of collaboration among the various persons who deal with the child and his or her education. Identifying present levels of performance is necessary so that there is a basis for judgment in establishing goals as well as for later evaluation and adjustment of goals and program.

A statement of annual goals and short-term instructional objectives. Goals and objectives should reflect present levels of performance and provide a way for educators and parents to track the child's progress in special education. They should not be confused with the goals and objectives that are normally found in daily, weekly, or monthly instructional plans. Otherwise there could be hundreds of educational goals for one IEP. Annual goals are statements that describe what a disabled child can reasonably be expected to accomplish within the framework of the school year. Short-term instructional objectives are measurable intermediate steps between a disabled child's present levels of educational performance and the annual goals that are established for the child. The objectives must be based on a logical breakdown of the major components of the annual goals and can serve as milestones for measuring progress toward meeting the goals (U.S. Department of Education, 1981). They are concrete elements that in total will guide the education process toward the achievement of particular goals.

A statement of the special education and related services to be provided to the child, and the extent to which the child will be able to participate in regular education programs. The statement of needed special education and related services is derived directly from the annual goals and short-term objectives. If necessary resources are unavailable within the school, the school must contract with outside agencies, individuals, or other school districts to ensure their provision. Parents, as part of the multidisciplinary team, must be included in the decision-making process that determines these resources. The law also requires a statement of the extent to which the child can participate in regular education with or without support services, underlining the importance of the process of developing the least restrictive environment for the child with disablities. This is the legal backing that is now being addressed in the inclusion movement.

The projected dates for initiation of services and the anticipated duration of the services. These time guidelines are established concurrently with the annual goals and initiation of services is proscribed by law. The length of duration of short-term objectives is, based upon an estimate of the time necessary for completion of the goals and objectives.

A statement of the needed transition services (to facilitate movement to post-secondary education, employment, or additional schooling or training) including, when appropriate, a statement of the interagency responsibilities or linkages before the student leaves the school setting (see chapter 1). Generally applying to students fourteen-and-a-half or older, transition services mean a coordinated set of activities for a student, designed within an outcome-oriented process, that promotes movement from school to postschool activities. The coordinated set of activities is based upon the individual student's needs, taking into account the student's preferences and interests.

It includes instruction, community experiences, the development of employment and postschool adult living objectives and, when appropriate, acquisition of daily living skills and functional vocational evaluation. Where a participating agency other than the educational agency would fail to provide agreed-upon services, the educational agency would reconvene the IEP team to identify alternative strategies to meet the transition objectives.

Appropriate objective criteria and evaluation procedures and schedules for determining, on at least an annual basis, whether the short-term instructional objectives are being achieved. Objective criteria are components of the child's behavior that may be observed and measured. Objective criteria may be used to compare the child's current performance with previous levels of performance or they may be compared with a classroom norm that is typical of children his or her age. The results of these comparisons indicate whether or not short-term objectives are being achieved or whether new and different objectives may be in order.

We may break down the steps that should be followed to arrive at those goals and objectives in the school social worker's contribution to the IEP. The steps represent a way of clarifying our own goals and involvement in developing the IEP.

The Presenting Problem

In order to be eligible for P.L. 104–476 funding, the problem must relate to the categories of disabilities written into the regulations. The fact that the child fits into one of the categories, for example, hearing-impaired, does not automatically make him or her a candidate for social work intervention. The inability to deal with stress, potential breakdown of social functioning, or needed improvement of social functioning are general reasons for referral to a social worker. The additional stress of a disability and the need for individualized environmental support systems are reasons that many exceptional children need social work help. The child with a particular disability may have difficulty coping with the educational and social skill demands of the school. He or she may need help in acquiring such skills and/or in dealing with experiences that are new.

A Hypothetical Case Study

Let us follow a simple referral for a case study evaluation, the IEP process, and service sequence through each of the stages of the process. The reader should keep in mind that this is a hypothetical case study and that the type and extent of the school social worker's involvement in a particular case will depend on the individual child's needs as determined by the multidisciplinary team. We may begin with the presenting problem. Jimmy is a multiply physically disabled twelve-year-old who is borderline educably mentally disabled. He was referred because of his teacher's concern that his excessive demands for attention were impeding his learning process in several regular education classes, particularly in gym. It should be noted that in this case we have deliberately used the example of a child who is taking a partial regular education program.

The problem as a whole. The school social worker's conference with teacher and parents resulted in a picture of a boy whose performance in school has been quite uneven and whose ability to function adequately in school has been hampered by parental overprotectiveness and disagreement on the degree of independence he should be allowed. He is currently enrolled in both special and regular education classes with poor adjustment to some of these classes, overwhelming needs for attention from adults, and withdrawal from relations with other children. In the family the parents have had difficulty agreeing on the tasks he could be involved in and on his expected level of self-care. As a consequence, Jimmy's participation in the family and in care of himself is considerably less than his potential. The parents are in conflict about this, and his two brothers and a sister reflect this ambivalence in their relationships with him. On the basis of this and other information gathered, the social worker makes a diagnostic statement that draws some connections between Jimmy's role in the family, the parents' feelings, and the way Jimmy has played out some of these family role interactions in school behaviors, particularly with parent-like school figures and teachers. The statement also includes alternative plans for working with the family, Jimmy, and his teachers. The results of the social worker's assessment, combined with the information gathered by the other team members, will be used by the team in the MDC and later to formulate the statement of present levels of educational functioning in the IEP.

The problem as it is experienced in the context of education. The next step is to define the problem as it is being experienced in the classroom and in relation to the goals of education. At the risk of oversimplifying, we may provide several social parameters of the educational problem. One parameter is that of engagement or withdrawal from educational tasks appropriate to the child's capabilities. The child may either engage in the learning process with distracting, attention-getting, inappropriately aggressive behavior or may withdraw from the process, attempting to compensate in other ways for the withdrawal. A second parameter is that of engagement or withdrawal from relationships with other children. Pupils need to learn social skills appropriate to their own maturational level. The learning of these social skills influences the performance of educational tasks. Thus, there is a direct relation between the learning environment and the child's social maturation.

To follow our example, the school wishes to place Jimmy in a particular gym class with nondisabled children. We can predict with some certainty that Jimmy will place high demands on the gym teacher and the other pupils, and that the parents, while accepting of the idea, might endanger the arrangement because of their own anxiety and worries about Jimmy. Failure in the gym class could generalize to several other classes where he has recently made some adjustment. There is particular concern with the gym class due to dressing, showers, and inherent physical competition. Any one of these factors might place Jimmy's use of what the school could offer him at risk. What we know about the problem allows us to predict with some degree of accuracy the chances of goal achievement within a behavior setting and some ability to generalize to the overall ecology of the school. This understanding allows us to move to the next stage, definition of the problem in behavioral terms.

The problem as behavior. The purpose of this stage is to state the school social worker's formulation of the problem in behavioral terms and to relate it to the educational goals established earlier. Behavioral terms are statements of the client's present functioning, or what Jimmy is presently doing. These terms establish a baseline for goals and objectives and must be specific.

Behavioral objectives risk fragmentation and meaninglessness if they do not flow from the process of problem definition discussed earlier. The school social worker may find him or herself in the position of choosing from a seemingly infinite range of behaviors for any child. Actually, a few well-chosen examples are much better, particularly if they may serve as indicators.

To go back to our example, Jimmy has difficulty dealing with a situation that seems competitive and draws attention to his poor functioning. Under stress he has tended to retreat into social relations with adults from whom he demands high levels of attention. He is particularly uneasy with the dressing and showering aspects of gym. His parents' anxiety reveals another set of needs in the situation. Teachers also can tend to overreact to the situation, increasing the chances of failure. To enumerate specific aspects of the problem:

1. Jimmy withdraws from situations involving physical competition. Without intervention, the pattern is expected to continue or increase in gym class.
2. Jimmy tends not to interact with nondisabled peers.
3. Social interaction with disabled peers is limited.
4. Jimmy has no close friends.

5. Jimmy makes excessive demands on adults, especially teachers, but doesn't function in the classroom up to his own capacities without constant support from the teacher.
6. Jimmy is particularly self-conscious concerning dressing and showering aspects of gym.
7. His parents have tended to protect Jimmy from situations that demand independence or involve any risking of self. Jimmy's home patterns are related to his school patterns.
8. Teachers have tended either toward excessive protection or excessive expectations of independence with Jimmy.

Annual goals, short-term objectives, and resources. Finally, we may define goals and objectives. Annual goals are specific statements of the skills the student should be progressing toward within the framework of the school year. Annual goals evolve out of the assessment of the child's needs and abilities and should be an index of student progress. Although there are different formats that may serve as examples for a particular child's individualized education program, most would probably contain:

1. The *direction* of change desired—to increase, to decrease, to maintain.
2. *Deficit* or *excess*—the general area that is identified as needing special attention.
3. *Present level*—what the child now does in deficit or in excess.
4. *Expected level*—where the child realistically could be or what he could gain, with proper resources.
5. *Resources needed*—to accomplish the needed level of performance. Resources could be specialists, materials, situations, or methods required to bring about the desired change.

In Jimmy's case, there are two major annual goals. The components are listed in brackets.

Annual Goal 1: For Jimmy to increase [direction] positive social relations with nondisabled peers [deficit] from limited [from] to more informal [to] through interaction experiences in a group with the social worker and regular social work contacts with the parents and teacher [resources].

Annual Goal 2: For Jimmy to maintain [direction] his current academic adjustment.

Note that the direction set in the second goal is maintenance of current functioning. Maintenance equates present and expected levels of functioning.

Short-term instructional objectives. Short-term instructional objectives can be thought of as steps toward achievement of the annual goals. These steps are really milestones through which progress toward the annual goals can be assessed. They should specify the conditions under which the behavior is to be exhibited by the student in his class, in unstructured group tasks, the lunchroom, gymnasium, etc. For the social worker, these can be indicators or changes in behavior and do not have to reflect every single objective that might be defined for that goal. For Jimmy, our hypothetical case example, some short-term instructional objectives might be:

1. Jimmy's level of class participation and quality of assignment completion in his regular education classes will be maintained at his current level through January 15.
2. Jimmy will interact compatibly with nondisabled peers in an unstructured group task by March 15.
3. Jimmy will interact comfortably and spontaneously with nondisabled peers in an unstructured lunchroom situation by May 15.
4. Jimmy will form casual friendships, with both disabled and nondisabled peers, by June 15.
5. Jimmy's distractibility and talking out in class will reduce by 50 percent by June 15.
6. Jimmy will be able to dress for gym without special arrangement by January 15.

Resources. There may be external barriers to Jimmy's accomplishing these goals and objectives.[1] For example, teachers and parents may need help to avoid overprotecting Jimmy or some modifications in the gym program may be necessary. A list of the specific educational services required must be written into the IEP so that the goals and objectives can be implemented. The list of services and persons responsible is essentially a resource statement. Parents have a right to request that educational services that are included in the IEP, but are not available in the school, be purchased by the school district for the child or otherwise be provided at no cost to the parents.[2] Examples of such services might include:

1. The social worker will see Jimmy once a week for a forty-five minute period with a group of other children with disabilities who are also dealing with a mainstreamed class. The appropriateness of whether Jimmy should continue in the group will be reevaluated on or about January 15.
2. The social worker will monitor Jimmy's group progress and act as liaison between the multidisciplinary team and the family service agency working with Jimmy's family, as well as informing Jimmy's parents of progress.

3. The teacher will monitor Jimmy's achievement of the above objectives, reinforcing independent and peer-affiliative behavior.

INVOLVING CHILDREN IN THE IEP

It is a good practice to involve the school child in IEP plans. Sometimes these goals may seem abstract and so a mechanism, such as the car-in-the-garage technique, developed by Fairbanks (1985), is useful. This technique involves the following steps:

1. The school social worker draws a rough sketch of a garage on a piece of paper, connects it to a road, indicates that the garage is to be the child's destination, and asks the child to identify what should be placed in the garage as goals.
2. The child tells the school social worker what changes are desired, and the social worker or the child writes these goals inside the garage.
3. The child places one or more cars at various points along the road to the garage, symbolizing how far away from the goals and objectives he or she is. Sometimes the child leaves one or more cars off the road completely, indicating extreme lack of progress toward the goals represented by those cars.
4. The social worker asks the child for additional information about the cars and records the responses. The child's stated goals and objectives then become part of the IEP that is formally drafted at the planning team meeting.
5. The child draws new cars on the road as treatment progresses, relocating the cars on the road either closer or farther away from the garage.
6. The child places one or more cars inside the garage when particular objectives are attained and either establishes a new set of objectives or terminates treatment.

Figure 1 illustrates use of the technique in clarifying initial objectives for Mike, age twelve, and Jerry, age eight, in a public school day treatment program. Following the clarification of objectives, the technique can be used to measure progress and change objectives. In some cases it can be used with a group, because the technique becomes a visual and verbal metaphor for their accomplishments.

THE INDIVIDUALIZED FAMILY PLAN (IFP)

The IEP framework addresses education with the parents as partners in developing the education program. For a family-oriented social worker this may seem incomplete. A number of social workers and educators, particu-

FIGURE 1 Using the Car-in-the-Garage Technique to Clarify Objectives

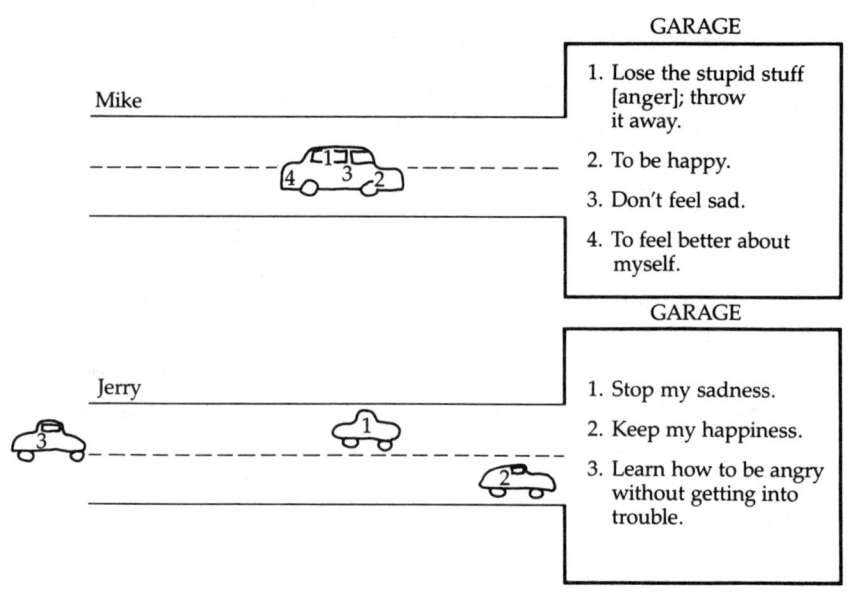

SOURCE: Nancy Mcdowell Fairbanks. 1987. Involving children in the IEP: The car-in-the-garage technique. Reprinted with permission from *Social Work in Education.* Vol. 9 (3).

larly Betty Welsh (1985), developed the Individualized Family Plan (IFP) as a supplement to the social work IEP. In Jimmy's case the problem in school was related to a long-established pattern of inconsistent expectations at home that caused Jimmy's self-care and participation in the family to be far below his capabilities. If parents and family are treated, not only as partners, but as the first educators and the first context for education of the child, a quite different approach to goal setting and consequent practice can be developed. The IFP is a formalized plan worked out with the family to assist it and the child with disabilities in accomplishing certain goals. In Jimmy's case the social worker works with the disabled child and the parents and indirectly with siblings to develop an agreement on specific aspects of participation and contribution in family, through chores, helping with younger siblings, learning more responsibility in maintaining his room, choosing his clothes, and dressing himself. These become objectives to the general goals of enhanced contribution to the family and self-care. In the process of planning with the parents and with Jimmy, some marital and family issues are touched upon. The family deals with aspects of these with reference to wanting to help Jimmy in his efforts to grow up. On the other hand, the persistence of these strains may prompt parents or family to go more deeply into marital counseling or family therapy in their efforts to deal with the problem. In any case, the IFP becomes a framework for a more focused family practice that is related to the goals of education (Welsh, 1985). Because in many situations the school absolutely cannot accomplish its goals without family involvement, the IFP becomes a necessary tool of the school social worker.

THE INDIVIDUALIZED FAMILY SERVICES PLAN (IFSP)

The IFSP grows out of early intervention programs for infants and toddlers and the obvious necessity of family involvement with children from birth through two years of age, especially children with multiple disabilities. The family often has heavy involvement with the health care system, and this system is often an important source of referral to early childhood or parent-infant programs. Parents are mourning the loss of the perfect child and of their hopes and expectations (Lachney, 1982). The heavy caretaking demands can split even well-established marital relations into overadequate and enmeshed roles or underadequate and disengaged roles, and these roles often follow conventional gender expectations. The resulting marital and family patterns are disruptive of other aspects of family living and may account for the higher rates of divorce, suicide, and child abuse among families of children with disabilities (Gallagher, Beckman, and Cross, 1983). Working with the parents while they are actively mourning their losses and when care patterns have not been completely solidified may prevent the most crippling effects of these disrupting patterns on the family and especially on the disabled child.

The IFSP must contain:

1. A statement of the child's present levels of development (cognitive, speech/language, psychosocial, motor, and self-help)
2. A statement of the family's strengths and needs relating to enhancing the child's development
3. The criteria, procedures, and timelines for determining progress
4. The specific early intervention services necessary to meet the unique needs of the child and family, including the method, frequency, and intensity of service
5. The projected dates for the initiation of service and the expected duration
6. The name of the case manager

7. Procedures for transition from early intervention into the preschool program

The IFSP must be evaluated at least once a year, and must be reviewed every six months or more, where appropriate.

Many of the principles underlying the IEP are also applicable to the IFSP and need not be repeated. There are several differences, because the IFSP is more comprehensive than the IEP and takes in a wider universe. The focus of the IFSP is first of all on *development,* rather than a more static focus, appropriate to the older child. This is evaluated through a variety of means and instruments. In addition, a statement of the family's strengths and needs relating to enhancing the child's development is needed. A statement of the family's strengths and needs requires a family assessment, and is best carried out by the school social worker. An agreement on goals, objectives, and tasks needs to emerge from this mutual assessment between social worker and family. Also, the coping and adaptation of parents, siblings, and support systems in an extended family and friendship network need to be assessed. A certain amount of inactivity associated with being overwhelmed and with mourning, and the potential distortion of relationships inherent in heavy care-giving demands often can be expected in these situations, and thus the risks should be assessed. The teaching role of parents can be distorted by the loss of hope implicit in a mourning process, and by the same relational distortions involved in the discussion of care-giving roles. Parents may be reluctant to accept help and may isolate themselves from other potential support systems in the process. Success in this process presupposes a good contact between the social worker and parents when the pressures and risks are discussed in a normalizing context. Thus, an agreement can develop with the family as the foundation for a statement of major outcomes expected to be achieved for the child and family.

MAJOR OUTCOMES EXPECTED TO BE ACHIEVED BY THE CHILD AND THE FAMILY

Based on the assessment and the particular contacts developed with the family, major expected outcomes now can be stated in a way that reinforces the primary roles of parents as educators as well as care givers and the appropriate assistance of the school in carrying out their mission. A key outcome will unavoidably be the family's participation in the teaching and care-giving roles and ability to use the case management process. The outcomes are largely based on (1) the assessments previously made of the child's present levels of development; and (2) the new coping and adaptation patterns becoming established in the family. Although educational and medical specialists have an important role in setting achievable developmental outcomes, social workers should be involved in setting achievable family outcomes and showing their relation to developmental outcomes.

These outcomes become more specific through (1) the criteria, procedures, and timelines for determining progress; (2) the specific early intervention services necessary to meet the unique needs of the child and family, including the method, frequency, and intensity of service; and (3) the projected dates for the initiation of services and the expected duration. As in the IEP, these set the parameters of the services to achieve the named developmental and family outcomes. Again, school social work services are the most appropriate (and available) external services in assisting families to meet the desired outcomes.

SERVICE COORDINATION

The IFSP must contain the name of the service coordinator from the profession most immediately relevant to the infant's, toddler's, or family's needs who will be responsible for the implementation of the plan in coordination with other agencies or persons. He or she coordinates services to the family of an infant or toddler with a handicap to assist in gaining access to early intervention services identified in the IFSP. Service coordination includes:

1. Coordinating assessments and participating in the development of the Individualized Family Service Plan
2. Assisting families in identifying available service providers
3. Coordinating and monitoring the delivery of services, including coordinating the provision of early intervention services with other services that the child or family may need or is receiving, but that are not required under this part
4. Facilitating the development of a transition plan to preschool services where appropriate (Federal Register, 52,222, November 18, 1987, 303.6)

The coordinator then assists parents in gaining access to these services. However, parents themselves should take responsibility as much as possible for the coordination roles (Garland, Woodruff, and Buck, 1988) or at least have a major role in the selection of a service coordinator. The social worker's role places him or her closest to the parents in carrying out service coordination responsibilities.

The final part of the IFSP is that of the child's transition from an early intervention program to the preschool program. Although this is frequently the domain of the educational specialists, the process and the timing of the entry of the child from a family context into a new program with new demands may be an area in which the school social worker needs to participate.

The family involvement projected in the IFSP need not be confined to infants and toddlers. When children present complex vulnerabilities and long-established patterns that inevitably affect the educational process, it is simply good practice to involve the parents in the work of the school. The IEP and the IFSP can be no better than the process of thinking, communication, and decision making they represent. They certainly are accountability documents, but they also are vehicles for collaboration with parents and for coordination of resources and development of the working agreements necessary for complex goals to be achieved. The IFSP and the IEP are challenges for social workers in developing clarity about what they will be offering students, parents, and the school, while providing an opportunity to work systematically with all of the influences on the full educational process. It is an opportunity that we cannot afford to let pass.

NOTES

1. See *Federal Register*, Education of Handicapped Children, Tuesday, August 23, 1977, 121a.552(d). "In selecting the least restrictive environment, consideration is given to any potentially harmful effect on the child or on the quality of services which he or she needs." While the concept of external barriers is not highlighted in the law, it is a traditional concept in dealing with persons with handicapping conditions. Lack of focus on such tangible or non-tangible barriers would be in effect "blaming the victim" for a condition which he or she did not create.
2. See *Federal Register*, Nondiscrimination on Basis of Handicap, Wednesday, May 4, 1977, Part IV, 84.33 for definition of a free, appropriate, public education. Also, *Federal Register*, Tuesday, August 23, 1977, 121a.126(b)(4) for a list of facilities necessary in a state to meet the goal of providing full educational opportunity for all handicapped children.

REFERENCES

Fairbanks, N. M. 1985. Involving children in the IEP: The car-in-the-garage technique. *Social Work in Education* 7(3):171–182.

Gallagher, J. J., Beckman, P., and Cross, A. H. 1983. Families of handicapped children: Sources of stress and its alleviation. *Exceptional Children* 50(1):10–18.

Garland, C., Woodruff, G., and Buck, D., 1988. Case management. *Division for Early Childhood White Paper*. Council for Exceptional Children: Reston, VA.

Lachney, M. E. 1982. Understanding families of the handicapped: A critical factor in the parent-school relationship. In Constable, R. T., and Flynn, J. P., (eds.). *School social work: Practice and research perspectives*. Homewood, IL: The Dorsey Press.

U.S. Department of Education. 1981. The Case Study Evaluation.

Welsh, B. L. 1985. The individualized family plan (IFP): A social work component to the IEP. Paper presented at the NASW School Social Work Conference, Philadelphia, PA.

CHAPTER 19

The Least Restrictive Environment and the School Social Worker

Mary Lou Rogoff
School Social Work Supervisor and Program Supervisor, Retired
Southwest Cook County Special Education Cooperative

Robert Constable
Professor, Loyola University of Chicago;
Former Editor, *Social Work in Education*

HISTORY

The Education of Handicapped Children Act, P.L. 94–142, and the latest version P.L. 101–476, Individuals with Disabilities Education Act (IDEA), require that children with disabilities receive their education in the least restrictive environment. The concept of *least restrictive environment* is defined officially in the federal regulations that require:

> special classes, separate schooling or other removal of children with disabilities from the regular educational environment occurs only when the nature or severity of the disability is such that education in regular classes with the use of supplementary aids and services cannot be achieved satisfactorily (Department of Health, Education, and Welfare, 1977a, 121a.550(b)2).

Prior to the passage of P.L. 94–142, the right to be educated in the least restrictive environment was recognized by the same landmark court decisions that acknowledged the child with disabilities' right to an education. "Among the alternative programs of education and training required by statute to be available, placement in a regular school class is preferable ... to placement in any other type of program of education and training" (PARC v. Commonwealth of Pennsylvania). The principle takes into account a variety of alternative learning environments in which the child may be educated. Thus, for the child with disabilities, there is a continuum of placement possibilities ranging from the least restrictive (that is, being placed in a regular classroom setting with ample opportunity to interact with children with no disabilities) through a variety of combinations of regular and specialized class assignments, to the most restrictive placement setting which might include a special school or even a non-public program, such as an institution with very little, if any, contact with children who are not disabled.

Current Interpretations

Federal regulations mandate that this continuum of placement possibilities be available through each local education agency for children with disabilities who live within their boundaries. The continuum of services must include instruction in regular classes, special classes, home instruction, and instruction in hospitals and institutions. Schools must also make provision for supplementary services, such as a resource room where a child may receive special instruction for learning disabilities, behavior disorders, speech and language instruction, and so on, or itinerant instruction to be provided in cooperation with regular class placement (Department of Health, Education, and Welfare, 1977a, 121a,441). In response to the court decisions and the federal regulations, states have further defined and established their own continua of placement alternatives.

The least restrictive environment amounts to a right to be educated to the maximum extent possible with children who are not disabled. When this process involves integrating such children into the regular classrooms, based on an ongoing, individually determined, education planning and programming process, it is called "inclusion." Factors idiosyncratic to school districts (such as organizational arrangements, technological differences in delivery systems, agency jurisdictional problems, and/or lack of adequate local, state, or federal financial support) may not be considered as reasons for abrogating the right to the least restrictive environment. Ultimately, school districts bear the responsibility for providing the least restrictive environment appropriate for each of their children with challenging educational needs, especially providing adequate supports for children to be educated in their regular classrooms.

We will be using Illinois as an example of the continuum of services developed by one state that adhered to the federal regulations. A list of program options available to children with disabilities in Illinois includes:

1. Standard program with modifications—the child receives his/her basic educational experience through the standard program. However, these experiences are modified through:
   a. Additional or specialized education from the teacher

b. Consultation to and with the teacher
c. Provision of special equipment and materials
d. Modification in the instructional program (for example, multiage placement, performance/output expectations, and so on).
2. Standard educational program with "resource programs" (see Taxonomy in Appendix) or "related services"—the child receives the bulk of his or her educational experiences in the standard program. However, these experiences are augmented by one or more resource programs or related services delivered either in the classroom or elsewhere, but at his or her local school.
3. Special educational program (self-contained)—the child receives most of his or her basic educational experience through an instructional program in a special class which is largely self-contained, or in a special school, but with inclusion or mainstreaming in those parts of the standard program that are appropriate, and related services as needed.
4. Cooperative community educational program—the child receives most of his or her educational experiences through either the standard or the special program of the public school. However, this educational curriculum is supplemented through work experience programs or shared agency involvement (sometimes a component of "transition planning" [i.e., school-to-work planning]).
5. Home or hospital educational program—the child who is eligible for either the standard or a special program, but is unable to attend such programs, receives instructional or resource programs and/or related services in the home or in the hospital.
6. State-operated or private program—the child whose exceptional characteristics are so profound or complex that no special education program offered by the public schools can adequately or appropriately meet his or her needs can be placed in either a state-operated or private facility, preferably one in the state, but in some cases in another state, for either a day program or full-time residential placement (Illinois Office of Education, 1979).

The placement of children with disabilities in the least restrictive environment has considerable benefits, provided that school personnel can adjust to any new procedures and adaptations necessary to support the child's educational needs. If, for example, developmentally disabled children are to be given the opportunity to acquire, maintain, and improve their life skills (adaptive behavior functioning), they may do this best by being placed with the main flow of students in the regular classroom in their neighborhood schools. Such placements could also allow their neighborhood groups to be more accessible to them. One of the most serious problems in placing students with disabilities in specialized school settings is that frequently these settings are further from home, creating for the students a feeling of isolation from their neighborhoods and regular school environments. Also, they routinely experience such a protected, controlled environment in these specialized settings that they may lose their ability to negotiate socially with the more freewheeling "regular" environment of their age-mates.

IDENTIFICATION OF CHALLENGES TO THE SCHOOL

Many children with special needs, as a result of these fundamental policy shifts, spend all or part of their school hours with children with no disabilities. The philosophy of mainstreaming a variety of students in the regular classroom necessitates adapting the environment of the school and the classroom on an ongoing routine basis to meet the special needs of children with disabilities. Certainly, students in the regular classroom are involved as part of the environment in which the student with specific needs resides. Because all children are unique, the ultimate payoff often becomes more effective educational environments for everyone. However, this new emphasis on more flexible programming, coupled with larger class size, can also create confusion, uncertainty, fear, and anxiety among school personnel, particularly the teaching personnel. The school social worker, who has traditionally dealt with socio-emotional factors that hinder or promote the process of education, has much to offer in helping education personnel learn to understand and adapt to this challenge.

There are three focuses in integrating children with disabilities with their peers who are not disabled: *temporal* integration, *instructional* integration, and *social* integration.

Temporal integration refers to the amount of time the child with disabilities spends with peers who are not disabled. The underlying assumption is that the greater the amount of time children with disabilities spend with peers without disabilities, the more socially adaptive will be their social and/or instructional growth experience. Children with disabilities need time and participation with all children to acquire essential socialization skills. Time spent with peers without disabilities is not necessarily formal instruction time. It may involve lunchroom, recess, a shared field trip, or other shared activities. Such programming also provides an opportunity for children with no disabilities to relate informally with children with disabilities and form friendships. Temporal integration is more than developing detailed schedules for both groups of children. It involves an informed estimate of how the groups of children will interact in informal situations. Occasionally, some preparation may be necessary for both groups and some monitoring of the experience is usually necessary.

Instructional integration refers to the extent to which a child with specific needs is integrated into the regular classroom instructional environment. Three conditions of compatibility must exist for instructional integration to occur. These conditions are:

- Compatibility between the child's needs and the learning opportunities available in the regular classroom
- Compatibility between the child with challenging physical or behavioral needs, learning characteristics and education needs, and the regular education classroom teacher's ability and willingness to modify instructional practices
- Provision by regular and special education personnel of an appropriate, coordinated, and well-articuated educational program

One of the tasks of the social worker in helping to meet conditions for instructional integration is to consult with the teacher regularly regarding the child's essential needs so that these can be met within a regular learning environment. An example of such consultation might be arranging for a volunteer parent, a classmate, or an older student to act as a tutor. Other examples might involve consultation regarding a child who needs a quiet place, a child who requires an opportunity for verbalizing, or the child who could benefit from more direct interaction with classroom materials or classmates. The social worker may help the teacher determine how he or she will provide these opportunities within the classroom to the benefit of the target student and often others as well.

Social integration refers to the placement of children with disabilities in situations where informal relations and friendships with their peer group with no disabilities is possible. Qualities of social integration may be expressed in terms of psychological and physical closeness, interaction with peers and the assimilation or acceptance of the children with disabilities in the regular classroom. In facilitating the social integration of children with identified needs into the regular classroom, the social worker's knowledge and expertise in social and emotional areas can be the key to maintaining them in an integrated environment.

The school social worker may assist the teacher in planning the physical location of the children within the classroom. Using the social worker's knowledge of patterns of interactions, the students may be regrouped to make the climate more conducive to learning for all students in the room. The social worker may be asked to utilize his or her skills to work directly with all of the children in the classroom in order to help them accept the child with disabilities and assist in the integration of that child into the group. The three basic formats that the social worker may use are (a) an educational format: films, bibliotherapy, or discussion of specific disabilities; (b) an affective educational approach to help children know and understand one another better so that they can function more comfortably as a group; and (c) a problem-solving approach through formal classroom discussions of problems that affect students. The social worker can enable the classroom teacher to develop the necessary skills to use these formats in the classroom by modeling and/or co-leading these groups with the teacher, or consulting regularly in a supportive, educative role.

ASSESSMENT OF THE SCHOOL ENVIRONMENT

The nature of the academic and social needs of a child with disabilities will greatly influence the opportunities for appropriate integration that can be provided. In addition to the physical restructuring of the educational setting to permit the integration of students with disabilities, there also is a need to adapt other elements of the educational environment for the same purpose. This restructuring of the classroom environment starts with an assessment of what staff are currently doing to create a climate for learning and what they can do to provide this for all students. With a better understanding of the strengths and weaknesses of each student, the available resources can be mobilized, including those of family and community, to assist schools in educating pupils in the least restrictive environment.

ROLES OF THE SOCIAL WORKER

The unique skills and abilities of the school social worker are now called upon as never before and he or she must be ready for the challenge. Research suggests that placement of children with disabilities in the regular classroom can be successful if teachers in regular education are able to modify or adapt their instruction to meet a wide range of student needs (Stainback et al., 1986).

School social workers have many skills to employ in assessing the degree to which environmental factors in the classroom and school milieu are effective in meeting the needs of children with disabilities. Social workers can make a careful appraisal of the child's environment, including the various situational and interactional processes in these behavior settings. Social workers need to shift their thinking from one child and one teacher to one child in many different groups and classroom situations, and how the child relates to the different students and teachers as well as how the different students and teachers relate to the child. Social workers need to assess the feelings of students in the regular classroom toward the student with special needs and how these, in turn, affect the child with disabilities, who may have previously experienced many negative feelings from peers and adults. As they assess the total environment of the child with disabilities, they must attempt to understand the dynamics of all groups within which the child is functioning and how they interact to influence the child. These groups can enhance or impede the child's potential for change. The possibility of providing alternative group experiences within the school may also be considered. Social workers can appraise these different situational factors and assist not only the child but also the other students in the involved groups. They must use a variety of skills that involve understanding individual personalities and the effect of the interactional processes upon each person involved.

School social workers can also effectively utilize student groups within the classroom to enhance the teacher's capabilities as a group leader. Groups can be used for many diverse purposes. As problems arise, a social worker can model some of these groups, such as discussion groups, for the teacher. Social workers frequently use the group setting to deal with students' social and emotional needs. In heterogeneous classrooms, where students are at various intellectual and achievement levels, the social worker can organize groups in which a variety of students can learn to share responsibilities and model experiences of helping one another. This can increase friendships and cooperation between the varied students. These groups can also offset stereotyping and stigmatization associated with diverse abilities, disabilities, and achievement levels among students. Students in regular education may need to be taught how to relate to students with special needs. The social worker and the teacher might implement a buddy system by which a classmate who is socially secure would befriend a student with disabilities and assist with various activities. The social worker, of course, may need to help them develop a good working relationship (Stainback, Stainback, and Forest, 1989, p. 134).

CONSULTATION WITH THE TEACHER

Social work consultation with the teacher and other professionals is also a relevant means for adapting the environment to better meet the special needs of children with disabilities. A social worker needs to take time to develop an empathic, supportive, and trusting relationship with the teacher, and to become knowledgeable about the problems between the child with disabilities and the regular education children with which the teacher is dealing. The social worker needs to listen to the teacher's perception of the situation, to be aware of the teacher's strengths, to be sensitive to his or her personality, and to be aware of the total educational milieu within which the teacher is functioning. Social workers must become knowledgeable about the educational process so that their unique skills and understanding of human interaction may be properly applied within the context of the educational situation. As experts in social functioning, social workers will be able to offer the teacher skills and techniques that will assist him/her in classroom management and in dealing with individual behavior, as well as supporting ongoing efforts at modification.

Interprofessional Cooperation

Mainstreaming students with widely diverse needs in a single classroom is a big task. Teachers often cannot deal easily with the wide array of students' needs simultaneously. The social worker and other support personnel may help most by forming teacher assistance teams. This team may provide a variety of individual and group interventions. For example, the social worker and speech therapist may conduct social skills groups. The psychologist, teacher, and social worker may offer role-playing exercises and include students as participants.

Any of these specialists may enhance classroom integration of the disabled student by adapting their interventions to current lessons. The social worker may use playtime as a social group learning experience in the classroom. In these ways the social worker and other specialists can provide students with activities and experiences that they can share or model with peers in the regular classroom through this team model. The support personnel can share their expertise with a wide array of other professionals, who can in turn share what they learn with others (Stainback, Stainback, and Forest, 1989, pp. 134-135; Welsh and Goldberg, 1979, pp. 271-284).

SPECIAL PROGRAMS

As the social worker appraises the child's total milieu, it may become apparent that environmental factors cannot be restructured sufficiently to meet the needs of this child. If the available resources of the regular classroom and teacher cannot be restructured sufficiently to meet the child's needs adequately, then continuing to retain the child in what was the least restrictive environment might adversely affect the student. For example, for the hearing impaired child if the environment is not sufficiently stimulating and there is insufficient social interaction through signing, an appropriate recommendation to consider may be to provide an environment with more hearing impaired children.

When a child requires a more restrictive program, the social worker's task as a member of the team should be to plan for a smooth transition and provide the necessary resources during this process. In planning this transition, it is essential to explore both the child's and his or her family's reactions, concerns, and general feelings about other recommended programs. With this knowledge, the social worker needs to work with the other staff personnel to identify an alternative environment appropriate to the child's adaptive needs to become educated. Next, the social worker's support and understanding can be key factors in helping the child to adjust satisfactorily to moving to another educational setting. If a child needs to spend time in a specialized setting, the social worker may see him or her individually. Also, the social worker may work with new teachers to help them understand how a particular child functions and how to deal with his or her needs. It must be stressed frequently that follow-up services are essential to the child, family, and teacher program, for a successful transition.

WORK WITH THE FAMILY

In addition to evaluating the educational environment of the child with disabilities, the social worker will have primary responsibility for assessing the nature of the child's interactions within the family environment. This involves understanding the family's expectations and their methods of child-rearing and determining whether these are conducive to the child's effective functioning in his or her current school placement. The social worker can be a vital factor in mobilizing the strengths of the family to help the child adjust to his or her disability and adapt to recommended school programs. He or she also is important in assessing the child's relationship structures outside the immediate family context. For example, babysitter, neighborhood, and peer-group relationships may affect the child's adjustment. The social worker needs to understand how the child with disabilities functions in each particular group and to assist him or her in fulfilling these roles. All of these factors will affect the child's adjustments in the classroom and the total educational environment.

WORK WITH THE PUPIL

The child with disabilities may have difficulty in accepting or participating in a plan that introduces new and different situational realities. If this occurs, it may be very helpful for the school social worker to provide a support base for the child to help him or her feel more comfortable in the new situation. In some cases, the social worker may need to work with the child on a regular basis over an extended period of time. Children with behavioral and emotional problems may need extensive counseling, which a school social worker may provide. If, in the social worker's judgment, the child requires an individual treatment relationship, there must be communication to staff regarding the needs of the child, the problems to be addressed, and how activities on the child's behalf can assist other team members.

PREVENTION AND INTERVENTION SYSTEMS

Research, particularly in the area of learning disabilities, suggests that referral for evaluation is often a function of variables other than the student's performance (Christenson, Ysseldyke, and Algozzine, 1982; Ysseldyke et al., 1983). Furthermore, once referred, there is a high probability that the student will be tested (92 percent nationally) and subsequently placed in special education (73 percent nationally) (Algozzine, Christenson, and Ysseldyke, 1982; Graden, Casey, and Christenson, 1985). Thus, a student may be placed in a system that tends to reinforce the initial problem and validate it by unduly labeling the child.

As a consequence of this research and of concurrently burgeoning numbers of mildly disabled students in all categories, numerous school systems throughout the country have developed prevention and intervention systems. These systems may consist of an informal problem-solving team and/or the provision of consultation prior to referral. In either case, when a child who is perceived to have mild difficulties is referred for placement, the goal is to encourage the classroom teacher to try different approaches with the child prior to referral. Serious effort must be made to serve the child in the environment of least restrictiveness, in this case the regular education classroom, prior to considering referral. An assessment of the transactions of the child in the learning environment with his/her peers needs to be made. The teacher remains in charge of the classroom conditions related to the problems of his/her own teaching. The goal of consultation is to assist the teacher in acquiring the knowledge, skill, self-confidence, and objectivity needed to deal with the needs of the pupil, the classroom situation, and the potential modifications. To some extent the conditions in the classroom, the teacher's reaction to the "problem child" (discouragement, anger, inappropriate expectations, etc.), or the teacher's need to acquire skills may be generating the referral; the consultant can provide assistance in the hope of remedying the problem without a more formalized procedure that could result in the identification of need for special education services. The social worker is particularly important here, because problems are often generated by relationship or group dynamic factors in the classroom or by factors in the family or community. The extent to which further help, on a continuum from consultation to work with the family and pupil, can remediate the identified problem is roughly the extent to which more restrictive placement can be avoided.

INCLUSION IN THE REGULAR CLASSROOM

Inclusion in the regular classroom presents unique opportunities for social workers. Some of the inadequacies in education that result in identification of children with problems in learning come from a system of education that sets norms according to grade level. According to Stainback et al. (1986), the assumptions of the grade system are:

1. All students of the same chronological age are ready to be taught the same objectives
2. All students require the same amount of time (i.e., an academic year) to master the predesignated objectives
3. All students can master the predesignated objectives for the grade level across all curricular areas during the same year

Each of these assumptions is directly refuted by experience and research. Learning environments that operate on different assumptions are developed in models, such as Adaptive Learning Environment Model, or ALEM (Wang and Birch, 1984a). In these models:

1. Students with specific and general education needs learn together
2. Programming is individualized for each child
3. "Special" students are delabeled and learning needs are described in instructional rather than categorical terms
4. Individually designated plans are developed to accommodate each student's learning strengths and needs
5. Self-management skills are taught to enable students to take increased responsibility for their learning
6. The classroom environment is organized as a cooperative group with mutual help among students who are strong or weak in different learning areas
7. Parents are involved as partners whenever possible

The results of experiments with this methodology are impressive. The Department of Education, many state education agencies, and many local districts have moved to develop similar programs. Particularly with children having mild disabilities, emotional disturbances or behavior disorders, the social worker can contribute a great deal to this model. However, the model can be accompanied by tension. Teachers often need consultants to learn/develop skills in setting workable educational goals, and students with disabilities often need preparation in moving from smaller to larger classes, often with fewer opportunities for engagement with a teacher, and the likelihood of initially diminished perception of self-worth. Other students in the classroom need preparation and guidance to accept the incoming student appropriately. Social workers may engage directly with a classroom, collaborating with the teacher in a trans-disciplinary model. Additionally, social workers may use group skills to teach students in areas such as acceptance of differences, and other related social skills. In a cooperative learning model, students may learn best from their peers, which may suggest to the social worker some very creative use of classroom group dynamics. Finally, teachers need to develop partnerships with parents. These partnerships can be accompanied by problems when a vulnerable family needs support. All staff need to be aware that for particularly stressed, vulnerable families, the school may even partially substitute for family functions at times.

School social workers have a special opportunity to make the educational process viable and beneficial to children. Let us be aware of the challenge, sharpen our skills, and gather our strengths. There are rights that cannot be denied. The issue for school social workers is not whether the intent of the law, educating each child of school age in the least restrictive environment possible, should be translated into practice, but to what extent the school social worker needs to contribute to this process to best serve the interests of children with disabilities.

REFERENCES

Algozzine, B., Christenson, S., and Ysseldyke, J.E. 1982. Probabilities associated with the referral to placement process. *Teacher Education and Special Education* 5(3): 19–23.

Christenson, S., Ysseldyke, J., and Lagozzine, B. 1982. Institutional constraints and external pressures influencing referral decisions. *Psychology in the Schools* 19: 341–345.

Graden, J.L., Casey, A., and Christenson, S. 1985. Implementing a prereferral intervention system: Part I, the model. *Exceptional Children* 51(5):377–384.

Illinois Office of Education. 1979. Rules and regulations governing special education. Springfield, IL.

Stainback, W., Stainback, S., Courtnage, L., and Jabel, T. 1986. Facilitating mainstreaming by modifying the mainstream. *Exceptional Children* 52(2):144–152.

Stainback, W., Stainback, S., and Forest, M. 1989. Educating all students in the mainstream of regular education. Baltimore: Paul H. Brookes.

Wang, M., and Birch, J. 1984a. Effective special education in regular class. *Exceptional Children* 50:390–399.

Wang, M., and Birch, J. 1984b. Comparison of a full time mainstreaming program and a resource room approach. *Exceptional Children* 51:33–40.

Welsh, B., and Goldberg, G. 1979. Insuring educational success for children-at-risk placed in new learning environments. *School Social Work Quarterly* 1(4):271–284.

Ysseldyke, J.E., Thurlow, M., Graden, J., Wesson, C., Algozzine, B., and Deno, S. 1983. Generalization from five years of research on assessment and decision making: The University of Minnesota Institute. *Exceptional Education Quarterly* 4:75–93.

CHAPTER 20

School-To-Work Transition Programs

Kevin Hollenbeck
Bridget F. Timmeney
W. E. Upjohn Institute for Employment Research

INTRODUCTION

The purposes of this chapter are to examine the school-to-work programs that have come into vogue and, in particular, to assess the adequacy of the support mechanisms that have been established. First described are the various models of programs that have been introduced. Next discussed are the four major issues that have emerged from critical examinations of the program variants. Two of these issues address content or instruction and the other two concern support mechanisms. The remainder of the chapter addresses the latter issues. The third section of the chapter reviews the literature concerning school-to-work programs to present what is known about program support mechanisms. Finally, it concludes with an assessment of the situation—what types of support mechanisms seem to be developing, for whom, and what types are missing and what should be done about them. The role of the school social worker in such program planning and delivery is also explored.

In June 1994, President Clinton signed into law the School-to-Work Opportunities Act. This legislation is intended to further a trend, some might characterize it as a movement, toward the use of work-based learning for young people as they make transitions from formal secondary schooling into careers. While this Act did not initiate the trend toward work-based learning, it did represent a quantum increase in resources and attention so such programs.

The notion of supplementing formal instruction with practical "hands-on" training in the workplace is not a new idea. Prior to the contemporary emphasis on school-to-work programs, the last time that education experienced a similar, broad initiative was the career education movement that received considerable attention in the 1970s before it lost popular support. Indeed, it can be argued that employers and worksite-based opportunities have been a part of public vocational education since its inception with the Smith-Hughes Act in 1917.

Having experienced the ebbs and flows of interest over the course of this century, the question might be asked as to why work-based learning is again attracting attention. We believe that it stems from two sources. First of all, the nation has been grappling with educational reform ever since the report entitled A *Nation at Risk* (National Commission on Excellence in Education, 1983) was released. Concomitantly, cognitive psychologists have made considerable strides in understanding and articulating the importance of students' learning styles in the teaching and learning process. Proponents suggest that appropriately structured work-based programs may facilitate learning, and thus educational outcomes, for students whose learning styles accommodate practical "hands-on" approaches. The second reason for the burgeoning interest in work-based learning is that such programs may ease the school-to-work transition of youth. International competition is more keen than ever, and the business community is concerned about the inefficient usage of productive labor when individuals between the ages of 18–28 have marginal attachments to the labor force, i.e., high rates of turnover and unemployment. Furthermore, the United States is seen as the only developed country without a formal system for assisting in the school-to-work transition. In short, work-based school-to-work transition programs are seen as a piece of the educational reform puzzle and as a way to facilitate the movement of young people into careers.

Implementation of "new" educational approaches, such as school-to-work transition programs, requires attention to both the structure of the programs *and* the support mechanisms needed by students to benefit from the programs. Without adequate and appropriate supports, students will not be able to benefit *fully* from even the best-designed programs. Similarly, if the content and instructional strategies are flawed, students will not benefit *fully* even with excellent support mechanisms. Our contention is that, to date, there has generally been a tradeoff between program structure and support mechanisms in school-to-work initiatives. However, a few exemplary programs have developed solid support mechanisms and it is to these programs that we need to turn for recommendations. School social workers have a natural role in program development, in consultation, and in assessment and service provision in these transition programs.

SCHOOL-TO-WORK TRANSITION PROGRAM MODELS

School-to-work transition programs have been established in many different settings and contexts throughout the country. Essentially, educators and other parties interested in smoothing the transition for youth into careers and jobs have customized programs that best fit their needs and resources. Programs differ in terms of credentials, extent to which post-secondary institutions are involved, extent to which learning takes place at a work site, whether or not work-based learning situations are paid, age of student, target populations, and other characteristics. We suggest that the following four key elements must be present in a program to classify it as a school-to-work transition program. The program:

- Constitutes an *identifiable, formal part* of a secondary and/or post-secondary curriculum with an explicit objective of facilitating the transition from formal schooling to work
- Involves active *participation* of employers
- Involves *actual or simulated* on-the-job *experience*
- Results in *formal or informal* certification of skills

The major types of programs that meet these criteria include *school-to-apprenticeships, youth apprenticeships or pre-apprenticeships, tech prep education, career academies, cooperative education, school-based enterprises, business-education compacts, employer certified programs, work site learning,* and *career exposure* programs.

Apprenticeships have been a significant feature of employment relationships for centuries (dating back, at least, to medieval craft guilds in Europe). Formally, apprenticeships are defined as "training programs operated by employers, employer associations, or jointly by management and labor, designed to provide workers entering the work force with comprehensive training by exposing them to the practical and theoretical aspects of the work required by the occupational area" (Michigan Departments of Labor and Education, 1993). Apprenticeships are usually characterized by requirements for a minimum number of hours of formal classroom instruction and a minimum number of hours on-the-job, by paid employment usually through a predefined wage progression, and by the implicit expectation that the sponsor will employ the apprentice upon successful completion. In the United States, apprenticeships have traditionally been limited to a few occupations, such as skilled construction trades and manufacturing trades, and apprentices have typically been males in their late twenties (Cook and Cairns, 1989).

Schools and agencies have been experimenting with *school-to-apprenticeship* programs that promote earlier entry to apprenticeships. Partial impetus for these programs comes from European training systems, and in particular, the German "dual" apprenticeship system. The Michigan Departments of Labor and Education (1993) formally define these programs as programs where "an employer, employer association, or the employer and the union establish programs that allow high school seniors to participate in registered apprenticeship programs while completing their requirements for graduation. Students would begin at age 16, with wages on a graduated scale, leading to journey status." The National Assessment of Vocational Education (NAVE) estimates that less than 5 percent of schools offer these kinds of programs (NAVE, 1994).

Youth apprenticeships or pre-apprenticeships are programs offered by schools to prepare young people for entry into formal apprenticeship programs. They emphasize developmental mathematics, reading and writing, and technical skills that individuals must show proficiency in to be admitted into an apprenticeship program. Furthermore, these programs introduce students to the apprenticeable occupations and industries.

Parnell (1985) developed the concept of *Tech Prep programs* that offer students a seamless articulation of secondary and postsecondary curricula that lead to an associate's degree in certain technical fields. These programs, also known as two-plus-two programs, formally begin in grade eleven and progress through a two-year postsecondary technical program. The Carl E. Perkins Technical Education Act in 1990 formalized these programs and used federal vocational education resources to support them. There are variations to the basic Parnell design, but most importantly, the Perkins Act requires significant employer involvement, encourages early career exposure, and allows the postsecondary component to be a formal apprenticeship program.

Career academices/magnet schools are defined as situations where "a large employer or a consortium of employers in an industry (or across industries regarding a specific occupation) lead in the design of a school (or school program). Employers look upon the school's program as a key source of potential entry workers and help in a wide variety of ways with equipment, consulting personnel, instructional materials, and part-time or summer employment opportunities" (Michigan Departments of Labor and Education, 1993). Large urban school systems seem to be most prominently involved in the career academy approach. Such schools in Philadelphia, New York City, Oakland, Los Angeles, and Dallas have received attention in the literature.

Cooperative education programs are "school-sponsored plans that help students gain competitive occupational skills at industry standards by linking the school's occupational programs/course of study with carefully supervised on-the-job training and performance" (Michigan Departments of Labor and Education, 1993). These programs occur at both the secondary and postsecondary level. Typically, students receive academic credit in lieu of compensation, although in some cases, they may receive both credit and pay. The employer commitment is just for the training period, although students are often employed after the school program ends.

NAVE (1994) defines *school-based enterprises* to be "school-based activities that produce goods or services for sale or use to people other than the students who produce them. Such enterprises include school restaurants, construction projects, child care centers, auto repair shops, hair salons, and retail stores." The advantage of these simulated work experiences is that they may be undertaken by schools in areas where there are not enough employers or there is insufficient employer interest to provide meaningful work-based opportunities.

Business-education compacts are formal agreements between the business and industry organizations in a locality and the school system(s). The business partners offer paid, part-time employment opportunities and on-the-job training to students, whereas the schools offer high-quality technical training, enhanced academics, and administrative services. Compacts usually involve several occupations and industries.

Closely related to cooperative education programs and to compacts are *employer certified programs*, where "an employer, or employer group, provides structured on-the-job training and paid employment. The training is closely linked to the instruction provided by a school partner" (Michigan Departments of Labor and Education, 1993.) As with cooperative education programs, the employer commitment is only for the duration of the training. However, retention of the students occurs frequently.

Work site learning programs are unpaid programs whose purposes are mainly to extend the learning environment to the work site. In other words, part of the formal curriculum of the school is delivered at a business or industrial site. Such programs vary in length; they can be a full semester in length, two or three weeks, or as short as a half-day. The students learn by observing or limited participation in productive activities.

Finally, *career exposure programs* are defined as "the active involvement of the community, business, industry, and labor to introduce and create awareness of job and career opportunities through career fairs, guest speakers, mentors, sponsorships, and field trips intended to increase all students' (grades K-12) knowledge of careers and the need for career planning" (Michigan Departments of Labor and Education, 1993). Job shadowing is a frequent career exposure activity.

In addition to the four characteristics that we have identified above as the defining elements of school-to-work transition programs—identifiable curriculum or instruction activity, active employer involvement, work experience, and formal or informal certification—the programs that are being offered include other important components. Some programs are targeted to educationally at-risk youths who are in danger of dropping out of school. These programs offer support mechanisms to help students succeed. Some programs integrate academic and vocational education. Some programs promote access for all students, while others set high standards as incentives for students to strive toward. Programs differ in terms of their means of student assessment and in their support of staff development. In short, no standardization of school-to-work programs has occurred and we feel that standardization is unlikely to occur. Schools and employers are customizing programs to fit their needs and to meet their levels of resources. Without systematic oversight, it is not surprising that significant issues are confronting programs and that support mechanisms for students have not been fully developed.

WHAT ARE THE ISSUES?

Our understanding of school-to-work programs suggests that there are four major issues being grappled with by program administrators and educational policymakers. The first two of these issues—integrating school-based and work-based learning meaningfully and providing effective incentives to employers to participate—relate to program content. The other two issues—assuring equal access to all students and providing appropriate ancillary instructional supports—are more concerned with program support mechanisms.

Issue #1: Meaningful Integration of School-based and Work-based Learning

The major strength of school-to-work programs is the involvement of "real-world" work-based learning situations. The advantages of these situations are at least threefold. First of all, students can gain employability skills and knowledge that are not typically emphasized in formal education. These skills include such attributes as punctuality, customer-orientation, quality, working in teams, and attention to detail. Second, workplaces can conceptualize learning. Students can see the applicability of skills such as communication, basic mathematics, reading, metrics, and problem solving. For students with learning styles that are facilitated by applied situations, work-based learning can improve learning and retention. Third, students are introduced to specific occupations and career possibilities; they will benefit from the information they acquire through improved career decision making.

At the same time, the greatest issue that school-to-work programs must address is the involvement of parties who are external to the formal education system. Many of the purported benefits of school-to-work transition activities rely on *integration* of school-based and work-based learning, but, in practice, coordination and joint planning by educators and employers is the exception, not the rule. Corson and Silverberg (1993) point out in their review of U.S. Department of Labor–funded school-to-work demonstration programs that almost no joint planning of educational objectives had occurred. Education took place in schools (often with considerable input from employers concerning content and equipment) and the training and work activities took place at the work site, often quite separate from what was going on in schools.

Meaningful integration of work-based and school-based learning implies that each must supplement or reinforce the other. For example, students may learn about angles in their geometry classes in school, and then apply that knowledge in the workplace by setting up machinery. Students may practice technical writing in school, and then prepare a work order at their work site. Achieving meaningful integration requires considerable coordination and planning between educators and employers. But because employers are outside of the school system and because teachers are not employed at the work site, there are few sanctions or incentives that can be used to promote such coordination.

Issue #2: Facilitating Employer Involvement in School-to-Work Programs

Providing work-based educational opportunities for students, particularly if the time opportunities are to be well-coordinated with school-based learning, requires employer time and resources. The payoffs to employers are tenuous. The primary benefit cited by employers is that school-to-work programs can provide a pipeline of trained, prescreened job applicants. However, this benefit is of little value to employers with low turnover rates, with few openings, or with openings that have skill demands that exceed what secondary or two-year postsecondary institutions can provide.

Bailey (1994) and Osterman (1994) suggest that the most significant barrier to increasing the scale of work-based learning programs will be finding enough employers to participate. The number of programs that have been implemented to date with significant employer participation is quite modest. It seems reasonable to assume that there is a continuum as to the receptivity and interest in supporting these programs among employers. Those with the greatest interest will be among the first to participate. However, if school-to-work programs are to reach a much larger share of schools and students, then they must involve more and more employers who have less and less interest.

The basic problem that must be overcome in attracting employers is that students who receive their work-based learning from one employer may never go to work for that employer and, worse still, may go to work for that employer's competitor. This is a problem that economists refer to as an externality—some or all of the benefits of the interaction between employer and student may accrue to an external, third party, namely the student's future employer. Theoretically, the solution to the externality problem is to have society provide the employer with financial incentives to undertake the training.

Germany, which has a much larger system of apprenticeship, solves the externality problem in two ways. First of all, there is an implicit assumption that the apprentice will be employed by the training firm (and Germany has lower turnover rates, so the implicit assumption is that the employment relationship will be long-term). Second, the apprenticeships are governed by employer associations and unions. Among employers, there is a strong expectation (peer pressure) that each company will participate in the system. Nevertheless, even in Germany, there is concern that there will not be enough "slots" to meet the demand (Osterman, 1994).

Issue #3: Ensuring Access to School-to-Work Programs for All Students

The number of high quality school-to-work programs is modest and the interest among students for such programs likely exceeds the number that can be served. Furthermore, the major benefit of such programs, as articulated by employers, is access to prescreened job applicants. The conditions are perfect for selecting only the most capable students to enter the program (sometimes referred to as "creaming" or "cream skimming"). The likelihood of inequitable participation and services is high. In large metropolitan areas, many suggest that pockets of poverty and the "underclass" result from an absence of jobs and employers, who have relocated to the suburbs or more amenable locations. Similarly, one could expect that effective school-to-work programs will be located where the employers and jobs are, leaving inner city students without such opportunities.

Furthermore the incentives are such that, within a school, only the most capable students will be selected for participation. Employers, seeing students as future employees, will want to work only with the capable students. School staff, attempting to solicit the participation of employers and knowing that businesspersons will be making judgments about the quality of the programs from perception about the quality of the students, will also funnel the most capable students into the program. At-risk populations will likely be left behind.

The Perkins Act (for Tech Prep) and the School-to-Work Opportunities Act (for other work-based programs) recognize this potential problem and attempt to address it. The seven elements that the Perkins Act identifies as essential in a fully implemented Tech Prep program include the following two:

- Equal access for special populations to the full range of Tech Prep programs including the development of services appropriate to the needs of such individuals
- Preparatory services to help all populations to participate in Tech Prep

The School-to-Work Opportunities Act will fund localities to undertake any of a number of activities that include the following (among many others):

- Establishing a graduation assistance program to assist at-risk students, low-achieving students, and students with disabilities in graduating from high school, enrolling in postsecondary education or training, and finding or advancing in jobs
- Integrating school-based and work-based learning into job training programs that are for school dropouts
- Obtaining the assistance of organizations and institutions that have a history of success in working with school dropouts and at-risk and disadvantaged youths in recruiting such school dropouts and youths to participate in the local School-to-Work Opportunities program

Clearly the legislative framework to assist all students through work-based education is in place. However the extent to which localities will emphasize program access as they develop their programs is yet to be determined. The pilot programs and demonstration projects that are in operation to-date seem to have focused on outcomes—and have yet to evolve to a place where they promote access.

Issue #4: Developing Support Mechanisms to Facilitate Success

The reliance on the work site as a learning location implies that students require certain ancillaries to participate and to succeed. For example, transportation between school-based and work-based activities must be secured. If work sites accommodate several students, then mass transportation such as buses or vans may be appropriate. However, securing resources to access and operate these vehicles may be difficult. Students in areas without a public transportation system may be unable to participate simply because of a lack of transportation. If work sites host only a single student or a small number of students, then other means of transportation are appropriate. To date, most programs have placed the onus of transportation to the work site on the student.

Having students engage in learning activities at work sites causes the students to take on the role of worker. An in this role, questions of liability and other worker protection issues arise. For example, are students covered by worker's compensation? But also issues such as safety, discrimination, harassment, training, wages, and fringe-benefit eligibility need to be addressed by the employer, the school system, or the students. It is incumbent upon school administrators to ensure that these issues and their implications are clearly understood by students and employers. Furthermore, legal arrangements and agreements may need to be enforced.

Vocational guidance is another important element of school-to-work programs. Many programs include a career exposure component, in which information about potential careers is conveyed to students prior to their secondary schooling. But in addition to such information, students need to have a credible source of information about the limits and opportunities that are associated with specific school-to-work programs. Students need to have reliable answers to questions such as the following: Does participation lead to postsecondary schooling opportunities? Does it lead to a credential? Of what value is that credential? To whom?

Of particular concern in this chapter are the latter two issues. These address head-on the question of adequate student support mechanisms. In the next section the literature concerning school-to-work programs is reviewed to see to what extent these support issues are being addressed.

HOW EXISTING PROGRAMS PROMOTE ACCESS AND SUPPORT STUDENT PARTICIPATION

Bailey and Merritt (1993) point out that an often overlooked school-to-work program has been around for a number of years and has developed successfully a number of student support mechanisms. Agricultural education, which follows the school-based enterprise concept, can be viewed as a successful program that integrates student supports. Key components of this model are the 4-H and Future Farmers of America (FFA) activities. Students in 4-H or FFA activities undertake twelve month projects to produce goods and services to fulfill applied agricultural requirements. These projects involve group activities and incorporate academic skills learned in school. Bailey and Merritt indicate that these organizations offer a solid, longstanding commitment of community participation. The authors also cite agricultural education as an effective blend of academic training with supervised occupational experiences and extracurricular activities that socialize students to the world of work.

Agricultural education is just one of many occupational areas that have constituted "traditional" vocational education at the secondary level. The literature suggests, however, that students who have pursued the "traditional" vocational education curriculum have been stigmatized and there is concern that this stigma will become associated with school-to-work programs. Educational tradition emphasized a two-tiered approach to career planning and entry. One tier was the college preparatory curriculum with more rigorous academic requirements and the other was a vocational track, which was perceived as less rigorous. Bailey and Merritt (1993) advocate that school-to-work programs should be structured to address the varying intellectual/cognitive styles of students regardless of their post–high school plans. They argue that applied learning strategies such as integrated school- and work-based learning (e.g., youth apprenticeships) offered to the broad range of students can bridge the gap between the two educational paths. They argue further that all students need educational content that addresses broader conceptual, social, and problem-solving skills absent in many educational curricula. They suggest that such a system would alleviate the labeling or categorization of students.

More and Waldman (1994) indicate that the school-to-work models envisioned and implemented as a result of recent legislative initiatives are placing more emphasis on providing for the broad participation of all youth. This includes youth who have traditionally been identified as at-risk. At the same time, the new programs are requiring greater accountability for proficiency in core academic subjects. The latter can only be accomplished through a more demanding curriculum that what had traditionally been offered to vocational education or general curriculum students. The authors suggest that schools will need to become more effective in instructing students from disadvantaged backgrounds in order to accomplish wider access and more rigor. Services suggested as necessary ingredients include child care, transportation, personal counseling, and case management; thus, an increasing role for school social workers is emerging because of such mandates for broad-based inclusion. Instructional supports suggested by these authors include academic tutoring, additional time in the summer or after school to increase proficiency in core courses, and access to courses that incorporate mathematical, scientific, and other higher order skills.

The literature describing provision of traditional support services is sparse. Specialized targeted programs appear to place more emphasis on supportive services. For example, a program for teen parents (Parmerlee-Greiner, 1993) included not only pre- and post-natal health services, child care, transportation, and case management in the program design but also parenting classes, intensive career counseling, and job placement counseling.

An important policy concern in the area of support is enhancing the enrollment rates of students in programs that are nontraditional for their sex. In a working paper released in cooperation with the American Youth Policy Forum, Milgram and Watkins (1993) explore the school-to-work opportunities for young women as part of the Wider Opportunities for Women (WOW) initiative. They examine the U.S. Department of Labor's model school-to-work demonstration sites and indicate that training continued to perpetuate gender bias and stereotyping even in these "state of the art" programs. The authors suggest that such bias results in a disparity in wages. Of the fourteen demonstration sites, six have either no or very few women. Most who are participating (90 percent) are enrolled in training for allied health careers, teaching and education, graphic arts, or office technology. The study supports the principle that broad career education strategies should be integrated into programs as a necessary support mechanism, and that opportunities for women must still be monitored for fairness.

A wide variety of reasons is offered to explain why young women are not participating at high rates in high tech or skilled trades areas. It is not due to lack of interest on the part of young women. Instead the authors attribute low enrollments to limited career counseling for females, an absence of role models in nontraditional fields, and limited recruitment due to bias. The Manufacturing Technology Program operated in Flint, Michigan targets the recruitment of women and includes a number of women in teaching and administrative positions, which the authors suggest results in relatively high participation rates of young women. Milgram and Watkins offer seven key components for success in programs that lead to nontraditional careers. These include:

- *Recruitment strategies* that compare salary ranges and promotion opportunities, that portray women in nontraditional jobs, and that over-enroll females
- *Non-biased assessment and career exploration activities* that focus on transferrable skills and that seek out opportunities to access role models. The authors found a number of assessment tools that evaluate interest and aptitudes based on past experiences, which tend to disadvantage women seeking nontraditional programs
- *Pre-vocational training* that targets specific math skills training, tool identification and use, and early physical conditioning
- *Survival skills training* to prepare for sexual harassment, to know rights on the job, and to learn techniques that prevent and diffuse harassment
- *Training of employers and union personnel in similar survival skills*
- *Training for vocational counselors and instructors*
- *Parent workshops*

A number of studies advocate career education and appropriate career guidance as the primary mode of school-to-work programming. Hamilton and Hamilton (1994) suggest that school-to-work initiatives must prepare students for careers rather than just work. A student's preparation must be for lifelong learning and for both education and employment. The authors argue that career guidance will best prepare students by encouraging them to take challenging courses rather than easy credits; for high risk students, of course, case management activities will be necessary to support this effort of the counselor by all other support services the student is receiving.

In a U.S. General Accounting Office (1993) study of the strategies states are developing to prepare students for jobs, career education is cited as the most common strategy within the four states studied (Florida, Oregon, Tennessee, and Wisconsin). However, the GAO finds that in all states other than Wisconsin, career planning and counseling is a fragmented component of the system. At the time of the study, some local schools had progressive self- and career-awareness programs, but this was not consistent across districts. Furthermore, most programs did not begin until the ninth grade. Uncertain resources were often viewed as the limiting factor for deficient programs and budget cuts were expected to further reduce the time and effort spent on career education.

The GAO report indicates that Wisconsin appeared to have the most comprehensive and uniform program. The school-to-work definition in this state included career education, preparation, and citizenship. A special counseling panel was appointed to propose a statewide system for guidance, counseling, and support systems. At the time of the report, the Wisconsin state legislature was creating a funding mechanism for these support mechanisms. One local site had adopted a particularly interesting model. This high school had contracted with a local social service agency for counseling services related to personal and social problems that created available time for regular in-school guidance counselors to direct their time toward student career guidance.

European models are often cited in the literature as much more integrated, accepted, and absent of stigma. For example, Weisberg and Partee (1994) offer the Swedish school-to-work program as a design that provides continuity in education and that offers appropriate student support. Once students have selected a vocational program, the students follow the same teachers and mentors over multiple years. This structure was cited as a means of establishing continuity in emotional and social supports through trusting and consistent relationships. The authors suggest that stigma is minimized in the Swedish system through credentialing. In addition, students can achieve a program's credentials by following alternative time frames, paths, and supports, which accommodates different interests, learning styles, and special needs.

Bailey and Merritt (1993) caution against relying too heavily on European comparisons. They suggest that differences in economic, cultural, and labor market conditions are considerable and do not allow for valid comparisons. Bailey and Merritt also indicate that although the German system, for example, is well advanced, it shows considerable signs of discrimination by ethnic and gender status. The authors use this as an important reminder that participation in school-to-work initiatives must be broad-based to not to be viewed as dumping grounds and instead as viable options for learning.

CONCLUSIONS

School-to-work programs resemble many other educational initiatives in the sense that they must find a balance between an emphasis on rigor and high quality and an emphasis on broad access (Hansen, 1993). To an extent, the joint involvement of the education community and employers makes it more difficult to achieve that balance. Our educational institutions are responsible for providing an education to all students. A prime motivation for employers, however, is to get access to the best and brightest students. Clearly, for both parties to accomplish their objectives the educational system needs to explore ways to ensure that all students have adequate preparation and supports to succeed in a work-based situation. This implies substantial remediation in basic skills, training in employability skills, survival training for individuals entering nontraditional programs, and aids for students with disabilities and other special populations. Beyond these traditional resources for students, adequate social skills training and other additional social/emotional supports must be available on an "as needed" basis. Herein lies the interface of functioning (identified in Chapter 4 by M. Monkman) which requires the ongoing services of the school social worker. Indeed, the success of the social worker in working with such vulnerable students may go far in ensuing the success or failure of such otherwise well-developed transition programs. However developed, such broad-based programs imply the need for considerable resources, not formerly provided when only the brightest and best were recruited to such programs.

School-to-work programs also face another tradeoff. Compared to schools, work sites are "unsupported." Employers have approached the work-based learning components of school-to-work initiatives much as they do any employment relationship. Students are expected to get to the work site, to provide their own child care (if necessary), and to navigate successfully the workplace environment including relationships with co-workers. As long as students are able to do so, then employers will provide them with skill training, compensation (in most cases), and, potentially, future jobs. If students cannot or do not meet employer expectations, the employers will take action to terminate the relationship as quickly as possible, just as the employer would do with any employee. On the other hand, schools are a much more supportive atmosphere. Education has a long tradition of counseling, tutoring, additional time and assistance from teachers, remediation, and social supports. The tradeoff that programs face is the extent to which support mechanisms should be brought into the workplace, and again the skills brought to such problems at this interface are directly in the province of school social work.

The case against such supports is that the work-based component of a school-to-work program is preparation for a career and employment. Students must get used to the work environment and its requirements for self-reliance. However, considering the work-based component as a learning experience argues for extending a school's support mechanisms into the workplace, and then gradually tapering such support off, as the transition becomes complete. Again, assessment of the student's progress in being able to tolerate such service withdrawal requires skills which school social workers need to provide.

No matter where programs emerge along the high quality versus broad access spectrum and no matter how extensively they support students at the work site, it is the case that programs must face the fact that vocational education and preparation have changed. The new paradigm emphasizes integration of vocational and academic skills and emphasizes considerable employer involvement, up to and including work-based learning. The technological demands of the economy have bypassed the traditional programs. Entry-level workers are expected to be able to work in teams, to solve problems, to communicate effectively, and to be technically literate. To effectively support students in the "new" vocational education will likely require change as well.

The good news is that legislative initiatives and governmental resources recognize the importance of achieving broad access and the need to develop appropriate support mechanisms to achieve such access. The additional good news is that some of the existing programs and demonstrations have achieved these ends. It will, however, take considerable diligence and attention to make sure that appropriate support mechanisms accompany the widespread growth in school-to-work programs in the near future. School social workers need to be involved at every level in such program development and delivery.

REFERENCES

Bailey, T. 1994. Barriers to employer participation in school-to-work transition programs. Prepared for Employer Participation in School-to-Work Transition Programs seminar, Washington, DC: The Brookings Institution. May.

Bailey, T., and Merritt, D. 1993. The school to work transition and youth apprenticeship: Lessons from the U.S. experience. NY: Manpower Demonstration Research Corporation.

Cook F., and Cairns, K. L. 1989. The impact of participation in apprenticeship. In 42nd Annual Proceedings of the Industrial Relations Research Association. Atlanta, GA. December.

Corson, W., and Silverberg, M. 1993. The school-to-work youth apprenticeship demonstration preliminary findings. Princeton, NJ: Mathematica Policy Research, Inc. October.

Hamilton, S.F., and Hamilton, M.A. 1994. Opening career paths for youth: What can be done? Who can do it? NY: Cornell University Youth and Work Program; American Youth Policy Forum and Jobs for the Future.

Hansen, W.L., 1993. The financial squeeze on higher education institutions and students. In E.P. Hoffman (ed.). Essays on the economics of education. Kalamazoo, MI: W.E. Upjohn Institute for Employment Research. pp. 139–62.

Michigan Departments of Labor and Education. 1993. School-to-work transition: Models for Michigan. Youth Apprenticeship Work Group. April.

Milgram, D., and Watkins, K. 1994. Ensuring quality school-to-work opportunities for young women. Working paper released in cooperation with the American Youth Policy Forum. March.

Moore, M.T., and Waldman, Z. 1994. Opportunities or obstacles? A map of federal legislation related to the school-to-work initiative. In *School-to-work: What does research say about it?* Washington, DC: U.S. Department of Education.

National Assessment of Vocational Education. 1994. Interim report to Congress. Washington, DC: U.S. Department of Education. January.

National Commission on Excellence in Education. 1983. A nation at risk. Washington, DC: U.S. Department of Education.

Osterman, P. 1994. Strategies for involving employers in school-to-work programs. Prepared for conference at The Brookings Institution. Washington, DC. May.

Parmerlee-Greiner, G. 1993. Job placement counseling and on-site child care. *Journal for Vocational and Special Needs* 15(2): 26–30.

Parnell, D. 1985. The neglected majority. Washington, DC: The Community College Press.

U.S. General Accounting Office. 1993. Transition from school-to-work: States are developing new strategies to prepare students for jobs. Washington, DC: Government Printing Office.

Weisberg, A., and Partee, G. 1994. Establishing quality designs and options for youth employment preparation. Presentation at the National Leadership Forum on School-to-Work Transition. Washington, DC. August.

CHAPTER 21
Promoting Children's Social Competence in the Schools

Craig Winston LeCroy
Arizona State University, Tucson

Kerry B. Milligan
CODAK-Behavioral Health Services

An increasing emphasis is being placed on a social competence model for understanding, preventing, and remediating the problems experienced by children and adolescents (LeCroy, 1983). This conceptualization asserts that problem behavior in children and adolescents can be understood in terms of youth not having acquired competencies or skills appropriate to specific situational demands. Children and adolescents may fail to develop appropriate social skills for many reasons; however, a deficit in skills can lead to problems in successful adaptation to life tasks.

Teaching children and adolescents social skills is a direct method of influencing how they are likely to interact with others in the future. The overall goal is to teach people the skills needed to sustain social interactions that will lead to positive outcomes. The strategy of social competence promotion is based on social skills training where the goal is to identify the skills needed and then choose a method for teaching the skills. Typically, children are taught skills in groups through the use of role-play practice with feedback from group members and the group leader. However, skills can also be learned by observing models, reviewing videotapes, reading stories that model the skills, playing games that emphasize the skills, and other methods.

SOCIAL SKILLS TRAINING IN THE SCHOOLS

School is the major socializing institution for children; in school children develop social behavior as well as learn academic skills. Although schools focus on children's educational or cognitive skills and capabilities, an important but neglected area of concern is the social skills of children. Unfortunately, to date, with few exceptions educational systems have neglected the development of systematic programs for promoting the social behavior of children.

The socialization of children could be facilitated by offering various social skills programs. Social skills classes could teach prosocial skills that will substitute for aggressive or withdrawn behaviors. Interpersonal skills can be taught to enhance communication with peers, parents, and authority figures. Stress management skills can be taught to help prevent future problems. Numerous opportunities exist for the implementation of various skill-based programs that can help facilitate the successful socialization of children and adolescents in our schools.

THE DEVELOPMENT OF SOCIAL SKILLS PROGRAMS IN THE SCHOOLS

The current proliferation of social skills programs is due to clinical observation and research that have found a relationship between poor peer relationships and later psychological difficulties (Hartup, 1983). Disturbances in peer relationships are one of the best predictors of psychiatric, social, and school problems. Research strongly suggests that social competence is essential for healthy normal development (Hartup, 1983). Child developmentalists stress that it is through a child's interactions with peers that many of life's necessary behaviors are acquired. For example, children learn sexual socialization, control of aggression, expression of emotion, and caring in friendship through their interaction with peers. When children fail to acquire such social skills, they are beset by problems such as inappropriate expression of anger, friendship difficulties, and/or an inability to resist peer pressure. It is this understanding that has led to the present focus on changing children's interpersonal behavior with peers. Since many of a young person's problem behaviors develop in a social context, the teaching of social skills in the classroom or in small group sessions elsewhere is one of the most promising approaches in remediating children's social difficulties.

Social skills can be defined as a complex set of skills that facilitate the successful interactions between peers, parents, teachers, and other adults. The "social" refers to interactions between people; the "skills" refers to making appropriate discriminations, i.e., deciding what would be the most effective response and using the verbal and nonverbal behaviors that facilitate interaction.

The conceptualization of social skills as training suggests that problem behaviors can be viewed as remediable deficits in a child's response repertoire (Asher, 1983; Hops, Finch, and McConnell, 1989). This focuses on building prosocial responses as opposed to an emphasis on the elimination of excessive antisocial responses. Children learn new options to problem situations. Learning how to respond effectively to new situations produces more positive consequences than past behaviors used in similar situations. This model focuses on the teaching of skills and competencies for day-to-day living rather than focusing on the understanding and elimination of defects. It is an optimistic view of children and is implemented in an educative-remedial framework.

A classic social skills training study by Oden and Asher (1977) sought to improve the social skills and peer relationships of third- and fourth-grade children who were identified as not well liked by their peers. The social skills program taught the following four skills: participation, cooperation, communication, and validation/support. The intervention consisted of a five-week program whereby each skill was 1) described verbally, 2) explained with examples, 3) practiced using behavior rehearsal, and 4) refined through feedback, coaching, and review of progress. The results of this study found that the children increased their social skills and that they had improved more significantly than a group of elementary school children who did not participate in the program. Particularly impressive was the finding that the children showed gains in how their classmates rated them on play and peer acceptance at a one year follow up.

THE SOCIAL SKILLS TRAINING METHOD

Social skills training is usually conducted in a group format that provides support and a reinforcing context for learning new responses and appropriate behaviors in a variety of social situations. The group is a natural context for social skills training because of the peer interactions that take place as the group members work together. Additionally, the group allows for extensive use of modeling and feedback that are critical components of successful skills training. Costin (1969) argued more than twenty-five years ago that there should be a broader application of group work method in the school setting. The following provides an overview of the process of developing a social skills training program appropriate to a school setting.

Developing Program Goals and Selecting Skills

The first step in the development of a successful social skills training program is to identify the goals of the program, based on the needs of the target population. For example, a program goal might be for withdrawn children to be able to initiate positive social interactions. Once the goals of the program are clearly defined, the next step is to select the specific skills that are to be taught.

Depending on the type of problem you are addressing, a number of different skills may be appropriate. Typical skills for withdrawn and isolated children include: greeting others, joining in ongoing activities, starting a conversation, and sharing and cooperation both things, e.g., toys, and idea (King and Kirschenbaum, 1992; LaGreca and Santogrossi, 1980; Ladd, 1981; Hops, Walker, and Greenwood, 1979). As a specific example, Gilchrist and Schinke (1983) have discovered the skills needed for preventing teen pregnancy: (1) discussing birth control, (2) asking for information, (3) refusing unacceptable demands, and (4) problem solving. Research has been helpful in identifying skills by studying behaviors that contribute to healthy social functioning in children and adolescents.

The process of social skills training requires continual attention to refining each skill that is to be taught. After identifying the broad social skills, it is important to divide each broad skill into its component parts so that they can be more easily learned. For example, LeCroy (1992, p. 136) breaks down the skill "beginning a conversation" into six component parts:

1. Look the person in the eye and demonstrate appropriate body language
2. Greet the person, saying one's own name
3. Ask an open-ended question about the person. Listen attentively for the response
4. Make a statement to follow up on the person's response
5. Ask another open-ended question about the person. Listen attentively to the response
6. Make another statement about the conversation

It is important to construct realistic social situations that demand the use of social skills you are teaching. It is preferable that the social situations and skills be determined empirically. For example, Freedman et al. (1978) constructed problematic situations that delinquents were likely to encounter, elicited responses to these situations, and then had the responses rated for effectiveness. This allows for a clear indication of what types of situations are problematic for delinquents and what constitutes an appropriate response to those situations. However, most practitioners must develop their own problematic situations or elicit them from the group during social skills training. For example, a problem situation for a substance abuse prevention program could be:

> You ride to a party with someone you've been dating for about six months. The party is at someone's house; their parents are gone for the weekend. There is a lot of beer and dope, and your date has had too much to drink. Your date says, "Hey, where's my keys—let's get going."

This situation ends with a stimulus for applying the skills of resisting peer pressure. An effective response to this situation would include the steps involved in resisting peer pressure: name the trouble, say no quickly, suggest alternatives, and leave the situation.

For additional information on assessment and selection of skills, see Cartledge and Milburn (1980), Goldstein et al. (1983), Rose and Edelson, (1987).

Any attempt to develop a social skills program will depend on its actual usefulness. School social workers need to assess carefully the programs they implement. For example, if one were to plan a series of social skills groups, one consideration would be the child's ability for language acquisition, which would have an impact on the program. Although provided in a group setting, social skills training should be sensitive to both individual and familial needs. Effective programs require good communication with students, teachers, and parents and make modifications based on their feedback.

Social skills programs also must be sensitive to racial and ethnic considerations. A standardized social skills program may not work for a Native American child living on a reservation or a Mexican-American child who speaks Spanish. The selection of social skills must address what constitutes an effective social interaction in a variety of cultures. If we remain sensitive to these issues then social skills training can help promote successful interactions in a variety of circumstances.

Guidelines for Practitioners

After program goals are defined and skills are selected, there is a sequential process for teaching social skills. The following seven basic steps delineate the process that leaders can follow (based on LeCroy, 1992). These guidelines were developed for social skills groups with middle school and high school students. Social skills groups with younger children would have to be modified; see King and Kirschenbaum (1992) for guidelines with younger children. Table 1 presents these steps and outlines the process for teaching social skills. In each step there is a request for group member involvement. This is because it is critical that group leaders involve the participants actively in the skill training. Also, this keeps the group interesting and fun for the group members.

Present the social skill being taught. The first step for the group leader is to present the skill. The leader solicits an explanation of the skill, for example, "Can anyone tell me what it means to resist peer pressure?" After group members have answered this question, the leader emphasizes the rationale for using the skill. For example, "You would use this skill when you're in a situation where you don't want to do something that your friends want you to do and you should be able to say 'no' in a way that helps your friends to be able to accept your refusal." The leader then requests additional reasons for learning the skill.

TABLE 1 A Summary of the Steps in Teaching Social Skills Training

1. Present the social skills being taught
   A. Solicit an explanation of the skill
   B. Get group members to provide rationales for the skill
2. Discuss the social skill
   A. List the skill steps
   B. Get group members to give examples of using the skill
3. Present a problem situation and model the skill
   A. Evaluate the performance
   B. Get group members to discuss the model
4. Set the stage for role playing the skill
   A. Select the group members for role playing
   B. Get group members to observe the role play
5. Group members rehearse the skill
   A. Provide coaching if necessary
   B. Get group members to provide feedback on verbal and nonverbal elements
6. Practice using complex skill situations
   A. Teach accessory skills, e.g., problem solving
   B. Get group members to discuss situations and provide feedback
7. Train for generalization and maintenance
   A. Encourage practice of skills outside the group
   B. Get group members to bring in their problem situations

Discuss the social skills. The leader presents the specific skill steps that constitute the social skill. For example, the skill steps for resisting peer pressure are: good nonverbal communication (includes eye contact, posture, voice volume), saying "no" early in the interaction, suggesting an alternative activity, and leaving the situation if there is continued pressure. Leaders then ask group members to share examples of when they used the skill or examples of when they could have used the skill but did not.

Present a problem situation and model the skill. The leader presents a problem situation. For example, the following is a problem situation for resisting peer pressure:

> After seeing a movie your friends suggest that you go with them to the mall. It's 10:45 and you are supposed to be home by 11:00. It's important that you get home by 11:00 or you won't be able to go out next weekend.

The group leader chooses members to role play this situation and then models the skills. Group members evaluate the model's performance. Did the model follow all the skill steps? Was his or her performance successful?

The group leader may choose another group member to model if the leader believes they already have the requisite skills. Another alternative is to present to the group videotaped models. This has the advantage of following the recommendation by researchers that the models be similar to the trainee in age, sex, and social characteristics.

Set the stage for role playing of the skill. For this step the group leader needs to construct the social circumstances for the role play. Leaders select group members for the role play and give them their parts to play. The leader reviews with the role players how to act out their role. Group members not in the role play observe the process. It is sometimes helpful if they are given specific instructions for their observations. For example, one member may observe the use of nonverbal skills, another member may be instructed to observe when "no" is said in the interaction.

Group members rehearse the skill. Rehearsal or guided practice of the skill is an important part of effective social skills training. Group leaders and group members provide instructions or coaching before and during the role play and provide praise and feedback for improvement. Following a role play rehearsal the leader will usually give instructions for improvement, model the suggested improvements, or coach the person to incorporate the feedback in the subsequent role play. Often the group member doing the role play will practice the skills in the situation several times to refine their skills and incorporate feedback offered by the group. The role plays continue until the trainee's behavior becomes more and more similar to that of the model. It is important that "overlearning" takes place, so the group leader should encourage many examples of effective skill demonstration followed by praise. Group members should be taught how to give effective feedback before the rehearsals. Throughout the teaching process the group leader can model desired responses. For example, after a role play the leader can respond first and model feedback that starts with a positive statement.

Practice using complex skill situations. The last phase deals with more difficult and complex skill situations. Complex situations can be developed by extending the interactions and roles in the problem situations. Most social skills groups also incorporate the teaching of problem-solving abilities. Problem solving is a general approach to helping young people to gather information about a problematic situation, generate a large number of potential solutions, evaluate the consequences of various solutions, and outline plans for the implementation of a particular solution. Group leaders can identify appropriate problem situations and lead members through the above steps. The problem-solving training is important because it prepares young people to make adjustments as needed in a given situation. It is a general skill with large scale application. For a more complete discussion on the use of problem-solving approaches, see Rose and Edelson (1987).

Train for generalization and maintenance. The success of the social skills program depends on the extent to which the skills young people learn transfer to their day-to-day lives. Practitioners must always be planning for ways to maximize the generalization of skills learned and promote their continued use after training. There are several principles that help facilitate the generalization and maintenance of skills. The first is the use of overlearning. The more overlearning that takes place the greater likelihood of later transfer of skills. Therefore, it is important that group leaders insist on mastery of the skills. Another important principle of generalization is to vary the stimuli as skills are learned. To accomplish this, practitioners can use a variety of models, problem situations, role play actors, and trainers. The different styles and behaviors of the people used produces a broader context in which to apply the skills learned. Perhaps most important is to require that young people use the skills in their real-life settings. Group leaders should assign and monitor homework to encourage transfer of learning. This may include the use of written contracts to do certain tasks outside the group. Group members should be asked to bring to the group examples of problem situations where the social skills can be applied. Lastly, practitioners should attempt to develop external support for the skills learned. One approach to this is to set up a buddy system where group members work together to perform the skills learned outside the group (for examples see Rose and Edelson, 1987).

SOCIAL SKILLS TRAINING EXAMPLES

Social skills training is being applied to several different children and adolescent populations including delinquents, behaviorally disordered children, and developmentally delayed children. Social skills training is also used extensively in prevention programs. As such, skills are reinforced for children in the general school population. In order to get a better understanding of the applicability of social skills training, some specific examples are described.

Aggressive Behavior

Verbal and aggressive behavior is frequently the genesis of a referral to the school social worker. Group social skills training increasingly is being used in response to such problems. From a social competence perspective, an aggressive child lacks the social skills needed to be competent in interpersonal relationships with peers. Social skills practitioners select several skill deficits to work on, such as recognizing interactions likely to lead to problems, interrupting others, bossing others, responses to negative communications (for example, teasing, criticism), and then making positive requests for behavior change.

Elder, Edelstein, and Narick (1979) developed a well-researched social skills program for aggressive behaviors. During each session, children role played various scenes designed to occasion interruptions, responses to negative communication, and requests for behavior change. The role play scenes were constructed from situations that the children identified as characteristic of daily troublesome encounters. An example of a scene designed to elicit a request for behavior change is, "You are reading a book and a fellow student turns his radio up very loud, which ruins your concentration. You...." Treatment consisted of providing instructions, modeling, and feedback for each role play scene. Results of the evaluation of this program and other similar programs indicate that the treatment was successful in teaching the children alternatives to aggressive behavior (Elder, et al., 1979; LeCroy, 1988). Feindler and Guttman (1994) describe a treatment manual they have developed for anger control that includes social skills training and cognitive therapy approaches.

Isolated and Withdrawn Behavior

Social skills training is frequently used for remediating the social skills deficits of isolated and withdrawn children. Children who are withdrawn are unpopular with their peers, and being unpopular is frequently linked to later problems in adaptive functioning (Hartup, 1983). However, teachers are not as likely to refer such children to social services as other more actively disruptive children (Hops, 1982). Since these children display behavior that is not intrusive—rarely initiating interactions, playing alone, and so forth, they rarely become a concern to teachers. Therefore, identifying these children for treatment is a critical task in developing an appropriate social skills training program.

Studies (Gottman, 1983; Greenwood, Todd, Hops, and Walker, 1982) have examined how withdrawn children differ in comparison to their peers and have identified the following characteristics: they make fewer social initiations, receive fewer initiations from peers, are less likely to respond to peer initiations when there is opportunity, talk less, spend less time in proximity to their peers, and spend more free time alone. This type of research helps identify more clearly what skills withdrawn children need to learn.

A well-known program in this area is the PEERS program that combines behavioral and social skills training interventions (Hops, Walker, and Greenwood, 1979). This program is designed to remediate the withdrawn behavior of young children by providing them with skills to enter the peer group mainstream. The program has several components: social skills tutoring where children learn skills such as initiating with others; recess intervention where during recess time children earn points for playing and talking with others; joint tasks where a peer works on a specific task with the child; and verbal correspondence where before recess the teacher asks the child who he or she plans to pay with and after recess has the child report back to the teacher on his or her progress. Research has supported the efficacy of this approach for treating social withdrawal (Paine, et al., 1982).

Substance Abuse Prevention

Many schools are concerned about the problems associated with substance abuse and are developing prevention programs to address this issue. In fact, the risk-taking behavior of young people is a serious national problem. Successfully confronting the pressures to become involved with sex, alcohol, and drugs is seen as a normal part of the process of growing up. Jackson and Hornbeck (1989, p. 833) state emphatically, "In our society, peer pressure to engage in early sexual activity and the availability of alcohol, drugs, and cigarettes virtually guarantee that every young American adolescent will be confronted with decisions about whether to engage in behaviors that could have life-long, if not lethal, consequences."

Many schools are developing substance abuse prevention programs based on social skills training. Young people often lack the skills needed to resist peer pressure to use alcohol and drugs. This focus on skill deficits has led to the development of many standardized skills-based programs that can be implemented in classroom settings. For example, Pentz (1985) developed STAR, Student Taught Awareness and Resistance. This program is based on the assumption that young adolescents get involved with drugs due to peer and parent social influences and poor social assertiveness skills needed to resist peer pressure to use drugs. This ten-session program uses a trained teacher paired with a program assistant and facilitated by peer leaders, who are identified by classmates. Specific social skills are taught using several social situations through modeling, rehearsal, and feedback. Program evaluation showed that children in this program increased their social competence and grades, and decreased drug use (Pentz, 1985). Research also indicates that the intervention is most effective when provided prior to major transitional times, such as the beginning of junior high school or the beginning of high school.

Hohman and Buchik (1994) describe a social skills program for adolescent relapse prevention. This program focuses on such skills as making friends who remain sober, coping with relapse, coping with internal urges, dealing with parents, and general problem solving and stress reduction.

A large part of the program is learning about "high risk" situations and developing coping skills for dealing with those situations.

Preventing Unwanted Adolescent Pregnancy

Research has shown that women who have unwanted pregnancies can be differentiated from never-pregnant women by lower measures on sensitivity, directness, control, empathy, and self-disclosure. Based on this and other research, Schinke, Blythe, and Gilchrist (1981) see unwanted pregnancy resulting from a deficit both in communication and in the interpersonal skills needed to regulate intimacy. They describe a school-based program designed to help adolescents learn new interpersonal responses, such as discussing birth control, asking for information, refusing unreasonable demands, and problem solving. As in other social skills programs, adolescents learn to respond to challenging social situations using the methods of social skills training.

Like many other skill-based prevention programs, this program recognizes that information and education programs can only go so far in addressing such problems. Simply being aware of the potential risks of involvement with sex and drugs is not enough. The strength of many skill-based programs is that young people learn the specific day-to-day skills needed to address many difficult social situations that may encourage them to be involved in high-risk behaviors.

Multiproblem Social Skills Training

While the previous examples have all examined a particular aspect of social skills, many practitioners use multiproblem social skills training in groups with children experiencing a variety of problems. For example, groups could include children with problems such as acting-out behavior, withdrawn behavior, fear, and so forth. Groups also can be designed for prevention purposes where the goal is to promote positive prosocial alternative behaviors (LeCroy and Rose, 1986). While social skills training will likely be the major component of the treatment, other treatment procedures also can be used. Treatment is conceptualized in several stages. The initial phase includes increasing group attractiveness, shaping problem solving and discussion skills, and learning how to complete assignments. The middle phase would introduce specific treatment procedures designed to help each child with his or her specific problem. The focus would be on developing role plays to address each child's individual problem, learning problem-solving skills, completing assignments to enhance learning and to further individualize the treatment, and modifying group patterns. The final phase focuses on termination and procedures to facilitate generalization of the learned behaviors.

SUMMARY

As school social workers work toward the goal of enhancing the socialization process of children, methods for promoting social competence, such as social skills training, have much to offer. Social workers can make an important contribution to children, families, and schools through preventive and remedial approaches like those described in this chapter. As we have seen, children's social behavior is a critical aspect of successful adaptation in society. The school represents an ideal place for children to learn and practice social behavior. It provides the needed multi-peer context and offers multiple opportunities for newly learned behaviors to be generalized to other situations and circumstances.

Social skills training provides a clear methodology for providing remedial and preventive services to children. This direct approach to working with children has been applied in numerous problem areas and with many child behavior problems. It is straightforward in application and has been adapted so that social workers, teachers, and peer helpers have successfully applied the methodology. Although we have emphasized the group application, social skills training also can be applied in individual or classroom settings. In general, research has supported the efficacy of social skills training; it is perhaps the most promising new treatment model developed for working with children and adolescents.

REFERENCES

Asher, S.R. 1983. Social competence and peer status: Recent advances and future directions. *Child Development* 54:1427–1434.

Cartledge, G., and Milburn, J.F. 1980. *Teaching social skills to children.* NY: Pergamon Press.

Costin, L.B. 1969. An analysis of the tasks of school social work. *Social Service Review* 43: 247–285.

Elder, J.P., Edelstein, B.A., and Narick, M.M. 1979. Modifying aggressive behavior with social skill training. *Behavior Modification* 3: 161–178.

Feindler, E.L., and Guttman, J. 1994. Cognitive-behavioral anger control training. In C. LeCroy (ed.). *Handbook of child and adolescent treatment manuals.* NY: Lexington Books.

Freedman, B.J., Rosenthan, C., Donahoe, C.P., Schlundt, D.G., and McFall, R.M. 1978. A social-behavioral analysis of skill deficits in delinquent and nondelinquent adolescent boys. *Journal of Consulting and Clinical Psychology* 48: 1448–1462.

Gilchrist, L.D., and Schinke, S.P. 1983. Coping with contraception: Cognitive and behavioral methods with adolescents. *Cognitive Therapy and Research* 7: 379–388.

Goldstein, A.P., Sprafkin, R.P., Gershaw, N.J., and Klein, P. 1983. *Skill-streaming the adolescent.* Champaign, IL: Research Press.

Gottman, J.M. 1983. How children become friends. *Monographs of the society for research in child development* 48: 410–423.

Greenwood, C.R., Todd, N.M., Hops, H., and Walker, H.M. 1979. Behavior change targets in the assessment and behavior modification of socially withdrawn preschool children. *Behavioral Assessment.* 4: 273–297.

Hartup, W.W. 1983. The peer system. In E.M. Hetherington (ed.). *Handbook of child psychology: Vol. 4. Socialization, personality, and social development.* NY: John Wiley and Sons.

Hohman, M., and Buchik, G. 1994. Adolescent relapse prevention. In C. LeCroy (ed.). *Handbook of child and adolescent treatment manuals.* NY:Lexington Books.

Hops, H. 1982. Children's social competence and skill: Current research practices and future directions. *Behavior Therapy* 14: 3–18.

Hops, H., Finch, M., and McConnell, S. 1989. Social skills deficits. In P.H. Bornstein and A.E. Kazdin (eds.). *Handbook of child behavior therapy.* Homewood, IL: Dorsey Press.

Hops, H., Walker, H.M., and Greenwood, C.R. 1979. PEERS: A program for remediating social withdrawal in school. In L.A. Hamerlynch (ed.). *Behavior systems for the developmentally disabled: I. School and family environments.* NY: Brunner/Mazel.

Jackson, A.W., and Hornbeck, D.W. 1989. Educating young adolescents: Why we must structure middle grade schools. *American Psychologist* 44: 837–840.

King, C.A., and Kirschenbaum, D.S. 1992. *Helping young children develop social skills.* Pacific Grove, CA: Brooks/Cole.

Ladd, G. 1981. Social skills and peer acceptance: Effects of a social learning method for training social skills. *Child Development* 53: 171–178.

LaGreca, A., and Santogrossi, D. 1980. Social skills training with elementary school students: A behavioral group approach. *Journal of Consulting and Clinical Psychology* 48: 220–228.

LeCroy, C.W. 1983. Social skills training with adolescents: A review. In C. LeCroy (ed.). *Social skills training for children and youth.* NY: Haworth Press, pp. 91–116.

LeCroy, C.W. 1988. Anger control or anger expression: Which is more effective? *Residential Care of Children.*

LeCroy, C.W. 1992. Promoting social competence in youth. *Structuring change.* Chicago, IL: Lyceum Press, pp. 167–180.

LeCroy, C.W. 1994. Social skills training. In C. LeCroy (ed.). *Handbook of child and adolescent treatment manuals.* NY: Lexington Books.

LeCroy, C.W., and Rose, S.D. 1986. Evaluation of preventive interventions for promoting social competence in adolescents. *Social Work Research and Abstracts* 22: 8–17.

Oden, S.L., and Asher, S.R. 1977. Coaching low accepted children in social skills: A follow-up sociometric assessment. *Child Development* 48: 496–506.

Paine, S.C., Hops, H., Walker, H.M., Greenwood, C.R., Fleischman, D.H., and Guild, J.J. 1982. Repeated treatment effects: A study of maintaining behavior change in socially withdrawn children. *Behavior Modification* 6: 171–199.

Pentz, M.A. 1985. Social competence skills and self-efficacy as determinants of substance use in adolescence. In S. Shiffman and T.A. Wills (eds.). *Coping and substance use*. NY: Academic Press.

Rose, S.D., and Edelson, J.L. 1987. *Working with children and adolescents in groups*. San Francisco, CA: Jossey Bass.

Schinke, S.P., Blythe, B.J., and Gilchrist, L.D. 1981. Cognitive-behavioral prevention of adolescent pregnancy. *Journal of Counseling Psychology* 28: 451–454.

CHAPTER 22

Developing School Social Work Consultation Programs in the Context of Special Needs Children

Christine Anlauf Sabatino
Assistant Dean, Assistant Professor,
National Catholic School of Social Service,
The Catholic University of America

Over the past seventy years, references to school social work practice have usually included consultation services as part of the practice repertoire. Over the past twenty years, statistical analyses of school social work tasks consistently identify that consultation continues to be an important school social work service (Oppenheimer, 1925; Allen-Meares, 1993; Carr, 1976; Costin, 1969; Kadushin, 1977; Lambert and Mullaly, 1982; Meares, 1977; Meares, 1982; Timberlake, Sabatino and Hooper, 1982). Consultation models have been applied to regular education teachers, special education teachers, and working groups of teachers (Sabatino, 1986; Drisko, 1993; Early, 1992).

For the 1990s and beyond, consultation theory, practice, and research have become even more critical components of the school social worker's knowledge base and practice skills. The necessity for building consultation programs has become increasingly apparent for several reasons.

Local and national efforts to balance the budget, reduce the deficit, control spending, and cut taxes have placed enormous burdens on governments at all levels to be fiscally responsible. Consultation programs are good policy and good practice because they are cost-effective while simultaneously providing primary prevention services. From just one consultation program an entire class, program, or school receives professional services that focus on its particular needs.

Beyond the budget problems, fundamental changes are occurring in public education philosophy and public education law in the United States. Special education policy and procedure have been built using both self-contained classrooms and pull-out programs. Basic changes have been proposed that could replace categorical services with either "total integration" of all special education students into regular classrooms or "partial integration" of the more mildly disabled. This educational philosophy is known as "inclusion" for special education students, and the proposed changes have been labeled the Regular Education Initiative. In response, several consultation models have been proposed, including the pre-referral model "whereby a teacher assistance team (TAT) is established, made up of regular education teachers, special education teachers, support services staff (for example, social workers and psychologists) and school administrators" (Blair, 1993, p. 235) to assess and design a plan for maintaining the special education child in the regular classroom.

Likewise, P.L. 99-457 represents the federal government's commitment to early identification and early intervention services for developmentally delayed infants, toddlers, preschoolers, and their families. Part B of the law extends all rights and privileges of the Education for All Handicapped Children Act of 1975 (P.L. 94-142) to children with disabilities between the ages of three and five. Part H "creates a discretionary program to help states plan, develop, and implement a statewide comprehensive, coordinated, multidisciplinary, interagency system of early intervention services for all eligible infants and toddlers from birth to three years who are disabled and their families" (Bishop, Rounds, and Weil, 1993, p. 36). In some states, public school preschool home resource teachers have been designated as the professionals who consult with private preschool directors and staffs regarding questions of developmental delay and referral for eligibility.

In view of these changes and their increasing importance, this chapter will review the theory and practice of consultation, and present a specific model of consultation applicable to the Regular Education Initiative. In addition, a paradigm of various consultation models will be presented as P.L. 99-457 moves them out of the schools into the community in an effort to identify developmentally delayed infants, toddlers, and preschoolers.

DEFINITION OF CONSULTATION

In this chapter, the term "consultation" is used in a specific way to mean a method of intervention that has the following characteristics: (1) it is a problem-solving process; (2) it takes place between a professional consultant and a consultee who have responsibility for the direct service to another person; (3) it is a voluntary relationship; (4) the objective is to solve a job-related problem of the consultee; (5) the consultant and the consultee share in solving the problem; and (6) the consultation helps the consultee to become better prepared to deal with similar problems in the future (Caplan and Caplan, 1993; Meyers, Parson and Martin, 1979; Zischka and Fox, 1985).

How is consultation distinguished from supervision? In a supervisory relationship, the supervisor holds an administrative position of authority in the agency hierarchy, which requires an ongoing evaluative relationship. Consultation services by definition exclude administrative authority and evaluation. Rather, the consultant collaborates with the consultee and both contribute to decisions and actions.

What is the nature of the consultative relationship? There is disagreement among authors whether or not the relationship between the consultant and consultee is the same or different from therapy (see Caplan, 1970; Bergen, 1977; Curtis and Zins, 1981). This is an important issue because it has a direct impact on the consultant's role performance. In a school setting the consultation relationship is defined as a coordinate professional relationship, not a therapy relationship. During consultation, material is discussed that is confidential in nature, personal to the teacher, and difficult to share. In other to meet the universally agreed-upon goal of solving job-related problems, it is not necessary for the consultant to stress examination of unconscious material or to foster the development of a transference relationship. In fact, these traditional elements of psychodynamic therapy may distract the teacher from focusing upon the identified educational problem and from preparing the teacher to act upon the problem.

STAGES IN THE CONSULTATION PROCESS

Many professionals assume that practice experience in a particular profession is adequate preparation to be a consultant. Helping others with their work problem is a more complex process than working directly with one's own cases. Specialized preparation is needed so that one understands the consultation process, the consultation phases, the different models of consultation, and the unique functions of the consultant's role.

Gallessich (1982) identifies the following phases of the consultation process. Awareness of these phases helps keep the consultant and the consultee focused and productive. There is fluidity among these phases and a phase may have several subphases. Each of the phases is presented with a series of questions that Gallessich might pose to help the consultant with his or her thinking while developing a consultation program.

1. Preliminary exploration
   What are the agency's needs?
   What are the consultant's qualifications regarding these needs?
   Is there a satisfactory "fit"?
   Are there any value conflicts among the parties?
2. Negotiation of a contract
   What are the terms for working together?
   Is this a formal/legal contract?
   Is this a informal/oral contract?

Does the contract include consultation goals, length of contract, consultant responsibilities, agency responsibilities, consultant's role and evaluation/termination procedures?

3. Entry

    Where will consultation take place?
    What physical barriers to entry are encountered?
    What social-psychological barriers to entry are encountered?
    What agency dynamics might be a barrier to being trusted and accepted in this social system?
    What tensions arise in the course of building a relationship with the consultee?

4. Diagnosis of problems or needs

    Do consultant and consultee collaborate in data collection?
    Is diagnosis seen as an ongoing activity?
    Has the entire context been scanned or is the assessment narrowly focused on the presenting problem?
    Have "hard" data and "soft" data been used?
    Has more than one theoretical perspective been used to sort and analyze the problem?
    Is further data gathering required?

5. Goal setting

    Who has proposed the goal(s)?
    Have the merits of a number of goals been weighed?
    Are there realistic solutions to the problem?
    If not, is the consultant prepared to terminate the consultation?
    Can the goals be reached by the staff without consultation?
    How urgent is it to achieve a goal?
    How successful might this goal be?
    How feasible is a goal?
    What is the cost of this goal in time and money?

6. Exploration of intervention alternatives and selection of one or more intervention strategies

    What is the best method for reaching the goal(s)?
    Have alternatives been generated and examined?
    Is there a clear definition of the objective?
    Is there a clear plan of action to reach the objective?
    What problems are anticipated?
    Which people are responsible for which actions?
    Have the consultant's role, function, and responsibility been delineated from those of the consultee's?

7. Implementation of intervention

    Does implementation involve the consultant?

(See the following section for discussion of implementing different models of consultation.)

8. Evaluation of outcome
   To what degree have the goal(s) been achieved?
   Is evaluation one of the consultant's functions?
   What factors contributed to positive and negative outcomes?
   Is the evaluation informal and anecdotal?
   Is the evaluation formal and quantifiable?
   Has the consultant's performance been evaluated?

9. Institutionalizing of change
   Have new procedures or behaviors been incorporated and routinized in the agency?
   Does this change require additional training and monitoring, or that incentives be institutionalized?

10. Termination of consultation
    What are the criteria for termination?
    What are the emotional reactions surrounding the termination?
    Will termination occur through a series of steps?
    Are there follow-up plans to termination?

The interpersonal relationships established during these phases will be crucial to the success of the consultation program. In the school setting it is important for the teacher to feel comfortable, accepted, and respected. The consultant may help to establish this atmosphere by being trustworthy, accepting, respectful, nonjudgmental, and collegial.

Throughout these phases, it is important to remember that it takes time for a teacher to build a relationship, to understand what consultation is, and to learn how to use it. For example, teachers need to learn how to present relevant information, what kind of help to expect from the consultant, and what the consultant has to offer.

Sometimes there is a hidden agenda in consultation. The consultant is invited into a conflict as an "expert" to support one person's viewpoint. Or the consultant is expected to share the emotional burden of making a difficult decision to enable someone to abdicate responsibility in a difficult case. Sometimes there is the wish to substitute consultation for administrative supervision.

In any case, there need to be several preliminary meetings to examine and understand the processes and phases, and to use them effectively. It is important that the teacher understand what consultation is and how it is to be used.

As Caplan and Caplan (1993) note, "resistance" may only be a lack of preparation for consultation. Or it may signal the belief that asking for consultation is an admission of professional incompetence. To overcome these barriers the teachers may be reminded that students' problems are often complicated and confusing and that the request for consultation services is a sign of professional competency. Most difficult, though, is to help teachers understand that no significant problems can be managed in a hurried manner.

ALTERNATIVE MODELS OF CONSULTATION PRACTICE

Reid (1979) defines a practice model as "rules for practitioners to follow in defining and assessing target problems and may delineate sequences of interventions to be used in attempts to alleviate problems . . ." (p. 216). A model organizes discrete principles, methods, and procedures into coherent strategies. Models are a bridge between theory and practice, the translation of theory into how-to-do-it descriptions of activities.

Mannino (1981) states "there is a broad array of theoretically and technically diverse approaches under the consultation label. It is, therefore, essential that the type of consultation studied be clearly described and defined" (p. 149). Meyers, Friedman, and Gaughan (1981) state that although there have been some attempts to describe consultation, "there have not been enough clear descriptions of procedures that could be replicated readily by researchers or practitioners in the schools" (p. 115).

There is a wealth of consultation literature (see Alpert and Silverstein, 1985; Brown, Pryzwansky, and Schultz, 1991; Herr and Fabian, 1993; Kurpius and Fuqua, 1993). Much of it is applied to the school setting (see Alpert, 1982; Conoley and Conoley, 1982, 1988; Gutkin and Curtis, 1990; West and Idol, 1987; and Zins and Ponti, 1990). Many, if not most professionals, however, are unaware there are a variety of specific consultation models. Gallessich identifies six:

- Educational Training Consultation
- Clinical Consultation
- Mental Health Consultation
- Behavioral Consultation
- Organizational Consultation
- Program Consultation

Gallessich provides a framework for analyzing these different consultation models using several different dimensions. The consultant is helped to see that data applied to one dimension naturally fits with data applied to other dimensions in a specific model of consultation. In other words, there is an internal consistency so that information on a number of dimensions leads the practitioner toward or away from choosing a specific model of consultation for implementation. The dimensions are as follows:

- Conceptualization or formulation of the problem
- Overall or broad goal of consultation
- Major methods used by the consultant
- Consultant's assumption about change
- Consultant's role or source of power
- Underlying value of the model

The six different models of consultation are compared and contrasted with these six different dimensions in the following section of this chapter. The purpose is to assist educational and pupil personnel to choose the most appropriate consultation model to consult with school-based and community-based programs and families as a result of P.L. 99-457, Part B.

Education and Training Consultation

In this model the assessed problem is the consultee's lack of technological knowledge, information, or skills. The consultant's goal is to provide the needed knowledge, information, or skills. Methods used may include lectures, multi-media, learning materials, structured laboratory experiences, small group discussions, modeling, and feedback measures. The consultant assumes that the consultee changes through cognitive learning. The consultant is viewed as an expert, who values the growing field of information and technology services to sustain the future of an organization, an agency, or a program. This model assumes that in a school the administrators have conferred with the faculty, and there is mutual agreement that staff may benefit from the proposed education and training.

Clinical Consultation

In this model the problem is the need for an expert diagnosis and authoritative recommendation regarding a client's disease of dysfunction due to the consultee's lack of technical expertise in the identified problem area. The consultant's goal is limited to the diagnosis and amelioration of the problem in this case, in order to restore normal social functioning or to remediate symptoms. The methods used include diagnosis, prescription, and treatment. It is assumed that the diagnosis is outside the consultee's range or competencies, and therefore, the consultant's expertise is essential for providing empirical knowledge to bring about change. The consultant may be collegial or directive in relating to the consultee, but in either case, the consultant values the healthy functioning of the client. This model assumes that the student's problem is so complex it requires a specialist for evaluation, disposition, and management.

Mental Health Consultation

In this model the problem is defined as the consultee's lack of knowledge, skill, self-confidence, or objectivity. The consultant's goal is to increase competencies and strengthen the consultee's professional functioning, with improvement in the client as a side effect. Methods that are used differ for each of these problem categories; however, all are part of education, facilitation, and support. The model assumes that the consultee has the capacity to solve the work problem with cognitive and emotional support. The consultant brings many sources of power to the role, so one becomes a model, teacher, resource, collaborator, and encourager. The consultant's primary underlying value is the diffusion of mental health concepts and principles as a form of mental health prevention. This model assumes that there is administrative sanction and support that provides the consultant and the consultee with the necessary time to analyze the identified problem, plan, and implement interventions.

Behavioral Consultation

In this model the problem is formulated in terms of dysfunctional behavior. The goal is to reduce or eliminate undesirable behaviors and replace or increase the frequency of desired behavior. The method used is the systematic application of cognitive learning principles. It is similar to methods of clinical consultation with its case-centered focus on the methods of diagnosis, prescription, and treatment. The method involves the following elements: defining the problem in behavioral terms; behaviors are observed and recorded; antecedents and consequences are analyzed; reinforcement contingencies are designed and implemented, the consultant withdraws, and the consultee assumes responsibility for the client's behavioral management program. This model assumes that change is possible with the consultant's empirical and rational expertise, which is the consultant's source of power. The behavioral consultation model places great value on technology and the scientific method. It assumes that the teacher is willing to collaborate with the consultant in the recording of observed behaviors, implementation of behavior modification strategies, the evaluation of behavioral changes, and the integration of a new behavioral management program in the appropriate settings.

Organizational Consultation

Problems in this model may fall into several domains: technology, structural, managerial, and/or human relations. In any case, the goal is to increase organizational productivity and morale. The methods used by organizational consultants vary widely depending upon the domain of concern, and in some instances teams comprised of consultants with different specialties are used. Consultants assume change is brought about by empirical knowledge and/or re-education. The consultant's authority comes from expert knowledge. In addition, the consultee usually identifies with the consultant's area of expertise and to the consultant's role performance. Organizational consultants base their models on the values inherent in technological information and human development services. As with education and training consultation, the model assumes that members of the organization agree that the services of a consultant are of value.

Program Consultation

Program consultation formulates the problem in terms of a lack of expertise needed to successfully carry out specialized services designed to benefit a target population. Methods used vary considerably due to the diversity of programs. Generally, they include some or all of the following: assessing needs, delineating clear goals, selecting methods to achieve identified goals, identifying resources, assessing benefits, identifying constituencies, defining administrative procedures, determining staffing needs, conforming to funding guidelines, evaluating program outcomes, and/or integrating new programs with existing services and agencies. The consultant assumes that theory and research is the foundation upon which changes are made to alter or plan a program. The consultant is viewed as an expert who values the scientific approach to program planning and/or the values reflected in the program.

AN APPLICATION OF MENTAL HEALTH CONSULTATION

The model of mental health consultation is now further discussed because it provides a flexible and rich framework for teachers and consultants to assist special education students who will no longer be served in pull-out programs, either because of financial constraints requiring staff downsizing or as a result of moving toward the new educational philosophy of "inclusion."

According to Caplan's consultee-centered case consultation category of mental health consultation theory, there are four reasons why a teacher might have a problem with a student: need for knowledge, need for skill, need for self-confidence, and need for objectivity (Caplan, 1970). These four reasons provide the core concept of this suggested model of school social work consultation that serves children returning from special education to the regular classroom.

Need for Knowledge

This problem arises when a teacher is lacking knowledge and information, which leads to an erroneous conclusion or misunderstanding about a child's unusual behavior. In some cases, the teacher has the theoretical knowledge necessary to understand the situation but does not see its relevance to this particular child and problem. The consultant responds by imparting missing information, sharing expertise, and, when appropriate, providing reading material.

Caplan takes the position that the need for knowledge should be the least frequent reason for consultation because the consultee is a trained professional. In a regular classroom setting, however, the teacher's primary training is in elementary or secondary education, not in mainstreaming special education students. Sometimes teachers are lacking in complex theoretical knowledge about the cognitive, emotional, social, or interactional processes that accompany a child's problem in the teaching-learning process. Other times a specific problem arises that would rarely be a part of a teacher's training or expertise. An in-service workshop may be the most economical way to impart knowledge about mainstreaming by using the education and training model of consultation.

Need for Skill

Here, the teacher's problem is not lack of knowledge but lack of skill in solving the presenting problem. There is a risk in this situation that the consultant might take on the role of supervisor and threaten the collegial relationship. The social work consultant may want to suggest to the teacher that he or she review the case with the principal who can supervise techniques of intervention.

There are instances when the type of skill required does not fall under the category of elementary or secondary education. One illustration of this involves modifying instructional designs, methods, and learning skills for managing a mildly autistic child placed in the regular classroom.

Need for Self-Confidence

When the teacher demonstrates knowledge and skill but does not use these abilities, the problem may be lack of self-confidence. This can be detected in the teacher's tentativeness and uncertainty. At its worst, it is seen in feelings of incompetence and worthlessness. When the teacher's problem manifests itself in this way, the consultant listens to the teacher describe how the situation was handled, then supports the teacher's good work, and ignores the teacher's self-depreciation. Another technique is to connect the teacher with another staff member who will be supportive of the teacher's work.

Some teachers have natural abilities in responding to the psychosocial needs of a child and do not question the plans they implement in order to assist the child. Other teachers need support because any actions that fall outside the traditional role of "teacher" engender in them a lack of self-confidence.

Need for Objectivity

This concept is defined as a teacher's loss of professional focus by becoming too close to or too distant from the child or a member of the child's family. When this occurs, conscious or unconscious factors invade the teacher's role functioning, distort perceptions, and cloud judgment. Caplan outlines five causes for loss of objectivity: (1) direct personal involvement; (2) simple identification; (3) transference; (4) characterological distortions; and (5) theme interference.

Direct personal involvement takes place when the teacher's professional relationship evolves into a personal relationship in which the teacher receives personal satisfaction rather than professional satisfaction in relation to the child. The task of the consultant is to help the teacher control the expression of personal needs in the workplace and develop professional goals and a professional identity.

One technique to use in these circumstances is to model for the teacher how he or she can be empathic while maintaining appropriate distance. Another is to recount a similar experience the consultant had in mastering personal feelings. When it is not feasible to discuss directly the teacher's overinvolvement and its negative qualities, the problem can be reversed. The teacher's actions can be discussed in terms of the child's wish to have a personal relationship with the teacher that excludes his or her classmates. In this way, it is easier to discuss the ramifications of a direct personal relationship.

A tendency toward simple identification with a pupil can be seen when the teacher describes a problem in such a way that one person is perceived in glowing, positive terms and the other person is perceived in derogatory, stereotypic terms. Sometimes the teacher shares a characteristic with the person who is seen in sympathetic terms. The consultant's task is to weaken the teacher's identification by having the teacher re-analyze the data concerning the entire situation. As this process occurs, the consultant helps the teacher to see the actors as separate and unique people rather than as extensions of the teacher.

Countertransference problems occur when the teacher imposes on the child a preordained set of attitudes, perceptions, or expectations derived from the teacher's own life experiences that block an objective assessment and the work with the child. The danger is that the teacher will use the child to act out or resolve the teacher's own unconscious conflict or fantasy. One way to detect this problem is the teacher's paucity of data to back up assertions made about the child. The consultant identifies the conflict that has stimulated the teacher's transference reaction, then influences the teacher to observe the child more closely in this area of conflict. Sometimes the newly collected observational data will help the teacher identify the conflict. In other cases, the best the consultant can do is offer emotional support, allow the teacher to vent feelings, and steer the teacher toward more appropriate outlets for the conflicts.

As in all professions, there are some teachers who have serious psychiatric problems, which Caplan labels "characterological distortions of perception and behavior" (1993, p. 119). The task of the consultant is to support the teacher's defenses and lower anxiety so that the teacher maintains optimal professional functioning. The goal is to inhibit regression and help the teacher maintain control over impulses and fantasies, and develop appropriate role boundaries.

During the ongoing contact with the school social worker, the teacher usually indicates whether he or she is in therapy. If the teacher is, the consultant can deflect regressive material by telling the teacher that the issues brought up are best reserved for the therapist. The teacher who has no therapist can be told that one of the key elements for the consultation contract precludes the consultant from taking on the role of therapist.

Theme interference is another form of transference. However, it is marked by a teacher's temporary ineffectuality in a limited segment of the work field. The teacher is suddenly confronted by a situation that is confusing and upsetting. Caplan postulates that an unresolved life experience or a fantasy persists in the consultee's "preconscious or unconscious as an emotionally toned cognitive constellation which we call a theme" (1970, p. 145). A major component of the theme is the repetitive quality that links an initial category to an inevitable outcome. The teacher is reminded of an unresolved conflict and associates it with the current situation. This condition is perceived to lead to one particular outcome, usually involving pain and suffering. For example, the teacher may say, "Children whose parents neglect them [initial category] are often failures in life [inevitable outcome]."

One technique used in dealing with theme interference is to influence the teacher to change his or her perceptions about the child so as to remove the initial category. This "unlinking" frees the child from the inevitable outcome. An unintended consequence of the technique, however, may be the consultee's displacement of the conflict onto another child. To avoid this problem the consultant can use a technique called "theme interference reduction." The consultant accepts the placement of the child in the initial category but, through examination of the specifics of this child's case, influences the teacher to see that the "inevitable" outcome is only one of several possible outcomes for the child. In fact, the data will often suggest a different outcome.

CONCLUSION

The emerging national policies and philosophical trends in education for special needs students encompass issues related to infancy, childhood, adolescence, and young adulthood. Effectively serving these students now requires school-based and community-based services.

Underlying this presentation of the consultation processes and models is the assumption that flexible and proactive consultation programs offer a powerful tool in meeting these needs. It provides a comprehensive continuum of services applicable to schools, families, and communities, that can provide education and training, expert evaluation, mental health supports, classroom behavior management, program planning and evaluation, and/ or delivery of services in an organization. Achieving successful outcomes for children and youth in today's world depends on developing consultation services as a part of one's school social work practice.

REFERENCES

Allen-Meares, P. 1993. Social work services in schools: A national study of entry-level tasks *Social Work* 39: 560–565.

Alpert, J. 1982. *Psychological consultation in educational settings*. San Francisco: Jossey-Bass.

Alpert, J., and Silverstein, J. 1985. Mental health consultation: Historical, present, and future perspectives. In J. Bergan (ed.). *Psychology in contemporary society*. Columbus, OH: Charles E. Merrill.

Bergen, J.R. 1977. *Behavioral consultation*. Columbus, OH: Charles E. Merrill.

Bishop, K., Rounds, K., and Weil, M. 1993. Preparation for social work practice with infants and toddlers with disabilities and their families. P.L. 99–457. *Journal of Social Work Education* 29(1): 36–45.

Blair, K. 1993. The regular education initiative and school social workers. *Social Work in Education* 15(4): 233–293.

Brown, D., Psyzwansky, W., and Schultz, A. 1991. *Psychological consultation: Introduction to theory and practice*. Needham Heights, MA: Allyn & Bacon.

Caplan, G. 1970. *The theory and practice of mental health consultation*. NY: Basic Books, Inc.

Caplan, G., and Caplan, R. 1993. *Mental health consultation and collaboration*. NY: Jossey-Bass.

Carr, L.D. 1976. *Report on survey of social work services in schools*. Washington, DC: National Association of Social Workers, mimeograph.

Conoley, J.C., and Conoley, C.W. 1982. *School consultation: A guide to practice and training*. Elmsford, NY: Pergamon Press.

Conoley, J.C., and Conoley, C.W. 1988. Useful theories in school-based consultation. *Remedial and Special Education* 9: 14–20.

Costin, L.B. 1969. A historical review of school social work. *Social Casework* 50(8): 439–453.

Curtis, M.J., and Zins, J.E. (eds.) 1981. *The theory and practice of school consultation*. Springfield, IL: Charles C. Thomas.

Drisko, J. 1993. Special education teacher consultation: A student-focused, skill-defining approach. *Social Work in Education* 15(1): 19–28.

Early, B. 1992. An ecological-exchange model of social work consultation within the work group of the school. *Social Work in Education* 14(4): 209–214.

Education for All Handicapped Children Act of 1975, P.L. 99–457, 89 Stat. 773.

Education of the Handicapped Act Amendments, P.L. 99–457, 100 Stat. 1145.

Gallessich, J. 1982. *The profession and practice of consultation.* San Francisco: Jossey-Bass.

Gutkin, T.B., and Curtis, M.J. 1990. School-based consultation: Theory, techniques, and research. In T.B. Gutkin and C.R. Reynolds (eds.). *The handbook of school psychology.* (2nd ed.). NY: Wiley.

Herr, L., and Fabian, E. (eds.). 1993. Consultation: A paradigm for helping. Consultation II: Prevention, preparation and key issues (Special issue). *Journal of Counseling and Development* 72(2).

Kadushin, A. 1977. *Consultation in social work.* NY: Columbia University Press.

Kurpius, D.W., and Fuqua, D.R. (eds.) 1993. Consultation: A paradigm for helping. Consultation I: Conceptual, structural, and operational dimensions (Special issue). *Journal of Counseling and Development* 71(6).

Lambert, C., and Mullaly, R. 1982. School social work: The congruence of task importance and level of effort. In R.T. Constable and J.P. Flynn (eds.). *School social work: Practice and research perspectives.* Homewood, IL: The Dorsey Press, pp. 72–84.

Mannino, F.V. 1981. Empirical perspective in mental health consultation. *Journal of Prevention* 1(3): 147–155.

Meares, P.A. 1977. Analysis of tasks in school social work. *Social Work* 22(3): 196–201.

Meares, P.A. 1982. A content analysis of school social work literature, 1968–1978. In R.T. Constable and J.P. Flynn (eds.). *School social work: Practice and research perspectives.* Homewood, IL: The Dorsey Press, pp. 38–41.

Meyers, J., Friedman, M., and Gaughan, E. 1981. The effects of consultee-centered consultation on teacher behavior. In M.J. Curtis and J.E. Zins (eds.). *The theory and practice of school consultation.* Springfield, IL: Charles E. Thomas.

Meyers, J., Parsons, R.D., and Martin, R. 1979. *Mental health consultation in the schools.* San Francisco: Jossey-Bass.

Oppenheimer, J.J. 1925. *The visiting teacher movement with special reference to administrative relationships.* (2nd ed.). NY: Joint Committee on Methods or Preventing Delinquency.

Reid, W.J. 1979. The model development dissertation. *Social Service Research* 3(2): 215–225.

Sabatino, C.A. 1986. The effects of school social work consultation on teacher perception and role conflict—Role ambiguity in relationship to students with social adjustment problems. *Dissertation Abstracts International* 46(11).

Timberlake, E.M., Sabatino, C.A., and Hooper, S.N. 1982. School social work practice and P.L. 94-142. In R.T. Constable and J.P. Flynn (eds.). *School social work: Practice and research perspectives*. Homewood, IL: The Dorsey Press, pp. 49-71.

West, J.F., and Idol, L. 1987. School consultation (part I): An interdisciplinary perspective on theory, models and research. *Journal of Learning Disabilities* 20: 388-408.

Zins, J.E., and Ponti, C.R. 1990. Best practices in school-based consultation. In A. Thomas and J. Grimes (eds.). *Best practices in school psychology-II*. Washington, DC: National Association of School Psychologists.

Zischka, P.C., and Fox, R. 1985. Consultation as a function of school social work. *Social Work in Education* (2): 69-79.

CHAPTER 23

Student Forums: Addressing Racial Conflict in a High School

Rita McGary
Retired School Social Worker, Fairfax, Virginia, Public Schools

During the 1984-85 school year, Falls Church High School, in northern Virginia, was the setting for serious racial incidents. The school's population of 1,612 students included three American Indians, 83 Hispanics, 139 blacks, 326 Asians, and 1,061 whites. Racial tension between black and white students developed in the 1960s as the county schools implemented their desegregation plan. By the mid-1970s, confrontations between blacks and whites abated, and although traces of institutionalized inequity may have continued, these were either tolerated or ignored for much of the decade between 1973-83.

An influx of immigrants from Southeast Asia, Central and South America, and Korea has rekindled racial tensions in the community. In general, the newly arrived minority groups have not been welcomed by the established residents. This has been especially true among the low socioeconomic groups, who perceive the new arrivals as competitors for resources and jobs. The immigrants, unsettled in a new environment, have not always known how to address their changed situation. Intergroup conflict ensued, and feelings of anger and frustration articulated at home have been acted out at school. Overt racial altercations reached alarming proportions by the spring of 1984.

In late February 1984, a serious altercation between two adolescents—one black and one Korean—occurred on the basketball court of a nearby elementary school. This was the first of several racial confrontations that occurred over the next three months. Students polarized along racial or ethnic

---

SOURCE: Reprinted with permission from *Social Work in Education*. Vol. 9, No. 3, 1987. Copyright 1987. National Association of Social Workers, Inc.

lines, and weapons were brought into the high school. The school took action. Two police officers worked with the Korean group and the author, a social worker, was asked to work with the black group. The incident on the basketball court culminated—as did several subsequent altercations—in formal mediation between the groups. Mediation as a method to address conflict was selected because the facilitators of both groups believed that its formal and controlled attributes were necessary to initiate and maintain communication among students who did not ordinarily interact. The facilitators provided training in communication and mediation. Five student representatives from each group were selected by their peers. Three sessions were held, the last being a social event. These sessions proved successful in eliminating conflict between the two racial groups.

From this beginning, with the school social worker acting as a catalyst, student forums were created. During the 1984-85 school year, six such groups existed. With the exception of one group that met for only two months, the groups met weekly throughout the year. Approximately seventy students participated. Four guidance counselors served as cofacilitators with the social worker. There was a forum for black male students; black female students; Hispanic students, coed; Korean students, coed; a group of representatives from the above four groups; and a group of white male students.

THEORY AND RESEARCH

The leaders used a sociological/anthropological approach that focused more on group activity than on individual behavior. They taught some theoretical concepts to students and simply included other concepts in their repertoire of techniques and strategies. The following considerations were especially helpful:

1. Adlerian psychological theory—particularly the concepts that all children's misbehavior has a purpose and does not occur ordinarily out of meanness or badness and that misbehavior is frequently a function of habit and habits can change. These two ideas served to prevent adults from making premature judgments about the behavior of the student participants.[1]
2. Small-group theory—especially the concept that groups, as human systems, have a life of their own and often must change before change in individuals can occur. Understanding such group attributes as group leadership roles, norms, goals, coherence, deviance, and juncture was a necessary part of this program. Only by focusing on the group as a system could the idiosyncratic behavior of the students be interpreted accurately.[2]
3. Analysis of the relationship between the helper and the person being helped—which needed conscious shaping in view of the stratification

issues inherent to the problems (that is, child/adult, minority/majority, nonwhite/white). Freire's analysis of the relationship between oppressor and oppressed provided the direction needed to establish productive dialogue within and between groups and with school personnel.[3]

4. The active involvement of the principal—which was crucial. Experience showed that the principal was the school person who could listen to the students' needs and have those needs acted on. Without this involvement, the rest of the program would have only been an exercise.[4]

OBJECTIVES

The immediate objective was to stop the violence but not to bury the racial issues in the process. Long-term objectives revolved around addressing the racial issues that had surfaced. The school provided a time and a place where students or groups of students could come to construct their own definition of themselves, clarify their needs and their goals, and, through the group process, have their needs acted on by significant others.

The objective here was not to stop the fighting per se. To suppress reactive behavior toward perceived inequity completely would be poor mental health practice. Instead, forums were used to look for less debilitating forms of resistance, if resistance was indeed necessary.

STRATEGIES

Certain students, usually the ones with the most visibility as leaders in times of conflict, were invited to talk to the author about what was going on at school. The first encounter involved two or three students, usually youngsters who were friends. At that first meeting, the need for more dialogue was rapidly established. The students agreed to come to a second meeting and to bring other interested students with them. From that point on, selection of students for participation was totally student-managed, with the result that friendship groups or gangs, as a unit, came to the forums. Friendship groups at Falls Church High School, no different from many other integrated high schools in the country, generally form along patterns of total or near-total resegregation.[5] Therefore, students who participated in a particular forum were, with a few exceptions, of the same race. Most of the participants were considered at high risk for behavioral deficits and poor achievement. In addition, the groups were already organized informally and group attributes and characteristics were fairly well set. Indeed, in most of the groups, coherence and norms were so strong as to preclude individual thought or movement.

Attendance

The groups met weekly. Regular attendance was not obligatory. Teachers were advised to keep their students in class if the group meeting conflicted with an important academic activity such as a test. It was understood that the purpose was to talk. There were no games and no lectures. Few students were absent from the meetings. Peer leaders maintained control and discipline, sometimes in creative ways. One group, for example, handled the disruptive behavior of some of its younger, lower status members by inviting more serious students to attend, thereby diluting the disruption. Meaningful deliberation, not a highly developed skill in the participants, came about very slowly, but it did occur and goal setting became possible. Some students attended a few meetings and used the forums to work out specific interpersonal conflicts, placing the other members in the role of mediators. The conflict was resolved after one or two sessions, and these students did not return.

Goal Setting

Students generated their own ideas for effecting change in themselves, their group, and/or the school environment. The minority student groups adopted the two-pronged goal of (1) removing violence from their lives and (2) avoiding suspensions from school. The white students' group was too invested in racial fighting as a pastime to want to give it up, indeed to arrive at any goal. Group meetings were used to provide insight into their emotions and behavior and to develop an understanding of the consequences of their behavior to themselves and to others. The leaders' agenda for all the groups was to help the students achieve their newly set goals and, looking beyond fighting, to help students become part of the mainstream as well as to maximize their engagement in the learning process. Initially, discussion centered around the ongoing conflicts and the latest confrontations and altercations. Gradually, discussion began to focus on why the fights were occurring. Social dynamics, intragroup and intergroup, were studied, both theoretically and from the students' experiential vantage point. The concept of displaced aggression clarified many reasons why minority students were fighting. They began to see that they were allowing others, either nonminority students or students from other ethnic/racial groups, to provoke them into fights and that their own frustration over perceived inequities provided the fuel for them to accept the challenge. They quickly realized that this reactive behavior was futile and could not improve their situation. They had to rethink the causes of their discontent and look for alternative behaviors. The group process entered its second phase.

Dialogue

Group meetings, in the second phase, while still focusing mainly on specific conflicts among peers, began to include dialogue on perceived racial discrimination at school. What the students reported as racist acts were studied and clarified. Discussion on the need for change and how to effect it was initiated by the group facilitators. The discussion included talking about the work of Dr. Martin Luther King, Jr. King's powerful methods of nonviolent revolution were compared historically to the methods of other revolutionaries (that is, the fathers of the American Revolution, and more recently—and of interest to the Hispanic students—Che Guevara in South America who believed that armed revolution was the only option for his time and place).

As the students broadened their perspective and their understanding of racial conflict, they devised new ways of addressing issues. The turning point occurred in the aftermath of an especially violent confrontation between groups of Vietnamese and white students. The next day, both sides were regrouping for another fight and both sides approached the black male group for reinforcement. The black group refused to participate and the fight did not occur. The black students were jubilant as they realized that the critical thinking they had engaged in had helped them assume some degree of control over their environment. They realized that proaction was just as effective as reaction.

It was at this juncture that the group facilitator's role expanded as well. Until this time, participants had been contained within the group and the adult leaders were mainly in the role of teacher and facilitator of the group process. However, the students' new awareness produced new behaviors. These behaviors began to make demands on the school. Their need to talk to the administration became very pressing. The adult leaders became enablers and negotiators to bring that about. Student conflict needed to be managed. The adult leaders served as mediators, sometimes with the help of administrators. The adult leaders also became chaperons or sponsors for some group projects. It was at this time that the involvement of the school principal became crucial. Students met with the principal to discuss relevant issues. They prepared for this by role playing how to communicate with authority figures. The principal, in turn, listened to the students and acted on their needs. Change occurred. This process soon replaced the students' original method of using physical force to maintain control over their lives at school.

RESULTS

Results of intervention with groups are not always tangible or measurable. Change does not occur immediately, nor is it the result of only one effort. Nevertheless, in the year and a half that the student forums operated, change was evident and positive effects on the students' lives were discernible. For one thing, interracial group fighting stopped. Students prevented rumbles from escalating. This work was done in the forums, sometimes at special meetings. As important as eliminating overt conflict, however, and certainly more far reaching, was the elimination of some institutionalized racist practices. Black male students played a leading role in rooting these out. For example, they addressed the practice that sent them to only one person, the black administrative aide, when they had any kind of concern or problem. They said that this practice deprived them of the help of other professionals and served to isolate them and make them feel different from the rest of the student body. This situation was discussed with the principal. Human-relations awareness training was given to faculty in the guidance department and the aforementioned practice was reduced significantly in the last half of the 1984–85 school year. Minority students received more attention and service from the grade administrators, the guidance counselors, and student services personnel. One sensed a change of attitude in these professionals as well.

A second issue addressed was the students' perception that black students were suspended from school more frequently and for longer periods of time than were other students. This perception was supported by national statistics, and it demanded investigation.[6] Using their new interactional skills, the students invited the administrators who they thought were perpetuating this practice to their meetings and discussed specific cases with them. This was helpful both to the students and to the administrators. (It is significant to note that the suspension rate dropped the next school year for all students.)

A third need surfaced quite unexpectedly. One of the forums had pressed for a school-sponsored college tour to a predominantly black college. This was arranged and, to everyone's surprise, 113 students, mostly minority students, signed up to go. When asked why they had signed up, many said that this was the first field trip they had had access to so far in their high school careers. The message was clear: low-track students, as many of them were, do not have field trips in their curriculum.

Another identified concern was the unique problem of Hispanic students who did not find a fit either in the Spanish curriculum or the Spanish Club. The Hispanic forum articulated a pressing need for the school to provide a Spanish curriculum for students whose first language is Spanish and to assist Hispanic youths in making a cultural contribution, jointly with non-Hispanic students, to the Hispanic activities of the school. At the time of this writing, the Spanish curriculum and extracurricular activities are for students who are learning Spanish as a second language. Thus, students from Vietnam or Afghanistan fit satisfactorily in these activities, because Spanish is a second language for them. This situation devalues the Hispanic student and must be addressed. Dialogue about this startling situation has already started, and the school is eager to search for a solution.

Other conditions and attitudes changed as well. Standardized test scores have gone up. The school now ranks third from the bottom out of twenty-five high schools, an improvement from ranking lowest for the previous three years. The test scores of minority students, particularly those of black girls, have gone up. Individual students have taken positive steps to invest more of their time and effort in learning. The school climate is calm, and one senses a new awareness. A survey taken by the Human Relations Department at the end of the 1984-85 school year showed a marked increase in positive student responses over the responses of 1983. Two items especially must be pointed out because the principal of the school attributes much of the increase to the student forums. The survey item "Adults in this school are willing to help me with my personal problems" went from 13.5 percent in 1983 to 69.9 percent in 1985 for black students and from 22.2 percent in 1983 to 63.6 in 1985 for Hispanic students. Another item, "I feel safe at school," was 55.9 percent in 1983 and 72.3 percent in 1985 for white students, 36.4 percent in 1983 and 69.9 percent in 1985 for black students. Most important, the school has taken new directions and acquired new sensitivities to the needs of minority students and majority students as well.

The process is evolving. Many of the students who participated in the forums have gone on to more mainstreamed activity and have less time to devote to the forums. Those students now understand that a multicultural school is not a static condition. Rather, it begs for the dynamic interchange that will make us all multicultural in the measure that we are able to interact with persons of cultures different from our own. The students who have reached this level of understanding agree that the forums must continue to provide service to students who need this type of intervention and to monitor the emotional climate of the school. Although constraints may prohibit their full participation in the forums, all want to assist the groups and the school in some way .

IMPLICATION FOR SOCIAL WORK

Student forums strengthened the social functioning of the participants, both within their groups and in the mainstream. They did not interfere with the participants' goals as minority students in a predominantly white society. The intervention at Falls Church High School benefited from, and owed much of its success to, social work concepts for practice. Identifying life tasks and then learning how to deal with one's life tasks, long the approach of the social work profession, served as the base for both the conceptualization and actualization of the students' involvement.[7] This project also supported the research of Slavin and Madden, which has shown the necessity of direct student involvement to affect interracial attitudes and behavior within a school environment.[8]

Finally, this endeavor represented a shift in social work practice from traditional casework to direct involvement in the internal life of the school. Although still using the casework method when indicated, the worker's role expanded to advocacy for minority students in their attempt to set a course of action for themselves. The student forums have been an effective tool toward providing equal treatment for all students and helping every person at Falls Church High School to become multicultural.

REFERENCES

1. For the application of individual psychology to adolescents, see D. Dinkmeyer and G. D. McKay. 1983. *Step/teen, systematic training for effective parenting of teens.* Circle Pines, MN: American Guidance Service.
2. Shepherd, C. R. 1964. *Small groups; some sociological perspectives.* NY: Chandler Publishing Co.
3. Freire, P. 1970. *Pedagogy of the oppressed.* NY: Seabury Press.
4. As an example of the principal's participation in programs to ensure success, see the following 1978 report to Congress: National Institute of Education. 1978. *Violent schools—Safe schools.* Washington, D.C.: U.S. Government Printing Office.
5. Cusick, P. A., and Ayling, R. 1982. Racial interaction in an urban secondary school. In J. W. Schofield and W. D. Francis, (eds.). An observational study of peer interaction in racially mixed "accelerated classrooms." *Journal of Educational Psychology* 74(5):p.724.
6. Several statistical studies confirm the disproportionate suspension rate for black students. Jurisdictions in suburban Washington, D.C. generally point to a ratio of 3 to 1. For national statistics the reader is referred to the Office for Civil Rights. 1980. *1980 Elementary and Secondary School Civil Rights Survey.* Washington, D.C.: Department of Education.
7. Bartlett, H. M. 1970. *The common base of social work practice.* NY: National Association of Social Workers.
8. Slavin, E., and Madden, N. E. 1979. School practices that improve race relations. *American Educational Research Journal* 16 (Spring): 169–180.

CHAPTER 24
Conflict Resolution

Shirley McDonald
Clinical Associate Professor, Jane Addams College of Social Work,
University of Illinois at Chicago

Anthony Moriarty
Principal, Homewood–Flossmoor High School,
Flossmoor, IL

INTRODUCTION

Conflict resolution—the skills needed to become an effective resolver of conflict and the learning of a formalized process of coming to resolution—has recently become recognized as a core social skill. These skills are now viewed as fundamental for effective participation in ordinary day-to-day negotiations between people, and also for negotiating those sometimes more serious, but hopefully less frequent, episodes in our lives which threaten to create major disruptions if not resolved. For elementary and high school students these skills play a major role in confirming their sense of social competence and, although some students seem to possess these skills naturally, most need some training and additional practice to be able to use them effectively (Moriarty and McDonald, 1991). The formal process of conflict resolution builds on the fundamental practice skills of social work. Since such skills are already part of our professional repertoire, the preparation required for teaching these skills is only the time required to learn the process of conflict resolution. This chapter will discuss a variety of methods for resolving conflicts, both formally and informally, and the skills necessary to achieve such resolutions. Finally, attention will be given to issues of training special student populations to become proficient in both the skills and the process. Such school programs already in place are widely recognized as having a positive impact on individual student's lives, as well as a positive impact on the climate of the school (South Suburban

Peer Network, 1993). When these skills are learned and modeled by teachers, administrators, parents, and community members, the process and skills learned are greatly reinforced, thereby producing family and community benefits.

CULTURE AND CONFLICT

How conflicts are handled in any society depends on community cultural norms, as well as individual perceptions of threats to personal safety in case of unsatisfactory resolution of the conflict (Combs and Snygg, 1959). For example, in many Asian cultures a third person is used as a go-between. Thus, the disputants need never directly acknowledge to each other that there is a difficulty, and may continue civil behavior as negotiations over the difficulty are in process (Sue and Sue, 1990). Clearly, the person acting as go-between will be selected because of a reputation for possessing skills of fairness, clear communication, and creative problem solving, all of which have the potential for obtaining a mutually agreeable solution. Peace may be preserved and the disputants can discard the previous concerns without acknowledging their feelings about the problem directly to the other. While the skills needed for an effective go-between in such cultures closely mirror the skills which describe an effective mediator in Western culture, the potential for problems with such a process may occur if the go-between is not perceived as fair, or may not communicate well in a particular dispute, and consequently, the outcome may or may not bode well for the concerned parties. Since the motivation for using a go-between is to resolve a dispute without the parties confronting each other directly, they are of course not able to hear the discussion with the go-between and the other disputant. Without this knowledge a process of checks and balances for correcting possible misinformation may be lacking. In Western society there is perceived honor in directly confronting one's accusers, and/or provocateurs. Certainly, this direct confrontation has many pitfalls and often follows similar patterns of avoiding direct confrontation, not dissimilar to those of Eastern cultures, but with no recourse to a go-between. Perhaps there is a combination of these two cultural patterns for solving conflict that draws on the best attributes of each.

Day-to-day attitudes toward conflict in most Western societies tend to be those of avoidance, despite the perceived honor of confronting one's foes or potential foes. This avoidance takes many forms. Some of these, as already discussed have cultural roots, some are socially driven, but all seem to have the common theme of desiring painless resolution of the dispute. Unfortunately, once it is clear that a controversy will not dissipate or dissolve, there seem to be very few alternatives but to stand one's ground and defend it, aggressively if needed (Fisher, Ury and Patton, 1991). One can avoid the difficulty if possible, at least for the immediate present, then stand firm against any challenges if the dispute does not dissipate.

CONFLICT AND EMOTIONAL EXPRESSION

Real feelings often are not easily expressed in our society, at least publicly. Revealing emotions may be perceived as being overly sensitive, insecure, unsure, vulnerable and/or manipulative. Each of these traits has its positive and negative attributes, but the interpretation of them, that is, the expression of emotion, is dependent upon the relationship of the person displaying the emotion and the interpreter of the experience. The potential is great for misunderstanding, and may leave the person showing emotion vulnerable to another's interpretation. Unfortunately, emotional displays are often discounted, apologized for, and perceived to be a weakness. Such negative interpretation is portrayed routinely in the media. The lesson learned most often is to withhold expression of feelings until one is in the safety of one's own space. For a child this is likely to be his/her home, room, or special secret hideaway.

An alternative reaction is to overreact aggressively early in the dispute's development as a warning that further incidents or perceived threats will not be taken lightly. This behavior can have the effect of rapidly escalating the emotional reaction to the dispute and physical aggression may be reverted to, especially by children and adolescents unless they are taught alternatives. In any case, the decision to warn of potential confrontation, or not to warn, has its own cultural and personal pressures. Societally, we continue to struggle with honest expression of feelings versus a sense of extreme vulnerability when emotional expression is experienced. This reluctance to confront negative reactions to others' behaviors exacerbates the difficulty of confronting others when their perceived actions cause discomfort. As school social workers, we routinely help students become more comfortable with their emotions and the productive expression of emotional responses. This skill must be achieved before a student is likely to profit from the process of conflict resolution.

Additionally, students need to be supported in demonstrating empathy to others' emotional responses. Next, there is a great need to explore mutually advantageous ways to defuse aggressive responses and to resolve the underlying problems before such potential conflicts escalate to physical assault. Finally, the social worker must incorporate teaching, coaching, reinforcing, and supporting of students in their ongoing use of conflict resolution skills.

A crucially important skill for a person in conflict is to learn to identify his or her feelings, and to be able to have sufficient empathic sensitivity to others' feelings, by observing their words, facial expression, tone of voice, body posture, and/or body language. This mutual ability to interpret emotional expression allows accurate communication to occur (Fast, 1970).

SKILL BUILDING FOR RESOLUTION

Once students show competence in the communication of feelings, the next step is expressing accurately how one feels, and communicating such feelings with non-pejorative language, such as "I messages" (Gordon, 1975). This gives the disputant the proper language and format with which the disputant can describe how she/he feels when the other disputant behaves in certain ways. For example, "When you (state behavior, e.g., 'ignore me') I feel (state feeling, e.g., 'worried') because I am (state effect, e.g., 'afraid you don't like me anymore')"; or using the "I message" the sentence might be, "When you ignore me I feel worried because I am concerned that you may not like me anymore." This non-accusing language may allow enough communication to occur so each disputant may experience how the other is feeling.

Listening skills are not natural talents for all people, certainly not for all young people. Unfortunately, they are seldom taught. The cliché "Just because you said it, does not mean she/he heard it" is testament to the ability to hear words, without "getting" the intended meaning. The child's game of telephone where a circle of children attempt to pass a message successfully around the circle without the message being changed is a second illustration of social awareness that messages are frequently distorted. Often the results are funny and seldom does the message stay intact around the circle. Therefore, real listening skills need to involve dialogue designed to "check out" the meaning of what was stated, such as "Can you be more specific," "Can you say that in another way," or the Rogerian reflective listening, "Let me tell you what I think I just heard you say, correct me if I am wrong. . . ."

Staying with one subject is also difficult for some children. They are easily distracted, either by something said or by their own thoughts. Teaching phrases such as "How does that relate to" (what the original subject was) may be helpful to reconnect the dialogue to the stated problem to be solved. Also, validating the student's new area of concern may be accomplished by teaching children to give assurances that the new topic will be returned to once the current topic is resolved.

Role playing is another aid in developing good listening skills once the skill has been taught and modeled by the instructor. Making up scenarios for role plays can be an enjoyable and useful exercise and personalizes the activity for the students. For younger children the use of puppets may be helpful to begin a dialogue leading to role playing.

Keeping the dialogue focused on the subject is essential to the process of conflict resolution. Since staying on task can be confounded by emotionality, it may help to coach children to avoid self-talk such as "I'm getting nervous," "I hope she/he still (likes me) (doesn't get any angrier) (doesn't tell my friends), etc." Such thoughts prevent the child from staying with the problem-solving task. Children can be encouraged to repeat phrases to themselves, such as "Keep it up," "Did I make that point clearly?" etc. However, much self-talk is negative and hinders the child's ability to concentrate and participate fully in the process.

PROCESS OF CONFLICT RESOLUTION

The actual process of conflict resolution has several components: 1) identification of the problem in specific language; 2) brainstorming possible solutions; 3) agreeing on a solution; 4) confirming intent to make the resolution work.

First, the student needs to learn to identify problems. They must specify problems, avoid general terms and "fuzzy" language (Moriarty, 1992), and then prioritize the problems according to level of seriousness or, in some cases, according to level of likelihood of being resolved. This is a personal skill that will serve the student in many arenas. To acquire this skill at a useful level, students first need to be able to state the presenting problem as specifically as possible, and then identify the most troublesome parts of the problem. At this point, it is important to introduce the idea of formulating what they feel they need from an agreement, if they are able to reach one. This is crucial if each disputant is going to be able to accept the outcome as fair. This process actually involves several components. The student needs to reconfirm his/her desire for a solution, that she/he wishes this solution to occur with a problem-solving process, and that this process may involve compromising on some points. Next, it is important for him/her to determine his/her "position," the problem, and, indeed, what the "bottom line" is—what is not negotiable (Fisher, Ury and Patton, 1991). These are often two different points. The student must learn that it is better to argue from a bargaining position that has some maneuverability. This is good strategy unless the student confuses what is needed from an agreement and what she/he is only using for bargaining. The next skill which students find difficult is focusing on the important issues—not getting side-tracked. When people get into arguments they normally have a sense of being threatened, and when this threat becomes too great, it is very common for the disputant to divert the argument by introducing extraneous information or additional complaints not directly related to the argument. For this skill to become highlighted, role plays are probably the most effective tool to demonstrate and practice the skill of staying with the core concern(s). Control of emotions is a skill that needs to be emphasized during the actual resolution process. It can be difficult, especially for younger students, but coaching students as they practice can quickly help them see how such control may operate often to their advantage if the real goal is resolution of the dispute.

SPECIAL STUDENT POPULATIONS

One fundamental reason for diverting arguments or at least getting off the subject is the fear of being exposed, either for faulty thinking, or over-emotionalism. These threats are often intensely felt by children who struggle in school because of developmental delays, learning disabilities, attention deficit disorder, or emotional disturbance/behavior disorders. Such children are already accustomed to being ridiculed for not succeeding, especially in cognitive areas, and for many, over-emotionalism is a persistent struggle as they attempt to become empowered. They need extra support in learning to sort the important from the unimportant and to stay with the main theme of the dispute. These students sometimes retain linear thinking processes longer than their age-mates who are not so disabled, and thus extra support in brainstorming for solutions may be necessary. This is not to say that such populations cannot benefit from conflict resolution training; in fact, the opposite is true and these students have some amazing assets and insights into the process, making them ideal candidates for such training.

Another population of students who need extra support are the students struggling with poor self-concepts and general problem-solving skills, sometimes identified as "at-risk" students. These students tend to cave in quickly to any challenge and are more likely to have difficulty staving off emotional responses that overwhelm their ability to think through problems clearly. However, the skills of conflict resolution can also enhance their sense of competence once they have successfully mastered them, and their ability to identify their "bottom line" needs in a dispute may be valuable to help them understand their rightful position in social encounters.

PROBLEM SOLVING PROCESS

The final skill that students need is a formalized process of problem solving to keep them on track to the end point of reaching an agreement. Problem solving is both a natural and a formal process. Most people go through a process of looking at a few options before making even small day-to-day decisions. This process may be barely conscious. A few options are considered and all but one ruled out. This becomes this person's decision about taking action or beginning an activity. This process works well if conflicting emotions are not significantly involved, and/or if the stakes are not very high. However, as the *outcome* of a decision increases in importance, the *process* becomes more important, and emotions are more likely to come into play, complicating the ability to think clearly and creatively. Also, the extent of an individual's routine use of formal operations in thinking patterns may further determine the "goodness of fit" of the resolution to the problem. Teaching a formal method of problem solving will certainly enhance the quality of life of students who receive such training, by giving them tools to use when under pressure to resolve a conflict at an early age. Such skill will carry over to their adolescent and adult years.

The steps to the problem solving process are these:

1. Identify the specific problem needing resolution;
2. Brainstorm potential solutions without criticizing any suggestions including some which may initially seem frivolous. All ideas are acceptable;
3. Discuss the positives and negatives of each possible solution that may have some potential;
4. Agree on one solution that has the most potential for satisfying both parties to the dispute, and that has the greatest potential of succeeding;
5. Agree on a timeline for trying the solution, even if it does not seem to be working very well at first. Stay with the proposed solution to give it a chance for success;
6. Evaluate whether the solution is meeting the needs of each disputant in resolving the identified and agreed upon problem, or whether some modifications need to be made or a new solution proposed.

Once the potential solution has been agreed to, the disputants and anyone helping to guide them through the process should congratulate each other on a successful outcome of the dispute. Older students will often shake hands as a sign of agreement. There should also be an understanding about not talking about the disagreement with outside parties, so that the privacy of all is respected (confidentiality).

ADAPTING THE PROCESS TO YOUR SETTING

Schools use conflict resolution in a variety of ways, but the process outlined above is essentially the same. The details are often quite different. Some school districts have instituted system-wide training in conflict resolution skills but have no formal program, such as a trained team of mediators or conflict resolvers. Other districts do some training with all students, but also train a cadre of students who are available in more difficult situations, especially when emotions are running high, or when there seems to be an imbalance in power and, therefore, care is required to ensure that each party to the dispute is respectful to the other. These specially trained students are often identified as a team and have regular meetings. Younger students may wear special vests on playgrounds and in lunchrooms, or during special functions where students are not being closely supervised. Other schools have students identified in each classroom who are the designated conflict resolvers and who may hold such dispute resolution sessions in the classroom, ideally in an area somewhat removed from the rest of the class. Other schools do not train all students, but rely on a cadre or team of conflict resolvers or mediators to deal with identified problems. In such schools there is likely to be a set policy regarding which types of problems are appropriate for referral to such specially trained teams. In all cases, the school must have a means to oversee the referral process so that mediators are at all times protected from serious problems or risks.

Any plan for using a formal conflict resolution program in schools needs administrative sanction and support, as well as occasional morale boosts in terms of recognition for a job well done. Any faculty or staff may choose to sponsor such efforts. The only real requirement for such sponsorship is that the adult be invested in conflict resolution and dedicated to the program.

EVALUATION

The usual measures to chart effectiveness of mediation programs have focused on one of three measures: 1) satisfaction of training as evaluated by the students who have been trained; 2) satisfaction ratings by disputants as they report back, usually a week or so after the conflict has been resolved (Moriarty, Marsfield and Leverence, 1992); 3) school impact studies measuring recidivism rates of individual students (whether the original identified problem has resurfaced, or not), or a global school profile regarding reduction of violent incidents and/or reduction in the number of disciplinary actions such as suspension rates (Tolson, McDonald and Moriarty, 1991).

Each of the above evaluations measure only part of the total impact of an established conflict resolution program. Perhaps a researcher in the near future will develop a more comprehensive method of evaluating the impact of such programs on students' lives, the climate of the school, and the contribution to the community made by graduating students who have developed skills in peacefully resolving conflicts.

CONCLUSION

Conflict resolution skills have proven to be basic, essential life skills that can be taught at all levels of school, and to children of both regular and special education categories. Teaching such skills includes: identification of actual problems amenable to being solved; helping student to control emotional reactions during the resolution process; identifying disputants' problem solving to find an acceptable solution. Fairness, the ability to compromise, staying on task, and the respect to all parties involved, as well as confidentiality, need to be addressed.

Conflict resolution is implemented in a variety of ways in different school districts. Some teach the same skills to all children. Some teach a modified curriculum to all and an enhanced training is then give to a selected group who are identified as conflict resolvers or mediators. Other schools only train a cadre of students who then are the designated mediators in specified categories that concern the school.

Teaching children such life skills serves them when they are students and later as adults. The school climate is enhanced when students better resolve their own personal problems, and a language of respect is developed when people in the school disagree. Thus, conflict need not be avoided as a personal threat and something dangerous, but conflict becomes an opportunity for positive change when the skills are at hand to resolve the conflict in a creative and lasting way.

The next chapter will address more specifically one approach to developing a conflict resolution program in a school setting. This more formal approach is frequently identified as "peer mediation."

REFERENCES

Combs, A., and Snygg, D. 1959. *Individual behavior: A perceptual approach to behavior.* NY: Harper & Row.

Fast, J. 1970. *Body language.* NY: Pocket Books.

Fisher, R., Ury, W., Patton, B. 1991. *Getting to yes.* NY: Penguin Books.

Gordon, T. 1975. *Parental effectiveness training.* NY: Bantam Books.

Moriarty, A. 1992. Training guide. Mimeograph.

Moriarty, A., Mansfield, V., and Leverence, W. M. 1992. Student satisfaction and peer-based mediation. *School Social Work Journal* 16(2): 32–35. Northlake, IL: IASSW.

Moriarty, A., and McDonald, S. 1991. April. Theoretical dimensions of school-based mediation. *Journal of Social Work in Education* 13(3): 176–18. Silver Springs, MD: NASW.

South Suburban Peer Network. Susan Kamba and Frank DuBois. Steering Committee Coordinators, Homewood-Flossmoor High School, Flossmoor, IL. Organized 1993.

Sue, D.W., and Sue, D. 1990 *Counseling the culturally different.* 2nd ed. NY: John Wiley and Sons.

Tolson, E., McDonald, S., and Moriarty, A. 1992. Peer mediation among high school students: A test of effectiveness. *Social Work in Education* 14(2). Silver Springs, MD: NASW.

CHAPTER 25

Mediation as a Form of Peer-Based Conflict Resolution

Anthony Moriarty
Principal, Homewood–Flossmoor High School, Flossmoor, IL

Shirley McDonald
Clinical Associate Professor, Jane Addams College of Social Work;
Past President, Illinois Association of School Social Workers

Increasingly large numbers of adolescents are becoming disenchanted with and alienated from the decision-making processes that are in common use in secondary schools (Rappoport, 1989). A major consequence of this disenchantment or outright alienation is an erosion of the student's personal investment in education. This takes place in large part because of students' inability to experience self-determination or to achieve self-responsibility, two powerful motivators for adolescents. If social workers are to play a significant role in helping schools to become more successful, they must assume much of the task of developing channels for school support systems which empower students (Germain, 1988). Rappoport (1989) suggests that in the general society today our accumulation of knowledge generates increasing numbers of experts and bureaucracies for the administration of this additional knowledge. The ordinary person becomes increasingly disempowered.

Possibly because of an emerging awareness of their perceived lack of power, and in a society driven by bureaucratic structures, students often are engulfed by a sense of personal disempowerment and subsequent alienation. They become increasingly vulnerable to a variety of adolescent problems, such as anxiety, stress, a sense of personal inadequacy, and low self-esteem. These alienated students frequently are involved in conflict and can be disruptive to the educational process. Social workers need to counter this alienation with strategies that reconnect and empower students in a positive manner.

Mediation is a structured attempt to involve individuals, in this case students, in the resolution of their own disputes.

There are many formats within which mediation can occur. Some are relatively structured and formal, especially those developed to intervene, and, it is hoped, prevent, legal confrontations, as in special education disputes (Gallant, 1982), or those developed for neighborhood or community disputes (Neighborhood Justice Center of Atlanta, Inc., 1982). The format used in our project, however, has been adapted to reflect the school milieu, the relative skill of secondary student mediators, and the types of disputes identified as amenable to student-to-student mediation. It is not the opinion of the authors, however, that there is significant difference in experience or quality of outcome of less-structured formats. In all cases, mediation is inherently democratic in its process, and it effectively balances concern for the needs of students with the needs of the institution.

Mediation is an effective model that provides a format for addressing problems that have a disruptive and negative effect on students' daily lives. Students, given the opportunity to pursue meaningful activity in school, are unlikely to experience the feeling of estrangement or alienation from that system. We have found that students who experience a personal sense of empowerment tend to demonstrate a greater capacity to assume responsibility for their own welfare than those who do not feel empowered.

Mediation helps keep students in school. If, alternatively, they are suspended, students are at increased risk for more serious problems, such as dropout or destructive behavior. They generally are without supervision either at home or in the community. They also are often angry at the school and cut off from social interaction with their peers. The dropout rate for students who have been suspended frequently significantly exceeds the rate of the general school population (National School Safety Center, 1988). Some authors believe that peer mediation in schools may be the most positive and effective means of intervention with students at risk for more serious problems (Wheelock, 1988). The process of mediation conveys a belief that students are indeed competent and therefore have the capacity and potential to resolve their own problems. School mediation significantly deters the serious side effect of alternative punitive interventions: student alienation.

Systems such as schools vary as to their receptiveness to change, and the organizational characteristics of the institution affect the degree to which mediation likely will function congruently within the school community. Systems in general are "open" or "closed," depending largely on the administrative ability to accept change. In a closed system, a rule infraction is dealt with according to a predetermined procedure and without a process of organizational reflection about possible change. In a more open system, rule infractions have prescribed consequences, but they also serve as an indicator of the effectiveness of the school's relationship with its students and the overall educational process. Consequently, in an open system, although infractions require a response, the school sees itself as capable of change and adaption to enable each individual student to better cope with the causes and circumstances of infractions. Mediation probably cannot function in an entirely closed school system. It requires a degree of flexibility and openness to creative problem solving. It also depends on the school philosophy reflecting a belief that everything that goes on between students in a school can be used for growth.

Peer mediation in the secondary school system significantly empowers students, but not without some reasonable control. A principle long recognized in government, and to some extent in industry, is that an individual's interpersonal conflicts are best resolved in a dialogue with his or her peers. Our judicial system is based on the principle that peers can make fair judgments on disputed questions. Secondary school students are at a developmental stage where they are interested in and value approval and sanction from their peers. Interpersonal disputes that appear to be unresolvable to the disputants often arise in a high school. Here, a growth-inducing settlement using peer mediation is more likely to have a positive long-term effect than a mandated solution imposed by an adult authority figure.

Mediation teaches the art of compromise, effective listening, judicious inquiry, rational thinking, and a skillful focus on areas of mutual concern and benefit. In an institution offering a dispute resolution program, assistance in the resolution of disputes is provided by trained peers who facilitate the resolution of problems brought to a neutral table. As a result, both the students who are trained as mediators and those who avail themselves of the process actively engage in a fundamentally democratic activity. In conflict resolution vernacular, the basic goal of mediation is to arrive at a "win-win" outcome rather than the traditional "win-lose" outcome of more closed styles of dispute resolution (Fisher and Ury, 1981). This process has proved to be an effective face-saving opportunity for students who find themselves caught in a web of peer conflict.

SELECTION CRITERIA FOR MEDIATORS

Mediation training does not require the teaching of entirely new skills. It is an inherently efficient process in that it redirects talents demonstrated by students. This is true especially of the talents developed in peer relationships. Mediation training builds on these demonstrated talents to develop the necessary elements of the mediation process. These skills are defined, identified, and sanctioned by the school as valuable and important. They are put to work for the greater good of the school community and the mediators themselves.

Identifying potential student mediators is a process that relies heavily on recognizing leadership traits and specific personal qualities. The students selected should be those who are sought out by others in times of personal difficulty, rather than those who have identified leadership characteristics resulting from academic, athletic, or social talent. Students who are able to serve effectively as mediators are found in every strata of student populations. They frequently are not well known to each other because they are the effective leaders of their separate social groups. Effective mediators do not emerge more frequently from any one particular type of activity or group in the school.

These students readily learn the fundamental interpersonal communication skills essential to the mediation process. Once students are selected for mediation training, the process of refining these preexisting skills begins. Indigenous leadership skills are shaped, and a degree of structure is imposed upon them. Thus, it is clear that teaching new skills is not a major focus of training. Training tailors skills students have brought with them to the job of conflict resolution.

THE DEVELOPMENT OF A MEDIATION PROGRAM

An example of a training program is the effort that began in the spring of 1988 to develop such a program at Rich East High School in Park Forest, Illinois. This effort was met with an impressive degree of acceptance by the students and an equal amount of success in its efforts to resolve interpersonal conflicts between students. The project was initiated in a two-day workshop for the students selected to serve as mediators. This training program described an approach to mediation that was a combination of several existing models. The specific components of this model will be described later.

The Selection Process

The first step in developing this specific model was a decision to proceed with the training program. Once this took place, students needed to be selected. It was important that students selected to be mediators should have "clout" with their peers. Such clout in a school has two relevant implications. First, it means influence or "pull"; and second, it implies power or "muscle." Deans and counselors were asked to recommend students they believed were sufficiently influential and whom they believed possessed clout. Surprisingly, the deans and the counselors largely recommended the same students, despite the seemingly vague definition of this criterion. All ten of the original nominees agreed to participate in the project. This level of agreement was a surprise to the project planners, who expected some students to decline to participate. However, the level of participation correlates with the characteristics of the students selected. When the general concept of the program was explained, all the students appeared to recognize the program to be a valuable contribution to the school, as well as an opportunity for personal growth and gain.

This group of students defied generalization. They were dissimilar in every category except that of age. Race, gender, grade-point average, extracurricular participation, and regular and special education defined no common characteristics. Some had problems themselves that had brought them to the deans' offices earlier in high school. Others were relatively unknown to the administrative staff. It soon was clear that students with identifiable clout came from a wide range of social and educational strata in the high school.

The Orientation Process

This group of fledgling mediators was given an orientation to the process of mediation and a series of structured steps to follow in the actual mediation process. Emphasis was placed on creating the proper atmosphere, personal demeanor, the structuring of the physical setting, and the preliminary remarks made by the mediators. Ensuring confidence and respect in the process by starting out with a well-delivered opening statement was seen as critical to the success of the experience. Consequently, time was spent helping each student develop the opening statement, make introductions, establish ground rules, and explain the process of mediation and rules of decorum. It also was essential that these content areas be explained in language compatible with each mediator's personal style.

Opening statements. Several elements are necessary in an appropriate opening statement. First, mediators need to structure a win-win environment. The disputants are told clearly that no one comes out of mediation a loser. This stimulates student interest and also lets them know early on that they are being provided a face-saving opportunity. Second, the principle of confidentiality is defined and its application to the mediation process is clearly established. Third, it is emphasized during the training sessions that a commitment to neutrality needs to be made clear in the opening statement. This is important for two reasons: the students in dispute need to know that the mediators are not going to take sides; and it is important for the protection of the mediators to reinforce the fact that mediators will not have any involvement with disputants outside the mediation session, at least in regard to the issue in dispute. Mediators must make it very clear that they will have no involvement with the problem or its solution outside of the mediation session, including any follow-up.

Finally, rules of order are introduced in the opening statement. The mediator requires appropriate decorum and specifically states what is and what is not appropriate behavior. In the pilot project the mediators quickly realized that full control of the mediation session is most effectively accomplished by insisting that all conversation be directed to and through the mediator. This style, while allowing each of the disputants to listen to the other's story, establishes equality and fairness in the disputants' opportunities to present their positions, and helps prevent interruptions.

Interpersonal skills. Disputes brought to mediation often are not thoroughly understood by the disputants. Mediation trainers need to discuss the concepts of "secondary" or "hidden" agendas and in this project there was concern that these concepts would be difficult for the students to grasp. The students quickly dissipated these worries. These ideas were readily grasped by the mediators, as were double-binding messages, reflective listening skills, and the general techniques of good therapeutic style, including the withholding of judgment, neutrality, the use of "I messages," and confidentiality. The students' affinity for these concepts seemed to be a natural by-product of their preexisting leadership abilities.

The skill-building component of the training focused on sharpening communication skills to serve the specific goals of the mediation process. The most effective mediators are those who are especially good at the use of reflective statements and those able to quickly ferret out hidden agendas. Reflective statements convey to the disputants that their issues are understood; the discovery of hidden agendas brings into focus why the disputants are clinging to their conflictual issues. The process transcends the angry and rigid presenting of positions and guides the students to their real agendas. In short, the mediators are learning basic techniques essential to good therapeutic intervention, and they come to appreciate and respect the power of good communication skills.

During the first year of this project, the mediators processed forty-seven referrals with a recidivism rate of zero. In every case, suspensions were prevented and the disputants eventually were able to take responsibility for the resolution of their own differences. Problems involved interpersonal relationships, space violations, and possession of property. Some issues were relatively minor. Others were potentially catastrophic. The significant point is that the students in dispute were themselves involved in developing the agreement that resolved the dispute. There was a follow-up component intended to monitor students' compliance with the terms of the agreements. Given meaningful responsibility, the students demonstrated an effective degree of competence and compliance.

Related School-System Developments

School suspension programs run counter to two relatively recent developments in secondary education. First, cooperative learning has assumed a significant role in education. Essentially, cooperative learning is a movement in education that has enjoyed a significant degree of success by devaluing the competitive aspects of classroom activity and focusing on the cooperative aspects (Johnson and Johnson, 1989). Outcome studies have indicated that it is a highly successful instructional model for today's adolescents (Block, 1983; Slavin, 1989). Second, in a study by Viadero (1988), students, when given an active, meaningful role within the school system in determining their destiny, proved to be significantly more responsible for what they learn. School suspension, the product of a unilateral decision-making process by the administration, requires only passive compliance by the student and tends to counteract any efforts by a school system to develop more student ownership and involvement in their educational experience.

MEDIATION AND SCHOOL SOCIAL WORK

The philosophy and process of mediation are compatible with the same tenets in social work. The only distinguishing characteristics of mediation that separate it from the fundamentals of social work practice are the relative formality and the degree of personal distance maintained by the mediators, as opposed to that of the usual social worker's more empathic response level. Also, the practical restrictions placed on mediators regarding their involvement in cases after the mediation is completed differs from good social work practice, where follow-up of cases is indicated when the need for this extended involvement is apparent. The process of mediation serves to facilitate a continuing thrust toward system change and effectively enables students to acquire more self-responsibility and competent independence within a complex system, a goal highly compatible with good social work practice.

The implementation of a program of student mediation in a secondary school has several benefits that affect the operation of the school and the effectiveness of the social worker in the school setting. First, it is congruent with the goals of social work in general. A program of student mediation is an effective vehicle for the promotion of mental health issues. Social workers are under an ongoing pressure to reach more students, and mediation helps to achieve this outreach goal.

Second, mediation also serves to increase general awareness in the school of the social worker's availability and effectiveness in program development. Such awareness is a prerequisite to encouragement of appropriate referrals of students for whom early interventions may be appropriate.

Third, the position of the social worker from a political perspective can be enhanced significantly by the implementation of a mediation program. The social worker's role is made easier once a position of relative indispensability is developed in the school system. Mediation is on the forefront of innovations compatible with a systems approach to school management, and school administrators, seeing their social worker on the cutting edge of innovation, may further consider their services essential to the effective administration of their school.

Fourth, the skills learned during mediation training, as well as the experience of mediation itself, have excellent carry-over value to other life situations involving dispute resolution. The experience of the authors has been that mediators do not leave these skills at school. They have found them useful in dealing with problems at home and in the community; and they use them regularly and, they report, effectively in off-campus settings.

Fifth, mediation is proactive. It serves to intervene and solve problems before disciplinary sanctions are required by the school. Consequently, a mediation program reduces suspensions, enhances student morale, and contributes to the overall positive operation of the school system.

Finally, mediators provide a significant service to the school. Mediation is serious business; the school runs better because of it. Mediators have a powerful experience in the building of their personal levels of self-esteem because they feel important to the school. Being important and doing an important job raise self-esteem as effectively as any activity the school can provide.

REFERENCES

Block, A. W. (ed.). 1983. *Effective schools: A summary of research*. Arlington, VA: Educational Research Service Press.

Fisher, R., and Ury, W. 1981. *Getting to yes: Negotiating agreement without giving in*. NY: Viking/Penguin Press.

Gallant, C. B. 1982. *Mediation in special education disputes*. Silver Spring, MD: National Association of Social Workers.

Germain, C. B. 1988. School as a living environment within the community. *Social Work in Education* 10(4).

Johnson, D. W., and Johnson, R. T. 1989. *Leading the cooperative school*. Edina: Interaction Book Company.

National School Safety Center. 1988. *Increasing student attendance: NSSC resource paper*. Malibu, CA: Pepperdine University Press.

Neighborhood Justice Center of Atlanta, Inc. 1982. *Dispute resolution in education*. The NJCA Mediation Model.

Rappoport, L. 1989. Entering the sacred: Prologue to a theory of transcendent consciousness. *Theoretical and Philosophical Psychology* 9(1):12–19.

Slavin, R. E. 1989. Research on cooperative learning. *Educational Leadership* 47(4): 52–54.

Viadero, D. 1988. Peer mediation: When students agree not to disagree. *Education Week*, May.

Wheelock, A. 1988. Strengthening dropout prevention: The role of school mediation programs. *The Fourth R: Newsletter of National Association for Mediation in Education*, 16.

CHAPTER 26

The No-Fault School: Understanding Groups— Understanding Schools

Joy Johnson[*]
Professor Emerita, Jane Addams College of Social Work,
University of Illinois at Chicago

Schools can be seen as complex organizations composed of groups. The education process takes place when loosely organized and often isolated groups of teachers interact with groups (called classes) of students within an administrative hierarchy. Surrounding these school-based groups are a wide variety of community organizations and families. Formal education clearly takes place in a multitiered social environment. The student is learning social skills concurrently with the academic content, and these skills are essential to satisfactory progress. In order to learn to function successfully in a setting almost entirely dominated by various group structures, essential learning must occur in the areas of communication, cooperation, consensus decision making, and democratic organizational structure in addition to the academic regimen.

This chapter examines the nature of group life in the education experience to discover how to use it constructively to create a more effective learning environment. Defining this experience adds another conceptual dimension to education from a social work perspective, and looking at the group process may assist in clarifying appropriate social work roles in these processes.

WHAT MAKES GROUPS WORK

I have consulted in numerous school systems with teachers, administrators, and pupil personnel team members about group issues. Usually I have been

---

[*]Revised and edited in collaboration with Shirley McDonald.

asked to assist with a group that was floundering. As I studied "what went wrong," I saw a pattern emerge that elucidated some of the factors that appear crucial to group performance. My thought was that if I could isolate the elements that were destructive, I might be able to formulate a conceptual structure of what makes groups work. Continuing in my attempt to move from what went wrong to how to make groups go right, I found my consultation moving from a problem-solving focus to a preventive one. For the past several years, I have been testing these formulations against actual groups—classroom and therapeutic, natural and formed—and have been able to find several consistent criteria for what it takes to make groups become cohesive, well-functioning units.

Perhaps the most important element in creating a positive group experience is the merging of purposes of why that group exists. The multiple goals of the various group members, of the group leader, and of the sponsoring school must be compatible. If these goals do not somehow mesh together, the group is doomed before it starts. That does not mean that the goals have to be the same, but they must be able to coexist. In one teachers' association there were some teachers who were power hungry, who needed to be recognized, who needed to be valued, and who very much wanted to take a strong leadership role to satisfy their personal needs. Although some teachers in that association looked for group cohesion and closeness with one another, others were interested in getting more pleasant working surroundings and higher salaries. These sets of goals, although very different, are compatible. They can exist together. One group may say to another, "Okay, you can have the power. We will help you feel important and significant if you also will keep our interests in mind."

Group composition is another important part of what makes groups work. Who are the members? How is the group composed? In a classroom group the composition frequently is arbitrary and you have little control. Understanding how the membership fits together is very important in any event. When you form groups yourself, either for therapeutic purposes or for task completion, you will want to think about some group process issues that will help you form efficient and compatible groups.

There are certain combinations of people that seem to work well together and others that do not. Before you compose a group you need to be aware of some general guidelines of composition. As you select your members, try to make sure that all of the basic maintenance roles are included—nurturer, subject changer, enabler, and leader. A group will not work well if everyone in the group tends to fulfill the same role. If you have a group of all leaders with no followers, that group is likely to be in a power struggle from beginning to end. If, on the other hand, you have a group of people who nurture a great deal but are not particularly strong leaders, people may feel good about each other but never get the task done.

There are some other basic issues with respect to composition for constructive group process. One is to try to avoid too many extremes; another is to try to avoid putting only one person from a particular category in a group. Let me explain what I mean. If I had a choice, I would never put just one poor child in a group of affluent children, nor just one black child in a group of white children, nor one girl in a group of boys, nor one slightly retarded child in a group of bright children. When one group member is quite different from the others, regardless of what the difference is, that person tends to be a built-in scapegoat and may get picked on or act out for the others. Whether you are composing a classroom, a therapeutic group, or a faculty committee, if you have a choice, try to find enough people who are representative of the various maintenance roles that are needed to form a helpful group and try to avoid setting up a situation that may inherently create one or more scapegoats.

There is another "golden rule" for forming a group in a school. Avoid putting people with similar problems together. This is true regardless of the type of group—whether it is a faculty committee or a therapeutic group of young people in a junior high school. If you put people with similar problems together, they will tend to integrate that problem as a group norm. Groups with members who have a variety of coping mechanisms greatly enrich the opportunities for members to view a variety of alternative behaviors. I was a member of a committee composed of people who all dealt with their frustrations by blaming the administration. We sat around and complained and nobody did anything to make it better. There was a dramatic change in that committee when we invited two people who were doers rather than complainers. They said, "Yes, you are right, it is intolerable, and what are we going to do about it?" This new, more active approach made all the difference in the world to the functioning of the committee.

Four Essential Qualities

Another consideration regarding what makes groups work is the issue of why, and when, people want to belong to a group. What are some of the qualities essential to voluntary participation in any group? What entices someone to decide to participate in group interaction? As I have studied groups, it has become clear that the qualities necessary for an individual to want to participate in a group are the very same qualities needed in a classroom for students to want to learn. These qualities are many and varied, and some differ from community to community and from person to person. Every socioeconomic and ethnic group represented in the schools with which I have worked has different expectations of the groups within their subculture and differing values for their members. However, there are four qualities that consistently are required for someone to want to participate in a group. The way these qualities are acted out may differ greatly, but the qualities themselves are universal.

Safety. For anyone to want to participate, the group needs to be a safe place. By that I mean emotionally and physically safe for everyone present. In a school where knives and guns are prevalent, it may not be physically safe to set foot in the classroom, or the school at all, and peoples' fears greatly inhibit learning. On the other hand, the fear within a classroom that is not emotionally safe also strongly inhibits learning and group participation. In any unsafe group, the goal moves from participation to survival, and the energies and efforts of the participants are focused to that end—survival. Many a teacher has said to me, "My only goal is to survive the rest of the school year." There are many reasons why a classroom or school may not be a safe place, emotionally or physically or both. This article attempts to help everyone who comes in contact with groups assist in making those groups safe.

You may think I am putting too much emphasis on the quality of safety, because adults do not need that much safety, especially emotional safety. You may feel that adults can take care of themselves. And yet I wonder what it would be like if you and I were sitting across from each other in a group session, I had encouraged you to be open, and then the first time you asked a question, I ridiculed you. Perhaps I could have said, "Boy, that was the dumbest question I have ever heard! Any more stupid questions?" That interaction might have caused you to get your dander up and fight back and say, "Hey, you can't talk like that to me!" My hunch is that you would do as I would have done—shut up and say to myself, "I better keep my mouth shut in this group; it is not safe to open it." Then, if I had a chance, I would probably leave at the first opportunity.

Another interesting dynamic about group safety is that if the group is not safe for everyone it is safe for no one. If I put you down, not only would the group feel unsafe for you, but for the other group members as well. They might think, "Forget it, I'm not going to take a risk either." This dynamic occurs in classrooms, faculty meetings, and groups of all kinds in schools. Time after time I have known safety to be a core issue.

Safety, or the lack of safety, passes not only from the teacher, leader, or facilitator to the group member, but also exists among the members themselves. If a bully in a group makes it unsafe for another member and if that is allowed to continue, the group becomes unsafe for everyone there, including the bully. If group members feel safe with one another, they protect one another from attack, from the leader or other sources. As a leader, therapist, teacher, or principal, whatever your role is in the school system, you need to help the school to be a safe place.

Something for you. Another dimension that makes one want to participate in a group is that the group provides something for all the members. If I am going to risk myself in my learning, in talking about myself, or in my teaching, there must be something in it for me. One of the first things that most people ask, whether they consciously think about it or not, is,

"What's in it for me? What do I get for making this investment?" In some classrooms what students get is teacher or parent approval or higher grades, and these certainly are of value. But there are additional things students can get out of learning. You may want to do some thinking about how you (being who you are) can help students make an investment in their learning. How can they get something back for themselves in addition to grades and approval? One of my prime goals as a teacher is to help each student find something that he or she can get excited about in whatever it is that I am teaching. This makes the learning itself inherently useful instead of merely a source of external recognition or rewards. I have what I call the "selfish approach" to learning and teaching. Everybody, including the teacher, ought to get something out of every learning experience.

That may be somewhat idealistic; there are courses, and some parts of most courses, that are not going to be exciting. Some material you have to learn just because you have to know it, and some content that is exciting to some students is boring to others. But, it is to be hoped, this is the exception to the rule. When the prevailing focus of a teacher is on motivating and exciting students about their learning, the more boring learning tasks do not loom as large. Other groups are also faced with unpleasant tasks at times, but you should not expect any member of a committee, any member of a therapeutic group, any member of a class, or anybody playing on the playground to participate constructively in the group unless there is something they get back for themselves; that is normal, natural, necessary, and, I think, kind of nice.

Something to contribute. Every person in every group should feel he or she has something to contribute. It is not enough to just take; a group member must feel that he or she has something to give. I vividly remember meeting with some high school students who had been in a treatment group for the majority of their junior year. As we reviewed at the end of the year what it was that made the group so successful in the eyes of the members, a consistent response (which each gave in his or her own way) was, "When I joined this group, I felt pretty crummy about myself, but when I found that I could be helpful to other people—could give advice and support when other people were hurting—I knew I wasn't as bad as I thought I was." This ability to give to other people turned out to be one of the prime curative factors in that group.

This is not necessarily the case in every group nor for all people. Many of you have had members in your group or class who did not seem to want to give. One teacher described two such students: "They don't want to give. They just think about themselves. They don't care about anybody else!" It is very difficult to work with people who appear to have this attitude, but it is important to find creative ways to help them to give, for them and for you. I worked with a group of delinquents who "ripped off" everybody and everything in sight and whose negative feelings about themselves and others led to their pretending they did not care about anything. When they were hired to manage a shelter for injured animals, this antagonistic attitude turned to one of deep concern. Discovery of their ability to give lessened their need to act out.

We have a responsibility as school personnel to see not only that our group participants get something for themselves, but also that everybody contributes something. Sometimes this is harder than seeing that everyone gets something, but it is even more important.

Someone cares. A final important quality is that every member in a group has to know that somebody cares whether he or she is there or not. As one teacher said, "There's nothing worse than being gone for a week with the flu and nobody noticing that you were gone." All of us need warm, caring relationships, both on and off the job, in and out of the classroom, whether we are teachers, administrators, or students. One of the things that makes it so hard for the young person in a classroom who is being made a scapegoat is that he feels that no one cares, and therefore he makes little investment in trying to get people to like him. Besides that, he probably does not like himself much either. My experience is that when caring can come through, when I am able to show a person who has no friends that I care, if indeed I do, then he has reason to think that he might be likable after all and may begin to care about himself, even just a little.

Striking a Balance

No group or class can always have all four qualities at one time. No class or group can always be safe, always have something in it for everyone, always help everybody contribute, and always help everyone feel cared for and significant. I have found, however, that when those qualities usually are present and the group is constructively functioning, during those rocky times when one or more qualities is missing, one of the others temporarily makes up the loss. In my own group treatment there were times when it was pretty scary, when it was not safe. At those times the caring that I experienced from the other members made that lack of safety temporarily manageable. Everyone has, at one time or another, sat through a boring, difficult lecture or class where there was absolutely nothing in it for you, but still you were required to be there. Perhaps you were able to tolerate it because you were sitting next to somebody you cared about with whom you exchanged complaining notes. I have gotten through many a faculty meeting or dull committee meeting by sitting with somebody I like.

Other Applications

Although this discussion has been related mostly to the classroom, the same dynamics are easily transferable to any other group within a school.

I wonder how many PTA presidents have thought of dealing with their dwindling attendance by asking all members to come to one meeting to discuss how to make it a more viable experience for everyone? How many principals, when things begin to go sour in the faculty, give the faculty the task of making it better for themselves? To do this, a principal runs the risk of getting honest feedback from the faculty about things he might be doing that get in the way of positive group functioning. (One of the problems of asking people what they think is that they might tell you.) My experience in a variety of settings shows that insistence on mutual assumption of responsibility and decision making is very important.

Your response to this discussion may well be, "It sounds very nice but what if it doesn't work? And what about the time that I get so angry I don't want to be rational?" These are good questions. You may want to find new ways to get yourself out of a bind you are in as well as try to stay out of the bind in the first place. As a teacher, I have my classes trained. If I temporarily lose control of myself or my feelings, or become irresponsible or irrational, the students not only let me know it, but they help me out. Even second graders can say, "Hey, Mrs. Johnson, you're yelling again." That can be a signal to me to take a look at what I am upset about. By sharing this with my class, I can then help them see what it is they are doing that gets me so angry. Then we can discuss what we can do about it to have a better day together.

A school is a system in which every individual who walks in the door ought to feel valued as a worthwhile human being. Too often, instead, people (students and faculty alike) feel that they are insignificant members of a huge bureaucracy. The groups of which you are a part contribute greatly to these positive and negative feelings. Your understanding of the dynamics and meaning of the things that happen in these groups is a key to making your life in school more satisfying.

Think about your school for a moment. Think of the number of groups that you are a part of, the number of different subgroups that you belong to, and think about what it does to you to be a part of these groups. Are there some groups in which you feel significant and valued? Are there others in which you feel frustrated and angry most of the time? When you close the door to your office, do you feel that the young people are expectant and excited about working with you? Or do you feel hostility as you close the door, both from you and from them? When you sit down in the faculty lunchroom, do you always sit with the same group of people? Do they make you feel valued and cared about? Are they people whom you trust? Can you take risks with them? Can you tell them where you "blew it" and still feel okay about yourself?

Now take a step back and look at your school as a whole. Which groups are functioning well? Which are having difficulty? What is it like to be in a faculty meeting in your school? A committee meeting? A curriculum planning meeting? A pupil personnel staffing? How are these groups functioning? What would you change if you could?

As you become more tuned into group dynamics, you will discover your power to help facilitate better group interaction. Every member of a group affects what is going on, whether he or she knows it or not. If you choose, you can play a conscious part in helping any group you are in to function in a more productive and satisfying way. You may also choose, as often as you like, to stay out of the group process and not try to help it function better. You may decide to protect yourself and avoid the pain of trying to interact. Or perhaps you do not know what would be most helpful. Whatever the reason, you have a choice once you understand what is happening within a group.

AN IDEAL SCHOOL

Knowing that it is an impossible one, let me share with you my dream of an ideal school. This dream has evolved over the course of ten years of consulting in different school districts and seeing some schools that function very well and others where the conflict and constant crises took so much time and energy that there was not much left over for teaching. My ideal school is a place where everyone's goal is to provide an environment in which growth and learning can take place, and where everyone who enters is respected for the contribution that he or she can make toward that goal. It is a school where people feel valued and significant and assume responsibility for helping others feel important. In the same way that I have advocated that school people work with students in cooperative ways, in this ideal school the principal respects the faculty, expects them to participate in the decision-making process, and freely shares with them his or her mistakes as well as his or her strengths. There is a mutual agreement that faculty will understand and support the principal's attempts to be a good administrator, in the same way they expect him or her to work with them regarding their strengths and weaknesses as teachers. If something goes amiss in this school, the parties involved meet together to figure out what went wrong and how they can work together to make it right.

The No-Fault School

This ideal school operates on what I would call a no-fault basis. The vast majority of schools I have visited are fault schools. In a fault school when something goes wrong, the important thing is to find somebody to blame. If there is a problem in the classroom, you try to find someone on whom to pin it. If you cannot find someone to blame, it might mean that there is something wrong with you, that it is your fault. Or perhaps the incident occurred because the principal did not give you enough support, so it is really his or her fault. This need to find fault that is prevalent in many schools is the essence of destructiveness when it comes to working cooperatively to provide a safe learning milieu.

In one high school where I was consulting, an incident occurred in which the fault finding progressed right down the line. A student made a remark that made the teacher extremely angry, and she threw the student out of class. Because she was so angry, the teacher immediately sent a "referral" down to the office requesting disciplinary action for that student. After class, the student came to the teacher, apologized for his behavior, and asked to be readmitted. Because this was a fault system, the teacher was in a bind. If she readmitted the student and withdrew the referral, she would be admitting that she had acted precipitously. Knowing how the vice principal had responded in the past to similar situations, she was afraid that he would judge her harshly. On the other hand, the teacher felt the student was genuinely sorry and deserved another chance. Not knowing what else to do, she let the student return to class and yet, feeling very guilty, allowed the referral to stand. The vice principal felt a responsibility to punish the young man in order to support the teacher, even though he felt the teacher was wrong. When I talked with the vice principal later about the incident and expressed my concern that the young person had been disciplined after the student and the teacher had already resolved the issue, he said, "Well, we have our eye on that teacher, and she may not have her contract renewed at the end of the year, but we have to support her in the meantime, even at the expense of the student."

It seems as if everybody lost and nobody won. Because the school environment did not permit mistakes, everybody got punished and everything that occurred was blamed on someone else. I wonder what might have happened if that same situation had taken place in a different school with a supportive environment? If the teacher had felt valued, she might not have lost control as quickly as she did over the insolence of the student. But if she had lost control and sent the referral prematurely, a supportive school system would have permitted her to go to the vice principal and say, "That student really got to me, but I don't think I want to continue with the referral. I'd like to work it out with him myself." That would have ended that administrative involvement and then she could have sat down with the student and talked with him about what had made her so angry. Instead of being punished, the student would have had to take responsibility for his own behavior and make plans to change the way he treated the teacher.

There is something about punishment that is positive and negative at the same time. On the one hand, particularly in a junior high school, some children need to have rules to test, to push against. For these situations, providing some form of repercussion may be helpful. On the other hand, punishment lets children "off the hook," and they may feel they do not have to assume responsibility for their behavior as long as they are willing to take the consequences.

I was amused one day when I walked into a junior high school and found a very angry principal walking up and down the hall among fifteen children who were sitting on the floor, writing fifty times each "I will not be tardy again." She had said that for every minute they were late they would have to write that sentence ten times. I found some young people outside plotting together about how many times they were willing to write that statement, so that they could be that many minutes late to school. One girl came in ten minutes late. She had written "I will not be tardy again" a hundred times at home so that she would have an extra ten minutes to finish watching a television show before she came to school. For her it was worth it.

You may think that behaving in this way is childish and irresponsible, and you may be right. But how many of us park in an illegal parking place because we are in a hurry, and it is worth paying the fine to have the convenience? I am not sure, but I think that kind of response to punishment is natural.

The School as a System—The Faculty as a Group

Because the tardiness in the junior high school in the above example was getting increasingly out of hand, I suggested to the principal that she inform the students that the punishment system was no longer in effect, and they would have to start coming to school on time. I also suggested that she ask each teacher to discuss with his or her class how frustrating it was to teachers when the students straggled in and to ask the students to assume responsibility for seeing that this did not continue to happen. With a great deal of skepticism, the principal agreed to try removing the punishment for students who were late and asked them to see that they came to school on time. Obviously, I would not have included this example if it had not worked so well. Within three days, instead of having fifteen students tardy, there were two or three with some very legitimate excuses, and peer pressure from class members helped these students get to school on time in the future. The fault system of schools, although it is a natural part of many bureaucracies, is not conducive to creating responsibility for behavior.

My ideal no-fault school is one where people share the excitement, planning, and responsibility. Students and faculty are free to make mistakes, and the expectation of the group members is that when someone makes a mistake, others will try to help, rather than sit back and blame. This attitude starts with the administration, and the sharing process of administrators and faculty needs to be two-way. A principal ought to be free to help faculty members who make errors in judgment and at the same time expect the staff to assist her or him if she or he gets into difficulty.

There are constructive ways to develop this mutual support system within a faculty group. An outside consultant is very helpful, but not essential. Principals or other administrators or school social workers can implement this process themselves. The no-fault system starts with the assumption that everybody who comes into the school is entitled to have a good day. Then the question is, what are some of the things that can help this come about? One principal asked this question on the first faculty institute day. In small groups the faculty was requested to draw up several sets of goals. One set included broad school goals. Another set of goals was for the faculty—what would make school a good place for them? Another set involved goals for the students—what is it that we want our students to learn? As the administrator helped the faculty outline these goals, she tried to assure that the four essential qualities for voluntary participation (safety, something for them, something to contribute, and someone caring) were all included, not only that day but in the future goal setting. These are just as important and significant for faculty and administration as for students. After she helped the faculty outline some basic goals and they decided what type of environment they wished the school to provide, they moved toward a plan of implementation by posing several questions:

1. What can we do together to develop these qualities?
2. What role do we want the principal to play?
3. What can each of us do to facilitate the desired outcome?
4. Knowing that it is going to take some time and that there is much that must be undone and begun, where should we start?

As these questions were discussed, the faculty developed a commitment to work toward a no-fault approach—a freedom to make mistakes as long as you learn from them—and a general agreement that faculty, staff, and students can support one another. This required some reworking of the old group norms that had operated in the faculty and had prohibited the openness discussed above.

Many faculties have norms, such as "Always be polite, even if you don't mean it," or "Never show a colleague how you really feel." These norms usually develop in a fault school where much of the complaining and arguing goes on behind people's backs. I can go into a school and in about thirty minutes tell you whether it is a fault or no-fault school. One of my prime diagnostic sources is the faculty lounge. In the faculty lounge I can see whether people are listening to one another, showing mutual concern, offering suggestions to teachers with problems, or whether it is a place where a great deal of nonproductive complaining and griping occurs with nobody offering any suggestions or attempting to make anything better. In the latter situation, if a teacher does something to make another teacher angry, the problem is rarely dealt with openly. The offended teacher usually goes to someone else to complain. How the faculty handles disagreements with one another and with the administration is an important indicator of their ability to function cooperatively as a group.

I am not saying that all faculty members have to like one another, socialize together, or be comrades and confidants. That is neither possible nor desirable. There will always be subgroups of people who like each other better than other people, and who trust each other more than the rest of the faculty; however, it is extremely important that these natural social friendships do not interfere with an overall atmosphere of mutual acceptance in the school.

The ladder concept. Once you feel you can make a mistake and still be valued as a teacher, you may want to think about developing the "ladder concept" in your school. The ladder concept gives each person in the school an imaginary ladder that can be used to help colleagues get down if they get stuck "up a tree." I believe that working with human beings is an extremely emotion-laden endeavor and that it is not possible to be a good teacher without sometimes having emotions take over. The times when I temporarily lose control of myself are the times when I would love to have somebody there with a ladder to help me get down out of the tree. That person must be someone who is not caught up in the incident, and who cares enough about me to see that I do not get myself further out on the limb than I already am.

A fourth-grade teacher was out of control, temporarily, in her fury at a girl in her class. This girl, Sara, had been irritating, insolent, and difficult to work with from the first day of school. The teacher, Mrs. S., had tried everything she could to reach Sara.

Sara not only seemed to be unreachable, but also able to make Mrs. S. feel inadequate. Sara's message was, "I'm not responding because you are not a good teacher," and there was a part of Mrs. S. that believed this, although the girl was wrong. The last straw came one day when Sara was late from recess, and Mrs. S. looked up as she came in asked her why she was late. Sara's defensive response was, "There was no reason to come to class—nothing interesting ever happens here." The teacher lost control, took Sara out in the hall, and started screaming at her. This strong emotional response was a very honest and natural one under the circumstances. How many teachers could have taken this all year without at some point letting it get to them?

A teacher who had been nearby realized that Mrs. S. was temporarily out of control and that she needed a ladder to get down out of her tree before she said or did something she would regret. Because this was a no-fault school, the teacher who was not upset was able to extricate Mrs. S. from the situation by going in and saying, "It looks like Sara has really gotten to you. Why don't you let me take her off your hands for a while?" This removed Sara from the wrath of Mrs. S. and gave each of them a chance to calm down. The helping teacher, the one with the ladder, walked off with Sara and without having to punish her or bawl her out was able to calmly comment, "You really made Mrs. S. furious. Is that what you wanted to do?" She then talked for a few minutes with Sara about what her goal was in relation to that teacher. After their talk, Sara came and sat in her classroom for a while until Mrs. S. sent word that she was ready to have the girl return.

This approach differs vastly from one where a teacher, trying to be supportive by not interfering, lets another teacher go on until real damage is done; or a colleague attacks the child in a false need to protect the angry teacher. The ladder concept is possible only when faculty members agree that these outbursts are normal and natural, and act as helping agents rather than judges. The ladder concept can also work among students in a classroom. Children can learn to help one another, but the tone must be set within the faculty. The guideline is: the person who is in control is the one responsible for helping make the situation better. As faculty members master this approach, they can educate their students to do the same thing—to carry ladders to help both students and teachers down from "trees" when they begin to do something that could be destructive to themselves or somebody else.

Conflict management. Even in an ideal school there will, of course, be conflicts. Some of these conflicts occur among subgroups; some of them may be theoretical in nature, others may be much more practical. Some conflict is healthy for a school and a good exchange of ideas and suggestions can be helpful. If conflicts are resolved in a supportive way, or there is consensus (or even agreement not to reach consensus), the school can exist with its conflicts without real difficulty. If, on the other hand, the conflicts are driven underground and acted out rather than talked out, there may be real problems with communication. If one conflict cannot be discussed openly, it is difficult for any conflict to be resolved. But because working in schools is emotionally laden, it is not unusual for a faculty not to want to have to deal with conflict. I talked with a teacher who said, "I just can't stand any more hassles. When two faculty members begin to argue, I want to get up and leave." I can certainly understand how she feels, and yet if a norm develops in that school that it is not acceptable to air differences, then the disagreements will be handled covertly, which will create another problem.

One district in which I consult has two high schools, each of which resolved the same conflict in a different way. The issue was whether or not to have a "smoking room" for students. Faculty differed greatly on the issue of students smoking in school. Some felt that smoking was dangerous and that to allow it was setting a bad example and was extremely destructive for students. Others felt that some young people were going to smoke anyway and rather than drive it into the washrooms, they would like to provide a smoking area on the condition that the students agreed (and kept the agreement) to confine all smoking to that one area. One of the reasons that this was a loaded issue was because there was conflict among the faculty themselves about whether or not they should smoke in school. Some teachers complained, "We can't even go into the teachers' lounge because the smoke is so heavy we have trouble breathing!" Others said, "Smoking is part of life and we ought to accept it."

In one of the two schools an agreement was reached that was satisfactory to everybody—something that everyone could live with—even though there were parts of the agreement that nobody liked. In the other school, a decision was made based on strong opinions that were expressed by a few vocal faculty members. Three-fourths of the faculty did not really agree; they were hesitant to challenge the other faculty, so they gave in rather than fight for their own beliefs. If I am pushed into acquiescing to a rule with which I really disagree, the likelihood that I will enforce it actively is not very great. Even though I know I should, I tend not to. In the school where the faculty really worked together to find a solution with which everybody in the school could live, all of the faculty supported the decision. In the other school, the solution worked only sporadically. Some faculty closed their eyes when they found children smoking and others became extremely rigid. There was no cooperative enforcement of the policy that had been developed in that school.

Now, exploration of the question of permitting smoking in school or anywhere else could easily fill another whole book. The point here is that the way the decision was made and the willingness and ability of the faculty to support it were inalterably intertwined.

THE VALUE OF DIVERSITY

This leads to the whole issue of how a school can accept and use differences among faculty to strengthen the program. One of the things that is exciting to me about some faculties is their diversity. I would hate to be in a school where everybody was the same and where norms were developed that said that we should all operate in the same mold. In my ideal school each faculty member would have some strengths and concerns of his or her own that would be known to and respected by other faculty members. Each faculty member would be free to develop his or her program, to utilize strengths, and to fit concerns within the broad overall curriculum and school goals. There would be a minimum of expectations for faculty members to act in the same manner. Of course fundamental school rules and state laws are mandates that all teachers have to enforce, but there are many rules that can differ from class to class. There is no reason why every classroom should have the same rules; in fact, there are contraindications for that structure.

Insisting that all teachers follow the same rules inhibits their freedom to teach in ways that are comfortable to them. Students know when a person is enforcing a rule in which he or she does not believe, and it can create mistrust in some students. On the other hand, students are able to adapt to different rules in different classrooms. They are not only aware of, but also responsive to, contrasting requirements of teachers.

One seventh-grade teacher said, "I know there is nothing wrong with chewing gum, but there is something about seeing all those young people with their mouths going all the time that drives me up a wall. I just can't stand it." Once she felt free enough to have her own particular bias, she was able to say to her students, "It may not make sense to you, but gum chewing is so annoying to me that when I see it I can't teach. I think more about your mouths going than I do about the subject, so in my class you can't chew gum." Of course, the students' immediate response was, "But Mr. Jones lets us chew gum in his class!" This teacher, fortunately, felt comfortable enough with herself, and Mr. Jones, to say, "Marvelous! I'm delighted that Mr. Jones lets you chew gum in his class. Chew all the gum you want there, but not here." It is this acceptance of yourself and your own expectations and desires in a no-fault school that frees you to set different rules for behavior in your classroom than there are in others. That is perfectly all right. What is not okay is for you to try to get *all* teachers to outlaw gum chewing because it is offensive to *you*. That is where schools run into difficulty. There are certain behaviors that some faculty expect from their students but others do not, and faculty members ought to have permission from one another as well as from the administration to formulate with their classes their own rules, based on the needs of the faculty member and desires of the students.

A CHALLENGE

Take a step back now and think about your school. What goes on in the teachers' lounge? What expectations do faculty have of one another and of the principal? What kind of support system exists? Do you have a desire to get away from backbiting and work toward mutual support? Is it possible for disagreements to be aired between the people who disagreed rather than pushed underground? These are all important questions and challenges. Take a look at your faculty as a group. How do you relate to one another, and how does the administration relate to you?

Such an analysis may seem like an overwhelming and insurmountable task. You might begin by asking yourself, "If I could walk into school tomorrow and have one thing different in the way the faculty relates to one another and to the administration, what would it be?" If you could only have one change, where would you start? Now think about whether you can go to school tomorrow and begin to effect that one change.

THE PROBLEM-SOLVING PROCESS: YOUR ALLY

One of the principles of "Human Education" is that children, teachers, principals, and school social workers are important human beings. Each is unique, special, and very human. Many schools give permission to children to be human, including the right to err. How many schools, however, see the teacher as having the right to make mistakes? One teacher bitterly stated, "I spend all day accepting both the strengths and weaknesses of the children in my class. I teach them, nurture them, value them, and help them learn from their mistakes. When is someone going to care about me? Why can't I make mistakes as the children do? I'm human too!"

Teachers do make mistakes, of course, as do administrators, psychologists, social workers, consultants, and all other people. The very human qualities that cause errors are the same ones that make teachers so responsive to the children. The ability to become involved with the children you serve is a great strength, and yet it leaves you vulnerable to being hurt, to letting your feelings get in the way, to err.

The problem-solving process is not for anyone who is perfect. It was designed to be used by those of us who make more mistakes than we choose to admit. Basically, it is an approach to problem resolution to use when difficulties occur between you and any other person or group of people within the school. The process assumes that most real problems are two-way, that both you and the other party are responsible. This means that you also have the power to use this process to change the way things are, to resolve the problem in some way or another.

Define the Problem

The first step in the problem-solving process is to define the various parts of the problem as you perceive them. What is wrong? What happened? How did it happen? How do you feel about what happened? What did it do to you as a person to have had this experience? You need to try to get in touch not only with the content of the problem and the process of how it happened, but also with your personal response to it. Then you can move beyond that to questions about the other people involved. What do you think happened to them personally? How do they feel?

One teacher kept a whole class after school because they had become "smart alecky" and defiant. Usually she could handle such an occurrence and settle the children down without becoming punitive. But this particular day she was feeling rotten physically, she had had a disagreement with her husband before school, and the material that she had carefully ordered for her lesson plan had not arrived. The combination of all of these aggravations, plus the obnoxious behavior of some of the children in the class, made her feel furious, sorry for herself, frustrated, and helpless. She was certainly entitled to those feelings. Her affective response was very real and relevant to the situation. But she felt bad about the way she had blamed and punished the children and asked me to help her understand what had happened. This incident had brought out a side of her that she did not like very much.

Sometimes keeping children after school can be helpful, but in this instance the teacher perceived it as her attempt to get even because the children had made her feel bad. When I encouraged her to take a look at the problem in its entirety, supporting her feelings both from within and without the classroom as being important, we were then able to move to another question. How could she help the children understand what had happened and regain a nonpunitive attitude in the classroom?

Accept Your Feelings and Fantasies

The second step of the problem-solving process is to accept your feelings and allow yourself to imagine what you would like to do. When the teacher was so angry, for instance, what would she have liked to do? Clearly, in this case, a part of the teacher wanted to get even because the pupils had hurt her feelings. Her desire to get even was perfectly natural. Many teachers, when they have been hurt, have vivid fantasies of methods of retaliation and relish them! Having fantasies is usually harmless yet potentially very helpful—it is what you do that matters.

I would like to digress a moment to talk about the tremendous therapeutic value for people within a school system of permitting themselves to have wild fantasies about ways to cope with disquieting situations. Fantasies do not cost anything, do not hurt, and can help a teacher experience his or her own legitimate feelings. Perhaps the teacher in the above illustration, had she allowed herself, would have fantasized some wicked way to get even with those demons in her class. One teacher used to enjoy fantasizing hanging pupils from the coat hooks in the closet. She never actually did this, but the fantasy helped her through some rough times with difficult children. Do not be afraid to have negative fantasies as well as positive ones and to allow yourself to experience your feelings.

Stop

Once you know what the problem is, once you know how you feel about it and have allowed yourself a fantasy, stop. Just stop. This is the third step in the problem-solving process. That pause gives you a chance to regain your equilibrium. Then, without giving up the relevance of your feelings, try to move beyond them and think about what it is that you would really like to have happen. What kind of rapport would you like to have with those young people? What kind of a relationship do you really want with your faculty if you are a principal? And in that stopping process, when your feelings are very evident and appreciated (but put aside for a few moments), you can set specific goals for what you would like to have happen next.

A word of caution. The goals you set must be limited enough so that they are attainable if you act in a different way. You cannot take a child who makes you furious when he continues to say how much he hates school and have as your goal to make him love school. This obviously is not realistic. But you may very well be able to take a small piece of that unrealistic goal and say, "Okay, if he hates school and I want him to like it, I'd like to start with finding out if we can have one good experience together in the classroom. Can we have a good day, or a good lesson, any one time that both of us would enjoy to set the tone for other things to come?"

Develop a Plan of Action

After you have set your limited goal, you then need to move to the fourth step, which is to develop a plan of action to attain that goal. Ask yourself, "If my goal is to help this youngster have a positive experience with me and for me to enjoy him, what are some of the things I can do to help that come about?" This is the time when you may want to pick up those feelings that you put aside in the "stop" phase and consider whether there is some way to use those feelings in a way to achieve your goal. Your plan of action should include helping the other people involved understand some of the things they did that upset you and what you can do to improve things together.

You, for example, in your anger and frustration at the boy who hates school might take him aside and share your frustration with him. Without blaming him, you can let him know that you are frustrated and that you know he must be too. Together you can develop a plan to try something new. Is it possible to have a good morning tomorrow? What could each of us do to enjoy our morning? This conversation might lead to some partialized, workable goals, agreeable to both student and teacher. The teacher who is so angry with her class that she becomes punitive may be able to use her anger in a helpful way. She might tell the class how angry she is, not blaming them, but as a way to get them involved. She can then ask them how they feel. What would they like to be different? After this mutual sharing of feelings, the students and teacher can put together what each of them can do to change the situation, or be ready for it if it begins to happen again.

Develop a Built-In Contingency Plan

The fifth step in the problem-solving process is what I call the "escape hatch." Suppose you get in touch with your feelings, you stop, you set a goal, you make a plan of action, and it falls flat. That is always a risk, so your next step is to ask, prior to putting your plan of action to work, "What if . . . ?" What if the plan does not work? What if the child does not respond? What if I cannot control my feelings? In this way you build in a contingency plan, which you can hold in reserve for use as necessary (as you would take a spare tire on an auto trip in case you need it).

Even if your plan of action does not work out the way you had originally intended, this contingency plan is a means by which most of your problem solving can be in some way successful. You will find as you begin to use this model that, in most instances, some of its methods work and some do not, and your contingency plan may help you cope with any negative outcomes.

Postpone Action

This problem-solving model works best when you are aware enough of your own feelings that you can creatively and spontaneously go through the process, which may take anywhere from thirty seconds to thirty minutes. There will be times, however, when your feelings are too intense, when you have been hurt too deeply, when you care too much to use this framework at the time. You may be too angry to care what the child thinks at that moment. You may be too hurt by another teacher to be able to understand how she feels. These are the times when the process needs to be put aside for a while. At these moments, the best and most helpful thing you can do is to acknowledge to yourself and to the people you are working with that you feel too intensely to make a decision right now about anything. That temporary inability to act is okay. In fact, when you feel that intensely, it is best not to act until things are in better perspective for you.

One faculty member, who had been called filthy names by a group of angry students, felt she had to act. She had tried very hard to reach these young people, and their abusive language hurt and upset her so much that she knew that to talk with them at that point would not be helpful to her or to the students. Instead, she said, "Kids, right now my feelings are so strong that I can't talk to you without saying some things I might be sorry I said. You've hurt me deeply, and we need to take a look at this and see what we're going to do about it. But I can't do it now. Come back after school, all four of you, and let's all sit down and see if we can figure out together what happened and how we can keep this from happening again. I don't like being hurt and I don't think you do either."

Not even that amount of objectivity showed a great deal of ability on the part of the teacher to share her feelings in a helpful way. Many of us cannot even say that much. We may just have to say, "Go away right now, I can't talk to you. Come back after school." Or, "I'll talk to you tomorrow." There are many ways a teacher or principal can create "cooling off time."

Sometimes it helps to ask the group of young people to write down what they think happened, using the time that they are writing as space to recoup, to get in touch with your feelings, and to get back into the problem-solving process.

Evaluate the Process

It is an impossible task to understand all of the things that go on in groups and also keep in touch with your own feelings and desires so as to be able to always use yourself in a helping way. Indeed, if you must succeed in order to feel good about your interventions, if they must work out the way you planned, then you may be frequently disappointed. In my own work in the schools with faculty and administrators, I have discovered that in order for this problem-solving approach to work, I have to change the way I evaluate myself. I used to evaluate my decisions and actions based on how successful I was at getting the outcome I desired. If noise was a problem in my class, I evaluated my success as a teacher by how quiet I was able to get the children to be. I do not do that anymore. Now I evaluate myself, not by the specific outcome, but by how much I am able to help the students in my class and myself find some common goal that all of us can support. This plan may not be the same as one I might develop on my own, but it is usually more successful because it was created by all of us together. I must, then, change my usual investment from the *end result* to the *process by which the result takes place*.

There are times, of course, when the end result becomes crucial and the process much less important. These are times when safety is involved, when prompt obedience and response is needed, or when the outcome is particularly important to the teacher or principal. If you are primarily a process person who lets your staff, students, or therapeutic group participate in the problem-solving process, the times that you have to say, "This is what it must be, you must follow me now," the group members will usually do so because they know you would not ask if it was not important. Because in the past they have not needed to act out against your authority, they probably will not need to now.

A further dimension involves how I evaluate myself overall in my role in school. As always, my prime measure is what people learn in an objective sense. But in other ways, I find I have to evaluate myself differently than I used to. I no longer can judge myself as a teacher by how perfect I am and how few mistakes I make. Instead, I evaluate myself based on how responsive I was to the class or to the staff. How well was I able to hear their point of view? How able was I to facilitate the respect for each other's rights, both theirs and mine? If I got into a power struggle, how quickly was I able to perceive that I was in a conflict with a student or students or other staff? How able was I to accept my piece of the power struggle?

How willing was I to be flexible so that it could be resolved? All of these questions are relevant to successful use of the problem-solving process in your work within a school system.

CONCLUSION

The roles of the school social worker, the teacher, the principal, the school secretary, the janitor, and the librarian are all different, but they all work together for and through one another to make the education process work, each contributing in his or her own unique way. When they do act, it is no longer a single role, but a cooperative effort whose success or failure will not be so much dependent on the talents of each person, but on their ability to interact and to work with each other. This is the quality about schools that is most often missed and, when missed, can lead to the breakdown of parts of, or all of, the process. The holistic perspective of the social worker can often make a more positive interaction possible and develop a living environment that can allow that which each person has to offer to be nurtured and supported.

CHAPTER 27

Analyzing the Organizational Context of Schools

Edith M. Freeman
Professor, and Chair of Clinical Practice Sequence, University of Kansas, Lawrence; Editor in Chief, *Social Work in Education*

A lack of formal knowledge about organizational theory on the part of many school social workers may affect the extent to which a systems approach develops in this practice area. In 1977, a study by Meares noted a shift in school social work away from the traditional casework approach toward systems-change models or those involving school-community relations.[1] The same study indicated that during this transition period, school social workers continued to focus on the individual student without placing sufficient emphasis on (1) identifying target groups of students who may be at risk for problems or (2) changing adverse conditions in the school or community that affect those problems.

Even when school social workers adopt a socioecological rather than a medical model perspective, they may not have the knowledge and skills necessary for doing the kind of critical analysis of the internal operations of the school and its components that is consistent with this perspective. This perspective is based on systems theory and the assumption that dysfunctional role performance occurs because of a misalignment between students' needs and the resources available in the environment.[2] School social workers are usually skilled in assessing the student, the family situation, and some relevant components of the school (such as the teacher's attitude toward the student), but they may be less skilled generally in knowing how to analyze the school itself as an organization and how to integrate that kind of analysis with the results of the student-familial assessment for developing an appropriate plan of action.

In addition to a lack of knowledge about organizational theory, other

---

SOURCE: Reprinted with permission from *Social Work in Education*. Vol. 7, No. 3, 1985. Copyright 1985. National Association of Social Workers, Inc.

complex interrelated issues may hinder this gradual and necessary shift away from using the traditional casework approach or clinical perspective. These include professional issues, such as how school social workers define their roles in this practice setting, and school context issues, such as role conflicts among interdisciplinary team members and demands for accountability for all professional schools. They also include some broad socioeconomic and political issues, such as inflation, which have resulted in decreased funding for support services and for other aspects of education programs.[3] Some of these issues have become priorities for school social workers because they directly affect their survival in this practice setting. Pressures related to organizational survival have made it more difficult for social workers in schools to be consistent in their attempts to analyze the effects that the organization itself can have on students' adjustment problems. Additional knowledge about organizational theory can help school social workers understand the school as an organization and the manner in which these issues and the needs of students are affected by the organization.

The primary purpose of this article is to describe a procedure for conducting an organizational analysis of the school and the school social work role at a building level.[4] This procedure focuses attention on positive and negative factors that may affect students' school adjustments, and it can be used in conjunction with student-familial assessments when appropriate. The need for school social workers to become skilled in this kind of analysis will be discussed, with reference to the literature on organizational theory. Finally, the discussion will deal with the kinds of special circumstances in which such a procedure could be used effectively in collaboration with other school professionals, and ways to plan for individual and organizational changes.

THE ORGANIZATIONAL CONTEXT OF SCHOOLS

Two categories of literature are particularly relevant to an understanding of the organizational context of schools. First, there are numerous research and theoretical articles on general organizational theory and systems change. A second category consists of articles focused specifically on organizational theory and change within the school context at a broad level. The following brief review of some of this literature will illustrate how it is relevant to and necessary for effective school social work practice.

Several articles on general organizational theory document the need for all professionals to understand the dynamics of organizations in which they are employed. For example, Resnick and Patti discuss the phenomenon of goal displacement "wherein institutions tend to become preoccupied with their own maintenance and survival over time so that their social purposes are replaced by latent goals such as protection of jurisdiction and program continuity."[5] Additionally, Hage and Aiken warn that practitioners should be sensitive to some of the personality characteristics of key individuals in organizations—such as their attitudes toward change.[6]

Goal displacement can occur in schools as it does in other organizations. For example, a principal may not want special education classes in the school because the students involved would not "fit in" with other students in the regular education program. The principal's goal may be to maintain the current achievement level among students and the standards of success in the building. This ignores the real purpose of schools: meeting the diverse needs of a wide range of students. If school social workers are aware of goal displacement as a common organizational phenomenon, they can better understand how some principals can focus more on program success than on the needs of the students for whom those programs were developed. They can engage a principal in a nonthreatening discussion about some of the pressures that encourage focus on program success and maintenance, and suggest ways to cope with some of those pressures.

Green notes that some professionals experience conflicts in balancing organizational/administrative needs against the needs of students because they go to polar extremes in their bureaucratic and professional orientations, identifying primarily with either the organization or the profession.[7] Those who are predominantly bureaucratically oriented give primacy to agency policies and procedures, whereas those with primarily a professional orientation give primacy to professional values, norms, and expectations. In the previously described example, school social workers with primarily bureaucratic orientations might misread clues that the principal and other school staff are resistive to mainstreaming special education students, and might not be able to help them to deal with their attitudes about those kinds of important changes.

School social workers with primarily professional orientations might magnify the conflicts within themselves and the organizational conflicts by labeling the principal as uncaring and unprofessional. This kind of attitude toward principals tends to set up an adversarial situation and limits the amount of collaborative problem solving that could be possible. In contrast, professionals with high professional and high bureaucratic orientations tend to experience minimal conflicts in organizations.

Hage and Aiken relate the rate of organizational change, as measured by the introduction of new programs, to four organizational characteristics.[8] They hypothesize that the rate of program change is positively related to job satisfaction and the degree of complexity or specialization and negatively related to the degree of centralization and formalization in an organization. School settings contain some conflicting conditions in relation to their vulnerability to organizational changes based on this assumption.

In the second category of articles—organizational theory and change related specifically to school settings—several authors stress the importance of school social workers involvement in organizational changes. For example, Steiner indicates that the question is not whether social workers in schools want to engage in school politics, since they are involved by virtue of being in schools, but whether they will do so in a responsible and well-planned manner. He also notes that many school social workers do not receive professional training that adequately prepares them for the realities of the schools' organizational dynamics and politics. Steiner proposes an interdisciplinary group planning procedure for handling problems at the building level that requires the social worker to consider whether the participants have a traditional, "illness," or socioecological perspective on problem etiology and resolution.[9]

Except for Steiner's article and others related to school climate analysis, most of the articles in this category focus on organizational theory and the implementation of changes in schools at district and state levels without much focus on the building level. For example, Meares's study focuses on how social work goals were attained within a given system. She found that the 269 school social workers in her study listed leadership and policy making seventh in importance among nine factors.[10] Assessing the child's problem was ranked first. Meares notes that these rankings emphasize continued use of the traditional casework approach and indicate a lack of understanding about how these two different activities are equally important to students' adjustment within the school's organizational context.

Barbaro, along with Smith and the present author, discussed the need for school social workers to understand models or procedures for decision making at higher administrative levels through the functions of district, state, and federal officials. This perspective requires knowledge of how input groups support and make demands on decision makers. Decision makers include district superintendents, boards of education, and commissioners of education. The groups that control inputs to these decision makers include interest groups; appointed community advisory groups; local, state, and federal government officials; and members of the media.[11]

> From this perspective, the [education] system is seen as being pluralistic and highly competitive, which suggests that politically astute social workers need not passively accept decisions but instead may help to shape them by allying themselves with politically active input groups and individuals.[12]

This also suggests that decision makers may have the authority to make decisions and shape policies, but they need the support of these input groups to maintain a stable organizational environment for themselves and to fulfill their stated objectives.

Although the articles described in this review contain essential information on organizational theory, some require some generalization to the specific context of schools and school social work practice whereas others require translation of goals for organizational changes at the broadest levels to specific activities at the building level. Furthermore, some of these articles describe procedures for analyzing components of schools, but none propose procedures for analyzing the complete organizational contexts. Therefore, additional discussion is needed on procedures for a systematic analysis of the total organizational context—for analyzing both the dynamics at the building level and the impact that dynamics at these broader levels have on the school's organizational context.

A PROCEDURE FOR ORGANIZATIONAL ANALYSIS IN SCHOOLS

To be useful for analyzing the organizational context of schools, a procedure must provide a framework for collecting and analyzing data in an orderly and systematic manner. The establishment of such a framework requires (1) a clear statement of the purpose for using the procedure, (2) a description of the procedure's components, and (3) a statement about how the procedure is to be used, under what specific circumstances, and by whom. Clarifying these three points can enable this particular procedure to be used effectively by school social workers.

Purpose

The purpose for using this procedure is threefold. First, it should assist the school social worker in identifying the building's organizational dynamics that can affect students' school adjustments. Second, the procedure should help them develop a plan of action for resolving problems related to the adjustment process of students. Finally, the procedure should help the school social worker and other school staff monitor any progress made in implementing the plan of action.

Components of the Procedure

The framework for this procedure consists of a face sheet and four major components. The face sheet requires certain important background information about the school involved, including (1) the racial-ethnic and socioeconomic background of students assigned to the school, (2) the racial-ethnic backgrounds of the school's staff, (3) the number of nonprofessional and professional staff, (4) the grade levels and types of education programs provided in the school (regular or special education classes), (5) the amount of time that the school social worker spends in the building, and (6) a description of certain physical, social, and political aspects of the surrounding community, such as its physical appearance.

The four major components cover (1) school policies, (2) school relations and environment, (3) school social work role, and (4) data collection; each component is subdivided into sections. (See table 1.) Each section within the first three components contains from seven to fifteen separate items

TABLE 1 Components of Procedure for Organizational Analysis

I. School policies component
   A. School practices: rules and enforcement of rules
   B. Instructional program: curriculum, instructional methods, extent of flexibility and creativity allowed
   C. Extracurricular program
II. School relations and environment component
   A. Staff-student interaction
   B. Staff-parent interaction
   C. Student-student interaction
   D. Staff-staff interaction
   E. School-community relations
   F. Physical environment
III. School social work role component
   A. School social work practice
   B. School social work interactions and communications
IV. Data collection component
   A. Data analysis
   B. Plan of action

---

in statement form, which will be rated for veracity by respondents. The items touch on a range of potential problem areas. For example, in the first two components there are items that relate to creativity and adequacy of instructional programs, how decisions are made about the school's operation and who has input into those decisions, the extent to which racial and sexist discriminatory practices exist, clarity and consistency in rule enforcement, how new students in the school are responded to, communication between members of the school and community, and the extent to which the educational needs of teachers are being met.

Items in the third component are shown in table 2. They focus on resources available to school social workers as well as their abilities to use both those resources and their practice skills effectively. This component also focuses on their understanding of organizational issues that are important in the change process, such as the need for periodic contact with district administrators, the need to share the goals for social work services in the school with the decision makers at that level, and the need to communicate effectively with all school personnel regardless of their racial-ethnic background, sex, age, and philosophy.

The data collection component requires that data from the other three components be analyzed by identifying the strengths and problem areas within the organization. The problem areas are then prioritized by identi-

TABLE 2 Some Examples of Items Included in the School Social Work Role (Component III) of the Organizational Analysis Procedure[a]

A. *School Social Work Practice*
   The social worker:
   1. Communicates to others both behaviorally and verbally the role of the school social worker.
   2. Explores opportunities to interact with students who have not been referred for service, in addition to those who have.
   3. Communicates effectively with all school personnel regardless of race, sex, age, philosophy.
   4. Meets with the principal on a regular basis.
   5. Has periodic contacts with district administrators (policymaking committees, problem-focused conferences, etc.)
   6. Is an advocate for students.
   7. Has adequate space to work with students individually and in groups.

B. *School Social Work Interactions and Communication*
   The social worker:
   1. Shares goals for social work services in the school with decision makers in the school.
   2. Explores opportunities for preventive problem solving by identifying target groups of students at risk for problems in addition to accepting and servicing referrals on students.
   3. Communicates effectively with parents.
   4. Is knowledgeable about community resources and community individuals who can be effectively involved in the school's operation.
   5. Encourages students to refer themselves for services or to "walk in" for discussion of their concerns.
   6. Is frequently used as a consultant by teachers, principals, and other school staff in identifying resources, developing programs, and providing staff development.
   7. Uses a variety of strategies and techniques when working with students.

[a]For each numbered item, the respondent is asked to indicate one of the following ratings for both "What Is" and "What Should Be": (1) almost always, (2) frequently, (3) occasionally, (4) almost never, or (5) not applicable. For a sample rating, see table 3.

fying those with the highest discrepancy scores (that is, those showing the greatest differences between what is and what should be). Table 3 lists the actual steps that should be taken in the data analysis component. A plan of action should be developed based on this analysis. Table 1 lists all of the areas that should be included in an effective plan of action.

Use of the Procedure

If this procedure is to be used effectively, it is important to clarify who should initiate its use and under what circumstances, who should complete

TABLE 3 Steps in Data Analysis

Data Collection Work Sheet

STEP 1: Compute and list the discrepancy for each item by subtracting the number circled in column 2 ("What Should Be") from the number circled in column 1 ("What Is"). The difference is the discrepancy. In this case, a significant discrepancy would be 2 or higher. Ignore any 5s (not applicable); any negative numbers that occur as a result of subtraction should be treated as if they were positive numbers.

EXAMPLE:

	1. What Is:					2. What Should Be:				
	Almost Always	Frequently	Occasionally	Almost Never	Not Applicable	Almost Always	Frequently	Occasionally	Almost Never	Not Applicable
	1	2	3	4	5	1	2	3	4	5
This school utilizes school social work services by making appropriate referrals to the social worker.	1	2	3	④	5	①	2	3	4	5

Subtract: 4 − 1 = 3 (the item discrepancy)

STEP 2: By all items for which a discrepancy of 2 or greater occurs, place a star to indicate the priority problems.

STEP 3: List all problem areas that are priorities (those that have a discrepancy score of 2 or higher). List all the strengths (those items with a score of 0 or 1) in order to present a complete analysis of the organization.

STEP 4: Compare scores among similar individuals (for example, the teachers in a particular school) and among different groups (teachers versus principal). It may be helpful to compute the mean scores when making these comparisons.

STEP 5: Develop the plan of action, collaborating with relevant individuals in the school organization at the building level or at higher administrative levels when appropriate. Include clear statements about factors that contribute to the problems, the goals, and activities for goal achievement; also include a schedule for periodic review and evaluation of the plan.

the items in each component and the process for doing this, and who should do the data analysis and the process to be used for this analysis.

School social workers are the most likely individuals to initiate use of this procedure because their professional mandate requires assessment and resolution of problems based on the person-in-environment perspective and is compatible with a focus on organizational dynamics as discussed earlier. This holistic perspective should allow them to identify patterns in problems within a particular school that implicate the organization as a possible contributor to those problems. Other school staff, such as principals, psychologists, and guidance counselors, also may initiate this procedure if they have enough expertise in personnel or administrative areas to become aware of and remain objective about relevant organizational dynamics. Even when the school social worker initiates this procedure, it should be done only with the sanction and involvement of the building principal.

There are two types of special circumstances that may call for this type of procedure. The first type involves any recent change in the student population or teaching staff, the educational program, school practices, or the school's physical setting. These kinds of changes can create disequilibrium in various components of the school's operation and can require a systematic analysis of the manner in which students, teachers, administrators, and others respond to and cope with them. The organizational analysis can also provide feedback on some of the conditions that have led to these changes and that can continue to affect the school's operations.

This procedure may also be useful when there are no major observable changes in the school's operation or program. In this second type of circumstance, referrals to support staff or other kinds of indicators may point to an increasing number of students who have similar problems or who seem to be at risk for these problems. An organizational analysis can identify the organizational factors involved in these problem areas (such as certain school practices) and the effects of those factors on individuals in the school.

When the procedure is initiated, there should be a formal agreement about who will be asked to complete each component. It is recommended that teachers, principals, and sometimes students be asked to complete the school policies, school relations/environment, and school social work role components. Unless the student and staff populations in a particular school are fairly small, it may be more practicable to ask only a random sample of the total number to complete items in these components. In elementary schools, younger students will not be able to respond to many of the items and should not be asked to do so. It may be helpful to have a small random sample of parents complete particular sections, such as those concerning staff-parent interactions and school-community relations. (See table 1.) One person should be responsible for distributing and collecting the completed forms in a manner that prevents respondents from collaborating while completing them. Ensuring anonymity of responses is equally important.

The completed forms can be scored easily by the school social worker and other staff designated by the principal. (See table 3.) Once it scores the forms, the same group can perform the data analysis by identifying the strengths, problem areas, and priorities among those problem areas, and by developing a plan of action. It may be helpful to compare certain responses during the analysis, such as those from teachers and the principal in the school practices section, those from students and teachers in the student-staff and student-student sections, and those from the school social worker and others in the school social work practice and communications sections.[13]

IMPLICATIONS FOR SCHOOL SOCIAL WORK

This section will present a case example to illustrate how this procedure for organizational analysis has been used effectively by school social workers in practice. Although the primary focus will be on the process and results of the organizational analysis, there will be some focus on the school social worker's role in integrating that analysis with the student-familial assessment.

> Millicent B. was an 8-year-old third-grade student who made average grades. Her teacher and the principal described her as a child who was not a troublemaker, but who was always on the fringes of trouble. For example, she didn't steal money from other children, but she had been able to talk another child into giving her money in one situation. The teacher's referral to the school social worker described her as being a social isolate and an abused child. She was at the school at least an hour early every morning and frequently stayed around unsupervised on the playground after school. Millicent was an only child. Both parents worked, and she was expected to get herself ready for school in the mornings and to stay in the house alone after school until her parents arrived home. When contacted about an interview, the parents were reluctant to meet. They stated they were unable to take time off from work to meet with the school social worker and that they were usually too busy each evening to meet them. They did agree to meet with the school social worker right after work at Ms. B.'s place of employment, since Mr. B. usually picked her up there each evening at that time. Essentially, the parents felt their plan for Millicent to "supervise herself" mornings and evenings was the best plan, even after the school social worker discussed some of the potential dangers involved. There was a neighbor whom Millicent had been instructed to call for any emergencies, and Ms. B. checked on Millicent by telephone each day. They also felt she was learning to be self-sufficient at a young age. They agreed to meet with the social worker again because they felt there was a communication problem with the school and that the teacher exaggerated Millicent's problem behavior at school.

The school social worker noted several problems in this case as he did his assessment of the student and her family during their first two interviews. They included the following: the parents seemed to be unaware of normal child development and were unrealistic about children's needs and the responsibilities appropriate for an 8-year-old (perhaps owing to their own childhood experiences with inadequate parenting); Millicent was not receiving adequate supervision or stimulation given her stage of development; the parents were having problems in managing time conflicts related to parenting responsibilities, work, community involvement, and their adult leisure-time activities; and Millicent's inability to express directly her feelings about being left alone and about not being able to play with other children after school resulted in their indirect expression through inappropriate behaviors at school.

The social worker's informal analysis of the dynamics at school related to this case indicated that Millicent's teacher was not knowledgeable about what constituted child abuse, neglect, or inadequate supervision and that she did not understand some of the difficulties that working parents have in managing their multiple role responsibilities. Consequently, when she made her frequent contacts with Millicent's parents about her concerns, it was obvious to the parents that she blamed them. Her frustrations over their "failure" to handle the problems made her over-react to Millicent's subsequent behavior problems at school.

ORGANIZATIONAL ANALYSIS AND SPECIFIC INTERVENTION

The school social worker also noted that the school staff in general seemed unaware that the school was in transition, even though they knew that students and teachers from two very different schools had been combined owing to a recent school closing. This resulted in a large number of new students in the school from dual-career two-parent families and families with employed single heads of household. The social worker knew that any changes in school policies to help deal with these problems had to be initiated at the principal's level to be effective. The case reminded the school social worker that the school nurse had expressed concern about the growing number of students who were left at school early each morning unsupervised. Also remembering that the principal often conferred with the nurse informally when making decisions because he respected her judgment, the social worker decided to talk with the nurse and enlist her support in getting the principal to hear and act on their concerns about students being left unsupervised and the possible effects on their school adjustments.

Their discussion with the principal led to the social worker's suggestion that the procedure described in this article be used to do an organizational analysis in order to identify the dynamics of the recent organizational changes and their effects on teachers and students such as Millicent. The principal was apprehensive about possible changes that this kind of procedure might indicate. However, he did feel it was very important for him to know as much as possible about his school, and the school social worker was able to reassure him that the analysis would provide him with more information on the new organizational context of the school. He noted also that he would help the principal interpret any needs that might be identified in the analysis, while the principal would be able to retain the authority for making decisions about how the school would respond to these needs. The procedure was used with the school social worker coordinating distribution and collection of the forms.

The data analysis indicated a number of needs, including the need for before- and after-school supervision for some students whose parents worked and who were left unsupervised, a need by most of the teachers for more knowledge about child abuse and related areas, a desire by some parents that the school encourage more involvement of working parents in the school and a need felt by some teachers for more input into the principal's decision-making process, especially in situations that concerned them directly. Although he could have developed a list of priorities through the scoring process for this procedure, this principal decided to circulate the list of eight needs identified in the data analysis among teachers so that they could participate actively in prioritizing them and suggesting solutions at the next staff meeting. This decision allowed the teachers to become aware of the strengths of the organization that had been identified in the data analysis, to have some input into this change process, and to have an opportunity to discuss other ongoing ways they could share their ideas with the principal.

Based on the data analysis, a plan of action was developed by the social worker, principal, school nurse, and two teachers chosen by their collegues. The plan involved changes in four major areas. First, a "latchkey" program was developed for students who needed before- and after-school supervision. The nurse and the social worker collaborated in planning and implementing the program. The content included health and safety tips, an activities program, tutoring, and discussion sessions about students' problems and feelings related to being on their own. A second part of the plan was an in-service program for teachers and the principal on child abuse. The program was developed to educate them about signs and causes of child abuse, neglect, and inadequate supervision; natural stresses in family life that parents experience (especially working mothers); and staff's legal responsibilities in reporting cases to protective services.

A third part of the plan of action was the development of a parents' group, which was co-led by the school social worker and school psychologist. This group was for parents who wanted help in coping with life transitions related to their children. The group experience lessened the emotional distance that parents had previously reported regarding the school. As a result, the group became an ongoing part of the school's services to parents.

A final part of the plan involved the decision-making process within the school. As noted previously, the principal gradually initiated an ongoing process for staff input based on the data analysis. The principal's responses about how district policies were decided and implemented at the building level indicated dissatisfaction and a negative attitude toward change. His bureaucratic orientation caused him to follow district policies, but his attitude toward those policies affected how he implemented them at the building level.

For example, a district policy had recently been enacted requiring principals to develop and consult with a school advisory committee made up of parents and other members of the community. The school social worker was able to consult with him about some of the advantages and disadvantages of the advisory committee, and alternative ways such committees could be developed and utilized. He enabled the principal to recognize how his strategy of delaying action in response to the district's making decisions without his input was similar to the teacher's reactions to his failure to obtain their input for his decision-making process. This consultive process helped the principal to develop and use this committee effectively by actively seeking and using their input. This improved the school's relationships with the community and resulted in fairer school policies. The five-member committee used the complete four-item plan of action to monitor the extent to which goals and specific tasks were accomplished over the following months.

In addition to performing the organizational analysis and interventions, the school social worker attempted to integrate those activities with the student-familial assessment and interventions; he attempted to identify related factors in both the school and home that were impinging on Millicent's problems. For example, he recognized that certain organizational dynamics, such as goal displacement and the school staff's attitudes toward change, may have prevented them from understanding the needs of new students like Millicent and caused them to exacerbate the problem by blaming parents. On the other hand, Millicent's parents' unrealistic expectations that she could supervise herself also contributed to the problem. Their expectations prevented them from recognizing the stress she was experiencing and from developing alternative ways to handle the supervision problem.

A two-step plan was developed based on the assessed needs in the case. First, the social worker helped the teacher understand the parents by explaining the time and role conflicts that they needed to resolve if they were to improve their parenting skills and understanding of Millicent's needs. He also provided support for the teacher in their consultation sessions by suggesting ways she could respond to Millicent's behavior problems at school more appropriately and consistently.

Second, the school social worker helped the parents understand Millicent's needs by reframing her behavior at school as a natural response at her age to inappropriate requirements for role performance that she could not fulfill. The parents agreed to have Millicent go to a neighbor's house after school until the latchkey program could be implemented. The parents began to see the development of this program as evidence of the school's concern for all students and not as just an attempt to single out Millicent, so they allowed her to become involved in the program. They were then able to own part of the responsibility for the communication problem within the school and to work on that and other problems identified in several additional sessions with the worker. They were later involved successfully in the parent's transitional group that had been developed at the school.

CONCLUSIONS

The following five practice principles can be generalized from this example and others that involve procedures for analyzing organizational dynamics. These principles require an understanding of organizational theory as well as knowledge of human behavior. They also require an understanding of the two kinds of special circumstances in which such procedures can be potentially useful.

1. The worker should ask appropriate individuals in the school to identify other students who are experiencing or seem to be at risk for the problem being observed or referred.
2. The worker should observe the formal and informal decision-making process in the building and identify the significant input groups or individuals and the decision makers who are involved.
3. An effort should be made to identify other individuals who have similar concerns about the problem situation—preferably among the significant input groups or individuals, but not restricted to them. Awareness of their own and others' organizational orientations and the use of collaborative skills can directly affect social workers' abilities to exert collective impact on decision makers. Additionally, school social workers need skills for clarifying decision makers' concerns related to problem areas, their attitudes toward change, and any organizational dynamics at the building or district levels that affect the problems.
4. The school social worker should meet with the principal or other decision makers to clarify the worker's role in collecting and analyzing data with this procedure and in deciding on ways in which the data can be used.
5. The worker should do a thorough organizational analysis involving as many of those individuals as possible who are affected by the problems and by any potential changes that result from the analysis. This final principle involves developing a plan of action through collaborative work with the principal and other school staff, integrating the needs identified in the organizational analysis and any student-familial assessments, and monitoring progress in implementing the plan.

By following these practice principles, school social workers can more effectively serve the total client system within the organization, including students, their families, teachers, and administrators.

REFERENCES

1. Paula Allen Meares. 1977. Analysis of tasks in school social work. *Social Work* May, pp. 196–201.
2. Joseph R. Steiner. 1979. Social workers in school politics. *Social Work in Education* 2 (October), pp. 41–57.
3. Fred Barbaro. 1980. School social work: The politics of professional survival. *Social Work in Education* 3(October), pp. 5–17. See also Meares, Analysis of tasks in school social work.
4. This procedure was developed in 1982 by the present author and Juanita Roland, Midwest Race Desegregation Assistance Center.
5. Herman Resnick and Rino J. Patti (eds.). 1980. *Change from Within: Humanizing Social Welfare Organizations*. Philadelphia: Temple University Press, pp. 4–5.
6. Jerald Hage and Michael Aiken. Program change and organizational properties. In Resnick and Patti (eds.). *Change from Within*, p. 163.
7. A. D. Green. 1966. The professional worker in the bureaucracy. *Social Service Review* 40 (March), p. 71.
8. Hage and Aiken. Program change and organizational properties.
9. Steiner. Social workers in school politics.
10. Meares. Analysis of tasks in school social work.
11. Barbaro. School social work; and Harrison Smith and Edith Freeman. 1980. Do school social workers neglect racially isolated minority children? *Social Work in Education* 3 (October), pp. 18–31.
12. Barbaro. School social work. p. 7.
13. Marlys Staudt and John L. Craft. 1983. School staff input in evaluation of school social work practice. *Social Work in Education* 5 (January), pp. 119–131.

CHAPTER 28

Resource Development and Coordination of Services

Robert Constable
Professor, Loyola University of Chicago; Former Editor, *Social Work in Education*

School social work began in the first decade of the twentieth century in New York City and Hartford, Connecticut. The Hartford social workers were part of a psychological clinic established by the schools; the New York workers were former settlement house workers who addressed themselves to the social and environmental conditions of children going to school. In both cases the unique social work perspective found a useful relation to the mission of the public schools. School social workers needed to address both the conditions school children encountered in their everyday lives and their ways of adjusting and adapting to these conditions. The two strains of intervention, with the environment and with the individual, were combined in one function. The later focus of social work would rest on separate and discrete methods of social casework, social group work, and community organization. These discrete methods theories would gradually narrow over the years to exclude much interaction with systems other than those the method addressed. There was little support in methods theory for the broadened role of the school social worker. Nevertheless, as present research seems to confirm, the conception, that the school social worker role encompassed more than one single method did persist. John Nebo (1963) attempted to express in the language of discrete methods what school social workers were doing in practice and wrote of the school social worker as a community organizer. The broadening of the school social worker's role in actual practice is confirmed through studies of the social worker's role, the most recent appearing in this volume.

From the very beginnings of practice school social workers had to find resources, get clients connected with them, make sure they were providing appropriate services, work out difficulties between different service providers, and develop new services or fight for their accessibility. The more severe the disability or the gap between home and school, the greater the need

343

for complex and individually constructed supportive resource systems. This component of practice has always been understood by school social workers. The movement to include more severely disabled youngsters in public education has created an even greater need for professionals who can develop these support systems. The current mandate of the school for provision of special education and related services creates a situation where the school is an even more important part of the network of services for children with disabilities. The schools are only now beginning to address the implications of their centrality in services for children with disabilities. There is an opportunity now for the school social worker to reaffirm an historic commitment and to develop a long-standing skill.

There are a number of long-standing reasons for the importance of resource development and coordination of services for school social workers. The service delivery system is segmented, divided by special functions within health care, child welfare, vocational rehabilitation, educational systems, mental health, and so on, in a seemingly unlimited array of services, each having particular functions, missions, and rationale for helping. Although family and school both have concerns that transcend the segmentation—with the whole child and his or her environment—both have natural roles in addressing the difficulty in accessing services for vulnerable children. The more vulnerable the child, the greater the need to coordinate services from different service providers and the greater the potential damage if something goes wrong. The more the services involved, the greater the likelihood that something will go wrong, and thus the greater the need for a problem-solving professional to address the configuration and delivery of services. The school is central to the child, and the school social worker is directly in the middle and is the person most likely to coordinate services and provide case management services.

The need for resource development and coordination of services has been recognized as crucial in working with diverse populations with profound and ongoing needs: the elderly, the physically disabled, the developmentally disabled, the chronically mentally ill, children experiencing neglect or abuse, and so on. Each area has developed a literature of its own in the areas of integration of services, coordination of services, and case management. In the schools there have been particular concerns for young children with severe disabilities and older disabled youngsters nearing transition from the world of the schools into the world of work. With both populations some case management is mandated, but with none of these populations can effective service be provided without the larger structure of *interagency agreements* and the smaller structures of *case management* that appropriately involve the family as well as resource persons in individual case plans.

The development of the NASW *Standards for Social Work Services in the Schools* (1978) and its subsequent review by school social work practitioners throughout the country confirmed this historical continuity of role. The essential skills of the school social worker included implementing of referrals to resources in the community, collaboration with agencies to solve specific problem situations or to develop new resources for pupils and their parents. A taxonomy of tasks for social work services in schools was divided into three areas—services to pupil and/or parents, work with school personnel, and school/community relations. Because they are directly relevant to resource development and coordination, the list of school-community relations tasks are worthwhile reviewing in their entirety. The standards have been most recently updated in 1992.

SCHOOL-COMMUNITY RELATIONS

Remedial

Identify children or target groups of children needing alternative educational planning or programs and support services.

Consult and collaborate with community representatives to identify effects of interacting school/community/pupil characteristics and develop resources to meet needs of child or target group.

Collaborate with community agencies in the development of alternative education programs and support services.

Clarify and interpret specific roles and responsibilities of the community in promoting school attendance.

Set objectives, monitor progress, and measure outcomes of service.

Crisis Resolution

Collaborate in community planning for crisis intervention services—drugs, rape, abuse and neglect, suicide, runaways, family violence, etc.

Set objectives, monitor progress, and measure outcomes of service.

Developmental

Aid in identification of child or target group of children needing preventive social services.

Aid in development of preventive social services to meet needs of child or target group.

Aid in collaborative planning to provide full range of services to target group.

Set objectives, monitor progress, and measure outcomes of service.

Resource development and coordination of service is clearly a part of the school social worker's function for several very practical reasons. First of all, the school and family often cannot really accomplish their own functions without specialized help from other agencies. These agencies might provide health services, counseling services, concrete assistance, respite care, summer camp, or other services necessary in modern society. School pupils may be involved with other systems in our society that have deeper claims on them, such as the juvenile justice system or the child welfare system.

INTERAGENCY AGREEMENTS

As schools have become more central to services to severely disabled children of all ages, but particularly the very young and those transitioning into the world of work, the demand for case management is accompanied by the need for interagency collaboration. Schools only gradually are seeing themselves, not as a world of their own, but as members of a larger community of services. They are not accustomed to thinking of themselves in terms of interagency coordination, although efficiency of service provision and indeed the effectiveness of any case management attempts will demand an agreement reached beforehand between various agencies serving particular populations. Some of these agencies are large public agencies with complicated structures and some are small grass roots operations. La Cour (1982) cites some of the difficulties in developing agreements:

- Lack of clarity on "first dollar" responsibility
- Lack of coordination of agencies' priorities
- Lack of coordination between state and local agencies
- Failure to coordinate budgets with service mandates
- Inconsistent service standards
- Conflicting views of constraints on confidentiality of information

He suggests that efforts to overcome these barriers be based first of all on an understanding of pertinent law and regulations. With this understanding the social worker needs to develop a network of informal connections to the leadership of the involved agencies. This may not be so formidable when the school social worker is well connected with those in a school district administration who often are in contact with their counterparts in the involved agencies. Because the social worker has a parallel relation with these agencies on a direct practice level, this also affords entry into the organization and an understanding of how the service is working in specific cases. The social worker needs to know how the agency is working from the inside. With this understanding, the social worker may identify the resources to be exchanged and point out the benefits of a resource exchange to the participating agencies. Building on reciprocity, an agreement can then be drafted.

A good interagency agreement needs to be written in simple and clear language. It should contain sections that (a) describe the reason for writing the agreement; (b) identify the responsibilities of each agency and the method for performing those responsibilities; (c) identify the standards each agency must meet when performing an activity; (d) describe the process of exchanging information on common clients; and (e) describe the method for modifying the agreement. The agreement should be flexibly written, focusing on the desired outcome rather than on the process for getting there. It should not jeopardize an agency's funding or turf. Instead the agreement should seek to clarify these issues. Finally, and obviously, the mutual benefit should be evident, enhancing the opportunity for future agreement as well as the full implementation of the current agreement (La Cour, 1982).

The paradox of service provision is that the more severe the need, the more difficult and complex the access. Children and parents often have multiple and complex involvements with these systems. When these systems provide resources at all, they are difficult and complex to access and accompanied by multiple and conflicting behavioral demands of their potential clientele. The more generally vulnerable the pupil, particularly the handicapped pupil, the greater the needs for external services, the greater the difficulty in getting these services, and, finally, the greater the likelihood of family breakdown in the face of these difficulties. Often parents are not even aware of what systems exist. Any commitment to vulnerable children places the school in the difficult and unwanted position of having to interact with community agencies in complex planning efforts. Educators generally are unprepared for this task. The school social worker is frequently the only member of the school team whose orientation and general skill development does include interaction with community agencies and so any coordination, if it is done at all, is and should be done by the school social worker. The social worker's investment of time in informing parents, removing barriers to service obtainment, and helping parents to utilize services has a high payoff in the child's adjustment to a learning situation.

Resource development and coordination is particularly important for the child with disabilities. These children often have difficulty and special needs in coping with other areas of their environment as well as school. The family's attempts to support the youngster and compensate for gaps in socialization and capability places it under pressure, particularly where the family is already vulnerable. Family units such as the single-parent household or the household where both parents work are particularly vulnerable. Whatever takes place in the family inevitably will affect what the pupil is able to do in school, and so it is artificial to draw a sharp boundary between what is educational and what is noneducational. The law has recognized to a degree the legitimacy and necessity of services that are going to help the child with disabilities to benefit from special education. Recent court interpretations around related services reveal a similar difficulty in distinguishing between educational and noneducational services. Related services are defined as services that are required to assist a child with disabilities to benefit from special education. Furthermore, the law, in firmly placing the responsibility for free, appropriate, public education of the child on the school, also places the school in the position of having to support more expensive and more restrictive alternatives for placement of the child with disabilities, if the network of family, informal support systems, and formal community resources breaks down. The need for coordination and service integration is dictated by the belief that it is better that children with disabilities remain with their families, and by simple economics, which makes remaining at home a less expensive educational alternative. Given the scarcity of regular and special education resources within school districts, the school faces the complex problem of bringing children and educational resources together in a appropriate environment and maintaining a support system.

Resources in the community can be divided into two groups: (a) those services available from formally constituted organizations, often purchased by either family or school, and, if not purchased, subject to complex eligibility determinations for entitlement, and (b) informal, helping networks of neighbors, community people, relatives, members of church and civic groups, local merchants, and other school children who may be willing and able to help in a variety of ways.

It would be unrealistic to assume that formal organizations by themselves will be able to meet the complex needs of children with disabilities and their families. The social worker may locate and help the family communicate with a variety of informal, helping networks that may exist in a community. Possible uses of such networks can be almost limitless. The social worker will often maintain an ongoing consultative relationship with some network members, so that they do not become disappointed or confused at the initial response of the child with disabilities and/or his family. The author has used volunteers, police officers, and a wide variety of other persons in many ways to provide structure, an element of caring, and vitally needed help for the handicapped child and his family.

New structures for collaboration are needed among public and private agencies having resources for handicapped children, with particular focus on the family of the disabled. A mixture of hard services (programs and tangible resources) and soft services (counseling, access to psychological support, and information), which help people to deal with stress, is needed. The traditional services for children with disabilities have been quite segmented and competitive, with different agencies dealing with different aspects of the disabled child's needs. Continuing this segmented system or dumping the responsibility on the schools would be grossly dysfunctional.

Because a variety of resources are being brought to bear on an individual child, the management problem is also quite different from the traditional model of educational administration, involving a building, an administrative hierarchy, a faculty, a group of pupils, equipment more or less in one place, and transportation primarily from home to school. With the decentralization of specialized personnel and equipment, the logistical problems faced by the school district or intermediate unit are complex. Proper utilization of resources both in and outside of school demands that the services be coordinated over a large area, that the services be integrated according to the needs of each child, and that there be accountability to assure that the services promised in the Individualized Education Program actually are delivered.

In Illinois the assumption of increased responsibility by the schools in the wake of P.L. 94-142 seems to lead to a lessening of responsibility for these children by other state agencies, if there was a possibility of school support for these services. The response of the state education agency to an increased burden was to develop a mandate for collaborative planning among agencies, each taking responsibility for its own area of service. Necessary services would in theory be available at no cost to the parents. Such a directive from the state level was necessary to conserve resources and to prevent unnecessary movement of children to more restrictive placements. It could not be implemented in the absence of structures on the local and regional level that develop the necessary interagency agreements. On the other hand, such fragile networks of agency agreements were not workable without state support.

For these networks to be viable, they had to include a commitment on the state level, a means of communication and development of network agreements on the local or regional level, as well as practitioners equipped to implement and coordinate service agreements on the direct practice level.

The movement to services based on legal entitlement has taken place, not only in the schools, but in most other agencies serving children with disabilities. In order to cope with the implications of this entitlement, laws have prescribed or agencies have developed case management approaches to the widened range of available services. These case management approaches have become instruments of compliance and management tools for assuring that clients are getting what they are entitled to and have the opportunity to be active, rather than passive, consumers of services. The approaches to case management are fairly similar. Each involves an individualized plan, founded on a data-based assessment of needs. They are driven by specific objectives to be attained, placed in a time frame with a date for specific initiation and duration of services and given expectations for

TABLE 1

Case Management Approach	Entitling Legislation or Framework
The Individualized Habilitation Plan	P.L. 94-103, for developmentally disabled
The Individualized Education Program	P.L. 94-142, for all children with disabilities
Individualized Written Rehabilitation Program	Rehabilitation Act of 1973
Individualized Service Plan	Title XVI for children with disabilities eligible for S.S.I.
Individualized Care Plan	For Title XIX Medicaid
Individualized Program Plan	Mandated by J.C.A.H.
Individualized Program Plan	Title XX, purchase of service

evaluation and review and participation in setting objectives and deciding upon appropriate resources. Table 1 illustrates six major case management approaches coming out of different enabling legislation or frameworks.

It is ironic that the plans, as developed, continue the same segmented approach to services but now with the grandiosity of a plan. Although such plans are worthwhile instruments for assuring appropriate service delivery, the next step would be to develop a single individualized plan that brings together all of the services needed by the client, but now with one focal case coordinator from one agency who would ensure the client's access to other services. Such an approach would need support at higher policy-making levels than any one agency could provide and on the other hand would need to be closely related to the needs of the family. It should come out of a coordinating structure that is not attached to any one agency. Schools and school services would have to play a major role in the development of any service network addressed to families and children.

CASE MANAGEMENT

Case management is a commonly accepted approach in social work to the delivery of service to populations having ongoing or fairly complex needs, necessitating that different services work together. It is an approach that requires considerable skill, because the social worker is working simultaneously with pupil, parent, teacher, school, and a network of agencies. Indeed, from a systems perspective the combination of small changes in each sector often makes broader changes that no one sector—pupil, parent, teacher, school, network—could ever accomplish on its own. Case management tasks described in the literature (Garland, Woodruff, and Buck, 1988; Compher, 1984; Eriksen, 1981; Austin, 1983) include:

1. Assessing client needs
2. Developing service plans
3. Coordinating service delivery
4. Monitoring service delivery
5. Evaluating services
6. Advocating on behalf of the needs and rights of the client(s)

In order to complete each step, the case manager needs to move beyond the confines of his or her agency and/or discipline. To coordinate the diverse segments of a service delivery system, the social worker needs to reach beyond the confines of agency and discipline and include other services with full respect for the differences they offer the totality. Two models of teamwork have emerged to meet the demands of case management: the transdisciplinary team and the transagency team.

Typically the transdisciplinary team, composed of the family and professionals from a variety of disciplines, collaborates in assessment and program planning. One individual, chosen from among the team, works in consultation with colleague specialists to carry out the individualized plan. Together with the family, the case manager integrates the information and skills of the entire team to work with the child and family on goals established, to ensure coordination and communication among providers, and to monitor services to make sure that services planned are actually provided. In the transdisciplinary model the case manager typically is both the primary provider and service coordinator.

The transagency team provides an alternative structure for case management, bringing together not only the many disciplines working within a single agency, but also a variety of agency representatives to assess needs and plan services. These are models in which the transagency team is created specifically for the purpose of a particular population, and the agencies represented on the team are determined by the nature of the program (Garland, Woodruff, and Buck, 1988).

THE TRANSAGENCY TEAM IN THE SCHOOLS

Schools offer a natural setting for the coordination of services among agencies. Schools are the central public institution dealing with the normal needs of children, and schools are now central to children with disabilities and crucial to development of mental health services. The transagency approach to services within its walls is a useful starting point for the development of more comprehensive models of service coordination and provision for children and families with complex needs.

We developed such a structure in the Chicago south suburban area. The area is heterogeneous, with patches of severe poverty mixed with blue-collar and middle-class suburbia. There are large populations of black and Hispanic minorities and white ethnics of Eastern or Southern European background. The area has experienced considerable development over the past twenty years, a development that had outstripped the capacities of the traditional service resources and provided the opportunity for a fairly innovative type of planning effort. An independent committee was established, composed of the major public and private agencies that are resources to families of children with disabilities. The committee has been given the neutral name of Regional Community Integration Resource Committee (RCIRC).

The RCIRC developed agreements on individualized service plans and provides a means of communication around resource issues affecting children with disabilities. A major focus of the committee was to develop agreements on individualized service plans for particular situations of need. With participation of the client/family/informal resource network, one particular agency would be designated as a focal agency and a particular worker from that agency would develop an agreement with the family about their overall goals and what they need to carry them out. This agreement would involve the client system, any appropriate informal support systems and the committee. The client and his or her family support system are recognized as the focus for all planning efforts and are included appropriately in the network. The social worker from the focal agency who works with the client/family/informal support system needs to be sufficiently skilled to:

Help the client and family define the problem, some resultant goals, and what resources, services, and supports are needed.

Define with the family the supportive network available to the client.

Involve the client/family/informal resource network in decision making by working with them individually, coordinating with other sectors, and bringing them together when they are ready to come to an agreement.

Identify formal resources needed, maintain a steady communication with the formal resource systems in the network, and do problem solving with these systems as questions arise.

Help the client/family and members of the informal resource network relate to the formal agency resources as collaborators, without a feeling of loss of dignity or control and with the assumption that agency actions must be related to client need.

Help client to use the situation of receiving service to identify his or her own aspirations for change and to enter upon a change process when his or her own aspirations and/or the need to adapt to realities in the environment point out a need for change in attitudes or accustomed ways of relating to others.

In providing means of communication around issues of service development and planning among agencies working with a particular clientele, the RCIRC focused on gaps in services, situations where the client was at high risk, had needs involving a number of agencies, and where coordination of services would be necessary. It could not represent any one agency if it were to carry out its function.

The social worker is the crucial link between planning processes. There is a duality in the social worker's role with a close relationship on the one hand to an individual client and his or her family/informal support system and, on the other hand, a working relationship for formal agency resources through the RCIRC. Members of the RCIRC generally did not have direct service responsibilities. They were to be far enough up on the agency hierarchy to deal with potential resource commitments and close enough to practice and service delivery to communicate with the direct service level of the agency. Several examples of these coordination arrangements can be given:

> Doris is an eighteen-year-old, severely disturbed adolescent whose reactivity to a symbiotic conflict with her mother and resultant self-destructive behavior has resulted in several hospitalizations. The school had found itself reacting to the behavior and programming for Doris rather than getting the mother and daughter into contact with help. Mother and daughter have now begun with a social worker in private practice. The school will now bring Doris into a one-hour-per-day class in ceramics with only the instructor present. If this can be established without incident, Doris will be involved with a pet zoo run by another agency. Because the situation between mother and daughter is potentially explosive, a shelter arrangement with a relative to be used in a crisis will be worked out. This would keep Doris in the community as long as possible. If the social worker is able to make further gains with the mother and Doris's school adjustment stabilizes, the next step is developing a program with the Illinois Department of Vocational Rehabilitation. The state agency is involved in the plan and will give special consideration to Doris's needs.

> Michael is a twenty-one-year-old severe and barely stabilized diabetic, legally blind, who lives in a nursing home because his single, working parent was unable to care for him. He is about to be graduated from his special education program because of his age. A plan is developed in the RCIRC to make it possible for him to return home through utilization of public assistance, medicaid, homemaker, and home health care services. Some further medical assessment is planned, and based on this assessment, some vocational assessment would be done. The social worker from the school will work with Michael and

the mother, coordinating with other agencies, with the goal of passing on case management responsibilities to another agency when the two have solidified their own direction and connections with other services.

Although such cases present complex need, they are not particularly unusual. In both cases a combination of resources could prevent institutionalization or make movement from an institutionalized setting possible. Furthermore none of the hard service provision, no matter how flexible, could have been effective or even possible without the soft services to parent and child to help them deal with the situation and to link their processes and needs with programs and resources. To make complex plans for families without their choice, involvement, and participation, indeed not to make the individual-in-family-unit the center of the decision process, is to court disaster and to set up an unproductive struggle around power and control.

The next decade is going to be an important one for schools and for school social workers. The impact of present school responsibility for children with disabilities will be generally felt among all agencies serving children, as the courts continue to clarify the extent of the child's entitlement. The decline in resources available in the education and social welfare sectors will make present segmented agency networks increasingly unworkable and inequitable for parents and children. The traditional involvement of school social workers in coordination of services in the interest of individual cases will need further development to meet the increased involvement of the education institution in planning for the needs of children in the community.

REFERENCES

Austin, C. 1983. Case management in long-term care: Options and opportunities. *Health and Social Work* 8(1):16–30.

Compher, J. V. 1984. The case conference revisited: A systems view. *Child Welfare* 63(5):411–418.

Eriksen, K. 1981. *Human services today.* 2nd Edition. Reston, VA: Reston Publishing Co.

Garland, C., Woodruff, G., and Buck, D. 1988. Case management, Division for Early Childhood White Paper. Reston, VA: Council for Exceptional Children.

Kurtz, L. F., Bagarozzi, D. A., and Pollane, L. P. 1984. Case management in mental health. *Health and Social Work* 9:201–211.

La Cour, J. A. 1982. Interagency agreement: A rational response to an irrational system. *Exceptional Children* 49(3):265–267.

National Association of Social Workers. 1992. NASW Standards for school social work services. Education Commission Task Force. Washington, D.C.: NASW.

Nebo, John. 1963. The social worker as community organizer. *Social Work* 8.

CHAPTER 29

Child Protection and the School Social Worker

Sally G. Goren
Jane Addams College of Social Work,
University of Illinois at Chicago

In helping children to benefit from educational opportunity, the school social worker uniquely promotes the protection of children, but this protective mission extends to the worlds of the child's family and community. In this way the school social worker shares common concerns with child protective service workers. To enable each child to fully use the educational opportunity the school provides, the child must be safe, nurtured, cared for, enjoy consistency and stability, and him/herself feel this level of support and security. The social worker must become an active participant in intervention and remediation efforts whenever the child's emotional or physical health is threatened or when expectations of teachers, administrators, parents, and others are beyond the child's developmental capacities. Additionally, new laws relating to child welfare policy, such as P.L. 103–66, The Omnibus Budget Reconciliation Act of 1993, also affect school social workers. This law provides funding for family support programs intended to increase family stability and enhance child development. Such community-based programs must include schools as centers for provision of services. Consequently, as access points and procedures change, school social workers will need to learn how to make effective referrals.

MANDATORY REPORTING OF ABUSE AND NEGLECT

All states now have mandated reporting laws for child abuse/neglect (Tower, 1993, p. 19). School professionals (teachers, principals, nurses, psychologists, and social workers) are required to report neglect or abuse and school districts are required to have a written policy regarding reporting procedures. Because the social workers are particularly familiar with the child welfare system, they would be the appropriate person to give leadership in developing such policies and procedures for reporting. Where abuse or neglect is suspected, school social workers often need to interpret the requirements for such reporting policies to teachers, administrators, and the school board to ensure conformity with the law and provide the best service to the child and family. They often consult with teachers who are concerned about any child who exhibits relevant symptoms or injuries, and collaborate with administrators and other pupil services personnel regarding actual reporting, dealing with family reactions, court appearances, or other events involved in suspected abuse or neglect.

Reporting often creates a significant emotional burden. A teacher, who is most frequently the first person to identify possible abuse or neglect, often needs support and guidance in the reporting process. The teacher's attitudes about protecting children, the sanctity of the family, government interference, or prior experience with the child welfare system might well influence a willingness to report. The possible consequences of a report of abuse, whether substantiated or not, will certainly stir feelings within the teacher to which the social worker must respond.

Sometimes teachers and administrators become frustrated when reports are unsubstantiated by the child protective system. Since only 32 percent of reports of sexual abuse reports are substantiated (U.S. Department of Health and Human Services, National Center on Child Abuse and Neglect, 1994, p. 11), the school social worker must be prepared to help school personnel understand why this occurs and to help them with their feelings of helplessness when they are convinced of the severity of danger to the child.

The entire educational system must be adequately informed regarding the requirements for protection of children at risk of physical harm through abuse or neglect. The school social worker must be aware of the multitude of system issues to be considered in preparing a program to respond to the legal and social requirements for protecting children. Disagreement between administration and staff regarding the discharge of this demanding responsibility could interfere with developing clear guidelines and effective reporting processes.

There may be concern about political implications as viewed by school boards and there often is administrative resistance to admitting that parents in a community may be capable of hurting or neglecting children. School faculty may not expect the state child protective service agencies to be helpful, and thus feel there is no value in reporting. The school social worker must be aware of the multitude of system issues to be considered in preparing a program to respond to the social requirement to protect children. Without such knowledge, the development of a plan may be seriously hindered. Both technical and attitudinal factors, as expressed by the school board, administrators, and/or teaching staff must be in concert for effective policy and procedure to be implemented. Without a holistic approach, the development of a plan may be seriously hindered.

THE PHYSICALLY ABUSED CHILD

Before identifying the characteristics of the physically abused child, it is important to note that there has been a clear shift in attitude regarding corporal punishment during this century. Such proverbs as "spare the rod spoil the child" reflect an earlier ethic that permitted or even encouraged the use of physical punishment to ensure obedience and respect for authority. Although Western cultural standards now deplore the use of physical force to control the child, we must remember that many cultures employ methods for punishing children that our predominant culture might consider abusive. The culture conflict encountered in situations beyond the norm might best be addressed by counseling the family and helping them to meet the standards of the community in which they now reside and to whose statutes they must now conform. Dealing with the pressure of assimilation and being without natural support systems, families exhibiting abusive behavior can easily be overwhelmed by the demands of children. Nonetheless, it is crucial to help such families to modify their disciplinary methods without compromising their cultural values.

The evidence of physical abuse often is clearly apparent, although there may be attempts to attribute the injuries to accidental falls, burns, carelessness, and so on, rather than to deliberate actions intended to hurt the child. Injury can indeed be accidental. It only becomes abuse when injury is inflicted by the actions or omissions of another person. Conversely, there may be no outward evidence of physical abuse, but more subtle behaviors could be a clue to the experience of abuse. The child may collude with the parent(s) to avoid detection of abuse by the child welfare system. Any child might sustain injuries while playing, but explanations of injuries by parent and child should be compatible with the child's age and development and type of injury received (Broadhurst, 1982, p. 157). Among the symptoms of physical abuse are bruises on the backs of legs, arms, chest, neck, head, or genitals, especially if the bruises appear to be inflicted by an object such as belt buckle, cord, or rope. There may be bite marks, scratches, or grab or pinch marks. Fractures, especially in children under three, breaks caused by twisting a limb, and dislocations at joints, point to physical abuse. Head injuries (skull fractures, subdural hematomas, retinal detachments, and black eyes) alert the school social worker to a dangerous degree of physical abuse. Finally, burn marks, especially those inflicted by cigarettes, are evidence of abuse, as are burns caused by immersion of a limb in scalding water and burns caused by a utensil such as an iron or poker (Tower, 1993, pp. 79–81).

The behavior of the child who experiences physical abuse includes an unusual degree of apprehension coupled with watchful observation of his or her surroundings, as if trying to determine where danger exists. There is obvious apathy, with little capacity for pleasure or fun. Such children often appear "old" for their age and have little or no facility for play. They may appear withdrawn but hyper-vigilant, have low self-esteem, and may have severe learning problems. These children may show symptoms of enuresis, encopresis, or exhibit temper tantrums or bizarre behaviors, especially younger age children (ages 2 to 6). As such children age, the added characteristic of "excessive adaptability" may increase. Fear of failure, verbal inhibition, and poor peer relationships often mark the behavior of an abused or previously abused child (Tower, 1993, pp. 82-84). Although these symptoms may be found in children who do not experience physical abuse, a multiplicity of the above symptoms strongly suggest the possibility of abuse.

Abusive parents often struggle with their own low self-esteem and their inability to control themselves or others. They may be impulse-ridden, in need of affection and approval, or are unable to tolerate delayed gratification. If their child is not instantly and appropriately responsive, they may see themselves as being rejected again, having another challenge to their competence or presuming themselves to be a failure. To assuage these feelings, and without the capacity to separate the feeling from action, abusive parents may wreak their wrath on the "frustrating" child. Although it is not the school social worker's role to act as the investigator of the suspected abuse, the worker likely will be the person to notify the parent about the concern, being as supportive as possible. It is crucial to remember that the parent, on some level, most likely wants to be a good parent. The report of suspected abuse likely confirms his or her sense of incompetence as a person and as a parent. It is frequently true that the kind of discipline the abusive parent uses is similar to the way he or she was treated as a child. The parent may be unable to perceive the inappropriateness of her or his actions because the parent received no protection from such abuse and he or she survived. Thus, the parent may honestly differ with the charges against her or him.

THE SEXUALLY ABUSED CHILD

The Child Abuse Prevention and Treatment Act as mandated in 1984 defines sexual abuse as:

1. The employment, use, persuasion, inducement, enticement, or coercion of any child to engage in any sexually explicit conduct (or any simulation of such conduct) for the purpose of producing any visual depiction of such conduct, or
2. The rape, molestation, prostitution or other form of sexual exploitation of children, or incest with children, under circumstances that indicate the child's health or welfare is harmed or threatened thereby (P.L. 98-457, 98th Congress, 9 October 1984).

Sexual abuse, considered to be significantly underreported, may occur in one of every three children (Costin, Bell and Downs, 1991, p. 345). Although it is commonly assumed that girls suffer a much higher rate of sexual abuse, it is estimated that the true ratio of sexually abused boys to sexually abused girls is equal (Tower, 1993, p. 143). If sexual abuse is perpetrated by a relative, it is termed incest. Offenders may be pedophiles, sexual addicts, neighbors, friends, or child-care workers, including babysitters.

The symptom picture of the sexually abused child may include the profiles already identified for the physically abused youngster. In addition, other symptoms may be seen, such as unwillingness to participate in physical activities because of genital pain, veiled or indirect allusions to a trusted teacher about their situation, regression to infantile behavior, or fantasies used to avoid the disturbing reality of their lives. A child may exhibit aggressive or delinquent behavior (especially adolescents) toward people or property as a reaction to the hostile attacks they are experiencing. Running away from home is a common action used to control the unavoidable trauma. Sexually abused children often are isolated and have poor peer relationships. They may be seductive or exhibitionistic with peers and adults as a learned means of winning attention. There is often a high rate of drug and alcohol abuse among these children in an attempt to handle guilt or anxiety resulting from the sexual abuse (Tower, 1993, pp. 397, 402).

The reporting of sexual abuse by the victim often creates a situation wherein the victim experiences further victimization and loss. The medical profession must perform intrusive and/or sometimes painful tests to verify the abuse. The child protective system may place the child away from its family or remove the offender from the home, creating further loss. The legal system may require the child to indict a family member or friend who is perceived by the child as having a great deal of power and for whom there may be feelings of love not related to the sexual episodes. The legal system, in order to provide a constitutionally guaranteed defense for the suspected perpetrator, may challenge the child's credibility. All this will certainly intensify the trauma the child has experienced. The social worker, who is expected to report suspected sexual abuse, needs to be aware of the potential backlash for the victim that reporting may create since the report is only the beginning of a longer process between the school, the child, the family, and the child protective agency.

Although there can be no assurance of cessation of the abuse unless it is reported and treatment is initiated as an outcome of the reporting, the social worker must be prepared to deal with a confused and potentially angry child. The child's world, however destructive, is the world she or he has known and now may seem to be shattered. Family members may be irate that the breadwinner has been removed from the home and can no longer support the family. The parent who remains in the home may be mourning the loss of the absent partner. Often the child may be free to continue with the school social worker, whom he or she feels is now the cause of his or her pain, and the social worker may need to look for other possible sources of support for the child.

THE NEGLECTED CHILD

Neglect involves the omission by a person responsible for the child's welfare of essential care required for a child's developmental, physical, or emotional needs. Lack of adequate food, clothing, or supervision, exposure to potentially dangerous conditions, and refusal to provide access to essential health care or to an education all could be construed as neglect. The courts have qualified and refined these definitions in different circumstances to the point of building a body of case law around the definition of neglect. However, unless neglect is flagrant, it is often difficult to prove because it is the omission of something that should be present. The social worker is obligated to report when there is evidence of neglect. However there are certain indications of a situation that a child and family are in need.

Since some of the need may be caused by neglect, certain indication should alert the social worker to follow a situation more closely. Such children may often appear apathetic, show indications of malnutrition, be dirty and ill-kept, demonstrate retarded growth, have poor motor and language development, have untended medical problems, or lack an ability to conceptualize at an age-appropriate level (Tower, 1993, pp. 105–110). The parents may show signs of immaturity, be retarded, be without supportive relationships, and/or lack judgment or knowledge regarding appropriate child care. Often, the parents' own paucity of social skills is reflected in their children's limited ability to interact with the other children in school. The neglected child may attend school sporadically because his or her parents do not observe a structured day, which includes rising in time to help get the child to school. The parents may regard education as unimportant, or they may be primarily concerned with simple survival.

Beyond the mandatory report to the child protective agency when there is evidence of neglect, the school social worker is in a key position to work with these situations. For interventions with the families of neglected children, the social worker's knowledge of community resources is her or his major asset. The need for referral for medical care, financial and vocational assistance, parent education, or psychological help requires advocacy, education, and experience in order to secure the necessary services. Depending on his or her age, it may be necessary to refer the neglected child to a child protective agency so that he or she receives the care needed to survive and thrive. It is far more desirable, and a tenet of public policy, that, if possible, the worker bring necessary resources to the parent to maintain and improve family integrity rather than simply facilitate the child's admission to the protective service system. Thus, it is important to attempt any interventions that appropriately may help the parent(s) develop the competence needed to create a home in which the child can remain safely.

SUPPORT TO STAFF

If we admit that reporting suspected abuse creates a great deal of tension for the social worker, we also must be aware of the effect on teachers and administrators involved in the reporting process and the kind of consultative support they may need from the social worker. They may have less theoretical understanding or personal tolerance for abuse and serious personal issues could be triggered. The social worker who has been involved in reporting must offer a period of contact to teachers or other school personnel to help them deal with their feelings about such an episode. The consequences noted above will have their effect on the child's school behavior and may create a more dysfunctional situation, at least temporarily, from that which existed before.

Child neglect or abuse occurs at all socio-economic levels and all demographic groups. School social workers, along with other special services personnel, can provide school staff with information regarding normal and pathological child development. School personnel need to be alerted to symptoms common at various stages along the developmental spectrum. Besides providing support and consultation on individual situations, school social workers can offer in-service programs to all school staff, alerting them to symptoms of child abuse or neglect that could be expressed in behavior or attitudes in the classroom. In-service programs can also address prospective reporters' concerns about the possible alienation of the child and family from the school as a consequence of the reporting process.

CHILDREN IN PLACEMENT

Another group of children in the schools who require particular attention from the school social worker are those children already in the foster care system. They may be living in foster homes, in kinship care, in group homes, or in large congregate institutions. Unless they already are attending an alternative school as part of the placement, these children are at risk for over-identification in the school for special education placement for behavioral, emotional, and learning disabilities. Although they may present symptoms of behavior disorders or learning disabilities, or both, it may be their stigmatized positions as "placed children" that prejudices school personnel to anticipate that their academic performance may be below expectations. The school social worker must be alert to these judgments and protect the identified children from inappropriate referrals to and placement in special education classes.

The placed child may require additional time from the school social worker, who will be expected to attend the interdisciplinary staffings at the protective service agency. The social worker may need to do additional paper work required by the agency. The school social worker needs to be aware of which children in her or his school are living in alternative settings. To flag these children for his or her own caseload list, or to offer consultation to teachers who may find these children more troubling, are other means of avoiding special education labeling. Working with teachers to help them develop effective in-class interventions, before referral for evaluation, likewise may help to avert consideration for more restricted placements. It is often possible to consult with the receiving teacher in a preliminary meeting prior to or soon after such a child enters the school without prejudicing the child's position.

RESPONSIBILITIES FOR PREVENTION

The school social worker may develop numerous preventive programs to forestall family and institutional breakdown that presages the need for protective services. Within the school, the worker may spearhead in-service programs for all school personnel to alert them to the symptoms of child neglect and abuse. Here too, outside speakers, especially those from child protection and child placement agencies, may offer the information and indicate how remediation occurs. The social worker should be available for consultation to teachers and administrators regarding any child of concern to the staff. The school social worker can meld family, cultural, and community issues to forecast the extent of danger to a particular child. He or she may become an advocate for school-based intervention programs such as Head Start, day care (both before and after school), and for volunteer services from people in the community who might provide a safe relationship to a child on school premises. The "lighted schoolhouse," for example, can become a safe place in the community for all children. Programs are needed for the families of the school-aged child in which effective parenting may be presented, concerns of parents can be addressed, and normal developmental stages and appropriate needs of children can be discussed. Many parents welcome such enrichment, and it can serve as a vital link between the school and the community. Neighborhood care programs and telephone access to foster grandparents for latchkey children can also help avoid potential danger to children.

The school social worker can prepare school personnel who work with children to be alert to the signs of victimization of those children at greatest risk. Other professionals in the school generally do not have the education and training to evaluate behavioral expressions that could be related to abuse, nor does the teacher normally possess the necessary assessment skills to identify a pathological situation. Consequently, the school social worker needs to initiate discussions with faculty, administration, and parents to define the serious consequences of child neglect and abuse, and the child's need for informed adults to help them deal with trauma.

Another important activity would be for a social worker to develop a collaborative curriculum to present to all faculty to teach protective behaviors to children. The social worker might team-teach this material with teachers if teachers can be found who are comfortable with it. For example, the social worker might deal with the affective components, while teachers might describe and teach techniques students can use to safeguard themselves from familiar adults as well as strangers. Social workers and/or teachers can offer support groups to enable children to share their fears and their experiences in these situations. If some teachers are unable to deal with this material, the social worker may present this curriculum with others from the pupil personnel services team, such as the nurse or psychologist.

BUILDING A COLLABORATIVE RELATIONSHIP WITH THE CHILD WELFARE SYSTEM

The school social worker needs to be able to work with the child welfare system and with child welfare workers. The objective of the child welfare or protective services worker (as he or she is often identified today) and that of the school social worker should be nearly identical. Unfortunately, this is not always the reality. There are circumstances that may create an adversarial situation between them, though the circumstances may be political or territorial in nature. A condition that most frequently breeds conflicts is a lack of understanding between the protective services worker and social worker of the demands, responsibilities, and limitations of the respective agencies that employ them. The protective service agency's practices may not reflect the law and may be unrelated to the school's involvement with the child. Conversely, the protective services worker may expect more flexibility and individualization of a child's needs than the school can offer. Thus, frustration, anger, and a sense of helplessness can result in an adversarial attitude that confounds collaboration. A lack of cooperation needs to be addressed by the workers and/or institutions, especially because children requiring the service of both school social workers and child protection workers are generally the most vulnerable of our children.

In order to develop a cooperative working relationship with the local child protective service agency, the school social worker must become familiar with the agency's criteria for referral and identify intake personnel with whom joint work must occur to make an acceptable referral. The school social worker also should be available for consultation following a referral and should learn the procedure for testifying in court, if that should be required. For this reason the school social worker would be wise to develop regular communication with the staff of the child protective agency. Such relationship building will increase the school social worker's comfort in making referrals and will facilitate appropriate service to the child and family for whom the referral is necessary. This preparation will also decrease the potential for misunderstanding between the school social worker and the protective service worker.

The school social worker and the protective service worker must collaborate in two major areas:

1. Identification of neglected and abused children and evaluation or remediation of the situations allowing such abuse and neglect to occur, and
2. Planning for the child who is living away from his or her biological family

Because the school social worker will be responsible for dealing with the child protective system, she or he should decide when to report developing concerns to the designated agency and develop a method for interaction with the agency. Most significantly, the social worker will need to become skilled at identifying children who are risk for abuse or neglect and at working with them and their families. The other mandated reporters in a school setting should be involved in some collaborative contact with child protective services or at least have the parameters of service described by the school social worker to avoid a sense of frustration should a reported case be unfounded or a less severe case be refused, even for investigation.

It is important to expand clinical skill in work with families. Biological families may require aggressive outreach and aggressive referrals. Home visits should be included in the interventive repertoire to emphasize the school district's concern for and interest in the child and family. Children in kinship care may need additional attention and school social workers must be prepared to deal with some of the ambivalence and/or conflict which relatives in caregiving roles may exhibit. Additional outreach to a relative giving care or foster families will also be appreciated by those who may cope with difficult behaviors but who have minimal access to the protective services worker. Such outreach should be negotiated with the worker and family to avoid overlap or conflicting guidance. This is another opportunity to act as advocate for the child who is in jeopardy of further life disruption.

Finally, the social worker can develop programs in the school that will provide more developed assistance to school personnel. The social worker might provide in-service training for teachers in identification of abuse, address the legal and emotional concerns of teachers, and demonstrate the social worker's participation in this process. The worker can cooperate with faculty and administration to provide curriculum on protective behaviors for children. Again, the school is an ideal center of belonging both before and after school. Presenting programs to PTA or other school groups to discuss social and legal components of abuse and neglect, to state the mandated reporting position on these requirements and the school's position on these requirements will inform the community of the responsibility the school has regarding children at risk. The school social worker may prepare presentation to the school board, identifying legal requirements and policies or plans developed by the district to meet the requirements.

It is important to evaluate community needs in order to identify those factors that intensify the need for protective services, such as poverty, unemployment, drug and alcohol abuse, prevalence of single-families, transiency, and so on. Following such an assessment, the school social worker can develop collaborative relationships with both formal and informal community resources that might alleviate the conditions leading to abuse and neglect. Schools, in conjunction with community agencies, can be a powerful force in moderating noxious causes. The school can serve as a center of stability for a community.

School social workers should be realistic about their own powers to change destructive environments for every child at risk for abuse and neglect. What may appear to be a modest change or gain may indeed alter the child's future. The fact that someone cared and tried may provide a child with a shred of hope and trust. Within the parameters of each situation, the courage of social workers to persist will reflect their professional values.

REFERENCES

Costin, L.B., Bell, C.J., and Downs, S.W. 1991. *Child Welfare policies and practices*. 4th Ed. White Plains, NY: Longman Publishing Group.

Hancock, B.L. 1982. *School social work*. Englewood Cliffs, NJ: Prentice Hall, Inc. (In Hancock, references by Broadhurst, p. 157.)

Tower, C.C. 1993. *Understanding child abuse and neglect*, 2nd Ed. Boston: Allyn and Bacon.

U.S. Department of Health and Human Services, National Center on Child Abuse and Neglect. 1994. *Child Maltreatment 1992: Reports from the States to the National Center on Child Abuse and Neglect*, Washington, DC: U.S. Government Printing Office.

SECTION FOUR
Research and Evaluation

CHAPTER 30

Research and Evaluation of Practice and Services in the Schools: An Overview

John P. Flynn
Professor Emeritus, Western Michigan University School of Social Work

Although the following articles deal particularly with research and evaluation of practice and services in the schools, there is no intent here to suggest any real separation of clinical practice and problem solving with the use of research and evaluation methods. The content of books on paper is necessarily provided in linear or serial fashion; only in digitized communication media can we "hypertext" and jump from one item to another and create our own links and real relationships. So we have saved this section on research and evaluation "for the end," when, in reality, the integration of clinical issues and techniques and service interventions are, of course, inextricably interwoven. Ideally, the process is iterative and circular. Each approach informs the other.

For purposes of this chapter, research and evaluation are seen as two distinct approaches to using "the scientific method" to examine practice and services. Some would say that evaluation is merely a subset of techniques under the more general rubric of research, mainly because the major elements (problem specification, assessment or identification, sampling, data collection and analysis, reporting, and the like) usually are shared. Perhaps that is so; however, we choose to define our conception as follows: *Research* is a method used to discover the state or nature of a particular activity. *Evaluation* is used to determine the value of a particular activity. Both employ the disciplined approach these steps or major elements suggest. Stated simply, research helps determine the size and shape or the present dimensions of a condition; evaluation helps to determine whether our values lead us to accept or reject that nature or state of something. As in all life, dichotomies and other classification schemes are never perfectly adequate to explain reality. Consequently, in real life research and evaluation usually go hand in hand, except when one explicitly launches a project aimed particularly at one or the other research or evaluation objective. It is a matter of emphasis at any moment in time or in any project at hand.

INFLUENCES DEMANDING RESEARCH AND EVALUATION OF PRACTICE AND SERVICES

There are a number of influences that demand research on and evaluation of social work practice and services in the schools. The first is that the age of accountability continues; stakeholders in America's educational institution, as in other American institutions, demand that outputs (i.e., activities) and outcomes (i.e., results) of their investments be made known. The utility and effectiveness of services supported by both private and public resources is more and more in question, pushed in part by dwindling available resources and in part by a diminution of society's collective willingness to provide automatic patronage.

The second influence is the mandate of the profession itself to integrate research and evaluation with the conduct of professional practice. Competition for scarce resources requires ways to affirm or confirm practitioners' credibility and viability; practice research and program evaluation can substantiate such claims and affirmations. People assume more and more that practice research and program evaluation can substantiate a profession's claims for status and legitimacy; hence, social work as a profession has its own self-interest in mind (and, by extension, the good of its clientele) in advancing its own "scientific" stature. There is abundant literature, of course, to show that the scientific approach and the profession's approach to change have much in common. As noted above, the similarities include specification of problem situations, objective means for assessment or problem identification, sampling of events or people or information, various means of data collection, and techniques for analysis and reporting that objectify the statement of findings and conclusions. Indeed, the practice of social work in the schools has now moved from having research and evaluation as ancillary functions of professional practice to using research, evaluation, and sound practice as a triumvirate that guides the fundamental orientation of a responsible professional person. Research and evaluation are moving from being add-ons to practice to being key elements in an amalgamated model of researcher/practitioner.

A third influence is the ethical mandate embraced by all human service professions to take ongoing responsibility to improve their practice methods and to examine the impact of their services. This has to do with a profession's obligation to "police itself," not only guarding against malpractice and the errors of its own members but also constantly striving to question and challenge its past and current practices.

A fourth influence, though perhaps the least conscious or purposeful, comes with ever-increasing specialization in the modern world. In all modern institutions, there is a trend towards particularistic and specialized approaches to problem solving. Examples in educational services include elementary-level teachers, secondary-level teachers, special education teachers, school nurses, psychologists, social workers, occupational therapists, audiologists and speech therapists, and the like, as well as, of course, subspecialties within those categories. Perhaps as much a *response* arising out of a need to communicate with one another as an *influence*, the methods or techniques of research and evaluation provide a *common language* that facilitates a shared dialogue and a common platform for the problem-solving tasks shared in the schools.

FOUR USES OF RESEARCH AND EVALUATION

There are at least four pragmatic uses of research and evaluation methods in school social work. The first use might be called the *codification of practice*. That is, research and evaluation methods are used to identify what social workers do and what works best under what conditions or at what particular times. Research and evaluation validate, through systematic and aggregated examination, what exists and what might have meaningful correlation with two conditions, if they do not establish an antecedent cause and a resultant effect. A number of task analyses have pointed out that social work's role in the ecology of schools has changed over time, moving from a focus on individual children to targeting at-risk populations to the provision of consultation as a means of providing maximum impact with minimal resources. Now the focus has shifted to examining the impact upon and the relationship with the family and even the community (see chapter 36). At the present time, the issue is the relative value of qualitative versus quantitative methodologies (each of which is considerably advanced in technique), and the volume of research aimed at codification is increasing rapidly. At any rate, a focus on the codification of practice centers on the building of a *professional knowledge base* so that the accumulated and verified experiences of professionals in the field can be captured and communicated to others, thus building a repertoire of knowledge and skill for those now in the field and for those yet to come.

A second function, and very close to that of the codification of practice, is the use of research and evaluation to develop guidelines for practice. Guidelines might be seen as one step below codification. Hypotheses have not yet been tested sufficiently and supported. Instead guidelines rely on what seems to work, what has been reported in the journals, what emerges as a hunch, or what colleagues find to be successful. Guidelines are, as the word implies, guides to practice in which practice wisdom not yet subjected to rigorous examination begins to enter the portfolio of "tricks of the trade." More explicit use of research and evaluation can help the practitioner to systematically examine those hunches or intuitive interventions and subsequently move their tests into the category of codification.

A third use of research and evaluation is to take the measure of an activity and determine how things are going, particularly in relation to how one desires things to be going. This use focuses on what one might value or prefer. Although presumably research of the type used in codifying practice or developing guidelines for practice might emphasize value-free preferences for intervention, this approach clearly examines what the practitioner or the service might value, or rank-order, or prefer, or desire compared to other possible activities or outcomes of service or practice. This use is more likely associated with program evaluation projects and with studies of service effectiveness.

Finally, a fourth use of research and evaluation is that research and evaluation are in themselves a method of practice and a method of service. Social workers might be said to engage primarily in clinical or interventive modes of professional presence in the schools. They do things with teachers, other school personnel, children, parents, or members of the community in which activity is aimed at intervening for the purpose of change directly with or on behalf of an individual client or group. However, social workers (as with other professionals) may also engage in research and/or evaluation as their primary activity in the schools. In reality, however, this latter characterization of social work practice is rare. It is hoped that there can be an integration of clinical or interventive practice and research and evaluation practice. The chapters in this section are based upon this view.

We always fail when we try to organize thoughts by classification schemes; however, divisions of reality can help communicate similarities and differences. The differences in uses here are based upon the emphasis given to the type of professional activity seen in a particular use of research and evaluation; the similarities are found in the fact that all approaches are aimed at emphasizing what works. All approaches are aimed at improving practice and services to help achieve goals and objectives that support the educational process for children and improve the school's contribution to the life of the community.

SUPPORT FOR RESEARCH AND EVALUATION

The field is presently presented with a dilemma. On the one hand, the age of accountability and the presumed return to "basic values" by our sponsors and patrons demand that the schools, social work services included, provide evidence of soundly guided practice and practice/service effectiveness. On the other hand, it is rare to see a line item in a school budget for any significant level of funding for research and evaluation of social work services. This dilemma seemingly presents a contradiction between expectation and support. Given this reality, the creative professional must redefine both the situation and the response.

One approach is to consciously take steps to more fully integrate research and evaluation with everyday practice. School social workers, as is true of other school staff, are generally now overburdened with expectations, increasing caseloads, and territorial responsibility. There is no recourse but to again redefine the paradigm guiding the nature of practice in the schools; the integrative approach suggested here and would not only *not* be radical, it would be reasonable and consistent with the direction of the field.

Given the busy nature of today's life for student support personnel in the schools, it is no wonder that the rate of research *production* on practice outside of the school is growing faster than the rate of research *consumption* or *utilization* within the schools. This imbalance, along with the lack of budgetary or "people-power" supports and the demand for accountability, suggests that modest, gradual, and targeted integration of practice with research and evaluation is needed. For example, a reasonable strategy might be a movement toward using such techniques as single-subject case studies or exploiting meta-analysis of project or program evaluations having some similarity in sampling or intervention method. We can also define our research and evaluation goals as identifying those interventions that have promise of showing near-term or intermediate-term payoff. These interventions can provide immediate reality checks on what works and what does not. Another approach is to use existing data that are already available within the schools or the community, saving valuable time and obviating the need for additional resources for data collection. Yet another is to tune in to current needs being expressed by the community that may, in fact, force us to redefine our priorities within the schools. Examples include the need to respond to new levels of teen violence, the relationship (or lack thereof) of the employment community to the school population, the demand for inclusive education for the developmentally disabled, or the need to organically integrate school social services with other community services, such as community mental health or services for the homeless.

These types of possible changes have to do not only with proving the worth of social work practice in the schools. They also have to do with sound ethical practice—using research and evaluation to guide and shape what we do and to form a professional style in which we build in a habit of always examining our practice.

CHAPTER 31
Initiating Change through Research and Evaluation

John P. Flynn
Professor Emeritus, Western Michigan University School of Social Work

Social workers are professionals with responsibility for bringing about planned change in individuals, groups, organizations, and communities. A characteristic of the practice of social work in schools is that school social workers carry out their professional activities as guests in host settings where education, not social work services, is the primary goal. There is constant competition for resources, policy support, and even the attention of potential clientele in this environment. This is especially problematic for school social workers when they restrict their activities to providing direct services to students and/or parents and attempt to ignore those influences that are external to a particular school building. It has been adequately demonstrated that environmental influences cannot be ignored in either practice or research in the schools (Bronfenbrenner, 1976).

Organizational change, to be effective and long-lasting, must be interconnected and interdependent at three levels: the policy level, the administrative level, and the level of direct practice or service delivery. A central premise of this chapter is that organizational development, peer consultation, and action research—three collaborative approaches to problem solving and system innovation—are powerful tools for mediating the goals and responsibilities of the policy, administrative, and direct services levels of school organization. The chapter encourages school social workers to develop their knowledge and skills as boundary workers among the policy, administrative, and service domains of a school system as well as to carry out their other duties in working with students and/or families. The concept of *boundary worker* is developed more fully later in the chapter.

This chapter describes three general approaches to innovation and change within schools. That information is then used to develop a research- and evaluation-oriented practice model, with particular emphasis given to the boundary work that social workers can perform in fostering system improvement.

TECHNOLOGIES FOR INNOVATION AND CHANGE

The following sections focus on technologies for bringing about organizational innovation and change in school social services. The literature on organizational development, peer consultation, and action research offers three useful technologies for school social work which will be discussed here. Person-to-person or individual change approaches have purposely been excluded, because the focus will be on the organization. Instead, research and evaluation processes for organizational change will be examined as particularly promising areas of the literature. There are, of course, other approaches to change, such as developmental research, operations research, the field of research development and diffusion, utilization-focused evaluation, the pursuit of outcome evaluation, and others (for a discussion, see Ketterer, Price, and Politser, 1980).

Organizational Development

In considering organizational innovation and change, the organizational development approach deserves attention. Richard Schmuck (1978, p. 137) characterizes organizational development as focusing primarily on a system as opposed to a particular problem or a particular decision. Schmuck identifies three approaches that are popular among educators: "(1) Expert technical assistance delivered by outsiders to the school district; (2) curriculum expertise offered by specialists within the school district; and (3) process consultation offered within the district but mostly on an ad hoc basis." In a review of a number of organizational development (OD) studies in schools, Schmuck observed that a school's potential for successfully implementing organizational development depends upon:

> readiness, duration of effort, and first phase activities. The readiness to benefit from O.D. is related to the support of the district administration, the acceptance to try O.D. by the principal of the school site, the staff members' interest and increased collaboration with colleagues, willingness to undergo some extra effort, and tolerance for individual differences within the faculty (p. 139).

One of the key issues is the extent to which consultants can help managers of human service organizations (administrators of school districts or directors of social work or special education services) manage the autonomy of the service domain of the workers while at the same time maintaining the sanction of the policy domain (the board or top-level administration). As cases in point, all key actors in the system may not be preoccupied with some of the issues presented as priorities in this book, such as concerns over lack of community involvement, problems in family inclusion in educational services, attention to cross-cultural affairs, and the like. That is, school managers constantly balance the mandates of policy and the constraints of resources with the exigencies of services provided by professional staff. This key issue is discussed later in some detail.

A Peer-Consultation Approach

Another promising area for planned change is found under the rubric of consultation. Consultation approaches have similarities with action research and organizational development. Alderfer and Brown (1975), for example, state that consultation involves a joint process of inquiry by client and consultant that generates valid information, an understanding of the consequences, and increased flow of information and communication.

Alderfer and Brown emphasize the flow of valid information, which is dependent on the open flow of information between the consultant and the client, and the development of a mutual relationship between them. They also stress the combining of both action and research.

A particular consultation approach emphasizes the use of peer cadres in organizational change. In fact, this approach may be especially appropriate in bringing diverse groups or opinions together, such as with fostering cross-cultural communication or problem solving or confronting gender issues in the organization. There are certain values inherent in peer consultation that are compatible with collaborative efforts at innovation and change. Central thrusts of peer consultation are: (a) the collaboration with clients in the design and implementation of plans; (b) providing assurances that researchers/evaluators and practitioners will not intrude without invitation; (c) fostering a norm in which researchers/evaluators and practitioners both take initiatives in introducing alternatives; and (d) making oneself available over extended periods of time (Schmuck, 1978).

Action Research

Another approach to planned innovation and change is commonly referred to as action research. *Action research* is "the application of the scientific method of fact-finding and experimentation to practical problems requiring action solutions and involving the collaboration and cooperation of scientists, practitioners, and laymen" (French and Bell, 1973, p. 87). Whereas some trace the origins of this approach to Collier in the 1940s or Lewin in the 1950s, the systematic application of action research has also been articulated by Ketterer, Price, and Politser (1980). The action research approach has been developed particularly by the Institute for Social Research, the National Training Laboratories, and the Tavistock Institute (England).

Action research is a rediscovery of an old idea that Carter (1959) developed for social work in the 1950s. She characterized action research as a process in which lay citizens and professional service providers act as decision makers engaged in a common effort to identify community need, arrive at a definition of a problem, collect and organize facts, and implement agreed-upon plans. In that context, action research is seen as complementary to classical community development approaches. Ernest Gullerud (1977) emphasized that action research allowed the social work practitioner to be both doer and evaluator. He emphasized the complementarity of research and practice in which research is conducted at the actual action/practice situation, the purpose of the research being to guide *decision making*. The approach characterized by Gullerud involved participants in all phases of the research process to the extent possible and emphasized the team approach between researcher and practitioner, both in the research process and in the use of data in making decisions. Action research replicates the steps involved in the scientific method of inquiry and has been characterized as both an approach to problem solving and a process or a series of activities and events. This use of research and evaluation technology may be particularly appropriate when *both the means and the ends* of participation are desirable, such as in fostering parental involvement in educational planning, dealing with conflict resolution in the schools or the organization, or in developing crisis-intervention services.

In community psychology, the argument has been made that community action research is that field's distinctive method of practice. It has been suggested that action research results in problem-solving work which is stimulated by community need, that theory then serves as a means and not just an end, that research becomes a tool for social action, that value issues are made explicit, and that the researcher then maintains the stance of giving rather than only taking from the field setting (Price and Cherniss, 1977).

In summary, organizational development, peer consultation, and action research are all *joint* ventures in which there is a recurring process of problem solving and collaborative relationships. Each technology is a tool for system change. In both research/evaluation- and practice-oriented activities, a scientific approach is utilized in a joint effort. The distinguishing characteristic of each approach is that organizational development and peer consultation emphasize the process aspects of communication and relationships, whereas action research emphasizes the problem or the decision. Each focus has its particular value.

A MODEL FOR THE INTRODUCTION OF SYSTEM CHANGE

A practical model for participatory organizational change based on using the methods and processes of research or evaluation would, it is hoped, include the central features of each of the three approaches discussed. That is, the model should give attention to (a) the problem to be solved or the decision to be made; (b) overall system structure and functioning; and (c) the process aspects of communication and relationships. Each of these must be taken into account in giving service or in collaborating with the components of a school system.

Models for organizational analysis in human service organizations (certainly a proper label for the service aspects of elementary and secondary schools) differ from models for understanding the industrial sector, however. Kouzes and Mico (1979) suggest that human service organizations are based in three distinct domains: policy, management, and service. Each domain operates by different principles and different success measures, is characterized by different structural arrangements, and has different work modes or technologies for carrying out responsibilities. Each domain is frequently in conflict, since dysfunction and discordance are natural conditions in human systems.

There are parallels of these three domains in school systems as organizations. Three kinds of actors in school systems that facilitate (or block) system changes are the board-level policy makers, top administrators (which includes department or unit heads), and direct service providers or practitioners (in this context, teachers, social workers, and other pupil personnel). There are other important components in the change system, such as the students, students' parents or other interested citizens, various funding and regulatory agencies in the external environment, and so forth. The present analysis, however, emphasizes the board policy makers, administrative staff, and direct service providers.

In regard to school staff, the top management level is responsible for policy development and the management of relationships with the environment; the middle management level develops and maintains the necessary internal linkages within the system; and the lower management level provides for service delivery. Social work personnel in the schools frequently shift levels, at one time providing for internal linkage between the service providers (for example, teachers) and top management, while at another time actually being direct service providers themselves. Perhaps the duality or multiplicity of these roles explains why school social work literature often deals with the identification of the proper role of the social worker, indicating that there is great diversity in the role conception and role expectation of social workers in the schools (see, for example, Alderson and Krishef, 1973; Costin, 1969; Flynn, 1976; Flynn and Gooding, 1979; Meares, 1977).

These "border connecting" roles of social workers in the schools can bring necessary elements together while focusing on particular problem-solving events. In fact, Kouzes and Mico (1979, p. 456) developed the concepts of *loose coupling* and *decoupling*, observing that:

Entities within social systems—specifically universities and public schools—do not share the same identities and are not closely attached to one another. Typical are the data from Meyer, "which show very low levels of distinctive consensus in describing school policies between superintendents, principals, and teachers in the same organization. These data in themselves show the decoupling characteristics of educational organizations."

This conceptualization of coupling and decoupling fits with the image held by Hearn and his colleagues that social workers essentially perform the function of boundary work (Hearn, 1969). The social worker-researcher has an excellent opportunity, then, to assume a boundary-working or coupling role among the three domains in the system, (a) the policy domain, (b) the management domain, and (c) the service domain.

The Role and Tools for System Innovation or Change

Taking direction from Hearn in viewing the social worker as boundary worker, with boundary worker as the *role* and action research, organizational development, or consultation as the *tools*, we have the essential dynamics for the introduction of innovation and change in a school system. Without this effort on the part of social workers and other change agents, there would be no countervailing force against the natural splintering of the domains from each other that inhibits development of a common vision (Kouzes and Mico, 1979).

One of the differentiating characteristics of each domain is a desire to maintain a separate identity. This phenomenon explains why different domains can be expected to view the organization from different vantage points and have different perceptions of reality (the so-called Rashomon effect). Each domain follows different norms, and its interrelationships with other domains are often characterized by discordance and tension. The domains routinely engage in struggles for power and control, have different rhythms of change based on their different attention to political and technological factors, and are all characterized by different environments of uncertainty. This explains why all those key elements who struggle with school-based issues are not routinely in concert, whether the issue is dealing with cultural diversity in policy or programs, introducing opportunities for mainstreaming, or whatever. To deal with these disparities, Kouzes and Mico, then, see the function of organizational development as creating opportunities for people to deal with the tensions caused by the interactions of disjunctive domains.

Kouzes and Mico speak of the creation of a *temporary domain* for the purpose of enhancing cooperation and bringing about joint endeavors. That time-limited entity (or domain) provides a vehicle for long-term interprofessional and intraorganizational relationships. A temporary domain, guided by principles of inquiry and experimentation, is a likely design for organizational development, peer consultation, or action research. To initiate change, such a temporary domain must be openly and purposively created by the participating actors. Furthermore, true collaboration (as opposed to manipulation) by the parties involved is essential.

If social work is typically a guest in a host setting in which service is seen as ancillary, a vehicle is needed that gives force and legitimacy to collaborative, planned change efforts initiated by social workers. For social workers, enlisting others into the process of inquiry and experimentation with other domains is one half of a two-pronged approach to collaboration. The other half is the technology: (a) organizational development; (b) peer consultation; or (c) action research. The scientific (purposeful, explicitly stated) approaches of these technologies not only provide force and legitimacy but also offer a means to depoliticize the process.

The Play of Power in Domain Relationships

Hierarchical relations between groups are often complicated by power differences. Although diversity and group differences are valuable in organizations, there are nevertheless imbalances in vertical intergroup relations, complicated by the distribution of power. Power is defined here as one group having access to and control over resources (for example, physical force, information, rewards, or legitimate authority) that can be used to control the other's behavior.

According to Brown (1978), various levels within a system generally overestimate and underestimate their own power. These imbalances create and are created by group perceptions. Individuals are seen as key elements in this development of perceived power, because some individuals are more active or assertive than others or are more likely to think in terms of strategies and tactics for change and development. These individuals, consequently, exert power, whether by design or by coincidence. The idea is to convert these individual activities to collaborative or horizontal uses.

The social worker in the school system, functioning as boundary worker with a set of organizational change tools, has the knowledge and skills to integrate efforts aimed at problem solving, decision making, and the development of effective system structure and process. The social worker's research or evaluation orientation as change agent and the creative use of horizontal and collaborative (rather than vertical or hierarchical) system power can be combined for the introduction of a legitimate and useful change role.

The *ability to be a strategist is the ability to have power*, and social workers are able to take the lead in engaging others in common efforts at organizational development, peer consultation, or action research. Through these collaborative processes, the distribution of power can become both democratic and technical, rather than manipulative and nontechnical or autocratic and intuitive.

Schmuck (1978, p. 141), referring to experiences in peer consultation for organizational development, has concluded that "if consultation and organizational development is to facilitate school improvement, it must break out of the mould of the traditional, hierarchical, expert relationship and move to reduce social distance between consultants and professional educators."

Horizontal redistribution of power through collaborative processes such as organizational development, peer consultation, or developmental activity may occur in an ad hoc temporary domain or a temporary action system for particular problem resolution. In such temporary arrangements, participants need not vacate their usual positions, roles, rights, or responsibilities. A temporary social contract can be established, and school social workers can be catalysts, initiators, or implementers of those contracts by initiating and/or orchestrating the temporary domain or action system for change.

GUIDELINES FOR ACTION

Organizational change results from an alteration (at least temporarily) in power relationships and a movement toward collaborative relationships. Foremost among the guidelines for producing change is that early development of openness and trust within the group seeking change is essential. Common expectations must then be identified, and a division of labor must be developed (Schmuck, 1978).

At the outset, there must be an emphasis on the potential and actual use of research or evaluation products. Strategies for utilization (the change process and/or its outcome) should be built into the overall research design via:

1. Reducing distance between researcher/evaluator and practitioner through collaboration with client and practitioners in defining scope, goals and methods.
2. The fostering of a broad rather than a narrow definition of utilization.
3. Engaging in multiple cycles of data feedback, increasing likelihood of the use of the fruits of the process or outcome.
4. Presenting findings in a clear, unified and unambiguous fashion (suggestion taken from Rothman, 1980) (Ketterer, Price, and Politser, 1989, p. 11).

Another point is to stress a "balanced emphasis" between the long-term as opposed to short-term objectives of the process (McFeely, 1975). That is, the participants must keep in perspective what can be achieved on both a short-term and a long-term basis. Inaccurate perspective may result in disappointment, misunderstanding, or disruption of morale.

Special attention must be given to those areas in which congruence of goals already exists between the individual and the organization and among groups and domains, and where there is agreement about shared paths of decision making. These are system strengths which can facilitate change (McFeely, 1975).

Herbert Shepard (1975) enumerates a number of "rules of thumb for change agents." He uses such adages as "don't build hills as you go," "work in the most promising arena," "build resources," "don't over-organize," "don't argue if you can't win," and a number of other practical admonitions. These suggest that one must have more than a single change target, that an optimistic outlook is more likely to result in success, and that appropriate timing is essential.

Brown (1978, p. 178) lists a number of activities that he characterizes as "third party tasks." He suggests that the action team:

1. Help mobilized or unmobilized lower groups to organize.
2. Create external boundaries.
3. Create internal structures.
4. Facilitate conceptualizing of issues.
5. Manage the mobilization of process.
6. Counter overmobilization (for example, play the devil's advocate).
7. Coordinate mobilization.
8. Control escalation tendencies.
9. Create temporary or permanent forums for safe communication.
10. Educate people regarding the dynamics involved.
11. Increase cross-group allegiances and mobility.
12. Increase or decrease interaction appropriately.
13. Develop mutual recognition of legitimacy.
14. Provide even-handed enforcement of the norms.

Lastly, attention should be given to the overall change process. Activities should aim at influencing the *stream of events* of collaboration efforts; the *structural* activities should aim at altering or influencing the *underlying conditions* that relate to the problem (Brown, 1978). The role of the social worker in a school, then, is to collaborate in developing, managing, or orchestrating the change process, converting vertical power relationships and processes among domains into positive, horizontal, collaborative power ties across domains aimed at innovation and change.

EXAMPLES

One example of change in school system relationships has been provided by Anderson (1974), who emphasized the maintenance of credibility and accountability in developing support for change. Anderson shows a negotiated selection of problems, using a team approach with faculty and students of a school of social work and persons from the student's field placement agencies (that is, public schools). The team, which also included psychologists, nurses, and counselors, focused on policy or program change in services affecting children. Recognizing that administrative staff had the power to hinder the efforts of the change agent, the action team gave particular attention to obtaining earlier administrative support by developing the change system's own credibility and accountability. They did this through careful recording, through regular communication with agency school administrators, through monthly or periodic reports, and through evaluation of their activities while in process. Administrators were thereby kept informed and were reassured. The change agents were monitored, and the overall system had a feeling of confidence and accomplishment. Time lines for change activity were established and the action group was held accountable for accomplishing clearly stated goals in the time specified. With this public and open process within the system, as well as the structure provided by the setting (time lines, reporting, and evaluation), the scientific approach to change obtained legitimacy. A similar approach aimed at legitimizing social work services is reported by Michals, Cournoyer, and Pinner (1979).

Another example (Flynn and Gooding, 1979) is one in which the subjects of the collection of research data were included in the consideration of the findings of the research. This is, perhaps, a less collaborative example than the one mentioned above. However, in a system in which the researcher and the system administration have shared needs for data, the findings are more likely to be utilized for something beyond academic or administrative purposes *if* the participants who serve as sources for data collection are given guarantees at the outset that the findings of the research process will be made available to them. In this example, an administrative advisory group, which included administrative decision makers responsible for the provision of services, was established. This advisory group reviewed the original research proposal and suggested items and modifications for constructing a task scale used to identify the various activities of a range of student support services personnel. This scale was used as a survey instrument in that project. Consequently, local decision makers were able to have early and meaningful input into the problem formulation and research design as well as to provide actual items in the data-gathering instrument that would relate to their own information needs. The group also assured those involved at the outset that the researchers would have the opportunity to meet in planned feedback sessions with each of the individual professional support services groups (psychologists, social workers, and speech therapists) who participated in the study survey. In that manner, the consideration of the research findings (if not the actual use of such findings) was structured in by contract during early negotiation and development of the research project.

A third and different approach is seen in a project (Western Michigan University, 1976) wherein a university research group made itself available to assist support services staff in a school district. The support services staff wanted help in clarifying the goals of their activities and in determining the barriers to achieving their own performance objectives with those activities. A graduate student research team joined a researcher in (a) identifying barriers to staff in achieving performance objectives and (b) determining with staff their perceived ability to alter those barriers. As a team, the research group and the school unit staff developed a model, an entire process, and a manual for a workshop aimed at identifying and assessing the manageability of barriers in achieving performance objectives in school social services. Rather than merely making observations and publishing a report, this collaborative action process of developing a workshop and a manual, by design, engaged staff in shaping the problem to be collaboratively explored as well as in utilization of the project findings. The project was helpful in clarifying the barriers that the group could reasonably expect to control and hence be accountable for. The action research process provided the opportunity to jointly engage in an effort to balance the mandates of accountability, on the one hand, with the realities of controllability, on the other.

In the first example noted above, the central principle was the development of credibility with administrators, with the intent that they would legitimate the process and utilize results. The second example illustrates the importance of early advisory group input, the development of ownership, and early contracting for the participation of important elements to consider findings. The third project illustrates that an organizational change project can actually be developed by the very targets of the desired change themselves, and that the action research or development project not only becomes a process, but can produce a product that is lasting for the participants.

CONCLUSIONS

This review and the research examples suggest a number of generalizations that may guide an organizational development, peer consultation, or action research approach to bringing about change in school systems. First, school system personnel are helpful and motivated participants in a planned change process when they are able to perceive that the effort has probable, immediate, or near-term benefits for them. Policy makers, administrators, and service staff place a high value on participation when the process and the product have relevancy for their day-to-day activities and responsibilities. Second, the use of research results or consultative process is more likely to come about when vertical power relationships are (for the task at hand) redefined for purposes of collaboration and/or coalition. The line worker and the administrator may still differ in their motivation for participation in a project or in their interpretation of the findings, but these differences can be minimized and need not dominate the process. Third, the results of the processes discussed may or may not be used in actual decision making over any sustained period of time. As with other organizational realities, there are many competing interests and intervening variables that affect the utilization of research or consultative findings. However, the techniques of organizational development, peer consultation, or action research, being based on the essential features and principles of a scientific (as well as a *democratic* or *participatory*) approach, tend to be durable because they are well-grounded in the realities of the school system. When developed in collaboration with the significant parties in the school system, the results of organizational development, peer consultation, or action research are most likely to find ready and lasting acceptance. These are approaches that school social workers can use to introduce system change in their places of employment.

REFERENCES

Alderfer, C., and Brown, L. D. 1975. *Learning for changing: Organizational diagnosis and development.* Beverly Hills, CA: Sage.

Alderson, J. J., and Krishef, C. H. 1988. Survey research for school social workers. In J. G. McCullagh and P. Allen-Meares (eds.), *Conducting research: A handbook for school social workers* (pp. 131–147). Des Moines, IA: Iowa Department of Education.

Anderson, R. J. 1974. Introducing change in school-community-pupil relationships: Maintaining credibility and accountability. *Social work in education* 2(3):2–3.

Bronfenbrenner, U. 1976. The experimental ecology of education. *Teachers college record* 78:157–204.

Brown, L. D. 1978. Toward a theory of power and intergroup relations. In C. Cooper and C. Alderfer (eds.), *Advances in experimental social processes.* London: John Wiley and Sons.

Costin, L. 1969. An analysis of the tasks in school social work. *Social service review* 43:274–85.

Flynn, J. P. 1976. Congruence in perception of social work-related tasks in a school system. *Social service review* 50: 471-81.

Flynn, J. P., and Gooding, R. Z. 1979. Differential role strain among student support personnel. *Social work in education* 1(2):47-57.

French, W., and Bell, C. H., Jr. 1973. *Organizational development.* NY: Prentice-Hall.

Gullerud, E. 1977. The search for the holy grail: Action research as the basic emphasis for research in social work practice. Paper presented at the Annual Program Meeting Authors' Forum, Council on Social Work Education, Phoenix, AZ, March 2, 1977.

Hearn, G. (ed). 1969. *The general systems approach: Contributions toward an holistic conception of social work.* NY: Council on Social Work Education.

Ketterer, R., Price, R. H., and Politser, P. 1980. The action research paradigm. In R. Price and P. Politser (eds.). *Evaluation and action in the social environment.* NY: Academic Press.

Kouzes, J. M., and Mico, P. R. 1979. Domain theory: An introduction to organizational behavior in human service organizations. *Journal of applied behavioral science* 15(4):449-469.

McFeely, W. M. 1975. Organization change and organization planning. In B. Taylor and G. L. Lippitt (eds.). *Management development and training handbook.* Maidenhead, UK: McGraw-Hill.

Meares, P. A. 1977. Analysis of tasks in school social work. *Social work* 22: 196-201.

Michals, A. P., Cournoyer, D. E., and Pinner, E. L. 1979. School social work and educational goals. *Social work* 24:138-141.

Price, R. H., and Cherniss, C. 1977. Training for a new profession: Research as social action. *Professional psychology* 8:222-231.

Rothman, J. 1980. *Using research in organizations: A guide to successful application.* Beverly Hills, CA: Sage.

Schmuck, R. A. 1978. Peer consultation for school improvement. In C. L. Cooper and P. Alderfer (eds.). *Advances in experimental social processes.* NY: John Wiley & Sons.

Shepard, N. A. 1975. Rules of thumb for change agents. *OD Practitioners* 7:1-5.

Western Michigan University. 1976. Action research with pupil personnel: A workshop on barriers to goal attainment. *Field studies in research and practice.* School of Social Work, Western Michigan University, Kalamazoo, MI. (mimeographed).

CHAPTER 32

An Ethnic-Sensitive Approach to Empirical School Social Work Practice

Lester B. Brown
Associate Professor, Department of Social Work, California State University

INTRODUCTION

School social work intervention has been carried out in various forms over the years. As with other areas of social work practice, as well as with other school support services, the need to systematically study its effectiveness has increased during the past decade. Although the number of studies is on the increase, social work in school settings is not yet securely grounded in empirical evidence about methods known to be effective at creating positive change. This chapter provides practice guidelines for school social workers who wish to follow an empirical approach to improve school performance and who wish to know whether their efforts are appropriately directed in ethnically sensitive practice.

Practice guidelines presented here provide a starting point and a method for guiding practice that utilizes available knowledge about change. The practice guidelines also provide practitioners with a foundation of knowledge about their clientele—school-aged children and adolescents—and the difficulties they encounter in school functioning, as well as the problem-specific methods needed to improve pupil functioning. School social workers need to ascertain whether change in client problems that occurs contiguously with workers' interventions is relatively simple, given the state of the art of research technology. Actually, all workers have the knowledge and skills to be ethnically sensitive as they examine the effectiveness of work with a degree of rigor.

A STRUCTURE FOR PRACTICE

All helping efforts require structure, which guides the efforts of the practitioner. The simplest structure for most social work practice efforts, the problem-solving process, largely was delineated by Dewey (1933) and further expanded by others in the helping professions (Perlman, 1958; D'Zurilla and Goldfried, 1971; Reid, 1978; Compton and Galloway, 1984; Epstein, 1988). If the problem-solving process is systematically followed, a worker can determine whether change is related to the interventions used. Following this process does not prove that the intervention used caused the change. It does, however, provide a worker with reportable data about changes in pupil problems, the apparent usefulness of an intervention in a particular setting, and awareness of obstacles to problem solving, possible gaps in services, and a beginning knowledge of how he or she seems to intervene best and most effectively. Front-line workers may not be able to test experimentally the effects of their interventions, but they can accumulate practice wisdom worth evaluating based on cumulative data about their interventions. For purposes of illustration, the task-centered model, a form of problem solving, will be used throughout this chapter to demonstrate ways of collecting data on intervention effects.

TARGETING AND SPECIFYING THE PROBLEM

The initial step in solving school malperformance is to identify the set of problems a given student is encountering. In school social work, the kinds of identifiable problems cover a wide range. To plan a strategy for problem solving, a worker needs to formulate and clearly define the particular problem(s) occurring in any case or client grouping. Thus the nature and identification of the pupil difficulty is fundamental. Some of the possible difficulties in a given situation area are: (1) a child deficit; (2) a child/child conflict; (3) a child/teacher conflict; (4) a teacher deficit; (5) a child's internal conflict; (6) a child/home conflict; (7) an organizational conflict or deficit; (8) a family conflict; (9) a family deficit; (10) a combination of these. This list is not exhaustive but gives some of the major problem areas that may affect a child's learning, performance, and opportunities. Once one has identified the problem area(s), one can determine and analyze the specifics of the problem situation. A careful assessment of the child, classroom, school and/or family contexts will enable the practitioner to accomplish this first task. Assessment procedures have been carefully outlined by Costin (1975) and Epstein (1988). A method for determining the specifics of the problematic situation has been developed (Brown and Levitt, 1979). The specifics of the problem situation provide baseline information with which a practitioner can determine whether change has occurred over the length of the intervention. In summary, the specifics of the problem will reveal who is involved and who is not, when and where the problem occurs and when and where it does not, what occurs, for how long, the intensity and duration of the disabling effects of the problem, what occurs before and after the problem, and so forth. For most of the problem types encountered by practitioners in school settings, these aspects will apply and careful collection of data about them will not only allow for measuring change but will also increase the specificity of the intervention activities, because the practitioner will have a clear idea of what and who needs to change to solve the problems.

BEGINNING WITH A SPECIFIC FOCUS

Examples of the importance of having specific information are readily available to any school social worker. Perhaps a child has been referred for certain behaviors he or she has been exhibiting. The eight-year-old seems sad most of the time and has on several occasions cried and asked to go home to be with his or her mother. One could speculate about many factors contributing to the child's inability to perform in class. Perhaps an aunt with whom the child had a close relationship died; the child's mother had a miscarriage, was hospitalized for several weeks, and is pregnant again; or the child's grandfather, who lives in his or her home, almost died and is now going to live elsewhere. Knowing what may be contributing to the child's sadness is important for designing an intervention program, as well as for the intervention itself and for the documentation of the changes that have occurred in the child's school performance. Before intervention the child cried and/or requested to go home a certain number of times a day. If the crying occurred at home, under what conditions have those occurrences and the nature of them changed? Exactly how have the child's affective response patterns changed over the course of the intervention? A careful assessment that details the nature and specifics of the problem situation provides a base for beginning the next phase of problem solving.

Another example might be an adolescent who is anxious and tearful. She shares freely, in confidence, that she is being encouraged by a boyfriend to become intimate and explains that she has never made love. She talks about her fears and her wishes not to lose his friendship. The worker talks with the young woman about abstinence and the reasons for it; she also talks about the risk of pregnancy. When the young woman mentions that her boyfriend has used intravenous drugs a few times with friends, the worker explains the added risks of being exposed to HIV (Human Immuno deficiency Virus) and of getting AIDS (Acquired Immuno Deficiency Syndrome). Also it is possible (because of other information sources) that the boys using drugs are part of a group that dates her best friends. All of them may be at risk for HIV/AIDS. If the worker identifies that each of the young women has a similar problem with respect to their boyfriends, she may try to use the same intervention with each one, or together as a group, if feasible. She may also decide to see whether the young men understand the risks of HIV, AIDS or pregnancy and whether they wish to work on changing. If there are five females and five males, the worker will have ten cases appropriate for intervention using a task-centered model. The effectiveness of the model used can be ascertained by using a single-subject design, to be explained more fully later. The first step is the specification of the problems for each of the ten adolescent clients. After determining this information, the worker and client can begin the next step.

GENERATING ALTERNATIVE STRATEGIES FOR PROBLEM SOLVING

This phase of problem solving is important for empirically oriented practice. In this phase the worker examines alternative strategies for problem solving and selects the highest payoff/lowest cost means of ameliorating the problem situation. At this juncture of helping, a practitioner can make informed choices about the best means to resolve problems in school functioning. The extensive, albeit insufficient, intervention research available provides clues as to what kinds of interventions have been found to work with particular kinds of problems and in what circumstances. Helping professionals need to have a working knowledge of this information or at least know how to gain access to the current knowledge regarding particular intervention strategies. Unfortunately, techniques have not yet been developed, tested, or proved sufficiently for practitioners to be able to identify specific interventions effective for each problem presented. However, available knowledge can help determine the kinds of interventions that may have more potential than others for effective helping.

The set of ten problems presented earlier may be dealt with in various ways. There are five general strategies for change efforts that encompass them all: (1) individual, family, or group counseling; (2) decreasing skills identified as counter-productive; (3) increasing skills identified as productive; (4) modifying teacher behaviors; and (5) modifying organizational hurdles (school policies, resources, programs and practices, and so forth). Most problem types can be changed through one or more strategies or a combination. The decision about which to use, given the state of intervention knowledge, is no longer a matter of pure guesswork. Personal preferences based on practitioners' awareness of what is possible in a given school and their particular expertise are still a necessary part of the decision-making process. As knowledge develops, choices about strategies will continue to need to be based on what we as a profession have done as well as what other helping professions have done that is related and relevant to our work.

There are excellent reviews of intervention research that can help a worker to select a strategy that is most appropriate and has the highest predictive effectiveness for the client or client group in question. The proliferation of research and numbers of research studies precludes each worker being aware of them all. However, reviews of research studies are done often enough that, when necessary, workers can refer to literature reviews to update their knowledge about potentially effective methods of helping.

Perhaps a primary basis for selecting a change strategy is the nature of the problem. This is determined by a thorough assessment of the situation. As one identifies the locus of the problem situation, one can determine whether intervention should be directed at the pupil, the classroom or teacher, the family, or some combination. As can be seen in the HIV/AIDS example, given the potential for teenage pregnancies or relationship difficulties, there is a range of strategies that can be taken. Schoolwide efforts can be made to decrease teen pregnancies and increase knowledge about HIV/AIDS. However, each of the ten adolescents may need individual or possible group intervention also. The ultimate goals are to help them help themselves to withstand the potential repercussions and to prevent them from making future misjudgments.

SENSITIVITY TO HUMAN DIVERSITY

Much has been written in the past decade about ethnic- and culturally sensitive social work practice (Brown, Oliver and Klor de Alva, 1986; Lum, 1986; Devore and Schlesinger, 1987; and Oliver and Brown, 1983). There is reason to believe that the use of problem-solving interventions and other strategies for helping individuals may be enhanced if one is also sensitive to different cultural and world views. Much literature indicates that clients are often unresponsive to intervention efforts whose intent is good and appropriate but whose implementation is insensitive to client belief systems and clients' usual ways of behaving. Much of the drop-out/discontinuance research (related to therapeutic efforts) indicates that clients do not perceive that practitioners are congruent with them; in fact, clients perceive that practitioners have some agenda that differs from that of the client (Garfield and Bergin, 1994).

Congruence between clients and practitioners about problem situations and the strategies for change is essential if one is to be sensitive to clients from other cultures, particularly those groups that traditionally have been oppressed in this country. The implementation of successful interventions requires a constant awareness of the fit between the practitioner's perceived actions and attitudes and the client's culture and belief system. When the practitioner is sensitive to culture and belief issues, the intervention selected can be designed so that conflict over these issues is minimized or obviated. Practitioners can become ethnically and culturally sensitive by learning about how their clients operate in their daily living. Such knowledge will help the practitioner understand how clients solve problems individually or together with others in their support networks, so that interventions designed for such client groupings will utilize existing structure to the greatest advantage for the client (Brown and Lewis, 1980; Brown, Oliver, and Klor de Alva, 1986; and Oliver and Brown, 1983).

The manner in which the worker in our example of adolescents taking risks through intimate behavior decides on the target and focus of intervention will partly be determined by the clients' religious, cultural, and familial beliefs. For example, some students may follow a religion that teaches that the use of artificial devices to prevent pregnancy or HIV infection is unacceptable. Although for some students these beliefs may not present a problem, others may have cultural beliefs that must be taken into account when helping them deal with their specific dilemmas.

INDIVIDUAL COUNSELING

Individual counseling may be selected for certain kinds of situations that relate to a student's concerns and that do not directly involve other persons. Frequently such work does involve others as collateral supports in a collaborative effort to help a child acquire new skills, and the like. At least two school social work studies have found that such intervention efforts can significantly reduce client-targeted problems (Reid, 1978; Reid, Epstein, Brown, Tolson and Rooney, 1980). In those studies, school performance was generally improved. Other studies of therapeutic work with children have also shown gains made (Garfield and Bergin, 1994). Although much of this work was not specifically directed toward school dysfunctioning, it is relevant. It suggests that children may frequently be helped by individual counseling efforts. These may be very structured, active forms of intervention, such as task-centered casework or behavioral treatments, or ego-strengthening treatments such as play therapy.

In our on-going example of adolescents, it is assumed that none of the ten subjects is willing to involve their parents in the counseling. When this is the case, intervention task development for each of the individuals would only involve each person in short-term, cognitively and task-focused work, possibly with some thoughtful access to the adult role models and/or other resources. Tasks most likely will be directed toward increasing each client's abilities to avoid harm.

FAMILY COUNSELING—CULTURAL CONSIDERATIONS

Family interventions as an adjunct focus of treatment for school dysfunctioning may be the treatment of choice when there is evidence that intrafamilial conflicts exist that are affecting the child's functioning in school. Familial difficulties take a variety of forms. There is voluminous evidence that family support interventions may, in the long run, strongly impact a child's academic functioning.

Family treatment is potentially one of the most culturally sensitive ways to help members of oppressed groups. African Americans, Native American Indians, Asian/Pacific Islander Americans, Hispanic Americans, and Arab/Chaldean Americans—all of these groups have immediate and extended family members, fictive and non-fictive kin, who play significant roles in problem solving. It is these extensive networks of support that help families maintain themselves and that help maintain their communities. By being aware of these support networks and by including them appropriately in the intervention process, enhanced outcomes may be more readily available.

GROUP COUNSELING

The use of group work in school settings has taken many forms, ranging from group treatment to deal with school adjustment, to group activities designed to increase social skills while engaging in play. Anecdotal reports attest to the efficacy of groups to help children and adolescents with school and personal difficulties that may affect school performance as well as general social functioning. Although there is limited research on the effects of group counseling in school settings, like other forms of counseling in schools, there is good reason to believe that such counseling can be efficacious (Cartwright and Zander, 1968; Kaul and Bednar, 1986; Hare, 1976; and Myers, 1986). Research on small group processes has indicated that groups formed in certain ways around specific tasks, issues, or activities may provide a positive learning experience for the members. One project trained previously counseled adolescents to serve as peer group counselors for other adolescents to help reduce school and personal problems (Rooney, 1977).

The eight-year-old child in our earlier example is mourning a number of losses in his/her life. Perhaps there are other children mourning significant losses or experiences in their lives and they can assist each other in a group. Task-centered groups provide an opportunity for members to help each other develop the strength to change. Group members become collateral "others," just as family members might be if they were involved. The support of others joined with oneself in change efforts makes it easier and less threatening to different ways of behaving. The experience of grief and loss work, and the experience of joining and helping in the group, have cultural components; thus the group can also foster increased cultural sharing around the most sensitive of human emotions.

DECREASING SKILL DEFICITS

Of the intervention strategies available for helping children with school dysfunctioning, this category is the most thoroughly researched, primarily by behaviorists. A wide range of techniques have been designed, executed, tested experimentally, and found to be effective in modifying child behavioral deficits and surfeits that are interfering with learning (Gambrill, 1976; Fischer and Gochros, 1975; Garfield and Bergin, 1994). The intervention research carried out in this area is so extensive that it is virtually impossible to keep up-to-date, let alone evaluate the efficacy of each. But clearly, behavioral techniques do exist for the widest range of behavioral problems encountered by children in school settings. The selective use of these methods by the social work profession is based primarily on personal preferences rather than a commitment to implementing strategies that are research-based and may have better clinically predictable results. However, since therapist variables do appear to have an effect on outcomes (Garfield and Bergin, 1994; Gurman and Razin, 1977), it is probably best that these tested technologies not be used by those uncomfortable with the assumptions of behavioral theories. Practitioner discomfort with a theoretical orientation would likely have a negative effect on the potential for helping. What is most important is that potentially effective methods are available as long as the therapist is comfortable with using the method as an addition to his/her repertoire of effective ways to help students and collateral support systems.

It is possible that the ten young people in our case example may need to increase certain skills or learn new ones. Those adolescent couples who wish to continue their relationship but remain sexually abstinent, need to learn the skills necessary to maintain close relationships while avoiding risk-taking behaviors. There are a range of skills that these adolescents may master to deal with these problems.

MODIFYING TEACHER BEHAVIORS

Modifying teacher behaviors, based on behavioral research (Fischer and Gochros, 1975; Gambrill, 1976), may take basically two forms. The practitioner may assist the teacher to modify interactions with a particular child, or may suggest the implementation of procedures for use in a classroom of children. For specific kinds of problems, either method has proven to have a positive effect on the learning performance of children in school settings.

Frequently, social workers in school settings tend to use teachers as collateral persons while working individually with a particular child. By developing new methods for interacting with the teacher and child, academic difficulties have decreased significantly (Reid, 1978; Reid, Epstein, Brown, Tolson, and Rooney, 1980). This process involves a change in a child's and a teacher's (and frequently parents') interactions related to the identified and specified problem situations or behaviors. A teacher's influence on a child's school performance is undeniably an important factor and needs to be seriously considered if practitioners wish to optimize learning experiences for school children.

MODIFYING ORGANIZATIONAL CONTEXT

Social work knowledge about educational practices, policies, and programs can add an important component to enriched opportunities for learning. As we develop more intervention knowledge for correcting the dysfunctional interaction of a child in the school context, we may also learn more about preventing obstacles to learning before they occur. As we practitioners advocate change in our host setting, we must be secure in our knowledge base, readily able to identify changes needed, and which changes are likely to be helpful. Perhaps our greatest expertise at this time is our ability to mobilize other school personnel to help with the children as a team.

IMPLEMENTATION OF THE SELECTED STRATEGY

Among the four categories of problem-solving strategies discussed, the strategy selected must be transformed into the specific acts needed to implement it. These various parts of the strategy are usually referred to as the *means* for problem solving. These *means* need to be developed as specifically and explicitly as is done with the targeting and specifying of the problems themselves. This process serves several important functions in empirically oriented practice. In the case example we are following, the means for implementing the selected strategy would be the *tasks* developed by the clients and worker to resolve the targeted problems. For example, the students might enhance little-used skills, or learn new ones, to avoid unwanted pregnancy or HIV infection. Learning the use of these skills might be the tasks developed.

If a worker is using previously experimentally verified techniques (such as task-centered in our example), it is essential that the necessary steps (means or tasks) be known and delineated beforehand to ensure that the process is being followed as tested. If the tested method is going to be used, such a process may increase the odds in favor of the method that works effectively with clients having similar kinds of problems. One can hardly judge the usefulness of a procedure if it is not being used correctly. Exact usage, on the other hand, will not guarantee the same outcomes achieved by others. A host of variables are always operating and can positively or negatively affect outcomes. These fluctuating circumstances test the effects of an intervention. The process of testing and verification occurs throughout problem solving, but to be most useful to practitioners and clients it needs to be done in an exacting fashion. As actions are taken to solve problems, the initial discomforts may lessen. Consequently, as the problem decreases there is a natural tendency to believe that successful problem solving is occurring. The importance of a deliberate and systematic verification process cannot be overemphasized. Without it, problem solving may fall short of the changes that are actually possible (Brown, 1980). If verification is spotty, imperfections in the strategy and/or its implementation may not be noticed or corrected in time to maximize the intervention process. Without verification the potentially useful feedback loop necessary for correcting imperfect strategies, for improving practice with clients, and for transmitting intervention to others may be lost or highly faulty.

Verification involves a step-by-step check of the fit between the delineation of the targeted problem, the intervention strategy selected, and its effect over the course of working with a client. This self-monitoring process can give practitioners more objective information about their work, the effects on client problem situation, and about ways to improve their intervention strategies.

In our case examples, it is important that the worker keep track weekly (or even daily) of the status of each problem while working with the ten adolescents or eight-year-olds suffering losses. If, for example, each adolescent client targets two problems, then the worker will be tracking twenty problems. Only by verifying change can the worker be sure that the intervention is working.

EMPIRICALLY ORIENTED PRACTICE KNOWLEDGE

The purpose of empirical practice is to enhance the functioning of clients. Empirical work encompasses those practice methods based on the results of observation and experiment. In other words, the helping process is based on what one thinks will work by virtue of previous observation or experiment. A package of techniques may have an advantageous effect on client problems without an explanation of *why* it is successful. This is true of the task-centered model, a particular social work model of practice that has been tested experimentally a number of times in the past decade (Reid, 1978; Epstein, 1988). The model was developed by combining many aspects of practice wisdom, previously observed occurrences, and variables experimentally tested and found associated with but not causally related to effective outcomes. The model has been further developed and tested as corrective feedback has been used and applied as obstacles to problem solving occurred and ways identified to obviate them. This kind of model development is a process that any practitioner may use in work with clients. Too much time, effort, and resources may be required to test each new innovation experimentally but the systematic development of one's own practice methods is entirely possible.

For some practitioners, small scale studies are possible, will be carried out, and will be reported. However, the efforts of front-line practitioners need to be known and understood if intervention research is to benefit clients (Epstein, 1988). The structure for practice as delineated here is one way to improve and enhance one's own practice. The incorporation into practice methods of factors found to be effective in experimental tests is an additional and crucial way to inform and develop empirically based practice methods. Reporting these findings through written accounts enhances our profession as a whole.

SINGLE SUBJECT DESIGN STUDIES

Data from working with the ten adolescents provides the information necessary for a solid single subject design study. The intervention, a task-centered model, was used in each case. The problems were specified, and therefore measurable during the course of the intervention (verification). At the end of each intervention, the school social worker can determine which and how many of the twenty targeted problems changed. However, the social worker cannot say that he/she or the intervention caused the change. In a clinical sense that is beside the point. The clients and worker are more often concerned about desired change than they are about experimental causation.

Single subject design is the research design of choice for a caseworker. This research design follows the problem-solving design, so there is no conflict between what the clinician does and what is needed for research. To help a client, one must define a problem. To determine through research if intervention helps, one must also define the problem before intervening.

Single subject design methodology has been used successfully in social work and in other professions for years. It has been developed so extensively that one can effectively design an experimental study using the single subject design (Alter and Evens, 1990; Barlow and Hersen, 1984; and Bloom and Fischer, 1982).

To continue our case examples as a single subject study, suppose a worker sees fifty individual cases a year using a task-centered approach (or some other form of problem solving). Each client has two targeted problems. At the end of the year, the worker has intervened with 100 problems. This is a single subject, multiple baseline study with 50 clients and 100 problems. This means of accumulating data about working with clients and the effects of that work can add to our knowledge about helpful efforts in school social work. The records of such data would enable us to know that certain kinds of problems occur with certain ethnically identified clients and not with others. Or that all groups have a similar problem sometimes, but strategies and tasks are different for each group: some have more positive outcomes with individual work and others with family or group work. One could also ascertain that some problems are quite amenable to the chosen intervention and that others are unaffected. The kinds of information available from single subject studies can help us do our work in ways that better the lives of our clients.

SUMMARY AND CONCLUSIONS

There is no need to argue that more intervention knowledge is needed to ensure that school social work practices optimize learning for children, particularly minority children. How that knowledge gets developed is not worthy of argument either. Front-line practitioners know best and most quickly what kinds of problems and kinds of clients respond best to interventions and in which social contexts. To develop the most effective practice methods, empirically oriented practitioners are needed in school settings. Further efforts to develop effective intervention methods need to utilize knowledge about human diversity. African-American, Hispanic, and Native American children drop out before completing high school at alarming rates. Interventions that are ethnically and culturally sensitive *and* effectively evaluated are needed in order to change these trends.

Most trained social workers already have the skills to provide the profession with empirical research observations about practice methods. However, these skills may not have been used to record systematically the research that would help achieve this objective. The structure of practice presented earlier can be used to achieve this, using single subject, multiple baseline designed studies and recording these faithfully and then reporting to other professionals. Other structures that can provide similar information for a worker and the profession, as a whole, are also needed. Without such efforts knowledge about effective intervention methods may come too slowly.

REFERENCES

Alter, C., and Evens, W. 1990. *Evaluating your practice: A guide to self assessment.* NY: Springer.

Barlow, D., and Hersen, M. 1984. *Single case experimental designs.* NY: Pergamon.

Bloom, M., and Fischer, J. 1982. *Evaluating practice: Guidelines for the accountable practitioner.* Englewood Cliffs, NJ: Prentice-Hall.

Brown, L., and Levitt, J. 1979. A methodology for problem system identification. *Social Casework* 60(7).

Brown, L., and Lewis, R. 1980. The task centered model in work with American indians. *Social welfare forum.* NY: Columbia.

Brown, L., Oliver, J., and Klor de Alva, J. 1986. *Sociocultural and service issues in working with Hispanic American clients.* Albany, NY: Rockefeller College, SUNY-Albany.

Cartwright, D., and Zander, A. 1968. *Group dynamics.* NY: Harper and Row.

Compton, B., and Galloway, D. 1984. *Social casework processes. Third edition.* Homewood, IL: Dorsey.

Costin, L. 1975. School social work practice: A new model. *Social Work* 20, March.

Devore, W., and Schlesinger, E. 1987. *Ethnic-sensitive social work practice.* Columbus, OH: Merrill.

Dewey, J. 1933. *How we think.* Lexington, MA: D. C. Heath.

D'Zurilla, T., and Goldfried, M. 1971. Problem solving and behavior modification. *Journal of Abnormal Psychology* 35: 549–61.

Epstein, L. 1988. *Helping people: A task centered approach.* Second edition. Columbus, OH: Merrill.

Fischer, J., and Gochros, H. 1975. *Planned behavior change.* NY: Free Press.

Gambrill, E. 1976. *Behavior modification: Handbook of assessment, intervention and evaluation.* San Francisco, CA: Jossey-Bass.

Garfield, S., and Bergin, A. 1994. *Handbook of psychotherapy and behavior change.* Fourth edition. NY: Wiley.

Gurman, A., and Razin, P. 1977. *Effective pscyhotherapy: A handbook of research.* NY: Pergamon.

Hare, A. 1976. *Handbook of small group research.* NY: Free Press.

Kaul, T., and Bednar, R. 1986. Research on group and related therapies. In Garfield, S., and Bergin, A. (eds.). *Handbook of pscyhotherapy and behavior change.* Third edition. NY: Wiley.

Lum, D. 1986. *Social work and people of color: A precess-stage approach.* Monterrey, CA: Brooks/Cole.

Myers, R. 1986. Research on educational and vocational counseling. In Garfield, S., and Bergin, A. (eds.). *Handbook of psychotherapy and behavior change.* Third edition. NY: Wiley.

Oliver, J., and Brown, L. 1983. *Sociocultural and service issues in working with Afro-American clients.* Albany, NY: Rockefeller College, SUNY-Albany.

Perlman, H. 1958. *Social casework: A problem solving process.* Chicago: University of Chicago Press.

Reid, W. 1978. *Task centered system.* NY: Columbia University Press.

Reid, W., Epstein, L., Brown, L., Tolson, E., and Rooney, R. 1980. Task centered school social work. *Social Work in Education* 2(2):7–24.

Rooney, R. 1977. Adolescent groups in public schools. In Reid, W., and Epstein, L. (eds.). *Task centered practice.* NY: Columbia University Press.

CHAPTER 33

Practical Approaches to Conducting and Using Research in the Schools

Sung Sil Lee Sohng
Assistant Professor, University of Washington, School of Social Work

Richard Weatherley
Professor, University of Washington, School of Social Work

The purpose of this chapter is to demystify a process generally considered the exclusive domain of professionally trained researchers and to suggest low cost research approaches that can be carried out by the school-based practitioners. A step-by-step guide to conducting research is obviously beyond the scope of this chapter. However, there are a number of excellent texts that can serve this function (Gabar and Grinnell, 1994; Neuman, 1994). Following an introductory discussion of research in the schools, we consider a range of alternative applications and discuss their relevance for the school-based practitioner. We outline guidelines for initiating research, and we identify several low cost methods for gathering and analyzing data.

THE CURRENT STATUS OF RESEARCH IN THE SCHOOLS

Research is something done more often to school personnel than by them. The growth of social programs in the 1960s spawned a new evaluation and research industry. While the popular view is that research is the product of the curiosity of individual academics, in reality the bulk of current research, evaluation, and data-gathering efforts in the schools is a response to federal and state legislative mandates. Legislative bodies demand strict accounting for the funds they appropriate, and even while decrying the regulations and paperwork, legislatures also contribute to the paperwork by imposing heavy reporting and evaluation requirements.

The volume of research and data gathering activities in public schools has reached such proportions that the federal government has found it necessary to impose some restrictions. There are rules to protect the research subjects, both students and personnel, from inappropriate intrusion by researchers. There have also been efforts to restrict the volume of research through federal review by the Office of Management and Budget (OMB). Federally mandated research must first be cleared by the OMB as well as by the Education Data Acquisition Council (EDAC), comprised of representatives of federal education agencies and members of the Chief State School Officers Association. Their task is to make sure that proposed research is relevant, necessary, and does not duplicate other ongoing or past research.

The impact of the research explosion on local schools, is of course, well known to practitioners. It shows itself in constantly growing paperwork requirements. School personnel at all levels spend much of their time completing forms and reports, a good deal of them seemingly irrelevant to day-to-day work concerns. The usual research role of school-based personnel is that of provider of data for research conducted elsewhere. Adding to the frustration of having to spend time completing forms is the fact that the information is seldom of direct use to the practitioner; furthermore, the practitioner rarely has any knowledge of why the data are needed or how they are to be used. From the local school's perspective, much of this data-gathering effort appears as little more than busy work.

Research tends to be defined as something that is done exclusively by academics, whose specialized language and methods are assumed to be necessary conditions for scientific validity. The use of complex statistical methods often limits the communication of research results, shutting out practitioners and the public. While methodological rigor is to be admired, all too often esoteric language and methods are worn as a badge of expertise and rationalized as necessary for scientific precision.

Local school personnel are themselves rarely involved in design research (let alone the parents, students or local community members), in assessing research products, or in suggesting applications. More often they are considered instruments for achieving organizational objectives. They are in this sense passive receivers of information and objects of administrative control. Furthermore, even the most rigorous research, designed from afar, may yield statistically significant findings that have little practical application (Oja and Smulyan, 1989; Sirotnik, 1987).

APPLICATIONS OF SCHOOL-BASED RESEARCH

If as suggested, externally-driven research is so often irrelevant to practice, then why should the practitioner be concerned with research at all? There are compelling reasons for school social workers and others to conduct their own research. Like it or not, this is the age of accountability. Schools are under pressure to demonstrate increased effectiveness, even without additional resources. Those who wish to regain some measure of control over their work environments must, of necessity, speak the language of accountability.

There are both defensive and affirmative reasons for conducting school-based research. Locally-initiated practitioner research can ward off top-down bureaucratic forms of accountability. Hierarchical management systems have proven inadequate for producing significant changes in program delivery at the school site (Elmore and McLaughlin, 1988; Sarason, 1971). Practitioner-based research can support a bottom-up change process and a collegial form of accountability. Recent educational reforms emphasize working toward the institutionalization of cooperative principles as the focus of school renewal (Holy, 1991; Reed, Mergendoller, and Horan, 1992). Rather than being passive consumers or clients, parents and community members can also become active partners in the collaborative network. Studies of educational innovations suggest that involvement of the local school community in research helps mobilize the capacity for internal regeneration of policies and strategies for school-driven improvement (Barth, 1988; Jones, 1991; Sirotnik, 1989).

Since school personnel spend their working lives with students, they are in an excellent position to identify educational issues first-hand. They are interested in what works and are sensitive to the practical constraints of school settings in ways that outside researchers may not be. The utilitarian, participatory, and localized nature of school-based research significantly reduces the gap between the discovery of what works and the practical applications of this knowledge (Elliot, 1991).

School-based research is the antithesis of externally-generated and externally-imposed change. Just as administrators and policy makers use research as a political resource, school social workers can do the same. Research in this sense is not the search for "objective" knowledge, but a political resource and adjunct to practice offering more immediate payoffs. Practitioners, including regular and special class teachers as well as school social workers, psychologists, and others can use research to ward off new programs and requirements which are unfeasible, impractical, or harmful to students. On the other hand, they can use research in a positive way to gain support for new program initiatives, to demonstrate the effectiveness of their services, to obtain additional resources, or to find out what kinds of interventions work best. School social workers can use research to move beyond traditional clinical roles to enlarge the arena of practice. Research can be used as an adjunct to consultation and as a way of demonstrating the potential of a more ecological social work role.

School social workers are in an especially advantageous position to develop collaborative school-based research. The profession has long been interested in effecting change through the empowerment, participation, and action of the people involved. The collaborative approach to research requires a different set of skills and knowledge—interactive skills, group decision-making, and conflict management skills necessary for negotiation among various constituents and interests. This kind of collaborative research is characterized by: 1) participation in problem-posing; 2) practitioner participation in data-gathering that answers questions relevant to *their* concerns; 3) collaboration among members of the school community as a "critical community." Here, research is aimed at generating data which can guide and direct planned change. It involves observation, assessment, interviewing, reading and analyzing reports and documents, and writing findings. These skills are already within the behavioral repertoire of school social workers. Below we will review how to do it. But first we examine some of the uses and potential benefits of practitioner-initiated school-based research.

Demonstrating the Effectiveness of Services

As practitioners, we generally know, or think we know, our effectiveness in the services we provide. We sometimes assume that because we are professionals, others should take us at our word when we make claims about the need for and benefits of our services. However, in the absence of convincing evidence, such claims may be dismissed by others as self-serving.

One school social worker, for example, was valued by the principals and teachers of the schools she served for her effectiveness in handling crisis situations—episodes of student acting out, students threatening violent and destructive behavior, and confrontations between students and teachers. She was frequently called upon to handle emergencies. She felt that this disruption of her regular work schedule was well worth the price, since her availability to handle crises gave her the credibility needed to get into the schools to do some of the more routine work. However, her crisis work was not officially recognized. It was not part of her job description, nor was it generally known by her superiors how much time it took or how much it was appreciated by the principals. Had she taken the time to document the number of such cases per month, to describe the circumstances and outcomes, and to record the feedback from the students and teachers, she could have used these data to gain official acknowledgment of an enlarged work role. She might also have gained greater insights into her work, recognition of her contribution, additional resources or decreased demands, or authorization for training school personnel in crisis intervention. As it stood, her work was appreciated by many but unacknowledged and unrewarded by administrators.

Fostering Collegial Accountability

School-based research, conducted by practitioners on practical concerns can foster a greater congruence between research and practice and help to demystify the research process. It can also contribute to building greater collegial, shared accountability. Let us assume, for example, that a social worker and a group of teachers have developed an alternative tutorial strategy, adding adult helpers to the classroom to work with a group of students, rather than taking these students out of class for remedial instruction. The team wants to examine the effect of this experiment. The results would be subject to some outcome measures, such as the students' progress, increase/decrease of tutoring time spent with each student, and the students' and teachers' assessment of the new procedures. Here, the purpose of the research does not necessarily require rigorous research procedures, but calls for collegial problem-identification and problem solving. The process of observing students and gathering data may also be an occasion for the team to examine and reflect upon their interaction and behaviors with students. By having the opportunity to experience and experiment with the research process, the team members may gain an increased appreciation of research and come to demand more of themselves, for example, to be more parsimonious and specific in the data they collect, and more clear about learning objectives.

Expanding Students' Involvement

Involving students in a research project can provide an excellent learning experience and meaningful participation in the school community. In Denmark, for example, one of the authors observed a high school class research project on birth control practices. The students had surveyed the student body, presented the findings to their peers, and then, working with the school administration, helped design a sex education program. Similarly, peer counseling programs have gained in appeal here as they involve students in real world concerns that are important to them. Students might, for example, participate in the assessment and evaluation of peer mediation programs with school staff. Guided by school staff, a group of students (or a class) might develop questionnaires, then collect and analyze data about specific school problems experienced by students. The process, as well as the findings, could serve as the basis for further joint student-teacher problem solving around these issues.

Establishing the Need for New Services

Arguments for the establishment of new services are all the more persuasive when supported by research data. Reluctant school administrators have become staunch supporters of services for pregnant students when staff demonstrated the increased state funding generated for average daily attendance (ADA) by retaining students who might otherwise drop out (Weatherley, et al., 1986).

Let us assume, for example, that the social worker and teachers feel that there is a need for a school breakfast program. This is resisted by school administrators, who are concerned about the cost as well as the administrative problems of implementing a program for which there may be little constituent demand. Requests for the program from teachers and social workers can easily be deflected by administrators in the absence of any other compelling reasons. When the request is accompanied by data showing support from the students and parents, the number of children who come to school without breakfast, well-documented reports of behavioral problems and the lack of attentiveness of such children, information on effects of nutritional deficits on learning, and data on the costs of the program, the request would be more seriously considered.

Establishing the Need for Additional Resources

School personnel are constantly seeking increased resources or reduced workloads in order to accomplish their work in keeping with professional standards. Administrators hear such requests so often that they are routinely discounted. Administrators like to sidestep conflicts between professional standards or official policy requirements and the limited resources available to meet them. This forces the practitioner to reconcile conflicting demands as best he or she can. For example, with the requirements of the Individuals Disabilities Education Act (IDEA), school social workers, psychologists, special class teachers, and other educational specialists are often expected carry out their regular work while accommodating time-consuming and cumbersome assessment and paperwork requirements for increased numbers of children. Administrators, themselves caught between federal and state requirements and limited resources, often thrust the problem downward, leaving it to school-based personnel to figure out how best to meet the new demands. School personnel work harder, taking paperwork home with them, forgo planning and preparation time, or routinize work tasks.

Another more proactive approach is to conduct team-based data gathering, documenting carefully the time required to perform specific tasks, thereby demonstrating the impossibility of completing them without sacrificing quality and deferring other responsibilities. Furthermore, the group involved in such data gathering and analysis can identify ways to reduce duplication and redundancy, and can recommend new procedures more relevant to the school community.

Fostering Collaborative Practice among Staff and Students

In settings where representatives of several different professions work together, professional dominance hierarchies develop, reflecting the respective status of the professions. The prototypical dominance hierarchy is that of doctors over nurses, social workers, and other professionals in medical settings (Friedson, 1974). In schools, social workers find themselves in a host setting administered and dominated by educators; social workers occupy a somewhat tenuous position. Their unique competencies are often neither recognized nor appreciated.

The use of research to demonstrate the effectiveness of services has already been mentioned. Advocating and organizing an interdisciplinary research project may be another way of highlighting the unique contribution of social workers. For example, a team consisting of the principal, social worker, counselor, and classroom teachers conducts focus group interviews of seventh graders near the end of the first middle school year. The students, selected to reflect the composition of the class in terms of ethnicity and ability, are asked what the school could do to help students make a more comfortable transition from grade school to middle school. The results are discussed by the team and reported to the faculty. Based on further faculty input, changes are made in the orientation and follow-up program for entering seventh graders.

Testing New Programs or Procedures

Often, new procedures are developed by administrators in response to mandates from Congress, the state legislature, or the local school board. This top-down approach, while customary, often results in new requirements being imposed with insufficient sensitivity to actual conditions within the schools. School-based personnel cope as best they can. However, it makes more sense to test new programs and procedures before they are implemented throughout the system. As an advocate for and participant in pilot tests, the school social worker can expand his or her role while indirectly contributing to the empowerment of all school-based staff.

Illuminating Practices Normally Hidden from View

In all organizations, schools being no exception, there generally are some practices tacitly accepted but at variance with official policy and not openly discussed. Research offers a way of bringing such practices out into the open by guaranteeing anonymity and confidentiality, thereby depersonalizing what may be very emotional issues. Examples include disciplinary practices, cultural sensitivity, or concerns about student-to-student sexual harassment. Teachers may be reluctant to discuss their own practices because they may violate official policy or because of the divisive nature of the issue. Such emotion-laden issues may be driven underground and beyond the scope of discussion. An anonymous survey might elicit responses that would never be brought out in open discussion and could serve to bring to the attention of administrators practices about which they might otherwise prefer not to know.

Forestalling the Implementation of an Undesirable Policy

A favorite method of politicians to avoid taking action is to call for a study of the issues. While outright opposition to an undesirable policy may be viewed by the administration as insubordination, proposing a study is a more constructive and conciliatory step that is harder for recalcitrant administrators to oppose. If, in fact, a study is undertaken, the results may help resolve differences about implementing a proposed policy.

HOW TO GET STARTED

We have discussed a number of ways in which research can be used to enhance the role of the school social worker and to support organizational change initiated from below. We turn now to the more difficult question of how to do it. In this section, we offer guidelines for getting started and suggest ways to augment limited resources. The concluding section provides a discussion of readily available data sources and methods of conducting research which do not require special research training.

Be Clear about Objectives

The first step in contemplating any research is clarity of objectives, both political and substantive. Are there specific group or organizational goals to accomplish by undertaking the research? Will these objectives be realized if the research is carried out? What are the costs in terms of both resources and possibly strained relations? If, for example, the objective is to encourage the implementation of a free breakfast program, would research findings in fact bring about that result?

It is important to distinguish between fairly broad goals and more specific objectives. A very useful resource in this regard is the now classic book by Mager (1984) on preparing instructional objectives. A frequent error of field researchers is to undertake a study with only vague objectives, hoping to make some sense out of the findings later. This approach is time-consuming and wasteful for researcher and subjects alike. For example, in approaching the issue of corporal punishment, one could try to find out about teacher, student, and parent attitudes as well as actual practices in the schools. But if current practices are the focus of concern, that is what should be studied. If teachers' support for a particular policy is at issue, then their attitudes and opinions may be a more appropriate focus. The objectives, framed as precisely as possible, should determine the direction of the research, not vice versa.

Don't Try for Too Much

When thinking in research terms, everything becomes a potential subject of research. One must guard against being overly ambitious and be realistic about the adequacy of the resources available to do the job. If one is planning to do a study without additional help, how much time realistically can be spent? Will this be sufficient to complete the study? One should estimate the time needed to accomplish each specific step. Even if it can be done, are the results likely to be worth the effort? If the answer to the latter two questions is no, then the research should not be undertaken.

Ask for Help

One way of extending available resources is to get additional help. This might mean seeking released time or volunteer assistance from colleagues and students. The greatest possible involvement of both colleagues and school community is desirable if the research objective is to bring about change.

Additional resources are available outside the school system. These include academics, student researchers, and advocacy groups. Advocacy groups have their own particular interest in practices within the schools, although their advocacy position may itself increase suspicions of administrators. Academics are often interested in consulting on practical issues and may even be willing to undertake the research themselves if offered an interesting research issue and access to a site. Students are often available from a number of academic disciplines—social work, education, psychology, sociology, political science, and public administration—to carry out research which satisfies their practicum requirements under academic supervision.

Involve Others at an Early Stage

There are two reasons to involve others at the early stage of a project. First, some might feel slighted, and justifiably so, if asked to join a project after the major directions have been decided by others. Second, and more important, the contributions of others enlarge the scope of issues considered and provide an essential source of new ideas. On the one hand, group process may complicate the orderly achievement of objectives, and groups are subject to group-think, which may constrain the consideration of alternatives. On the other hand, research aimed at changing current practices should be undertaken with a view of building constituencies of support to help implement the findings.

LOW COST, STRAIGHTFORWARD METHODS

Most social research is an extension of logical processes used in everyday life. In shopping for new clothes, getting estimates for car repair or home improvement, or planning a vacation, the customary first step is to gather data on the reliability of the seller, the quality of the merchandise or service, and its availability and price. Prior to the data-gathering stage, there may be some assessment of the need and ability to pay. Similarly, when contemplating research in the work setting, a first step is to specify the objectives of the research and then develop a research plan. This involves a determination of the information needed, its availability, the methods required to obtain it, and the relative costs of time, materials, and other resources.

There are several research approaches that require a minimum of time, some of which may be undertaken using readily available data. (On the use of existing data sources, see Webb, 1981.) While it is generally desirable to enlist the support of administrators and colleagues in undertaking research, there occasionally may be situations in which some administrators are threatened by the proposed research and withhold permission or seek in other ways to block it. In such instances, it is still possible to gather data using records and documents that are public information and available to any citizen.

Perhaps the most straightforward kind of research involves the analysis of existing data. Schools are constantly compiling reams of data on every conceivable activity. Much of this information is funneled to state and federal agencies to meet reporting requirements but is not necessarily analyzed for local administrative purposes. Examples include aggregate data on pupil characteristics, family income, attendance, grades, achievement test scores, the numbers receiving free lunches, the incidence of visual or dental problems, the prevalence of handicapping conditions, the numbers in special classes or programs, the incidence of problems requiring disciplinary action, and so forth. Other data are available with respect to class size and case loads of social workers and other educational specialists. Frequently, when caseload sizes are examined in relation to the performance requirements, a discrepancy between expectations and the reality of the work load is immediately apparent. The fact that a class for children with special needs contains 15 children of differing ages and levels of ability and is taught by one teacher with no aide offers prima facie evidence of a resource deficiency. Or if a particular school has an unusually high incidence of violence, there may be cause to investigate further.

Another invaluable source of information is the school district's budget.

The budget is a planning document which gives a good picture of what the district actually does and what its priorities are, as represented by the commitment of resources. An examination of the budget permits a comparison of stated objectives with the actual allocation of resources to achieve those objectives.

Other public documents which may shed light on local practices are federal and state laws, administrative codes and regulations, court decisions, state agency policy and procedural statements, and state and local education agency reports. A reading of the state or federal requirements may reveal a discrepancy between these requirements and local practices. Some administrators intentionally keep information about the specific state and federal requirements from those school personnel who must implement them. Knowledge of deliberate violations of law can give school-based staff a powerful tool for advocating change. School practices with regard to discipline, suspensions, and expulsions, and the notification and involvement of parents in placing children in special programs may be at variance with the law and/or district policy. If so, change can be encouraged by a range of interventions, all the way from judicious questioning to encouraging advocacy groups to file suit.

Another powerful kind of analysis is estimating the costs of procedures and practices. For example, it is a humbling exercise to calculate the cost of a single meeting in relation to its objectives and results. When one counts the dollar value of the participants' time, the costs can be quite substantial. Certain reporting requirements are costly, yet the costs are rarely calculated. In processing paperwork, one must consider both the actual cost of completing the forms and reports, as well as other hidden costs. These include the costs of printing the forms, moving the paper through the organization, handling and storing it, and the time of those who must read it, comment on, and analyze it. Cost comparisons of alternative procedures can be used to support one alternative rather than another.

Chances are good that most problems have been encountered elsewhere and subjected to some kind of analysis or research. Therefore, a good starting point in any research activity is the library. University librarians are generally helpful in locating studies and reports. There are now a number of excellent computerized reference files that can produce a list of titles and abstracts on specific subjects at nominal cost.

Academic specialists in schools of education and social work, and departments of psychology and sociology, may be familiar with specific bodies of literature and be willing to share their expertise with practitioners. For just about any problem which can occur in a public school setting, there are likely to be some interested specialists. In addition to academic departments of universities, educational specialists are found in the federal department of education, in state departments of education, in contract research firms, and on the staffs of interest groups, such as state chapters of Children's Defense Fund, Council for Exceptional Children, National Association of School Boards, Council of Chief State School Officers, National Association of Social Workers, and so on. A few phone calls are generally sufficient to access such networks and learn what work has already been done in a specific problem area. For example, if one is investigating student discipline, the Children's Defense Fund may be able to provide a number of references to completed studies, summaries of legal opinions and pertinent laws, and suggestions about model programs. The state teachers' union may maintain a research staff and have access to information on many school issues. Newspaper articles provide another source of data about school policies. In larger cities, local newspapers often have reporters who specialize in educational concerns and who develop expertise in particular educational areas. The papers themselves frequently maintain clipping files, as does the school administration. This is an important documentary record which should not be overlooked. The school board minutes are available to the public and also supply a documentary record of actions taken and contemplated.

Other methods for gathering data about school activities include surveys, structured observation, and interviews. Questionnaires are advantageous for gathering information that safeguards anonymity, and providing a structured format for analysis of responses. The disadvantages are that they restrict the amount of data that can be gathered and analyzed, and questionnaire responses may be at variance with actual behavior. Face-to-face interviews offer an opportunity to gather information in greater depth. The interviewer can probe, ask additional questions, and clarify responses. Furthermore, some structure may be maintained through the use of an interview schedule, a listing of topics or questions.

Structured observations are those in which there is some purposeful gathering of data according to predetermined categories. Observational techniques can get very sophisticated and complicated, as with the use of interaction scales to record information about who initiates and responds in a group meeting. More straightforward, simple observational methods will usually suffice. Very simple categorization and computations will sometimes reveal profound meanings. In one of the author's research on Individualized Educational Programs (IEPs), the number of participants in, as well as the duration of IEP meetings, were recorded and counted. It was observed that in one school system, the meetings lasted several minutes and involved only three or four participants, whereas in another system, the meetings averaged nearly an hour and involved six or seven individuals (Weatherley, 1979). This difference in itself revealed a great deal about the quality of the assessments in these two school systems. Sometimes it is also possible to enlist others in making observations. For example, all school social workers may agree to keep records of certain activities or to record observations of meetings in which they participate for subsequent analysis.

A final stage in the process is the compilation of data and the preparation of a report or position paper. The format will depend on the purpose of the research and the objectives sought. If one is attempting to block the initiation of a new policy or procedure, the report would necessarily differ from that used in attempting to compare two alternative procedures, neither of which is particularly preferred. The guidelines offered earlier for initiating the research will also serve in planning the report; one should be clear about objectives, avoid being overly ambitious, keep it simple, involve others, and seek the help of those with expert knowledge. In writing the report one should avoid pejorative language, cast the findings in objective or neutral terms, and let the facts make the argument. Brevity and clarity are the watchwords.

CONCLUSION

Research is too important to be left entirely to researchers. This chapter shows some of the ways practitioners can conduct and use research and, in the process, enhance their practice roles. Perhaps the most difficult step is getting started, particularly in view of the widely held perception that the proper conduct of research requires expertise that comes only from years of specialized training and experience. Such a view effectively rules out many of the more relevant applications of research in schools. However, as shown in this chapter, the school-based practitioner can rescue research from researchers, and by so doing, assume a more affirmative role in shaping school policy.

REFERENCES

Barth, R. 1988. School: A community of leaders. In A. Lieberman (ed.). *Building a professional culture in schools* (pp. 129–147). NY: Teachers College Press.

Elliott, J. 1991. *Action research for educational change.* Philadelphia, PA: Open University Press.

Elmore, R. F., and McLaughlin, M. W. 1988, February. *Steady work: Policy, practice and the reform of American education.* Santa Monica, CA: The Rand Corporation.

Friedson, E. 1974. Dominant professions, bureaucracy, and client services. In Hasenfeld, Y., and English, R. A. (eds.). *Human service organizations.* Ann Arbor, MI: University of Michigan Press.

Gabor, P., and Grinnell, R. 1994. *Evaluation and quality improvement in the human services.* Boston, MA: Allyn and Bacon.

Holy, P. 1991. From action research to collaborative enquiry; the processing of an innovation. In O. Zuber-Skerritt (ed.). *Action research for change and development* (pp. 36–56). Brookfield, VA: Gower Publishing Co.

Jones, J. 1991. Action research in facilitating change in institutional practice. In O. Zuber-Skerritt (ed.). *Action research for change and development* (pp. 207–223). Brookfield, VA: Gower Publishing Co.

Mager, R. F. 1984. *Preparing instructional objectives.* Revised 2nd ed. Belmont, CA: Lake Management & Training.

Neuman, W. L. 1994. *Social research methods: qualitative and quantitative approaches.* Boston, MA: Allyn and Bacon.

Oja, S. N., and Smulyan, L. 1989. Collaborative action research: A developmental approach. London: Falmer Press.

Reed, C., Mergendoller, J. and Horan, C. 1992. Collaborative research: A strategy for school improvement. *Crossroads. The California Journal of Middle Grades Research,* Spring: 5–12.

Sarason, S. B. 1971. *The culture of the school and the problem of change.* Boston, MA: Allyn and Bacon.

Sirotnik, K. A. 1987. Evaluation in the ecology of schooling: The process of school renewal. In J. I. Goodlad (ed.). *The ecology of school renewal: Eighty-six yearbook of the National Society for the Study of Education* (pp. 41–62). Chicago: University of Chicago Press.

Sirotnik, K. A. 1989. The school as the center of change. In T. J. Sergiovanni and J. H. Moore (eds.). *Schooling for tomorrow: Directing reforms to issues that count* (pp. 89–113). Boston, MA: Allyn and Bacon.

Weatherley, R. 1979. *Reforming special education: Policy implementation from state level to street level.* Cambridge, MA: MIT Press.

Weatherley, R., Perlman, S. B., Levine, M. H., and Klerman, L. V. 1986. Comprehensive programs for pregnant teenagers: How successful have they been? *Family Planning Perspectives* March/April 18: 73–78.

Webb, E. J. 1981. *Nonreactive measures in the social sciences.* 2nd ed. Boston, MA: Houghton Mifflin.

CHAPTER 34

Needs Assessment in a School Setting

Lyndell R. Bleyer
Director, Community Information System, Western Michigan University*

Kathryn Joiner
Associate Director, Community Information System,
Western Michigan University*

Needs assessment is a crucial skill in school social work. It provides a systematic means of gathering data about a problem experienced by more than one student in the school. It provides a broader context for the problems which students are experiencing in school. It provides a data-based means of communicating about this broader context in a way school administrators, teachers, and community members can understand. It provides school social workers with a powerful, data-based means of custom-tailoring their roles to fit the needs of a particular school or district. In a time when such decisions are becoming increasingly decentralized to the school and to the district, it is clear that the skill of doing needs assessment will become an important component of every school social worker's professional responsibility. This chapter is intended as a jargon-free introduction to needs assessment for school social workers.

WHAT IS A NEEDS ASSESSMENT?

According to a 1975 report funded by the former U.S. Department of Health, Education and Welfare, a human need is any identifiable condition which limits a person as an individual in meeting his or her full potential. Human needs are

---

*The Community Information System (CIS) staff have been providing technical assistance to schools, municipalities, health agencies, and human service organizations for seventeen years. In addition to providing data and statistics, CIS conducts an average of six needs assessments and four program evaluations per year and provides consultation to those wishing to conduct their own studies.

usually expressed in social, economic or health related terms and are frequently qualitative statements. Needs of individuals may be aggregated to express similar needs in quantified terms (United Way of America, 1982).

Many have attempted to define human need, from *Erikson's* (1968) eight critical stages of development, to *Maslow's* (1970) concept of motivation based on a hierarchy of needs. J. A. *Ponsioen* (1962) stated that every society's first duty is to take care of the basic survival needs of its citizens, which include the biological, emotional, social, and spiritual aspects. According to this view, each society must establish a level below which no person must fall. These levels vary from society to society, and change over time within the same society (United Way of America 1982, p. 7). Therefore, "need" is a normative concept involving value judgements, and is greatly influenced by social, political, and economic conditions. The change in political power during the mid-1990s will challenge the standards established during the mid-60s War on Poverty. For example, according to the Center for Budget and Policy Priorities, if the proposed welfare reforms are implemented, more than five million children currently receiving assistance would be ineligible for benefits (Michigan League for Human Services, 1995, p. 1). This will place more responsibility for creative solutions and interventions on our communities and our schools.

A needs assessment is a data gathering and planning activity to inform decision making. The data describe the characteristics, achievements, knowledge, behaviors, desires, needs, and/or opinions of a group of persons or an entire community.

Why Conduct a Needs Assessment?

The data gathered in a needs assessment are used to:

- help understand the nature of a problem; its characteristics, magnitude, or consequences;
- provide clues about causes and possible interventions;
- compare your students with other students or other schools;
- document the need to be included in a problem statement of a grant proposal;
- convince school officials that a problem exists that warrants the allocation of resources;
- demonstrate the need for programs threatened by budget cuts;
- document the support for new programs or interventions;
- provide information to assist with planning or developing new services/programs;
- influence legislation.

A needs assessment can be as simple as examining existing data, or as complex as a multi-year, multi-phase study involving the design of questionnaires to collect new data. Designing and administering surveys is time-consuming and expensive. Explore and use existing data before considering any type of new data generation. Collecting existing data can be very effective and schools generally have a wealth of data on hand.

Types of Data

There are a variety of sources that form the substantive elements of need. Some examples are:

- *Characteristics* describe the group or population being studied and include ascribed characteristics like age, gender, and race, and achieved characteristics like family income, poverty status, highest grade completed, and so forth.
- *Counts and rates* provide data on the incidence and prevalence of conditions. For instance, the teen birthrate is a measure of the number of births to teenage mothers compared to the number of female teenagers, while prevalence is the total number of cases in a given population at a point in time, such as the number of suicides that occurred during 1994 in your community (Simons and Jablonski, 1990, p. 5).
- *Knowledge* might include reading comprehension levels, math proficiency, standardized test scores, or street-smarts, and so on.
- *Beliefs and opinions* range from concepts like self-esteem or knowing right-from-wrong and the value placed on education, to conceptions like believing boys are better at math and science.
- *Behaviors* might include: eating habits, use of alcohol, participation in sports, number of hours worked per week by full time students, absences, number of students suspended or expelled by reason, and so forth. Normative behaviors fall within expected/acceptable ranges.
- *Desires* are what people want (or think they want) but don't have, while *needs* can encompass things missing that are self-perceived or perceived by others. *Needs* might be determined by directly asking the intended audience, observed, or inferred from available data, whereas *desires and opinions* are usually gathered directly from questions on a survey and/or are gathered through observation, interviews, focus groups, or community forums.

PLANNING YOUR NEEDS ASSESSMENT

Determine What You Want to Know

The first step is determining what you want to know, then deciding what information you really need to make an informed decision. The second step is determining the best source, balancing accuracy and reliability against cost and time restraints. Often as you and/or a committee begin to explore doing a needs assessment, the list of questions to be answered keeps growing. To expedite the process, make a checklist and decide which data are critical to your goal, which data would be helpful to clarifying issues, which would be interesting to have, and which will not add any insight to the problem being studied. As part of your checklist, include a source column. This may help you narrow your choices. Remember to look at existing data first before gathering new data.

In the next example, a school district wants to know if a school breakfast program is a worthwhile pursuit. First, they need to know whether or not nutrition makes a difference in school performance, then what percent of the students currently do not eat a nutritious breakfast, what their current performance is, and perhaps, how many children would be eligible for a subsidized breakfast program.

Information which may be useful in planning school services or programs are:

- the number of children living in your community and the percentage that those children represent of the total population;
- how many children live in poverty; how many are homeless;
- how many have disabilities;
- how many live in single-parent families;
- mobility/consistency—what percent of students attend the same school in June that they attended in September;
- reported incidence of crimes by juveniles, violent, serious, and misdemeanor;
- the services and resources already available to meet the specific need you are addressing.

Discuss the project with school administrators, teachers, parent and student representatives to develop a clear idea of the purpose of the needs assessment and what you hope to learn/achieve. One way to encourage cooperation among all the involved parties is to form a small committee to help you formulate an action plan. In addition to promoting ownership of the project, involving others in the planning stage is a good way to make sure you have not overlooked important details. Having the scope of the activity agreed upon by a majority of those involved will reduce hurdles.

Write a Proposal or Plan

After you and/or your committee have determined the scope of the needs assessment, develop a written plan. In the proposal include the following:

TABLE 1 Types of Data or Questions and Associated Sources or Methods

Type of Data or Questions	Source and Method	Essential	Helpful	Interesting	No Use
Breakfast's impact on learning—does it make a difference?	Literature review via: State Dept. of Educ. U.S. depts. of Educ., Health & Human Serv.	✓			
How many of our children eat a nutritious breakfast?	Students and/or parents via log, diary, or question	✓			
What are eligibility guidelines for subsidies?	U.S. Dept. of Health & Human Serv.; census		✓		
How many of our school's children are eligible?	School records: i.e., now eligible for free milk or lunch subsidy; census data on poverty		✓		
Are there any differences in achievement between:	*Grades and test scores plus:*				
Our children who do and don't eat breakfast?	students &/or parents, teacher observation	✓			
Our children from single vs. two parent homes?	school records			✓	
Our children who get <7 vs. >7 hours sleep?	students &/or parents log/diary, teacher observation			✓	
Our children with parental review of homework?	parent signature on homework			✓	

- Methodology of the study.
- Tasks to be performed and by whom.
- Project time-line. Don't set short deadlines. Give yourself enough time to collect data, review it, and produce a well-written summary.
- Develop a budget for the project based on the activities and time needed to carry them out. In addition to personnel, other expenses might included copying of questionnaires and summary reports, computer time, phone, postage, and resource materials.

In writing your needs assessment plan, be realistic about whether or not you and other school staff have the time and the expertise to carry out *all* elements of the project and what level of data fit the time available and the need. Keep in mind the impact school breaks will have on your project. You may have a fairly good grasp of basic research concepts and techniques from your masters level courses. On the other hand it may be that you will want to perform certain tasks, but will need to engage additional help from other professionals to perform certain functions. If there are colleges or universities close by, you may be able to work out a plan for a graduate-level or upper-level undergraduate class to take on all or portions of your study as their semester project. Many colleges and universities have research centers that provide technical assistance and consultation to nonprofit organizations at cost. Large corporations may have research staff that they are willing to "loan" for committee work or consultation. If you intend to carry out the needs assessment yourself, consider whether or not you will need or can get release time.

IMPLEMENTING THE ASSESSMENT

Accurate information is key to successful planning. Having reliable data can help you prove your point and persuade others. Think of the group or groups which will be the beneficiaries of the needs assessment, and also think of the groups that will be potential funding sources or will make the decision to allocate resources to address the need. Gather data with both audiences in mind.

If, for example, you are concerned about the need for enhanced substance abuse prevention education, you could provide a number of statistics regarding substance use and abuse, e.g., the age at which children begin to smoke, use drugs and alcohol; the number of teenagers and young adults who smoke or use alcohol; gender differences in drug usage; changes in use/ abuse patterns over time, the number of automobile accidents attributed to substance abuse by age of driver, and so forth. Existing data might be in previously compiled reports or could be gathered by observation. Some data may only be readily available at state or national levels. You may cite the data as found, or you can provide a rough estimation of local incidence by applying state or national rates to local populations.

Gathering *Existing* Data

Be sure to make use of your own organization. Most school districts have data on absences, suspensions, number of students repeating a grade, standardized test scores, student turn-over (migration in and out of school district or building), and immunization records. Also check with the regional or intermediate school district and the state department of education. Local libraries also provide a wealth of data. If materials are not available at your library, the librarian may be able to assist with interlibrary loans, searches of other libraries' catalogs, and computer searches of various databases. This provides access to many federal and state resources.

- Do a literature review or search to find out what other studies or data exist.
- Establish a profile of the student population affected by the problem.
- Determine if there are any programs/services currently in place to meet the need.
- Describe your organizational structure, goals, and objectives.
- List current programs, services, and resources.

Identify sources of existing data (see list at end of chapter for additional information):

Federal—U.S. Census Bureau, Department of Health and Human Services, Department of Education, and other federal agencies.

State—Department of Education, Department of Public Health, state data centers, state human service leagues, special interest/lobby groups, etc.

Local—Public, college and university libraries, police or public safety departments, chambers of commerce, school boards, technical consulting with local universities, computer-based search techniques via such systems as the Internet. Many hospitals maintain medical libraries which may be open to the public.

Other—Children's Defense Fund, Child Welfare League of America, and many non-profit foundations which fund programs and research about children and teens.

Other potential sources of data include: teacher and guidance counselor records, evaluation forms and reports done for accreditation review, and standardized test scores.

Gathering *New* Data

Exhaust existing sources of data before determining if you need to collect any new data. If you determine that you need additional data that can only be gathered firsthand, several methods are possible including: (1) observation, (2) focus groups, (3) key informant interviews, and (4) use of surveys. Surveys may be used with in-person or phone interviews, or can be distributed by mail, or at meetings or other gatherings.

As an example of data gathered through observation, one measure of cigarette use and/or exposure to second-hand smoke would be to count the number of students entering each homeroom that smell of smoke or have tell-tale nicotine-stained fingers. This measure would be crude, as it depends on the sensitivity and accuracy of the observer. Some might perceive observation as invasion of privacy.

Consider which of the following might be most successful and provide the best results for your specific project:

Focus Groups. These small informal groups, led by a facilitator, gather information from audiences similar to those who would fill out a questionnaire (teachers, students, parents, school administrators). You usually have a script or a short questionnaire to serve as a guide; however, the advantage of a focus group is that people build on the ideas of others (brain-storm, think-tank), and therefore, the group may explore ideas that you or the committee never anticipated.

Key Informant Interviews. Key informants are persons in a position to know or be aware of the problem you are studying. They may include the same people you would invite to a focus group: teachers, administrators, parents, other professionals, and/or students. A questionnaire is used, but the format enables the interviewer to follow-up and clarify responses, as well as explore areas that were not on the original questionnaire. This procedure is best when there are a limited number of issues to be discussed, a limited number of people to interview, and there are interviewers who are well-trained not to be judgmental or to allow their own opinions to influence the outcome.

Using Existing Instruments. If an appropriate instrument or questionnaire already exists and has been tested, it may be the best use of time to obtain permission to use that instrument.

Designing New Survey/Questionnaire Instruments (mail, phone, or in-person interviews and focus group scripts). If you decide to design a new instrument, develop your questions with data analysis and output in mind. Try to make it as easy as possible for respondents to answer. Keep in mind that a large number of open-end questions that require the person to write answers rather than circle answers on a provided list will add considerable time to your data analysis process. Then you will have to categorize and synthesize these responses. However, if you don't want to provide the respondent with answers, an in-person or telephone interview in which the interviewer reads the questions but not the checklist of answers is often a good compromise.

If time permits, pilot-test your questionnaire on a small group (12 to 20 people) to help you anticipate the range of responses for checklists, and to see if some questions are too ambiguous or poorly worded. At the very least, make sure the person analyzing the data looks at the questionnaire from that perspective.

Suggestions for getting the most out of each method. *Focus Groups*—Carefully identify those individuals you want included to be as representative as possible to reduce bias or skewing of results. Schedule in advance. Hold the sessions at a location convenient for those attending. Offer an incentive for attending. Have someone experienced lead the focus group. If possible, tape-record your sessions so you will not have to concentrate on note-taking and have a back-up tape recorder.

Key Informant Interviews—Schedule the interviews in advance and have your questions prepared. Let those being interviewed know how long the interview will take and stick to that time frame.

Mailed Survey—Allow adequate time for the return mail, and if possible, time for follow-up if the initial response rate is low. Including a "business-reply envelope" or stamped self-addressed reply envelope will increase the response rate. This method tends to be the least expensive. However, response rates are lower than other methods unless you offer an incentive or have a hot topic about which people want to express their opinion.

Phone Survey—Try to schedule phone calls at the most likely time to reach your specific population. For example, during the day for stay-at-home moms or retirees, or evenings for working parents. This method tends to be expensive, unless you have volunteers, such as PTA members to make the calls. Phone interviewers must be trained so that questions are asked in a standard format. You will need approximately ten phone numbers for every three surveys you hope to complete assuming that you attempt each phone number at least three times on different days and different times. It takes approximately six nights, with twelve interviewers to complete 300 to 350 four-page questionnaires.

In-person Survey—Use interviewers who are friendly and outgoing. Keep the questions short so those being interviewed do not have to remember long sentences or lists of things. Use 3 by 5-inch cards for answer scales, that can be handed to the person (i.e., 1 = strongly agree, 5 = strongly disagree). Do the surveys at a time when those you want to reach are not rushed. Pick your interview location carefully. For example, if you want to talk to students, a good place might be a quiet room near a study hall or the library. Bad timing for the survey would be during midterm or final exams.

ANALYZING YOUR DATA

Unless your study is funded by a major foundation or a federal or state agency which requires detailed documentation, you may be able to analyze your data by looking at the frequency or prevalence of conditions. How many students come from families with incomes below poverty? Where do they live? Or examine the frequency of opinions, such as, how many parents believe their children are receiving a strong foundation in the three R's. If, however, you need to provide more extensive data analysis, many of today's computerized software packages will provide you with an assortment of statistical measures and tests that are appropriate for various types of data. If you feel your data analysis skills are rusty, consider using a consultant to provide this level of analysis for you. However, it is important for the consultant to review your data collection methodology, including the questionnaire *before* you begin collecting data. Contact local colleges and universities for consultants within educational leadership, social work, statistics, and other disciplines that specialize in research.

Depending on the size of the sample, data can be hand-tabulated (under 50 respondents), or entered into a computer and analyzed by a statistical analysis software package such as SPSS (Statistical Package for Social Sciences), SAS (Statistical Analysis System), or other packages. For small sample sizes (50 to 200 respondents), manually enter the responses in a table or chart and calculate any desired percentages. For larger samples (over 200 respondents), consider using an optical scan form for questionnaire responses. With this method, answer sheets are optically scanned instead of manually input into a computer file. The optical scan format for data gathering and analysis generally saves time and money with large size samples. Customized scan forms which allow the respondent to read the question and make their answer next to each question have the highest degree of accuracy. However, the minimum fee for printing customized forms is $1,000, making it more cost-efficient for surveys involving 500 or more respondents.

REPORTING YOUR FINDINGS

Reporting findings is a critical element to the success of your needs assessment. Present your results in a manner that is easy to understand. Do not lose sight of the audiences to whom you are presenting. Focus your attention on the specific issue you have studied, and use your data to show that the changes proposed will make a difference. If you want to convince your audience regarding effective programs or services, it is helpful to cite examples of other successful programs or efforts.

Many times lengthy narratives are not the best way to report findings. You may find that a simple summary accompanied by charts, graphs, or tables that show your data in easy-to-interpret formats is the best way to present the results. Table 2 illustrates one method of displaying standardized test scores. The key statistic is the percent of students with satisfactory test scores. School districts evaluate strengths and weaknesses in their curricula by looking at these data over time. Comparing your own school or school district with others in your county or state provides a measure of where your district stands in relation to others.

If, for example, you collected data on the number of children who ate breakfast before coming to school and the data varied widely by grade level, an effective way to display this result might be in a bar chart with each bar representing the number or percent of children in that grade level who

TABLE 2 Michigan Education Assessment Program (MEAP), Fictitious County: 1993–94

	Students with Satisfactory Scores		
Grade Level	4th	7th	10th
Reading	47.5%	44.2%	43.5%
Math	49.9%	46.8%	33.0%
Grade Level	5th	7th	11th
Science	70.0%	61.9%	58.1%

do not have breakfast. Instead of wading through paragraphs of narrative, the reader could see at a glance that the problem is not common across all grade levels and then you may be permitted to target limited resources where they are most needed.

SUMMARY

Needs assessment is a systematic data collection and analysis process. Its purposes are (1) to discover and identify the resources and services the community is lacking in relation to generally accepted standards and (2) the transmittal of that information to those who make resource allocation decisions (United Way of America 1982, p. 10).

The choice of data-gathering methods will depend on both data availability and on the topic of need being explored. Using existing data will help conserve time and funds. Using focus groups and/or key informants will provide information on the level of support and help rank needs by your audience's opinion of their importance. Questionnaires, while more costly and time intensive, enable you to directly measure the desires, beliefs, knowledge, and opinions of your intended beneficiaries and benefactors.

DATA SOURCES

The following are some possible sources of data that are already available:

NATIONAL AND FEDERAL SOURCES

U.S. Census Bureau Customer Services. Bureau of the Census, Washington, D.C. 20233-8300. (301) 457-4100. Customer services has phone numbers for the following data sources:

Depository Libraries—1,400 libraries that have selected publications and some computer files on CD-ROM from the U.S. Government Printing Office and Census Bureau.

State Data Centers—usually state government agencies (and assorted affiliates—often state universities) with data services. Centers receive Census Bureau data for their areas and make them available to the public. Found in all states.

National Census Information Centers—nonprofit centers that often serve the interests of various racial and ethnic groups.

National Clearinghouse for Census Data Services—vendors that provide specialized services.

U.S. Census Bureau Publications:

Census Catalogue & Guide: 1994. (A 360-page bibliography that covers everything from mid-1988 through 1993, including phone numbers and addresses for easy access to information and assistance.)

1990 Census of Population Reports, Characteristics of the Population. (There are several different volumes in this series: General Social and Economic Characteristics; Detailed Population Characteristics; Living Arrangements of Children and Adults, Household and Family Characteristics; Money Income and Poverty Status in the United States.) The population census is conducted once every ten years; 1990 is the most recent.

County and City Data Book: 1994. (May 1988) Provides selected characteristics about counties and cities above 50,000 in population.

Statistical Abstract of the United States: 1994. 1,040 pgs. $32. PB94-20985 National Technical Information Service.

Package special on *County and City Data Book* plus *U.S. Statistical Abstract*. Order from National Technical Information Service, 5285 Port Royal Rd., Springfield VA 22161. Tel: (703) 487-4650. Cite order # PB95-123972LKB $58 + $6 P&H.

More Education Means Higher Career Earnings. 2 pgs, single copy free. SB-94-17

Dollars for Scholars-Postsecondary Costs and Financing: 1992. 2 pgs, single copy free. SB-94-21

Dollars for Scholars-Postsecondary Costs and Financing: 1990–91. 76 pgs, $4.50. GPO-SN-803-044-00028-7.

U.S. Department of Education, Washington, D.C. *State Education Performance Chart.* (Shows percentage of students who graduate from high school.)

National Center for Education Statistics. *Digest of Education Statistics.* (Gives per pupil expenditures.)

National Foundation for the Improvement of Education and National Education Association, Washington, DC. *Teacher Centers and Needs Assessment.* 25 pgs. LB1745.E32

U.S. Department of Health and Human Services, Public Health Service, Centers for Disease Control, National Center for Health Statistics. *Vital and Health Statistics.* Washington, D.C.

U.S. Department of Labor, Bureau of Labor Statistics, Washington, D.C. *Employment and Earnings.*

United Way of America, *Needs Assessment: A Guide for Planners, Managers and Funders of Health and Human Care Services.* Alexandria, VA, 1982.

PRIVATE AND NONPROFIT SOURCES

Children's Defense Fund, 25 E. Street N.W., Washington, D.C. 20001. Tel: (202) 662-3652.

> *The Adolescent and Young Adult Fact Book. 1991.* (Comprehensive reference on America's 10- to 20-year olds. Includes family income, family types, health status, school enrollment, causes of death, sexual activity, and more.)
>
> *The State of America's Children Yearbook 1994.* (Annual analysis of the status of children.)
>
> *Where to Find Data About Adolescents and Young Adults: A Guide to Sources.* November 1989, CDF's Adolescent Pregnancy Prevention Clearinghouse report.

Council of Chief State School Officers, One Massachusetts Avenue, N.W., Suite 700, Washington, DC 20001. *Family Support, Education and Involvement: A Guide for State Action: 1989.*

Harvard Family Research Project, Cambridge, MA 02138.

> Weiss, H. B., *Raising Our Future: Families, Schools, and Communities Joining Together:* A Handbook of Family Support and Education Programs for Parents, Educators, Community Leaders, and Policy Makers, 1992.
>
> Weiss, H. B. et al. *Innovative Models to Guide Family Support and Education Policy in the 1990's: An Analysis of Four Pioneering State Programs—Connecticut, Maryland, Minnesota, Missouri,* 1990.
>
> Weiss, H. B., and Halpern, R. *The Challenges of Evaluating State Family Support and Education Initiatives: An Education Framework,* 1989.

AVAILABLE ON THE INTERNET

Gopher: gopher.census.gov
FTP: ftp.census.gov (ftp = file transfer protocol)
EMAIL: gatekeeper@census.gov or call 301-457-1242
            County and City Data Book (rankings only)
            Financial data on state and local governments and schools
            News releases
            Population estimates and projections
            State level statistical briefs

Gopher: gopher.fldc.cornell.edu Family Life Development Center

REFERENCES

Erickson, E. H. 1968. *Identity, Youth and Crisis.* New York: W. W. Norton.

Maslow, A. H. 1970. *Motivation and Personality.* New York: Harper & Row Publishers.

Michigan League for Human Services. 1995. *The Human Services Connection.* January, p. 1.

Ponsioen, J. A. 1962. *Social Welfare Policy: Contributions to Theory.* Publication of the Institute of Social Studies, Vol. 3. The Hague: Mouton & Co.

Simons, J., and Jablonski, D. 1990., *An Advocate's Guide to Using Data.* Washington, D.C.: Children's Defense Fund.

United Way of America. 1982. *Needs Assessment: A Guide for Planners, Managers and Funders of Health and Human Care Services.* Alexandria, VA: November, p. 8.

CHAPTER 35

Differential Ethical Orientations to Practice and Research in School Social Work

Joseph R. Steiner
Professor, Syracuse University School of Social Work*

Thomas Pastorello
Associate Professor, Syracuse University School of Social Work*

INTRODUCTION

The relationship between social workers in practice roles and those in research roles often is an uncomfortable one, and few social workers have been able to fulfill both roles comfortably in one setting, although progress is being made. The inclination to place an emphasis on the fulfillment of practice or research roles versus the integration of practice and research roles is especially evident in school settings. Here, the overwhelming majority of social workers identify themselves as practitioners who, for the most part, feel isolated from social work researchers, applied research methodologies, and relevant research findings. Most are trained in programs in which extensive emphasis was given to remedial practice methodologies designed for work with individuals.

Failure to incorporate practice and research knowledge, skills, and activities is problematic in school social work. Strong personal, professional, and organizational imperatives to do so exist. School social workers face increasing pressure to practice effectively and to demonstrate this by speci-

---

*The authors wish to acknowledge and thank Brenda Hartman-Souder and Janine Hunt for their assistance in updating the literature review.

fying plans to reduce or prevent problematic conditions, to describe what was done, and to analyze and communicate the results of the efforts. Most school social workers also are committed to being ethical, whether they are in practice roles, research roles, or both. Perceptions of ethical practice and research are closely related to perceptions of high-quality practice and research.

This chapter discusses how social work practice and research duties and consequences relate to professional identity and the development of both school social workers and school social work. The concepts *duties* and *consequences* will be defined and associated with ethical imperatives that guide school social work practice and research. These concepts and the ethical imperatives (thoughts) associated with them will be illustrated with examples taken from school settings and from the social work code of ethics. It is hoped that a fuller understanding and acceptance of contrasting ethical orientations to social work practice and research in schools also will help increase collaboration between those in practice and research roles and reduce intrarole conflict within individuals who attempt to integrate both roles.

DUTIES AND CONSEQUENCES: CONTRASTING ETHICAL EMPHASIS IN SCHOOL SOCIAL WORK PRACTICE AND RESEARCH

Many school social workers evaluate the ethical acceptability and the quality of their performance primarily in relation to fulfillment of duties or in relation to the consequences of their efforts. The Rogers-Skinner debate was in part a debate between a person who was strongly committed to the duties of practitioners and another who was equally committed to the consequences of practitioners. Rogers believed strongly in moral imperatives associated with means—the rightness of conducting interviews and relating to clients in a certain way. Skinner believes strongly in moral imperatives associated with outcomes—the rightness of specifying consequences and finding effective means to achieve them (Rogers and Skinner, 1956). These arguments symbolize the contrasting emphasis associated with duties and consequences found within school social work.

The technical meaning of *duties* and *consequences* and the contrasting emphases given to them by different ethical orientations (Reamer, 1987) provide new insights into intraprofessional conflicts within school social work. The concept of duties, in this chapter, grows out of a deontological ethical orientation. It refers to ethical imperatives to perform in certain ways, irrespective of the results or outcomes of this performance. Duties by definition are limited to those means that ought to be carried out because they are believed to be right in and of themselves, not because of their consequences. Duties may grow out of the requirements of one's professional role (for example, school social workers ought to respect a student's right to speak with them confidentially), one's promises to others (for example, to meet someone at a specific time and place), and/or one's belief in a moral rule (for example, one should love one's neighbor as one's self).

The concept of consequences, in this chapter, grows out of a utilitarian ethical orientation. It refers to ends or outcomes that ought to occur, irrespective of whether the means used to achieve them were also duties. Consequences may have a moral or nonmoral nature (Taylor, 1978), but there is, by definition, an ethical imperative to achieve them. Consequences may be immediate and/or long term; they may be direct or indirect. For example, direct consequences of one-to-one social work services to drug-abusing students may be less drug abuse. Indirect consequences associated with this same service could be reduced rates of faculty and staff turnover. Defined and planned outcomes are referred to as intended consequences; unanticipated and unplanned outcomes are referred to as unintended consequences. Ethical imperatives associated with practice consequences may be derived from the worker's own sense of oughts or the sense of oughts communicated by the social work profession, school personnel, parents, and children.

Much unnecessary dissension exists between social workers who base their professional practice primarily upon ethical imperatives associated with duties and those who rely primarily upon ethical imperatives associated with consequences. School social work practices that are supported by a fuller integration of the ethical imperatives of both duties and consequences have the strongest ethical support. (See Frankena, 1973, 1978, and Taylor, 1978, for a more elaborate development of deontological, utilitarian, and ethical pluralism theories that support the key ideas presented in the section.)

THE PROFESSIONAL IDENTITY OF SCHOOL SOCIAL WORKERS

In this chapter, the identity of school social workers refers to their role(s) and the ethical imperatives that guide their professional activities. The new social work code of ethics, more clearly than the former code, mandates that social workers ought to fulfill practice and research duties and achieve practice and research consequences. The authors believe that this change in the code's emphasis symbolizes development of the social work profession and prescribed further development for most individual social workers. Some authors have questioned the current ability of many school social workers to perform both practice and research roles (Bok, 1980, and Meares, 1980), but these authors advocate school social workers' performing both professional roles. In addition, Gallant (1978) reveals that P.L. 94-142 widened the dimensions of the school social work role to include both research

FIGURE 1 A Typology of Professional Identity of School Social Workers

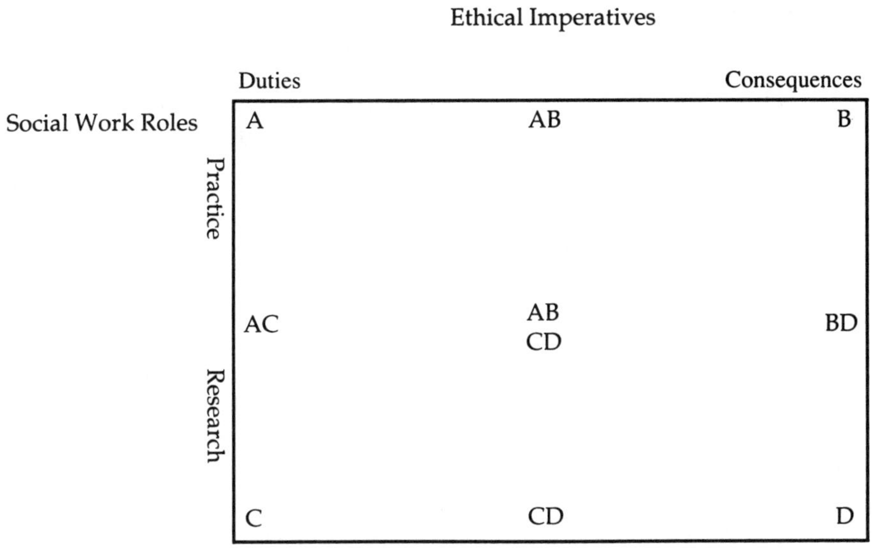

Ethical Imperatives

	Duties		Consequences
Practice	A	AB	B
	AC	AB / CD	BD
Research	C	CD	D

Social Work Roles (rows: Practice, Research)

and practice. She encourages workers to develop and operationalize practice and research knowledge and skills in schools.

Figure 1 is designed to help readers assess their own professional identity—what it is and what they would like it to be. Each area on this figure represents a somewhat different type of professional identity; the weight given to practice and research duties and consequences varies by area. The corners represent four extreme theoretical types. There are social workers in schools whose recurring patterns of performance represent one of these extremes, but most school social workers' professional activities represent areas somewhat between the four corners (that is, between the four extremes).

The ethical imperatives associated with corner A (practice duties) are manifested in those who are committed only to fulfilling their duties as social work practitioners. Such persons give little emphasis, at least in terms of overt manifestations, to the consequences of their practice activities, to duties associated with research, and to the consequences of research—communicating information that in turn has consequences. Persons who practice with an emphasis upon duties alone make little attempt to articulate favorable outcomes (consequences) for their practice activities. Much more emphasis is placed on the nature and quality of the relationship (or processes) than on the outcome (or product). Such persons generally value process recordings in their attempt to assess the goodness or badness of social work practices; little or no attention is given to consequences.

NASW has released (1992) *Standards for School Social Work Services* with specific attention paid to the ethical performance of the tasks of school social workers. In general, the social work code of ethics gives much attention to the duties of practitioners. For example:

- The social worker should not participate in, condone, or be associated with dishonesty, fraud, deceit, or misrepresentation.
- The social worker should under no circumstances engage in sexual activities with clients.
- The social worker should provide clients with accurate and complete information regarding the extent and nature of services available to them.

These are duties, to the extent that they ought to be done by social workers whether or not the consequences are favorable. Directly related to school social work, Fritz (1978, p.39) revealed commitment to practice duty imperatives when she wrote: "Social workers practicing in schools generally look with disfavor upon the widely used method of punishment known as paddling. It is indeed a practice that is contrary to social workers' belief in the dignity and worth of the individual, since it involves the use of physical force by an adult toward a minor." To persons with this orientation, corporal punishment is not right, irrespective of whether results are assumed to be favorable or unfavorable.

Persons whose behavior represents only ethical imperatives associated with practice duties (corner A of figure 1) may be interested in the results of their practice activities as well as the duties and consequences of the research role, but the ethical imperatives that determine their professional behavior consistently are associated only with practice duties. Some critics, responding to other cells on this figure, believe that such a pattern is unethical because it does not give sufficient attention to the consequences of one's practice and to the efficiency of achieving these consequences. Anderson's appeal (1979) for school social workers to describe their work in terms of "product" rather than "process" exemplifies the importance of considering consequences more closely in school social work practice. Other critics may claim that social work based only upon practice duty imperatives is unethical because it does not give sufficient attention to research duties and consequences. School social work literature has emphasized a duty orientation. Chavkin (1985) notes that little has changed since 1969: the field's focus is still on an analysis of casework tasks in school social work. Chavkin's position is reiterated by independent literature reviews (Allen-Meares and Lane, 1985; Fisher, 1988).

Persons who manifest behavior associated only with the ethical imperatives of corner B (practice consequences) give much emphasis to obtaining favorable consequences in practice. The means they use to obtain these consequences may or may not involve fulfilling the duties of a social work practitioner or the duties or consequences associated with a research role. Their interest in practice behavior is limited to how effectively it does (or does not) achieve practice consequences. Process recordings are of little value to persons with this orientation, beyond the fact that they may help reveal information about what means were (or were not) effective in achieving consequences. Such persons generally value the degree to which consequences are achieved in their attempt to assess the goodness or badness of social work practice. The means that were used are not valued in and of themselves.

Lela Costin (1978, p. 55) argued against the use of corporal punishment from a practice-consequences perspective when she said: "A number of hazards attend the use of corporal punishment, not the least of which is the danger that the child will suffer serious physical injury. Psychological injury is also a frequent concomitant of the humiliation and loss of self-respect that most children feel when they are subject to painful physical punishment. This is particularly true when they are punished in the presence of classmates and other witnesses." Some school personnel may argue for corporal punishment on the basis of its consequences. Evaluative research is especially helpful in deciding whether corporal punishment, like any other means used to achieve ends, does lead to favorable or unfavorable results. Many authors (Bok, 1980; Lewis and Moore, 1974; Meares, 1980; Pool, 1980; Radin, 1980; Welsh and Goldberg, 1978) advocate that school social workers give more conscious attention to the consequences they are seeking and to the most effective means to achieve them. Michals, Cournoyer, and Pinner (1979) illustrated the importance of consequences for school social workers when they revealed the importance of social work activities in one setting in relation to reduced absenteeism and tardiness and also to improved grades. The words *evaluation, accountability,* and *efficiency* are used as political slogans to advocate that social workers pay more attention to practice consequences, although these words also could be used to encourage fulfillment of practice duties.

The social work code of ethics has numerous ethical imperatives for social workers related to practice consequences:

- The social worker should make every effort to foster maximum self-determination on the part of clients.
- The social worker should not engage in any activity which violates or diminishes the civil rights of clients.
- The social workers should act to prevent and eliminate discrimination against any person or group. . . .
- The social worker should act to expand choice and opportunity for all persons. . . .
- The social worker should promote conditions that encourage respect for the diversity of cultures which constitute American society.

Anderson (1980, p. 2) advocates that school social workers give more attention to consequences by means of a sports analogy: "The evaluation in sports is consistent with the final score, the important product." It is not important how you play the game; it is important whether you win or lose. Persons with a practice duty perspective may disagree by claiming that how one plays the game is much more important than the final score.

Ethical arguments based on imperatives to fulfill practice duties irrespective of consequences have little meaning to those who base their assessment of professional activities only upon ethical imperatives associated with practice consequences (corner B of figure 1). Critics of those whose behavior manifests only corner B ethical imperatives (practice consequences) may call such practice behavior unethical, even if it is successful, when ethical imperatives associated with practice duties have to be compromised. An example of this might occur when a school social worker has to disclose confidences or misrepresent the truth in order to bring about more favorable consequences. Some social workers would call such behavior unethical, even if the consequences were favorable. In addition, other critics may claim that too little attention is given to research duties and consequences, although many school social work practitioners with a consequences orientation fulfill research duties as they practice.

To better guarantee the consequences of free and appropriate education, social workers equally invested in the ethical imperatives of practice duties may conceive of duties in addition to the proscriptions of the law, and beyond the context of the school to related family and community systems. Such duties may encompass the provision of family support services, as well as the education and training of family members on issues of sensitivity to children with disabilities and community advocacy. The social worker who integrates duties and consequences orientations may be more likely to see the roles that families of children with disabilities can play in the community for the elimination of physical barriers, e.g., the possible lack of hydraulic lifts on school buses, and its consequential contribution to free and appropriate education. School social work of this type is well in keeping with the recommendations of a resource and planning guide for school social work recently published by the Wisconsin State Department of Public Instruction (1991) for the purpose of enhancing the interrelationships of child, family, school, and community.

The area of figure 1 identified as AB represents school social workers who attempt to respond equally to the ethical imperatives associated with practice duties and consequences. This may be difficult in specific situations, but it does represent a practice ideal. A recent review of trends in school social work (Radin, 1989) describes movement toward an AB ideal as stimulated by the passage of Public Law 94-142 (The Education for All Handicapped Children Act) and by the growing emphasis on the duty of school social workers to participate as members of interdisciplinary teams.

The act itself dictates that school social workers guarantee certain consequences, e.g., free and appropriate education. Amendments to the act emphasize preventive intervention activities. Perhaps it is the area of prevention that will necessarily stimulate conscious integration of duties and consequences.

The ethical imperatives associated with corner C (research duties) in figure 1 are manifested by social workers who are committed to carrying out their duties as social work researchers. The social work code of ethics indicates that social work researchers ought to warn research participants of any danger; obtain their consent; treat information about persons confidentially; take credit only for work they, not others, have done; and follow the conventions of scientific inquiry.

Important conversations of scientific inquiry for social workers are commitment to objectivity and rationality. This involves reflective consciousness about one's own biases to help ensure value neutrality in data collection and presentation. Commitment to provide pro and con information, as opposed to marshaling evidence in favor of one position, is clearly a research duty. In addition, researchers have a duty to make their procedures public, to develop precise definitions, and to ensure that data collection is objective. The approach is to be systematic and cumulative, and findings are to be presented in such a way that they are replicable. In short, social work researchers have a duty to maximize both internal and external validity of their research, while respecting the dignity of research participants. At one time, researchers argued the ethical merits of their research duties on the basis of the conventions of scientific inquiry alone, even if those conventions abused the dignity of the physical or emotional well-being of participants. Classic examples of this kind of abuse include "The Godzieher Study," which involved the dissemination of placebos, for experimental purposes, to Mexican-American women who thought they were receiving genuine birth control pills, and "The Tuskegee Study," which involved the deceptive denial of treatment, for experimental purposes, to black men suffering from syphilis (Smith, 1975). These are not acceptable models for social work research, and research review boards are helping to ensure that human subject abuses do not happen in any area of social science.

Persons who identify closely only with ethical imperatives associated with research duties (corner of figure 1) give little emphasis to ethical imperatives associated with the consequences of their research (that is, the knowledge they communicate and its resulting consequences) and to those associated with social work practice roles. Critics might call this "research for its own sake" and might also claim that social work researchers who do not give sufficient attention to the knowledge they present and its consequences are unethical because of the harm it may do to individuals, a school program, or a local community.

Social workers who manifest a pattern of behavior associated only with corner D, ethical imperatives (research consequences), emphasize how one prepares and communicates knowledge in order to obtain favorable outcomes (consequences). Presenting information in a way that increases the chance of funding a "good" program is a common example. The pattern of behavior symbolized by corner D is not influenced significantly by the duties of researchers or the duties or consequences of practitioners.

The phrase *advocacy research* is sometimes used to describe one's response to ethical imperatives associated with research consequences. Persons who do advocacy research are much more aware of the consequences they hope to achieve, beyond just representing information, than are researchers limited to a research duties perspective. *Political savvy* is sometimes used to describe someone who prepares knowledge in a way that obtains favorable outcomes, even if research and practice duties have to be compromised. The word *Machiavellian* sometimes is used to describe those who manifest a more extreme rejection of the ethical imperatives associated with corners A, B, and C of figure 1, especially if the outcome is one of self-aggrandizement.

Selective interpretation or use of data with an eye toward consequences is not acceptable practice to those with a strong commitment to research duties. Adhering strongly to research duties is not acceptable to those with strong commitment to research consequences when adherence to research duties threatens the achievement of valued outcomes. The conflicts between (and within) school workers with strong commitment to research duties and those with an equally strong commitment to research consequences are as intense as the conflicts between practitioners committed to duties and those committed to consequences.

Coughlin (1980, p. 27) cautions school social workers that, "The frequent failure of evaluation to effect change or alter purpose in education is the result not of a lack of credibility or accuracy, but rather a lack of political savvy...." He goes on to say:

> It behooves the evaluator to develop a keen political sense of the major elements in the structure of power. The social science researcher must recognize that educational policy within American education is essentially determined in a Machiavellian atmosphere, not through Aristotelian logic... school social workers ... must reflect a skepticism of the hidden agendas of the institution, and they must look outside of education for their most sincere support. Only then will professional assessment become a significant instrument of ideological change (p. 37).

In brief, school social workers should give attention to corner D, ethical imperatives (research consequences), as well as research duties if they are to fulfill their mission. Giving equal attention to research duties and consequences is symbolized by the letters CD on figure 1. Doing this in specific situations sometimes is difficult, but it represents a professional ideal.

Critics may charge that responding only to corner D, ethical imperatives (research consequences), is unethical because this pattern does not give sufficient attention to the duties of researchers and/or the duties and consequences of practice. And yet, social work researchers are committed to many of the same consequences as are social work practitioners. Is it worse for social work researchers to minimize duties in their pursuit of consequences than it is for social work practitioners to do this? We believe that minimizing practice or research duties is not ideal, although we recognize that it happens.

The professional identities of specific school social workers are equated with the ethical imperatives that determine their professional behavior. School social workers, like other social workers, have their professional identities shaped in part by the settings in which they work. It is not uncommon for school social workers to feel much strain and discomfort when the demands of a job require them to respond to ethical imperatives to which they are unable or unwilling to respond.

For example, school personnel may expect social workers to achieve consequences, even if it means that duties have to be compromised; or, equally frustrating, school personnel may expect social workers to carry out certain activities over and over again, as if they were duties, even though the results of these activities may not be favorable. In recent years much more emphasis in social work literature and education has been given to practice accountability and efficiency and research activities. These are attempts within the profession to have individual social workers broaden the range of the ethical imperatives that determine their performance as professionals. Social workers should not lose sight of their duties as they become more concerned with achieving consequences.

THE PROFESSIONAL DEVELOPMENT OF SCHOOL SOCIAL WORK

The professional development of school social work is closely related to the general development of social work and the specific development of school social workers. Professional development, as presented here, is defined as increasing the range of school social work duties one fulfills and/or the consequences one achieves in practice and/or research. We assume that most school social workers, like other social workers, are interested in professional development. Failure to develop professionally is closely related to low morale, burn out, and professional degradation. An integrated response to practice and research duties and consequences (corners A, B, C and D) represents the highest level of professional development discussed in this paper.

Persons generally acquire their professional identities at a time when one social work role, oriented toward either duties or consequences, becomes dominant. This represents the lowest level of professional development discussed in this chapter. Some social workers manifest this pattern throughout their careers, but most attempt to broaden the ethical support for their professional behavior.

Social workers who respond to the ethical imperatives associated with more than one corner (as symbolized in figure 1) face the likelihood of intra- and inter-role conflict in their roles as practitioners and/or researchers. For example, some school social workers manifest responses to the ethical imperatives that can be represented by two corners (that is, A and B, practice duties and consequences; A and C, practice and research duties; B and C, practice consequences and research duties; B and D, practice and research consequences; C and D, research duties and consequences; and A and D, practice duties and research consequences). Some of these combinations tend to cause more role conflict and accompanying strain for school social workers than other combinations. There are seldom (perhaps never) conflicts associated with the integration of practice and research consequences (corners B and D); there may (or may not) be conflicts associated with the integration of practice duties and consequences (corners A or B) and of research duties and consequences (corners C and D). There is seldom (perhaps never) conflict associated with the integration of practice consequences and research duties (corners B and C), and there is frequently (nearly always) some conflict associated with the integration of duties of practitioners and researchers (corners A and C). Nevertheless, the integration of roles, which is the hallmark of professional growth, can be accomplished with the successful management of conflict. The mutually supportive and conflict-free integration of practice consequences and research duties is well illustrated by the recent emphasis in social research on what is referred to as formative or developmental research. This type of research gives form to or helps to develop appropriate and responsive practice interventions to social problems. Key descriptive terms employed in developmental research include *consumer driven research, planning research* and *involvement of diverse community groups as stake-holders* (e.g., Hooper-Briar, 1990; Stockdill, et. al. 1992).

Conflict between the duties of practitioners and researchers is common and sometimes viewed as practice or research intrusiveness (Thomas, 1978). This is true whether the person in practice and research roles is one person or two. In talking about direct practice, Rosenblatt (1968, p. 58) recognized the conflicting duties of practice and research when he said, "The clinician must believe in himself if he is to inspire hope of recovery in his clients. . . . The researcher, in contrast, must maintain a questioning attitude about practice." In addition, practitioners have a duty to individualize treatment procedures based upon the needs of clients; researchers may have a duty to standardize treatment procedures based upon the research design. Practitioners have a duty to provide service promptly; researchers may have a duty to gather baseline data before treatment begins. Practitioners have a duty to collect data needed to work with their clients; researches may have a duty to collect additional information that the practitioner may feel distracts from practice activities. Practitioners have a duty to provide more than one service, based upon the needs of clients, and these additional services may be confounding variables that will lower internal and/or external validity, limiting how well research duties can be fulfilled. Finally, practitioners have a duty to maintain confidentiality about clients, whereas researchers have a duty to gather information about clients. This conflict is felt in many practice settings, but Macarov and Rothman (1977) claim that this last conflict is a false one and that it grows out of the inability of social workers to distinguish adequately among anonymity, confidentiality, and secrecy.

Resolution or successful management of these and other conflicts between the duties of social work practitioners and researchers (corners A and C) becomes more likely if practitioners see research as a valuable tool in practice, and researchers see their role in terms of service to students and other school personnel, including social role practitioners. (That is, they see the need to temper the dictates of corner C, ethical imperatives, in light of other duties and consequences defined as desirable—corners A, B, and D.)

Resolution or successful management of conflicts between the duties of practitioners and researchers (corners A and C) also is facilitated by an understanding of the perceptions and misperceptions of researchers and practitioners in regard to what Thomas (1978) has called *service intrusiveness* and *research design intrusiveness*. Service intrusiveness is perceived by the researcher when the effects of service delivery appear to reduce or limit the internal or external validity of research. Design intrusiveness is perceived by the practitioners when research appears to affect service delivery adversely. Service can be seen as intrusive by the researcher if delivery of service becomes incompatible with the researcher's execution of two basic duties: the implementation of a research design (which maintains the integrity of the independent variable) and the implementation of an information management system (which allows for useful analysis of data). It is often the case that practitioners feel duty-bound to provide multiple services to their clientele in immediate response to established needs. These duties define the basis for the perception of design intrusiveness on the part of practitioners.

Conflict at times is inevitable between the duties of researchers and practitioners: thus, conflict management rather than conflict resolution becomes the goal. For example, to the extent that a researcher has defined one particular program as an independent variable (for example, casework services to acting-out adolescents) and the design calls for a control group (that is, not providing casework services to acting-out adolescents) conflicts with practitioners providing casework services may be inevitable. In addition, although researchers expect it, practitioners may not be able to complete data collections for every case and may not have time to check the consistency of data-collection methods with colleagues. Again, this causes conflicts.

The classical canons of basic research demonstrate little flexibility for responding to conflicting imperatives associated with practice duties and consequences and research consequences (see Kushler and Davidson, 1979). And yet much flexibility regarding research duties is being shown in the growing movement of applied research in social work, including school social work (Jayaratne, 1977, 1978; Thomas, 1978; Meares, 1980; Nuehring and Pascone, 1986). This permits resolution of possible conflicts between the duties of social work practitioners and those of researchers and also helps social work practitioners give more conscious attention to the relationship between duties and consequences. These kinds of research include single-subject and group designs, demonstration research, assessment and placement research, consumer- (client-) oriented research, and formative (planning and program-modification) research. Where service requirements dictate the immediate delivery of service, applied researchers are equipped to adapt quasi-experimental designs, eliminating the necessity of a control group (Cook and Campbell, 1979). Where service requirements dictate the changing of program characteristics during the course of research, applied researchers are equipped to adapt formative research designs to field conditions (Rutman, 1977). Staudt and Craft (1983) have argued strongly that continued successful school social work intervention outcomes are contingent upon ongoing evaluation research.

Correspondingly, movement toward conflict resolution requires information management flexibility on the part of practitioners. In fact, this information management flexibility more accurately could be called a practice duty because practitioners have a duty to collect data as they practice in order to carefully assess client needs and monitor progress.

Given the new directions in applied social work research and given practitioner refinement of information-collection skills, the potential for managing or resolving conflicts between practice duties and research duties is high. For example, a school social work practitioner may feel duty bound to prohibit the use of aversive stimuli, in spite of clear research evidence that the introduction of aversive stimuli reduces fighting in schools (that is, that aversive stimuli achieve consequences that the social worker supports). The social worker may continue the prohibition of aversive stimuli while using formative research to plan and implement strategies to achieve the same consequences (reduced fighting in schools) in more acceptable ways. Underlying successful management or resolution of conflicts between those in school social work practice and those in research roles is a level of professionalism that integrates concern and demonstrates performance in keeping with practice and research duties and consequences.

Professional development that reveals significant commitment to practice and research duties and consequences represents a major challenge for social workers, as it does to other social workers. This high level of development and the responsibility associated with it are accompanied by conflict and strain, which some may wish to avoid, but they are also accompanied by the greatest opportunities for service to students, to the school, to the profession of social work, and to the larger society.

SUMMARY

This chapter provides a framework based upon practice and research duties and consequences that is designed to remind school social workers of the professional roles and ethical imperatives that determine their performance in schools (their professional identity). This framework is also associated with professional development ideals. It is hoped that, as school social workers become more mindful of their professional identity, they will also be more mindful of what it could and should be. In addition, it is assumed that this framework may be utilized equally well by social workers in other settings. The development of social work, like the development of the social work profession, is dependent on more social workers making the attempt to integrate practice and research duties and consequences.

REFERENCES

Allen-Meares, P., and Lane, B. A. 1985. Practitioners have differing views of school social work? *Social Work in Education* 5(3):141–155.

Anderson, R. J. 1979. Accountability, means, and ends. *Social Work in Education* 1(2):2–4.

Anderson, R. J. 1980. Honey bees and social work education. *Social Work in Education* 2(3):2–3.

Bok, M. 1980. External vs. internal evaluation. *Social Work in Education* 2(3):5–17.

Chavkin, N. F. 1984. School social work practice: A reappraisal. *Social Work in Education* 8(1):3–13.

Cook, T., and Campbell, D. 1979. *Quasi-experimentation: Design and analysis issues for field setting.* NY: Rand McNally.

Costin, L. B. 1978. The dark side of child rights: Corporal punishment in the schools. *Social Work in Education* 1(1):53–63.

Coughlin, A. V. 1980. Technology of school practice: Implications for evaluation. *Social Work in Education* 2(3):25–39.

Fisher, R. A. 1988. Clinical aspects of school social work. *School Social Work Journal* 13(a):13–22.

Frankena, W. K. 1978. Deontological theories. In T. L. Beauchamp and L. Walters (eds.). *Contemporary issues in bioethics.* Belmont, CA: Wadsworth Publishing.

Fritz, A. 1978. Alternatives to corporal punishment. *Social Work in Education* 1(1): 39–54.

Gallant, C. 1978. New skills for public law 94-142. *Social Work in Education* 1(1): 29–38.

Hooper-Briar, K. 1990. The convergence of the mentally disordered and the jail population. *Journal of Offender Counseling, Services and Rehabilitation* 15(1):47–162.

Jayaratne, S. 1977. Single subject and group designs in treatment evaluation. *Social Work Research and Abstracts* 13(3):35–42.

Jayaratne, S. 1978. Analytic procedures for single-subject designs. *Social Work Research and Abstracts* 14(3):30–40.

Kushler, M., and Davidson, W. 1979. Using experimental designs to evaluate social programs. *Social Work Research and Abstracts* 15(1):27–32.

Lewis, A., and Moore, F. M. 1974. A comprehensive compelling program effecting relevant change in socially maladjusted adolescent girls. In N. Bellos, G. Gross, and J. Steiner (eds.). *Innovative projects in school social work practice*. (Vol. 1). Syracuse University School of Social Work.

Macarov. D., and Rothman, B. 1977. Confidentiality: A constraint on research. *Social Work Research and Abstracts* 13(3):11–16.

Meares, P. 1980. Interrupted time series design and the evaluation of school practice. *Social Work in Education* 2(3):50–61.

Michals, A. P., Cournoyer, D. E., and Pinner, E. L. 1979. School social works and education goals. *Social Work* 24:138–141.

National Association of Social Workers. 1992 *NASW Standards for School Social Work Services*. Washington, D.C.: National Association of Social Workers.

Nuehring, E., and Pascone, A. 1986. Single subject evaluation: A tool for quality assurance. *Social Work* 31(5):359–365.

Pool, L. D. 1980. Evaluation as an opportunity to improve goal-directed services. *Social Work in Education* 2(3):62–71.

Radin, N. 1989. School social work practice: Past, present, and future trends. *Social Work in Education* 11(4):213–255.

Radin, N. 1980. Evaluation of performance: Where does it fit in? *Social Work in Education* 2(3):39–49.

Reamer, R. G. 1987. Values and ethics. In A. Minahan (ed-in-chief). *Encyclopedia of Social Work* (18th edition). Silver Spring, MD: National Association of Social Work. pp. 806–807.

Rogers, C., and Skinner, B. F. 1956. Some issues concerning the control of human behavior. *Science* 124:1057–1065.

Rosenblatt, A. 1968. The practitioner's use and evaluation of research. *Social Work* 13(1):53–69.

Rutman, L. 1977. *Evaluation research methods: A Basic guide*. NY: Sage.

Smith, H. W. 1975. *Strategies of social research*. Englewood Cliffs, NJ: Prentice-Hall.

Social Work Code of Ethics. 1980. NASW News 25(1):24–25.

Staudt, M. M., and Craft, J. L. 1983. School staff input in the evaluation of school social work practice. *Social Work in Education* 5(2):119–131.

Stockdill, S., Duhon-Sills, R., Olson, R., and Patton, M. 1992. Voices in the design and evaluation of a multicultural education program: A developmental approach. In Madison, A. (ed.) *New Directions for Program Evaluation: Minority Issues in Program Evaluation* (No. 53). San Francisco, CA: Jossey-Bass Publishers.

Taylor, P. 1978. Utilitarianism. In T. L. Beauchamp and L. Walter (eds.). *Contemporary issues in bioethics.* Belmont, CA: Wadsworth Publishing.

Thomas, E. 1978. Research and service in single-case experimentation: Conflicts and choices. *Social Work Research and Abstracts* 14(4):20–31.

Welsh, B. L., and Goldberg, G. 1978. Insuring education success for children-at-risk placed in new learning environments. *School Social Work Quarterly* (4):271–284.

Wisconsin State Department of Public Instruction. 1991. *School social work: A resource and planning guide.* (Bulletin No. 91464). Madison, WI: Wisconsin State Department of Public Instruction.

CHAPTER 36
Research in School Social Work: To Survive and Thrive

Christine Anlauf Sabatino
Assistant Professor, National Catholic School of Social Service,
The Catholic University of America

Elizabeth March Timberlake
Ordinary Professor, National Catholic School of Social Service,
The Catholic University of America

The 1994 midterm elections have captured the nation's attention. Voters have elected a majority of candidates whose campaigns centered on instituting conservative economic principles and social policies. This conservatism aims at: amending the budget process, anticrime measures, welfare reform, family supports including strengthening the rights of parents in their children's education, tax codes, national security, senior citizen earnings taxes, job creation/wage enhancements, legal reforms, and legislative term limits (Republican National Committee, 1994). For the school social worker, this newly conservative political climate raises questions about federal legislation, education reform, the regular education initiative, and choice in education. For example: will public laws continue to provide resources for school social work services for targeted student populations (Freeman, 1994)? Will public education become decentralized with site-based management? Will there be a restructuring of all special education programs and the return of special education services to the regular classroom (McDonald, 1992)? Will choice promote equity, access, school improvement, and accountability (Koppich, 1992)?

Amidst this political and fiscal conservatism, school social workers must prepare to meet the needs of the increasingly diverse and disadvantaged student population anticipated in the twenty-first century. For example, although it is projected that the total number of children under 18 will decline only slightly to 62,644,000 in the year 2010, it is anticipated that the percentage of minority children will increase from 31.1 percent to 38.2 percent of the total and that the minority child will be in the majority (over 50.0%) in seven states (Hawaii, New Mexico, Texas, California, Florida, New York, Louisiana) and the District of Columbia (Wetrogen, 1989). It is also estimated that 82 percent of all children today have working mothers and that this percentage is not likely to decline (Wetrogen, 1989). Child poverty increased 21 percent between 1979 and 1989 (Children's Defense Fund, 1991) and a decrease is not predicted any time soon.

And school social workers must meet needs with fewer resources, critical lacunae in the knowledge base of school social work, and greater practice accountability to multiple constituents. Yet in the most recent national study of entry-level school social work tasks, Allen-Meares (1994) found that the tasks of leadership and policymaking continue to receive the lowest mean rating despite the challenges and problems facing schools. This reluctance to become involved in policy and planning coupled with the long standing reluctance to theoretically frame and empirically test practice (Task Force on Social Work Research, 1991) is a combination the profession can no longer afford. School social workers must substantiate what they do, document their effectiveness, and be accountable to client consumers, communities and school boards. To assist school social workers in increasing their capability for planning and accountability in a time of high uncertainty, this chapter highlights the critical role which needs to be played by practice research if school social work is to survive and thrive in the twenty-first century. In doing so, the chapter first grounds school social work practice within the social work ecology in the school setting and explores the current context of this field of practice before addressing methodological and substantive dilemmas in knowledge development and practice accountability.

CURRENT CONTEXT OF SCHOOL SOCIAL WORK PRACTICE

School social work practice is conducted in an environment that is both limited and fostered by the ecology of a particular school. Practice is also influenced by the philosophical, political and fiscal climate of the times.

Social Work Ecology in the School

The traditional function of school social work services has been to support the school in its mission by helping children reap the full benefit of their education. Thus, as one might expect, historical analyses of school social work practice tasks reflect trends associated with the political climate, educational legislation, and professional social work practices operant at the time. For example, when Costin undertook the first national study in 1969, the federal government had not yet begun to pass public laws demonstrating a commitment to public education for children with disabilities and their families. Consequently, the findings of her task analysis identified service to individual children as the most frequently preferred service. Allen-Meares' 1977 replication came at a time when the ecological perspective was being introduced into social work practice and when federal legislation had begun to target at-risk student populations. Consequently, the interplay of her research findings and professional knowledge development led her to introduce the service paradigm of home/school/community. Timberlake, Sabatino, and Hooper's 1982 research was conducted during a period of economic recession and shrinking resources. Thus, it was not surprising that the findings of their task analysis identified consultation, a service requiring minimal resources for great impact, as a dominant task.

Today, federal legislation and the increased family systems perspective of the social work profession are shifting the school social work task paradigm once again. In 1986, passage of PL 99-457, the Education of the Handicapped Act (EHA), authorized an early intervention school program for children with disabilities ages 3-5 and their families. In 1991, PL 94-142, the Education for All Handicapped Children Act, was re-authorized as PL 102-119, the Individuals with Disabilities Education Act (IDEA). Together, these two laws represent a new and unique paradigm shift for schools and school social work services. By law, today's educational and social service ecology in the schools has expanded to incorporate family and community support systems. In addition, the laws have expanded the educational service ecology by giving the family a place in their child's assessment and intervention and, in the instance of preschoolers, by identifying the family as the central milieu through which educational prevention, amelioration, and rehabilitative services occur. This major paradigm shift is now codified in practice as the individualized educational plan (IEP) established in PL 94-142 and the individual family service plan (IFSP) established in Part H of IDEA.

Over time, school social work services have moved from a unidimensional perspective on the child to a person-in-environment ecological perspective to a new multidimensional, legislatively driven model mandating educational partnership and collaboration with families. Thus, the old school social work practice models and language of service must be amended to incorporate the new practice tasks of collaboration. While this new role task builds on previous practice and research, it requires development of a new synergistic intervention model whereby parents are recognized as having a role position with authority vested in them as parents. The major difference is that this model institutes a new role for parents in their children's education and mandates their involvement to an extent never before implemented. In the past, professionals primarily collaborated with each other in assessment and intervention. At present, the law redirects the collaboration to include parents as partners in assessment and intervention designed to enhance the child's educational performance. Thus, the current and future educational ecology requires a partnership model which includes the central practice tasks of collaboration, consultation, mediation, and empowerment as driving forces in the school social work ecology.

Conservative Climate For Practice

School social workers are attempting to cope with this practice paradigm shift within today's highly pressurized practice context. Multiple events have suggested to American citizens that their nation is out of control and devoid of human values and are fueling a rise in philosophical, political, and fiscal conservatism.

Violence has dramatically increased and appears all pervasive and invasive. Guns and gangs exist in every region of the country and in both urban and rural settings. African American youth, however, remain the most vulnerable, constituting 17.7 percent of all homicide victims in 1992 even though only 1.3 percent of the U.S. population (*Washington Post*, 1994). The violence and aggression in schools mirrors the record numbers of reported cases of domestic violence, street crimes, and homicides impacting on family and community.

Economic deprivation is a growing concern. One fifth of U.S. children live in poverty (Children's Defense Fund, 1991); an estimated 500,000 to 750,000 school-age children are homeless (National Coalition for the Homeless, 1990) and another million are runaway and homeless youth (National Network of Runaway and Youth Services, 1991). In addition, unprecedented numbers of middle- and upper-income wage earners have been displaced through private sector downsizing of corporations and businesses and public sector layoffs and their school-age children thrust into economic instability.

Intolerance of difference in others and exclusion because of difference have taken on many facets. California's legislative Proposition 187 intends to deny public social services and educational services to illegal immigrants and their children. Hate crimes include neo-Nazi slogans, racial and religious epithets, and other acts conveying intolerance of cultural and ethnic group diversity. This intolerance blames the victim and is undergirded with the expectation and demand for personal responsibility and individual achievement. It is replete with a philosophy of individualism which elevates personal responsibility for self over communal responsibility for others. In the schools, this intolerance is especially apparent in the inclusion/exclusion debates about the integration and mainstreaming of children with disabilities. It is also apparent in the debates about politically correct, values-based curricula which are part of the back-to-basics approach to educational philosophy and curriculum development apparent at one end of school reform movements. At the other end is the philosophical and curriculum thrust that emphasizes multiplicity in educational approach and advocates for a multiple levels of intelligence framework and use of multisensory and multidimensional methods of teaching.

As a result of these pressures, it is anticipated that state departments of education and local school boards will set their own particularized agendas for dealing with these issues in their communities and that these agendas may differ from some prevailing federal policies and programs. "Policy formulation and debate ... have drawn on relevant research when it was available, but all too often these discussions have revealed critical gaps in convincing research-based knowledge" (Inouye, Ell, and Ewalt, 1994). Thus, school social workers must monitor local, state, and federal policies, planning efforts, and administrative programming in relation to local school service practices so that so that the findings of their practice research remain current and relevant.

METHODOLOGICAL DILEMMAS IN KNOWLEDGE DEVELOPMENT AND ACCOUNTABILITY

Professional choices and preferences for appropriate means of intervention are constantly developing. Interventive methods are influenced by an expanding knowledge base and shifts in value emphases within the field. These changes demand the development of new guidelines for practice.

Professional Knowledge Base

Throughout the twentieth century, social workers have debated the usefulness, credibility, and hierarchical status of professional knowledge derived through practice wisdom disseminated in the oral tradition of supervision, and professional knowledge derived through scientific method and disseminated through publications (Richmond, 1917; Flexner, 1915). Although appearing in various forms, the core of the earlier debate centered around three questions: (1) Is scientific practice knowledge generated by research or cumulative practice wisdom about what works more valid and reliable? (2) Which is more credible, relevant, and useful in the real world of practice? (3) Which establishes the credibility of the social work profession with consumers and with colleagues in other professions? In recent years, social workers appear to have tacitly accepted the need for a scientific knowledge base for the profession and have virtually ignored practice wisdom. Yet neither type of practice knowledge by itself is adequate. Nor does this tacit resolution appear to have addressed the place of theory in professional practice. Thus, for the foreseeable future, the professional knowledge base for school social workers is perhaps best defined as comprising a network of propositions which have originated in practice experience, theory, and research, and are grounded in both the social work profession and the school practice setting. For school social work researchers, the knowledge development issue becomes: What constitutes credible social work knowledge and validly informed social work practice in the face of constantly evolving state-of-the-art knowledge and an uncertain practice context?

Paradigm Debate

In the past decade, debates about knowledge development methodology have polarized around identifying the best paradigm for establishing a social work knowledge base and determining accountability: Is the primary research design to incorporate quantitative or qualitative methodology (Guba, 1990; Hudson and Nurius, 1994; Luborsky, et al. 1988)? More recently, this polarized debate has been eschewed in favor of multimethod research designs which employ multiple theoretical perspectives, embedded or nested designs, multiple measures, multimodal analyses, and within/ across group replications to offset the weaknesses of one approach with the strengths of another (Brewer and Hunter, 1989; Timberlake and Sabatino, 1994). These validity and reliability debates and the multimethod solution, however, beg the critical issue underlying the choice of design in school social work research. Rather than being chosen simply to cross-validate findings through a counterbalancing of methodological strengths and weaknesses, research design is ideally selected because it: (1) best enables the researcher to address the research problem and question at hand; (2) provides a means of corroborating the findings: (3) generates evidence which fills in knowledge lacunae; and (4) permits the researcher to build explanatory and intervention models that are adequate, acceptable, accessible, and accountable to the multiple stakeholders in the outcomes of school social work practice—child and parent consumers, social work service providers, educator colleagues, boards of education, and the tax-paying public. For it is increasingly clear that professional truths in explanation and intervention are established by agreement among constituent communities of consumers, practitioners, and payors rather than by the research community alone.

Generating Meaningful Data

In a host setting such as a school, social work services are secondary services and a considerable expenditure of resources for communities. As such, it has been difficult to document service effectiveness because social workers employ different criteria and measures than educators in evaluating outcomes. Educators use ability tests, performance measures, report card grades, and attendance, outcomes not associated directly with school social work services. Social workers, by contrast, conceptualize observed changes in psychosocial functioning to evaluate service outcomes as:

- Improved appropriateness of classroom behavior and lowered probability of identification of students as academically deficient (Owen and Sabatino, 1989);
- Decreased separation anxiety and improved school adjustment in transitioning from home to school; or
- Age-specific task achievements and developmental phase-specific accomplishments associated with increased attention to the teaching-learning process.

It is important to note that although the practice models may vary and change over time the desired outcomes change little as they remain closely tied to the ultimate outcome measure driving all professions employed in the school setting—the success or failure of a child's classroom performance.

When the research paradigm is an integral part of school social work service design and delivery, research questions are concerned with the impact of the specified intervention on outcomes meaningful to the school setting—changes in children's attitudes and behaviors in the classroom, environmental structures and processes in the school setting, the fit of children with their classroom environments, and the critical outcome of improvement in academic achievement. The choice of specific dependent and independent variables is dependent on the practice problem addressed, the research question relating to the point of service provided, and the explanatory and change theories employed.

The goal of school social work practice research is capturing the reality of what actually exists but doing so often proves difficult. For example, the theoretical orientation of the research may not take into account the actual experiences of the children, the parents, or the teachers. Or a lack of cultural understanding or insensitivity to diversity in the schools might impose dominant cultural norms on the data collected (Marin and Marin, 1991). For example, data collection tools may not capture the specificity of the behaviors, attitudes, and situations that are the foci of intervention. The measurement or observation may miss important aspects of children's classroom behavior or well-being in school that are affected positively or negatively by the intervention. Or, the assumptions in the selected measures may differ from those in the practice intervention. In these instances, the research does not measure what the school social worker thought it would measure and provides invalid answers to the questions asked. In other instances, the demonstration project and outcome research may not yield the same answers upon repetition and, thereby, may raise reliability issues of intervention replicability as well as stability, accuracy, and error of measurement.

Thus, it is clear that conceptualizing, implementing, and assessing school social work practice is a matter for careful clinical framing, operationalization in practice, and systematic evaluation.

Methodological Guidelines

Given the profession's thrust toward documenting its theory and practice and the federal laws that increasingly affect their practice in the schools, school social workers are beginning to develop a theoretically-framed and empirically-based practice. In moving forward with this task, it is important that their research studies in the aggregate:

- Employ valid and reliable single subject and aggregate experimental research designs in actual educational settings;
- Develop and test social work intervention models that represent discrete points of service responsive to specific problems and target populations of interest to both social workers and educators;
- Develop and test social work intervention models that variously incorporate child-focused, family-focused, and community-focused approaches germane to educational settings;
- Develop and test social work intervention models that represent discrete points of service responsive to specific problems associated with organizational development, empowerment, advocacy, school reform, and policy development;
- Develop and test individual and group intervention models for psychosocial dysfunction, psycho-educational models for normative problems as well as empowerment, consultation, collaboration, and mediation models;
- Explore and refine the change processes occurring within their social work intervention models;
- Select problem explanations and intervention methodologies that are appropriate, theoretically driven, based in conceptually integrated evidence (as opposed to eclectic summarizations), and germane to the educational setting;
- Use theoretical frameworks and research methodologies sensitive to cultural, socioeconomic, age, and gender diversity in order to build a body of knowledge that translates into increased understanding of school population heterogeneity, expanded social service technology and skills, and additional ways to facilitate school personnel's understanding and handling of classroom diversity; and
- Acknowledge and accept pragmatic circumstances associated with issues of resource allocation that, at times, may dictate the timing, focus, or rank ordering of experimental research projects.

However, a word of caution is in order. Unless the research problem and proposed interventions can be described and discussed in terminology meaningful to the mission of this host setting, the outcomes of school social work services cannot be assessed by administrative, instructional, or special education personnel in terms of their cost/benefit ratio—their usefulness, effectiveness, efficiency, and financial outlay. Nor can they be used as justification for allocating scarce resources. Indeed as Constable (Chapter 1, this volume) reminded,

> The social worker is a catalyst for the personal, familial, and institutional work to be done for the best match between resources and tasks, in accord with the essential values of human nature. . . . The school social worker makes education possible for many children who otherwise would have difficulty coping with an educational process as it takes place and is defined in school.

Value and Ethical Commitments

In their practice research, school social workers confront a dual set of professional value and ethical commitments. On the one hand, they are accountable to the values and ethics of the social work profession as codified by state licensure/certification laws and the *Code of Ethics* (NASW, 1980) of the National Association of Social Workers. On the other, they are accountable to the value and ethical constraints of the educational institution as their practice setting. At times, these dual value and ethical commitments are congruent. Both profession and educational institution, for example, would concur that school work practice should routinely be evaluated. Both would concur that making embedded values and ethical reasoning conscious and explicit is essential in school social work practice and would include the following ethical conventions:

- Concern for the dignity and privacy of all participants;
- Protection of participants from discomfort, danger, and deprivation;
- Explication of risk/benefit consequences for voluntary, informed participation by children and families;
- Assurance of confidential handling of information and security of computerized data;
- Protection of participants from value influences and bias in assessment and intervention methodology;
- Development and testing of assessment and intervention models which incorporate the best empirical evidence of effectiveness;
- Recognition of value influences and bias embedded in research methodology and interpretation of findings; and
- Assurance of fairness in access to and utilization of research and demonstration service projects.

Both profession and institution would also concur that children have the right to receive services and would question whether the anticipated research benefit of long range improvement of children's well-being would ever justify delaying service provision in the short term. Thus, experimental comparison groups designed to answer the research question "which treatment works better?" would be preferable to experimental designs with treatment groups and no treatment control groups which address the research question "does treatment work better than no treatment?"

Value dilemmas or conflicts may, however, arise in relation to social work's and education's preferred conceptualizations of children, families, and schools; preferred instrumentalities for assessing and intervening with children and parents within the educational institution; or preferred service outcomes in school social work practice (Levy, 1973). For example, P.L. 94-142 presents an instrumental value dilemma at the point of initial service—individualized educational assessment and planning. The law specifies that families have a right to obtain a copy of all public school system evaluations of their children but does not specify the method of providing this information. It is this method which may become a source of value conflict among multidisciplinary team members. For example, some team members placed emphasis on the content and substance of the report, believing that furnishing a written copy of an evaluation report satisfies the legal requirements and constitutes the whole point of the initial service. School social workers, by contrast, traditionally have placed emphasis on both content and process, valuing the professional intervention process of assessment, planning, and reporting as the whole point of the initial service. In other words, school social workers value the family's right to participate in and respond to the evaluation process, findings, and recommended plan. To explore this professional value dilemma in service delivery, school social workers might pose the following research: Do different styles and levels of family participation in individualized assessment and planning affect their response to and use of the process, findings, recommendations, and outcome? If so, which families are affected? In what ways?

Accountability

National standards and rigorous assessment of student learning and achievement are being promoted in an effort to establish accountability of educators, schools, and school systems. Thus, it seems likely that a comparable process will be put in place to explore the hidden costs and benefits of school social work services. Yet the central definitional questions remain: How is accountability of school social workers to be defined, rigorously assessed, and enforced? One part of this definitional issue is clearly accountability to whom—child, parent, school, school system? The other part is establishing practice standards and exploring costs and benefits in relation to these standards. At this time, school social workers have the option of either allowing others to set standards for them or accepting the challenge to specify their practice standards and goals, develop ways of evaluating the outcomes of their practice, develop ways of assessing costs/benefits, and conduct program and practice evaluations. This option seems preferable to abdication as school social workers are clearly in a better position than educators to take responsibility for explicating the scope, costs/benefits, and quality of service offered and establishing accountability criteria for the public and private resources absorbed.

SUBSTANTIVE DILEMMAS IN KNOWLEDGE DEVELOPMENT AND ACCOUNTABILITY

The pursuit of many goals simultaneously presents certain dilemmas for the field. Among them are the need to use resources for both long term planning and policy impact studies. At the same time, limited resources must still be used for immediate and short-term interventions.

Epidemiological Studies and Long Range Planning

Philosophically, school social workers espouse universal social work services to address the psychosocial problems of children and youth which interfere with school learning and performance. With conservative economic and social policies, however, programs and services are likely to be based on local and state school priorities and available funding sources. The actual scope of the need and the school social work services provided need to be made clear: Who is being served? For what problems? Under what circumstances? At what costs/benefits? And conversely: Who is not being served? For what problems? Under what circumstances? At what costs?

An epidemiological study, for example, might address the question of children's needs for school social work services, including the nature and severity of the problem and the numbers of children involved. One such study (Sabatino, Timberlake, and Zajicek-Farber, 1992) found no difference on these variables when comparing inner-city and suburban elementary school students. This finding and others served to undo the stereotype that inner-city children were experiencing more psychosocial functioning problems in the classroom and pointed to functional strengths in resourcefulness in coping of inner-city children. Another epidemiological study (Timberlake and Sabatino, 1994) explored the nature and severity of the problem of homelessness to children and found that school attendance mediated their self-esteem and loneliness. These findings paved the way for program development to meet their service needs.

School social workers also need an epidemiological data base to help in predicting behavior of children and their parents that is likely to be dangerous to self or others. Community and administrative pressure and increased legal liability are pressing school social workers to pay increased attention to their clinical data, inferred practice implications, and predictions about the future behavior of children, youth and parents (Gambrill, 1990; Murdock, 1994). For example: Is this child likely to attempt suicide? Is this parent likely to abuse? Is this adolescent likely to harm another child? School social workers are accustomed to making clinical predictions informed by social case history, current behavior patterns, and psychosocial assessment. They are not, however, accustomed to using a template whose aggregate data provides information about the statistical likelihood that certain behaviors will occur. Such aggregate data bases can facilitate more systematic clinical prediction and decision making by expanding their knowledge base and pointing to harmful behavioral outcomes likely to be associated with:

- Historical behavior patterns—degree to which history of assault is predictive of future violent behavior or a history of suicide threats is predictive of a future suicide attempt; or
- Demographic factors—degree to which age, gender, race, diagnosis, and marital status are predictive of destructive behavior.

While data which can function as useful indicators or predictors have been compiled into actuarial tables for use in selected mental health situations calling for clinical judgment, such tables have not yet been developed for school social work.

In addition to programmatic needs assessment and clinical prediction, epidemiological research sets the stage for long-range planning. By juxtaposing a broad-based client characteristics and needs data set, a school social work service provision data set, and a data set of school social work services utilized, epidemiological research can provide both the desired specificity about, and fuller understanding of, school social work practice.

Model Development and Effectiveness Studies

The new accountability paradigm with its underlying conservative philosophy makes it clear that school social workers no longer have the luxury of simply describing and conceptualizing what they are doing in their espoused models of practice. They must move toward greater specificity in what they actually do and test for its effectiveness.

In providing services, school social workers are accountable not only to their clients, themselves, and their profession, but also to the school as an educational institution within which their practice occurs. As competent practitioners, they are responsible for providing adequate evidence of the extent to which their clients have benefited from intervention and of ongoing efforts to improve their practice. That is, they are responsible for establishing the effectiveness of both service delivery programs and individual practice efforts.

Studies of program effectiveness establish the degree to which a particular school social work program meets its goals and objectives in terms of: types of problems addressed, number of clients served, barriers to service utilization, overall results achieved, cost/benefit ratio, and the congruence of results with the core educational mission of the school setting. Since school social work programs are not static entities, establishing their effectiveness is not a onetime event. Rather, program evaluation is an ongoing dynamic process as school social work programs are continually evolving entities. Decisions about actual program delivery should be based on evidence, not arguments of ideology, theory, or authority (Hasenfeld, 1992). Clinically and statistically significant evidence is based on information derived from: (1) substantive programmatic variables which operationalize multidimensional program structures, program activities, and client outcomes; (2) contextual variables such as program history, educational and social work norms, community expectations, and political pressures; and (3) client variables such as demographic characteristics, diversity, and family involvement. For example, Timberlake, Sabatino, and Hooper (1979) explored decisions about the educational placement of handicapped children in order to understand the contribution of the social case history to multidisciplinary team decision making and evaluate the effectiveness of this practice tool.

Studies of practice effectiveness address the outcomes expected when intervention is provided under the real world conditions of school settings and with all of the variations apparent among children, families, educators, and social workers. Practice effectiveness studies link substantive questions of service provision, conceptual issues of explanatory and change theories, the intervention practices, specific outcome questions, and cost/benefit analyses. In the practice research, it is important to ask questions which provide adequate evidence useful in making practice decisions. Simply counting is not sufficient. It is the practitioner's task to translate the meaning of the evidence to parents, educators, and children. For example, using consultation services as a conceptual framework for practice, Drisko (1993) developed but did not test a model of school social work consultation with special education teachers that profiles student skills and teacher intervention strategies while enhancing teacher empathy and understanding. Sabatino (1986), by contrast, not only developed a model of school work practice but incorporated as a major component of the practice an effectiveness measure. Using a quasi-experimental design with pre- and post-measures of teacher perception of children's classroom behavior, she provided teacher-centered mental health case consultation services and found statistically significant differences between teachers who received consultation services and those who did not. The identified children whose teachers received consultation also received statistically significant higher grades on their report cards for non-academic performance of "listens to and follows teacher's directions."

Thus, program and practice effectiveness research involves assessing both the statistical significance and clinical meaningfulness of the findings obtained. It involves both systematic data collection using sound research design and continuous data collection using sound practice methodology.

Policy Impact Studies

According to Prigmore and Atherton (1979), policy decision making requires choosing from among various alternatives. These choices reflect social values and preferences. Thus, public values heavily influence how politically viable and publicly acceptable a particular social policy will be. Today, dominant conservative political norms and values call into question continued use of value-based analyses of policy barriers to service delivery. The new accountability paradigm with its underlying conservative philosophy makes it clear, however, that school social workers no longer have the luxury of simply relying on federal policies as the legal basis for practice in school settings. They must move toward policy analysis guided by social work, economic and educational precepts, and providing an evidentiary data base for decision making and refinement. In such an approach, a policy impact assessment would, at minimum, focus on analyzing each of the four elements of entitlements, goals, service delivery, and financing (Chambers, 1993) from a perspective that takes into account social work, education, and economics. While heavy emphasis would be placed on economic cost/benefit analysis, such analysis would be framed and anchored within the school social work mission.

The childhood educational disability legislation provides a case in point. As noted in the *Washington Post* (1994), the Department of Education reported that in 1992/93 nearly 95 percent of the nation's 5,017,000 students with disabilities received education and related services in a regular school setting for some part of the day. Of these disabled students ages 6 to 21, 52.4 percent were assessed as having specific learning disabilities; 22.2 percent, speech/language impairment; 10.9 percent, mental retardation; and 8.3 percent, emotional disturbance. These figures, however, are flat and yield minimal information about programmatic successes or failures. On the one hand, these figures suggest that the educational system is providing comprehensive assessment services and, by extrapolation, that the system is moving disabled children toward normalization in the regular classroom. On the other hand, the psychosocial and economic cost/benefits were not discussed. Without cost/benefit data, practitioners and planners have no nuanced evidentiary base for evaluating the policy's operationalization into programming and practice.

For example, Seligman and Darling (1989) assert that: (1) the availability of supportive community resources is the most important determinant of normalization for most families of disabled children; and (2) the ability of children to achieve a normalized lifestyle is determined by their access to resources, their opportunity structure. Although it is clear that 95 percent of these children now spend part of their time in mainstream classrooms, school social workers do not know if schools and families see this as a resource and normalization of children's lives.

During the 1970s and 1980s, three major pieces of federal legislation sought to remove barriers to normalization in the schools. Specifically, PL 94-142, PL 99-457, and PL 102-119 mandate that preschool and school age children with targeted disabilities receive a free and appropriate public education in the least restrictive environment. Policy impact studies, however, have not yet assessed the degree to which the promise of normalization within the least restrictive environment has become reality and at what costs with what benefits.

CONCLUSION

The 1994 elections appear to reflect an enormous amount of anxiety about whether Americans are up to the task of handling the nation's social, economic, and educational problems. Now is the time to put school social work knowledge, skills, and values into research-based practice activities to help alleviate these anxieties and to guide services to school children and their families across the threshold into the next century. New practice approaches and research paradigms are the seeds of the future—the way to survive and thrive.

REFERENCES

Allen-Meares, P. 1994. Social work services in schools: A national study of entry-level tasks. *Social Work* 39(5):560–565.

Allen-Meares, P. 1977. Analysis of tasks in school social work. *Social Work* 22:196–201.

Brewer, J., and Hunter, A. 1989. *Multimethod research*. Newbury Park, CA: Sage Publications.

Chambers, D. 1993. *Social policy and social programs*. NY: Macmillan.

Children's Defense Fund. 1991. *Child poverty in America*. Washington, D.C.: Author.

Costin, L. 1969. An analysis of the tasks in school social work. *Social Service Review* 43:274–285.

Drisko, J. 1993. Special education teacher consultation: A student-focused, skill-defining approach. *Social Work in Education* 15:19–28.

Flexner, A. 1915. Is social work a profession? In *Proceedings of the National Conference of Charities and Corrections.* Chicago. pp. 576–590.

Freeman, E. 1994. School social work report card. *Social Work in Education* 16(4): 203–206.

Gambrill, E. 1990. *Critical thinking in clinical practice.* San Francisco, CA: Jossey-Bass.

Guba, E. 1992. *The paradigm dialog.* Newbury Park, CA: Sage.

Hasenfeld, Y. 1992. *Human services as complex organizations.* Newbury Park, CA: Sage.

Hudson, W., and Nurius, P. 1994. *Controversial issues in social work research.* Boston, MA: Allyn and Bacon.

Inouye, D., Ell, K., and Ewalt, P. 1994. Social work research and social policy. *Social Work* 39:629–631.

Koppich, J. 1992. Choice in education: Not whether, but what. *Social Work in Education* 14(4):253–257.

Levy, C. 1973. The value base of social work. *Journal of Social Work Education* 9: 34–42.

Luborsky, L., Crits-Cristoph, P., Mintz, J., and Auerbach, A. 1988. *Predicting therapeutic outcomes.* NY: Basic Books.

Marin, G., and Marin, B. 1991. *Research with Hispanic populations.* Newbury Park, CA: Sage.

McDonald, S. 1992. Special education through the lens of the regular education initiative. *Social Work in Education* 14(1):63–67.

Murdock, A. 1994. Avoiding errors in clinical prediction. *Social Work* 39:381–386.

National Association of Social Workers. 1980. *Code of ethics.* Silver Spring, MD: Author.

National Coalition for the Homeless. 1990. *Homelessness in America: A summary.* Washington, D.C.: Author.

National Network of Runaway Youth Services. 1991. *To whom do they belong? Runaway, homeless, and other youth in high risk situations in the 1990s.* Washington, D.C.: Author.

Owen, M., and Sabatino, C. 1989. Effects of cognitive development on classroom behavior: A model assessment and intervention program. *Social Work in Education* 11:77–88.

Prigmore, C., and Atherton, C. 1979. *Social welfare policy: Analysis and formulation.* Lexington, MA: Heath.

Republican National Committee. 1994. *Contract with America.* Washington, D.C.

Richmond, M. 1917. *Social diagnosis.* NY: Russell Sage Foundation.

Sabatino, C. 1986. The effects of school social work consultation on teacher perception and role conflict-role ambiguity in relationship to students with social adjustment problems. *Dissertation Abstracts International* 46:11.

Sabatino, C., Timberlake, E., and Zajicek-Farber, M. 1992. Psychosocial coping of urban children. *Social Thought* 17:35–47.

Seligman, M., and Darling, R. 1989. *Ordinary families, special children.* NY: Guilford Press.

Task Force on Social Work Research. 1991. *Building social work knowledge for effective services and policies: A plan for research development.* Rockville, MD: NIMH. Publication contact. D. Austin, School of Social Work, University of Texas at Austin.

Timberlake, E., and Sabatino, C. 1994. Homeless children: Impact of school attendance on self esteem and loneliness. *Social Work in Education* 16:9–20.

Timberlake, E., Sabatino, C., and Hooper, S. 1982. School social work practice and P.L. 94-142. In R. Constable and J. Flynn, (eds.). *School social work practice and research perspectives.* Homewood, Ill: Dorsey Press, 49–67.

Timberlake, E., Sabatino, C., and Hooper, S. 1979. Decisions made in educational placement of handicapped children. *Journal of Social Service Research* 3:187–200.

Washington Post. 1994. Special education students in the mainstream. December 13.

Washington Post. 1994. Homicide. December 9.

Wetrogen, S. 1989. *American demographics: Projections of the populations of states by age, sex, and race: 1988–2010.* Washington, D.C.: Bureau of the Census.

APPENDIX

Taxonomy of Terms Which School Social Workers Encounter

Shirley McDonald, Sally G. Goren, Carol Massat

ACLD—American Council on Learning Disabilities

Adaptive Behavior Assessment—Standardized instrument measuring seven areas of functioning other than educational achievement

ADD—Attention Deficit Disorder

ADHD—Attention Deficit Hyperactivity Disorder

AFT—American Federation of Teachers

AIDS—Auto-immune deficiency syndrome

Annual Review—Interdisciplinary yearly meeting required under Public Law 94-142, and subsequently Public Law 101-476, to review progress of each identified student needing special education services.

Anorexia—Eating disorder marked by serious distortion of body perception and excessive avoidance of food. Intense fear of becoming fat.

Autism—Distortion of skills and function marked by social non-responsiveness, impaired or peculiar language, and bizarre responses to the environment.

BD—Behavior Disorder—characterized by difficult to manage acting-out behaviors

Case Study Evaluation—An educational evaluation of a child referred for possibility of receiving special education services which includes among other components a Social Development Study

CEC—Council for Exceptional Children

Confidentiality—Social work value respecting and guaranteeing privacy of client communication, within the parameters of the law.

DD—Developmental Disability

DSM-IV—Diagnostic and Statistical Manual, Fourth Edition (published by the American Psychiatric Association)

ED—Emotional disturbance

EH—Educationally handicapped

EMH—Educable mentally handicapped

EMI—Educably mentally impaired (same as EMH)

GED—General equivalency diploma

HHS—U.S. Department of Health and Human Services

HI—Hearing Impaired

Host Setting—Setting in which social work is a support service, rather than the primary service

ICD-X—International Classification of Diseases, Tenth Edition

IEP—Individualized Education Program

IFSP—Individualized Family Service Plan

IGAPP—Iowa General Assessment of Pupil Performance

Inclusion—Movement which grew from the REI (Regular Education Initiative) concept, placing all students possible in regular education classrooms in their home district

LD—Learning disability

LEA—Local Education Agency (school district)

Low Incidence—Disabilities which affect fewer than one-tenth of one percent of the population (.1% or fewer)

LRE—Least Restrictive Environment—Educational placement most closely resembling a regular education placement, in which student may maximize his/her educational experience

Mainstreaming—The practice of placing students from self-contained classrooms into one or more regular education classrooms for regular education instruction

MBD—Minimal brain dysfunction

MDC—Multi-disciplinary conference—mandated conference to determine a student's eligibility for special education programming

Mediation/Conflict Resolution—Process of identifying real issues in a dispute and discovering acceptable compromise solutions to original conflict

MLD—Moderate learning disability

MMI—Moderately mentally impaired

MR—Mental Retardation

Multipli-Disabled—More than one significant disabling condition affecting a person

NEA—National Education Association

OT—Occupational therapist

Peer Support—Any of a variety of programs using a teaching/learning model which relies on student-to-student communication

PH—Physically handicapped

P.L. 94-142—The Education for All Handicapped Children Act of 1975, amended as:

P.L. 99-457—Early Childhood Amendments, and

P.L. 101-476—Individuals with Disabilities Education Act (IDEA)

PMI—Profoundly mentally impaired

PT—Physical Therapy

REI—Regular Education Initiative—movement to integrate special education students into the regular educational environment

Related Services—Instruction given a student by specially trained professionals within the special education domain, not primarily related to regular educational instruction

Resource Room—A separate environment within a regular education setting within which the student receives special education services on a limited basis

Resource Services—Services delivered to a student who spends more than 50 percent of his/her time in a regular education classroom

Self-Contained—Classrooms in which students designated as special education students receive over 50 percent of their daily educational instruction

SDS—Social developmental study, includes an assessment of adaptive behaviors and assessment of cultural environment, as mandated by P.L. 94-142 and P.L. 101-476

SLD—Severe learning disability

SMI—Severely mentally impaired

SSWAA—School Social Work Association of America. National association, organized officially in 1994, to support national legislation, sponsor national conferences focused on issues relevant to school social work, to support the formation and particular interests of regional state organizations, and to support the professional needs of individual school social workers.

Standard Education Placement—Placement in a regular education school setting

TMH—Trainable mentally handicapped

VI—Visually impaired

INDEX

abused children. *See* child abuse
accountability
   collegial accountability, 403-4
   methodological dilemmas in, 448-54
   as political slogan, 433
   research to demonstrate accountability of schools, 401-2
   of school social workers, 62, 453-54
   staff accountability if child does not meet IEP objectives, 113
   substantive dilemmas in, 454-58
achievement, coping behaviors for, 44-45, 48, 161
action research approach to change, 376-77
adaptation, 31, 41, 184, 203-4
adaptive behavior assessments, 203-4, 461
Adaptive Learning Environment Model (ALEM), 235
Addams, Jane, 5, 6, 101
Adlerian psychological theory, 283
adolescence
   adolescents becoming disenchanted with secondary schools, 299-300
   stresses in early, 33-34
   See also teenage mothers
advocacy research, 436
affiliation, coping behaviors for, 44-45, 48, 161
aggressive behavior
   remediation of, 260-61
   violence in schools, 70, 447
agricultural education, 246
alcohol use, 70, 78, 262-63
ALEM (Adaptive Learning Environment Model), 235
Amber Tatro et al. v. Irving (Tx.) Independent School District et al., 136, 143n35
American Indians, revisions to IDEA regarding, 116, 119, 124

Anderson, R. J., 35
appeals process in special education placement, 112, 138
apprenticeships, 239
Argonne School (Milan, Italy), 188
assessing as social work activity, 53, 54
attendance officers, 18, 19
attorneys, 137-38, 144n43
autism, 104, 461

back-to-basics approach, 448
Bartlett, Harriet T., 6, 7, 28
battered child syndrome, 167
behavioral consultation, 274
behavioral modification, 393-94
bilingual-bicultural families, 168
block grants, 78-79
Board of Education of the Hendrick Hudson Central School District Bd. of Ed., Westchester County, et al., v. Amy Rowley, et al., 135, 141n6
Boston, 18
boundary workers, 374, 379, 380
Brown v. Board of Education of Topeka, Kansas, 3, 185
business-education compacts, 241

California: Proposition 187, 447
car-in-the-garage technique, 219, 220
career academies/magnet schools, 240
career education movement, 237-38
career exposure programs, 241
Carl E. Perkins Technical Education Act, 240, 244
case management, 350-51
   of Individualized Family Services Plans, 223-24

response to entitlement laws, 349–50
  tasks of, 351
case study evaluation, 461
casework
  generic base and specific practice of, 6–7
  as major method of school social work, 55
  replacing home-school liaison and attendance officer's role, 19
  service coordination services, 126–27
  single subject design studies in, 397–98
certification for school social workers, 80
change, organizational
  action research approach to, 376–77
  examples of school system change, 383–84
  guidelines for action, 381–83
  initiating through research and evaluation, 374–86
  factors influencing rate of, 330
  model for introducing system change, 377–81
  organizational development approach to, 375–76
  peer-consultation approach to, 376, 381
  technologies for, 375–77
charter schools, 79
Chicago, 18
child abuse
  battered child syndrome, 167
  identification and reporting by teachers, 356, 361, 364
  mandatory reporting of, 355–57
  physical abuse, 357–58
  programs for school personnel on, 339
  school's responsibilities in cases of, 167
  sexual abuse, 358–60
Child Abuse Prevention and Treatment Act, 358
child neglect, 360–61
  mandatory reporting of, 355–57
  school's responsibilities in cases of, 167
child welfare system, 363–65
children
  child-school interface, 29–30
  child welfare system, 363–65
  developmentally delayed children, 47, 48, 117–18
  exceptional children, 44, 89
  increasing percentage of minority children, 444–45
  needs of in postmodern society, 13–14

  in placement, 361–62
  promoting social competence in schools, 253–66
  school social workers and protection of, 355–65
  vulnerability of, 189–90
  See also adolescence; child abuse; child neglect; children with disabilities; children with special needs; peers; pupils
children with disabilities
  defined by IDEA, 104
  early identification of disabilities, 98
  educational mandates for, 103–15, 132–40
  educational objectives for, 90
  equal educational opportunities for, 27
  evaluation of, 97, 106–8, 206–7, 461
  full inclusion for, 141
  Handicapped Children's Protection Act, 138
  home environment of, 187
  Individualized Education Programs for, 90, 108–9, 113, 139–40, 210–19
  integration of, 228–30
  placement procedures for, 108–12
  public education mandated for, 74, 87, 88–93, 132
  resource development and coordination for, 347
  segregation of prohibited, 133–34
  seriously emotionally disturbed children, 104–5
  social worker's support in accepting new realities, 233
  stress in families of, 183–84
  surrogate parents for, 112
  suspension and expulsion of, 136–37
  traditional services for, 348–49
  trend toward inclusion for, 147–55, 268
  See also Education for All Handicapped Children Act; Individuals with Disabilities Education Act; infants and toddlers with disabilities; related services; special education
children with special needs
  buddy system for, 231
  identification of, 134–35
  mainstreaming of, 228–32
  school social work consultation programs for, 267–81
  social development study of, 197–208

classroom behavior
  environmental influence on, 12
  in school social work evaluation, 450
clean intermittent catheterization (CIC), 136
clinical consultation, 273-74
Coalition of Essential Schools, 79
Comer, James, 79-80
communication
  in organizations, 50
  as social work activity, 53
communities
  community-school interface, 30-31
  conflict with schools for control of education, 27
  obligation to ensure families can face their responsibilities, 190
  resources in, 348
  school as a community of families, 187-89
  in school-based research, 402, 403
  school-community tasks for social work, 345
  social workers as link between clients and, 127
  as unit of attention, 194-95
community psychology, 377
community services, 24, 166
competence, social. *See* social competence
Comprehensive School Health Programs, 77-78
compulsory school attendance laws, 5, 18
"Concern for Community" program, 33
confidentiality, 206-7, 461
conflict resolution, 290-98
  adapting the process to your setting, 296-97
  conflict and emotional expression, 292-93
  conflict management in no-fault schools, 319-20
  in conflicts between school social work practice and research, 439-41
  culture and conflict, 291-92
  defined, 462
  evaluation of, 297
  problem solving process in, 295-96
  process of, 294-95
  role playing in, 293, 294
  skill building for, 293-94
  See also mediation
consequences
  defined, 430
  practice consequences, 432-34
  research consequences, 436-37

conservative political climate, 444, 447-48
  "Contract With America," 78
consultation. *See* school social work consultation
"Contract With America," 78
cooperative education programs, 240
cooperative learning, 304-5
Coordinating Council for Handicapped Children, 145n56
coordination of services, 343-54
coping, 40-41
  categories of, 44-45
  mediating factors for, 31
  related to access to support systems, 184
  as transactional phenomenon, 32, 161
corporal punishment, 357, 432, 433
counseling
  family, 392-93
  group, 393
  individual, 392
credentialing of school social workers, 21-22
Crime Bill, The (Violent Crime Control and Law Enforcement Act), 74
culture
  bilingual-bicultural families, 168
  and conflict, 291-92
  cultural sensitivity in family counseling, 392-93
  culturally-sensitive social work practice, 391-92
  effect on school social work research, 450
curriculum planning, 95-96

decentralization of special education, 152-54
decoupling, 378-79
decreasing skill deficits, 393-94
deinstitutionalization in mental health, 151
Dellmuth v. Muth, 141n10
developmental research, 438
developmentally delayed children
  defining developmental delay, 117-18
  matching person and environment, 47, 48
discrimination
  coping with, 41
  defined for education, 90
  ideal of democracy masking realities of, 3
  and racial conflict in schools, 285-86
  reinforced in public schools, 19
diversity
  sensitivity to human, 391-92
  value of, 320-21

domains in organizations, 378
  desire by domains to maintain separate identity, 379
  temporary domains, 379–80
dropping out of school
  by children of teenage mothers, 69
  clients perceiving practitioners as not congruent with them, 391
  by minorities, 70
drug use, 70, 78, 262–63
due process hearings, 110–12, 133, 138–39
duties
  defined, 429
  practice duties, 431–34
  research duties, 435–37

early adolescence, stresses in, 33–34
early intervention services
  for infants and toddlers, 74–75, 118–19
  requirements for statewide system for, 119–20
  transition to preschool program, 223
ecological perspective
  defined, 28
  the family and its institutional ecology, 184–85
  on the school, 11–12
  on school social work, 26–37, 445–47
  on social work, 43
  See also environment
Edison Project, 79
Educating Students with Learning Problems—A Shared Responsibility (Will), 149–51
education
  agricultural education, 246
  back-to-basics approach, 448
  as a civil right, 3, 185
  comprehensive education agenda of 1994, 66
  conflict between communities and schools over control of, 27
  cooperative learning, 304–5
  curriculum planning, 95–96
  decline in U.S. educational performance, 70–71
  discrimination defined for, 90
  dynamic relation with school social work, 8, 11
  excellence in, 21, 182
  the grade system, 234
  Headstart Program, 15, 73, 168, 188
  homework, 185, 186
  mandates for children with disabilities, 103–15
  parents' influence on educational productivity, 186–87
  as reflection of state of society, 3
  school social workers' contribution to, 17–25
  school-to-work transition programs, 237–51
  social factors influencing American education, 69–71
  social policy for, 87
  splitting the difference in considering student abilities, 150
  traditional model of educational administration, 349
  values in, 95–96
  vocational education, 238, 246, 251
  See also public education; school reform; school-to-work transition programs; schools; special education
Education Alternatives Inc. (EAI), 79
education and training consultation, 273
Education for All Handicapped Children Act (P.L. 94-142)
  ethical consequences for school social workers, 434–35, 446
  on inclusion, 149
  Individualized Education Program, 90, 108–9, 113, 125, 209
  Individualized Family Service Plan, 209
  influence on school social workers, 20
  least restrictive environment required by, 74, 90, 225
  mandating public education for children with disabilities, 74, 88, 89–91
  policy impact studies on, 458
  provisions of, 103–15
  reforms brought about by, 95
  school social work services expanded due to, 61
  social development studies referred to in, 200
  in social work knowledge, 44
  values expressed by, 97–98
  See also Individuals with Disabilities Education Act
Education of the Handicapped Act Amendments (P.L. 99-457), 74–75, 87, 116, 209, 458
education reform. *See* school reform

ego psychology, 29
emotional expression and conflict, 292-93
employer certified programs, 241
Empowerment Zones and Enterprise Communities, 74
environment
　categories of, 45-47
　expectations, 45-46
　the home environment, 187
　matching persons and, 47-49, 161
　quality of the impinging, 41-42, 45-47
　See also laws and policies; resources
epidemiological studies, 454-55
Erikson, Erik, 29
ethics in school social work, 428-43
　consequences defined, 430
　contrasting emphases in practice and research, 429-30
　duties defined, 429
　ethical commitments in research, 452-53
　ethical imperatives associated with professional identity, 430-37
　Machiavellianism, 436
　political savviness, 436
　practice consequences, 432-34
　practice duties, 431-34
　research consequences, 436-37
　research duties, 435-37
　selective interpretation of data, 436
evaluating
　as approach to scientific method, 369
　"evaluation," as political slogan, 433
　influences demanding evaluation of practices and services, 370-71
　initiating change through research and, 374-86
　school social work practice and services, 369-73
　school social workers, 64
　as social work activity, 54
　support for, 372-73
　uses of, 371-72
evaluation of children with disabilities, 106-8
　case study evaluation, 461
　independent, 107-8
　nondiscriminatory, 97, 106-7
　preplacement, 106-7
　in social development study, 206-7
exceptional children, 44, 89
　See also children with disabilities
expectations, 45-46

faculty, the. *See* teachers
families
　bilingual-bicultural families, 168
　community's responsibility to support, 190
　family-centered approach of Part H of IDEA, 125, 127-30
　family-centered social work, 126
　family counseling, 392-93
　the home environment, 187
　Individualized Family Plan, 219-21
　Individualized Family Service Plan, 120-22, 125-26, 221-24
　institutional ecology of, 184-85
　mobilizing strengths of to help the child, 233
　as most important mediating system, 184
　necessary arrangement in relations between schools and, 189-91
　needs of in postmodern society, 13-14
　resource development and coordination for, 347
　school social work facilitating home-school partnerships, 182-96
　school social worker interpreting school and family to each other, 166
　schools as communities of families and school personnel, 14-16, 187-89
　school's influence compared to that of, 11
　schools isolated from, 15
　stress in families with children with disabilities, 183-84
　as unit of attention, 193-94
　See also parents
family background, in social development study, 203-4
family counseling, 392-93
Family Preservation and Support Programs, 74
Family Service Centers, 167
FAPE (free, appropriate, public education), 133, 160, 167
Fetal Alcohol Syndrome (FAS), 70
field experience, 13
Flexner, Abraham, 26
free, appropriate, public education (FAPE), 133, 160, 167
full inclusion, 141

Gary A. v. New Trier High School District and the Illinois State Board of Education, 141n10

Gary B. v. Cronin, 91
general systems model, 49, 58
goal displacement, 329–30
Goals 2000: Educate America Act (P.L. 103–227), 66–68
    content of, 72
    intent of, 22
    provisions on coordinated services, 77
    school social work included in, 75
    threat of budget cuts to, 78
Godzieher Study, 435
Gordon, William E., 6, 7, 9, 28
grade system, assumptions of, 234
group counseling, 393
groups, 307–27
    applications of, 312–14
    caring relationships in, 312
    essential qualities for voluntary participation in, 309–12
    everyone having something to contribute to, 311–12
    the faculty as a group, 316–20
    group composition, 308–9
    members with a variety of coping mechanisms, 309
    merging of purposes in, 308
    providing something for all members, 310–11
    safety in, 310
    striking a balance in, 312
    what makes groups work, 307–9

Handicapped Children's Protection Act, 138
Hartford (Connecticut), 5, 18, 79, 343
Headstart Program, 15, 73, 168, 188
health care reform, 77–78
High School and Beyond survey, 186
high schools (secondary schools)
    addressing racial conflict through student forums in, 282–89
    adolescent disenchantment with, 299–300
    effect of mandatory attendance laws on, 5
home environment, 187
homework, 185, 186
Honig v. Doe, 136, 143nn 31, 36
human service organizations, 378

IASA (Improving America's Schools Act; P.L. 103–382), 72–73, 75, 77
IDEA. *See* Individuals with Disabilities Education Act

IEP. *See* Individualized Education Program
IFP (Individualized Family Plan), 219–21
IFSP. *See* Individualized Family Service Plan
Illinois
    Chicago, 18
    classifying children with special needs, 142n18
    increased burden on schools in fulfilling mandates, 349
    least restrictive environment options in, 226–27
    local school system's role in, 134
    school social work credentialing standards, 21
    the social development study in, 198, 205
    statute implementing IDEA, 144n44
Illinois Special Education Policy and Procedures Training Manual, 151–52
Illinois State Board of Education, 150–51, 198
implementing as social work activity, 54
Improving America's Schools Act (IASA; P.L. 103–382), 72–73, 75, 77
inclusion
    defined, 462
    Education for All Handicapped Children Act on, 149
    full inclusion, 141
    learning environment models for, 234–36
    least restrictive environment and, 147, 149, 226
    trend toward, 147–55, 268
    See also mainstreaming
independent evaluation, 107–8
Indiana, 142n18
individual counseling, 392
individualized education, 97
Individualized Education Program (IEP), 139–40, 210–19
    annual goals and short-term objectives, 211, 212–13
    car-in-the-garage technique, 219, 220
    contents of, 212–14
    developing agreements and integration of resources for, 211–12
    hypothetical case study of, 214–19
    involving children in, 219
    mandated by P.L. 94–142, 90, 113
    meeting to develop, 108–9
    parents in development of, 213
    Part H of IDEA on, 125, 133

the presenting problem, 214
when changing schools, 139
Individualized Family Plan (IFP), 219–21
Individualized Family Service Plan (IFSP), 221–24
  case management of, 223–24
  contents of, 221–22
  major outcomes expected by, 222–23
  Part H of IDEA on, 120–22, 125–26
Individuals with Disabilities Education Act (IDEA; P.L. 101–476)
  defining civil rights for children with disabilities, 88
  educational mandates for children with disabilities, 103–15, 132–140
  effect on school social work task paradigm, 446
  Individualized Education Program, 209
  Individualized Family Services Program, 209
  least restrictive environment mandated by, 133, 225
  policy impact studies on, 458
  purpose of, 104
  reforms brought about by, 95
  revised as P.L. 102–119, 116, 125
  school social work services expanded due to, 61
  social development studies referred to in, 200
  social service provisions in, 74, 75
  in social work knowledge, 44
  state plan required by, 133
  values expressed in, 97–98
  See also Education for All Handicapped Children Act; Part H of IDEA
infants and toddlers with disabilities, 116–30
  defined by IDEA, 117–18
  early intervention for, 74–75, 118–20
  Individualized Family Service Plan for, 120–22, 125–26, 221–24
  procedural safeguards for, 122–23
  transition to preschool program, 223
innovation
  action research approach to, 376–77
  organizational development approach to, 375–76
  peer-consultation approach to, 376
  technologies for, 375–77
  See also change, organizational
instructional integration, 228–29
instrumental values, 51, 52

interagency agreements, 346–50
Interagency Coordinating Councils, 123–24
isolated and withdrawn behavior, 261–62
judicial review, 138–39
junior high school
  punishment in, 315–16
  stresses in entering, 34

Kelly McNair v. Oak Hills Local School District, 142n24
knowledge
  building a professional knowledge base, 371, 448–49
  empirically-oriented practice knowledge, 396–97
  methodological dilemmas in developing, 448–54
  required for social work, 43–44
  substantive dilemmas in developing, 454–58
  values distinguished from, 52–53

ladder concept, 318–19
latchkey programs, 339
laws and policies, 46–47
  case management approaches to entitlements, 349–50
  for children with disabilities, 87–94
  effect on school social work task paradigm, 446–47
  policy impact studies, 457–58
  as source of data for school-based research, 410
LEA. *See* local school agency
least restrictive environment (LRE), 225–36
  benefits of, 227
  challenges to the school of, 228–30
  current interpretations of, 226–28
  defined, 462
  Education for All Handicapped Children Act on, 74, 90, 225
  full inclusion not mandated, 141
  as IDEA mandate, 133, 225
  and inclusion, 147, 149, 226
  as value of special education, 97
listening skills, 293
local school agency (LEA)
  affirmative action required of, 142n14
  role in special education, 134
  See also school systems
loose coupling, 378–79

LRE. *See* least restrictive environment

magnet schools, 240
mainstreaming
  challenges to the school of, 228–32
  in the conservative political climate, 447
  defined, 462
  See also inclusion
mandatory school attendance laws, 5, 18
Mann, Horace, 5
Marcus, Grace, 6
marijuana, 70
Max M. v. Thompson, 143n26
Mayson by Mayson v. Teague, 141n9
mediating systems, 184
mediation
  defined, 300, 462
  developing a mediation program, 302–5
  in disputes between schools and families of children with disabilities, 137, 144n39
  hidden agendas in, 304
  in high school racial conflict, 283
  mediation training, 301
  orientation of student mediators, 303–4
  peer-based conflict resolution, 299–306
  related school-system developments, 304–5
  school social work and, 305–6
  selection criteria for student mediators, 301–2, 302–3
Medicaid, 77
mental health
  deinstitutionalization in, 151
  mental health consultation, 274, 275–78
Meyer, Carol, 9
Midwest School Social Work Council, 21
Milford Conference, 6
Millicent B., case of, 337–41
Mills v. District of Columbia, 88, 89
minorities
  bilingual-bicultural families, 168
  dropout rate for, 70
  increasing percentage of minority children, 444–45
  poor educational performance of, 71
  as proportion of public school students, 71
  in racial conflict in high school, 282–89
multidisciplinary teams (transdisciplinary teams)
  in case management, 351
  individualized family service plan development, 121, 127

  involvement in special education and related services, 98
  in placement process, 108
  social worker as coordinator of, 211

Nation at Risk, A (National Commission on Excellence in Education), 238
National Alliance of Pupil Services Organizations, 76
National and Community Service Trust Act (P.L. 103–82), 73
National Association of Social Workers (NASW)
  formation of, 7
  report on psychosocial components affecting school performance, 68
  school social work conferences, 20
  in school social worker certification, 80
  standards for school social work, 99, 432
  state school social work committees, 21
NEA Code of Ethics, 96–97
needs assessment, 414–27
  analyzing the data, 422–23
  defined, 414–15
  determining what you want to know, 416–17
  gathering existing data, 419–20
  gathering new data, 420–22
  implementing, 419–22
  planning, 416–19
  possible data sources, 424–27
  reasons for conducting, 415–16
  reporting the findings, 423–24
  types of data for, 416
  writing a proposal or plan, 417–19
neglected children. *See* child neglect
networks, social, 50
networks of service organizations, 50–51
New American Schools Development Corporation, 79
New York City, 5, 18, 343
no-fault schools, 314–20
  conflict management in, 319–20
  ladder concept in, 318-19
  sharing excitement, planning, and responsibility in, 316
nondiscriminatory evaluation, 97, 106–7
Northeastern Coalition, 21

OBRA (Omnibus Budget Reconciliation Act; P.L. 103–66), 74, 355

Oliverez, Jorge, case of, 162–65
Omnibus Budget Reconciliation Act (OBRA; P.L. 103-66), 74, 355
operational values, 99
Oppenheimer, J., 18–19
organizational analysis in schools, 328–42
　five practice principles derived from, 341–42
　implications for school social work, 337–38
　organizational context of schools, 329–32
　a procedure for, 332–37
　and specific intervention, 338–41
organizational consultation, 274–75
organizational development approach to change, 375–76
organizations, 49–50
　climate of, 49–50
　communication in, 49
　domains in, 378, 379–80
　human service organizations, 378
　modifying organizational context, 395
　organizational change, 330, 374–86
　organizational environment, 50
　organizational structure, 49
　systems theory of, 49, 58

parent advocates, 137–38, 144n40
parent-sponsored schools, 16
parents
　abusive parents, 358
　attending placement meeting, 109–10
　disagreements with school regarding placement, 110–11
　in due process hearings, 110–12, 133, 138–39
　IDEA on maximizing involvement of, 133
　in Individualized Education Program development, 213
　on Interagency Coordinating Councils, 123–24
　mourning loss of the ideal child, 183, 221
　of neglected children, 360
　parent advocates, 137–38, 144n40
　parent-school interface, 30
　parental involvement and school effectiveness, 185–86
　partnership with teachers, 235
　procedural safeguards of Part H of IDEA for, 122–23
　resisting that their child is low-functioning, 145n51
　right to review evaluation material, 110
　school-parent programs, 187
　special education at no cost to, 106, 136
　stress in parents of children with disabilities, 183
　surrendering parental rights to obtain funding for special education, 135
　surrogate parents, 112
　See also teenage mothers
Parks v. Pavkovic, 142n12, 143nn 27, 32
Part H of IDEA, 116–31
　early intervention services defined by, 74–75, 118–19
　implications for social workers, 127–30
　individualized family service plan defined by, 120–22, 125–26
　infants and toddlers with disabilities defined by, 117–18
　Interagency Coordinating Council mandated by, 123–24
　philosophy of, 124–25
　procedural safeguards of, 122–23
　purpose of, 116–17
　requirements for statewide system to implement, 119–20
　service coordination in, 126–27
peer-consultation approach to change, 376, 381
peers
　influence of, 50
　peer-based conflict resolution, 299–306
　peer friendship, 189
　peer leaders maintaining control and discipline, 285
　resisting peer pressure, 256, 262
　teaching social skills regarding, 254
PEERS program, 261–62
Pennsylvania Association of Retarded Children (PARC) v. Commonwealth of Pennsylvania, 88–89, 225
Perkins, Carl E., Technical Education Act, 240, 244
personal practice model, 13
personal values, 51, 52
physically abused children, 357–58
Piaget, Jean, 29
P.L. 94–142. See Education for All Handicapped Children Act
P.L. 99–457 (Education of the Handicapped Act Amendments), 74–75, 87, 116, 209, 458
P.L. 101–476. See Individuals with Disabilities Education Act

P.L. 102-119. *See* Individuals with Disabilities Education Act
P.L. 103-66 (Omnibus Budget Reconciliation Act; OBRA), 74, 355
P.L. 103-66 (Student Loan Reform Act), 73
P.L. 103-82 (National and Community Service Trust Act), 73
P.L. 103-227. *See* Goals 2000: Educate America Act
P.L. 103-252 (Headstart Program Reauthorization), 73
P.L. 103-239 (School-to-Work Opportunities Act), 73, 237, 244
P.L. 103-382 (Improving America's Schools Act; IASA), 72-73, 75, 77
placement procedures for children with disabilities, 108-12
  appeals process, 112, 138
  due process hearings, 110-12, 133, 138-39
  impartial hearing officers, 111
  meetings for, 108-10
  multidisciplinary teams in, 108
planning as social work activity, 53
Police-or-Prevention Block Grants Bill, 79
policy, social. *See* laws and policies
policy impact studies, 457-58
poverty, 69, 183, 447
power
  in domain relationships, 380-81
  school social workers identifying the power structure, 59-60
pre-apprenticeships (youth apprenticeships), 240
pregnancy, adolescent. *See* teenage mothers
preplacement evaluation, 106-7
prevention and intervention systems, 233-34
primary prevention in school social work, 31-34
problem solving, 322-27
  accepting your feelings and fantasies, 323
  in conflict resolution, 295-96
  defining the problem, 322-23
  developing a built-in contingency plan, 324-25
  developing a plan of action, 324
  evaluating the process, 326-27
  generating alternative strategies for, 390-91
  implementing the selected strategy, 395-96
  importance of having specific information, 389-90
  postponing action, 325-26
  in school social work, 388-90
  stopping once you know what the problem is, 323-24
  targeting and specifying the problem, 388-89
  testing and verifying the procedure, 395-96
procedural due process, 97
  due process hearings, 110-12, 133, 138-39
professional values, 52
program consultation, 275
Proposition 187 (California), 447
psychotherapy, 91-92, 143n26
public education
  attacks on, 19
  changes in philosophy and law of, 267-68
  characteristic focus of the school social worker in, 38-56
  for children with disabilities, 74, 87, 88-93, 132
  FAPE, 133, 160, 167
  mandate of, 3, 5, 11
  ratio of minorities in, 71
  ratio of poor children in, 69
  See also schools
punishment, 315-16
  corporal punishment, 357, 432, 433
pupils (students)
  classroom behavior, 12, 450
  conflict resolution skills for, 290-91
  fostering collaborative practice between staff and, 405-6
  involvement in research, 404
  National Alliance of Pupil Services Organizations, 76
  school-community-pupil relations model, 19-20
  school social work helping pupils use available services and resources, 161
  smoking by, 319-20
  special populations needing extra support, 295
  student forums for addressing conflict, 282-89
  as unit of attention, 194

racial conflicts in high school, addressing through student forums, 282-89
Rashomon effect, 379
Regional Community Integration Resource Committee (RCIRC), 352-54

Regular Education Initiative (REI), 147-55
 consequences of decentralization, 152-54
 defined, 463
 deinstitutionalization in mental health compared to, 151
 and *Educating Students with Learning Problems—A Shared Responsibility*, 149-51
 encouraging movement back to regular classroom, 87, 268
 history of, 149
 implementing, 151-52
related services, 90-92
 clean intermittent catheterization as, 136
 defined, 463
 defined by IDEA, 105-7, 134
 defined in terms of provider, 142n24
 educational and noneducational services, 92, 348
 psychotherapy as, 91-92, 143n26
 which services schools must provide, 135-36
relating as social work activity, 53
research. *See* school social work research
research design intrusiveness, 438, 439
resource room, 463
resource services, 463
resources, 45
 in the community, 348
 concepts for analyzing, 49-51
 for Individualized Education Program, 211-12
 resource development in school social work, 343-54
 the social worker as a resource, 54-55
Richmond, Mary, 5, 6, 27
Rochester (New York), 18
Rogers-Skinner debate, 429
role playing, 259, 293, 294
roles, 46

Safe and Drug-Free Schools Program, 78
school administrators, 63
school-based enterprises, 240-41
school-based health centers, 77
school-based research, 400-413
 applications of, 401-7
 asking for help, 408
 being clear about objectives, 407-8
 as collaborative, 402-3
 community involvement in, 402, 403
 compilation of data and preparation of the report, 411
 current status of, 400-401
 for demonstrating effectiveness of services, 403
 for establishing need for additional resources, 405
 for establishing need for new services, 404-5
 for estimating cost of procedures, 410
 for forestalling implementation of undesirable policies, 407
 for fostering collaborative practice between students and staff, 405-6
 for fostering collegial accountability, 403-4
 getting started, 407-9
 for illuminating practices normally hidden from view, 406-7
 interviews in, 411
 involving others at early stage, 408-9
 laws and policies as source of information, 410
 libraries as resource for, 410
 low cost, straightforward methods for, 409-12
 not trying for too much, 408
 as political resource, 402
 questionnaires in, 411
 restrictions on, 401
 the school district's budget as source of information, 409-10
 structured observation in, 411
 student involvement in, 404
 for testing new programs or procedures, 406
 using available data in, 409
school-community-pupil relations model, 19-20
school history, in social development study, 203-4
school-linked services, 76-77
school-parent programs, 187
school personnel
 accountability if child does not meet IEP objectives, 113
 administrators, 63
 anxiety about children with special needs, 228
 becoming aware of disabling conditions, 134
 in child abuse cases, 361

child abuse programs for, 339
fostering collaborative practice between students and, 405–6
research by, 400, 401, 402
school as community of families and, 14–16
See also teachers
school reform (education reform)
comprehensive legislative package for, 71–74
cooperative principles emphasized by, 402
highlighting of problems in U.S. education, 68
ignoring effects of social ills, 20–21
increased expectations from children at risk, 14
private efforts at, 79–80
school social work affected by, 75–77
second wave focusing on students-at-risk, 69
threats to repudiate federal reform, 78–9
school social work
behavioral modification techniques in, 393–94
casework as major method of, 55
common case for, 174–81
conflict between practice and research, 438–41
the conservative climate for practice, 444, 447–48
coordination of services in, 343–54
current context of practice of, 445–48
defining the practice of, 10–13
developing networks of services and support systems, 161
dual function of, 27–31
dynamic relation with education, 8, 11
ecological perspective on, 26–37, 445–47
education reform's effect on, 75–77
empirical findings on role of, 191
as entitlement for children with disabilities, 8
ethical orientations to practice and research, 428–43
ethnic-sensitive approach to empirical practice, 387–99
facilitating home-school partnerships, 182–96
family counseling, 392–93
as field of practice, 4–5
general perspectives on, 1–84
glossary of terms of, 461–63

group counseling, 393
health care reform's effect on, 77–78
helping pupils use available services and resources, 161
historical analysis of, 5–8, 17–23
implications of organizational analysis in schools, 337–38
implications of student forums, 288–89
individual counseling, 392
integration with community services, 24, 166
interagency agreements in, 346–50
interface position of, 28–31, 32, 35
mandated foundations for service delivery, 85–155
mediation and, 305–6
modifying organizational context, 395
modifying teacher behavior, 394
NASW standards for, 99, 432
new model of required, 14
personal practice model for, 13
in postmodern society, 13–14
practice and service delivery, 157–365
primary prevention in, 31–34
problem solving in, 388–90
professional development of, 437–41
professional knowledge base for, 371, 348–49
professional status of, 27
resource development in, 343–54
school-community tasks for, 345
service delivery overview, 159–65
services as secondary services, 449
social work values' application to, 23
and the special education system, 132–46
a structure for practice, 387–88
task-centered model for, 396, 397
tasks of, 18–19, 23
theoretical introduction to practice of, 8–10
three components of learning, 13
values guiding, 51–53
See also school social work consultation; school social work research; school social workers; social work
School Social Work Association of America (SSWAA), 21, 463
school social work consultation, 267–81
alternative models of, 272–75
behavioral consultation, 274
clinical consultation, 273–74

476 Index

consultation defined, 268–69
education and training consultation, 273
hidden agendas in, 271
mental health consultation, 274, 275–78
organizational consultation, 274–75
program consultation, 275
stages in consultation process, 269–72
with teachers, 231–32, 234, 269, 271, 275–78
school social work research, 369–460
advocacy research, 436
as approach to scientific method, 369
conflict between practice and, 438–41
in the conservative political climate, 444–60
cultural influences on data analysis, 450
delaying service provision for research purposes, 453
developmental, 438
differential ethical orientations to practice and, 428–43
epidemiological studies, 454–55
ethnic-sensitive approach to empirical practice, 387–99
flexibility required in, 440
generating meaningful data in, 449–51
goal of, 450
influences demanding, 370–71
initiating change through evaluation and, 374–86
methodological dilemmas in knowledge development and accountability, 448–54
methodological guidelines for, 451–52
model development and effectiveness studies of school social work, 455–57
needs assessment, 414–27
overview of, 369–73
paradigm debate in, 449
quantitative or qualitative methodology in, 449
policy impact studies, 457–58
research design intrusiveness, 438, 439
research for its own sake, 435
school-based research, 400–413
selective interpretation of data, 436
single subject design studies, 397–98
substantive dilemmas in knowledge development and accountability, 454–58
support for, 372–73
uses of, 371–72
value and ethical commitments in, 452–53
School Social Work Specialist (SSWS), 80

school social workers
accountability of, 62, 453–54
assisting in making schools work as communities, 15
assisting parents accept that their child is low-functioning, 145n51
assuming an advocacy role, 35
attendance officers, 18, 19
availability of, 60
as boundary workers, 374, 379, 380
centralizing tendencies in social work opposed by, 7
certification of, 80
challenging boundaries between school and home, 15–16
characteristic focus of, 38–56
child protection and, 355–65
child welfare system collaboration, 363–65
children in placement and, 361–62
choosing the unit of attention, 191–92
congruence between client and practitioner, 391
contribution to education, 17–25
controlling the definition of the role of, 62
counting contacts, 64
credentialing of, 21–22
in defining the school community, 16
defining within the system, 58
employed in special education, 75
evaluating, 64
first, 5
function of, 5, 159–65
identifying children with special needs, 134
identifying the power structure, 59–60
Individualized Education Program and Individualized Family Services Program and role of, 209–24
influences on role of, 20
interpreting family and school to each other, 166
least restrictive environment and, 225–36
legitimacy of, 5
multiple roles of, 160
national credential examination for, 21–22
as necessary for special education, 8
organizational analysis of schools by, 328–42
prevention programs, 362–63
problems confronting, 4
professional identity of, 430–37

referenced in special education legislation, 74, 75
relations with administrators, 63
as a resource, 54–55
School Social Work Specialist, 80
in school-to-work transition programs, 250
shifting levels within the system, 378
as spanning boundary between home and school, 15
state associations of, 21
supervision of, 63–64
supporting staff in child abuse cases, 361
teaming with teachers, 48
three-decade chronology of a, 166–73
total agency concept of, 57, 62
understanding organizations, 49–50
value of, 62–65
values of, 99
viability of, 60–62
visibility of, 58–60
See also school social work
school suspension, 304–5
of children with disabilities, 136–37
school systems
examples of change in, 383–84
local school agencies, 134, 134
a model for introducing change in, 377–78
organizational domains of, 378
school-to-apprenticeship programs, 239–40
School-to-Work Opportunities Act (P.L. 103-239), 73, 237, 244
school-to-work transition programs, 237–51
agricultural education, 246
benefits to employers, 243
career education movement, 237–38
cream skimming in, 244
ensuring access to, 244–45
European models of, 249
facilitating employer involvement in, 243–44
German programs, 243–44
how existing programs promote access and participation, 246–49
integrating school-based and work-based learning, 242–43
issues regarding, 242–46
key elements of, 239
models of, 238–42
preparing students for careers not just work, 248
school social workers in, 250
support mechanisms for, 245–46, 247, 250

vocational guidance in, 245–46
Wisconsin's programs, 248–49
for women, 247–48
work sites as unsupported, 250
worker protection issues in, 245
schools
as adaptive organizations, 58
balancing organizational and student needs, 330
bringing children and resources together, 348
broadening traditional focus of, 88
career academies/magnet schools, 240
charter schools, 79
child-school interface, 29–30
as communities of families and school personnel, 14–16, 187–89
community-school interface, 30–31
conflict with communities for control of education, 27
diversity in, 320–21
dropouts, 69, 70, 391
ecological position of, 11–12
as essential institution for families with children, 184
first social workers in, 5
goal displacement in, 330
as groups, 307–27
innovation and change within, 374–86
junior high school, 34, 315–16
least restrictive environment requirement's challenges to, 228–30
mandatory attendance laws, 5, 18
mission of, 185
as natural setting for social work intervention, 11
necessary arrangement of relations between families and, 189–91
needs assessment in, 414–27
needs of in postmodern society, 13–14
no-fault schools, 314–20
openness of, 58
organizational analysis in, 328–42
parent-school interface, 30
parent-sponsored schools, 16
parental involvement and school effectiveness, 185–86
related services that must be provided by, 135–36, 142n24
requesting due process, 145n51
Safe and Drug-Free Schools Program, 78
the school as a system, 316–20

school-based research, 400–13
school-community tasks for social work, 345
school program as unit of attention, 192–93
school social work facilitating home-school partnerships, 182–96
school social worker interpreting school and family to each other, 166
social skills training in, 253–66
stress in entering for first time, 33
substance-abuse in, 70
suspension, 304–5
suspension and expulsion of children with disabilities, 136–37
transagency teams in, 351–54
violence in, 70, 447
See also education; high schools; pupils; school personnel; school reform; school systems
scientific values, 52
SDS. See social development study
secondary schools. See high schools
seriously emotionally disturbed children, 104–5
service coordination services, 126–27
service intrusiveness, 438, 439
service organizations, 50–51
sexually abused children, 358–60
single subject design studies, 397–98
skill deficits, decreasing, 393–94
skills, social. See social competence
Skinner-Rogers debate, 429
small-group theory, 283
smoking by students, 319–20
social competence (social skills), 253–66
　aggressive behavior remediation, 260–61
　complex skill situations, 259–60
　components of, 29
　conflict resolution as, 290–98
　defined, 254
　development of social skills programs, 254–55
　examples of social skills training, 260–64
　the group as context for training in, 255
　guidelines for practitioners, 257–60
　isolated and withdrawn behavior remediation, 261–62
　multiproblem social skills training, 263–64
　program goals, 255–57
　racial and ethnic considerations in programs for, 257
　role playing in training for, 259
　social skills training in schools, 253–54
　the social skills training method, 255–60
　steps in teaching, 258
　substance abuse prevention, 262–63
　teen pregnancy prevention, 256, 263
　training for generalization and maintenance, 260
social development study (SDS), 197–98
　adaptive behavior assessments in, 204–6, 461
　components of, 201–7
　confidentiality of, 206–7
　defined, 463
　evaluation in, 206–7
　family background in, 204
　guarding against inappropriate labeling of a child, 199–200
　purposes of, 198–200
　references to in P.L. 94-142 and P.L. 101-476, 200
　school history in, 203–4
　the SDS report, 201–3
　social history compared to, 198
social history, 198
social integration, 229–230
social networks, 50
social policy. See laws and policies
social skills. See social competence
social work
　activities of, 53–54
　characteristic focus of, 38–43, 48
　as dealing with values, 9
　defining the point of intervention of, 39–40
　dual function of, 27–28
　ecological perspective on, 43
　family-centered practice, 126
　fundamental orientation of, 9
　implications of Part H of IDEA for, 127–30
　interface position of, 28
　knowledge required for, 43–44
　as a mediating function, 26, 27
　practice of as matching, 42–43, 44
　professional status of, 26–27
　purpose of social work activity, 44
　social work education, 6, 12
　social worker as catalyst, 10
　social worker's contribution diagrammed, 31

social workers as link between client and community, 127
as strengthening adaptive potential and improving environments, 31
values of, 23
See also school social work; social work services
Social Work (journal), 7
social work services
coordination of, 343–54
delaying service provision for research purposes, 453
paradox of service provision, 347
service intrusiveness, 438, 439
See also related services
Southern School Social Work Council, 21
special education
"at no cost" to parents, 106, 136
centralized, 148, 152
changes in philosophy and law of, 267–68
consumer involvement in, 97
decentralization of, 152–54
defined by IDEA, 105
IDEA mandates for, 132–40
individualized education, 97
legislation on, 74–75, 88–93
local school system's role in, 134
multidisciplinary involvement in, 98
number of social workers in, 75
placement procedures, 108–12, 133, 138–39
qualified staff mandated for, 97
related services that schools must provide, 135–36
school social work and, 132–46
school social workers as necessity for, 8
staff accountability if child does not meet IEP objectives, 113
transition from regular classroom to, 232
trend toward inclusion in, 147–55, 268
values associated with, 95–102
See also Individualized Education Program; least restrictive environment
Spielberg v. Henrico County, 141n6
stay-put provision, 138–39
stress, 31–32, 41, 254
student forums in addressing racial conflict, 282–89
implications for social work of, 288–89
objectives of, 284
results of, 286–88
strategies of, 284–86

theory and research behind, 283–84
Student Loan Reform Act (P.L. 103-66), 73
students. *See* pupils
substance abuse
alcohol and drug use, 70, 78, 262–63
prevention programs, 262–63
in schools, 70
Safe and Drug-Free Schools Program, 78
surrogate parents, 112
surviving, coping behaviors for, 44–45, 48, 161
systems
open and closed, 300–301
the school as a system, 316–20
systems theory, 49, 58
task-centered model, 396, 397
Task Force on Specialization, 9, 10
tasks, 46
teacher assistance team (TAT), 268
teachers (faculty)
adapting instruction to variety of student needs, 230
anxiety about children with special needs, 228
bringing expectations into line with children's coping behavior, 46
faculty lounge as diagnostic source, 317
faculty norms, 317–18
as a group, 316–20
identifying and reporting child abuse, 356, 361, 364
modifying teacher behavior, 394
partnership with parents, 235
social work consultation with, 231–32, 234, 269, 271, 275–78
social workers teaming with, 48
Tech Prep programs, 240, 244
teenage mothers
educational problems of children of, 69
no longer excluded from schools, 169
teaching skills for preventing teen pregnancy, 256, 263
Transactions Individuals Environment approach to, 47–48
temporal integration, 228
theme interference, 277, 278
Tillich, Paul, 9
Timothy W. & Cynthia W. v. Rochester, N.H. School District, 136, 143n28
toddlers with disabilities. *See* infants and toddlers with disabilities

Town of Burlington v. Dept. of Education, 139, 144n42
transactions, 40, 44, 161
Transactions Individuals Environment (TIE), 44–49
  framework of diagrammed, 34
  research evidence for, 47
transagency teams, 351–54
transdisciplinary teams. *See* multidisciplinary teams
transference, 277, 278
transition services, 213–14
traumatic brain injury, 104
Tuskegee Study, 435
ultimate values, 51, 99
unit of attention
  choosing, 191–92
  community as, 194–95
  family as, 193–94
  pupil as, 194
  school program as, 192–93

valued qualities of a well-functioning person, 99
values, 51–53
  in education, 95–96
  knowledge distinguished from, 52–53
  in school social work research, 452–53
  of social work, 23
  types of, 51–52
  in special education, 95–102
  value conflicts, 99–101
violence in schools, 70, 447
Violent Crime Control and Law Enforcement Act (The Crime Bill), 74
vocational education, 238, 246, 251
Vocational Rehabilitation Act of 1973, 88, 89, 90

Western Alliance of School Social Workers, 21
White, Robert, 29
Whittle, Christopher, 79
Wisconsin, 248–49
work site learning programs, 241

youth apprenticeships (pre-apprenticeships), 240

zero reject, 97